PRE·ALGEBRA

Second Edition

Larry Hall

Kathy Kohler

Mark Wetzel

bju press®

Greenville, South Carolina

Note:

The fact that materials produced by other publishers may be referred to in this volume does not constitute an endorsement of the content or theological position of materials produced by such publishers. Any references and ancillary materials are listed as an aid to the student or the teacher and in an attempt to maintain the accepted academic standards of the publishing industry.

PRE-ALGEBRA

Second Edition

Larry Hall, MS

Kathy Kohler, MEd

Mark Wetzel

Contributing Authors
Bonney Block
David Brown, PhD
Larry Lemon, MS
Kathy Pilger, EdD

First Edition Author
Hal C. Oberholzer II, MA

Editor
Mary Schleifer

Bible Integration
Bryan Smith, PhD

Project Manager
Kevin Neat

Consultants
Tami Knisely
Pam Litzenberger

Composition
Publication Services
Dzign Associates, Patricia Tirado

Designer
David Siglin

Cover Design
Aaron Dickey

Illustrators
Hattie Bopp
Amber Cheadle
Courtney Godbey
Preston Gravely
Akane Kibayashi
Kathy Pflug
Lynda Slattery

Photo Acquisition
Rita Mitchell
Holly Nelson

Technical Consultant
Dzign Associates, Patricia Tirado

Photograph credits appear on page 646.

Produced in cooperation with the Bob Jones University Division of Mathematical Sciences of the College of Arts and Science, the School of Education, and Bob Jones Academy.

© 2010 BJU Press
Greenville, South Carolina 29614
First Edition © 1994 BJU Press

ISBN 978-1-59166-546-5

15 14 13 12 11 10 9 8 7 6 5 4 3

Our Commitment.
Your Confidence.

CONTENTS

INTRODUCTION

Consider the following tasks: using negative numbers when balancing a checkbook, measuring the length and width of a piece of fabric for a set of drapes, calculating the amount of fertilizer required for the yard, creating a culinary masterpiece in the kitchen, determining the number of square yards of carpet needed, and finding the volume of a truck bed or the amount of cement required for a building project. All of these tasks use the math covered in a pre-algebra course.

Do you think you will ever need to do these types of things? If so, then you will find this course useful. To accomplish these tasks, you will need a thorough knowledge of fractions, decimals, and percents. You will also need to know the basic formulas for calculating area and volume and how to use various measuring instruments. You will need skill in estimating quantities as well as in converting units, such as quarts to pints and inches to feet.

Man has a God-given dominion over the plants.

But maybe you're one of those people who hate math. You may be thinking, "No matter how useful math is, I'm not interested. There's got to be some way to get through life without having to know math." In that case, you need to consider what God says about our place in His world.

Our Calling in God's World

God created the human race with a job to do. Shortly after making the first man and woman, He commanded them, "Be fruitful, and multiply, and replenish the earth, and subdue it: and have dominion over the fish of the sea, and over the fowl of the air, and over every living thing that moveth upon the earth" (Gen. 1:28). Everything in this world exists to declare the glory of God—to reveal how great He is and how good He is (Ps. 19:1; Rom. 11:36). Humans, however, play a special role. We declare the glory of God by being like Him. He is the King of the universe, and He has called us to be stewards over His earth.

If we are to exercise good stewardship over the earth, we will have to know a good bit of math. The earth is a place where things need to be counted, divided, and measured. If we refuse to take math seriously, we will not be able to exercise dominion over our place in God's world. In time that place will exercise dominion over us, and the end result will be that, in important parts of our lives, we will not be declaring the glory of God.

Man has a God-given dominion over the animals.

But if we take math seriously (even if we never become a physicist or a math teacher), we can declare God's glory in areas that many humans ignore. We can responsibly manage our finances, our earthly possessions, and our health. A person who is totally devoted to the Lord declares the glory of God not just when he is singing hymns at church but also when he is at home balancing his checkbook, seeding his lawn, or renovating his kitchen.

Christian Love

Jesus taught that Christians are to live by love (Mark 12:30–31). All that we do should be motivated by love for God and love for our fellow humans. This implies that you should be generous in the way you handle your possessions. If you have enough to be comfortable, you have enough to share. But you will not have enough to share unless you are wise. And where will this wisdom come from? In part, it will come from the math you learn in this course. Love is the chief Christian virtue, but for love to function well it must be shaped by knowledge and good judgment (Phil. 1:9–11). Properly understood, math is much more than a school subject—it is a powerful tool for Christian love.

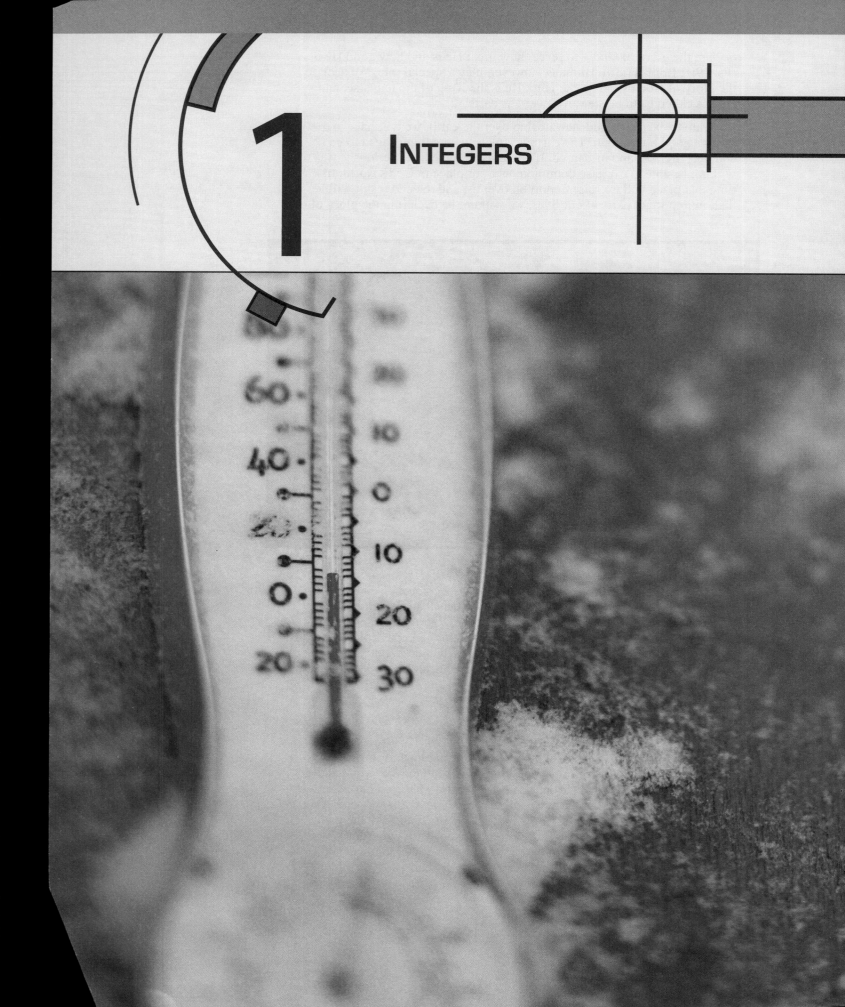

You may have heard one of your parents say, "you have a temperature" or "you have a fever." We all have a temperature, because the normal temperature for a human is 98.6°F (37°C). Any body temperature several degrees above normal is referred to as a *fever*, and any body temperature several degrees below normal is referred to as *hypothermia*. Either situation can be dangerous to a person's health. We can survive only a short time in an environment that is significantly above our normal temperature because our body's cooling system breaks down. However, we can live in temperatures much lower because we can put on layers of warm clothing to protect us from freezing. The polar regions of the earth are the coldest places, and the deserts are the hottest places. Although there are many people living on the fringes of deserts and the Arctic Circle, humans generally do not spend much time in either of these places. Most of the earth's inhabitable land lies within the temperate zones of the earth, although many people live in the tropical zones of Africa and South America.

God made us to manage what He has made (Gen. 1:28). Knowing how to use math is an important part of managing a world of changing weather. Although we cannot alter the weather, we can use math to predict it, and we can then plan our lives accordingly. In this chapter, you will use your math knowledge to answer questions that are important to the work of exercising dominion over God's earth.

After this chapter you should be able to

1. find opposites (additive inverses) and absolute values.

2. order integers from smallest to largest and vice versa.

3. add, subtract, multiply, and divide integers.

4. express numbers in exponential form.

5. multiply and divide powers with like bases.

6. simplify using the order of operations.

7. express numbers in scientific notation.

1.1 Opposites and Absolute Value

Negative numbers are used in everyday life. Temperatures below zero, a loss of company funds, an overdrawn bank account, and a loss of points in a game all require the use of negative numbers.

The set of *integers*, designated by the symbol $\mathbb{Z}$, is written as

$$\mathbb{Z} = \{\ldots, -3, -2, -1, 0, 1, 2, 3, \ldots\}.$$

The three dots indicate that the set continues in like manner.

The set of integers can be represented on a number line. Positive integers lie to the right of zero on the number line, and negative integers lie to the left of zero.

A magnet has a north and a south pole; opposites attract.

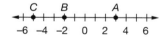

Notice that negative integers are indicated with a negative sign, such as –4, but the positive integers do not require a sign. Zero is neither a positive nor a negative integer.

Example 1   Write the integers for points *A*, *B*, and *C* on the number line.

Answer

A: 3   Point *A* is 3 units to the right of 0.

B: –2   Point *B* is 2 units to the left of 0.

C: –5   Point *C* is 5 units to the left of 0.

Skill Check 1

Draw a number line and mark the origin with a zero. Place the letter associated with the given coordinate in the proper place on the line.

1. *X*: –1   2. *Y*: 4   3. *Z*: –4

The term *opposite* has several meanings. It could refer to mutually exclusive things, such as the opposite sexes, or things that are altogether different in nature, such as night and day. The Bible describes life in terms of opposites. Everything a person does will be either godly or ungodly. Nothing is neutral. Jesus said, "He that is not with me is against me" (Matt. 12:30*a*).

"Opposite" can also mean located directly across from something. Observe below that 3 and –3 are located the same distance from zero on a number line but in opposite directions. Negative 3 and 3 are called *opposites*.

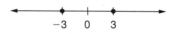

Opposites are two numbers located the same distance from zero on the number line but in opposite directions. The opposite of a number is also called its *additive inverse*.

The number zero is its own opposite.

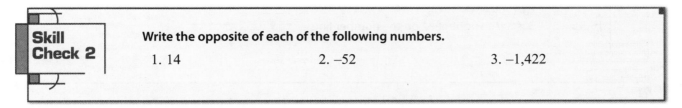

Skill Check 2

Write the opposite of each of the following numbers.

1. 14   2. –52   3. –1,422

The *absolute value* of an integer tells its distance from zero on the number line. Absolute value is concerned only with the number of units between the number and zero, regardless of direction. Since distance is a positive quantity, absolute value is always positive.

The **absolute value** of a number x is its distance from zero on the number line. It is indicated by the symbol $|x|$ and is read "the absolute value of x."

Example 2   Find $|3|$ and $|-3|$.

Answer

$|3| = 3$ The distance from 0 to 3 is three units.

$|-3| = 3$ The distance from 0 to –3 is also three units.

Example 3   Write the absolute value of each of the following.

a. $|-9|$ b. $|0|$ c. $|4|$

Answer

a. $|-9| = 9$ –9 is nine units from 0.

b. $|0| = 0$ 0 is zero units from 0.

c. $|4| = 4$ 4 is four units from 0.

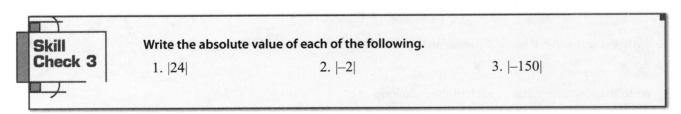

Skill Check 3

Write the absolute value of each of the following.

1. $|24|$ 2. $|-2|$ 3. $|-150|$

You can compare positive and negative integers using the inequality symbols <, meaning "is less than," and >, meaning "is greater than." A help that you may want to use to avoid confusing the symbols is to consider that the *less than* arrow points *left*. Both "less than" and "left" begin with the letter *l*. This may help you to remember which symbol is which.

On the number line, the integer located farther to the left is always the lesser number. Always place the *small* end of either symbol pointing toward the *smaller* number.

Example 4   Compare the following numbers by using < or >.

a. −3 and 2   b. 3 and −2

Answer

a. −3 < 2   −3 is to the left of 2 on the number line, so it is less.

b. 3 > −2   3 is to the right of −2 on the number line, so it is greater.

Skill Check 4

Compare the numbers by using < or >.

1. −4 _____ 0   2. −6 _____ −11   3. 3 _____ −9

You can also use inequality symbols to arrange a set of integers in order from least to greatest or from greatest to least.

Example 5   Write the integers −1, 3, and −5 in order from least to greatest by using <.

Answer

−5 is farthest to the left on the number line. It is the least number.

3 is farthest to the right on the number line. It is the greatest number.

−1 is between −5 and 3 on the number line. It is greater than −5 but less than 3.

−5 < −1 < 3

Skill Check 5

1. Write the integers −3, 5, and −7 in order from least to greatest by using <.

2. Write the integers 8, −6, 0, and −1 in order from greatest to least by using >.

■ **A. Exercises**

Draw a number line, and place each given letter where the integer falls on the line.

1. *A*: 3   2. *B*: −3   3. *C*: 2   4. *D*: −4

Write the opposite of each of the following numbers.

5. 8 −8   6. −16   7. $\frac{1}{2}$

Write the absolute value of each of the following.

8. |−7| 9. |3| 10. |0| 11. |−152|

Compare by using < or >.

12. 9 > −3   13. −2 > −13   14. −4 _____ 2

15. −5 _____ 1   16. 0 _____ 18   17. −15 ≤ −10

■ B. Exercises

Write the integers in order from least to greatest by using <.

18. –3, 0, 1

19. –4, –7, –9

20. 7, –4, 6 $-4 < 6 < 7$

21. –2, –5, 3

22. –15, 11, 8 $-15 < 8 < 11$

23. –11, 0, –19

Simplify.

24. –|5|

25. |17 – 9|

26. –|5 – 3|

27. –|–6|

Write the integers in order from greatest to least by using >.

28. –3, –9, –5, –17

29. –4, |–2|, 5, 3 $-2 < -4 < 3 < 5$

30. –2, 6, –7, 2

31. –18, |11|, –4, |–23|

Fill in the blank to make a true statement.

32. The opposite of a positive integer is a(n) _____ integer.

33. The additive inverse of a negative integer is a(n) _____ integer.

34. The integer _____ is neither positive nor negative.

35. The absolute value of every nonzero integer is a(n) _____ integer.

36. What is the symbol used for the set of integers?

37. What is another name for the set of natural numbers, {1, 2, 3, …}?

38. Should a plus sign be used to indicate that a number is positive?

39. What is another name for two numbers that are opposites?

40. Define opposite numbers.

41. What is the sum of a number and its opposite?

42. What number has a negative absolute value?

■ C. Exercises

Simplify; then write the simplified numbers in order from least to greatest by using <.

43. –|–3|, |7 – 2|, |6 – 6|, –|5|

44. |2|, –|–2|, |2 – 2|, |2 · 2|

45. |–8|, |–8| – |–8|, –|8|, |8| · |–8|

46. |6 + 3|, |6 – 3|, |6 · 3|, –|6 ÷ 3|

47. |–10| · |8|, |10| – |–8|, |10| + |–8|, |10 – 6|

1.2 Adding Integers

The addition of integers can be pictured on a number line. An arrow to the right indicates a positive integer, and an arrow to the left indicates a negative integer.

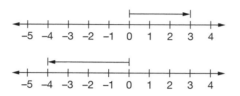

The abacus is used for arithmetic calculations and predates our number system.

Example 1 Add the following integers on number lines.

a. $1 + 4$

b. $-1 + (-4)$

Answer

a. $1 + 4 = 5$

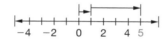

Start at 0 and draw an arrow 1 unit to the right, representing 1. From that point, draw a second arrow 4 units to the right, representing 4. The end of the second arrow, 5, is the sum.

b. $-1 + (-4) = -5$

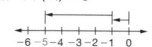

Start at 0 and draw an arrow 1 unit to the left, representing −1. From that point, draw a second arrow 4 units to the left, representing −4. The end of the second arrow, −5, is the sum.

Parts of an Addition Problem

Addend	−5
Addend	+ −4
Sum	−9

In Example 1, notice that the sum of two positive integers is positive and the sum of two negative integers is negative. This suggests a rule for adding integers with like signs.

Adding Integers with Like Signs

1. Add the absolute values of the addends.
2. Use the sign of the addends for the sum.

Example 2 Add.

a. $-3 + (-4)$

b. $-4 + (-6) + (-2)$

Answer

a. $-3 + (-4) = -7$ $|-3| + |-4| = 3 + 4 = 7$; insert a negative sign for the sum, giving -7.

b. $-4 + (-6) + (-2) = -12$ $|-4| + |-6| + |-2| = 4 + 6 + 2 = 12$; insert a negative sign for the sum, giving -12.

Skill Check 1

Add the following integers on number lines.

1. $5 + 3$

2. $-2 + (-7)$

Add the following numbers without number lines.

3. $-2 + (-6)$

4. $8 + 3$

5. $-3 + (-9) + (-2)$

Examine the number line additions shown in Example 3. The addends are integers with unlike signs.

Example 3 Add the following integers on number lines.

a. $-3 + 7$

b. $4 + (-6)$

Answer

a. $-3 + 7 = 4$

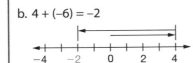

Start at 0 and draw an arrow 3 units to the left, representing -3. From that point, draw a second arrow 7 units to the right, representing 7. The end of the second arrow, 4, is the sum.

b. $4 + (-6) = -2$

Start at 0 and draw an arrow 4 units to the right, representing 4. From that point, draw a second arrow 6 units to the left, representing -6. The end of the second arrow, -2, is the sum.

Notice that the absolute value of the sums in Example 3 (4 and 2) could be obtained by finding the difference of the absolute values of the addends.

$$|7| - |-3| = 7 - 3 = 4$$
$$|-6| - |4| = 6 - 4 = 2$$

But how do you determine the signs for the sums? Notice that the sign of the sum is the same as the sign of the addend with the greater absolute value. In part a, $|7| > |-3|$, so the sum is positive. In part b, $|-6| > |4|$, so the sum is negative. This suggests the following rule for adding integers with unlike signs.

Adding Integers with Unlike Signs

1. Find the difference of the absolute values of the addends.

2. Use the sign of the addend with the greater absolute value for the sum.

Example 4   Add.

a. −9 + 3   b. −4 + 12   c. 8 + (−6)

Answer

a. −9 + 3 = −6 |−9| − |3| = 9 − 3 = 6, and |−9| > |3|, so the answer is negative.
b. −4 + 12 = 8 |12| − |−4| = 12 − 4 = 8, and |12| > |−4|, so the answer is positive.
c. 8 + (−6) = 2 |8| − |−6| = 8 − 6 = 2, and |8| > |−6|, so the answer is positive.

Skill Check 2   Add.

1. −15 + 9   2. −5 + 18   3. 24 + (−32)

■ A. Exercises

Add the following integers on number lines.

1. −4 + (−2)   2. 5 + (−3) = −2   3. −4 + 2

Add the following numbers without number lines.

4. −6 + (−9) −15   5. −8 + 2 = −6   6. 4 + 7 = 11

7. 12 + (−5)   8. −16 + 3 −13   9. −14 + (−6)

10. 19 + (−15) −34   11. 17 + 4   12. −25 + 11 − 14

13. −22 + 0   14. 19 + (−8) = 8   15. −17 + (−9)

■ B. Exercises

Add.

16. 18 + (−30)   17. 26 + (−17)   18. 31 + (−31) =

19. 74 + (−18) − 56   20. −45 + 32 = −13   21. 123 + (−96)

22. 35 + (−17) + (−24)   23. 23 + (−17) + 9 + (−2)   24. −37 + 18 + (−18) + 37

25. −12 + 44 + (−33) + (−5)   26. 54 + 13 + (−26)   27. −7 + 11 + (−14) + 3 + 12

28. A submarine dives to a depth of 650 ft. below the surface of the ocean. Later it climbs 150 ft. before descending an additional 80 ft. Use an integer to represent the depth of the submarine.

29. Mr. Jackson owned 650 shares of stock in the McBlock Corporation. On Monday he sold 75 shares, on Tuesday he sold 65 shares, on Wednesday he purchased 320 shares, and on Thursday he sold 280 shares. How many shares of the stock did he then own?

30. The high temperature yesterday was 6°F. It fell 17° overnight and rose only 5° by noon today. Find the overnight low and today's noon temperature.

31. Mr. Beeson has $220 in the bank and $12 in his billfold. He has bills of $76 and $188 to pay. Use an integer to express his total balance.

32. An elevator goes up to the seventh floor. It then travels down five floors. From there it goes up three floors. Write a sum of integers that could be used to determine the location of the elevator. Give the last floor on which the elevator stops.

■ C. Exercises

Find the integer that would be substituted for the variable to make a true statement.

33. $7 + y = -7$

34. $-15 + z + (-8) = -8$

35. $-8 = -4 + x$

36. $a + |-23 + 6| = -32$

37. Substituting both −9 and 33 for y in the equation $|-12 + y| + (-4) = 17$ makes a true statement. Verify that both of these numbers give a true equation and explain why there are two numbers that can be substituted for y.

■ CUMULATIVE REVIEW

Write the additive inverse of each of the following integers. [1.1]

38. 52

39. −8

40. −23

41. 69

Write the absolute value of each of the following. [1.1]

42. $|-87|$

43. $|32|$

44. $|9|$

45. $|-134|$

Write the integers in order from least to greatest by using <. [1.1]

46. 4, −4, 2, −1

47. 7, 2, −3, 4

MIND OVER MATH

How many complete squares can you count in the drawing?

The operation of subtraction is related to addition. Examine the problems below.

Subtracting	Adding the Opposite
$3 - 2 = 1$	$3 + (-2) = 1$

Subtracting 2 from 3 and adding the opposite of 2, or –2, to 3 give the same results. Thus, subtraction can be defined in terms of addition.

> **Definition**
>
> **Subtraction** is adding the opposite. In symbols, $a - b = a + (-b)$ for any real numbers a and b.

If sea level is assigned zero, this diver's elevation is in the negative range.

The symbols in the definition above should be read "a minus b equals a plus the opposite of b."

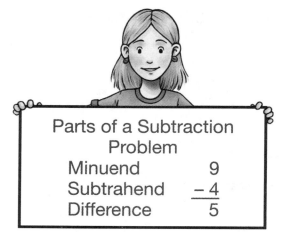

Parts of a Subtraction Problem

Minuend	9
Subtrahend	– 4
Difference	5

Example 1   Rewrite the following subtraction problems as addition problems.

a. $9 - (-7)$ b. $-5 - 9$ c. $8 - 15$

Answer

a. $9 - (-7) = 9 + 7$ Add the opposite of –7, or 7, to 9.

b. $-5 - 9 = -5 + (-9)$ Add the opposite of 9, or –9, to –5.

c. $8 - 15 = 8 + (-15)$ Add the opposite of 15, or –15, to 8.

Of course, if you are subtracting a smaller positive number from a larger number, such as 20 – 8, you do not need to apply the definition of subtraction; just subtract the whole numbers.

Skill Check 1

Rewrite the following problems as addition problems.

1. 4 – 9 $4 + -9$

2. 9 – (–8) $9 + -8$

3. –8 – (–4) $-8 + -4$

4. –6 – 3 $-6 + 3$

Example 2   Subtract 9 from –7.

Answer

Notice that the 9 is subtracted from –7. This means that –7 is the minuend and 9 is the subtrahend.

–7 – 9 = –7 + (–9) = –16   Add the opposite of 9, or –9, to –7.

Example 3   Subtract –5 from 8.

Answer

–5 is subtracted from 8. Therefore, 8 is the minuend and –5 is the subtrahend.

8 – (–5) = 8 + 5 = 13   Add the opposite of –5, or 5, to 8.

By now it should be obvious to you that the minus sign has various meanings. It denotes subtraction, indicates a negative number, and designates the opposite of a number. You need to be comfortable with all three uses of the minus sign and be able to convert to a plus sign when applicable. For example, –(–4) means the opposite of –4, which is 4. Therefore, any time you are subtracting a negative, you can add the positive instead. $n - (-4) = n + 4$, for any number n.

Skill Check 2

Subtract.

1. –5 – 7

2. –3 – (–5)

3. 2 – 8

4. 4 – (–6)

5. –2 – 8 – (–7)

6. 12 – 7 – 6

7. Ryan's score is –57 and Martin's score is 173. By how many points is Martin ahead of Ryan?

8. Mr. Hastings wrote a budget for the month that required $4,525, but his monthly take-home pay is only $3,970. Find the balance that will occur at the end of the month if no adjustments are made.

A. Exercises

1. Write the definition of subtraction in symbols.

2. Write the definition of subtraction in words.

Rewrite the following problems as addition problems.

3. $8 - 3$

4. $-12 + 4 = -8$

5. $15 + (+8) = 7$

6. $6 + 9 = 13$

7. $7 - 18$

8. $4 + 11 = -7$

9. $-7 + 8 = -1$

10. $-5 + (+17) = +12$

11. $32 - (-19)$

12. $3 + (+5) = +2$

13. $12 - 19 = -7$

14. $-18 - 20$

B. Exercises

Subtract.

15. $-9 - (-13)$

16. $-3 - (-9)$

17. $-27 - 38$

18. $4 - (-11)$

19. $-9 - 8$

20. $-14 - (-3)$

21. $-19 - (-24)$

22. $-23 - (-18)$

23. $-17 - (-28)$

24. $47 - 63$

25. $-79 - 14$

26. $-6 - 8 - (-14)$

27. $8 - 15 - 6$

28. $-20 - (-17) - 4$

29. $-42 - 82 - (-7)$

30. $18 - 46 - (-21)$

31. A bank customer had a balance of $47, on which he wrote a check for $101. What is his new balance?

32. At 5:00 PM the temperature was 13°F. By midnight it had fallen 29°. What was the temperature at midnight?

33. The price of a stock was quoted at $83 per share at the beginning of the day. Due to a bad day on the stock market, the price fell to $65 by the end of the day. Use an integer to represent the change in the value of the stock.

34. A football team is given four downs to move the ball 10 yd. On first down the Bears gained 5 yd. On second down they lost 9 yd. On third down they completed a pass for 8 yd. How many yards must they gain on fourth down to keep possession of the ball?

35. A store item with a regular price of $72 was reduced by $18 for the big sale. During the sale, it incurred a scratch and was reduced another $15. What was the final reduced price?

C. Exercises

Simplify.

36. $340 - (-147) - 809$

37. $-81 + (36 - 110)$

38. $74 - (99 + 12)$

39. $88 + (-14) + (15 - 21)$

40. $(-27 + 70) - 39 + (-4)$

41. $950 - (-661 + 46)$

■ Dominion thru Math

Three different scales are used to measure temperature. The Fahrenheit scale sets the freezing point of water at 32° and the boiling point at 212°. The Celsius scale sets the freezing point at 0° and the boiling point at 100°. Scientific work often uses the Kelvin scale, which has the same size units as the Celsius scale; but it sets absolute zero (0 K) at –273° on the Celsius scale. Thus, to convert between Kelvin and Celsius, use the formulas $C = K - 273$ and $K = C + 273$. Also, use the following formulas to convert between Fahrenheit and Celsius: $C = \frac{5}{9}(F - 32)$ and $F = \frac{9}{5}C + 32$.

42. The normal body temperature for a human is 98.6°F. Write the normal human body temperature using the Celsius scale and the Kelvin scale.

43. On the Fahrenheit scale, what integer expresses a temperature 48 degrees below freezing?

44. On the Celsius scale, what integer expresses a temperature 48 degrees below freezing?

45. What integer expresses absolute zero on the Fahrenheit scale? Round to the nearest degree.

46. If water is the densest at 4°C, what is this on the Fahrenheit scale? Round to the nearest degree.

47. What would a temperature of –40°F be on the Celsius scale?

48. The core temperature of our sun is 15,000,000 K. Express this temperature in degrees Fahrenheit. Round to the nearest million degrees.

CUMULATIVE REVIEW

Write the additive inverse of each of the following integers. [1.1]

49. 82

50. –49

Write the integers in order from greatest to least by using >. [1.1]

51. –8, –2, –10, 0

52. 6, –1, –6, 4

Evaluate. [1.1–1.2]

53. $|{-7} + 5|$

54. $|18 + (-12)|$

55. $4 + (-10)$

56. $-11 + 5$

57. $9 + (-4)$

58. $-3 + (-9)$

S. Josephine Baker, Physician and Public Health Worker

S. Josephine Baker was a woman pioneer in the field of medicine.

Sara Josephine Baker was born in Poughkeepsie, New York, on November 15, 1873. She grew up in a home that placed a high premium on education. Josephine's father died of typhoid fever, leaving her with the responsibility of providing for her mother and sister. Her father's death emphasized to her the need for skilled doctors. Josephine decided to be one, an almost unheard-of ambition for a woman during her day.

After studying biology and chemistry on her own, Josephine was accepted as a student at the Women's Medical College of the New York Infirmary for Women and Children in New York City. This college was founded by Dr. Elizabeth Blackwell, the first woman to earn a doctorate in medicine. Josephine worked hard and received a high ranking in her class.

Upon graduation in 1898, Dr. Baker discovered that no hospital at which she applied would hire her. They said no one would want to be treated by a woman doctor. Finally, she secured a position as a medical intern at Boston's New England Hospital for Women and Children. There she learned firsthand about the sickness and squalor in city slums.

In 1899 Dr. Baker returned to New York City with her friend Dr. Florence Laighton. They set up a private practice and waited for patients to come. By year's end, Dr. Baker had earned only $185. Refusing to quit, she set out to find a way to supplement her income. She was offered a position as a medical inspector for the city's health department. Unlike many inspectors, Dr. Baker personally visited the slum apartments and schools to examine the children.

At the turn of the century, thousands of children were dying each year because of poor health conditions. During the summer of 1908, Dr. Baker instituted a program in one of the East Side slums to teach mothers of newborn infants how to care properly for their children. At summer's end there were 1,200 fewer deaths than during the previous summer. One of her most interesting contributions to New York City health care was her role in tracking down Mary Mallon (Typhoid Mary), who spread typhoid fever while working as a cook in several households over a period of seven years.

The city officials were impressed with her work, and they decided to form the Division of Child Hygiene. This was the first tax-supported agency in the world dedicated solely to children's health care. After Dr. Baker was appointed director of the bureau, she influenced many states to establish similar child health care departments. She faithfully served for fifteen years in this capacity.

To serve in such a responsible administrative position as the one S. Josephine Baker held, you would need to apply mathematics to such financial matters as budgeting the government funds allocated to the bureau and formulating payrolls for the workers. You would need to track health care statistics and use them both to determine where to spend the government funds and to make a case for more funds. Health care workers must know the metric system so they can handle the purchase, distribution, and dosages of medicine.

Dr. Baker published five books and over two hundred articles during her professional career. She died in 1945 after a distinguished career as a physician and public health worker.

1.4 Multiplying Integers

Multiplication is a way of expressing repeated addition. The product 4×2 is the same as the sum of four 2s.

$$4 \times 2 = 2 + 2 + 2 + 2 = 8$$

Likewise, the product of $4 \times (-2)$ is the sum of four –2s.

$$4(-2) = -2 + (-2) + (-2) + (-2) = -8$$

Examine the product of a negative integer and a positive integer in the examples below.

$$4(-2) = -2 + (-2) + (-2) + (-2) = -8$$
$$3(-2) = -2 + (-2) + (-2) = -6$$
$$2(-2) = -2 + (-2) = -4$$
$$1(-2) = -2 = -2$$

These examples illustrate that the product of a positive integer and a negative integer is negative. Remember from your study in previous math courses that multiplication is commutative. This means that the order of the factors is not significant. Therefore, $3(-2) = -6$ and $-2(3) = -6$. The product of a positive integer and a negative integer is negative, regardless of the order of the factors.

This panel has $6 \times 6 = 36$ individual tiles.

Parts of a Multiplication Problem

Factor	9
Factor	× 4
Product	36

Multiplying Integers with Unlike Signs

1. Multiply the absolute values of the factors.
2. The product is negative.

Example 1   Multiply –4 by 7.

Answer

$|7| \cdot |-4| = 7 \cdot 4 = 28$ 1. Multiply the absolute values of the factors.

$7(-4) = -28$ 2. If two integers have unlike signs, their product is negative.

Example 2 Multiply 5 by –4.

Answer

$|-4| \cdot |5| = 4 \cdot 5 = 20$ 1. Multiply the absolute values of the factors.

$-4(5) = -20$ 2. If two integers have unlike signs, their product is negative.

Skill Check 1

Multiply.

1. 4(–3)   2. –6(5)   3. 7(–1)

The product of two positive integers is always positive, so 4 × 2 = 8. But what type of product do you get when you multiply two negative integers, such as –4 × (–2)? Notice in the examples below that each time the multiplier decreases by one, the product increases by two. By continuing this pattern, you see that the product of a negative integer times a negative integer is a positive integer.

$3(-2)$ = -6
$2(-2)$ = -4
$1(-2)$ = -2
$0(-2)$ = 0
$-1(-2)$ = 2
$-2(-2)$ = 4
$-3(-2)$ = 6
$-4(-2)$ = 8

Multiplying Integers with Like Signs

1. Multiply the absolute values of the factors.
2. The product is positive.

Example 3 Multiply –9 by –6.

Answer

$|-6| \cdot |-9| = 6 \cdot 9 = 54$ 1. Multiply the absolute values of the factors.

$-6(-9) = 54$ 2. If two integers have like signs, their product is positive.

Skill Check 2

Tell whether the product is positive or negative.

1. 9(–8)   2. –5(–2) +   3. –4(3) –

Multiply.

4. –5(8) – 40   5. 7(–5) – 35   6. –4(–6) + 12

7. –4(3) = –12   8. –2(–11) + 22   9. –3(–9) + 27

Example 4   Multiply –6(–2)(–3).

Answer

–6(–2)(–3) = 12(–3)   1. Multiply –6 times –2; the product is positive.
            = –36   2. Multiply the remaining two numbers; the product is negative.

Example 5   Multiply 4(–3)(–5).

Answer

4(–3)(–5) = –12(–5)   1. Multiply 4 times –3; the product is negative.
          = 60   2. Multiply the remaining factors; the product is positive.

When multiplying more than two factors, you can determine the sign of the product by counting the number of factors with negative signs. If there is an even number of negative factors, the product is positive. The negative factors can be paired, and each pair will have a positive product. Thus, the final product will be positive. When you attempt to pair up an odd number of negative factors, one of them will remain, making the final product negative. The problems in Examples 4 and 5 could have been solved using this approach.

Example 6   Multiply –6(–2)(–3).

Answer

6(2)(3) = 12(3) = 36   1. Multiply the absolute values of the factors.
–6(–2)(–3) = –36   2. There is an odd number of negative factors; the product is negative.

Example 7   Multiply 4(–3)(–5).

Answer

4(3)(5) = 12(5) = 60   1. Multiply the absolute values of the factors.
4(–3)(–5) = 60   2. There is an even number of negative factors; the product is positive.

Take note of the different ways of indicating multiplication. You need to be familiar with each of these.

$$6 \cdot 5 \qquad\qquad 6 \times 5 \qquad\qquad 6(5)$$

When negative integers are involved, parentheses will be used to separate the negative sign from the operational sign.

$$-9 \cdot (-4) \qquad\qquad -9 \times (-4) \qquad\qquad -9(-4)$$

Skill Check 3

Tell whether the product is positive or negative.

1. –2 · (–4) · (–4) · (–9)   2. –14(3)(–5)(–2)

Multiply.

3. 5 × (–2) × 3 × (–1)   4. 2(–6)(12)(3)

5. –4 · (–3) · 5 · 0 · (–11)   6. –8 × (–1) × 3 × (–2)

■ A. Exercises

1. Give three ways to signify multiplication, using the numbers 4 and 10.

Tell whether the product is positive or negative.

2. 2(–5)

3. –4(7)

4. –5(–9)

5. 8(–2)(–1)

6. –5 × (–2) × (–60) × (–8)

7. –3 · 4 · (–12) · 6 · (–11)

8. 1(–2)(3)(–4)(5)

9. 6 × 8 × (–3)

Multiply.

10. 8 · 6 = 48

11. –4(–3)

12. –7(–11)

13. –1 × 8

14. 4(–7) = –28

15. 3(–15)

16. –9(5) = –45

17. –2 × 0

18. –4 · 12 = –48

■ B. Exercises

Multiply.

19. 5(–13)

20. –10(–24)

21. 12(–35)

22. –6 · 18

23. –16(17)

24. –21(–28)

25. 8(16)

26. 3(–117)

27. 4(–19)

28. –5(–253)

29. –3(5)(–4)

30. –9(–5)(–18)(–1)

31. –2(–7)(–9)

32. –1(–2)(–3)(–4)(–5)

33. 8(–2)(5)

34. –6(–5)(4)(–3)(–2)

35. –7(2)(0)(–5)(3)

36. –2(3)(–4)(0)(–6)

37. 2(–14)(–3)(–10)

38. –4(5)(–2)(25)(3)

39. A football team lost 4 yd. on each of two consecutive plays. Use an integer to reflect the result of these two plays.

40. A trust fund has a balance of $8,974, from which ten siblings will each receive a check for $620. Find the balance in the trust fund after the checks are distributed.

41. In your own words, explain the multiplication rules for integers.

42. In your own words, explain how to determine the sign of the product by looking at the factors.

■ C. Exercises

Perform the indicated operations, and then compare by using <, >, or =.

43. –8(17) and –14(7)

44. –13(140)(–2) and –11(150)(6)

45. 44 – (13 · 7) and 6(–9)

46. –45(–7)(3) and 28(–16)(–3)

47. 17(–14)(–3) and –7(–8)(15)

48. 4(–14) and (–8 + 2) × [–(14 – 26)]

Compare by using <, >, or =.

49. 35(–458)(87) ____ 35(0)(–1,236)

50. –12(–34)(–23)(–17) ____ 347(–127)

■ **Dominion thru Math**

The chart below gives either the Celsius or Fahrenheit temperatures of various locations where extremely hot or extremely cold temperatures have been recorded. Find the equivalent temperatures of the other scale for each one. Round to the nearest degree. (Review the conversion formulas in Section 1.3, Dominion thru Math.)

Global Extreme Temperatures					
Cold Temperatures			Hot Temperatures		
Location	°C	°F	Location	°C	°F
51. Rogers Pass, MT	−57		54. El Azizia, Libya		136
52. Prospect Creek, AK	−62		55. Death Valley, CA		135
53. Oimiakan, Russia	−73		56. Timbuktu, Mali		130

CUMULATIVE REVIEW

Perform the indicated operations. [1.2–1.3]

57. $5 + (-7)$

58. $8 - 21$

59. $-4 - 12$

60. $-16 + 9$

61. $42 - (-18)$

62. $-31 + (-29)$

63. Simplify $|-3 - 5| - |-3| - |-5|$. [1.1–1.3]

64. Write the opposite of -255. [1.1]

65. If $a + b = c$ and a and b are additive inverses, then c equals what? [1.1]

66. If $c + d = 0$, then c and d are called what? [1.1]

1.5 Dividing Integers

Division is related to multiplication. When a product is divided by either of its factors, the result is the other factor. Since $4(-2) = -8$, we can conclude that

$$\frac{-8}{-2} = 4 \text{ and } \frac{-8}{4} = -2.$$

The first division problem shows that a negative integer divided by a negative integer is positive. The second problem shows that a negative integer divided by a positive integer is negative.

It is also true that $-4(-2) = 8$. The division problems that result are

$$\frac{8}{-4} = -2 \text{ and } \frac{8}{-2} = -4.$$

These examples illustrate that a positive integer divided by a negative integer is negative. The rules for dividing integers with like and unlike signs are similar to those for multiplying integers.

You can divide a lot of firewood with this tool.

Dividing Integers with Like Signs
1. Divide the absolute values of the integers.
2. The quotient is positive.

Dividing Integers with Unlike Signs
1. Divide the absolute values of the integers.
2. The quotient is negative.

Example 1 Divide −32 by −4.

Answer

$\dfrac{|-32|}{|-4|} = \dfrac{32}{4} = 8$ 1. Divide the absolute values of the numbers.

$\dfrac{-32}{-4} = 8$ 2. Since the integers have like signs, the quotient is positive.

Example 2 Divide 45 by −9.

Answer

$\dfrac{|45|}{|-9|} = \dfrac{45}{9} = 5$ 1. Divide the absolute values of the numbers.

$\dfrac{45}{-9} = -5$ 2. Since the integers have unlike signs, the quotient is negative.

Example 3 Divide −36 by 12.

Answer

$\dfrac{|-36|}{|12|} = \dfrac{36}{12} = 3$ 1. Divide the absolute values of the numbers.

$\dfrac{-36}{12} = -3$ 2. Since the integers have unlike signs, the quotient is negative.

Skill Check 1

Divide.

1. $-30 \div (-6)$ 2. $\dfrac{-40}{-5}$ 3. $-18 \div 2$

4. $\dfrac{-141}{1}$ 5. $-75 \div (-25)$ 6. $\dfrac{36}{-6}$

Division of integers is shown by the standard symbol (÷) or by the fraction bar. The fraction bar appears frequently in algebra, since answers are often left in rational form as improper fractions rather than being changed to mixed numbers.

$$19 \div (-8) \qquad \dfrac{19}{-8}$$

A negative fraction can be indicated with the negative sign in front of the fraction or in either the numerator or the denominator. Therefore, $\dfrac{19}{-8} = \dfrac{-19}{8} = -\dfrac{19}{8}$.

When you multiply and divide integers in succession, the operations must be performed left to right as you come to them. The sign of the answer to a multiplication or division problem can be determined by the number of negatives in the problem. An expression with an odd number of negatives will have a negative answer, and an expression with an even number of negatives will have a positive answer.

| **Example 4** | Simplify $-3(8) \div (-12)$. |

Answer

$-3(8) \div (-12) = -24 \div (-12)$ 1. Multiply first.
$= 2$ 2. Perform the remaining division.

| Parts of a Division Problem |
| Dividend   Divisor   Quotient |
| 15 $\div$ 3   =   5 |

| **Example 5** | Simplify $-30 \div (-2)(-3)$. |

Answer

$-30 \div (-2)(-3) = 15(-3)$ 1. Divide first.
$= -45$ 2. Perform the remaining multiplication.

Remember that if an operation appears in parentheses, you should complete that operation first.

Skill Check 2

Perform the indicated operations.

1. $-4 \cdot (-6) \div 2$ 2. $-6 \div [-2 \times (-3)]$

3. $14 \div [-2(3) \div (-3)]$ 4. $6 \times 2 \div (-3) \times 8$

5. $(-22 \times 16) \div (-11 \times 4)$ 6. $-75 \div (-3)(-5) \times 2$

■ A. Exercises

Divide.

1. $\dfrac{-48}{-6}$ 2. $64 \div (-8)$ 3. $\dfrac{35}{-7}$ 4. $\dfrac{115}{-5}$ 5. $-80 \div 4$ 6. $\dfrac{-144}{-8}$

7. $\dfrac{-24}{-8}$ 8. $34 \div (-2)$ 9. $156 \div 13$ 10. $-42 \div 7$ 11. $\dfrac{-72}{-9}$ 12. $\dfrac{-132}{11}$

13. $-49 \div (-7)$ 14. $\dfrac{-70}{5}$ 15. $\dfrac{120}{8}$ 16. $75 \div (-5)$ 17. $\dfrac{36}{18}$ 18. $\dfrac{-162}{9}$

■ B. Exercises

Perform the indicated operations.

19. $-24 \div (-3) \div (-2)$ 20. $-48 \div 2(8)$

21. $8(-5) \div 10$ 22. $\dfrac{-3-7}{-5}$

23. $-46 \div 2 \cdot 8$ 24. $8(-7) \div 2(-6)$

25. $(2 - 11) \div 3$ 26. $18 \div 2 \times (-3) \times (-4 + 6)$

27. $2 \times (-10) \div [-92 \div (-23)]$ 28. $\dfrac{-3(8)}{2}(-2)$

29. Three partners in a business venture have incurred a debt of $9,876. Use an integer to express the amount of debt for each one.

30. What is the quotient of 948 divided by the product of 79 and –3?

31. Find the average of the following low temperatures during a week in January: –5°F, –10°F, –13°F, –11°F, –8°F, 0°F, 3°F. Round the answer to the nearest tenth.

32. A game results in either a positive or a negative score for the player during each turn. One player had a total score of –288 points after nine turns. What was his average score per turn?

■ C. Exercises

Perform the indicated operations.

33. $-718 \div (-4) \div 0.5$

34. $1,976 \div (-4)(-2) \div (-64 \div 16)$

35. $-2[-88 \div (-2)(2)] \times (-17 \div 2)$

36. $\dfrac{-273 \div (-3)}{52(-2)}$

You are planning an all-day trip to an amusement park for your youth group. There are thirty-one people going on the trip, including four chaperones and a bus driver. The park offers group discounted tickets at $39 and admits the bus driver free of charge. In addition to paying for admission, each member of the youth group is expected to bring at least $24 in cash. This includes $5 for bus fare and the remainder for two meals.

37. How much must each young person spend for tickets if the youth group is sharing the cost of the chaperones' tickets?

38. The additional $24 is to cover two meals and the bus fare. How much is allotted for each meal?

■ Dominion thru Math

39. At 1 PM the temperature in Bangor, Maine, was 52°F; but a severe storm moving into the area caused the temperature to start dropping at 4°F per hour. If the storm lasted through the night, when did the temperature reach freezing, and when did it reach 0°F?

40. During the first half hour after the start of a thunderstorm the air temperature dropped 4°F every 10 min., and during the second half hour it dropped 2°F every 15 min. During the next half hour it dropped 0.5°F every 15 min. If the temperature was 88°F at the start of the storm, what was the temperature $1\frac{1}{2}$ hr. into the storm?

41. The air temperature in a certain Midwestern city is 49°F at 7 AM and continues to rise to a maximum of 84°F at 2 PM. Then it falls over the next few hours to 68°F at 6 PM. Use integers to express the change during the first seven hours and the change during the next four hours of the day. Calculate the change per hour for each of the periods.

■ CUMULATIVE REVIEW

Evaluate. [1.1–1.4]

42. $16 - (-48)$

43. $5(-15)(-2)(-3)$

44. $-27 + (-31)$

45. $47 + (-83) - 14$

46. $3(-8)(2)(5)$

47. $-12 - (-8) + 6$

48. $49 - 82$

49. $-7(2)(-3)(-4)$

50. $|-21| - |-35|$

51. $6(-4)(-2)$

1.6 Exponents

Just as repeated addition can be expressed in simpler form using multiplication, so repeated multiplication can be expressed in simpler form using exponents. An *exponent* indicates how many times a number is used as a repeated factor.

Definition

An **exponent** is a positive integer superscript written to the right of a number telling how many times that number is used as a factor. The repeated factor is the *base*.

$$2 \cdot 2 \cdot 2 \cdot 2 = 2^4 \leftarrow \text{exponent}$$

factors   base

When no exponent is written, the exponent is understood to be one.

$$2 = 2^1$$

The second and third powers of a number have special names. The area of a square is found by multiplying a side length times itself. The square shown has an area of $5 \times 5 = 5^2$. Therefore, a number with an exponent of 2 is read as the number squared. For example, 5^2 is read *five squared*.

The volume of a cube is found by multiplying length × width × height, or using the length of an edge as a factor three times. The cube shown has an area of $5 \times 5 \times 5 = 5^3$. Therefore, a number with an exponent of 3 is read as the number cubed. For example, 5^3 is read *five cubed*.

Example 1   Write $6 \times 6 \times 6 \times 6$ using exponential notation.

Answer

$6 \times 6 \times 6 \times 6 = 6^4$ The exponent 4 indicates that the base 6 is used as a factor four times.

Exponents can be used with variables as well as with numbers. In algebra, a variable is generally a lowercase letter.

Definition

A **variable** is a symbol used to represent an unknown number.

Example 2   Write each of the following in expanded form. Simplify if possible.

a. 5^2 b. x^6 c. $(-4)^3$

Answer

a. $5^2 = 5 \times 5 = 25$ b. $x^6 = x \cdot x \cdot x \cdot x \cdot x \cdot x$ c. $(-4)^3 = -4(-4)(-4) = 16(-4) = -64$

When a negative number is raised to a power, the number is written in parentheses. For example, –3 squared is written $(-3)^2$. If the parentheses are omitted, the expression means the opposite of 3^2.

$$(-3)^2 = -3(-3) = 9$$
$$-3^2 = -(3 \times 3) = -9$$

Skill Check 1

Write each of the following using exponential notation.

1. $c \cdot c \cdot c \cdot c$

2. $-1(-1)(-1)(-1)(-1)(-1)(-1)$

Write each of the following in expanded form. Simplify if possible.

3. 10^3

4. b^5

5. 7^4

6. -2^6

Example 3   Simplify each of the following.

a. $3^4 - 4^2$

b. $-5^2 + (-2)^2$

c. $4(15^1)(2^3)$

Answer

a. $3^4 - 4^2 = (3 \times 3 \times 3 \times 3) - (4 \times 4)$
   $= 81 - 16$
   $= 65$

b. $-5^2 + (-2)^2 = -[5(5)] + (-2)(-2)$
   $= -25 + 4$
   $= -21$

c. $4(15^1)(2^3) = 4(15)(2 \times 2 \times 2)$
   $= 60(8)$
   $= 480$

Skill Check 2

Simplify.

1. $3^2 + 4^2$

2. $2(2^4 - 3^1)$

3. $(5^2 + 3^3) \div 2$

4. $5(-2^2 + 3)$

Numbers expressed in exponential form can be multiplied and divided if they have like bases. To multiply, you must add the exponents. Examine the example below.

$$3^2 \cdot 3^3 = (3 \cdot 3) \cdot (3 \cdot 3 \cdot 3) = 3^5$$

The sum of the exponents, $2 + 3 = 5$, indicates the total number of factors.

Multiplication Property of Exponents

For any number x and integers a and b, $x^a \cdot x^b = x^{a+b}$.

Example 4   Multiply $2^3 \cdot 2^4$. Leave the answer in exponential form.

Answer

$2^3 \cdot 2^4 = 2^{3+4} = 2^7$

What happens when you raise an exponential expression to a power? Simplify $(2^4)^2$.

$$(2^4)^2 = (2^4)(2^4) = (2 \times 2 \times 2 \times 2)(2 \times 2 \times 2 \times 2) = 2^8$$

Since you end up with eight factors of 2, it simplifies to 2^8. Notice that the two exponents in the expression multiply to equal the exponent of the answer: $4 \times 2 = 8$. This illustrates the Power Property of Exponents.

Power Property of Exponents

For any number x and integers a and b, $(x^a)^b = x^{ab}$.

Skill Check 3

Simplify the following. Leave the answers in exponential form.

1. $2^2 \cdot 2^4$

2. $(7^3)^5$

3. $d^3 \cdot d$

4. $(x^2)^3 \cdot x^4$

5. $(b^4 \cdot b^2)^3$

6. $10^4 \cdot 10^7 \cdot 10^2$

Powers with like bases can also be divided. This allows you to simplify expressions such as $\dfrac{2^5}{2^3}$.

$$\frac{2^5}{2^3} = \frac{2 \cdot 2 \cdot \overset{1}{\cancel{2}} \cdot \overset{1}{\cancel{2}} \cdot \overset{1}{\cancel{2}}}{\underset{1}{\cancel{2}} \cdot \underset{1}{\cancel{2}} \cdot \underset{1}{\cancel{2}}} = 2^2$$

The difference of the exponents is the exponent of the quotient.

Division Property of Exponents

For any number x and integers a and b, $\dfrac{x^a}{x^b} = x^{a-b}$.

Example 5   Simplify the following. Leave the answers in exponential form.

a. $\dfrac{3^5}{3^2}$

b. $\dfrac{y^7}{y}$

Answer

a. $\dfrac{3^5}{3^2} = 3^{5-2} = 3^3$ Subtract the exponents.

b. $\dfrac{y^7}{y} = \dfrac{y^7}{y^1} = y^{7-1} = y^6$ Subtract the exponents.

Skill Check 4

Simplify the following. Leave the answers in exponential form.

1. $\dfrac{7^8}{7^5}$

2. $5^9 \div 5^4$

3. $\dfrac{x^7}{x \cdot x^2}$

4. $(y^4 \cdot y^6) \div y^3$

The division property can be used to verify that any number to the zero power equals 1.

$$\frac{3^4}{3^4} = \frac{\overset{1}{\cancel{3}} \cdot \overset{1}{\cancel{3}} \cdot \overset{1}{\cancel{3}} \cdot \overset{1}{\cancel{3}}}{\underset{1}{\cancel{3}} \cdot \underset{1}{\cancel{3}} \cdot \underset{1}{\cancel{3}} \cdot \underset{1}{\cancel{3}}} = \frac{1}{1} = 1$$

$$3^{4-4} = 3^0$$

Therefore, you can conclude that $3^0 = 1$.

Properties of Exponents

1. $x^a \cdot x^b = x^{a+b}$

2. $(x^a)^b = x^{ab}$

3. $x^a \div x^b = x^{a-b}$

Any nonzero number to the **zero power** equals 1. In symbols, $n^0 = 1$ for any real number n, where $n \neq 0$.

The base of 0 cannot be raised to the zero power. 0^0 is undefined.

The Division Property of Exponents allows you to simplify the expression $\dfrac{4^2}{4^5}$.

$$\frac{4^2}{4^5} = 4^{2-5} = 4^{2+(-5)} = 4^{-3}$$

You can also simplify the same expression in the following manner.

$$\frac{4^2}{4^5} = \frac{\cancel{4} \cdot \cancel{4}}{4 \cdot 4 \cdot 4 \cdot \cancel{4} \cdot \cancel{4}} = \frac{1}{4^3}$$

Therefore, $4^{-3} = \dfrac{1}{4^3}$. This example illustrates the definition of a *negative exponent*.

Negative exponent: for any nonzero number x and any integer a, $x^{-a} = \dfrac{1}{x^a}$.

Example 6   Write the expression 2^{-3} without exponents and simplify.

Answer

$2^{-3} = \dfrac{1}{2^3}$ 1. Change to positive exponent form.

$\phantom{2^{-3}} = \dfrac{1}{2 \cdot 2 \cdot 2}$ 2. Expand the denominator.

$\phantom{2^{-3}} = \dfrac{1}{8}$ 3. Write the standard numeral.

Example 7   Write the expression $(-2)^{-5}$ without exponents and simplify.

Answer

$(-2)^{-5} = \dfrac{1}{(-2)^5}$ 1. Change to positive exponent form.

$\phantom{(-2)^{-5}} = \dfrac{1}{-2(-2)(-2)(-2)(-2)}$ 2. Expand the denominator.

$\phantom{(-2)^{-5}} = \dfrac{1}{-32}$, or $-\dfrac{1}{32}$ 3. Write the standard numeral.

Example 8   Write the expression $\dfrac{1}{x^5}$ with a negative exponent and simplify.

Answer

$\dfrac{1}{x^5} = x^{-5}$

Write each expression using exponents. Do not write as fractions.

1. $-4(-4)$

2. $\dfrac{1}{7 \cdot 7 \cdot 7 \cdot 7}$

3. $\dfrac{1}{9 \cdot 9 \cdot 9}$

4. $\dfrac{c^7}{c^3}$

5. $3 \times 5 \times 3 \times 5 \times 3$

6. $\dfrac{7^5}{7}$

Write each of the following as a standard numeral.

7. 3^{-2}

8. $(-2)^{-4}$

9. $(-5)^3$

■ A. Exercises

Write in exponential form without fractions.

1. $2 \cdot 2 \cdot 2$

2. $a \cdot a$

3. $\dfrac{1}{a}$

4. $5 \cdot 5 \cdot 5 \cdot 5$

5. $h \cdot h \cdot h$

6. $\dfrac{1}{x \cdot x \cdot x}$

Write in expanded form. Simplify if possible.

7. x^3

8. 13^2

9. x^{-2}

10. y^5

11. $(-7)^3$

12. 5^{-3}

13. 6^1

14. $1{,}243^0$

15. 10^4

16. $x^2 y^3$

■ B. Exercises

17. Tell what each of the following equals: 3^0, 0^3, and 0^0.

Simplify.

18. $c^4 \cdot c^7$

19. $p^3 \cdot p$

20. $m^6 \cdot m^2 \cdot m^9$

21. $x^4 \cdot x^5 \cdot x^2$

22. $y \cdot y^7$

23. $(z^2)^3$

24. $15^4 \div 15^3$

25. $\dfrac{a^{10}}{a^2}$

26. $y^9 \div (y^2 \cdot y^5)$

27. $\dfrac{b^4}{b}$

28. $\dfrac{8^4 \cdot 8^3}{8^6 \cdot 8}$

29. $(x^4)^2 \div x^5$

30. $\dfrac{x^4 y^5}{x^3 y^2}$

31. $(z^a)^b$

32. $y^{3a} \cdot y^b$

33. $\dfrac{x^{4a}}{x^{2b}}$

Write each of the following as a standard numeral.

34. $2^3 + 2^2$

35. $3^2 + 3^4$

36. $(-2)^2 \cdot 2^3$

37. $-2^2 \cdot 2^3$

38. $5^2 + 5^3$

39. $2^3 + 3^2$

40. $2^3 \cdot 3^2$

41. $-2^3 \cdot 2^2$

42. $(-2)^2 + 2^2$

■ C. Exercises

Write an expression for each of the following quantities. Express all answers in exponential form.

43. the volume of a cube that is 6 units on an edge

44. the area of a square that is 5.2 units on a side

45. the perimeter of square that is 8 units on each side

46. the surface area of a cube with edges 6 units long; the volume of the cube

47. the volume of a rectangular prism 25 units by 5 units by 5 units

■ Dominion thru Math

The moon takes 29.5 earth days to go through its phases and thus make one revolution about its axis. This is called a lunar day.

48. The average temperatures on the moon range from 100°C at noon to –173°C half a lunar day later. What is the change in average temperature during this half lunar day?

49. How many earth hours are in a half lunar day? What is the temperature change on the moon in degrees Celsius per earth hour?

CUMULATIVE REVIEW

Simplify. [1.2–1.5]

50. $-7 + 9 - 3$

51. $-63 \div 3 \div (4 - 7)$

52. $3 - 8 + 9 + (-1)$

53. $7 - 2 - 32 + (-14)$

54. $(78 \div 3) - (2 \cdot 11)$

55. $-8(-2)(4)(8)$

56. Mt. Everest is 8,850 m high. The Dead Sea reaches a depth of 400 m below sea level. Find the difference between the height of Mt. Everest and the depth of the Dead Sea. [1.3]

57. What is 18 more than –45? [1.2]

58. A multiple choice test is graded based on the following: correct answer = 5 points, incorrect answer = –2 points, no answer = –1 point. If a student answers fifteen questions correctly, answers four questions incorrectly, and does not give an answer for two questions, how many points will he earn? [1.2, 1.4]

59. Find the quotient of –456 and –8. [1.5]

Over three thousand people have climbed Mt. Everest's 29,029 ft.

PROBLEM SOLVING

Introduction

George Polya was born in Budapest, Hungary, in 1887. He was of Jewish ancestry, though his parents converted to the Roman Catholic Church before he was born. Before moving to the United States in 1940 because of the persecution of Jews in Europe, Polya wrote a book called *How to Solve It*. This book, originally written in German, was translated into English and sold over one million copies. It has been translated into seventeen different languages. Polya died in Palo Alto, California, in 1985.

Most math textbooks have strategies used for solving problems, including guessing, trial and error, plausible reasoning, and so on. But Polya's book *How to Solve It* introduced a general strategy that has been used in many math textbooks ever since. His four problem-solving steps are as follows:

1. Understand the problem.
2. Devise a plan to solve the problem.
3. Carry out the plan.
4. Look back.

The second step, devising a plan, seems to be the most difficult step for most math students. Planning a solution requires creative mathematical thinking to bring together an effective and efficient plan. The problem-solving features throughout this book highlight different strategies of problem solving that can assist you in designing your solution.

The *four-point checklist* is a set of problem-solving guidelines designed to help you solve word problems. It comes directly from Polya's four problem-solving steps.

The Four-Point Checklist
1. **Read** to understand the question and identify the needed data.
2. **Plan** what to do to solve the problem.
3. **Solve** the problem by carrying out the plan.
4. **Check** to make sure the solution is reasonable.

The most important aspect of step 1 is identifying the question. Ask yourself, "What am I trying to find?" Step 2 requires you to use your mathematical knowledge to create an effective plan. For some questions, this may involve identifying only the correct operations to perform. Once you have a plan, step 3 directs you to actually carry out that plan. Step 4 verifies the accuracy of your calculations. Use estimation to be sure your answer is reasonable.

You may be asked to write out the plan for the solution before solving the given problem. The example on the next page shows the method expected when identifying each step.

| Example | Tickets for the school play cost $5 for adults and $2.25 for children. If 94 adults and 141 children attended the play, what was the total amount of ticket money collected? |

Answer

1. **Read**: Determine what the question is and identify the given information.

    Question: How much money was collected for tickets?

    Given information: Ticket prices were $5 for adults and $2.25 for children; 94 adults and 141 children attended the play.

2. **Plan**: Determine how the given information relates to what you are trying to find.

    Let c be the total cost.

    c = (number of adult tickets × cost per ticket) + (number of child tickets × cost per ticket)

3. **Solve**: Use the plan to answer the question.

    $c = (94 \times 5) + (141 \times 2.25)$

    $= 470 + 317.25$

    $= \$787.25$

4. **Check**: Is your answer reasonable? Use estimation to check the answer.

    $(90 \times 5) + (150 \times 2) = 450 + 300 = 750$

    The answer is reasonable.

■ Exercises

Solve the following by writing out the four steps according to the four-point checklist.

1. Amy bought a 10 lb. bag of potatoes for $4.29, 3 lb. of apples at $1.29/lb., and a honey-baked ham for $16.25. How much change did she receive from a $50 bill?

2. Whitewater Rentals has 39 canoes and 25 solo kayaks. The canoes rent for $45 for a six-hour trip. The solo kayaks rent for $49 for the same trip. One day 8 canoes and 4 kayaks were not rented. How much money was collected for rentals that day?

3. Twenty-five men volunteered to lay 1,450 pieces of sod around a new church building. If each man was given an equal number of pieces, how many pieces would each man get?

4. Karina purchased 5 yd. of fabric costing $7.99/yd., two spools of thread at $1.25/spool, and a pattern costing $5.75. What was the total amount of her purchase before tax?

White water like this is not for the faint of heart.

5. Dan bought a 5 lb. bag of sugar for $2.19, 2 lb. of apples at $1.09/lb., and a 20 lb. box of laundry detergent for $16.59. How much change did he receive after paying with a $20 bill and a $10 bill?

6. The eighth-grade class plans to produce a three-act play. The set for the play will cost $420, the play scripts will cost $250, and the costumes for the play will cost $175. What will be the total cost of the play? If tickets for the play cost $3 and 350 people attend, what will be the total income from the play? Find the profit or loss for the class on this venture.

7. The soccer team plans to take five trips to visit schools for games this season. The roundtrip mileage for the five trips is as follows: 44 mi., 126 mi., 60 mi., 188 mi., and 244 mi. What is the total mileage for the trips? If the school budgets $0.42/mi. for gasoline, what will be the total budgeted for the trips?

8. Tri-City Rent-All has six mowers and three tillers that can each be rented for $29 per day. One day two mowers and one tiller were not rented. How much money was collected in rent for the machines that day?

1.7 ⌐ Order of Operations

Our God delights in orderliness and regularity (1 Cor. 14:40). God's love for order is evident in every part of His creation. If we are to do a good job of managing God's world, we have to learn about the orderliness of that world and learn how to work within it. The importance of order is especially apparent when working with mathematical operations.

Without a designated order of operations, the following expression could be simplified to several different values.

$$2 + 8 \cdot 3 - 6 \div 2$$

The batter "on deck" is next in the batting order, and the player on the dugout steps who follows him is "in the hole."

One person may get 27, another may get 12, and yet another may get 10. All of these are incorrect calculations based on the *order of operations* agreed upon by mathematicians.

Order of Operations
1. Symbols of grouping—evaluate quantities within symbols of grouping first.
2. Exponents—evaluate a term with an exponent before performing other operations.
3. Multiplication and division—perform these operations in order from left to right.
4. Addition and subtraction—perform these operations last, in order from left to right.

Consider the numerical expression $3 + 4 \cdot 5$. Performing the operations from left to right in the order that they are listed gives the answer 35. If the multiplication is done before the addition, the result is 23. According to the order of operations, 23 is the correct answer.

Incorrect
$3 + 4 \cdot 5$
$7 \cdot 5$
35

Correct
$3 + 4 \cdot 5$
$3 + 20$
23

Skill Check 1

Which operation should be performed first?

1. $4 \cdot 6 + 2$ 2. $15 - 8 \cdot 5$ 3. $4 + 6 \div 2$

4. $16 \div 8 \cdot 2$ 5. $4(5 - 2)$ 6. $2 \cdot 3^2$

Example 1   Simplify $2 + 8 \cdot 3 - 6 \div 2$.

Answer

$2 + 8 \cdot 3 - 6 \div 2$

$2 + 24 - 3$ 1. Perform the multiplication and division from left to right. Since they are not dependent on one another, both operations can be done in the same step.

$26 - 3$ 2. Perform the addition and subtraction in order from left to right.

23

Example 2   Simplify $2 + 3^2 \times 4$.

Answer

$2 + 3^2 \times 4$

$2 + 9 \times 4$ 1. Eliminate the exponent first.

$2 + 36$ 2. Multiply before adding.

38 3. Add.

Parentheses ( ), brackets [ ], and braces { } are common grouping symbols. A fraction bar and absolute value sign are also considered symbols of grouping. It is customary to use parentheses for groupings unless you have a grouping within a grouping, such as $2[5 + 3(12 - 4)]$. If grouping symbols contain more than one operation, as in $3 + (2 - 18 \div 3)$, evaluate within the parentheses using the order of operations. In this case the division is done before the subtraction.

Example 3   Simplify $(12 + 9) \div 3$.

Answer

$(12 + 9) \div 3$

$21 \div 3$ 1. Perform the operation inside the parentheses first.

7 2. Divide.

Example 4   Simplify $3 + (13 - 2^3)$.

Answer

$3 + (13 - 2^3)$

$3 + (13 - 8)$ 1. Simplify the exponent first.

$3 + 5$ 2. Perform the operation inside the parentheses.

8 3. Add.

Example 5   Simplify $14 - 3(17 - 4) + (12 - 5)^2$.

Answer

$14 - 3(17 - 4) + (12 - 5)^2$

$14 - 3(13) + 7^2$ 1. Perform the operations inside the parentheses. They can be done simultaneously since they do not affect one another.

$14 - 3(13) + 49$ 2. Evaluate the exponential term.

$14 - 39 + 49$ 3. Multiply.

$-25 + 49$ 4. Subtract.

24 5. Add.

Simplify.

1. $18 \div 6 + 24$ 2. $(3 - 7)^3$ 3. $13 - 2(4 - 7)$

4. $48 \div (8 + 4)$ 5. $9 - 5^2$ 6. $5(8 - 3) - 2(3 - 8)$

Example 6   Simplify $4^2 - \{7[-16 + (-3)(-5)] - 8\}$.

Answer

$4^2 - \{7[-16 + (-3)(-5)] - 8\}$

$16 - \{7[-16 + 15] - 8\}$ 1. Simplify the exponent. The multiplication inside the brackets can also be done because it is not affected by the exponent.

$16 - \{7[-1] - 8\}$ 2. Add inside the brackets.

$16 - \{-7 - 8\}$ 3. Multiply inside the braces.

$16 - \{-15\}$ 4. Subtract inside the braces.

31 5. Subtract.

Example 7   Simplify $\dfrac{7 + 9}{2(4)}$.

Answer

$\dfrac{7 + 9}{2(4)}$

$\dfrac{16}{8}$ 1. The fraction bar is a symbol of grouping. Do what is grouped in the numerator and denominator before dividing.

2 2. Divide.

Example 8   Simplify $|-4 + 3(-6)| - 5(-7 + 3 \cdot 6)$.

Answer

$|-4 + 3(-6)| - 5(-7 + 3 \cdot 6)$

$|-4 + (-18)| - 5(-7 + 18)$ 1. Multiply inside the absolute value sign and inside the parentheses.

$|-22| - 5(11)$ 2. Do the addition inside the absolute value sign and inside the parentheses.

$22 - 5(11)$ 3. Evaluate the absolute value of -22.

$22 - 55$ 4. Multiply.

-33 5. Subtract.

Simplify.

1. $2[-4(20 - 3 \cdot 5) + 7]$ 2. $\dfrac{28 \div 4}{2 + 12}$

3. $24 \div 2|4 - (3 + 7)|$ 4. $2\{[(2 + 3)^2 - 15]^3 - 50\}$

⊕ Invention

The first truly mechanical calculator was invented in 1641 by the French mathematician Blaise Pascal. Prior to this invention only the Chinese abacus and the Japanese soroban could be identified as calculators, and they simply used beads on a wire. The Pascaline (named after the inventor) consisted of a series of eight dials, each with the digits 0 through 9, interconnected so that each dial from right to left increased by a power of ten. For example, one complete turn of the units dial would click the adjacent tens dial one number. The operating principle of this calculator matches what is used even today in a car odometer or the registers of a water meter. Mechanical calculators were still used into the mid-twentieth century, when the invention of the microchip prompted a revolutionary change in calculators.

■ A. Exercises

Simplify.

1. $-3 \cdot 7 - 5$
2. $12 + 4 \cdot 22$
3. $(10 - 2) \div 4$
4. $37 - 2(9 + 3)$
5. $180 \div 6 + 7$
6. $21 \div (9 - 6)$
7. $7 + 3(2)$
8. $9(15 - 82)$
9. $8(9) - 25$
10. $11 + 24 \div 8$
11. $13 - 6 + 8$
12. $8 \cdot 9 \div 12$
13. $12 - 81 \div 3$
14. $24 - 5(4)$

■ B. Exercises

Simplify.

15. $16 + (3 \cdot 14 - 17)$
16. $35 \div (24 - 17) + 12$
17. $\dfrac{11 + 3}{2 - 9}$
18. $13(7 - 18 \div 6)$
19. $16 + [(21 - 13)33]$
20. $(20 + 4 \cdot 7) \div 8$
21. $2(4) + 3(-6)$
22. $15 \cdot 4 - 18 \div 2 + 3$
23. $4 - 1 + 10 \div 2$
24. $18 - 15 \div 3 + 7 \cdot 2$
25. $8 + 12 \div 4 \cdot 5$
26. $3 + 9(5) - \dfrac{8}{2}$
27. $|15 \cdot 4 - 18| \div (-2)$
28. $2^5 - (6 + 8 \div 4) + 8^2$
29. $\dfrac{24}{8} + 4(9) - 15$
30. $(36 \div 3 + 4) \cdot |3 - 5|$
31. $(18 - 8 \cdot 2)(4 + 3 \cdot 7)$
32. $24 - [(3 + 2)(11 - 8)]$
33. $\dfrac{8(29 - 7 \times 4)}{4 + 7 - 8 + 1} - 3(2) \div 6$
34. $\dfrac{2^4 + 4(5 - 3)}{18 - 4 \times 3 + 6} + 3^5$

■ C. Exercises

Simplify.

35. $-15 + 21(-3 - 4) + |(3 - 5) \cdot 4| \div (-4)$

36. $8 + (-4)^{-2 + 5} - |-7 - 4|(-2) + [6 - (3 - 4)]$

37. John has 6 packages of baseball cards with 9 cards per pack. If he sells 19 cards and then buys another pack, how many cards will he have?

38. Stenson has 39 baseball cards. If he buys 7 more packages with 12 cards per pack and 2 packs are left out in the rain and ruined, how many cards will he then have?

39. While at the seashore, Joanie collected 28 clam shells and 16 sea urchins and then gave half of each to her sister. Jake gave Joanie $\frac{1}{4}$ as many sea urchins as she originally had. How many shells and sea urchins total did Joanie take home?

CUMULATIVE REVIEW

Write in expanded form. [1.6]

40. x^4

41. $x^6 y^2$

Simplify. Leave the answers in exponential form. [1.6]

42. $a^3 \cdot a^5$

43. $(x^5)^3$

Simplify. [1.6]

44. $4^2 - 4^3$ 45. $(3^2)^{-1}$ 46. $7^2(7)$ 47. $2^3 - 3^2$

Simplify; then write the simplified numbers in order from least to greatest by using <. [1.1, 1.6]

48. $17, |3 - 18|, 4^2, 19(-1)$

49. $2^4, 3^2, 2^3, 3^3$

1.8 Scientific Notation

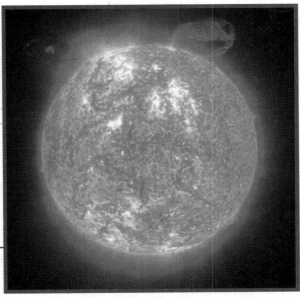

The sun has a surface temperature of about 6,000°C or 11,000°F.

You cannot exercise dominion over God's world unless you are able to measure its various parts. One challenge faced in measuring God's world is that it is huge. The numbers you have to deal with are large and difficult to manage. For example, the distance from the earth to the sun is about 93,000,000 mi. (about 150,000,000 km).

Numbers as large as those above require a simpler way to write and calculate with them. Scientific notation is used to express very large or very small numbers in a convenient form.

Definition

A number is in **scientific notation** if it is expressed as the product of a number between 1 and 10 and a power of ten.

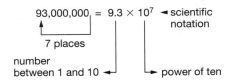

$93,000,000 = 9.3 \times 10^7$ ◄ scientific notation

7 places

number between 1 and 10 ◄

► power of ten

In the previous example, the decimal point was placed after the 9 to form a number between 1 and 10. The power of ten is 7 because 9.3 must be multiplied by 10,000,000, or 10^7, to equal the original number. Seven is also the number of places the decimal must move to the right to return 9.3 to 93,000,000.

If a decimal numeral between 0 and 1 is expressed in scientific notation, negative exponents are used. Consider the following example.

The decimal point is placed after the 4 to form a number between 1 and 10. Multiplying 4.5 by $\frac{1}{100,000}$, or $\frac{1}{10^5}$, gives the original number. Since $\frac{1}{10^5} = 10^{-5}$, the power of ten is negative.

$$0.000045 = 4.5 \times \frac{1}{100,000} = 4.5 \times \frac{1}{10^5} = 4.5 \times 10^{-5}$$

Example 1   Write the following numbers in scientific notation.

a. 1,670,000

b. 0.00059

Answer

a. $1{,}670{,}000 = 1.67 \times 10^6$ Place the decimal point after the 1 to form 1.67, a number between 1 and 10. The number must be multiplied by 10^6 to obtain the original number. (The decimal point must move 6 places to the right.)

b. $0.00059 = 5.9 \times 10^{-4}$ Place the decimal point after the 5 to form 5.9, a number between 1 and 10. The number must be multiplied by 10^{-4} to obtain the original number, so the power of ten is negative. (The decimal point must move 4 places to the left.)

Skill Check 1

Write the missing exponent.

1. $39{,}000 = 3.9 \times 10^?$

2. $0.00031 = 3.1 \times 10^?$

Write the missing factor.

3. $72{,}500{,}000 = \underline{\quad} \times 10^7$

4. $0.00009 = \underline{\quad} \times 10^{-5}$

Write the following numbers in scientific notation.

5. 0.00000321

6. 640,000,000

To change a number written in scientific notation into standard form, multiply by the power of ten. The exponent tells how many places the decimal point is moved. If the power of ten is positive, move the decimal point to the right. Multiplying by a negative power of ten is the same as dividing by the positive power of ten. Therefore, move the decimal point to the left. Annex zeros as needed.

Example 2 Write the following numbers in standard form.

a. 6.37×10^5

b. 8.4×10^{-3}

Answer

a. $6.37 \times 10^5 = 637{,}000$ 6.37 is multiplied by 10^5, so move the decimal point 5 places to the right.

b. $8.4 \times 10^{-3} = 0.0084$ 8.4 is multiplied by 10^{-3}, so move the decimal point 3 places to the left. This is the same as dividing by 1,000.

Skill Check 2

Write the following numbers in standard form.

1. 4.9×10^3 2. 3.1×10^{-2} 3. 6×10^6

The monumental increase in technology has led to the need for additional units to describe very large and very small quantities. The following example deals with a very small length. The prefix "nano" (one billionth) is used.

Example 3 Write the following distances in scientific notation.

a. the speed of light, about 186,000 mi./sec.

b. 3.6 nanometers in meters (a nanometer is one billionth of a meter)

Answer

a. $186{,}000 = 1.86 \times 10^5$ mi./sec.   Place the decimal point to the right of the 1 to form a number between 1 and 10. Multiply 1.86 by 10^5 to obtain the original number.

b. 1 nanometer $= 0.000000001$ m   Express 1 nanometer in terms of meters. Change the decimal
                $= 10^{-9}$ m   value to a power of ten.

    3.6 nanometers $= 3.6 \times 10^{-9}$ m   Multiply 3.6 by the number of meters in 1 nanometer. The expression is in scientific notation since it is a number between 1 and 10 times a power of ten.

■ A. Exercises

Write the missing exponent.

1. $98.1 = 9.81 \times 10^?$

2. $-0.00000737 = -7.37 \times 10^?$

3. $0.057 = 5.7 \times 10^?$

4. $6{,}530{,}000 = 6.53 \times 10^?$

5. $1{,}050{,}000{,}000 = 1.05 \times 10^?$

6. $-0.00000000089 = -8.9 \times 10^?$

Write the missing factor.

7. $56{,}300 = ? \times 10^4$

8. $8.7 = ? \times 10^0$

9. $0.0101 = ? \times 10^{-2}$

10. $-12{,}700 = ? \times 10^4$

11. $630{,}000 = ? \times 10^5$

12. $-0.000601 = ? \times 10^{-4}$

■ B. Exercises

Write the following numbers in scientific notation.

13. 63   14. 0.0703   15. −34,700   16. −0.0000924

17. 0.00481   18. 5,120   19. 700   20. 0.00000032

Write the following numbers in standard form.

21. -9.32×10^{-7} 22. 3.75×10^{-3} 23. 3.84×10^{4} 24. -8.2×10^{5}

25. 7.66×10^{0} 26. -4.29×10^{3} 27. 2.87×10^{-2} 28. 5.02×10^{2}

29. The average distance of Earth from the sun is 149,500,000 km. Write this in scientific notation.

30. The average distance of Mars from the sun is 227,000,000 km. Write this in scientific notation.

31. If NASA launched an Earth-to-Mars expedition when the two planets are farthest apart, the mission would have to travel more than 376,500,000 km. Write this in scientific notation.

32. If NASA launched an Earth-to-Mars expedition when the two planets are closest, approximately how far would it have to travel? Write this in scientific notation.

■ C. Exercises

33. If the Earth-to-Mars spaceship averages 35,000 km/hr., to the nearest hour, how long would it take to travel from Earth to Mars when they are farthest apart (exercise 31)? State your answer in hours, and then convert it to days (round to the nearest whole number).

34. If the Earth-to-Mars spaceship averages 35,000 km/hr., to the nearest hour, how long would it take to travel from Earth to Mars when they are closest (exercise 32)? State your answer in hours, and then convert it to days (round to the nearest whole number).

35. Rewrite $(4.02 \times 10^{5}) + (3.19 \times 10^{5})$ using the Distributive Property and simplify.

36. Use the Commutative and Associative Properties of Multiplication to show how to multiply the numbers $A \times 10^{a}$ and $B \times 10^{b}$ in scientific notation. Show all steps with the property used.

37. Use the appropriate properties to show how to divide $A \times 10^{a}$ by $B \times 10^{b}$ in scientific notation. Show all steps with the property used.

CUMULATIVE REVIEW

Simplify. [1.7]

38. $|-12| + (-7)$ 39. $2^{3} + 3^{2}$ 40. $5^{2} - 7(4 + 2) + 14$

41. $|3 - 2^{4}| + 25 \div 5$ 42. $6[-3 - 2^{3} \cdot 4(1 - 6)] + 4$ 43. $(32 \times 10 - 32) \div 3$

44. $5 - 2^{3} + 7(9) - 18 \div 6$ 45. $3(-4 - 11)^{2} + (11 - 4)^{2}$ 46. $4 - 2(3)(5 - 17)^{3}$

47. $-3(5 - 6^{3} \cdot 2)$

MATH & SCRIPTURE

Daniel's Influence

Archeologists have found several hundred clay tablets written in cuneiform that provide a clear understanding of Mesopotamian, or Chaldean, mathematics (about 1800–1600 BC). This system of numeration, called the Babylonian system, continued in use for centuries, until around 586–583 BC. Daniel no doubt had to learn and use the Babylonian system of numeration during his time in Babylon.

In Daniel 1:20 the Scriptures declare that Daniel and his three friends were far superior in wisdom and understanding to the wise men of Babylon. Daniel became the governor and leader of this highly educated society (Dan. 2:48), influencing many people. Probably one of his purposes in writing the book of Daniel was to influence a non-Jewish audience. Most of chapters 2–7 were written in Aramaic, the main international language of that time.

Consider the following verses that relate to Daniel and his three friends as captives in Babylon and answer the related questions.

1. What is the reason given in Daniel 1:17 that Daniel and his three friends were superior?

2. According to Daniel 5:12, what qualities of intellect did Daniel possess?

3. According to Daniel 6:4, how good was Daniel in doing his duties for the king?

Considering what Daniel writes in Daniel 7:1–14, answer the following questions based on Matthew 2:1–12.

4. The "wise men" in Matthew 2 were magi, descendants of religious scholars who were part of the Medo-Persian empire Daniel served later in his life. What prompted these wise men to make their long journey?

5. What title did they give to Christ?

6. What does Daniel say the "Son of man" receives from the "Ancient of days" in Daniel 7:13–14?

7. What gifts did the visitors give to Christ?

8. What do these gifts suggest about the economic status of the visitors?

9. What could have prompted the reaction of these visitors as recorded in Matthew 2:10?

In light of the topics in this lesson, consider the following events God brought about so that the times were ready (full) for the coming of the Messiah (Gal. 4:4–5).

• The warning of an angel of the Lord (Matt. 2:13) made it necessary for Joseph and Mary to flee with Jesus. This protected Jesus from Herod's murder of the babies less than two years of age.

• This flight and the following time spent in Egypt required money, which was provided by the gifts of the wise men.

• The wise men knew about the Messiah from a source in their own country. This source was very likely the prophecies of Daniel, who came to Babylon as a young captive from Jerusalem.

Infinite Truths

As for these four children, God gave them knowledge and skill in all learning and wisdom.
*Daniel 1:17*a

Chapter 1 Review

Vocabulary

absolute value	integers	squared
additive inverse	negative exponent	subtraction
cubed	opposites	variable
exponent	scientific notation	zero power

Write the opposite of each of the following numbers.

1. 15

2. –7

Write the integers in order from least to greatest by using <.

3. 9, –8, –9

4. –15, –21, 0

Write the absolute value of each of the following.

5. |–62|

6. |32|

7. Show the following addition on a number line: $4 + (–7)$.

Add.

8. –19 + 12

9. –23 + (–17)

10. 42 + (–51)

11. –17 + (–12)

12. 22 + (–8) + 3

13. –8 + 4 + (–7)

14. Write the definition of subtraction in words and symbols.

Subtract.

15. 9 – 15

16. –7 – 2

17. 3 – (–6)

18. –14 – (–7)

19. 12 – (–12)

20. 72 – (–58) – 62

21. 29 – (–8)

22. –4 – 9

23. 8 – 14

Multiply.

24. 4(–6)

25. –7(2)(6)

26. 9(–12)(5)(–8)

27. State a rule for multiplying integers based on the signs of the factors.

Divide.

28. –48 ÷ 6

29. –72 ÷ (–4)

30. $\frac{125}{–5}$

Simplify.

31. (–15 – 13) ÷ (–7)

32. –56 ÷ (–4) ÷ (–2)

33. –9 + 3(–4) – 6

Write in exponential form without fractions.

34. $9 \cdot 9 \cdot 9 \cdot 9$

35. $\dfrac{x \cdot x \cdot x \cdot x \cdot x \cdot x}{x \cdot x \cdot x \cdot x \cdot x \cdot x \cdot x}$

36. $\dfrac{1}{m \cdot m \cdot m \cdot m \cdot m}$

Simplify.

37. $x^8 \cdot x^2$

38. $\dfrac{n^9}{n^5}$

39. $4^2 + 2^4$

40. $y^6 \cdot y^2 \cdot y^4$

41. $(–3)^4 – 3$

42. $–3^4 – 3$

43. $4^3 \cdot 3^2$

Simplify.

44. $3 \cdot 6 + (-5) - 7$

45. $-21(4 + 5 \cdot 2) + (-16)$

46. $|-8 + (-5)|(-2) + 6 \div 3$

47. $\{[3 + 5(-2 - 9) - 8] - 3\} \div 3^2$

Write the following numbers in scientific notation.

48. 0.00000038

49. 749,000,000

Write the following numbers in standard form.

50. 3.95×10^{12}

51. 9.8×10^{-9}

52. Give the mathematical significance of Daniel 1:17a.

2

EXPRESSIONS

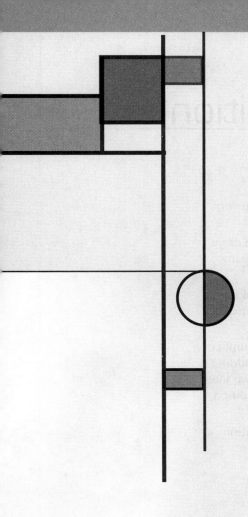

We are reminded in 1 Corinthians 6 that our bodies are the temple of the Holy Spirit and that we are to glorify God in our bodies. We are also told in 1 Corinthians 10:31 that whether we eat or drink or whatever we do, we are to do it all to the glory of God. Glorifying God in our bodies refers not only to our activities, but to our lifestyle and care of these temples.

Are you physically fit? The President's Council on Physical Fitness reports that at least 15% of American youth are overweight or obese. There are serious consequences in our country from poor nutrition and physical inactivity. The annual cost in the United States because of obesity is $117 billion, along with an annual cost for type 2 diabetes of $132 billion. Christians who are not physically fit not only hinder their service for Christ but also are at a risk for multiple diseases. The command to exercise dominion (Gen. 1:28) is not about fish, trees, and birds only. It also concerns self dominion—learning to manage our own bodies for the glory of God and the benefit of others. In this chapter you will work Dominion thru Math exercises that will help you determine your fitness to serve and help you improve and strengthen your mind.

After this chapter you should be able to

1. identify uses of and apply the properties of real numbers.

2. apply the Distributive Property to expand or simplify a mathematical expression and to find products mentally.

3. evaluate algebraic expressions.

4. simplify algebraic expressions.

5. write word phrases as mathematical expressions.

6. round numbers to a given place value.

7. estimate sums, differences, products, and quotients.

2.1 Properties of Addition

Principles are basic truths or laws. There are many types of principles that govern our lives, such as scientific, mathematical, and biblical principles.

A biblical principle often called the golden rule is found in Luke 6:31—"And as ye would that men should do to you, do ye also to them likewise." It is necessary to know biblical principles to be able to apply them to your life.

It is also necessary to know mathematical principles, such as the properties of numbers, in order to understand and work with expressions. The following properties describe how integers behave under the operation of addition.

The *Closure Property of Addition* applies to some sets of numbers. A set of numbers is *closed* for addition if you add any pair of numbers from the set, including adding a number to itself, and the sum is also in the set. For example, if you add any two integers, the sum will be an integer. Therefore, the set of integers is closed for addition.

Not all sets of numbers are closed for addition. Consider the set of odd integers. Since $3 + 3 = 6$, an even number, the set of odd integers is not closed for addition.

Closure Property of Addition
For all integers a and b, $a + b$ is an integer.

In previous math courses you learned several properties that apply to addition. The *Commutative Property of Addition* allows the order of the addends to change without affecting the sum.

$$9 + 2 \; ? \; 2 + 9$$
$$11 = 11$$

Commutative Property of Addition
For all integers a and b, $a + b = b + a$.

Applying the Commutative Property to $-5 + 3$ gives $3 + (-5)$. This expression has two consecutive signs, $+$ followed by $-$. It is not in simplest form. The expression $-5 + 3$ is also *equivalent* to $3 - 5$, which is in simplest form. "Equivalent" means that two expressions represent the same value. Follow the steps below to verify that the expressions $-5 + 3$ and $3 - 5$ are equivalent.

1. $-5 + 3 = 3 + (-5)$ Commutative Property of Addition
2. $3 - 5 = 3 + (-5)$ definition of subtraction
3. $-5 + 3 = 3 - 5$ Since both $-5 + 3$ and $3 - 5$ are equal to the same quantity, they must equal each other.

This example shows that adding a negative is equivalent to subtracting its opposite.

Example 1   Use the Commutative Property to write an equivalent expression for each of the following. Be sure it is in simplest form.

a. $-9 + 4$

b. $x + 9$

  Answer

a. $-9 + 4 = 4 + (-9) = 4 - 9$ Adding a negative is equivalent to subtracting.

b. $x + 9 = 9 + x$

The *Associative Property of Addition* allows you to change the grouping when adding three or more numbers. Parentheses are often used to show grouping. Notice that the order of the addends does not change, only the grouping.

$$(2 + 5) + 6 \; ? \; 2 + (5 + 6)$$
$$7 + 6 \; ? \; 2 + 11$$
$$13 = 13$$

Associative Property of Addition
For all integers a, b, and c, $a + (b + c) = (a + b) + c$.

Example 2   Use the Associative Property to write an equivalent expression for each of the following.

a. $(-8 + 17) + 43$

b. $-9 + (7 + x)$

  Answer

a. $(-8 + 17) + 43 = -8 + (17 + 43)$ Change the grouping to 17 with 43.

b. $-9 + (7 + x) = (-9 + 7) + x$ Change the grouping to 7 with -9.

Skill Check 1

Name the property or properties of addition illustrated by each of the following.

1. $-5 + 9 = 9 - 5$

2. $(a + x) + 9 = (x + a) + 9$

3. $8 + (3 + y) = (8 + 3) + y$

4. $(-4 + b) + 3 = -4 + (3 + b)$

5. Is the set of whole numbers closed for subtraction?

6. Is the set of negative integers closed for addition?

Using one of the properties above, write an equivalent expression for each of the following. Be sure it is in simplest form.

7. $7 + h$

8. $(8 + m) + (-4)$

Zero is unique in the operation of addition: when you add zero to any number, you get that number. Therefore, zero is called the *identity element of addition*.

$$429 + 0 = 429$$

Identity Property of Addition

For any integer a, $a + 0 = 0 + a = a$.

To find the sum $4 + (-4)$, you take the difference of their absolute values.

$$4 + (-4) = |4| - |-4| = 4 - 4 = 0$$

When two numbers have a sum of zero, they are called *additive inverses*. Four and -4 are additive inverses. The term *opposite* is another name for additive inverse, as you learned in Chapter 1.

Definition

Additive inverses are two numbers whose sum is zero.

Inverse Property of Addition

For any integer a, $a + (-a) = -a + a = 0$.

Notice that adding a number and its additive inverse results in zero, the identity element of addition.

Example 3

What are the additive inverses of 17 and -14?

Answer

-17 is the additive inverse of 17, since $17 + (-17) = 0$.
14 is the additive inverse of -14, since $-14 + 14 = 0$.

Example 4

Use the properties of addition to find the value of each variable. Name the properties used.

a. $x = 6 + (-6)$
b. $y + 0 = 19$
c. $(9 + 2) - 6 = x + (2 - 6)$

Answer

a. $x = 6 + (-6)$
   $x = 0$

Inverse Property of Addition—the sum of a number and its additive inverse is zero.

b. $y + 0 = 19$
   $y = 19$

Identity Property of Addition—the sum of any number and zero equals that number, so $y + 0 = y$.

c. $(9 + 2) - 6 = x + (2 - 6)$
   $9 + (2 - 6) = x + (2 - 6)$
      $x = 9$

Associative Property of Addition—change the grouping on the left side to make it similar to the right side. This makes the value of x easy to identify.

Skill Check 2

Give the additive inverse of each number.

1. -54
2. -6
3. 114

Use the properties of addition to find the value of each variable.

4. $-8 + a = 0$
5. $(4 + 8) - 5 = b + (8 - 5)$
6. $2 + (-2) = c$
7. $12 + 8 = 8 + d$

The table below summarizes the properties of addition. Study this table to obtain a good understanding of these important properties.

Property of Addition	Description	Example
Closure For all integers a and b, $a + b$ is an integer.	The sum of any two integers is an integer.	$5 + 9 = 14$; 14 is an integer.
Commutative $a + b = b + a$	Changing the order of the addends does not change the sum.	$8 + 4 = 4 + 8$
Associative $(a + b) + c = a + (b + c)$	Changing the grouping of the addends does not change the sum.	$(-5 + 4) + 6 = -5 + (4 + 6)$
Identity $a + 0 = 0 + a = a$	The sum of any integer and zero equals the original integer.	$-2 + 0 = 0 + (-2) = -2$
Inverse $a + (-a) = -a + a = 0$	The sum of any integer and its additive inverse equals zero, the identity element of addition.	$6 + (-6) = -6 + 6 = 0$

Skill Check 3

Name the property of addition illustrated by each of the following.

1. $(13 + 4) + 7 = 13 + (4 + 7)$ 2. $8 + 6 = 6 + 8$

3. $4 + 0 = 4$ 4. $-24 + 24 = 0$

Use the properties of addition to find the value of each variable. Name the property used.

5. $3 + a = 3$ 6. $(2 + 9) + 4 = 2 + (9 + b)$

7. $c + 5 = 5 + 7$ 8. $d + 32 = 0$

■ A. Exercises

1. What is the identity element for addition?

2. What is the sum of two numbers that are additive inverses?

3. What is the additive inverse of 23?

4. What number is its own additive inverse? Why?

Name the property of addition illustrated by each of the following.

5. $2 + 3 = 3 + 2$ 6. $-5 + 0 = -5$

7. $-3 + (2 + 7) = (-3 + 2) + 7$ 8. $-12 + 12 = 0$

9. Since -3 and 5 are integers, $-3 + 5$ is an integer.

10. $-8 + 5 = 5 - 8$

■ B. Exercises

11. In your own words, explain the Closure Property of Addition.

12. Is the set of even integers closed for addition?

13. Is the set of odd integers closed for addition?

14. Is the set of integers closed for subtraction?

15. Is the set of positive integers closed for subtraction?

Name the property or properties of addition illustrated by each of the following.

16. $(x + y) + 3 = x + (y + 3)$ 17. $3(4 + x) = 3(x + 4)$

18. $(x - 3) + (3 - x) = 0$ 19. $2(0 + 5) = 2(5 + 0)$

20. $(-2 + 3) + 0 = -2 + 3$ 21. $7x + (y - 2z) = (7x + y) - 2z$

22. $-y + (x + z) = (x - y) + z$

Using the numbers –3, 4, and 7, write an equation that illustrates each property of addition.

23. Identity 24. Associative

25. Inverse 26. Commutative

Use the properties of addition to simplify the following.

27. $3 + (-7 + y)$ 28. $-3 + x + 12$

29. $-3 + (x + 5) + 3$ 30. $(-5 + z) + (5 + y)$

■ C. Exercises

The table below is an addition table for a set represented by {*a*, *b*, *c*}.

+	a	b	c
a	b	c	a
b	c	a	b
c	a	b	c

31. Is the set closed? Why?

32. Is the set commutative? Why?

33. Which element is the identity element? Why?

34. What is the inverse of a? Why?

35. A clock has no zero on it. What number serves as the identity number for adding clock times?

36. Based on your answer to exercise 35, what is the inverse of 7 on a clock?

■ Dominion thru Math

One of the simplest measures of body weight is the Body Mass Index (BMI). It is defined by the following ratio: BMI $= \dfrac{\text{weight in kilograms}}{(\text{height in meters})^2}$. For adults, a BMI of 18.5–24.9 is considered normal, 25.0–29.9 is overweight, and 30 or more is obese. (The BMI is not accurate for children and teens who are still growing.)

If a customary measurement is given, convert it to a metric unit using one of the conversion factors below.

$$2.2 \text{ lb.} \approx 1 \text{ kg} \qquad 0.0254 \text{ m} \approx 1 \text{ in.}$$

37. Find the BMI (to the nearest tenth) for the adults listed below. Rate them as normal, overweight, or obese.

   a. Megan is 5 ft. 2 in. and weighs 120 lb.
   b. Richard is 5 ft. 5 in. and weighs 152 lb.
   c. Jason is 5 ft. 9 in. and weighs 184 lb.
   d. Cynthia is 5 ft. 6 in. and weighs 122 lb.

38. Find the weight in pounds (to the nearest tenth) or height in feet and inches of the adults listed below.

   a. Wendy: BMI = 19.5 and 5 ft. 3 in. tall
   b. William: BMI = 28.2 and 6 ft. 2 in. tall
   c. Soledad: BMI = 22.4 and 128 lb.
   d. Gene: BMI = 31.2 and 198 lb.

■ CUMULATIVE REVIEW

Simplify. [1.7]

39. $(-4 - 7) + 8 \cdot 6 + 2^3$

40. $|-15| + 7(2 + 1)^2 - 6$

41. $9(-2)^3 + [(3 - 5) \cdot 7](2)$

42. $24 \div 6 + (-4) - 7(-2)^2$

Write the absolute value of each of the following. [1.1]

43. $|-40 + 17|$

44. $||-21| - |32||$

Write the following numbers in scientific notation. [1.8]

45. 245,000,000

46. 0.00006

47. 0.000115

48. 1,890,000

Joseph, Ruler of Egypt

Joseph was the eleventh son of Jacob and his father's favorite son (Gen. 37:3). Because of this favoritism his brothers hated him. One night in a dream, God told Joseph that his brothers would one day bow down to him (Gen. 37:5–8). When he told his brothers of the dream, they hated him even more. Their hatred led them to sell Joseph into slavery and trick their father into believing that he was dead.

As a slave in Egypt, Joseph found favor with his Egyptian master, Potiphar, and was made manager of Potiphar's household. After being thrown into prison on false charges, Joseph found favor with the keeper of the prison, who eventually entrusted all the prisoners to Joseph's care. Through all of these circumstances, Joseph continued to trust God to take care of his future.

While in prison, Joseph interpreted dreams for Pharaoh's chief butler and baker, and the dreams came true. If Joseph had not been in prison with Pharaoh's chief butler, he would have missed the chance to interpret Pharaoh's dreams. Because of the famine coming to the land, Joseph told Pharaoh to find a wise man and give him the authority to collect and store grain throughout all Egypt. After consulting with his advisers, Pharaoh decided that Joseph was that man. At the age of thirty, Joseph was appointed ruler of the land, second only to Pharaoh.

During the seven good years when the grain was as plenteous "as the sand of the sea" (Gen. 41:48–49), Joseph used his math skills to collect one-fifth of all the people's grain to put into storage for the lean years. When the famine came, Joseph bought their land in exchange for grain. He established an exchange rate of land for grain, allowing the people to stay on the land for a fifth (20%) of all they produced (Gen. 47:24).

Regardless of what happens in your life, you will do well to follow the example of Joseph and never allow hardships to make you bitter. Through all his trials, Joseph's main concern was that he not sin against God (Gen. 39:9). Even in the worst of circumstances, God has a plan for you. Jeremiah 29:11 says, "For I know the thoughts that I think toward you, saith the Lord, thoughts of peace, and not of evil, to give you an expected end." Since you do not know the nature of God's plan, you should prepare for the future by doing your best each day in school. Everything you learn—including math—may become important one day!

2.2 Properties of Multiplication

The properties of multiplication are similar to the properties of addition. You will study the Closure, Commutative, Associative, and Identity Properties in this section. The Inverse Property will appear in Chapter 6, since it involves the use of rational numbers rather than just integers.

If you multiply any two integers together, the product is an integer. This is the essence of the *Closure Property of Multiplication*.

If you plant half a bushel of grain to the acre and harvest 30 bu. per acre, that is a sixty-fold return.

Closure Property of Multiplication

For all integers a and b, ab is an integer.

Does the set of integers have a closure property for division? Divide the integers 3 and 4.

$$3 \div 4 = \frac{3}{4}$$

Since $\frac{3}{4}$ is not an integer, the set of integers is not closed for division.

If you change the order when multiplying two numbers, the product remains the same. Consider the example below.

$$
\begin{array}{r}
28 \\
\times\ 13 \\
\hline
84 \\
28 \\
\hline
364
\end{array}
\qquad
\begin{array}{r}
13 \\
\times\ 28 \\
\hline
104 \\
26 \\
\hline
364
\end{array}
$$

This example demonstrates the *Commutative Property of Multiplication*.

Commutative Property of Multiplication

For any integers a and b, $ab = ba$.

Earlier we discussed three ways to indicate multiplication: $2 \cdot 3$, 2×3, and $2(3)$. When multiplying a number times a variable or two variables, you can write them next to one another without a symbol between them. The notation ab means a times b. The product of 7 and x is written $7x$. Note that the numerical factor is written first. Do not write x times 7 as $x7$.

> **Example 1**   Use the Commutative Property to write an equivalent expression for each of the following.
>
> a. 6(–9)   b. xy
>
> Answer
>
> a. 6(–9) = –9(6)   b. $xy = yx$

When more than two factors are being multiplied, you can change the order of the multiplication by using grouping symbols. This change in grouping does not change the product. Consider the following example.

$$(12 \cdot 25)3 = 300 \cdot 3 = 900$$
$$12(25 \cdot 3) = 12 \cdot 75 = 900$$

This example illustrates the *Associative Property of Multiplication*.

Associative Property of Multiplication

For any integers a, b, and c, $(ab)c = a(bc)$.

> **Example 2**   Use the Associative Property to write an equivalent expression for each of the following.
>
> a. $(-7 \cdot 8)4$ b. $3(5n)$
>
> Answer
>
> a. $(-7 \cdot 8)4 = -7(8 \cdot 4)$ b. $3(5n) = (3 \cdot 5)n$. This could be simplified to $15n$.

Skill Check 1   Write an equivalent expression for each of the following.

1. 8(–4)   2. $m(nt)$

Zero is the identity element of addition because adding zero to any number gives that number. Multiplication also has an identity element. You can multiply any number by one, and the product is identical to the original number. For example, $1 \times 28 = 28$. Thus, one is the *identity element of multiplication*.

Identity Property of Multiplication

For any integer a, $a \times 1 = 1 \times a = a$.

> **Example 3**   Use the Identity Property to write an equivalent expression for each of the following.
>
> a. 1(–42)   b. $1x$
>
> Answer
>
> a. 1(–42) = –42   b. $1x = x$

Even though zero is not the identity element of multiplication, it does have a unique property. The product of zero and any integer is always zero.

Zero Property of Multiplication

For any integer a, $a \times 0 = 0 \times a = 0$.

Skill Check 2

Name the property or properties of multiplication illustrated by each of the following.

1. $47(-9) = -9(47)$

2. $39 \times 1 = 39$

3. $-15[2(-8)] = [-15(2)](-8)$

4. $-1,892(5-5) = 0$

5. $8(6a) = (6 \times 8)a$

Use the properties of multiplication indicated to write an equivalent expression for each of the following.

6. $4(5)$; Commutative

7. $18(7n)$; Associative

8. $4[5(-130)]$; Associative and Commutative

The table below summarizes the properties of multiplication.

Property of Multiplication	Description	Example
Closure For all integers a and b, ab is an integer.	The product of two integers is an integer.	$-7(2) = -14$; -14 is an integer.
Commutative $ab = ba$	Changing the order of the factors does not change the product.	$-6(-5) = -5(-6)$
Associative $(ab)c = a(bc)$	Changing the grouping of the factors does not change the product.	$[-5(4)]9 = -5[4(9)]$
Identity $a \times 1 = 1 \times a = a$	The product of any integer and one equals the original integer.	$-7(1) = 1(-7) = -7$
Zero $a \times 0 = 0 \times a = 0$	The product of any integer and zero equals zero.	$0(5,210) = 5,210(0) = 0$

■ A. Exercises

1. What is the identity element of multiplication?

2. What is the product of any number and zero?

Name the property of multiplication illustrated by each of the following.

3. $2(3) = 3(2)$

4. $-5(0) = 0$

5. $-3(2 \cdot 7) = (-3 \cdot 2)(7)$

6. Since -3 and 5 are integers, $-3(5)$ is an integer.

7. $-9(-7) = -7(-9)$

8. $-3(5 \cdot 7) = (-3 \cdot 5)7$

9. $-8(1) = -8$

10. $-7 \cdot 0 + 8 = 0 + 8$

11. $(a + c)(1) = a + c$

12. $4(-6 \cdot 3) = (-6 \cdot 3)4$

■ B. Exercises

Name the property or properties of multiplication illustrated by each of the following.

13. $(x + 3)(x - 1) = (x - 1)(x + 3)$

14. $2x(3 + 5x) = 2x(5x + 3)$

15. $9y(0) = 0$

16. $[-x(-4x)]5 = -x[-4x(5)]$

17. $1(-3x \cdot 8) = -3x(8)$

18. $(2 \cdot 3)(-4) = (3 \cdot 2)(-4)$

Use the properties of multiplication to simplify the following.

19. $x(-4)$

20. $3[x(-6)]$

21. $-3a(4^0)$

22. $[x(-5)](-6)$

23. $5b(2c)(0)(-4d) + 2^0$

24. $x(3)(x)$

25. $4x(6x)$

26. $[2x(9x)](3x)$

27. In your own words, explain the idea of closure with respect to multiplication in the set of integers.

28. Is the set of natural numbers $\{1, 2, 3, 4, \ldots\}$ closed for multiplication?

29. Is the set of negative integers closed for multiplication?

Write an equation that illustrates each property of multiplication.

30. Commutative

31. Identity

32. Associative

33. Zero

■ C. Exercises

The following is a multiplication table for the set {d, e, f}.

×	d	e	f
d	d	d	d
e	d	e	f
f	d	f	g

34. Is the set closed for multiplication? Why?

35. Is the set commutative? Why?

36. Find $(f \times e) \times d$.

37. Find $f \times (e \times d)$.

38. Find $(e \times f) \times (d \times f)$.

39. Why is the set not associative for multiplication?

The following is a multiplication table for the set {i, j, k}.

×	i	j	k
i	i	i	i
j	i	j	k
k	i	k	j

40. Is the set closed? Why?

41. Is the set commutative? Why?

42. Which element is the identity element? Why?

■ Dominion thru Math

43. Jose is 6 ft. tall and weighs 215 lb. How many pounds will he need to lose (to the nearest tenth) to reach his target BMI of 24 (see Section 2.1, Dominion thru Math)?

44. Inge is 5 ft. 5 in. tall and weighs 160 lb. How many pounds will she need to lose to reach her target BMI of 20?

Simplify. [1.6–1.7]

45. $8(3 - 17) + |-9| \div 3$

46. $-7 - 3[4(2 + 5) - 8]$

47. $(7^0)(3 - 9) + 4[4(-8 + 2) - 1]$

48. $4^8 \cdot 4^{-6}$

Name the property of addition illustrated by each of the following. [2.1]

49. $a + 8 = 8 + a$

50. $6 + (-6) = 0$

51. $7 + 0 = 7$

52. $(3 + 1) + 9 = 3 + (1 + 9)$

53. $6 + 9$ equals an integer.

54. $-12 + 8 = 8 - 12$

2.3 Distributive Property

The *Distributive Property* involves both multiplication and addition. It is also known as the *Distributive Property of Multiplication over Addition*. This property is used frequently in simplifying algebraic expressions and solving equations.

Distributive Property
For any integers a, b, and c, $a(b + c) = ab + ac$.

The following example illustrates the Distributive Property.

$$3(2 + 5) = 3 \cdot 2 + 3 \cdot 5$$
$$3(7) = 6 + 15$$
$$21 = 21$$

Because subtraction is defined as adding the opposite, the Distributive Property also applies to multiplication over subtraction.

$$a(b - c) = ab - ac$$

For example,

$$3(8 - 5) = 3 \cdot 8 - 3 \cdot 5$$
$$3(3) = 24 - 15$$
$$9 = 9$$

The Distributive Property is useful for finding a product mentally. Suppose you want to calculate 3×82. The 8 in the tens place really represents 80, so split 82 into $80 + 2$ and multiply each part by 3.

$$3(82) = 3(80 + 2) = 3(80) + 3(2) = 240 + 6 = 246$$

Aid workers arrive by helicopter to distribute disaster relief.

Practice Mental Math
$7 \times 42 = 7 \times 40 + 7 \times 2$
$= 280 + 14$
$= 280 + 10 + 4$
$= 294$

You could also express 82 as 90 − 8 and apply the Distributive Property of Multiplication over Subtraction.

$$3(82) = 3(90 − 8) = 3(90) − 3(8) = 270 − 24 = 246$$

Example 1   Use the Distributive Property to write an equivalent expression. Then simplify if possible.

a. −5(2 − 7)

b. 4(m + n)

Answer

a. $−5(2 − 7) = −5 \cdot 2 − (−5) \cdot 7 = −10 − (−35) = −10 + 35 = 25$

b. $4(m + n) = 4m + 4n$

Skill Check 1

Use the Distributive Property to write an equivalent expression. Then simplify if possible.

1. −5(x + 6)

2. −4(3 − y)

3. 8(12 − 4)

4. 6(−4 + 2)

Use the Distributive Property to calculate.

5. 5(76)

6. 9(58)

Sometimes the Distributive Property is used in reverse. You need to recognize the expanded form and be able to write its equivalent expression. Notice that *a* is a common factor in both parts of the addition problem on the left side of the equation. Thus it is the factor that you will multiply by the sum when you apply the Distributive Property.

$$ab + ac = a(b + c)$$

Example 2   Use the Distributive Property to write an equivalent expression.

a. 4(−8) + 4(32)

b. −3(7) − 3x

Answer

a. $4(−8) + 4(32) = 4(−8 + 32)$ The common factor is 4.

b. $−3(7) − 3x = −3(7) + (−3)x$ Apply the definition of subtraction. Then identify the common
        $= −3(7 + x)$ factor, −3.

The common factor could appear after the sum. Applying the Commutative Property of Multiplication to the expression $a(b + c)$ gives $(b + c)a$. Using the Distributive Property will give the expression $(b + c)a = ba + ca$.

Example 3   Write an equivalent expression for (5 + x)y.

Answer

$(5 + x)y = 5y + xy$

Use the Distributive Property to fill in the blanks.

1. $5(x + y) = 5\_\_\_ + 5\_\_\_$

2. $(4 \cdot 3) + (4 \cdot 5) = \_\_\_(3 + 5)$

3. $3(\_\_\_ + \_\_\_) = (3 \cdot 2) + (3 \cdot 7)$

4. $9x + 2x = (\_\_\_ + \_\_\_)x$

Use the Distributive Property to write an equivalent expression.

5. $(2 + 3)y$

6. $(4 \cdot 3) + (6 \cdot 3)$

■ A. Exercises

Use the Distributive Property to fill in the blanks.

1. $7(x + y) = 7\_\_\_ + 7\_\_\_$

2. $-5 \cdot 3 + (-5) \cdot 2 = \_\_\_(3 + 2)$

3. $8(\_\_\_ - \_\_\_) = (8 \cdot 4) - (8 \cdot 7)$

4. $-10x + 2x = (\_\_\_ + \_\_\_)x$

Use the Distributive Property to find the value of each variable.

5. $2(7 + 11) = 2n + 2(11)$

6. $6(3 + 15) = 6(3) + 6z$

7. $8(b - 7) = 8(6) - 8(7)$

8. $-5(4 + a) = -5(4) + 5(12)$

9. $(w + 8)15 = 5(15) + 8(15)$

10. $(2 + 13)17 = 2(17) + c(17)$

■ B. Exercises

Use the Distributive Property to write an equivalent expression. Then simplify if possible.

11. $2(8 + 7)$

12. $5(3 + 19)$

13. $(5 + 7)4$

14. $(6 + 11)4$

15. $6(2 + b)$

16. $7(d + 5)$

17. $(r + 2)13$

18. $(4 + n)15$

Use the Distributive Property to compute the following products mentally.

19. $5(14)$

20. $4(7) + 4(3)$

21. $8(34)$

22. $6(24) + 6(6)$

23. $7(2) + 7(8)$

24. $9(53)$

25. $-7(x + 22)$

26. $3(40) + 3(60)$

27. $-3(x - 35)$

■ C. Exercises

Identify the property used for each step in simplifying the following. If an arithmetic operation is performed, write *arithmetic fact*.

28. $6 + 3r + 5 = 3r + 6 + 5$
$= 3r + 11$

29. $4n + 2m + 9n = 4n + 9n + 2m$
$= (4 + 9)n + 2m$
$= 13n + 2m$

30. $2x + 3y - 4x + 8 = 2x - 4x + 3y + 8$
$= (2 - 4)x + 3y + 8$
$= -2x + 3y + 8$

31. $2(h + 3) + h = 2h + 6 + h$
$$= 2h + h + 6$$
$$= 2h + 1h + 6$$
$$= (2 + 1)h + 6$$
$$= 3h + 6$$

32. $(5b + 6) - 2b = (6 + 5b) - 2b$
$$= 6 + (5b - 2b)$$
$$= 6 + (5 - 2)b$$
$$= 6 + 3b$$
$$= 3b + 6$$

■ Dominion thru Math

For maximum benefit, an exercise program needs to be at 60–70% of a person's heart rate (HR) reserve. This is called the training range (TR). The following steps show how to establish a person's training range and target heart rate.

Determining Target Heart Rates
1. max HR = 220 – age (use 226 for women)
2. HR reserve = max HR – resting HR
3. training range (TR): upper TR = 70% × HR reserve   lower TR = 60% × HR reserve
4. target HR (upper or lower) = TR (upper or lower) + resting HR

33. Find the lower target heart rate for Darren, who is 12 and has a resting HR of 60. Round to the nearest whole number.

34. Find the upper target heart rate for Melissa, who is 13 and has a resting HR of 62. Round to the nearest whole number.

CUMULATIVE REVIEW

Write the following numbers in scientific notation. [1.8]

35. 32,000

36. 0.000056

Name the property or definition illustrated by each of the following. [2.1–2.2]

37. $xy = yx$

38. $5 + (2 + 3) = (5 + 2) + 3$

39. $6 \cdot 1 = 6$

40. $z - y = z + (-y)$

41. $4 \cdot 0 = 0$

42. $x + 0 = x$

43. $x + 8 = 8 + x$

44. $9(3 + 7) = (3 + 7)9$

2.4 Evaluating Expressions

A *numerical expression* is a string of numbers and operational signs that names a number. Consider the numerical expressions below.

$$9 + 2 \cdot 6 \qquad \frac{3+9}{9-5} \qquad 6 - (4+3)$$

As discussed in Section 1.7, numerical expressions are evaluated using the order of operations. When a variable is used in place of a number in a mathematical expression, the expression is an *algebraic expression*. The properties of addition and multiplication, as well as the Distributive Property, are used to simplify algebraic expressions.

A grocery bill involves using addition, multiplication, and subtraction in the proper order.

Definition

An **algebraic expression** is a mathematical expression containing numbers, variables, and operational signs.

To evaluate an algebraic expression, replace the variable with a given number and evaluate the resulting numerical expression.

Example 1 Evaluate $n + 6$ when $n = 8$.

Answer

$$\begin{aligned} n + 6 &= 8 + 6 \\ &= 14 \end{aligned}$$

1. Substitute 8 for n.
2. Add.

Example 2 Evaluate $a + 7$ when $a = -12$.

Answer

$$\begin{aligned} a + 7 &= -12 + 7 \\ &= -5 \end{aligned}$$

1. Substitute -12 for a.
2. Add.

Example 3 Evaluate $-7 - n$ when $n = -3$.

Answer

$$\begin{aligned} -7 - n &= -7 - (-3) \\ &= -7 + 3 \\ &= -4 \end{aligned}$$

1. Substitute -3 for n.
2. Apply the definition of subtraction (add the opposite).
3. Add.

Evaluate.

1. $n + 6$ when $n = -13$ 2. $m - 8$ when $m = -9$

Example 4   Evaluate $x - (y + 7)$ when $x = 9$ and $y = 3$.

Answer

$x - (y + 7) = 9 - (3 + 7)$	1. Substitute 9 for x and 3 for y.
$= 9 - 10$	2. Follow the order of operations (parentheses first).
$= -1$	3. Subtract.

Example 5   Evaluate $2x - \frac{y}{3}$ when $x = -3$ and $y = 12$.

Answer

$2x - \frac{y}{3} = 2(-3) - \frac{12}{3}$	1. Substitute -3 for x and 12 for y.
$= -6 - 4$	2. Multiply and divide in order from left to right.
$= -6 + (-4)$	3. Apply the definition of subtraction (add the opposite).
$= -10$	4. Add.

Example 6   Evaluate $2ab - 3b$ when $a = -2$ and $b = -3$.

Answer

$2ab - 3b = 2(-2)(-3) - 3(-3)$	1. Substitute -2 for a and -3 for b.
$= 12 - (-9)$	2. Multiply in order from left to right.
$= 12 + 9$	3. Apply the definition of subtraction (add the opposite).
$= 21$	4. Add.

Skill Check 2

Evaluate.

1. $y + 17$ when $y = -6$ 2. $(n + 9) - 6(3)$ when $n = 5$

3. $24 - 5r$ when $r = 2$ 4. $-3n + \frac{m}{2}$ when $n = -4$ and $m = 14$

⊕ Invention

Invented in 1852 by Frenchman Jean-Bernard-Léon Foucault, the *gyroscope* became a critical instrument in the areas of navigation and autopilot for aircraft, even though it came more than 150 years before airplanes. The gyroscope consists of a weighted disk rotating on its axis and suspended in an apparatus called *gimbals* so that it is free to move in all directions. Since the plane of the spinning disk always maintains its direction (attitude) in space, it will indicate any change in the attitude of the support system—which in the modern case might be an airplane. Airplanes might have a dozen gyroscopes, the space station has at least eleven, and the Hubble Space Telescope has many. A bicycle wheel or a free-wheeling Yo-Yo can be used to simulate a gyroscope.

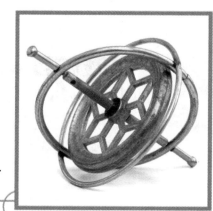

■ A. Exercises

Evaluate.

1. $7a$ when $a = -4$

2. $\dfrac{2n}{-8}$ when $n = 16$

3. $5m$ when $m = 9$

4. $\dfrac{5t}{3}$ when $t = 21$

5. $a - 3$ when $a = -8$

6. $x + 33$ when $x = -51$

7. $-15 + b$ when $b = 4$

8. $-26 + y$ when $y = 48$

9. $-12 + c$ when $c = 21$

10. $z - 52$ when $z = -29$

11. $d + 18$ when $d = 49$

12. $w + 63$ when $w = -87$

13. $8z$ when $z = 12$

14. $\dfrac{18x}{6}$ when $x = 3$

15. $\dfrac{c}{3}$ when $c = -21$

16. $\dfrac{-7d}{2}$ when $d = 6$

17. $\dfrac{-28}{k}$ when $k = 7$

18. $\dfrac{4y}{16}$ when $y = -20$

19. $\dfrac{p}{2}$ when $p = 38$

■ B. Exercises

Evaluate.

20. $7 + \dfrac{y}{2}$ when $y = -12$

21. $\dfrac{3b}{2}$ when $b = 8$

22. $\dfrac{m - 6}{3}$ when $m = 24$

23. $9 - \dfrac{d}{3}$ when $d = 6$

24. $\dfrac{c + 40}{12}$ when $c = -16$

25. $6t - 1$ when $t = 5$

26. $\dfrac{n}{3} + 4$ when $n = 18$

27. $12 - 3b$ when $b = 2$

28. $2x + 5$ when $x = -5$

29. $\dfrac{30 - r}{7}$ when $r = -5$

30. $2a + 5b + 7$ when $a = 3$ and $b = 2$

31. $15 + bc$ when $b = 6$ and $c = 9$

32. $7m - 4 + 3n$ when $m = 4$ and $n = 2$

33. $\dfrac{3a}{c + 1}$ when $a = 8$ and $c = 5$

34. $18 - 3s - 4t$ when $s = 3$ and $t = -1$

35. $\dfrac{2xy}{14}$ when $x = 3$ and $y = -7$

36. $4xy$ when $x = 3$ and $y = -5$

37. $\dfrac{2r + 8}{s - 2}$ when $r = 11$ and $s = 7$

38. $6r - 2s$ when $r = -7$ and $s = -4$

39. $\dfrac{3x - 3}{y + 4}$ when $x = -5$ and $y = 2$

■ C. Exercises

Evaluate each expression when $a = 2$, $b = 3$, $c = 4$, $d = 5$, $w = 7$, $x = -3$, $y = -2$, and $z = 5$.

40. $(ax - 3)(bd - yc)$

41. $6w - \dfrac{9c}{a} + 4ax$

42. $\dfrac{dy + ax + 20}{cz - w}$

43. $\dfrac{2d + 8b + 2}{3w - 3x}$

■ Dominion thru Math

To be physically fit, you must maintain a healthy weight. Use the calorie usage table and the definitions of various levels of exercise for exercises 44–46.

Calorie Usage by Weight and Gender		
Bodily Activity	Calories burned per pound of weight per hour	
	Male	Female
Moderate exercise	2.5	2.3
Active exercise	3.5	3.2
Very active exercise	4.8	4.1

Moderate exercise: bicycling, hiking, mowing the yard, fast walking

Active exercise: tennis, jogging, cheerleading, backpacking

Very active exercise: running, swimming laps, soccer, basketball

44. How many calories will Monique burn on a 2 hr. bicycle trip if she weighs 115 lb.?

45. Curtis weighs 150 lb. and runs 5 mi. every morning before breakfast. His pace is very close to 7.5 min./mi. How many calories does Curtis burn when he runs each morning?

46. Anisha weighs 120 lb. and has a target HR of 160. At the Workout Express she knows that maintaining her target HR for 24 min. burns about 200 calories. At what exercise level is her workout?

CUMULATIVE REVIEW

Simplify. [1.6]

47. $x^4 \cdot x^{-7}$

48. $a^6 \div a^3$

49. $(x^2 y^5)^3$

50. $x \cdot x \cdot x \cdot x \cdot x \cdot y \cdot y \cdot y$

Name the property or definition illustrated by each of the following. [2.1–2.3]

51. $5(x + 1) = 5x + 5$

52. $7 + (3 + 8) = (7 + 3) + 8$

53. $8 \cdot 0 = 0$

54. $9 - 14 = 9 + (-14)$

55. $12 + 0 = 12$

56. $45 + 27 = 9(5 + 3)$

2.5 Simplifying Expressions

Food is transferred from large containers to smaller ones for sale and use.

You will use the properties of addition and multiplication, as well as the Distributive Property, to simplify algebraic expressions. For example, the expression $2(3n)$ is simplified by applying the Associative Property of Multiplication.

Example 1 Simplify $2(3n)$.

Answer

$2(3n) = (2 \cdot 3)n$ 1. Regroup, using the Associative Property of Multiplication.

$= 6n$ 2. Multiply the numbers inside the parentheses.

You can also simplify algebraic expressions using the Associative Property of Addition.

Example 2   Simplify $(x + 2) + 9$.

Answer

$(x + 2) + 9 = x + (2 + 9)$ 1. Regroup, using the Associative Property of Addition.

$= x + 11$ 2. Add the numbers inside the parentheses.

Skill Check 1

Simplify.

1. $5(7b)$
2. $6(9 \cdot n)$
3. $4(13r)$
4. $(m + 5) + 8$
5. $(a + 17) + 6$
6. $(s + 4) + 12$

Definitions

A **constant** is a number whose value does not change.
A **term** is a constant, a variable, or the product of a constant and one or more variables. Terms are always separated from each other by a plus or a minus sign.
The **numerical coefficient** is the number factor (constant) accompanying the variable in a term.

The algebraic expression $3x + 2y - 4$ has three *terms*. Since the terms of an expression are separated by plus or minus signs, the terms in this expression are $3x$, $2y$, and -4.

Notice that the minus sign preceding the 4 made the term negative. Since subtracting 4 is adding a negative 4, the term is considered to be -4 rather than just 4.

$$3x + 2y - 4 = 3x + 2y + (-4)$$

The term without a variable factor is the *constant* term. In this expression the constant term is -4. The terms that contain variables have *numerical coefficients*, often just called *coefficients*. In this expression, 3 is the coefficient of the first term and 2 is the coefficient of the second term.

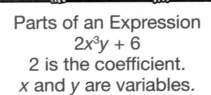

Parts of an Expression
$2x^3y + 6$
2 is the coefficient.
x and y are variables.
3 is an exponent.
6 is a constant.

Example 3   Use the expression $-6xy + \dfrac{x}{2} - z$ to answer the following questions.

a. What are the terms of the expression?
b. Does the expression have a constant term?
c. What are the coefficients in the expression?

Answer

a. The expression has three terms: $-6xy$, $\dfrac{x}{2}$, and $-z$.
b. There is not a constant term. All terms contain a variable factor.
c. The coefficients are -6, $\dfrac{1}{2}$, and -1. $\dfrac{1}{2}$ is a coefficient since $\dfrac{x}{2} = \dfrac{1}{2}x$. -1 is a coefficient since $-z = -1z$.

If two terms of an expression have the same variable or variables with the same powers, they are called *like terms*. Study the examples below.

Like Terms	Unlike Terms
$5x,\ -7x,\ \frac{1}{2}x$	$4x,\ 4x^2$
$5xy^2,\ -xy^2,\ 0.75xy^2$	$6xy,\ -8xy^3$

Definition

Like terms are terms that have the same variable (or variables) with the same exponents.

Recall that the Distributive Property is as follows.

$$a(b + c) = ab + ac$$

The factor a can be written on the right side of each factor by applying the Commutative Property of Multiplication.

$$(b + c)a = ba + ca$$

Switching sides of the equation results in another form of the same equation.

$$ba + ca = (b + c)a$$

This form of the Distributive Property allows you to combine like terms by adding the coefficients.

$$3x + 5x = (3 + 5)x = 8x$$

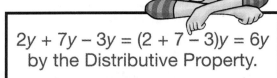

$2y + 7y - 3y = (2 + 7 - 3)y = 6y$
by the Distributive Property.

Example 4   Simplify $7x + 4x$.

Answer

$7x + 4x = (7 + 4)x$ 1. x is the common factor of the addends 7 and 4 (reverse Distributive Property).

$ = 11x$ 2. Add the numbers in the parentheses (the coefficients).

Combining like terms is simply adding the numerical coefficients and keeping the same variable factor.

$$5x + 13x = 18x$$

Skill Check 2

Use the expression $2xy + 4y + z - 7$ to answer the following questions.

1. How many terms are in the expression?

2. What is the coefficient of z?

3. What is the constant term?

Simplify.

4. $3y - 7y$

5. $2xy + 7xy$

6. $-3z + 5z$

7. $5x + 8x - 3x$

To simplify longer expressions, you can use the Commutative and Associative Properties to group like terms before you combine them.

| Example 5 | Simplify $2x + 7y + 3 - y + 5x$. |

Answer

$$2x + 7y + 3 - y + 5x = (2x + 5x) + (7y - y) + 3$$ 1. Group like terms.
$$= (2 + 5)x + (7 - 1)y + 3$$ 2. Apply the Distributive Property to combine like terms.
$$= 7x + 6y + 3$$ 3. Simplify.

When writing the terms of an algebraic expression, follow the guidelines below.
1. Write the terms in descending order according to the power of the variables.
2. Write the terms in alphabetical order according to the variables.
3. Write the constant term last.

Skill Check 3

Simplify by combining like terms.

1. $2x - (-5x)$
2. $7 + 9a + 4$
3. $b + 19 + 5b - 7$
4. $y - 11 + 5y - 4 + 3y$
5. $-7m - 3m + 1$
6. $4 + 9p + 2 + 3p$
7. $5r - 8s - 2r - 7s$
8. $2w + 8x - 6w + 3 + 4x$

■ A. Exercises

Simplify.

1. $5(7b)$
2. $4(13r)$
3. $(8d)44$
4. $6(9n)$
5. $3(28w)$
6. $(79k)56$
7. $(m + 5) + 8$
8. $(s + 4) + 12$
9. $(119 + m) + 47$
10. $(a + 17) + 6$
11. $(a + 34) + 28$
12. $(56 + p) + 135$

■ B. Exercises

Simplify.

13. $2x + 5x$
14. $b + 19 - 5b - 7$
15. $7m - 3m + 1$
16. $5r + 8s - 2r + 3s$
17. $-7 + 9a + 4$
18. $y + 11 - 5y + 4 - 3y$
19. $4 + 9p + 2 + 3p$
20. $6w - 8x - 2w + 3 - 4x$

Simplify. Then evaluate when $a = 3$, $b = 4$, $c = 2$, $x = -6$, $y = 8$, and $z = -5$.

21. $2c + 5 + 7c$
22. $6c + 9 + 7c - 4$
23. $6x - 4 - 2x$
24. $-5a + 3z + 2a + 6z$
25. $7 + 4y - 6y$
26. $8c + 5y - 2c + 9y$
27. $7a - 3 + 5a$
28. $7c + 4b - 8 - 3c + 5b$
29. $-7a + 3 + 2a + 15$
30. $4a + b + 2a - 13b + 7a$

■ C. Exercises

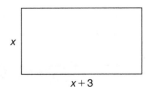

31. A rectangle has consecutive sides that are represented by x and $x + 3$. Find the expression that represents the perimeter of the rectangle.

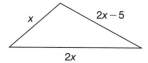

32. The sides of a triangle are represented by x, $2x$, and $2x - 5$. Find the expression that represents its perimeter.

33. A farmer has a rectangular pasture with dimensions x by $2x$. If he places posts 15 ft. apart, how will he represent the distance between each post on the shorter side? on the longer side?

34. Each side of a regular octagon (all sides equal in length) is represented by $14x$. Find the expression that represents the perimeter of the regular octagon.

35. The side of a square is 4 in. shorter than one side of a given rectangle. The side of the rectangle is represented by $2x + 3$. Find the expression that represents the perimeter of the square.

■ Dominion thru Math

Time expressed in hours, minutes, and seconds (written 4:13:10 to mean 4 hr. 13 min. 10 sec.) must sometimes be changed to hours.

All the events in the following exercises are to be taken as very active exercise (see Section 2.4, Dominion thru Math). Round the answers to the nearest calorie.

36. The Olympic Triathlon event includes a 1.5 km swim, a 40 km bicycle ride, and a 10 km run. How many calories did the men's gold medalist expend if his time was 1:51:07 and he weighed 170 lb.?

37. How many calories would a 54 kg woman expend during a sprint triathlon if her time is 1:13:45?

38. A full-distance triathlon requires a 2.4 mi. swim, a 112 mi. bicycle ride, and a 26.2 mi. run (marathon). Suppose a contestant weighed 172 lb. and had a time of 8:40:59. How many calories did he expend?

CUMULATIVE REVIEW

Use the Distributive Property to write an equivalent expression. [2.3]

39. $-9(z - 8)$

40. $3x + 3y$

41. $45x + 30$

42. $6(x - 1)$

Name the property or definition illustrated by each of the following. [2.1–2.2]

43. $4(x + 9) = (x + 9)4$

44. $a + (a + b) = (a + a) + b$

Evaluate. [2.4]

45. $-10(x + 2)$ when $x = -8$

46. $a + 4b - c$ when $a = -6$, $b = -2$, and $c = 4$

47. $x(4 + y)$ when $x = -1$ and $y = 5$

48. $6(m - 5n) - 6m$ when $m = 4$ and $n = 6$

PROBLEM SOLVING

Select the Operations

"Select the operations" is a common strategy that can be used to solve word problems. To apply this strategy, decide which operations are needed to solve a problem and determine in what order to apply them. Consider the following example.

| Example | The August electric bill was $168.40. This was $49.30 more than the July electric bill. The September bill was half the August bill. What was the total cost of electricity for the three-month period? |

Answer

Think: Use the four-point strategy for problem solving. First, read the problem and determine what needs to be found.

Read: Find the question and given information.

Question: What was the total paid for the three-month period?

Given: The August bill of $168.40 was $49.30 more than the July bill. The September bill was half the August bill.

Think: Determine a plan to use the given information to answer the question. Then carry out the plan.

Plan what must be found.	Plan the operations.	Solve; do the computations.
First—July electric bill	subtraction	168.40 – 49.30 = $119.10
Second—September bill	division	168.40 ÷ 2 = $84.20
Third—total cost	addition	119.10 + 168.40 + 84.20 = $371.70

Think: Is this answer reasonable? Check the results by estimating, inverse operations, or an alternate method for solving the problem. The use of inverse operations is shown here.

Check the subtraction by adding: 119.10 + 49.30 = $168.40.

Check the division by multiplying: 2 × 84.20 = $168.40.

Check the total by adding in reverse order: 84.20 + 168.40 + 119.10 = $371.70.

■ Exercises

Devise a plan and solve the following problems. Write down your thought process in working toward a solution for exercises 1–4.

1. Mrs. Taylor bought a gift box containing four half-pound boxes of gourmet coffee for $29.95 plus $1.50 in sales tax. She paid $4.95 to have it shipped to her mother for Mother's Day. How much of her $40 did she have left after mailing the package?

2. Hearty Chili is on sale for three cans for $5.59. The regular price is two cans for $3.99. How much can be saved by buying a dozen cans at the sale price?

3. Twice as many students got Bs as Cs on the math test. The number of Ds is $\frac{1}{4}$ the number of Bs. There is one more A than the number of Ds, and one student got an F on the test. If the teacher says that six students got a C on the test, how many students are in the class?

4. Mr. Hess paid the entrance fee into the amusement park for himself, his wife, and their five children. The children's ages were 16, 11, 8, 5, and 2. Children ages 2 and under are free, ages 3–5 cost $18, ages 6–15 cost $30, and adults (ages 16 and over) cost $40. What was the total entrance fee for the family? Mr. Hess allows up to $15 per person for food for the three younger children and $20 for himself, his wife, and the two older children. What is the amount needed for the day at the amusement park?

5. James takes inventory of the books on his bookshelf. He discovers that he has thirty-six books. There are half as many joke books as historical fiction and three times as many mysteries as historical fiction. The rest of the books are westerns. If he has two joke books on his shelf, how many of each of the other kinds of books does he have?

6. The March telephone bill was $89.28. The February bill was half as much as the March bill. The January bill was $23.49 less than the March bill. What was the total cost of the telephone use for these three months?

7. Beth Haven's youth group is planning a ski trip for grades 7–9. There are twice as many eighth graders as seventh graders and six more ninth graders than eighth graders. If there are four seventh graders, what is the total number of young people planning to go on the trip?

8. Judson's cell phone bill reveals that he spent 23 more minutes talking to Bryce than to Donovan. His time talking to Grady was three times as much as to Donovan. If he talked to Grady for 24 min., what was the total number of minutes he used his cell phone during the month?

2.6 Translating Word Phrases

When translating word phrases into numerical or algebraic expressions, it is important that you look for key words. Certain words will indicate the arithmetic operation being performed.

Addition Key Words	Subtraction Key Words	Multiplication Key Words	Division Key Words
added to	subtracted from	multiplied by	divided by
sum	difference	product	quotient
increased by	decreased by	times	ratio of
more than	less than	twice (× 2)	halved (÷ 2)
plus	minus	doubled (× 2)	
	less		

The phrase "5 more than a number" means that the number is increased by 5. Thus, it would be expressed as $x + 5$. Since addition is commutative, it would be equivalent to use $5 + x$ to represent the algebraic expression.

However, subtraction is not commutative, and care must be taken when the words "less" or "less than" are used.

"x less 5" means $x - 5$. You begin with x and subtract 5 from it.

"x less than 5" means $5 - x$. You begin with 5 and subtract x from it.

Do not confuse the phrase "less than" with the phrase "is less than." "Less than" indicates subtraction, but "is less than" indicates an inequality.

"5 is less than x" means $5 < x$.

| 7 less than x | "$x - 7$" |
| 7 less x | "$7 - x$" |

Example 1 Write "9 decreased by 5" as a numerical expression.

Answer

$9 - 5$ The phrase "decreased by" indicates subtraction.

Example 2 Write "the product of 9 and 5" as a numerical expression.

Answer

9×5 The word "product" indicates multiplication.

Skill Check 1

Write each word phrase as a numerical expression.

1. 6 increased by 31
2. 14 less than 54
3. the quotient of 75 and 3
4. 2 more than 5
5. 17 times 61

If a variable is required to translate a word phrase, the result is an algebraic expression.

Example 3   Write "a number is increased by 2" as an algebraic expression.

Answer

$n + 2$ Let n represent the unknown number. The phrase "increased by" indicates addition.

Example 4   Write "the quotient of a number and 3" as an algebraic expression.

Answer

$\dfrac{x}{3}$ Let x represent the unknown number. The word "quotient" indicates division.

Example 5   Write "7 more than the opposite of a number" as an algebraic expression.

Answer

$-n + 7$ The phrase "opposite of a number" means the additive inverse of the number.

Skill Check 2

Write each word phrase as an algebraic expression.

1. the sum of a number and 12
2. a number decreased by 4
3. 8 times a number
4. a number subtracted from 11
5. 81 divided by a number

You can also write numerical or algebraic expressions to represent real-life situations.

Example 6   Write each as a mathematical expression. Bill has $46. How much will he have if he does the following?

a. spends $5
b. earns y dollars

Answer

a. $46 - 5$ Spending money decreases the initial amount. Therefore, subtract 5 from 46.
b. $46 + y$ Earning money increases the initial amount. Therefore, add y to 46.

Example 7 Write each as a mathematical expression. Rhonda saves $18. How much will she have if she does the following?

a. saves twice as much

b. saves *n* times as much

c. divides her savings evenly among 3 people

d. divides her savings evenly among *n* people

Answer

a. 2×18 b. $18n$ c. $\dfrac{18}{3}$ d. $\dfrac{18}{n}$

Skill Check 3

Write an expression to represent each of the following situations.

1. Thomas has 15 candy bars left to sell. He has already sold *m* candy bars. Write an algebraic expression representing the number of candy bars he originally had in his box.

2. Brad is twice as old as his sister, Peggy. If Peggy is *n* years old, how would you represent Brad's age?

A word phrase may suggest a combination of operations. For example, the phrase "3 more than twice a number" suggests the operations of multiplication and addition.

Example 8 Write "3 more than twice a number" as an algebraic expression.

Answer

Let *n* represent the number.

$2n$ 1. "Twice a number" indicates multiplication.

$2n + 3$ 2. "3 more than" signifies that 3 is added to the previous amount.

Skill Check 4

Write each word phrase as a mathematical expression.

1. 6 times the sum of 7 and 4

2. 15 divided by the difference of a number and 3

3. the product of 8 and a number, decreased by 7

4. the sum of a number divided by 7 and 6

■ A. Exercises

Write each word phrase as a numerical expression.

1. 7 less than 3

2. twice 5

3. 12 less than 19

4. increase 8 by 9

5. 15 decreased by 4

6. 4 more than the opposite of 6

Write each word phrase as an algebraic expression.

7. a number increased by 5

8. 6 plus a number

9. 12 multiplied by a number

10. the quotient of a number and 21

11. 8 subtracted from a number

12. one-third more than x

13. 19 decreased by a number

14. 4 less than a number

15. the difference of 7 and a number

■ B. Exercises

Write each word phrase as an algebraic expression.

16. one-fifth of a number, decreased by 10

17. 6 times a number, increased by 7

18. the sum of 27 and twice the opposite of y

19. 9 more than the product of 5 and x

20. 33 decreased by the quotient of x and 7

21. 3 times the sum of x and 5

22. 1 less than the quotient of z and 12

Jenny is 11 years old. Write an expression to represent each of the following situations.

23. How old will she be in two years?

24. How old will she be in n years?

25. How old was she five years ago?

26. How old was she m years ago?

Raymond earned \$85. How much money will he have if the following situations occur?

27. he gains r dollars

28. he receives a gift of m dollars

29. he spends s dollars

30. he gives t dollars to a missionary

Mr. Roberts handed out n tracts last week. How many tracts will be handed out this week if the following situations occur?

31. he gets two other people to help and they each pass out n tracts

32. he hands out 7 more than one-half as many

33. he hands out 4 less than twice as many

■ C. Exercises

If the letter _n_ represents a positive integer {1, 2, 3, 4, …}, write an algebraic expression for each of the following.

34. the next consecutive integer

35. an even integer

36. the integer 2 more than _n_

37. an odd integer

38. the integer preceding _n_

39. three consecutive integers

40. Three boys decide to share a pizza and divide the cost. They will each leave a $0.50 tip. Write an expression for how much each boy will have to pay.

CUMULATIVE REVIEW

Simplify. [2.5]

41. $4x + 7 - 3x + 9$

42. $12x - x + 5y + 3y - 5x$

43. $8(2x - 9) + 4(x + 4)$

44. $-3x - 5y + 8x - 6z$

45. $-7(x - 3) + 6x + 1$

46. $3 - 4y - 9 + 7y$

47. $-2(y - x + 3) + 5y$

48. $6(x - 2y) - 4(x + 9)$

Evaluate. [2.4]

49. $x + 7y$ when $x = 2$ and $y = -4$

50. $|x| - y + 6z$ when $x = -8$, $y = -4$, and $z = -1$

MIND OVER MATH

A man is stranded on one side of a river with a fox, a goose, and a bag of corn. He finds a boat, but it is too small to carry more than him and one of the above items. To complicate matters, he must make sure that the fox does not eat the goose and the goose does not eat the corn. How can he safely transport all three items to the other side of the river?

2.7 Estimating

Estimation is an important mathematical tool. It can be used to help you determine whether answers to problems are reasonable. It is also a practical tool in everyday life. When shopping, you can estimate the sum of your purchases. When dining at a restaurant, you can estimate an appropriate tip. When planning a meal, you can estimate the amount of food needed.

Sums, differences, products, and quotients can be estimated using rounding. The procedure for rounding numbers is given below.

Rounding Positive Numbers
1. Identify the place to which you are rounding.
2. Look at the digit to the right of the place to which you are rounding. If it is 5 or greater, increase the place to which you are rounding by 1. If it is less than 5, do not change the digit in the place to which you are rounding.
3. Change all digits to the right of the rounding place to zeros.*

*Dropping zeros that follow the rounded digit behind a decimal does not change the value of the decimal.

Example 1   Round 7,384 to each indicated place.

a. thousand
b. hundred
c. ten

Answer

a. 7,384 ≈ 7,000   The digit to the right of 7 is less than 5. Do not increase the 7.
b. 7,384 ≈ 7,400   The digit to the right of 3 is greater than 5. Increase the 3 to a 4.
c. 7,384 ≈ 7,380   The digit to the right of 8 is less than 5. Do not increase the 8.

Example 2   Round 15,469.7482 to each indicated place.

a. tenth
b. ten thousand
c. hundredth

Answer

a. 15,469.7482 ≈ 15,469.7   The digit to the right of 7 is less than 5. Do not increase the 7.
b. 15,469.7482 ≈ 20,000   The digit to the right of 1 is 5. Increase the 1 to a 2.
c. 15,469.7482 ≈ 15,469.75   The digit to the right of 4 is greater than 5. Increase the 4 to a 5.

Skill Check 1

Round each number to the indicated place.

1. 78 (ten)

2. 628.0625 (hundredth)

3. 24,763 (thousand)

4. 0.305219 (hundred-thousandth)

You can use rounded numbers to approximate sums and differences. Study the procedure for estimating sums and differences using rounding.

Estimating Sums and Differences Using Rounding

1. Round each number to its highest place value unless a specific place is indicated.

2. Use the rounded numbers to compute the estimate.

Example 3 Estimate the sum of 17,436 + 43,519 by rounding each addend to its highest place value.

Answer

```
  20,000    Round 17,436 to 20,000.
+ 40,000    Round 43,519 to 40,000.
  60,000
```

Example 4 Estimate the difference of 60.09241 − 3.0483 by rounding each number to the nearest hundredth.

Answer

```
  60.09    Round 60.09241 to 60.09.
−  3.05    Round 3.0483 to 3.05.
  57.04
```

Skill Check 2

Estimate by rounding to the highest place value.

1. 64 + 37

2. 7,791 − 486

3. 1,913 + 979

4. 5,354 − 1,619

Estimate by rounding to the nearest thousand.

5. 9,423 + 2,731

6. 43,625 − 8,251

Estimate by rounding to the nearest tenth.

7. 5.9401 − 2.064

8. 5.372 + 1.805

Rounding is also useful for estimating products and quotients. To estimate a product, round each number to its highest place value.

Example 5 Estimate the product by rounding.

a. 42 · 87

b. 942 × 78

Answer

a. 42 ≈ 40   1. Round each factor to its highest place value.
   87 ≈ 90
   40 · 90 = 3,600   2. Multiply the rounded numbers.
b. 942 ≈ 900   1. Round each factor to its highest place value.
   78 ≈ 80
   900 × 80 = 72,000   2. Multiply the rounded numbers.

Rounding numbers for estimating quotients will vary slightly. The goal is to obtain compatible numbers so that the division will not have a remainder.

Example 6 Estimate the quotient by rounding.

a. 263 ÷ 9

b. 1,149 ÷ 34

Answer

a. 263 ≈ 270   Do not round the single-digit divisor. Round 263 to 270, since 27 is divisible by 9.
   270 ÷ 9 = 30
b. 34 ≈ 30   Round the divisor to 30. Then round the dividend to a number compatible with
   1,149 ≈ 1,200   the rounded divisor. 12 is divisible by 3.
   1,200 ÷ 30 = 40

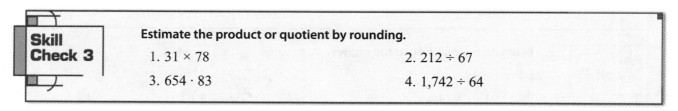

Skill Check 3

Estimate the product or quotient by rounding.

1. 31 × 78   2. 212 ÷ 67

3. 654 · 83   4. 1,742 ÷ 64

Front-end estimation is another strategy that can be used to estimate sums and differences. It works best if the numbers have the same number of digits. Front-end estimation uses the digits in the highest place value of the numbers, making the other digits zeros. The estimation obtained can be adjusted by examining the digits in the next highest place value and adding or subtracting to obtain a more accurate estimate. Study the examples below.

Example 7 Estimate the sum of 373 + 224 using front-end estimation. Then adjust the answer to get a more accurate estimate.

Answer

Initial Estimate

300 + 200 = 500   1. Add the first digits. Make the other digits zero.

Adjustment

70 + 20 = 90   2. Add the digits in the tens place, making the other digits zero. Add
500 + 90 = 590   this sum to the original estimate to get a more accurate estimate.

Example 8 Estimate the difference of 34,289 – 18,192 using front-end estimation. Adjust to get a more accurate estimate.

Answer

Initial Estimate

30,000 – 10,000 = 20,000

1. Subtract the first digits. Make the other digits zero.

Adjustment

4,000 – 8,000 = –4,000

20,000 – 4,000 = 16,000

2. Subtract the digits in the thousands place, making the other digits zero. Since the difference is negative, the estimate is too large. Subtract 4,000 from the original estimate.

Note that if the difference of the digits in the thousands place were positive, it would indicate that the estimate was too small. In that case, 4,000 would be added to the 20,000.

Skill Check 4

Estimate the sum or difference using front-end estimation. Adjust to get a more accurate estimate.

1. 5,861 + 7,469

2. 34,578 – 11,845

■ A. Exercises

Round to the nearest ten.

1. 47

2. 63.54

3. 592

Round to the nearest hundred.

4. 336

5. 7,854

6. 89,073

Round to the nearest thousand.

7. 6,793

8. 16,329

9. 121,592

Estimate the sum or difference by rounding to the highest place value.

10. 32 + 75

11. 463 + 215

12. 87 – 36

13. 731 – 584

14. 375 + 521

15. 419 – 153

16. 6,378 + 841

17. 7,429 – 2,965

■ B. Exercises

Estimate the sum or difference by rounding to the nearest thousand.

18. 7,642 + 1,526

19. 14,261 – 4,758

20. 42,839 + 26,173

21. 35,384 – 14,732

Estimate the product or quotient by rounding.

22. 37 × 91

23. 895 × 216

24. $\frac{296}{21}$

25. 84(53)

26. 348(469)

27. $\frac{803}{38}$

28. 66 · 28

29. 763 · 948

30. $\frac{629}{93}$

31. 675 × 33

32. 479 ÷ 6

33. $\frac{4,213}{61}$

34. 54(329)

35. 244 ÷ 4

36. $\frac{2,397}{372}$

37. 79 · 513

38. 719 ÷ 8

39. $\frac{8,092}{904}$

Estimate the sum or difference using front-end estimation. Adjust to get a more accurate estimate.

40. $321 + 197 + 278$

41. $7,209 + 6,298$

42. $403 + 258 + 341$

43. $6,815 - 2,289$

44. $9,275 - 4,194$

45. $53,027 - 15,985$

■ C. Exercises

46. Mr. Brown drove his new car for 76,845 mi. He sold the car to his brother, who drove it for 34,923 mi. Estimate the total mileage to the nearest thousand miles.

47. Mr. Wilson bought a new car for $19,875. He later sold the car for $9,495. Estimate the difference in the prices to the nearest hundred dollars.

48. Mr. Ricks test-drove a car that was on sale for $15,990. He asked the dealer to add optional equipment costing $899. Estimate the total cost to the nearest hundred dollars.

49. Use front-end estimation to estimate the total cost of Jesselyn's lunch. Then give a more accurate estimate. She purchased a cheeseburger for $3.59, French fries for $1.44, a fruit cup for $1.39, and a soft drink for $0.99.

CUMULATIVE REVIEW

Write each word phrase as an algebraic expression. [2.6]

50. a number less 22

51. the product of a number and 5

52. a number increased by 17

53. the quotient of a number and 12

54. one-third of a number, decreased by 6

Name the property or definition illustrated by each of the following. [2.1–2.3]

55. $6(x - 7) = 6x - 42$

56. $7xy = 7yx$

57. $(7 + 9) + 2 = 7 + (9 + 2)$

58. $29 \cdot 1 = 29$

59. $3 \cdot 6$ is an integer.

MATH
& SCRIPTURE

Joseph's On-the-Job Training

The Egyptian system of numeration did not have place values. It was a set of hieroglyphic symbols representing powers of ten that were summed to find the value of the number. This cumbersome system makes it all the more remarkable that the pyramids were built or that Joseph kept track of selling the huge stores of grain he collected during the seven years of plenty (Gen. 41, 47). It is likely that Joseph began his study of Egyptian math while a slave in Potiphar's house, and perhaps he continued to hone his math skills while falsely imprisoned.

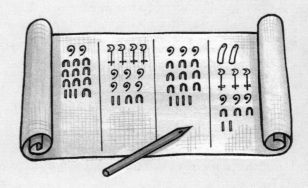

Read Genesis 39:1–6, 21–23; 41:25–57, and answer the following questions.

1. Why did Potiphar give Joseph complete charge of everything pertaining to his house and fields?

2. What are some things that Joseph would have managed in a large, prosperous estate?

3. Which of your answers in exercise 2 would have required mathematical skills?

4. Ultimately, what reason did Pharaoh give for promoting Joseph over all the land of Egypt?

5. Did Pharaoh's stated reason for promoting Joseph lessen Joseph's need for knowledge and understanding of mathematics, agriculture, and building?

6. In Genesis 41:56–57 Joseph is presented with a mathematical challenge. What was that challenge?

7. Read Genesis 41:34–35. What percent of the harvest did Joseph suggest saving for the time of famine? Why do you suppose this could be sufficient to sustain the land for the seven years of famine?

8. Read Genesis 41:48–49. Where was the excess grain stored until it was needed? How much grain was stored?

Infinite Truths
Go to the ant, thou sluggard; consider her ways, and be wise: which having no guide, overseer, or ruler, provideth her meat in the summer, and gathereth her food in the harvest. *Proverbs 6:6–8*

Chapter 2 Review

Vocabulary

algebraic expression

Associative Property of Addition

Associative Property of Multiplication

Closure Property of Addition

Closure Property of Multiplication

Commutative Property of Addition

Commutative Property of Multiplication

constant

Distributive Property

front-end estimation

Identity Property of Addition

Identity Property of Multiplication

Inverse Property of Addition

like terms

numerical coefficient

term

Zero Property of Multiplication

Name the property or definition illustrated by each of the following.

1. $9 + 0 = 9$

2. $7 + (-7) = 0$

3. $0 \cdot 12 = 0$

4. $(5 + 8)6 = 6(5 + 8)$

5. $6 + 9$ is an integer.

6. $4[-3(-7)] = [4(-3)](-7)$

7. $(-4 + 7) + 8 = 8 + (-4 + 7)$

8. $15(x + 2) = 15x + 30$

9. $(3 + 6) + 2 = 3 + (6 + 2)$

10. $5(-9) = -9(5)$

11. $-4(x + 2) = -4(2 + x)$

12. $1(x + 3) = x + 3$

13. $2(3)(4) = 2(4)(3)$

14. $x - y = x + (-y)$

Use the Distributive Property to write an equivalent expression.

15. $8(7 + 6)$
16. $3(5x - 7)$
17. $-9(x + 4)$
18. $y(y + 19)$

Simplify.

19. $5(x + 8) + 2(x + 10)$
20. $y(2y - 4) + y(y + 6)$

21. $4(x + y) - 3(x - y)$
22. $a(b + d) + b(a - d) + d(b - a)$

Evaluate.

23. $2a - b$ when $a = -7$ and $b = 12$

24. $5(m - 7n)$ when $m = -2$ and $n = -6$

25. $\frac{5 - b}{3c}$ when $b = 11$ and $c = 1$

26. $19 + 5x - y$ when $x = -9$ and $y = 5$

27. $xy + 5y$ when $x = 8$ and $y = -3$

28. $\frac{m - n}{n}$ when $m = -20$ and $n = 5$

Identify the terms, constants, and coefficients in the following expressions.

29. $5x^2 - 3x + 9$

30. $a + 5ab - 7b$

Simplify.

31. $-4x + 9 + 6x - 24$

32. $5(a - 4b) + 3b$

33. $a + 3b - 4a + 8b$

34. $6(-2b) + 3b - 14 + 9b$

35. $5x + 9 - 8x - 3x + 12$

36. $-3(m - 7) + 6(8m) - 16$

37. Give three words that indicate multiplication.

38. Give three words that indicate subtraction.

Write each word phrase as an algebraic expression.

39. the product of -9 and n

40. 8 less than the quotient of x and 2

41. 23 increased by twice m

42. the difference of 12 and a

43. 64 less the product of 5 and p

44. the quotient of z and v, decreased by 28

45. Round 82,596 to the hundreds, tens, thousands, and ten thousands.

Estimate by rounding.

46. $72 + 89$

47. $8,352 - 6,724$

48. $517(28)$

49. $9,859 \div 192$

50. Give the mathematical significance of Proverbs 6:6–8.

3

BASIC
EQUATIONS AND
INEQUALITIES

Environmental engineers and scientists are concerned with pollution of the air, rivers, lakes, and ground water. Not only do they have to measure the type and amount of pollution in the environment, but they must design appropriate treatment methods to eliminate problems or lessen the impact on nearby residents' quality of life.

In the past, the United States Environmental Protection Agency (EPA) has allocated vast sums of money to clean up toxic waste sites where extreme pollution existed. Some of these environmental disasters came through ignorance of the hazards of certain chemicals, but many were motivated by greed. Many of the polluters were industries that buried the toxic wastes or dumped them in nearby streams with little regard for the consequences. The state of New Jersey alone has 116 such sites.

When the Lord gave man the Creation Mandate in Genesis 1:28, His command also included the implied responsibility of caring for the earth so that all that God made would not be destroyed. If people turn away from polluting practices, then significant healing of the environment can take place. At one time Lake Erie was so polluted no one could swim there or eat its fish, but recently great strides have been made toward cleaning up the lake and protecting it from further damage. The Christian has the best reason for being concerned about the environment. He knows the earth is important because it is God's creation. He also knows his fellow humans are precious (Gen. 1:27; Mark 12:31). By caring for the earth, he can obey God's mandate and help meet the needs of others.

After this chapter you should be able to
1. solve one-step and two-step equations.
2. translate a word sentence into an equation and solve it.
3. write an equation from a word problem and solve it.
4. determine the solution set for a one-step inequality.
5. write an inequality from a word problem and solve it.

3.1 Solving Equations by Adding or Subtracting

An equal sign indicates that the expressions on both sides of a math sentence represent the same number. This type of math sentence is an *equation*.

The equation $x - 5 = 9$ contains a single variable, x, and is true only when $x = 14$. The number 14 is the *solution* to the equation.

Definitions

An **equation** is a mathematical sentence that contains an equal sign.
A **solution** is a number that, when substituted for a variable, makes a mathematical sentence true.
Inverse operations are operations that undo one another.

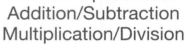
Inverse Operations:
Addition/Subtraction
Multiplication/Division

Addition and subtraction are inverse operations. This is because adding and subtracting the same amount from some number will always give the original number.

$$15 + 7 - 7 = 22 - 7 = 15$$

Consider again the equation $x - 5 = 9$. The expression $x - 5$ means 5 less than x. Adding 5 to $x - 5$ gives x. That is, $x - 5 + 5 = x$. But attempting to solve the original equation by adding 5 to one side of the equation destroys the equality. x does not equal 9. To maintain the equality, it is necessary to add 5 to both sides of the equation.

$$x - 5 = 9$$
$$x - 5 + 5 = 9 + 5$$
$$x = 14$$

In the same way, if one side of an equation contains $x + 5$ instead of $x - 5$, you can "undo" the addition of 5 by subtracting 5 from both sides.

$$x + 5 = 9$$
$$x + 5 - 5 = 9 - 5$$
$$x = 4$$

Whatever is done to one side of the equation must be done to the other side. This keeps the two sides equal.

The property used when solving equations by adding or subtracting from both sides of an equation is the *Addition Property of Equality*.

Addition Property of Equality

For all integers a, b, and c, if $a = b$, then $a + c = b + c$.

In the above property, any of the variables can be negative. The Addition Property of Equality signifies that if the same amount is added to (or subtracted from) both sides of an equation, then the quantities are still equal. It is not necessary to write a separate subtraction property. If you subtract the same amount from both sides of an equation, you are using the addition property above.

Example 1 Solve $x - 6 = 10$, and check the solution.

Answer

$x - 6 = 10$

$x - 6 + 6 = 10 + 6$ 1. To undo the subtraction, add 6. Since 6 is added to the left side, it must
$x = 16$ be added to the right side also.

Check: $16 - 6 = 10$ 2. Check by substituting 16 for x in the original equation.

Example 2 Solve $a + 39 = 17$, and check the solution.

Answer

$a + 39 = 17$

$a + 39 - 39 = 17 - 39$ 1. To undo the addition, subtract 39 (same as adding a negative 39)
$a = -22$ from both sides of the equation. This is an application of the Addition
                    Property of Equality.

Check: $-22 + 39 = 17$ 2. Check by substituting -22 for a in the original equation.

To solve an equation involving addition or subtraction,

1. determine what operation must be performed in order to isolate the variable on one side of the equation;

2. undo addition by subtracting or undo subtraction by adding;

3. remember that what you do to one side of the equation you must do to the other side also.

Skill Check 1

Name the inverse operation, including the quantity, that would be used to solve each equation.

1. $x + 18 = -46$ 2. $b - 25 = 87$

3. $125 = s + 87$ 4. $-162 = c - 48$

Solve.

5. $x + 18 = -46$ 6. $b - 25 = 87$

7. $125 = s + 87$ 8. $-162 = c - 48$

If the variable is on the right side of an equation, the sides of the equation can be switched to place the variable quantity on the left side.

$15 = y + 11$ is equivalent to $y + 11 = 15$.

The *Symmetric Property of Equality* allows us to do this. Since we read from left to right, it is convenient to apply this property before beginning to solve an equation. We will write solutions with the variable on the left side.

Symmetric Property of Equality
If $a = b$, then $b = a$.

If stating this as a property seems obvious, consider the relationship *greater than*. The Symmetric Property does not hold for greater than: $7 > 5$, but $5 < 7$.

Example 3 Solve $47 = m + 3$, and check the solution.

Answer

$$47 = m + 3$$
$$m + 3 = 47 \qquad \text{1. Apply the Symmetric Property of Equality.}$$
$$m + 3 - 3 = 47 - 3 \qquad \text{2. Subtract 3 from both sides of the equation.}$$
$$m = 44$$

Check: $44 + 3 = 47$ 3. Check by substituting 44 for m in the original equation.

The definition of subtraction can be used to simplify an expression when a plus or minus sign is followed by a negative integer.

$$3 - (-6) = 3 + 6 \qquad \text{Subtracting a negative is the same as adding a positive.}$$
$$3 + (-6) = 3 - 6 \qquad \text{Adding a negative is the same as subtracting a positive.}$$

The next two examples use this technique.

Example 4 Solve $y - (-7) = -18$, and check the solution.

Answer

$$y - (-7) = -18$$
$$y + 7 = -18 \qquad \text{1. Apply the definition of subtraction by changing from subtracting a negative to adding a positive.}$$
$$y + 7 - 7 = -18 - 7 \qquad \text{2. Subtract 7 from both sides of the equation.}$$
$$y = -25$$

Check: $-25 - (-7) = -25 + 7 = -18$ 3. Check by substituting -25 for y in the original equation.

Example 5 Solve $z + (-32) = -19$, and check the solution.

Answer

$$z + (-32) = -19$$
$$z - 32 = -19 \qquad \text{1. Apply the definition of subtraction by changing from adding a negative to subtracting a positive.}$$
$$z - 32 + 32 = -19 + 32 \qquad \text{2. Add 32 to both sides.}$$
$$z = 13$$

Check: $13 + (-32) = -19$ 3. Check by substituting 13 for z in the original equation.

Skill Check 2

Solve.

1. $n - (-28) = 73$
2. $115 = v + 34$
3. $m + (-41) = 87$
4. $98 = r - 69$

In the real world, applying algebra involves writing equations and solving them. Problems are expressed in words and the worker is expected to translate them into equivalent mathematical terms in the form of equations. The best way to simulate this process is to translate information from word problems into usable mathematical equations. The Problem Solving feature in Chapter 1 introduced the four steps of problem solving. They are reproduced here with an expansion of step 2 to cover writing equations.

The Problem-Solving Four-Point Checklist
1. **Read** to understand the question and identify the needed data.
2. **Plan** what to do to solve the problem.
a. Choose a variable to represent the unknown.
b. Write an equation to express the conditions of the problem.
3. **Solve** the problem by carrying out the plan.
4. **Check** to make sure the solution is reasonable.

Before writing equations, study Examples 6 and 7 to review how to change word phrases to mathematical expressions.

Example 6 Write each word phrase as a mathematical expression. Use *n* for the variable.

a. four more than a number

b. a number increased by ten

c. five less than a number

d. a number decreased by seven

e. seventeen decreased by a number

Answer

a. $n + 4$

b. $n + 10$

c. $n - 5$

d. $n - 7$

e. $17 - n$

Example 7 Write an algebraic expression for the number of nickels Sergei has and the number Kimberly has, if Sergei has eight more than Evan and Kimberly has six fewer than Evan. Use *x* for the variable.

Answer

Let $x =$ the number of nickels Evan has.

Sergei has $x + 8$ nickels.

Kimberly has $x - 6$ nickels.

Write each word phrase as an algebraic expression.

1. three decreased by a number

2. the sum of a number and nine

3. five more attended the meeting this month than last month

4. twelve more athletes than we had last year

5. forty-five less than a number

The verb generally indicates the location of the equal sign in the equation. The text before the verb is translated into symbols followed by the equal sign. The symbols representing the text that comes after the verb are written to the right of the equal sign.

Example 8   Write an equation for the sentence "A number decreased by three is sixteen."

Answer

Let n = the number.

$n - 3 =$

$n - 3 = 16$

1. Read the sentence carefully. Choose a variable for the unknown.

2. Identify the verb. Represent the words before the verb with an algebraic expression. The equal sign takes the place of the word *is*.

3. Sixteen is the only thing after the equal sign. Place it on the right side of the equation.

Example 9   Write an equation for the sentence "Seven dollars more than the cost of the shoes is ninety-eight dollars."

Answer

Let c = the cost.

$c + 7 =$

$c + 7 = 98$

1. Read the sentence carefully. Choose a variable for the unknown.

2. Identify the verb. Represent the words before the verb with an algebraic expression. The equal sign takes the place of the word *is*.

3. Place 98 to the right of the equal sign.

Write an equation for each of the following sentences.

1. The sum of a number and eighteen is thirty-one.

2. Twenty-three less than a number is six.

3. Eight dollars more than the total electric bill is seventy-six dollars.

4. The total bill was $118. The shoes cost $12 more than the dress.

■ A. Exercises

Name the inverse operation, including the quantity, that would be used to solve each equation.

1. $x - 12 = -49$
2. $s + 8 = 7$
3. $-16 = c - 42$
4. $a - 17 = -2$
5. $-8 + x = 23$
6. $b + 15 = 80$

Solve.

7. $x + 3 = 17$
8. $b - 19 = 8$
9. $17 + y = 6$
10. $x - 200 = 87$

■ B. Exercises

Solve.

11. $x - 19 = -3$
12. $x + (-3) = -3$
13. $x - (-14) = -2$
14. $32 = z - 17$
15. $w - (-7) = 31$
16. $14 + x = -33$

Write an equation using *n* for the variable for each sentence below. Solve the equation.

17. A number decreased by 8 is 27.

18. The sum of a number and 32 is 43.

19. 45 less than a number is 118.

20. 15 less than a number is -4.

21. 12 added to a number is 25.

22. The difference between a number and 9 is 34.

23. A number increased by 53 is 96.

24. -20 added to a number is -5.

25. A number decreased by 130 is -42.

Specify what the variable stands for, and then write an equation. Solve it and show your work.

26. A fisherman caught 27 fish, 18 of them before noon. How many did he catch after noon?

27. Mr. Blaine was overdrawn by $27 after writing a check for $163. What was his bank balance at the time he wrote the check?

28. A rectangular picture frame was made from one 8 ft. long board with nothing left over. The two lengths of the frame total 6 ft. What is the total for the two widths?

29. The home team scored 80 points and won by 19. How many points did the opposing team make?

30. This week's groceries cost $9 more than last week's groceries. This week's bill was $104. How much was spent on groceries last week?

31. Maura was twelve years old five years ago. How old is she now?

32. Fourteen absentees subtracted from the total number of choir members leaves 64 present. How many choir members are there?

33. The sum of the number of teachers and five teacher's aides is 32. How many teachers are there?

34. There are 96 cows in all, of which 73 are Herefords. The rest are Angus. How many Angus cows are there?

■ C. Exercises

Solve.

35. $-5 + (s + 2) = -9(8)$

36. $(17 - 12) - (-a) = 125 - 250$

37. $-6y + 9 + 7y - 4 = -8 + (-41)$

38. $23 + c - 7 + 2 = 7 - 61$

39. $d + [17 - (-12)] = 5 - (-58)$

■ Dominion thru Math

Levels of pollution in a water course are expressed in mg/L of the particular substance. The discharge from sewage treatment plants can potentially introduce significant amounts of pollutants into streams and rivers. For this reason, regulatory agencies set limits for the maximum amount of each type of potential pollutant that may be discharged.

Use these conversion factors to help you solve the following problems: 1 g = 1,000 mg; 1 kg = 1,000 g; 1 m^3 = 1,000 L; and 1 gal. = 3.785 L.

40. The discharge to a stream of a certain pollutant is 840 g/day and the flow rate is 4,500 m^3/day. Find the pollutant discharge in mg/day, the flow rate in L/day, and the concentration of the pollutant in mg/L.

41. A bypass sewer used for emergencies discharged 15,000 gal. of untreated wastewater with a concentration of 240 mg/L of chemical oxygen demand (COD). Find the total amount in liters of wastewater discharged during this emergency, the amount of COD discharged in kg/L, and the total amount of COD in kilograms.

42. The bypass sewer in exercise 41 also discharged 635 mg/L of suspended solids (SS). What was the total amount of SS in kilograms discharged during this emergency?

⌐■ CUMULATIVE REVIEW ■⌐

Simplify. [2.5]

43. $3x + 2 - 5x + 8$

44. $4 - 7y + 12 + 15y$

45. $17 - 2x - 8$

46. $-8 + 7x - 4$

Write the following numbers in standard form. [1.8]

47. 4.5×10^7

48. 3.67×10^{-3}

49. 2.45×10^4

50. 6.8×10^{-6}

Simplify. [1.7]

51. $6 - 8 \times 4$

52. $7 \times 5 - 8$

PROBLEM SOLVING

Guess and Check

You may use the strategy "guess and check" to solve some word problems. In this strategy you begin by guessing the answer. Then you check your guess to see whether it satisfies the conditions of the problem.

Example 1   A pet store has four more dogs than cats. If the number of cats were doubled and then reduced by one, the result would be equal to the number of dogs. How many dogs and how many cats does the pet store have?

Answer

Think: If I guess that the number of cats is 3, then the number of dogs is $3 + 4 = 7$. Does this produce the correct result? If not, try another number for the number of cats.

Guess: Step 1	Guess: Step 2	Check
Guess the number of cats.	Find the number of dogs $(c + 4 = d)$.	Is 2 times the number of cats minus 1 equal to the number of dogs $(2c - 1 = d)$?
3 cats	$3 + 4 = 7$ dogs	$2 \times 3 - 1 = 5; 5 \neq 7$
4 cats	$4 + 4 = 8$ dogs	$2 \times 4 - 1 = 7; 7 \neq 8$
5 cats	$5 + 4 = 9$ dogs	$2 \times 5 - 1 = 9$

The pet store has 5 cats and 9 dogs.

Think: As you look back at the original problem, does the answer fit the statements and facts in the problem?

This answer fits perfectly, so it must be correct.

An interesting math problem called "Guess My Rule" involves finding a rule that will take a given number (usually labeled x) and, after using the rule on it, will produce another given number (usually labeled y). The guess-and-check strategy can be used to solve these problems.

Example 2 Find a rule that will produce –6 from –2, 6 from 1, 2 from 0, and –2 from –1.

Answer

Think: Guess an operation that would produce –6 from –2. Check to see if it is correct for the other pairs. If not, try another operation that will produce –6 from –2. Keep checking until you find the correct answer.

Guess	Check	Check	Check
Guess the rule.	Does the rule work for the second pair of numbers?	Does the rule work for the third pair of numbers?	Does the rule work for the fourth pair of numbers?
$-2 - 4 = -6$ $y = x - 4$	$1 - 4 = -3 \neq 6$; no		
$4(-2) + 2 = -6$ $y = 4x + 2$	$4(1) + 2 = 6$; yes	$4(0) + 2 = 2$; yes	$4(-1) + 2 = -2$; yes

The rule that works for all four pairs of numbers is $y = 4x + 2$.

Think: This rule works for all of the given pairs of numbers, so it is correct.

■ Exercises

For each of the following problems, devise a plan for finding the solution and carry out the plan.

1. Matt scored three more goals than Mark during the soccer season. If the number of goals Mark scored were doubled and then decreased by one, the result would equal the number of Matt's goals. How many goals did Mark score? How many did Matt score?

2. A bookstore has twice as many biographies as autobiographies. The store has 81 biographies and auto-biographies combined. How many books of each type does the store have?

3. Three consecutive integers have a sum of 24 and a product of 504. What are the integers?

4. Jessica found that the bill for 16 mugs ordered by the restaurant had digits blurred by water damage. She could read the cents part on the price per mug (50¢) but not the dollar amount. The total cost was an even dollar amount. She was sure that both digits on the total cost were the same, but she was not sure what the numbers were. What do you think the total price was? Explain your answer.

5. Guess a rule that when applied to the set of numbers {2, 4, 6, 10} gives the set of numbers {7, 11, 15, 23} respectively.

6. There are emus and llamas in a fenced field of an exotic animal farm. Melody tells Amber that she counts 60 feet and 18 heads behind the fence. How many of each animal are in the field?

7. Peanuts cost $3.25/lb. and cashews cost $6.15/lb. If a 20 lb. mix of these two nuts is made and costs a total of $85.30, how many pounds of each type of nut are in the mix?

Llamas are beasts of burden. A 300 lb. llama can carry from 75 to 90 lb.

3.2 Solving Equations by Multiplying or Dividing

Multiplication and division are inverse operations. If a number is multiplied by 5 and then the product is divided by 5, the result is the original number.

$$15 \times 5 \div 5 = 75 \div 5 = 15$$

Consider the equation $\frac{x}{3} = 8$. The expression $\frac{x}{3}$ means x divided by 3. Multiplying $\frac{x}{3}$ by 3 would give x. That is, $3\left(\frac{x}{3}\right) = x$. But multiplying one side of the equation by 3 destroys the equality. x does not equal 8. To maintain the equality, it is necessary to multiply both sides of the equation by 3.

$$\frac{x}{3} = 8$$

$$3\left(\frac{x}{3}\right) = 3(8)$$

$$x = 24$$

If one side of the equation contains $3x$ instead of $\frac{x}{3}$, you can undo the multiplication by its inverse operation, division by 3.

$$3x = 24$$

$$\frac{3x}{3} = \frac{24}{3}$$

$$x = 8$$

As before, whatever is done to one side of the equation must be done to the other side. This keeps the two sides equal.

The property used to solve equations involving multiplication or division is the *Multiplication Property of Equality*.

Multiplication Property of Equality
For all integers a, b, and c, if $a = b$, then $ac = bc$.

In the above property, a, b, or c can be fractions; and division is equivalent to multiplication by the reciprocal. Therefore, there is no need to state a separate division property of equality. Division is equivalent to multiplying by the reciprocal. Whether you multiply or divide both sides of the equation by a quantity, you are using the multiplication property above.

Example 1   Solve $\frac{x}{-4} = 14$, and check the solution.

Answer

$$\frac{x}{-4} = 14$$

$$-4\left(\frac{x}{-4}\right) = -4(14)$$ 1. Multiply both sides by –4, since x is divided by –4.

$$x = -56$$

Check: $\frac{-56}{-4} = 14$ 2. Check by substituting –56 for x in the original equation.

The fractions $-\frac{a}{b}$, $\frac{-a}{b}$, and $\frac{a}{-b}$ are all equivalent. If an equation contains the fraction $\frac{-x}{5}$ or $-\frac{x}{5}$, you can treat it as $\frac{x}{-5}$ and multiply both sides of the equation by –5 to isolate the variable.

Example 2   Solve $9y = 72$, and check the solution.

Answer

$$9y = 72$$

$$\frac{9y}{9} = \frac{72}{9}$$ 1. Since y is multiplied by 9, undo the multiplication by dividing by 9. The right side must also be divided by 9.

$$y = 8$$

Check: $9(8) = 72$ 2. Check by substituting 8 for y in the original equation.

To solve an equation involving multiplication or division,

1. determine which operation must be performed in order to isolate the variable on one side of the equation;

2. undo multiplication by dividing or undo division by multiplying;

3. be sure to perform like operations on both sides of the equation to keep it balanced.

Skill Check 1

Name the inverse operation, including the quantity, that would be used to solve each equation.

1. $12b = 24$ 2. $\frac{r}{35} = -9$

3. $-27n = 81$ 4. $\frac{x}{-3} = 6$

Solve.

5. $12b = 24$ 6. $\frac{r}{35} = -9$

7. $-27n = 81$ 8. $\frac{x}{-3} = 6$

The equation $-n = 37$ is equivalent to $-1n = 37$. Therefore, to solve this equation, multiply both sides by –1.

$$-n = 37$$
$$-1(-n) = -1(37)$$
$$n = -37$$

You could also divide both sides by −1 instead, as shown in the following example.

Example 3   Solve $-n = 37$.

Answer

$-n = 37$

$\dfrac{-n}{-1} = \dfrac{37}{-1}$ Divide both sides by −1.

$n = -37$

Before writing equations, study Examples 4 and 5 to review translating word phrases into mathematical expressions.

Example 4   Write each word phrase as a mathematical expression. Use n for the variable.

a. twice a number

b. four times a number

c. one-third of a number

d. quotient of a number and eight

e. quotient of eight and a number

Answer

a. $2n$

b. $4n$

c. $\dfrac{n}{3}$ or $\dfrac{1}{3}n$

d. $\dfrac{n}{8}$ or $\dfrac{1}{8}n$

e. $\dfrac{8}{n}$

Example 5   Write an algebraic expression for the ages of Jon and Eileen, if Jon's age is twice Joyce's and Eileen's age is one-fourth of Joyce's.

Answer

Let x = Joyce's age.

Jon's age is $2x$.

Eileen's age is $\dfrac{x}{4}$ or $\dfrac{1}{4}x$.

Skill Check 2

Write each word phrase as an algebraic expression.

1. a number tripled

2. the quotient of sixty and a number

3. the quantity m dozen eggs

4. one-fifth of this year's team

5. sixty-one students decreased by the number of visitors

6. Which of the following are equivalent: $\dfrac{2x}{3}$, $\dfrac{2}{3x}$, $\dfrac{2}{3}x$?

Example 6   Write an equation for the sentence "Nineteen dollars is the result of dividing the cost of a tennis racket by three."

Answer

Let c = the cost.	1. Read the sentence carefully. Choose a variable for the unknown.
$19 =$	2. The verb *is* indicates the equal sign. Nineteen is to the left of the equal sign.
$19 = \dfrac{c}{3}$	3. Represent the phrase following the verb and place it to the right of the equal sign.
$\dfrac{c}{3} = 19$	4. You can rewrite the equation with the variable on the left. This is a use of the Symmetric Property of Equality.

Example 7   The advertised cost for three items is $69. What is the unit price?

Answer

Let x = the price per unit.	1. Read the sentence carefully. Choose a variable for the unknown.
$3x =$	2. The verb *is* indicates the equal sign. The total cost is three times the cost per unit.
$3x = 69$	3. Place 69 to the right of the equal sign.
$\dfrac{3x}{3} = \dfrac{69}{3}$	4. Divide both sides of the equation by 3.
$x = 23$	5. The unit cost is $23.

Skill Check 3

Write an equation and solve.

1. The quotient of a number and twelve is eight. Find the number.

2. The bill for coffee selling for $7/lb. was $42. How many pounds of coffee were purchased?

3. The offering of $8,428 was divided equally among the missionary families at the conference. Each family received $2,107. How many missionary families were there?

■ A. Exercises

Name the inverse operation, including the quantity, that would be used to solve each equation.

1. $\dfrac{y}{5} = -14$ 2. $-3z = 39$ 3. $4x = -36$

4. $7x = -49$ 5. $-\dfrac{a}{16} = 8$ 6. $3p = 18$

Solve.

7. $4x = 96$ 8. $\dfrac{z}{7} = 40$ 9. $-7x = 28$ 10. $-c = -13$

11. $-9x = 27$ 12. $25 + y = -10$ 13. $\dfrac{a}{2} = 16$ 14. $17y = -51$

■ B. Exercises

Solve.

15. $63 = -7b$ 16. $-240 = -20a$ 17. $-3y = 783$ 18. $\dfrac{x}{3} = -33$

19. $52 = -13x$ 20. $-4w = -68$ 21. $31a = -527$ 22. $\dfrac{z}{-12} = 19$

Write an equation using *n* for the variable for each sentence below. Solve the equation.

23. One-half of a number is 84.

24. Seventeen multiplied by a number is 68.

25. The quotient of a number and 7 is 44.

26. The product of 5 and a number is 215.

27. A number divided by 14 is 7.

28. Nineteen times a number is 361.

29. If the original number is doubled and then that number is tripled, the result is 138.

30. One-thirteenth of a number is 1,157.

Specify what the variable stands for, and then write an equation. Solve it and show your work.

31. Mr. Shaw tithes one-tenth of his income. His last tithe check was $213. How much income did he tithe on?

32. Find the cost per yard if 5 yd. of material cost $65.

33. The high-school track team won first place in one-third of the events in the meet. If the team won five events, how many events were there?

34. The 364 mi. automobile trip was finished in 7 hr. What was the average speed?

35. The school's top running back gained 126 yd. in the game. If his average was 6.0 yd. per carry, how many times did he carry the ball?

36. A farmer sold ears of corn for $4 a dozen and took in $304. How many dozen ears did he sell?

37. Find how many candy bars costing $0.69 each can be bought with a $20 bill.

38. The grand prize of $7,500 was divided equally among all the entrants who had tied for first place in the competition. Each received $1,250. How many tied for the prize?

■ C. Exercises

39. Write an equation and solve: Eighty increased by the sum of three times a number and nine is one hundred ten.

40. On a 627 mi. work trip, Mr. Johannson traveled by airplane, automobile, and bicycle. He traveled seven times farther by plane than by car and one-seventh as far by bicycle as by car. Express the three distances without using fractions; then use them to write the resulting equation. Find each distance traveled.

41. Write the following sum as a single fraction: $2n + \dfrac{n}{3}$.

42. For what values of the variable or variables would (a) $\dfrac{5}{x}$ be negative and (b) $\dfrac{y}{z}$ be positive?

Dominion thru Math

43. During an 8 hr. shift a factory discharges 5.95 g of a moderately toxic chemical into a stream. The flow rate of the discharge averages 14 L/min. Will the factory meet the mandated standard of no more than 0.25 mg/L of the chemical?

44. A wastewater stream with a concentration of 4 mg/L of COD discharges 3.4 kg/day into the nearby stream. What is the discharge flow rate of this wastewater stream in liters (a) per day and (b) per minute?

CUMULATIVE REVIEW

Perform the indicated operations. [1.2–1.6]

45. $-6 - (-19)$

46. $115 \div (-23)$

47. $-17 + (-44)$

48. $-91(-3)$

49. -3^4

50. $(-3)^4$

Write each of the following using only positive exponents. [1.6]

51. x^{-3}

52. $\dfrac{x^{-4}}{y^{-2}}$

53. $a^2 b^{-5}$

54. $\dfrac{1}{c^{-3}}$

3.3 Solving Two-Step Equations

In Sections 3.1 and 3.2, one-step equations were solved by undoing a single operation. Suppose an equation has two operations in it, such as $3x - 8 = 28$. Before solving this two-step equation, you must decide which inverse operations should be used and in what order.

The key to solving an equation like $3x - 8 = 28$ is to do the inverse operations in reverse order of the way you would evaluate the expression if you were given a value for the variable. Suppose you evaluate the expression $3x - 8$ when $x = 5$.

$$3x - 8 = 3(5) - 8$$
$$= 15 - 8$$
$$= 7$$

When solving equations, undo the last operation first.

The operations performed were multiplying by 3 and then subtracting 8. To solve the equation $3x - 8 = 28$, you undo the subtraction first, since it was the last operation performed. Then you undo the multiplication.

$$3x - 8 = 28$$
$$3x - 8 + 8 = 28 + 8$$
$$3x = 36$$
$$\frac{3x}{3} = \frac{36}{3}$$
$$x = 12$$

Study the following table, comparing columns 2 and 3 for each equation.

Equation	Order of Operations Performed on the Variable	Undoing These Operations
$2n + 7 = 25$	First n is multiplied by 2; then 7 is added to the product.	Subtract 7 from both sides; then divide both sides by 2.
$3x - 4 = -10$	First x is multiplied by 3; then 4 is subtracted from the product.	Add 4 to both sides; then divide both sides by 3.
$\dfrac{z - 3}{2} = 9$	First 3 is subtracted from z; then the difference is divided by 2.	Multiply both sides by 2; then add 3 to both sides.
$\dfrac{x}{4} + 6 = 20$	First x is divided by 4; then 6 is added to the quotient.	Subtract 6 from both sides; then multiply both sides by 4.

Examples 1–4 following Skill Check 1 offer written solutions to the above four equations.

The steps for solving equations in which two operations have been performed on the variable are summarized below.

Solving Equations with Two Operations
1. Determine the order in which the operations have been performed on the variable.
2. Undo the operations in reverse order by performing the inverse operations on both sides of the equation.

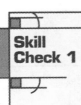

Skill Check 1

Name the inverse operation, including the quantity, that would be used first to solve each equation.

1. $4a + 7 = 34$

2. $\dfrac{r - 3}{12} = 2$

3. $\dfrac{k}{2} - 9 = 5$

4. $2x - 5 = 17$

Example 1 Solve $2n + 7 = 25$, and check the solution.

Answer

$2n + 7 = 25$

$2n + 7 - 7 = 25 - 7$ 1. Subtract 7 from both sides.

$2n = 18$

$\dfrac{2n}{2} = \dfrac{18}{2}$ 2. Divide both sides by 2.

$n = 9$

$2(9) + 7 = 25$ 3. Substitute 9 for n in the original equation to check the solution.

$18 + 7 = 25$

$25 = 25$

Example 2   Solve $3x - 4 = -10$, and check the solution.

Answer

$$3x - 4 = -10$$

$$3x - 4 + 4 = -10 + 4$$ 1. Add 4 to both sides.

$$3x = -6$$

$$\frac{3x}{3} = \frac{-6}{3}$$ 2. Divide both sides by 3.

$$x = -2$$

$$3(-2) - 4 = -10$$ 3. Substitute −2 for x in the original equation to check the solution.

$$-6 - 4 = -10$$

$$-10 = -10$$

Example 3   Solve $\frac{z - 3}{2} = 9$, and check the solution.

Answer

$$\frac{z - 3}{2} = 9$$

$$2\left(\frac{z - 3}{2}\right) = 2(9)$$ 1. Multiply both sides by 2.

$$z - 3 = 18$$

$$z - 3 + 3 = 18 + 3$$ 2. Add 3 to both sides.

$$z = 21$$

$$\frac{21 - 3}{2} = 9$$ 3. Substitute 21 for z to check the solution.

$$\frac{18}{2} = 9$$

$$9 = 9$$

Example 4   Solve $\frac{x}{4} + 6 = 20$, and check the solution.

Answer

$$\frac{x}{4} + 6 = 20$$

$$\frac{x}{4} + 6 - 6 = 20 - 6$$ 1. Subtract 6 from both sides.

$$\frac{x}{4} = 14$$

$$4\left(\frac{x}{4}\right) = 4(14)$$ 2. Multiply both sides by 4.

$$x = 56$$

$$\frac{56}{4} + 6 = 20$$ 3. Substitute 56 for x to check the solution.

$$14 + 6 = 20$$

$$20 = 20$$

Example 5   Solve $5 - x = 10$, and check the solution.

Answer

$$5 - x = 10$$
$$5 - x - 5 = 10 - 5$$ 1. Note that 5 has been added to $-x$, and subtract 5 from both sides.
$$-x = 5$$
$$x = -5$$ 2. Taking the opposite of both sides produces the same result as multiplying or dividing both sides by -1.
$$5 - (-5) = 10$$ 3. Substitute -5 for x to check the solution.
$$5 + 5 = 10$$
$$10 = 10$$

The subtraction of x in the last example can cause confusion. Adding 5 to both sides will not undo this subtraction. Rewriting the equation as $5 + (-x) = 10$ or $-x + 5 = 10$ can clarify the need to subtract 5 from both sides.

Skill Check 2

Solve.

1. $3n - 5 = 16$ 2. $2x + 8 = 4$

3. $\dfrac{x - 5}{-12} = 2$ 4. $\dfrac{t}{7} + 2 = -6$

5. $\dfrac{a}{9} - 11 = 13$ 6. $7 - x = 12$

The following examples show equations set up and solved for word problems.

Example 6   This year the team won three more than twice as many games as last year. This year they won 75 games. How many games did they win last year?

Answer

Let g = games won last year.   1. Read the problem carefully. Choose a variable for the unknown.

$$2g + 3 = 75$$ 2. The first two sentences begin with the words "This year." Both refer to the same quantity. Write an expression for the first sentence followed by an equal sign and the value from the second sentence.

$$2g + 3 - 3 = 75 - 3$$ 3. Subtract 3 from both sides.
$$2g = 72$$
$$\dfrac{2g}{2} = \dfrac{72}{2}$$ 4. Divide both sides by 2.
$$g = 36$$ 5. They won 36 games last year.

| | Example 7 | Tony bought a trumpet for $498. He made a down payment of $46 and arranged to make payments of $55 per month. How many months will it take him to pay for the trumpet? |

Answer

Let m = the number of months.   1. Read the problem carefully. Choose a variable for the unknown.

$55m + 46$ 2. Write an expression to represent the total payment ($55 per month plus the down payment).

$55m + 46 = 498$ 3. The expression representing the total amount paid must equal the cost of the trumpet.

$55m + 46 - 46 = 498 - 46$ 4. Subtract 46 from both sides.

$55m = 452$

$\dfrac{55m}{55} = \dfrac{452}{55}$ 5. Divide both sides by 55.

$m \approx 8.2$ or 9 months

Skill Check 3

Write an equation and solve.

1. Mr. Gage wants to buy new car A but is considering used car B. Car A costs $2,500 less than twice as much as car B. If car A costs $20,800, what is the cost of car B?

2. The shadow of a vertical pole on level ground is 10 ft. more than one-third the height of the pole. If the shadow is 19 ft. long, how high is the pole?

■ A. Exercises

Name the inverse operation, including the quantity, that would be used first to solve each equation.

1. $7a + 6 = 34$
2. $\dfrac{b}{-5} - 15 = 100$
3. $3(x + 17) = 21$
4. $\dfrac{s + 7}{5} = 11$

Solve.

5. $2k + 3 = 15$
6. $\dfrac{c}{6} - 7 = 1$
7. $8k + 8 = -16$
8. $\dfrac{n}{9} + 5 = 14$

9. $6z - 5 = 19$
10. $8s - 2 = 70$
11. $4x - 8 = 12$
12. $-2n + 9 = 17$

13. $3 = \dfrac{r}{9} - 4$
14. $7x - 9 = 19$

■ B. Exercises

Solve.

15. $4b - 7 = -47$
16. $\dfrac{p}{13} - 4 = 26$
17. $9 - x = 27$
18. $\dfrac{w}{5} + 3 = -11$

19. $\dfrac{x + 7}{9} = 6$
20. $18 = \dfrac{x + 12}{6}$
21. $\dfrac{s + 7}{5} = 23$
22. $\dfrac{t + 11}{4} = -6$

23. $\dfrac{9 - m}{3} = 19$
24. $\dfrac{x - 5}{2} = 17$
25. $\dfrac{b - 18}{11} = 9$

Write an equation and solve.

26. Samuel has saved $223, part in ten-dollar bills and $43 in other bills. How many tens does he have?

27. Mrs. Brand spent $50 on a sewing project. She bought 4 yd. of material and $6 worth of notions. What is the price per yard that she spent on the material?

28. Mr. Jenks spent $527 for a new mower and three equally priced hand tools for use in his garden. The mower cost $470. What was the cost for each hand tool?

29. Mrs. Jung bought two bottles of perfume, each costing the same amount. She presented a $10 off coupon and $140 cash. What was the regular cost per bottle of the perfume?

30. A shopper bought four shirts, all at the same price, and spent $75 on ties. The total cost was $155. What was the cost per shirt?

31. $800 is allotted to perform a play. There are two expenses: stage prop construction and costumes. The necessary stage props cost $416. How much is available per costume for the eight members of the cast?

32. A landscaper is buying a tree costing $96 and wants to buy shrubs at $8 each. He has to keep the total amount spent to a maximum of $200. How many shrubs can he buy?

33. A homeowner has budgeted $10,000 for some home remodeling. A contractor has told him the labor and the cost of materials will be about the same amount. The homeowner wants to have about $3,000 left over for furnishings. How much will the homeowner be able to spend on labor and on materials?

34. A budget calls for $200 less than one-third of the clothing portion of the budget to be spent on the man of the house. If the man's needs are estimated at $600 for the year, how much should be budgeted for the entire family for the year?

35. A business is closing down. Each of eight workers is to be given a severance package from an account containing $22,840. From this account, four workers are to be given $500 each and the other four $1,000 each. From the remainder, each of these workers is to receive an equal share. How much will each worker get?

■ C. Exercises

Solve.

36. $\dfrac{4a + 5}{9} = -3$

37. $\dfrac{-6x + 6}{7} = -18$

38. $-9z - 36 - 6 = 48$

39. $\dfrac{-y}{4} + 3 = 8$

40. $\dfrac{2x}{13} - 6 = 4$

■ Dominion thru Math

The amount of water carried by pipes of various sizes must be determined for many different conditions when engineers design treatment facilities to reduce pollution. The flow of water in pipes falls under two categories: gravity flow (such as sewers) and pressure flow (such as water distribution piping). Gravity flow is too complicated for our present consideration, but flow in pressure piping is simpler. All that is needed is the formula $Q = AV$. Q is the flow rate in ft.^{3}/sec. A is the cross-sectional area of the circular pipe in ft.^{2}, which is found by the standard formula $A = \pi r^2$. V is the velocity of the water in the pipe in ft./sec. The velocity in the pipe depends on the pressure available and the roughness of the inside of the pipe.

41. What is the flow rate in a 12 in. diameter pipe with a velocity of 7 ft./sec.?

42. What is the flow rate in a 6 in. diameter pipe with a velocity of 7 ft./sec.?

43. Find the ratio of the flow rate in a 12 in. pipe to the flow rate in a 6 in. pipe. Even though the ratio of the diameters is 2, explain why the ratio of the flows is not 2.

CUMULATIVE REVIEW

Evaluate each expression when $x = -4$, $y = -7$, and $z = 8$. [2.4]

44. $2x - 3y$

45. $x^2 - 2z$

46. $3(2x - y)$

47. $z(4 - x)$

48. $3 - xyz$

49. $\dfrac{z}{2x}$

Perform the indicated operations. [1.3–1.5]

50. $-3(-7)(-4)$

51. $14 - 2(-5)$

52. $-12 \div 2$

53. $-17 - (-8) - 5$

3.4 Simplifying Before Solving

As equations become more complicated, solving them requires more steps. The Distributive Property is often used to simplify one or both sides of an equation before proceeding to solve it. Example 1 reviews combining like terms.

| Example 1 | Simplify the expression $12y + (4y - 5)$ by combining like terms. |

Answer

$12y + (4y - 5)$

$(12y + 4y) - 5$ 1. Group the like terms together using the Associative Property of Addition.

$(12 + 4)y - 5$ 2. Use the Distributive Property to express $12y + 4y$ as $(12 + 4)y$.

$16y - 5$

Simplify.

1. $5m + 3m$

2. $14x + 2y - 18x + z$

3. $-6z + 9z + 8 - 3z$

4. $-13n - 24n - 2$

Example 2 Solve $2x - 9x = 343$.

Answer

$2x - 9x = 343$

$-7x = 343$

$\dfrac{-7x}{-7} = \dfrac{343}{-7}$

$x = -49$

1. Mentally apply the Distributive Property: $2x - 9x = (2 - 9)x = -7x$.

2. Divide both sides of the equation by -7.

Example 3 Solve $9x - 6 - 6x + 12 = 33$.

Answer

$9x - 6 - 6x + 12 = 33$

$(9x - 6x) + (-6 + 12) = 33$

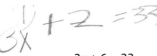

$3x + 6 = 33$

$3x + 6 - 6 = 33 - 6$

$3x = 27$

$\dfrac{3x}{3} = \dfrac{27}{3}$

$x = 9$

1. Use the Commutative and Associative Properties to group the numbers on the left side. Notice that the minus sign in front of the term 6 makes the term negative when it is written as the first term of the expression.

2. Combine like terms.

3. Subtract 6 from both sides.

4. Divide both sides by 3.

Example 4 Solve $-5x + 7x + 12 = -8$.

Answer

$-5x + 7x + 12 = -8$

$2x + 12 = -8$

$2x + 12 - 12 = -8 - 12$

$2x = -20$

$\dfrac{2x}{2} = \dfrac{-20}{2}$

$x = -10$

1. Mentally apply the Distributive Property: $-5x + 7x = (-5 + 7)x = 2x$.

2. Subtract 12 from both sides.

3. Divide both sides by 2.

Solve.

1. $4x - 7x = 69$

2. $8x + 3 - 7 = -12$

3. $8x + 13 - 11x = 7$

4. $4x + 5x + 12 - 1 = -16$

Once an equation is used to model the situation in a word problem, the equation can be solved to answer the question.

| Example 5 | The concession stand sold twice as many 16 oz. sodas as they did 12 oz. sodas and gave two large (16 oz.) sodas to the referees. If they used 30.5 gal. (3,904 oz.) of soda during the ball games, how many sodas of each size did they sell? |

Answer

Let s = the number of small sodas and $2s$ = the number of large sodas sold.

1. Read the problem carefully. Choose a variable for the unknown.

$12s + 16(2s) + 2(16) = 3,904$

2. Each small soda was 12 oz., each large soda was 16 oz., and the sodas sold plus the two large sodas for the referees totaled 3,904 oz.

$12s + 32s + 32 = 3,904$
$44s + 32 = 3,904$

3. Simplify the equation.

$44s + 32 - 32 = 3,904 - 32$

4. Subtract 32 from both sides of the equation.

$44s = 3,872$

$\dfrac{44s}{44} = \dfrac{3,872}{44}$

5. Divide both sides of the equation by 44.

$s = 88$

88 small and 176 large sodas were sold.

6. Answer the question posed by the problem.

⊕ Invention

So what is a microwave? It is a type of electromagnetic radiation with a wavelength in the range of 1 mm to 30 cm, which is about the same as that used for radar. In 1946 a Raytheon Corporation engineer named Dr. Percy LeBaron Spencer invented the microwave oven as a consequence of his radar research. After several experiments with foods such as popcorn and eggs, Dr. Spencer realized that he had a completely new way to cook food. He set up his laboratory experiment to direct microwave energy into the oven so that the electromagnetic field did not escape. In 1946 Raytheon Corporation filed a patent and began testing the microwave oven's use in commercial restaurants. By 1967 development had progressed to the point that the Amana Division of Raytheon was able to offer the public a reasonably priced compact microwave oven called the Radarange. Today more than 95% of US homes have a microwave.

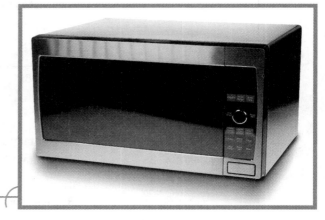

■ A. Exercises

Simplify.

1. $7x + 5x$

2. $-4y + 17y$

3. $-z - 5z$

4. $15g - 28g$

5. $9 - 5c + 8$

6. $8x + (-6x) - x$

7. $8p - 4p - 6$

8. $3a + 4a - b$

9. $12 - 6r + 3r - 4$

10. $6t - 5 + 2t$

Solve.

11. $7x - 2x = 25$ 12. $18x - 4x = 70$ 13. $7z - 4z = -9$ 14. $2x + x = -45$

Write an equation and solve.

15. A number decreased by twice the number is –60.

16. A high-school football team played nine games. It won twice as many as it lost. How many games did the team lose?

17. The sum of two numbers is twenty-five. The larger number is four times the smaller number. Find the numbers.

18. One number is one more than twice another number. Their sum is 91. Find the numbers.

■ B. Exercises

Solve.

19. $72 = 2x + 16x$ 20. $18x - (-x) = 95$ 21. $-18 = -4y + 7y$

22. $-132 = -3a - 9a$ 23. $120x - 1,000 + 32x = 64$ 24. $6x - 8x + 3 = 41$

25. $20 - 8y + 3 = -129$ 26. $-16 = 9k + 7k$ 27. $2x + 3 - 8x + 9 = 0$

28. $-5y + 2y - 9 + y = -25$ 29. $9x - 5x - 3 = 401$ 30. $2x + 19 - 17 + 14x = 2$

Write an equation and solve.

31. A builder purchased four identical doors for a building on Monday and then seven additional doors at the same price on Thursday. The total bill came to $1,386. What was the price per door?

32. A Laundromat owner bought eleven new washing machines and eight new dryers. He paid the same amount for a dryer as for a washer. His final cost was $10,450. What was the cost per machine?

33. A barbeque stand sold twice as many regular size sandwiches as large sandwiches. The regular ones sold for $4 each and the large sandwiches sold for $5 each. The total sales amount was $585. How many of each kind were sold?

34. On a multiple choice exam, a college instructor gives 2 points for a correct answer and –1 for a wrong answer. No points are given for an unanswered question. A student received 82 points on the test. If he left two questions unanswered and missed six, how many did he get right? How many questions were there on the exam?

35. A grocery shopper bought 6 lb. of steak and 20 lb. of ground beef. The steak cost $5/lb. more than the ground beef, and the total bill was $82. What was the price per pound for each type of meat?

36. A consumer bought two items on credit with zero interest for set monthly payments of $250 and $90. Both items were financed for the same length of time. How long would it take to pay them off if the total amount of the combined purchases was $3,060?

37. A shopper bought eight identical garden shrubs. Later she returned and bought twelve additional more expensive shrubs at twice the price. The total spent on shrubs was $256. How much did she spend for each type of shrub?

38. It took twice as long to go from Jones Corner to Summer Town as it did from home to Jones Corner. The whole trip required one hour and nine minutes. How long did it take to go from home to Jones Corner?

39. The trailer cost one-fourth as much as the boat. The total cost of both was $4,000. How much did each cost? Explain how to avoid the use of fractions in setting up the problem, and then work it.

40. Denny, Jamal, and Bobby are saving up quarters. Denny has one-fifth as many as Bobby, and Jamal has three fewer than twice as many as Denny. All three of them combined have 61 quarters. Find how many each has.

■ C. Exercises

Solve.

41. $74 - (x - 19) = 0$

42. $\dfrac{x + 2x}{3} - 16 = 45$

43. $\dfrac{2(3x + 2)}{5} = 8$

44. $\dfrac{3}{7}(x + 49) + 8 = 35$

45. An investor bought shares of stock in blocks of 100 shares. The cost per share was $45, and the broker's fee was $200. Two days later he bought twice as many shares for $47 per share. This time the broker's fee was $225. The total spent on the two investments was $42,125. How many total shares did he buy?

■ Dominion thru Math

Detention time in large tanks in a sewage treatment plant is very critical in order to provide proper reduction of pollutants. Detention time in minutes is calculated by dividing the capacity of the tank (expressed in cubic feet) by the flow rate into the tank (expressed in ft.^{3}/min.). Of course the SI units (metric) for capacity and flow rate can also be used as long as they are compatible units, such as m^3 and m^3/min.

46. A 48 ft. diameter circular clarifier has a capacity of 22,320 ft.^{3}. If the flow rate into this tank is 186 ft.^{3}/min., find the detention time in minutes and hours.

47. Four rectangular aeration basins, each with a capacity of 50,000 ft.^{3}, receive the treatment plant inflow of 8 million gal. per day. What is the detention time through each treatment unit in minutes and hours? (1 ft.^{3} of water = 7.48 gal. of water.)

CUMULATIVE REVIEW

Simplify. [1.1, 1.3]

48. $|32 - 14|$

49. $|14 - 32|$

50. $|32| - |14|$

51. $|14| - |32|$

Write the following numbers in scientific notation. [1.8]

52. 6,700,000,000

53. 0.00000725

54. 20,300,000,000

55. 0.000000032

Name the property illustrated by each of the following. [2.1, 2.3]

56. $(-6 + 39) + (-4) = -6 + [39 + (-4)]$

57. $-2[14 + (-7)] = -2(14) + (-2)(-7)$

David, King of Israel

David lived from about 1040 to 970 BC. He was a man of many talents. As a young man he gained a reputation as one "cunning in playing [music], and a mighty valiant man, and a man of war, and prudent in matters, and a comely [handsome] person" (1 Sam. 16:18). Although David was a wise ruler, on one tragic occasion he disobeyed God and used math for a wrong purpose.

David succumbed to Satan's temptation and ordered Joab to number the people of Israel (1 Chron. 21:2–3). (Perhaps David desired to find out how much God had multiplied the nation under his rule so that he would know how many soldiers he could call to arms for battle.) Joab, the captain of the army, realized that David's motive was pride and warned him not to do it. But David refused to listen to him. When Joab finished his count, he reported to David that there were 800,000 men of war from Israel and 500,000 from Judah (2 Sam. 24:9). So the total number of fighting men was 1,300,000.

After he had numbered the people, David's heart was stricken with guilt. He realized that he had sinned and asked the Lord for forgiveness. God gave David his choice of three punishments—famine, defeat in battle, or a plague. When David chose the plague, 70,000 men were wiped out in three days. From this experience, David learned that sin has awful consequences—not only in the sinner's life but also in the lives of others.

You can use the math skills that you learn to honor God or to further your own selfish ends. The choice is yours. In making your choice, consider the life of David. When he realized his sin in counting the people, he confessed to God, "I have sinned greatly in that I have done: and now, I beseech thee, O Lord, take away the iniquity of thy servant; for I have done very foolishly" (2 Sam. 24:10).

With all his heart, David wanted to serve God and to receive forgiveness when he failed. In spite of his mistakes, the Lord praised David as "a man after mine own heart, which shall fulfill all my will" (Acts 13:22). Could the Lord say the same thing about you?

3.5 Using Equations

Problems are a fact of life. Learning to solve problems efficiently makes you a valuable member of society, of the workforce, of a church, and of a family. The four-step problem-solving approach can be applied to personal problems as well as word problems.

When facing challenges in life, you should **Read** the Bible to find God's **Plan**. Then carry out His plan to **Solve** your problem. Afterwards, you can **Check** to see how God led you through the situation. Consider God's command to Joshua: "This book of the law shall not depart out of thy mouth; but thou shalt meditate therein day and night, that thou mayest observe to do according to all that is written therein: for then thou shalt make thy way prosperous, and then thou shalt have good success" (Josh. 1:8).

The purpose of algebra is not to write equations, but to solve problems. A variable is chosen, and the words are translated into an equation using the variable. Then the equation must be solved. The following examples are real-life word problems and their solutions.

Example 1 A contractor charges $50 for a service call plus $60 per hour for his work. How long will he have to work to earn $350?

Answer

Let w = the number of work hours.

1. **Read** the problem carefully. Choose a variable for the unknown.

$$50 + 60w = 350$$

2. **Plan** how to represent the words with an algebraic equation. He receives $50 plus $60 times the number of hours worked. He wants that to total $350.

$$50 + 60w - 50 = 350 - 50$$
$$60w = 300$$
$$\frac{60w}{60} = \frac{300}{60}$$
$$w = 5 \text{ hr.}$$

3. **Solve** the resulting equation.

$$50 + 60(5) = 50 + 300 = \$350$$

4. **Check** to make sure that the answer is reasonable and correct.

Example 2 One hundred twenty feet of fence is needed to enclose a rectangular garden that is twenty feet wide. What is the length of the garden?

Answer

Let x = the length.

1. **Read** the problem carefully. Choose a variable for the unknown.

$2x + 2(20) = 120$

2. **Plan** how to represent the words with an algebraic equation. There are two lengths and two widths in a rectangle. The sum of all sides is the perimeter, the distance around the rectangle.

$2x + 40 = 120$

3. **Solve** the resulting equation.

$2x + 40 - 40 = 120 - 40$

$2x = 80$

$\dfrac{2x}{2} = \dfrac{80}{2}$

$x = 40$ ft., the length

$2(40) + 2(20) = 80 + 40 = 120$ ft.

4. **Check** to make sure that the answer is reasonable and correct.

The perimeter equals the amount of fencing available.

Example 3 Corey bought six of the same kind of pastry and a loaf of sourdough bread costing $4. If the total cost was $16, what was the cost of each pastry?

Answer

Let x = the cost per pastry.
$6x$ = the total cost of pastries.

1. **Read** the problem carefully. Choose a variable for the unknown, cost per pastry.

$6x + 4 = 16$

2. **Plan** how to represent the words with an algebraic equation. You represented the cost of all the pastries as $6x$. Add the cost of the bread. Set the sum equal to the total cost of $16.

$6x + 4 - 4 = 16 - 4$

3. **Solve** the resulting equation.

$6x = 12$

$\dfrac{6x}{6} = \dfrac{12}{6}$

$x = \$2$ each

$6(2) + 4 = 12 + 4 = 16$

4. **Check** to make sure that the answer is reasonable and correct.

Skill Check 1

Solve using the four-point checklist.

1. Stephanie made gifts by mixing peanuts with cashews. She used twice as many pounds of peanuts as cashews in each bag. If the total weight of her gifts is 27 lb., how many pounds of each did she use?

2. A school play was attended by 64 adults. Tickets cost $5 for adults and $2 for children. The total amount collected for tickets was $556. How many children attended the play?

The distance that an object travels is determined by its speed and the amount of time it travels. If an object travels in a straight line at a constant rate of speed, it is said to be in *uniform motion*. The equation used for uniform motion problems is $d = rt$, where d = distance traveled; r = rate of travel, or speed; and t = time traveled. The rate of an item is determined by the units in which distance and time are measured: $r = \dfrac{d}{t}$. Examples of rates are mi./hr., ft./sec., and km/min.

Example 4

Luis left his house at 9:00 AM and arrived at Marcus's house at 9:30 AM. If it is 15 mi. to Marcus's house, what was Luis' average rate of speed?

Answer

$$d = rt$$
$$15 = r\left(\frac{1}{2}\right)$$
$$\frac{r}{2} = 15$$
$$2\left(\frac{r}{2}\right) = 2(15)$$
$$r = 30 \text{ mi./hr.}$$

1. Use the uniform motion equation.
2. Substitute the distance traveled and the time into the equation. The time is $\frac{1}{2}$ hr.
3. Multiply the variable times the fraction. Use the Symmetric Property of Equality to move the term with the variable to the left side.
4. Multiply both sides by 2.

Example 5

Jackie is walking from one airplane departure gate to another. She walks on a moving walkway at a rate of 6 ft./sec., and the walkway itself moves at a rate of 10 ft./sec. How long will it take her to go 160 ft.?

Answer

$$d = 160 \text{ ft.}$$
$$r = 6 + 10 = 16 \text{ ft./sec.}$$

$$d = rt$$
$$160 = 16t$$
$$\frac{16t}{16} = \frac{160}{16}$$
$$t = 10 \text{ sec.}$$

1. Determine the given information. Since Jackie and the moving walkway are traveling simultaneously, add their rates to obtain the total rate of travel.
2. Use the uniform motion equation.
3. Substitute the known values into the equation.
4. Apply the Symmetric Property of Equality and solve the equation.

Skill Check 2

Solve using the four-point checklist.

1. Determine the average speed in miles per hour if it takes 20 min. to travel the 12 mi. to school.

■ A. Exercises

Specify what the variable stands for, write an equation, and solve.

1. Mr. Groves traveled 636 mi. in 12 hr. Find his average rate of speed.

2. If the Alexanders completed the 735 mi. trip in 15 hr., what was their average rate of travel?

3. Mr. Jones eats out at his favorite buffet restaurant every Friday night. If the cost is $9 and he budgets $42 for the month, how many times will be able to eat at this restaurant?

4. A store sells rakes for $9 each. If the sale of the rakes totaled $171, how many rakes were sold?

5. A farmer has 1,200 lb. (60 bushels) of seed wheat. If he sows 20 lb. per acre, how many acres can he sow?

6. If Ben buys 24 items at $3 each, how much change will he receive from a $100 bill?

7. A bicycler traveled 45 mi. at an average speed of 6 mi./hr. How long did the ride take?

8. If it takes 6 hr. for a 2,400 mi. flight from Philadelphia to Los Angeles, what is the average speed of the plane?

9. A store inventory showed the stock of a particular item as 52 after 18 were sold earlier that day. What was the inventory at the beginning of the day?

10. A stock inventory of an item was 65 Monday morning. At the close of business on Friday, the inventory level was 18. How many were sold during the week?

11. If an airplane travels 1,350 nautical miles in 6 hr., what is its average speed in knots (nautical miles per hour)?

12. How many 6 in. fence slats are required to make an 8 ft. long section of privacy fence?

13. A 66 in. 1" × 4" board is to be cut so that the result is four equal pieces of maximum length. Each piece must also be a whole number of inches in length. How long will each piece be?

14. A bakery advertises doughnuts at $5 per box. When the coach bought doughnuts for his employees, he received 52 doughnuts for $20. How many boxes did he get, and how many doughnuts were in each box?

■ B. Exercises

Specify what the variable stands for, write an equation, and solve.

15. A man bought a $250 suit and four shirts for $398. How much did he spend per shirt?

16. A customer returned a light fixture to the store in exchange for a $53 light fixture and three gallons of paint at $29 each. He had to pay $112. How much had he paid for the first light fixture?

17. Joe mows a lawn, for which he charges $30, and does some one-time cleanup work, for which he is paid $60. How many times will he have to mow the lawn before he makes a total of $300?

18. A sewing project requires material costing $44 plus some tassels. If the material and tassels are to be purchased with four $20 bills, how many tassels can be purchased if they cost $2.40 each?

19. The Dicksons drove for 6 hr. at 55 mi./hr. on the first day of their 570 mi. trip. How many hours do they need to drive on the second day of their trip if they can average 60 mi./hr.?

20. Jacques ran at 880 ft./min. for the first 10 min. of the 3 mi. race before slowing his pace to finish the race with a total time of 20 min. What was his pace (in feet per minute) for the second part of the race?

21. Erin has a $20 bill with which to buy coffee. If she buys 2 lb. of ground coffee at $4/lb. and spends the rest on gourmet coffee at $8/lb., how many pounds of gourmet coffee can she buy?

22. The 80 eighth graders took a trip to Washington DC. The boys numbered 16 fewer than twice the number of girls. How many of the eighth graders are girls?

23. Mr. Hays bought a 5 gal. bucket of paint costing $175 and five identical paintbrushes for a total bill of $215. How much did he pay per paintbrush?

24. A buyer spent $164 for two loads of mulch at $22.50 per load, $35 worth of flowers, and 42 landscaping blocks. Find the cost per block.

25. Victor has $20 cash. If he spends $7 to wash his car and uses the balance to buy gas at $2/gal., how much gas can he buy?

26. Mr. Jansen budgeted $400 for clothes. If he buys a new suit for $290 and a tie for $35, how many shirts can he buy at $25 each?

27. Ted makes $18/hr. painting houses and $12/hr. power-washing houses. If he painted for 27 hr. last week and made a total of $738, how many hours did he spend power-washing houses?

28. A mechanic billed a customer for 4 hr. labor plus $215 for parts. The total bill was for $375. How much did the mechanic charge for labor per hour?

29. Tickets to a high-school play were $5 for adults and $2 for students. Twice as many adults as students attended. How many students attended the play if it took in $960?

30. Elisabeth took 13 min. less than twice as long as Heather to solve the puzzle. If their total time together was 23 min., who took less time to solve the puzzle? How much less?

31. The boat traveled up the river at 15 mi./hr. To reach their campsite 90 mi. up the river, the Rogerses traveled twice as long in the afternoon as they did in the morning. How long did they travel in the morning?

32. Jeffery biked to the store at 12 mi./hr. but took his time on the way home, going 8 mi./hr. If it took him 20 min. to get to the store, how many minutes did it take him to get back?

■ C. Exercises

Specify what the variable stands for, write an equation, and solve.

33. A carpenter bought 16 boards at $2.95 each and an additional 20 boards, some at $5 each and the rest at $8 each. How many $5 boards and how many $8 boards did he buy if his total bill was $171.20?

34. The sides of a triangle are in the ratio of 1 : 2 : 3, and the perimeter is 24 ft. Find the lengths of the sides of the triangle.

35. Machine A produces twice as many gadgets as Machine B. Machine C produces 50 more than Machine B. If at the end of the day 6,170 gadgets are produced, how many does each machine produce?

36. Greg is 5 yr. older than Randy, who is 3 yr. older than Wilson. The sum of their ages is 32. How old is Greg?

37. Two ships are 120 nautical miles apart, and they are traveling toward one another. The rate of the one ship is 4 knots greater than the rate of the other. If it takes them 3 hr. to meet, find the rate of each ship.

38. How much inflow in cubic feet per minute can a treatment tank receive from an incoming pipe if the tank has a volume of 160,000 ft.³ and requires 5 hr. of detention time?

39. If the pipe feeding the tank in the previous problem flows at a velocity of 4 ft./sec., what is the largest sized pipe that can bring the wastewater into the tank? Give the diameter to the nearest 2 in. size.

CUMULATIVE REVIEW

Define the following terms. [2.1–2.2]

40. additive inverses

41. multiplicative inverses

Simplify. [2.5]

42. $3x - 2y + 18y - 4x$

43. $x + 8 + 5x - 10$

44. $2x - 9 + 4x - 8$

45. $2x + 5 - 3(4x + 1)$

Estimate by rounding. [2.7]

46. $37 + 24 + 12 + 46$

47. 52×47

48. $4,905 \div 72$

49. $324 \div 8$

3.6 Sets of Numbers and Inequalities

In your study of mathematics, the first set of numbers you encounter is the set of *natural numbers*, or counting numbers. This set is represented by the symbol $\mathbb{N}$. Including zero with the natural numbers gives a different set called the set of *whole numbers*, symbolized by $\mathbb{W}$. These two sets are shown below.

$$\mathbb{N} = \{1, 2, 3, 4, \ldots\} \quad \text{Natural numbers}$$
$$\mathbb{W} = \{0, 1, 2, 3, 4, \ldots\} \quad \text{Whole numbers}$$

Two things should be noted about them. First, both sets are infinite. The three dots indicate that the pattern continues forever. Neither set has a largest number. Second, every natural number is also a whole number. This means that set $\mathbb{N}$ is a *subset* of set $\mathbb{W}$, symbolized as $\mathbb{N} \subseteq \mathbb{W}$.

The set of whole numbers can be expanded by including the additive inverses (opposites) of the natural numbers. This set is the set of *integers*, as introduced in Chapter 1. The set of integers is symbolized using $\mathbb{Z}$ (for *Zahlen*, the German word for "number").

$$\mathbb{Z} = \{\ldots, -3, -2, -1, 0, 1, 2, 3, \ldots\} \quad \text{Integers}$$

The set $\mathbb{W}$ is a subset of $\mathbb{Z}$, since every whole number is also an integer.

$$\mathbb{W} \subseteq \mathbb{Z}$$

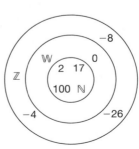

The solution to an equation such as $6x = 5$ is not found in the set of integers. Fractions are needed for the solution, since $x = \frac{5}{6}$. Including all fractions that are ratios of integers with the set of integers forms the set of *rational numbers*, represented by the symbol $\mathbb{Q}$. This symbol comes from the phrase "quotient of integers."

The numbers contained in the set of rational numbers cannot be given in a list format. This is because no matter how close together two rational numbers are, there are still an infinite number of rationals between them. Therefore, the following definition is given for the set of rational numbers.

$$\mathbb{Q} = \left\{ \frac{a}{b} \;\middle|\; a \in \mathbb{Z},\, b \in \mathbb{Z},\, \text{and } b \neq 0 \right\} \qquad \text{Rational numbers}$$

Notice that the denominator of the fraction cannot equal zero. Division by zero is impossible.

The integers are a subset of the rationals.

$$\mathbb{Z} \subseteq \mathbb{Q}$$

The Venn diagram to the right shows the relationship of natural numbers, whole numbers, integers, and rational numbers. All of the previous sets are subsets of $\mathbb{Q}$.

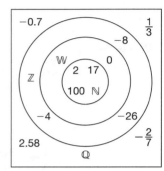

It is not possible to express every number as a quotient of integers, as required by the definition of rational numbers. These other numbers are called *irrational numbers*. None of the previously studied sets are a subset of the irrationals, nor are the irrationals a subset of any of them. The rationals and irrationals are *disjoint sets* since they have no common element. The rational and irrational numbers combined form the set of *real numbers*, designated by $\mathbb{R}$.

The Venn diagram below shows the relationship of these six sets of numbers.

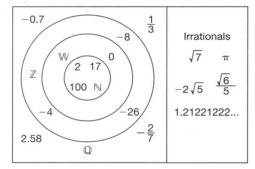

Real Numbers
Rationals $\cup$ Irrationals

Example 1   Place the given numbers in the correct set on a Venn diagram. Be as specific as possible when classifying them: $-15;\ 0;\ \frac{3}{2};\ 1{,}290;\ -\frac{2}{5};\ \sqrt{12}$.

Answer

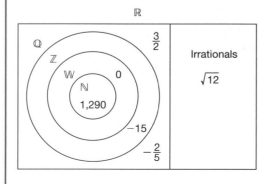

1,290 is a natural number.

0 is a whole number.

−15 is an integer.

$\frac{3}{2}$ and $-\frac{2}{5}$ are rational numbers.

$\sqrt{12}$ is an irrational number.

Skill Check 1

Copy the Venn diagram and place the given numbers in the correct set.

1. 53

2. −4

3. −493

4. $\frac{7}{4}$

5. 0.919919991...

6. $\frac{56}{11}$

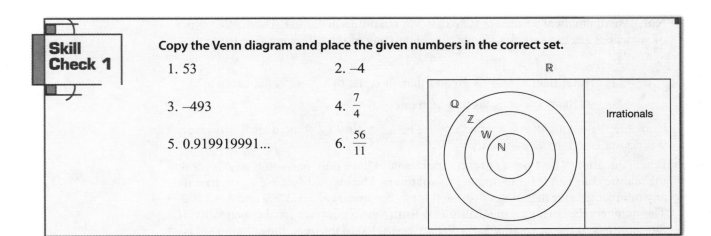

In real-world problems numerical answers generated by the process of solving an equation may not be true solutions. For example, suppose the solution to a problem represents a number of people. If the solution found is 4.5 people, there is a problem since the number of people must be a whole number. Likewise, if the problem asks for the length of a figure, a solution of −20 ft. makes no sense. Measurements must be positive numbers. However, they do not need to be natural numbers. A rational number, such as $\frac{3}{4}$ in., is a legitimate measure of length.

The equation $x + 6 = 1$ has no solution over the set of whole numbers. It does, however, have a solution over the larger set of integers: $x = 1 − 6 = −5$.

$3y = 2$ has no solution over the set of integers, but it does have a solution over the larger set of rational numbers: $y = \frac{2}{3}$.

Example 2 Do the following equations have solutions over the set given? If yes, solve.
a. $3x = 39$ over the set of whole numbers
b. $7y = 48$ over the set of integers

   Answer
a. Yes; dividing both sides by 13 produces $x = 13$, a whole number.
b. No; dividing both sides by 7 produces a rational number that is not an integer.

Skill Check 2

Do the following equations have solutions over the set of integers? If yes, solve.

1. $−4x = 28$

2. $x − 9 = 8$

3. $5x = 26$

Do the following equations have solutions over the set of whole numbers? If yes, solve.

4. $3x = −33$

5. $7x = 55$

6. $x − 8 = −3$

Not all mathematical sentences state that two quantities are equal. These other types of sentences are *inequalities*. They will contain one of the following five inequality symbols.

> "is greater than" ≥ "is greater than or equal to" ≠ "is not equal to"

< "is less than" ≤ "is less than or equal to"

Compare the inequalities $x \geq 9$ and $x > 9$. The inequality $x \geq 9$ includes 9. However, 9 is not included in the inequality $x > 9$.

Linear equations (first power of the variable only) have only one solution. Algebraic inequalities have an infinite number of solutions. The inequality $x + 3 > 9$ is true if any number greater than 6 is substituted for x. For instance, $7 + 3 > 9$ and $8 + 3 > 9$. The numbers that make an inequality true form the solution set for the inequality. If the solutions to the inequality $x + 3 > 9$ are restricted to integers, the solution set is written as $x \in \{7, 8, 9, 10, \ldots\}$. If the solutions can be any type of real number, the solution set is written as $x > 6$.

Definitions

An **inequality** is a mathematical sentence expressing the relative size of two quantities that may or may not not be equal.
All the numbers that make an inequality true form the **solution set**.

Example 3	Which numbers are members of the solution set for the inequality $3x < -6$: $-5, -3, -1, 0,$ or 2?

Answer

Substitute the given values into the inequality and check to see if they make it true.

$3(-5) = -15$; $-15 < -6$; true
$3(-3) = -9$; $-9 < -6$; true
$3(-1) = -3$; $-3 < -6$; false
$3(0) = 0$; $0 < -6$; false
$3(2) = 6$; $6 < -6$; false

The solution set would contain -5 and -3.

Skill Check 3

Which numbers are members of the solution sets for the given inequalities?

1. $7x \neq 105$; $-3, 5, 15, 18$

2. $-4m > -12$; $-2, 0, 2, 4, 6$

3. $9y \leq -18$; $-4, -2, 0, 2, 4$

4. $x + 2 < -3$; $-6, -3, 3, 6$

■ A. Exercises

Copy the Venn diagram and place the given numbers in the correct set.

1. 406

2. -2

3. 26

4. $\dfrac{65}{16}$

5. $-\dfrac{4}{9}$

6. π

7. -8

8. $\dfrac{7}{8}$

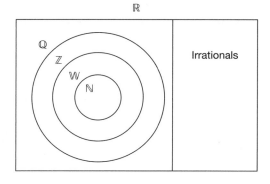

Do the following equations have solutions over the set of whole numbers? If yes, solve.

9. $3x = 17$
10. $8x = 32$
11. $y - 8 = 17$
12. $y + 20 = 8$

Do the following equations have solutions over the set of integers? If yes, solve.

13. $x + 8 = 3$
14. $4y = 18$
15. $14x = 2$
16. $\frac{x}{5} = 2$

■ B. Exercises

Do the following equations have solutions over the set of rational numbers?

17. $x^2 = 28$
18. $3x = 2$
19. $4x = -20$
20. $-5x = -8$

Which numbers are members of the solution sets for the given inequalities?

21. $x - 8 < 20$; 10, 20, 30, 40
22. $7x > 49$; 4, 8, 10, 11

23. $-9x \neq 72$; -8, 0, 8, 16
24. $\frac{x}{4} \geq 3$; -7, 10, 12, 15

25. $x + 4 \geq 7$; -1, 0, 2, 3
26. $13 > \frac{z}{3}$; -8, 20, 39, 40

27. $x + 82 < 75$; -10, 10, 20, 100
28. $-4x \leq 20$; -10, -5, 5, 10

29. $y + (-4) \leq -8$; -4, 0, 4, 8
30. $-32 > \frac{y}{7}$; -200, 0, 100, 200

31. $36 > y - 17$; 19, 60, 71, 90
32. $42 \geq \frac{y}{10}$; 4.2, 10, 100, 420

■ C. Exercises

Write an equation whose solution is as indicated.

33. a rational number
34. a natural number

35. a negative integer
36. an integer that is not a natural number

37. a rational number that is not an integer
38. a whole number that is not a natural number

39. Write the minimum and maximum values for the inequality $-5 \leq x \leq 3$.

■ Dominion thru Math

40. How much flow in gal./min. can a 3 million gal. treatment pond handle if the detention time must be a minimum of 9 hr.?

41. How much flow in L/min. can a 50 m³ clarifier handle and still provide at least 2.5 hr. detention time (1 m³ = 1,000 L)?

CUMULATIVE REVIEW

Solve. [3.1–3.2]

42. $x - 4 = 10$
43. $\frac{x}{3} = -4$
44. $18 - x = 12$
45. $3x = 51$

Simplify. [1.7]

46. $2 - [3(14 - 20)]$
47. $-4 - 7(18 - 4)$
48. $(-12)^3 \times 2 - 17$
49. $3[(4 - 7) + 2(6 - 4)]$

Write each word phrase as an algebraic expression. [2.6]

50. four less than twice a number
51. the square of four more than a number

Kyle is making a map of his state and wants to color the counties that are adjacent to each other different colors. A county is adjacent to another county if it has a common border, not just a common point. What is the least number of colors that Kyle can use on his map?

3.7 □ Solving Linear Inequalities

Recall from Section 3.6 that inequalities have an infinite number of solutions. The inequality $x + 3 > 9$ is true if x is any real number greater than 6. To list all the numbers greater than 6 is impossible. Therefore, it is useful to picture solution sets on number lines.

Example 1   Graph $x > 6$.

Answer

```
◄──┼──┼──┼──┼──○──┼──┼──►
  -2  0  2  4  6  8  10
```

The inequality indicates that x can be any number greater than 6. This includes the fractions between 6 and 7 and any irrational numbers that fall between 6 and 7. Place a small circle at 6 as a boundary and shade to the right of 6 on the number line.

Example 2   Graph $x \le -3$.

Answer

```
◄──┼──●──┼──┼──┼──┼──►
  -6  -4  -2  0  2  4
```

The "equal to" part of the inequality indicates that x could be −3 or anything less than −3. Place a dot at −3 on the number line to include −3 and shade everything to the left of −3.

Example 3 Graph $x \neq 2$.

Answer

All numbers on the number line except 2 would satisfy this inequality. Place a circle at 2 and shade both to the right and to the left of 2 on the number line.

The properties of inequality needed to solve one-step inequalities are similar to the properties of equality discussed in Section 3.1. The properties hold for all types of inequalities, but for simplicity's sake the statement of each property will contain only the less than symbol.

Addition Property of Inequality

If a and b are real numbers, such that $a < b$, and c is any real number, then $a + c < b + c$.

As in the case of the Addition Property of Equality, any of the variables a, b, and c can be negative. Recall that according to the definition of subtraction, $a - 5 = a + (-5)$ and $b - 5 = b + (-5)$.

Like the Addition Property of Equality, the Addition Property of Inequality signifies that if the same amount is added to (or subtracted from) both sides of an inequality, then the quantities are still equal. It is not necessary to write a separate subtraction property. If you subtract the same amount from both sides of an inequality, you are using the addition property above.

Example 4 Solve $x - 5 \geq -2$, and graph the solution set.

Answer

$$x - 5 \geq -2$$
$$x - 5 + 5 \geq -2 + 5$$
$$x \geq 3$$

1. Apply the Addition Property of Inequality by adding 5 to both sides.
2. Graph the solution set on the number line.

Example 5 Solve $x + 8 < -12$, and graph the solution set.

Answer

$$x + 8 < -12$$
$$x + 8 - 8 < -12 - 8$$
$$x < -20$$

1. Subtract 8 from both sides of the inequality.
2. Apply the definition of subtraction:
   $-12 - 8 = -12 + (-8) = -20$.
3. Graph the solution set.

The Symmetric Property does not apply to inequalities. If $a > b$, you cannot switch sides of the inequality and conclude that $b > a$. When the quantities change sides, the inequality sign must change direction. It is true to say that if $a > b$, then $b < a$.

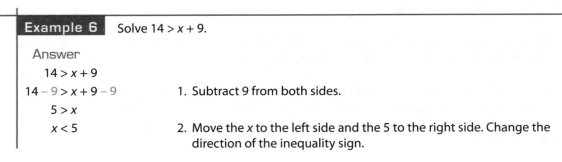

Example 6 Solve $14 > x + 9$.

Answer

$14 > x + 9$

$14 - 9 > x + 9 - 9$ 1. Subtract 9 from both sides.

$5 > x$

$x < 5$ 2. Move the x to the left side and the 5 to the right side. Change the direction of the inequality sign.

Of course you could have reversed the statement of inequality before solving it, by reading it right to left as $x + 9 < 14$.

Skill Check 1

Graph the following inequalities.

1. $x < 7$ 2. $x \neq -4$ 3. $x \geq 0$

Solve and graph the solution sets.

4. $y - 12 \geq -15$ 5. $-2 > y + 5$

The Multiplication Property of Inequality does not always work like the Multiplication Property of Equality. Examine the following examples to find the differences.

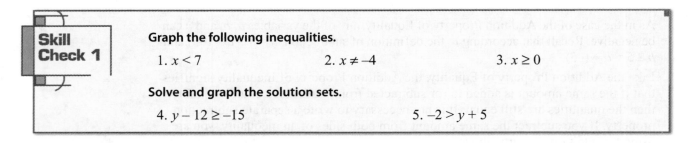

$2 < 4$			$2 < 4$	
$2(2) < 2(4)$	Multiply both sides by 2.		$-2(2) < -2(4)$	Multiply both sides by -2.
$4 < 8$	True		$-4 < -8$	False
			$-4 > -8$	True

$2 < 4$			$2 < 4$	
$\dfrac{2}{2} < \dfrac{4}{2}$	Divide both sides by 2.		$\dfrac{2}{-2} < \dfrac{4}{-2}$	Divide both sides by -2.
$1 < 2$	True		$-1 < -2$	False
			$-1 > -2$	True

When both sides of the inequality are multiplied (or divided) by the same positive number, the resulting inequality is true. But when both sides are multiplied (or divided) by the same negative number, the direction of the inequality sign must be reversed. Less than must be changed to greater than, or vice versa.

Multiplication Property of Inequality
If a and b are real numbers, such that $a < b$, and c is any positive real number, then $ac < bc$.
If a and b are real numbers, such that $a < b$, and c is any negative real number, then $ac > bc$.

Since a, b, and c in the above property can be any real number, and division is multiplication by the reciprocal, no separate division property is needed. When you divide both sides of an inequality by the same number, you are using the multiplication property above.

Reverse the inequality sign <u>only</u> when multiplying or dividing by a negative.

Example 7   Solve.

a. $-5x \geq 35$

b. $\dfrac{y}{3} < -4$

Answer

a. $-5x \geq 35$

$\dfrac{-5x}{-5} \leq \dfrac{35}{-5}$ Divide both sides by −5. The inequality sign must change direction since the

$x \leq -7$ divisor is negative. $\geq$ becomes $\leq$.

b. $\dfrac{y}{3} < -4$

$3\left(\dfrac{y}{3}\right) < 3(-4)$ Multiply both sides by 3. The inequality sign does not change direction since the

$y < -12$ multiplier is positive.

Skill Check 2

Will you reverse the inequality sign when solving the following inequalities?

1. $-2x > 20$ 2. $x - 5 < -7$ 3. $\dfrac{x}{4} \geq -16$ 4. $x + 6 \leq 10$

Solve.

5. $x + 8 \neq -3$ 6. $-3x \leq -9$ 7. $12 < x - 6$ 8. $\dfrac{x}{2} \geq -7$

The Addition and Multiplication Properties of Inequality also can be applied to inequalities requiring two-step solutions. These applications are shown below in Examples 8 and 9.

Example 8   Solve $2x - 9 < 15$.

Answer

$$2x - 9 < 15$$
$$2x - 9 + 9 < 15 + 9 \qquad \text{1. Add 9 to both sides.}$$
$$2x < 24$$
$$\frac{2x}{2} < \frac{24}{2} \qquad \text{2. Divide both sides by 2.}$$
$$x < 12$$

Example 9   Solve $-\frac{x}{4} + 7 \geq 20$.

Answer

$$-\frac{x}{4} + 7 \geq 20$$

$$-\frac{x}{4} + 7 - 7 \geq 20 - 7 \qquad \text{1. Subtract 7 from both sides.}$$

$$-\frac{x}{4} \geq 13$$

$$-4\left(\frac{x}{-4}\right) \leq -4(13) \qquad \text{2. Multiply both sides by } -4. \text{ The inequality sign must change direction.}$$
$$\qquad\qquad\qquad\qquad\qquad \geq \text{ becomes } \leq.$$

$$x \leq -52$$

Skill Check 3

Solve.

1. $3x + 8 \leq 50$ 2. $\frac{x}{4} + 3 \geq 11$ 3. $7 - 4x > 23$ 4. $12 - \frac{x}{5} < 20$

■ A. Exercises

Graph the following inequalities.

1. $x \geq 3$ 2. $x < -2$ 3. $x \leq -4$

4. $x \neq 2$ 5. $x > -2$ 6. $x \leq 4$

Solve.

7. $x - 6 \leq 1$ 8. $x + 4 < 2$ 9. $15 > x + 7$

10. $y - 2 < -3$ 11. $y + 8 < -9$ 12. $z - 6 > -4$

Solve.

13. $6z \le 18$ 14. $2y \ne 20$ 15. $3 \ge -\frac{x}{12}$ 16. $-7x \ge 14$

17. $3x \ge -15$ 18. $\frac{x}{5} > -6$ 19. $-4x > 28$ 20. $-7x \le -14$

■ B. Exercises

Solve.

21. $-2x + 4 > 10$ 22. $4x - 8 \le 32$ 23. $-\frac{x}{5} + 2 < 20$ 24. $\frac{x}{3} - 5 \ge 100$

25. $-\frac{y}{5} - 10 \ne 6$ 26. $7 - \frac{z}{3} < 8$ 27. $8 - 3x \ge 23$ 28. $5 + \frac{x}{8} < 4$

■ C. Exercises

Solve.

29. $3x - 7x < -4$ 30. $(-5 + 7) - (8 + 4) > -5x$

31. $|2 - 7|x \le |-17 - 13|$ 32. $-[79 - 3(18)]x \ge -5^3$

33. What integers would make the inequality $|x| < 5$ true?

34. What values of x would make the inequality $|x| > 3$ true?

■ Dominion thru Math

35. The typical household in the United States uses 100 gal. of water per person per day with about 90% reaching the sewage treatment plant (STP). How much water would the STP receive from a city with a population of 243,950?

36. What is the required capacity in gallons of the primary clarifiers of the STP from the previous problem, if the detention time needs to be 2.5 hr.?

CUMULATIVE REVIEW

Simplify. [1.6]

37. $-7^2(-3)^2$ 38. $[(-2)^4]^2$ 39. $(2x^6)^3$ 40. $(-7)^2(-3)^2$

Name the property illustrated by each of the following. [2.1–2.3]

41. $2(x + 3y) = 2x + 6y$ 42. $(7 + 8) + 3 = (8 + 7) + 3$

43. $[5(7)](9) = 5[7(9)]$ 44. $7 + (-7) = 0$

Write an equation that illustrates each of the following. [2.1–2.2]

45. a and b are additive inverses.   46. c and d are multiplicative inverses.

3.8 Using Inequalities

Problems that indicate that a quantity is more or less than something require inequalities. Key phrases that indicate an inequality include *more than*, *less than*, *at least*, and *at most*.

The phrase *at least* indicates that it could be that amount or greater. If Jordan has at least 180 stamps in his collection, then he has 180 or more stamps. The inequality that expresses "a number that is at least 180" is $x \geq 180$.

If a word problem uses the phrase *at most*, then it could be that number or less. Suppose Katie says she will make at most 7 puppets. She means that she will make 7 puppets or fewer than 7 puppets. So "a number that is at most 7" is expressed as $x \leq 7$.

Example 1 Write an inequality for each of the following.

a. Five more than a number is at most sixteen.

b. Janice has three times as many nickels as Tom. Janice has fewer than 24 nickels.

Answer

a. $x + 5 \leq 16$ "At most" indicates less than or equal to.

b. $x = $ Tom's nickels   Assign a variable for the unknown you are trying to find. Represent
    $3x = $ Janice's nickels   Janice's nickels in terms of Tom's nickels. The number of Janice's nickels
    $3x < 24$ is less than 24.

Skill Check 1

Write an inequality for each of the following sentences.

1. The difference between a number and 25 is greater than 82.

2. How long can Jennifer drive at 60 mi./hr. if she wants to travel at most 720 mi.?

3. Hadessah wants a job that pays at least $8.50 per hour.

4. Until further notice, all employees will restrict their time on the clock per week to less than full time (full time is considered to be 40 hr.).

Example 2   Elissa knows that she has at least $120 in her savings account. She wants her savings split into three categories with equal amounts in each category. What is the least amount that she has available to spend in each category?

Answer

Let x = the amount in each category.

1. **Read** the problem carefully. Choose a variable for the unknown.

$3x \geq 120$

2. **Plan** how to represent the words with an algebraic inequality.

$\dfrac{3x}{3} \geq \dfrac{120}{3}$

3. **Solve** the resulting inequality.

$x \geq 40$

Elissa has at least $40 in each category.

If she spent all of her money in all categories, she would spend at least $3(40) = \$120$.

4. **Check** to make sure that the answer is reasonable and correct.

Example 3   Mr. Haney has taken a job where he earns $2,570 per month. He tithes 10% of his income. How long will it take him to earn more than $23,000, excluding his tithe? Round your answer to the next full month.

Answer

Let m = the number of months.

1. **Read** the problem carefully. Choose a variable for the unknown.

$2,313m > 23,000$

2. **Plan** how to represent the words with an algebraic inequality. His monthly pay after tithe is $2,570 - 257 = \$2,313$.

$\dfrac{2,313m}{2,313} > \dfrac{23,000}{2,313}$

3. **Solve** the resulting inequality.

$m > 9.9$

He must work 10 months.

$10(2,313) = \$23,130 > \$23,000$

4. **Check** to make sure that the answer is reasonable.

It is reasonable.

Example 4   A car buyer wants to finance a car for 24 months and keep his monthly payments less than $300. He has $1,500 available for a down payment. Will he be able to buy an $8,988 car and meet his goal?

Answer

Let m = the number of months.

1. Choose a variable for the unknown.

$1,500 + 24m \geq 8,988$

2. Represent the words with an algebraic inequality.

$24m + 1,500 - 1,500 \geq 8,988 - 1,500$

3. Solve the resulting inequality.

$24m \geq 7,488$

$\dfrac{24m}{24} \geq \dfrac{7,488}{24}$

$m \geq \$312$

No, he will not be able to make his goal.

$20(300) + 2,000 = 6,000 + 2,000$
$= \$8,000$

4. Use estimation to check to make sure that the answer is reasonable.

It is reasonable.

Example 5 A will contains the provision that the estate, worth $64,892, be divided equally among six relatives. However, at least $12,500 is to be held in trust for a missing son for up to one year. If he is not found within that time, the money will go to the deceased's favorite charity. How much will each of the six relatives get?

Answer.

Let x = the amount per relative.

1. Choose a variable for the unknown.

$$64,892 - 6x \geq 12,500$$

2. Represent the words with an algebraic inequality.

$$64,892 - 6x - 64,892 \geq 12,500 - 64,892$$

3. Solve the resulting inequality.

$$-6x \geq -52,392$$

$$\frac{-6x}{-6} \leq \frac{-52,392}{-6}$$

$$x \leq 8,732$$

Each of the six relatives will receive at most $8,732.

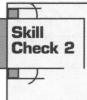

Skill Check 2

Write an inequality, solve it, and express the answer in words.

1. Kelly wants to consume at most 2,300 calories per day. If she has already consumed 800 calories today, how many more can she eat?

2. Mrs. Grant says to her class, "I am thinking of an integer. If it is multiplied by –5, the result is at least 360." Write an inequality that expresses all possible numbers that Mrs. Grant could use.

3. A sales advertisement states that if a customer buys three pairs of ladies' shoes, with a total cost of at least $135, she can choose a fourth pair for free. What must the average price per pair be on the first three pairs to get the fourth pair free?

Life is full of inequalities. People have different abilities in various areas. Some people can sing well, and others cannot. Some people can paint beautiful pictures, and others cannot. It is not for us to worry about these inequalities but to develop each talent that God has given us to the fullest. Matthew 25:14–30 tells the story of servants who have been given various amounts of money. The conclusion of the story is that all of the servants are commended if they have been faithful in using what their master had given them. Those who are faithful hear their lord say, "Well done, thou good and faithful servant." But the servant who did not use what he had been given is punished. Even now as a student you need to work to develop what God has given you.

■ A. Exercises

Write an inequality and solve.

1. The owner of a used car lot wants to buy as many cars at an auction as he can while not spending more than $20,000. If he expects the average price to be $4,000, how many would he expect to be able to buy?

2. A farmer wants to sell enough grain to get at least $2,400. If the selling price is $3 per bushel, how many bushels must he sell?

3. The sum of the two shorter sides of a triangle must be greater than the longer side. The shortest side of a triangle is 8 in. and the longest side is 18 in. How long must the third side of the triangle be?

4. A merchant is bagging potatoes that he will sell for $5 a bag. He wants to take in at least $400 for them. How many bags should he prepare?

5. Daniel has 40 points and Zeke has 75. The opposing team has 150. It is Daniel's turn. How many points must Daniel make to put him and his teammate ahead?

6. Some land sold for $4,000 per acre, and the price was over $60,000. How many acres were sold?

7. The width of a rectangle is 6 m, and the area is at least 840 m². How long must the rectangle be (area = length × width)?

■ B. Exercises

Write an inequality, solve it, and express the answer in words.

8. Four times a number is less than 56. Find the largest integer that satisfies the inequality.

9. A number increased by 15 is greater than 124. Find the smallest integer that satisfies the inequality.

10. A person's daily fat intake should be at most 600 calories from fat. Justin consumed 270 calories from fat during breakfast. On average, how many more fat calories can he consume per meal for the rest of the day?

11. Mr. Jenkins wants to save at least $5,000 over the next three years to apply to the cost of a car. How much should he save each month (rounded to the nearest dollar) to achieve his goal?

12. A football coach set a goal of keeping opposing teams to an average of less than 200 yd. of total offense per game. After three games the opposing teams had gained a total of 701 yd. How many yards can the next opponent gain and the coach's goal still be met?

13. An advertisement says that during a sale you can save at least $50 on a suit. The most expensive suit sold for $249 during the sale. How much did the suit sell for before the sale?

14. Fifteen less than three times an integer is at most 54. What is the largest integer that could be used for the number?

15. Mr. Kirkland receives $13/hr. for regular time (8 hr./day) and double pay for working on holidays. He worked on Friday even though it was a holiday. If his week's pay was at least $650, how many hours did he work on Friday?

16. Jenn's mother bought her two shirts (identical except for color) and a small jewelry box that cost $8. She spent less than $30 for the gifts. How much did each shirt cost?

17. Mr. Barnes is going on a business trip. His meals will be furnished at the cafeteria of the company he is visiting for a flat fee of $135, but he will need to stay at a motel for three nights. He does not want to spend more than $350. What is the most he should he pay for each night's stay? Express your answer in whole dollars.

18. A junior basketball player has a goal of scoring at least 1,000 points during his high-school career. His team plays twenty games per year, and after two years he has 320 points. To be successful, how many points does he have to average per game over his last two years?

19. The dress cost twice as much as the shoes. Together they cost more than $200. What is the minimum cost for each item (to the nearest dollar)?

20. Leanna finds a "buy two, get one free" sale at her favorite store. Her purchases cannot exceed $100. A skirt originally sells for $22. What is the greatest number of skirts that she can get?

■ C. Exercises

Write an inequality, solve it, and express the answer in words.

21. The suit cost $10 more than four times as much as the shoes. The suit cost at least $480. What is the least amount paid for the shoes? Round up to a whole dollar.

22. Kate has ten more than twice as many marbles as Mary. Together they have more than a hundred marbles. What is the smallest number of marbles that Mary and Kate can have?

23. When playing a game, Emily had six more properties than Terry. Together they owned at least twenty of the properties. What is the smallest number of properties that Terry had?

24. The length of the rectangular lot is 25 ft. longer than twice the width. If the perimeter of the lot cannot exceed 350 ft., what is the greatest width possible?

■ Dominion thru Math

25. If the diameters of two pipes have a ratio of 2 : 6 and the smaller pipe has a flow rate of 150 gal./min. at 5 ft./sec., what is the flow rate of the larger pipe at the same velocity?

■ CUMULATIVE REVIEW

Simplify. [2.5]

26. $3x - 4 - 8x + 9$ 27. $3(x - 7) - 4x$ 28. $(3x + 5) + (7x - 8)$ 29. $3 - 4(5x - 3)$

Estimate by rounding. [2.7]

30. $29 + 82 + 41$ 31. $719 - 296$ 32. 81×21 33. $2,900 \div 32$

Write each word phrase as an algebraic expression. [2.6]

34. sixteen less than four times a number

35. three more than one-third of a number

MATH & SCRIPTURE

King David's Unwise Census

The numbering of the people by King David is presented in 2 Samuel 24 and in 1 Chronicles 21. These accounts show an interesting example of conflicting numbers for the census. By carefully considering other passages, one can show that the Word of God is accurate in presenting this account from the pens of two different inspired authors. In this lesson you will examine the numbers to come up with an accurate account of the census.

Read 2 Samuel 24 and 1 Chronicles 21 and answer the following questions.

1. Give the two different reasons for David's census.

2. Which verses indicate that what David did was a sin?

3. What group within the nation did Joab actually take a census of (see also 1 Chron. 27:23)?

4. How long did it take Joab and his officers to conduct the census?

5. What tribes did Joab leave out of the census?

6. Give the total number of the census for Israel from each of the passages.

7. Give the total number of the census for Judah from each of the passages.

8. What is the discrepancy in the count for Israel?

9. What is the discrepancy in the count for Judah?

Reconciling Israel's Census

10. According to 1 Chronicles 27:1–15, how many fighting men of Israel were in David's regular rotating militia?

11. Combining the census for Israel from 2 Samuel 24 with the rotating militia gives how many fighting men?

12. How many more fighting men are needed to reconcile the count from exercise 11 with the count from 1 Chronicles 21?

13. Many scholars have studied these passages, and many of them believe the writer of Chronicles wrote after the Babylonian exile and probably rounded to the nearest hundred thousand. How many soldiers were in the rotating militia if the number is rounded this way? Does this reconcile the two accounts?

Reconciling Judah's Census

14. What possible explanation for the discrepancy in the census for Judah can be found in 2 Samuel 6:1, especially if the context and geography suggests that the men were from Judah?

15. What other explanation can be found in 2 Samuel 8:6 and 8:14, even though no actual numbers are given?

16. If the 1 Chronicles value for Judah is rounded to the hundred thousands place, what is the count for Judah?

Infinite Truths
Let me be weighed in an even balance that God may know mine integrity. *Job 31:6*

Chapter 3 Review

Vocabulary

Addition Property of Equality	irrational numbers	real numbers
Addition Property of Inequality	Multiplication Property of Equality	solution
disjoint sets		solution set
equation	Multiplication Property of Inequality	subset
inequality	natural numbers	Symmetric Property of Equality
inverse operations	rational numbers	whole numbers

Name the inverse operation, including the quantity, that would be used to solve each equation.

1. $x + 9 = 15$

2. $5x = 35$

3. $\dfrac{x}{2} = -8$

4. $a - 6 = 14$

5. $-7x = 28$

6. $12 + m = -21$

Name the property of equality illustrated by the first step in the solution of the following equations.

7. $\quad x + 8 = 12$
   $\quad x + 8 - 8 = 12 - 8$

8. $\quad y - 15 = 32$
   $\quad y - 15 + 15 = 32 + 15$

9. $\quad \dfrac{a}{2} = 7$
   $\quad 2\left(\dfrac{a}{2}\right) = 2(7)$

10. $8m = 56$
    $\dfrac{8m}{8} = \dfrac{56}{8}$

Solve.

11. $x - 5 = 82$

12. $3m + 6 = 18$

13. $a + 9 = -16$

14. $\dfrac{5x}{3} = 20$

15. $\dfrac{n}{6} = 18$

16. $6n - 9 = -27$

17. $-14p = -322$

18. $7x - 8 + 2x = -71$

19. $y - 7 + 8y - 16 = -14$

20. $6x + 8x - 27 - 2x + 18 = -81$

Write an equation for each of the following sentences.

21. Three times a number is 52.

22. A number decreased by 24 is 93.

23. The quotient of a number and –3 is 16.

24. Sixty-two is four times the sum of a number and 3.

25. Twice a number decreased by 42 is –18.

26. The quotient of the difference of a number and 48, and twice the number is 31.

Specify what the variable stands for, write an equation, and solve.

27. Asa is collecting insects for his science project. He has six fewer beetles than twice the number of other insects. If he has a total of eighteen insects in his collection, how many beetles does he have?

28. The eighth-grade class is selling candy bars to raise money for a charity project at Thanksgiving. Each candy bar that they sell provides a profit of $0.50. How many candy bars do they need to sell to reach their goal of $500?

29. Pastor Jeffers has a box of 600 gospel tracts. The youth group plans to canvass the neighborhood around the church. The high-school students are given 114 less than twice the number of tracts that the middle-school students are given. If all of the tracts are distributed, how many did each group hand out?

30. Eli read four more biographies than historical fiction books during the semester. He also read two fewer mysteries than historical fiction books. If he read a total of eleven books during the semester, how many of each type did he read?

Determine which numbers are members of the solution set for each inequality: –4, –2, 0, 1, 5.

31. $2x < 8$

32. $x + 9 > 2$

33. $-x - 2 > -4$

34. $4x - 8 \geq 12$

Graph the following inequalities.

35. $x \geq -7$

36. $x \neq 3$

37. $x < 0$

38. $x \leq 5$

Solve.

39. $x + 21 > 52$

40. $4x \leq -36$

41. $5x - 4 \neq -54$

42. $\dfrac{x}{-4} + 3 > 17$

Write an inequality, solve it, and express the answer in words.

43. The difference of a number and 46 is at most 153. What is the largest integer that could be used for the number?

44. Vanessa must earn at least 360 points to make an A in her Pre-Algebra class. If she currently has scores of 82, 91, and 89 points from her first three tests, how many more points does she need to make an A?

45. The band has been selected to march and play in the holiday parade. The 105 members must raise at least $49,500 for the trip. What is the least amount that each one needs to raise (to the next whole dollar)?

46. All of the cars a company sells require a down payment of $2,000 and 48 monthly payments. The contract amount for any of the cars is at least $19,940. What is the amount of the monthly payment (to the next whole dollar)?

47. A particular type of TV is being sold for $1,200 cash or for $500 down with 24 monthly payments. Find the amount of the monthly payment if the plan results in charges of at least $1,484 over the life of the contract. Find the amount of interest paid if the monthly payment plan is chosen.

48. State the mathematical significance of Job 31:6.

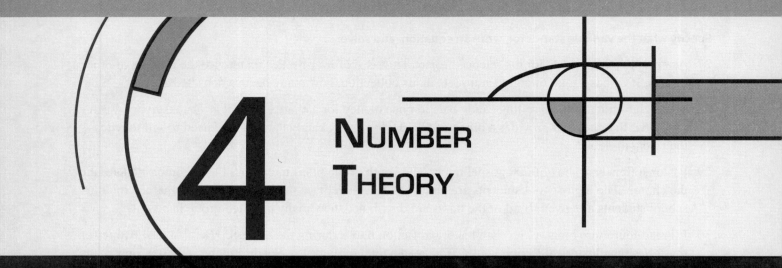

4 NUMBER THEORY

Companies that do business on the Internet must protect their clients' personal information. In this electronic age, keeping personal information secure from identity theft and other invasions requires sophisticated encryption methods. *Encryption* is the process of taking a message and transforming it into unreadable text, called *cipher text*. However, there must also be a way for authorized personnel to recover the original message. A *cipher* is used to transpose or substitute letters, symbols, or numbers of the original text to form the encrypted text. Most modern ciphers rely on modular arithmetic and very large prime numbers to encrypt a message. Modular arithmetic can be thought of as arithmetic on a circle or a clock rather than on a number line. If you consider the question "What time is it five hours after 9:00?" you get the answer 2:00. This is because the number 12 acts as a zero. The numbers on a circle or clock face need not go to 12, but it is necessary to have a number that acts as a zero. For example, you can draw a circle that goes only from zero to four. On such a circle, $3 + 4 = 2$.

A *key* is the tool used to decrypt the message. To *break* a code or cipher means that the original text is retrieved without the key by techniques called *cryptanalysis*. The process of breaking a cipher relies on high-speed computing.

Modular arithmetic, one aspect of number theory, also plays a significant role in the determination of valid numbers such as ISBNs (International Standard Book Number), UPCs (Universal Product Code), and credit card numbers. When people use these numbers in the course of various transactions, mistakes can be made in transcribing the numbers. Transposing two digits is the most common mistake. Each number includes a check digit at the end that makes it fairly easy to determine whether the number is valid.

In this chapter you will learn the principles that guide many of the mathematical processes in algebra.

After this chapter you should be able to

1. determine whether a number is prime or composite.

2. find the prime factorization of a composite number.

3. use prime factorizations to find the GCF and LCM of numbers and algebraic expressions.

4. distinguish between arithmetic and geometric sequences.

5. write recursive definitions for sequences and apply them to find individual terms.

6. write explicit formulas for sequences and apply them to find individual terms.

7. express base 10 numbers in other bases and vice versa.

8. perform addition and subtraction in bases other than 10.

4.1 Prime and Composite Numbers

Definition

A **multiple** of an integer is the product of that integer and any natural number.

Consider the multiples of 2, 5, and –9 listed below.

Multiples of 2	Multiples of 5	Multiples of –9
$1 \times 2 = 2$	$1 \times 5 = 5$	$1 \times (-9) = -9$
$2 \times 2 = 4$	$2 \times 5 = 10$	$2 \times (-9) = -18$
$3 \times 2 = 6$	$3 \times 5 = 15$	$3 \times (-9) = -27$
$4 \times 2 = 8$	$4 \times 5 = 20$	$4 \times (-9) = -36$

A cake is cut into many pieces. Likewise, a number is made up of many prime factors.

Example 1 List the first four multiples of each number.

a. 7   b. –5

Answer

a. Multiples of 7   b. Multiples of –5

   $1 \times 7 = 7$ $1(-5) = -5$

   $2 \times 7 = 14$ $2(-5) = -10$

   $3 \times 7 = 21$ $3(-5) = -15$

   $4 \times 7 = 28$ $4(-5) = -20$

Integers that are multiplied together to obtain a product are called *factors* of the product. For example, since $3 \times 7 = 21$, both 3 and 7 are factors of 21. A number divided by one of its factors has a quotient that is an integer. When this is the case, the factor is said to "divide the number." For example, 3 divides 21 and 7 divides 21.

$$7\overline{)21} \quad \begin{array}{r} 3 \\ \hline \end{array} \qquad 3\overline{)21} \quad \begin{array}{r} 7 \\ \hline \end{array}$$

$$\begin{array}{r} 3 \\ 7\overline{)21} \\ \underline{-21} \\ 0 \end{array} \qquad \begin{array}{r} 7 \\ 3\overline{)21} \\ \underline{-21} \\ 0 \end{array}$$

← remainder →

Definition

A **factor** of an integer is any integer that divides the given integer with no remainder. We will limit our discussion of factors to positive integers unless otherwise stated.

Seven is a factor of 21 because there exists an integer 3, such that $7 \cdot 3 = 21$. If a number a is a factor of a second number b, then there must exist an integer k such that $a \cdot k = b$. This fact gives us a means of defining the term *divides*.

Definition

The integer a **divides** the integer b (written $a|b$) if and only if $b = a \cdot k$ for some integer k.

Example 2   Is 8 a factor of 104?

Answer

$$\begin{array}{r} 13 \\ 8\overline{)104} \\ \underline{8} \\ 24 \\ \underline{24} \\ 0 \end{array}$$ Divide 104 by 8. Check that the remainder is zero.

Yes, 8 is a factor of 104 because $8 \cdot 13 = 104$.

Example 3   List all the factors of 18.

Answer

$1 \times 18 = 18$ You can find all the factors of 18 by listing all the pairs of natural numbers that have
$2 \times 9 = 18$ a product of 18.
$3 \times 6 = 18$

The factors of 18, in order of size, are 1, 2, 3, 6, 9, and 18.

Divisibility tests can be used to quickly determine if 2, 3, 4, 5, 6, 8, 9, or 10 are factors.

	Divisibility Tests
2	the integer ends in an even digit: 0, 2, 4, 6, or 8
3	the sum of the integer's digits is divisible by 3
4	the number formed by the last two digits of the integer is divisible by 4
5	the integer ends in 0 or 5
6	the integer is divisible by both 2 and 3
8	the number formed by the last three digits of the integer is divisible by 8
9	the sum of the integer's digits is divisible by 9
10	the integer ends in 0

Finding all the factors of a number may seem like an arduous task. It can be simplified, however, if you consider a few facts about the factors of numbers.

Examine the factors of 36.

$1(36) = 36$ $2(18) = 36$ $3(12) = 36$ $4(9) = 36$ $6(6) = 36$

The factors of 36 are 1, 2, 3, 4, 6, 9, 12, 18, and 36.

When a small factor is found, the other factor is large. You can stop looking for possible factors when you reach the dividing point between the small and large factors. This is the place where the two factors are equal; in the case of the factors of 36, the equal factors are 6×6. Remember from your earlier studies that one of a number's two equal factors is the square root of the number.

$$\sqrt{36} = 6, \text{ since } 6 \times 6 = 36.$$

Therefore, finding or approximating the square root of a number gives the dividing point between the small and large factors. The square root is the largest number that you will have to test in order to find all the factors of a number.

Example 4   List all the factors of 58.

Answer

Since $7^2 = 49$ and $8^2 = 64$, you know that $7 < \sqrt{58} < 8$. You need to check numbers up through 7.

| $1(58) = 58$ | $2(29) = 58$ | 3, 4, 5, 6, and 7 are not factors of 58. |

The factors of 58 are 1, 2, 29, and 58.

Skill Check 1

True or false

1. 20 is a multiple of 4.   2. 35 is a factor of 7.

3. 6 is a factor of 18.   4. 9 is a multiple of 45.

List the first four multiples of each number.

5. 3   6. 8

Is the first number a factor of the second?

7. 7, 28   8. 6, 32

List in order all the factors of the given number.

9. 12   10. 30

Definitions

A **prime number** is a natural number greater than one that has exactly two positive factors: one and itself.

Any natural number greater than one that has positive factors other than one and itself is called a **composite number**.

The number one is neither prime nor composite because it is not greater than one.

To determine whether a number is prime or composite, you can list its factors. If you find any factor other than one and itself, the number is composite.

> A prime number is > 1 and has two factors (1 and itself).

Number	Factors	Prime or Composite
1	1	neither
2	1, 2	prime
3	1, 3	prime
4	1, 2, 4	composite
5	1, 5	prime
6	1, 2, 3, 6	composite

| Example 5 | State whether 17 is prime, composite, or neither. |

Answer

$1 \times 17 = 17$ Find the factors of 17.

Since 17 has exactly two positive factors, 1 and 17, it is prime.

| Example 6 | State whether 57 is prime, composite, or neither. |

Answer

$1 \times 57 = 57$ Find the factors of 57.

$3 \times 19 = 57$

Since 57 has factors other than one and itself, it is composite.

The process of finding prime factors of a composite number is a fundamental skill that is used within other mathematical problems. The application of basic number theory principles builds a sure foundation of mathematical concepts. Similarly, the Bible builds a sure foundation for spiritual life in the believer. Hebrews 5:12–6:1 indicates that there are certain basic "first principles" of doctrine that believers build upon as they grow in their knowledge of God through His Word (1 Pet. 2:2).

Skill Check 2

List in order all the factors of the given number.

1. 11   2. 16   3. 23   4. 24

State whether the given number is prime or composite.

5. 16   6. 13   7. 18   8. 35   9. 47   10. 69

■ A. Exercises

List the first four multiples of each number.

1. 2   2. 9   3. 12

4. 90   5. –3   6. –10

Is the first number a factor of the second?

7. 3, 18   8. 7, 44   9. 4, 122

10. 5, 75   11. 4, 344   12. 7, 94

13. 5, 310   14. 9, 217   15. 8, 552

Write which of the following numbers are factors of the given number: 2, 3, 4, 5, 6, 8, 9, 10, or none.

16. 3,620   17. 270   18. 7,139   19. 9,876

■ B. Exercises

List in order all the factors of the given number.

20. 14   21. 20   22. 49

23. 32   24. 63   25. 75

State whether the given number is prime, composite, or neither.

26. 1	27. 3	28. 19	29. 31	30. 35	31. 47
32. 51	33. 59	34. 60	35. 61	36. 73	37. 77
38. 91	39. 97	40. 100			

■ C. Exercises

41. List the first ten prime numbers.

One way to express 21 as a sum of three prime numbers is 21 = 3 + 7 + 11. Express each of the following primes as a sum of three prime numbers.

42. 14   43. 35

■ Dominion thru Math

Modular arithmetic provides a way to change an infinite set of numbers into a finite set of numbers. The set of positive integers with respect to modulus 5 is {0, 1, 2, 3, 4}. In modulus 5 (abbreviated "mod 5"), every positive integer is said to be congruent to one of these five numbers. Think of five bins labeled 0–4. Zero and every positive integer will each be placed into one of the bins. To find the correct bin, convert an integer to mod 5 by dividing the integer by 5 and considering only the remainder.

For example, $7 \div 5 = 1 \text{ r } 2$; therefore, 7 goes in the bin labeled #2. This is expressed as follows: $7 \equiv 2 \pmod 5$ (read "7 is congruent to 2 mod 5"). The numbers 12 and 17 also go in this bin since $12 \div 5 = 2 \text{ r } 2$ and $17 \div 5 = 3 \text{ r } 2$.

$26 \div 5 = 5 \text{ r } 1$; therefore, 26 goes in the bin labeled #1. We say $26 \equiv 1 \pmod 5$ (read "26 is congruent to 1 mod 5").

To do arithmetic in mod 5, add, subtract, or multiply the numbers; then change the answer to mod 5. For instance, $(4 + 3) \pmod 5 = 7 \pmod 5 \equiv 2 \pmod 5$.

Change the following numbers to mod 7.

44. 64   45. 128   46. 517   47. 6,563,924

Do the following calculations in mod 7.

48. $(3 + 2 + 5 + 1) \pmod 7$ 49. $(5 \times 6) \pmod 7$ 50. $(32 - 6) \pmod 7$

51. What set of numbers is used for mod 11?

Change the following numbers to mod 11.

52. 51   53. 239   54. 594   55. 9,205,326

Do the following calculations in mod 11.

56. $(5 + 9 + 3 + 7 + 2) \pmod{11}$ 57. $(9 \times 6 \times 4) \pmod{11}$

58. $[8 \times (6 + 3)] \pmod{11}$ 59. $(14 \times 6 - 3 \times 9) \pmod{11}$

Consider the following table, which illustrates the addition of integers mod 3.

+	0	1	2
0	0	1	2
1	1	2	0
2	2	0	1

60. Is the table closed with respect to addition?

61. Is there an additive identity? If so, what is it?

62. What is the additive inverse of 1? How do you know?

Solve. [3.1–3.4]

63. $x + 9 = -23$

64. $6 = y - 8$

65. $3w + 9 = -15$

66. $-6x - 12 = -24$

67. $5(x - 1) = -45$

68. $4 + x + 1 = 8$

69. $3(y + 2) + 6y = 51$

70. $-6x + 3 - 7x + 8 = 37$

71. $4(3z + 4) + 9 = -47$

72. $69 = 5w + 2(w + 6) + 8$

4.2 Prime Factorization

A mathematical theorem is a statement that can be proved by a logical series of true statements. The Bible says, "Prove all things; hold fast that which is good" (1 Thess. 5:21). This verse means that a Christian should compare all influences and behavior with Scripture to see whether they are to be held onto, avoided, or discarded.

The Fundamental Theorem of Arithmetic is an important building block in the study of integers. Its proof uses math induction and is beyond the scope of this text.

The factorizations above suggest that, if the order of the prime factors is ignored, every composite number can be written as a unique product of two or more prime numbers. This product is called the *prime factorization*. This is exactly what the Fundamental Theorem of Arithmetic states.

Fundamental Theorem of Arithmetic
Every composite integer greater than one can be written as a product of prime factors in exactly one way (though the order of the factors may vary).

For convenience, we will write prime factorizations in ascending order. There are a variety of procedures for factoring composite numbers. Common methods include a factor tree and a factor ladder. Example 1 uses a factor tree, and Example 2 uses a factor ladder. You may choose the method you like better for the exercises.

Example 1   Write the prime factorization of 42.

Answer

$$42$$
$$2 \cdot 21$$
$$2 \cdot 3 \cdot 7$$
$$42 = 2 \cdot 3 \cdot 7$$

1. 42 is even, so it is divisible by 2.
2. 21 is divisible by 3.
3. Write the factors in ascending order.

When the same prime number occurs more than once in a prime factorization, use exponents to indicate the number of times each prime factor occurs. The factorization $2 \cdot 2 \cdot 3 \cdot 5 \cdot 5 \cdot 5$ would be written $2^2 \cdot 3 \cdot 5^3$.

Example 2   Write the prime factorization of 126.

Answer

$$\begin{array}{r|r} 2 & 126 \\ \hline 3 & 63 \\ \hline 3 & 21 \\ \hline 7 & 7 \\ \hline & 1 \end{array}$$

1. 126 is even, so 2 is a prime factor. The quotient is not even.
2. Use the divisibility test for 3 to determine that 3 is a prime factor of 63. The quotient is 21.
3. 21 is also divisible by 3. The quotient is 7, a prime number.

$$126 = 2 \cdot 3^2 \cdot 7$$ 4. Using exponents, write the factors in ascending order.

The ladder method employs division repeatedly to find the prime factorization of a number. In this method, always use the smallest prime number divisor first and observe the following rules.

1. Check to see if the number is even; if so, divide by 2.

2. Check the quotient to see if it is even; if so, divide by 2 again and continue until the quotient is no longer even.

3. Apply the divisibility test for 3. If it is divisible by 3, divide. Continue dividing by 3 until the quotient is no longer divisible by 3.

4. Apply the divisibility test for 5. If it is divisible, continue dividing until the quotient is no longer divisible by 5. Then continue with the next lowest prime.

5. When the quotient is a prime, you are finished. All the divisors comprise the prime factors in order. Write the result as a product using exponents.

Example 3   Write the prime factorization of 90.

Answer

$$\begin{array}{r|r} 2 & 90 \\ \hline 3 & 45 \\ \hline 3 & 15 \\ \hline 5 & 5 \\ \hline & 1 \end{array}$$

1. 90 is even, so divide by 2.
2. 45 is not even. Since $4 + 5 = 9$, which is divisible by 3, 45 is divisible by 3.
3. 15 is also divisible by 3.

$$90 = 2 \cdot 3^2 \cdot 5$$ 4. Using exponents, write the factors in ascending order.

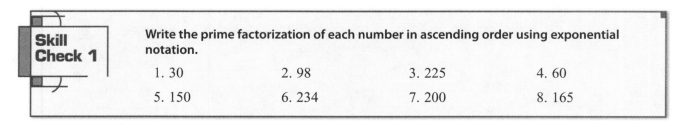

Skill Check 1

Write the prime factorization of each number in ascending order using exponential notation.

1. 30	2. 98	3. 225	4. 60
5. 150	6. 234	7. 200	8. 165

■ A. Exercises

Find the number whose prime factorization is given.

1. $2 \cdot 3 \cdot 7$ 2. $2^2 \cdot 3 \cdot 5$ 3. $2 \cdot 3^2$ 4. $2 \cdot 5 \cdot 11$ 5. $2^2 \cdot 5^2$ 6. $3^2 \cdot 5 \cdot 7$

Write the prime factorization of each number.

7. 33   8. 28   9. 66   10. 90

11. 36   12. 64   13. 63   14. 40

■ B. Exercises

Find the number whose prime factorization is given.

15. $2^3 \cdot 3^2$ 16. $3^3 \cdot 5^2$ 17. $2^4 \cdot 7^3$ 18. $2^2 \cdot 3 \cdot 7^2$

19. $3^2 \cdot 5^3 \cdot 11$ 20. $5 \cdot 7 \cdot 13^2$

Write the prime factorization of each number.

21. 175   22. 308   23. 279   24. 135

25. 231   26. 594   27. 198   28. 294

29. 338   30. 525

■ C. Exercises

Solve each equation to find the missing prime factor.

31. $273 = s \cdot 7 \cdot 13$ 32. $105 = 3 \cdot 5 \cdot n$ 33. $418 = 2 \cdot c \cdot 19$

34. $935 = 5 \cdot 11 \cdot y$ 35. $238 = 2 \cdot t \cdot 17$ 36. $1{,}235 = y \cdot 13 \cdot 19$

■ Dominion thru Math

Prior to 2007, books cataloged in the Library of Congress were required to have a 10-digit ISBN. (Now books are published with a 13-digit ISBN.) This number gives certain identifying information, such as the language the book was written in, the publisher, and the publisher's specific title number of the book. The last digit is a check number so that a certain representation of the ISBN will be equivalent to 0 (mod 11). The checking of an ISBN code helps ensure the accuracy of orders placed with publishers.

The Library of Congress is the world's largest library.

Suppose the ISBN is 1-57924-892-6. A check for validity could be as follows. (The check for 13-digit ISBNs is different but follows a similar process.)

Multiply each digit by an integer from 1 to 10, beginning from the right side of the number. Add these products. The sum must equal 0 (mod 11) if the ISBN is to be valid. The table below demonstrates this process.

ISBN digit	1	5	7	9	2	4	8	9	2	6	
Factor	10	9	8	7	6	5	4	3	2	1	**Sum**
Product	10	45	56	63	12	20	32	27	4	6	275

$1(10) + 5(9) + 7(8) + 9(7) + 2(6) + 4(5) + 8(4) + 9(3) + 2(2) + 6(1)$
$= 10 + 45 + 56 + 63 + 12 + 20 + 32 + 27 + 4 + 6 = 275$

$275 \div 11 = 25$ r 0, so $275 \equiv 0$ (mod 11). Therefore, the number is valid.

37. Is 1-57924-235-7 a valid ISBN?

38. Is 1-75924-345-0 a valid ISBN?

39. Is 0-13-113948-7 a valid ISBN?

40. In the valid ISBN 1-57924-386-X, what number must the letter X stand for?

41. Find the check number that is needed to make 0-618-40137-? a valid ISBN.

42. What happens to the ISBN in exercise 39 if the digits 3 and 9 are transposed: 0-13-119348-7?

CUMULATIVE REVIEW

Name the property illustrated by each of the following. [2.1–2.3]

43. $1b = b$

44. $ax + ay = a(x + y)$

45. $az = za$

46. $c + 0 = c$

Solve. [3.1–3.4]

47. $x - 7 = -26$

48. $36 = 3z + 12$

49. $-8w - 4 = -132$

50. $6(y + 7) = -12$

51. $3x + 2 - 5x = 10$

52. $-5(2x - 7) + 3x = 42$

When you find the prime factorization of a number, you break the number down until you find the prime factors that make up the number. This ability to find the parts that make up a whole is important in living your life for the Lord. As problems arise, you need the ability to break down issues in order to determine the right course to follow. This ability is called discernment. The Greek word for *discern* means "to take apart thoroughly." Through studying the Bible, which is "sharper than any twoedged sword" (Heb. 4:12), you learn to "discern both good and evil" (Heb. 5:14). Are you using the mighty sword that God has placed in your hand?

4.3 Greatest Common Factor

"**C**ommon" means sharing a characteristic. People have all sorts of common characteristics, such as two eyes, a nose, and ten fingers. There is one common characteristic that all people share: every person is born with a sin nature. We are all sinners. Romans 3:23*a* says that "all have sinned." Because of our sin, we all need Jesus Christ as our Savior. All who come to Him in faith He will cleanse from sin. This truth is confirmed in 1 John 1:7: "the blood of Jesus Christ his Son cleanseth us from all sin." Since we all have the common problem of sin, we all need Jesus Christ, the Savior.

Consider the factors of 12 and 18 listed below.

Factors of 12: 1, 2, 3, 4, 6, 12

Factors of 18: 1, 2, 3, 6, 9, 18

The *common factors* of 12 and 18 are numbers that are factors of both 12 and 18. These are 1, 2, 3, and 6.

Definition

The **greatest common factor** (also known as the **greatest common divisor**) is the largest number that is a factor of all the given numbers.

The above list of common factors indicates that the greatest common factor of 12 and 18 is 6, since 6 is the largest factor they have in common.

Skill Check 1

Find the GCF of each pair of numbers by listing all the common factors.

1. 6 and 15   2. 8 and 14   3. 16 and 20   4. 20 and 30

The greatest common factor (GCF) can be found by using prime factorizations. An outline of the procedure follows.

Factoring to Find the Greatest Common Factor
1. Write the prime factorization of each number.
2. Identify the prime factors common to all the given numbers.
3. Find the product of the common prime factors.

Example 1   Find the GCF of 24 and 36.

Answer

$24 = 2 \cdot 2 \cdot 2 \cdot 3$ 1. Find the prime factorization of each number.

$36 = 2 \cdot 2 \cdot 3 \cdot 3$

$GCF = 2 \cdot 2 \cdot 3 = 12$ 2. Find the product of the common prime factors (two 2s and one 3).

Example 2   Find the GCF of 180 and 600.

Answer

$180 = 2 \cdot 2 \cdot 3 \cdot 3 \cdot 5$ 1. Find the prime factorization of each number.

$600 = 2 \cdot 2 \cdot 2 \cdot 3 \cdot 5 \cdot 5$

$GCF = 2 \cdot 2 \cdot 3 \cdot 5 = 60$ 2. Find the product of the common prime factors (two 2s, one 3, and one 5).

If numbers do not have any common prime factors, then the GCF is one. This is true because one is a factor of every positive integer. The prime factorization of 9 is 3^2, and the prime factorization of 16 is 2^4. They do not share a common prime factor. However, if you list all the factors of 9 and 16 and examine them for common factors, one is the only factor that appears in both lists.

Factors of 9: 1, 3, 9
Factors of 16: 1, 2, 4, 8, 16
The GCF of 9 and 16 is 1.

Definition

Numbers are **relatively prime** if their greatest common factor is one.

When two integers are consecutive, they are always relatively prime.

Example 3   Find the GCF of the three numbers 1,764; 630; and 252.

Answer

$1{,}764 = 2 \cdot 2 \cdot 3 \cdot 3 \cdot 7 \cdot 7$ 1. Find the prime factorization of each number.
$630 = 2 \cdot 3 \cdot 3 \cdot 5 \cdot 7$
$252 = 2 \cdot 2 \cdot 3 \cdot 3 \cdot 7$
$\text{GCF} = 2 \cdot 3 \cdot 3 \cdot 7 = 126$ 2. The GCF is the product of the common prime factors (one 2, two 3s, and one 7).

The greatest common factor can also be found for two or more algebraic expressions. For example, the expressions $4x$ and $4x^2$ each contain a factor of 4, but they contain one and two factors of x respectively. Their GCF is $4x$; that is, $4x$ is a divisor of $4x^2$ (just as 5 is a divisor of 15).

The expressions $3ab^2$ and $5a^2b$ have no common numerical factor other than 1. However, $3ab^2$ contains one factor of a and two factors of b, while $5a^2b$ has two factors of a and one factor of b. Both expressions contain at least one factor of a and one factor of b. The GCF of $3ab^2$ and $5a^2b$ is ab.

The expressions $3y$ and $4z$ contain no common numerical factor and no common algebraic factor. Their GCF is 1, so they are relatively prime.

Example 4   Find the GCF of $15x^3y$ and $21x^2$.

Answer

$15x^3y = 3 \cdot 5 \cdot x \cdot x \cdot x \cdot y$ 1. Find the prime factorization of each expression.
$21x^2 = 3 \cdot 7 \cdot x \cdot x$
$\text{GCF} = 3 \cdot x \cdot x = 3x^2$ 2. Each expression contains one factor of 3 and at least two factors of x.

Skill Check 2

Use prime factorizations to find the GCF of each pair of numbers.

1. 40, 100   2. 12, 15   3. 24, 30   4. 18, 24

Use prime factorizations to find the GCF of each pair of expressions.

5. $12x^2y^3$, $15xy^4$ 6. $60xy^2z$, $48yz^3$

■ A. Exercises

Find the GCF of each pair of numbers.

1. 16, 18   2. 12, 40   3. 14, 84   4. 35, 75   5. 21, 58   6. 27, 36

7. 40, 50   8. 28, 35   9. 12, 30   10. 36, 48   11. 14, 21   12. 40, 60

■ B. Exercises

Use prime factorizations to find the GCF of each set of numbers.

13. 42, 70   14. 60, 84   15. 90, 104   16. 81, 189   17. 10, 25, 40   18. 12, 18, 24

19. 8, 12, 28   20. 27, 45, 54   21. 28, 42, 56

Use prime factorizations to find the GCF of each set of expressions.

22. a^2b^5, a^3b

23. $9c^3d^5$, $12c^4d^4$

24. $4j^5g^3$, $6j^4h^3$

25. $m^{18}n^2$, $m^{15}p^6$

26. $10r^3s^2t$, $25r^2s^3$, $40s^2t^2$

27. $16x^5y^2z^4$, $64x^3yz$, $36x^5y^7$

Is each pair of numbers relatively prime?

28. 14, 15

29. 15, 18

30. 27, 40

■ C. Exercises

Find the GCF of these numbers given in factored form.

31. $2^3 \cdot 3^2$ and $2^2 \cdot 3^3$

32. $2 \cdot 3^2 \cdot 11$ and $3 \cdot 5 \cdot 11^2$

33. $2^2 \cdot 3 \cdot 5^2$ and $2^2 \cdot 5^2 \cdot 7$

34. $3 \cdot 5$, $2^2 \cdot 5$, and $2^3 \cdot 3$

35. $2 \cdot 3^2$, $2 \cdot 3 \cdot 5$, and $2^2 \cdot 3 \cdot 5$

36. $2^3 \cdot 5^2 \cdot 11$, $2^2 \cdot 5 \cdot 7^2$, and $2^4 \cdot 5^3 \cdot 7$

■ Dominion thru Math

Checking the validity of credit card numbers is very important. People entering card numbers manually are prone to mistakes. The algorithm for checking credit card numbers is more sophisticated than the 10-digit ISBN method, though the right-hand digit is still a check digit. To verify the card numbers in this exercise, follow the directions below.

Highlight every other digit starting at the second from the right. Double all the highlighted digits and add the resulting digits to the check digit. The sum must equal 0 (mod 10). If a doubled number has two digits, such as 9 × 2 = 18, treat it as two separate digits and add a 1 and an 8 rather than an 18. Study the following example to make sure you understand the process.

Credit cards are very convenient, but credit card theft is a constant threat.

Determine whether 6011 5432 2121 9292 is a valid credit card number. Highlight every other digit beginning with the second digit from the right—6 0 1 1 5 4 3 2 2 1 2 1 9 2 9 2. Double the highlighted digits—12 0 2 1 10 4 6 2 4 1 4 1 18 2 18 2. Add all the highlighted digits and the check digit 2 at the far right: $(1 + 2) + 2 + (1 + 0) + 6 + 4 + 4 + (1 + 8) + (1 + 8) + 2 = 40 \equiv 0$ (mod 10); the number is valid.

37. Determine the validity of this credit card number: 5491 3482 1992 7254.

38. Is 4235 6442 0980 5237 a valid credit card number?

39. Is 5238 4382 2225 1999 a valid credit card number?

40. Is 6011 9595 0302 2586 a valid credit card number?

CUMULATIVE REVIEW

Estimate the sum or difference by rounding to the nearest hundred. [2.7]

41. $315 + 821$ 42. $219 - 793$ 43. $4{,}578 + 321$ 44. $-3{,}929 - 2{,}285$

Write an equation using *n* for the variable for each sentence below. [3.5]

45. A number decreased by 16 is 52. 46. −28 multiplied by a number is 252.

47. The sum of a number and 97 is 26. 48. 319 less than a number is 498.

49. The product of 19 and a number is 456.

50. 38 subtracted from the number of seventh graders gives 63 students.

4.4 Least Common Multiple

The following table shows a comparison of the multiples of 3 and 4. The first common multiple is 12. However, 24 is also a common multiple. If the multiples are continued, there will be an infinite number of common multiples. A useful multiple is the *least common multiple* (LCM). The LCM of 3 and 4 is 12.

	1 ×	2 ×	3 ×	4 ×	5 ×	6 ×	7 ×	8 ×
Multiples of 3	3	6	9	(12)	15	18	21	(24)
Multiples of 4	4	8	(12)	16	20	(24)	28	32

Definition

The **least common multiple** of two or more numbers is the smallest number that is a multiple of each of the given numbers.

Example 1   List multiples to find the LCM of 10 and 12.

Answer

Multiples of 10: 10, 20, 30, 40, 50, (60), 70, …
Multiples of 12: 12, 24, 36, 48, (60), 72, 84, …
The LCM of 10 and 12 is 60.

For any set of numbers, LCM > GCF.

Using Listing to Find the Least Common Multiple

1. List the multiples of each number.
2. Identify the first common multiple in each list of multiples.

Skill Check 1

Use the given multiples to find the LCM.

1. 2, 4, 6, 8, …
   3, 6, 9, 12, …

2. 6, 12, 18, 24, 30, …
   8, 16, 24, 32, 40, …

List multiples to find the LCM of each pair of numbers.

3. 6, 10

4. 9, 15

The least common multiple can be found without listing multiples of the given numbers. Prime factorizations make it possible to find the LCM of two numbers by multiplying all the factors used in either or both factorizations. This is done most easily when the prime factorization is written in exponential form. Examine the procedure explained in the table below and used in Example 2.

Using Exponential Form to Find the LCM

1. Write the prime factorization of each number in exponential form.
2. Identify all the prime factors, both common and different prime factors, that appear in the factorizations.
3. Find the product of all the prime factors, using only the highest power of each that appears in any of the factorizations.

Example 2   Find the LCM of 30 and 45.

Answer

$30 = 2 \cdot 3 \cdot 5$ 1. Find the prime factorizations of 30 and 45.

$45 = 3 \cdot 3 \cdot 5 = 3^2 \cdot 5$

$LCM = 2 \cdot 3^2 \cdot 5 = 90$ 2. Identify the prime factors used in any of the factorizations: 2, 3, and 5. Use the highest power found in any of the factorizations.

The LCM is divisible by each of the given numbers. For the LCM to be divisible by 30, the prime factors of 30 must appear in the factorization that produces the LCM. Likewise, to be divisible by 45, the LCM must include the prime factors of 45.

Example 3   Find the LCM of 12, 28, and 75.

Answer

$12 = 2 \cdot 2 \cdot 3 = 2^2 \cdot 3$ 1. Find the prime factorizations in exponential form.

$28 = 2 \cdot 2 \cdot 7 = 2^2 \cdot 7$

$75 = 3 \cdot 5 \cdot 5 = 3 \cdot 5^2$

$LCM = 2^2 \cdot 3 \cdot 5^2 \cdot 7$ 2. Use the highest power of each of the prime factors.

     $= 4 \cdot 3 \cdot 25 \cdot 7$

     $= 2,100$

In order for the LCM to be a multiple of 12, it must contain two 2s and a 3. In order for the LCM to be a multiple of 28, it must also have a factor of 7. In order for the LCM to be a multiple of 75, it must additionally contain two factors of 5.

The least common multiple can also be found for two or more algebraic expressions. Consider the expressions $4x$ and $4x^2$. The least common multiple of the numeric factors is 4. The first expression has one factor of x, and the second contains two factors of x. Two factors of x are required in the LCM for $4x^2$ to divide into it, so the LCM is $4x^2$.

The LCM of $3ab^2$ and $5a^2b$ must contain a factor of 3 and a factor of 5. The LCM must contain two factors of a if $5a^2b$ is to divide into it, and it must contain two factors of b if $3ab^2$ is to divide into the LCM. Therefore, the LCM is $15a^2b^2$.

Since $3y$ and $4z$ are relatively prime (contain no common factor other than one), their LCM is $3y \cdot 4z = 12yz$.

Example 4   Find the LCM of $15x^3y$ and $21x^2$.

Answer

$15x^3y = 3 \cdot 5 \cdot x \cdot x \cdot x \cdot y$ 1. Find the prime factorization of each expression.

$21x^2 = 3 \cdot 7 \cdot x \cdot x$

$3 \cdot 5 \cdot 7 = 105$ 2. Find the numeric portion of the LCM.

x^3 and y 3. Find the highest power of the variable x and the highest power of the variable y.

$\text{LCM} = 105x^3y$ 4. Multiply to find the LCM.

Skill Check 2

Use the given prime factorizations to find the LCM.

1. $10 = 2 \cdot 5$
   $15 = 3 \cdot 5$

2. $20 = 2 \cdot 2 \cdot 5 = 2^2 \cdot 5$
   $50 = 2 \cdot 5 \cdot 5 = 2 \cdot 5^2$

Use prime factorizations to find the LCM of each pair of numbers.

3. 9, 12

4. 7, 21

Use prime factorizations to find the LCM of each pair of expressions.

5. $8x^2y$, $12y^2z$

6. $14a^3b$, $35a^2c$

■ A. Exercises

List multiples to find the LCM of each pair of numbers.

1. 3, 5   2. 4, 6   3. 6, 10   4. 10, 20   5. 10, 15   6. 8, 12

Find the LCM of these numbers given in factored form.

7. $2 \cdot 3 \cdot 3 \cdot 5$ and $3 \cdot 3 \cdot 5 \cdot 5$ 8. $3 \cdot 5 \cdot 7$ and $3 \cdot 3 \cdot 7 \cdot 7$ 9. $2^2 \cdot 7$ and $3 \cdot 7^2$

10. $3 \cdot 5^2 \cdot 7$ and $5^2 \cdot 7$ 11. $5 \cdot 19$ and $5 \cdot 17$ 12. 2^4 and $2^5 \cdot 3$

13. $2 \cdot 17$ and $2 \cdot 19$ 14. $2^4 \cdot 3$ and $2^3 \cdot 3^2$ 15. $5^2 \cdot 7$ and $5 \cdot 7^3$

16. $2^2 \cdot 3 \cdot 19$ and $2 \cdot 3^2 \cdot 17$

■ B. Exercises

Use prime factorizations to find the LCM of each pair of numbers.

17. 4, 14   18. 6, 20   19. 15, 25   20. 18, 28   21. 42, 49   22. 45, 28

Use prime factorizations to find the LCM of each set of numbers.

23. 2, 4, 5

24. 4, 8, 12

25. 8, 16, 20

26. 4, 6, 25

27. 8, 15, 18

28. 36, 54, 81

Use prime factorizations to find the LCM of each set of expressions.

29. a^2b^5, a^3b

30. $9c^3d^5$, $12c^4d^7$

31. $4g^3j^5$, $6h^3j^4$

32. $m^{18}n^2$, $m^{15}p^6$

33. $10r^3s^2t$, $25r^2s^3$, $40s^2t^2$

34. $16x^5y^2z^4$, $64x^3yz$, $36x^5y^7$

■ C. Exercises

Find the GCF and LCM of each set of numbers.

35. 36, 48

36. 12, 18, 24

37. For any two numbers, what would be the *least* common factor? (Hint: List the common factors of 8 and 10.)

38. For any two numbers, what would be the *greatest* common multiple?

39. When you reduce fractions such as $\frac{350}{400}$, are you using an LCM or a GCF? How?

40. When you add fractions such as $\frac{1}{6}$ and $\frac{1}{8}$ to get $\frac{7}{24}$, are you using an LCM or a GCF? How?

■ Dominion thru Math

You can use the table below to encrypt a message by finding the desired letter in the second row and writing the letter below it. To encrypt a number, find each digit in the top row and write the number below it in the bottom row. (Insert a space between the codes for consecutive digits.) To decrypt a message, find the letter in the third row and replace it with the letter above it. To a decrypt number, find the number in the bottom row and replace it with the digit above it in the top row.

1	2	3	4	5	6	7	8	9	10	11	12	13	14	15	16	17	18	19	20	21	22	23	24	25	26
A	B	C	D	E	F	G	H	I	J	K	L	M	N	O	P	Q	R	S	T	U	V	W	X	Y	Z
I	J	K	L	M	N	O	P	Q	R	S	T	U	V	W	X	Y	Z	A	B	C	D	E	F	G	H
9	10	11	12	13	14	15	16	17	18	19	20	21	22	23	24	25	26	1	2	3	4	5	6	7	8

The above table was obtained by using the formula $C(n) = (n + 8)$ (mod 26). Each letter of the alphabet was assigned a number from 1 to 26, starting at $A = 1$ and continuing in order to $Z = 26$. The bottom two rows were obtained by adding 8 to each number and expressing it mod 26. For example, $T = 20$ and $(20 + 8)$ (mod 26) $\equiv 2$ (mod 26). Therefore, the second letter, B, is the substitute for T, and 2 is the substitute for 20. If a value turns out to be 0 (mod 26), use 26 instead of 0, since no letter of the alphabet has been assigned the 0.

41. Encrypt the message "Meet me at 9 PM at the clubhouse on 53 Steel Road."

42. Encrypt the message "Chocolate chip cookies and milk in room 364."

43. Decrypt the message "JZQVO 11 14 LWCOPVCBA BW BPM UMMBQVO."

44. Decrypt the message "AQZ JMIV QA BPM OZMMV SVQOPB WN KIUMTWB."

Do the following equations have solutions over the set of whole numbers? If yes, solve. [3.6]

45. $8x = -24$ 　　　 46. $14x = 28$ 　　　 47. $y - 12 = 49$ 　　　 48. $3y + 5 = 16$

Do the following equations have solutions over the set of rational numbers? [3.6]

49. $-9x = 49$ 　　　 50. $6x = \dfrac{-5}{7}$ 　　　 51. $5x = -85$ 　　　 52. $-\dfrac{2}{3}x = 6$

Solve. [3.7]

53. $x - 19 \leq -43$ 　　　 54. $x + 12 < 27$ 　　　 55. $-7 > x + 11$ 　　　 56. $y - 37 < 3$

4.5 Arithmetic Sequences

Understanding patterns and seeing relationships is extremely important to problem solving. Knowing the pattern for living that Jesus Christ exemplified in the Bible is even more important in the Christian's life. A careful study of God's Word, the Bible, is necessary for a Christian to be able to follow the pattern Christ set forth. First Peter 2:21 says, "For even hereunto were ye called: because Christ also suffered for us, leaving us an example, that ye should follow his steps."

A *sequence* is a set of objects in a definite order (pattern). The objects can be a multitude of items such as pictures or colors. However, in the context of pre-algebra, the objects will be sets of numbers that are placed in a definite order.

> ### Definition
>
> A **sequence** is a set of numbers, ordered according to a distinguishable pattern. The set can be either finite or infinite.

By carefully studying sequences, you can make conjectures about their patterns. A *conjecture* is a generalized statement that seems to be true at all times. Mathematicians look at patterns and sequences regularly and make conjectures or predictions about what they think always seems to be true. To do this, they look at specific examples and generalize to a conclusion that seems to be true. A good mathematician will then attempt to use logical deduction to prove the statement true. This is how mathematics is discovered and theory is developed.

You have used sequences of numbers for many years. The set of natural numbers (counting numbers) that you learned at a very early age is an example of a sequence.

$$1, 2, 3, 4, 5, 6, 7, \ldots$$

The marking ... is called an *ellipsis*; it indicates that the pattern continues in the same manner.

A number in a sequence is called a *term* of the sequence. The positions of the terms are identified by natural numbers. An arbitrary term of a sequence is called the *n*th term.

Consider the sequence of the multiples of three. The table below shows the terms of the sequence and their positions. The fourth term of the sequence is 12. An individual member of a sequence can be represented as a_n, where n is the position of the term. In the sequence of the multiples of three, $a_4 = 12$ and $a_6 = 18$.

Position of the Term	1	2	3	4	5	6	...
Term	3	6	9	12	15	18	...

When you inspect the sequence of the multiples of three, what pattern do you see? Each term of the sequence is three more than the term that precedes it. This is an example of a special type of sequence called an *arithmetic sequence*. The difference between the consecutive terms of an arithmetic sequence is called the *common difference* and is indicated by a lowercase d.

Definitions

A sequence of numbers, each differing by a constant amount from the preceding number, is an **arithmetic sequence**.
The **common difference**, d, is the difference between successive terms of an arithmetic sequence.

Arithmetic Sequence
Terms differ by a constant addend d.
$$a_n = a_{n-1} + d$$

Example 1

Find the following values for the sequence 5, 9, 13, 17, 21, 25, 29, 33, ...

a. d b. a_1 c. a_5 d. a_{10}

Answer

a. $d = 4$ The difference between each pair of consecutive terms is 4.
b. $a_1 = 5$ The first term of the sequence is 5.
c. $a_5 = 21$ The fifth term of the sequence is 21.
d. $a_{10} = 41$ The ninth term is $33 + 4 = 37$, so the tenth term is $37 + 4 = 41$.

The common difference, d, in an arithmetic sequence can be negative as well as positive. If the common difference is negative, then the terms of the sequence decrease as n increases.

Example 2

Write the first six terms of the sequence in which $a_1 = 20$ and $d = -2$.

Answer

$a_1 = 20$
$a_2 = 20 + (-2) = 18$
$a_3 = 18 + (-2) = 16$
$a_4 = 16 + (-2) = 14$
$a_5 = 14 + (-2) = 12$
$a_6 = 12 + (-2) = 10$
The first six terms of the sequence are 20, 18, 16, 14, 12, and 10.

Find d, a_1, a_4, and a_7 for each of the following sequences.

1. 5, 8, 11, 14, 17, …

2. –9, –5, –1, 3, 7, …

3. 22, 19, 16, 13, 10, …

A formula can be used to derive the terms of a sequence from previous terms. If each successive term is three more than the previous term, then the formula $a_n = a_{n-1} + 3$ can be used to find successive terms of the sequence. Suppose $n = 8$. Then $n - 1 = 7$, and the formula says that $a_8 = a_7 + 3$, or the eighth term is three more than the seventh term.

Definition

A **recursive formula** specifies the step by which each term of the sequence is generated from the preceding term or terms.

The sequence 3, 9, 15, 21, 27, 33, … is shown in the following table. Do you recognize a pattern in the sequence? Each term is six more than the preceding term, so the common difference, d, is 6. The recursive formula is written $a_n = a_{n-1} + 6$.

Position of the Term	1	2	3	4	5	6	…
Term	3	9	15	21	27	33	…

Example 3

Write the first five terms of the sequence defined by $a_1 = 2$ and $a_n = a_{n-1} + 9$.

Answer

$a_1 = 2$

$a_2 = a_1 + 9 = 2 + 9 = 11$

$a_3 = a_2 + 9 = 11 + 9 = 20$

$a_4 = a_3 + 9 = 20 + 9 = 29$

$a_5 = a_4 + 9 = 29 + 9 = 38$

The first five terms of the sequence are 2, 11, 20, 29, and 38.

Example 4

Write the recursive formula for the sequence 28, 25, 22, 19, 16, …

Answer

$a_1 = 28$ 1. Identify the first term of the arithmetic sequence.

$d = -3$ 2. The successive terms differ by –3.

$a_n = a_{n-1} + (-3)$, or $a_n = a_{n-1} - 3$ 3. Each term is three less than the previous term.

Skill Check 2

Write the first five terms of the following recursively defined sequences.

1. $a_1 = -8$; $a_n = a_{n-1} + 6$

2. $a_1 = 3$; $a_n = a_{n-1} - 9$

3. $a_1 = -3$; $a_n = a_{n-1} - 4$

Write the recursive definition for the following sequences.

4. 7, 12, 17, 22, 27, ...

5. –15, –7, 1, 9, 17, ...

The terms of an arithmetic sequence can also be described by a formula that uses n, the position of the term. This type of formula is called an *explicit formula*. Using the explicit formula allows you to find a_{20} in a sequence without knowing all of the previous nineteen terms.

Consider the sequence 3, 9, 15, 21, 27, 33, ... Six is added to the first term once to get the second term: $3 + 6 = 9$. The third term is obtained by adding 6 twice to the first term: $3 + 2(6) = 15$. To get the fourth term, 6 is added to the a_1 value three times: $3 + 3(6) = 21$. How many times would you add 6 to the first term to find the twentieth term? Six must be added $n - 1 = 20 - 1 = 19$ times. Therefore, $a_{20} = 3 + 19(6) = 3 + 114 = 117$.

The pattern for the term of the sequence based on the position of the term is shown below.

Position of the Term	Term
1	3
2	$3 + 1(6) = 9$
3	$3 + 2(6) = 15$
4	$3 + 3(6) = 21$
5	$3 + 4(6) = 27$
6	$3 + 5(6) = 33$
$\vdots$	$\vdots$
n	$3 + (n - 1)6$

Notice that the number of 6s added to 3 is always one less than the position of the term. If the position of the term is n, then the term is $3 + (n - 1)6$.

Definition

The **explicit formula for an arithmetic sequence** is $a_n = a_1 + (n - 1)d$, where n is the position in the sequence and d is the difference between terms.

This formula allows the calculation of any term based on the first term and the difference between consecutive terms.

Example 5 The explicit formula for the sequence 10, 15, 20, 25, 30, 35, ... is $a_n = 10 + (n - 1)5$. Find a_{60}.

Answer

$a_{60} = 10 + (60 - 1)5 = 10 + (59)5 = 10 + 295 = 305$

Example 6 Write the explicit formula for the sequence $-7, -4, -1, 2, 5, 8, \ldots$ Then use the simplified form of the explicit formula to find a_{72}.

Answer

$a_1 = -7; d = 3$ 1. Identify the first term and the common difference.

$a_n = a_1 + (n-1)d$ 2. Substitute the values into the explicit formula for an arithmetic sequence
$\quad = -7 + (n-1)3$ and simplify the expression.
$\quad = -7 + 3n - 3$
$\quad = 3n - 10$

$a_n = 3(72) - 10$ 3. Evaluate the expression for $n = 72$.
$\quad = 216 - 10 = 206$

Skill Check 3

Find each term using the explicit formula.

1. a_{12} if $a_n = 4 + (n-1)2$ 2. a_{51} if $a_n = 4n - 7$ 3. a_{27} if $a_1 = 6$ and $d = -3$

Invention

On October 7, 1952, Joseph Woodland and Bernard (Bob) Silver received a US patent for their version of a *barcode* system. In reality, no system for quickly scanning information for product identification would become viable until computers reached a level of development where their size and economy would make it happen. The grocery industry and the railroads were begging for this invention. The US Postal Service was also a ripe candidate for barcodes for letter handling. By 1973 laser scanners and computer technology had advanced enough, and the industry adopted the IBM-developed Universal Product Code. Computers could manage well its array of vertical bars encoded with binary information. This beautiful marriage of mathematics and electronics stands as the most historically significant invention in the history of logistics.

■ A. Exercises

1. If the difference between terms is a constant, the sequence is called _____.

2. The difference between succeeding terms is called the _____.

3. A(n) _____ formula specifies the step by which each term of the sequence is generated from the preceding step.

4. A(n) _____ formula allows you to find any term in the sequence without knowing the preceding term.

Find the following values for the sequence 2, 9, 16, 23, 30, ...

5. a_1 6. d 7. a_4 8. a_7

Write the first five terms of the following sequences.

9. $a_1 = 6$; $d = 7$

10. $a_1 = -8$; $d = 3$

11. $a_1 = -10$; $d = 4$

12. $a_1 = 20$; $d = -8$

■ B. Exercises

Write the first five terms of the following recursively defined sequences.

13. $a_1 = 2$; $a_n = a_{n-1} + 5$

14. $a_1 = -1$; $a_n = a_{n-1} + 8$

15. $a_1 = -3$; $a_n = a_{n-1} + 5$

16. $a_1 = 6$; $a_n = a_{n-1} - 5$

17. $a_1 = -1$; $a_n = a_{n-1} + 5$

18. $a_1 = -1$; $a_n = a_{n-1} - 5$

19. $a_1 = 3$; $a_n = a_{n-1} + 31$

Write the recursive definition for the following sequences.

20. 3, 7, 11, 15, 19, …

21. –6, 0, 6, 12, 18, …

22. –2, –6, –10, –14, –18, …

23. 30, 18, 6, –6, –18, …

24. –2, 6, 14, 22, 30, …

25. 4, 2, 0, –2, –4, …

Write the simplified form of the explicit formula for the following sequences.

26. 7, 11, 15, 19, 23, …

27. –3, 7, 17, 27, 37, …

28. 11, 8, 5, 2, –1, …

29. –4, –9, –14, –19, –24, …

30. –8, –2, 4, 10, 16, …

31. 19, 28, 37, 46, 55, …

Find a_1 and d for each sequence; then find a_{50} and a_{89}.

32. –16, –3, 10, 23, …

33. 2, 9, 16, 23, 30, …

34. 8, 3, –2, –7, –12, …

35. 10, 4, –2, –8, …

36. –25, –21, –17, –13, …

37. 60, 45, 30, 15, …

■ C. Exercises

38. If the house numbers on one side of a street form an arithmetic sequence where the first house number is 2, the second house number is 4, and the third house number is 6, how many houses are along that side of the street if the last house number is 38?

39. The first house number in a block is 13, and the twelfth house number is 90. Assuming the numbers form an arithmetic sequence, what is the number of the fourth house?

40. Locust Street has sixteen lots for new houses. If the planners are laying out the numbers for the addresses of the new homes on that street and they are to form an arithmetic sequence, what is the largest common difference that could be used if the numbers cannot go above 50?

■ Dominion thru Math

41. Complete the bottom two rows of the cipher table. Use the formula $C(n) = (19 - n)$ (mod 26).
    (See Section 4.4, Dominion thru Math.)

1	2	3	4	5	6	7	8	9	10	11	12	13	14	15	16	17	18	19	20	21	22	23	24	25	26
A	B	C	D	E	F	G	H	I	J	K	L	M	N	O	P	Q	R	S	T	U	V	W	X	Y	Z

42. Use the table in exercise 41 to decrypt the message "J GDWN CDCPDAE REO CNREXY QXYYNA."

43. Use the table in exercise 41 to encrypt the message "If wishes were horses, beggars would ride."

Evaluate. [2.4]

44. $-7a$ when $a = -12$

45. $\dfrac{9n}{5}$ when $n = -4$

46. $8r - 3 + 5r$ when $r = 6$

47. $-18a + 4b + 21$ when $a = 3$ and $b = 2$

48. $-7 + bc$ when $b = -2$ and $c = 15$

Solve. [3.1–3.3]

49. $8x = 24$

50. $x - 42 = 83$

51. $-12x = 156$

52. $9x + 3 = 75$

53. $47 = 23 - 4b$

4.6 Geometric Sequences

The following sequence exhibits a pattern, but it is not an arithmetic sequence. See if you can identify the pattern.

$$3, 6, 12, 24, 48, 96, \ldots$$

Each number in the sequence is two times the previous term. When the terms of a sequence are found by multiplying the previous term by a common factor, the sequence is a *geometric sequence*. The common factor is called the *common ratio*, denoted r, of the geometric sequence. The common ratio of a geometric sequence can be any real number—even a fraction or a negative number.

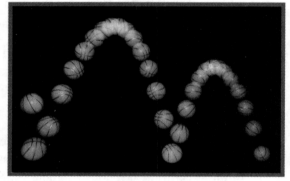

The height of a bouncing ball above the ground is a decreasing sequence.

Definitions

A **geometric sequence** is a sequence of numbers whose successive terms differ by a constant multiplier.
The constant multiplier for a geometric sequence is called the **common ratio**, r.

Example 1	Write the first six terms of the geometric sequence in which $a_1 = 1$ and $r = 3$.

Answer

$a_1 = 1$
$a_2 = 1 \cdot 3 = 3$
$a_3 = 3 \cdot 3 = 9$
$a_4 = 9 \cdot 3 = 27$
$a_5 = 27 \cdot 3 = 81$
$a_6 = 81 \cdot 3 = 243$

The first six terms of the sequence are 1, 3, 9, 27, 81, and 243.

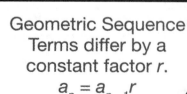

Geometric Sequence
Terms differ by a
constant factor r.
$$a_n = a_{n-1} r$$

Example 2 Find the following values for the sequence 2, 6, 18, 54, 162, 486, …

   a. a_1 b. r c. a_3 d. a_8

  Answer

  a. $a_1 = 2$ The first term of the sequence is 2.

  b. $r = 3$ Each term is multiplied by 3 to find the next term.

  c. $a_3 = 18$ The third term of the sequence is 18.

  d. $a_7 = 486 \cdot 3 = 1{,}458$ Multiply the sixth term by 3 to find the seventh term.

     $a_8 = 1{,}458 \cdot 3 = 4{,}374$ Then multiply by 3 again to find the eighth term.

Skill Check 1

Write the first five terms of the following sequences.

1. $a_1 = 4; r = -2$ 2. $a_1 = 972; r = \dfrac{1}{3}$

Find a_1, r, a_4, and a_6 for each of the following sequences.

3. 2, 6, 18, 54, …   4. –7, 14, –28, 56, …

5. 256, 128, 64, 32, …

The above methods for finding the terms lead us to recursive formulas for geometric sequences. The general recursive formula for a geometric sequence is $a_n = a_{n-1} r$.

Example 3 Write the first five terms of the sequence defined by $a_1 = -4$ and $a_n = 3a_{n-1}$.

  Answer

$a_1 = -4$

$a_2 = 3(-4) = -12$

$a_3 = 3(-12) = -36$

$a_4 = 3(-36) = -108$

$a_5 = 3(-108) = -324$

The first five terms of the sequence are –4, –12, –36, –108, and –324.

Example 4 Write the recursive formula for the sequence 729, 243, 81, 27, …

  Answer

$a_1 = 729$ 1. Identify the first term of the sequence.

$r = \dfrac{1}{3}$ 2. Determine the common ratio that when multiplied by a term of the sequence produces the next term of the sequence: $\dfrac{243}{729} = \dfrac{1}{3}$; $\dfrac{81}{243} = \dfrac{1}{3}$; $\dfrac{27}{81} = \dfrac{1}{3}$; etc.

$a_n = \dfrac{1}{3}a_{n-1}$ 3. Write the recursive formula that expresses each term of the sequence as one-third of the previous term.

Skill Check 2

Write the recursive formula for the following sequences.

1. 1, 6, 36, 216, 1,296, …   2. –2, 6, –18, 54, –162, …

Write the first five terms of the following sequences.

3. $a_1 = 12; r = \dfrac{1}{2}$ 4. $a_1 = -10; r = -2$

In the sequence 3, 6, 12, 24, 48, 96, ..., the second term is found by multiplying 3 by one factor of 2. The third term is found by multiplying 3 by two factors of 2: $3(2)^2 = 3(4) = 12$. The fourth term is found by multiplying 3 by three factors of 2: $3(2)^3 = 3(8) = 24$. Notice the progression to the general nth term given below.

Position of the Term	Term
1	3
2	$3 \cdot 2^1 = 6$
3	$3 \cdot 2^2 = 12$
4	$3 \cdot 2^3 = 24$
5	$3 \cdot 2^4 = 48$
6	$3 \cdot 2^5 = 96$
$\vdots$	$\vdots$
n	$3 \cdot 2^{n-1}$

Notice that the power of two in each calculation above is one less than the position of the term. This reveals a formula for the nth term of a geometric sequence.

Definition

The **explicit formula for a geometric sequence** is $a_n = a_1 r^{n-1}$, in which a_1 is the first term and r is the common ratio.

This formula allows the calculation of any term based on the first term and the ratio.

Example 5
Write the explicit formula for the sequence $-5, -15, -45, -135, -405, \ldots$

Answer

$a_1 = -5$ 1. Identify the first term of the sequence.

$r = 3$ 2. Each successive term is found by multiplying the previous term by 3.

$a_n = -5(3)^{n-1}$ 3. Write the explicit formula.

Skill Check 3

Write the explicit formula for the following sequences.

1. 2, 8, 32, 128, ...   2. $-250, 50, -10, 2, \ldots$

State whether the following sequences are arithmetic, geometric, or neither.

3. 81, 27, 9, 3, ...   4. 6, 10, 14, 18, ...   5. 2, 22, 222, 2,222, ...

■ A. Exercises

1. If each term of a sequence is a constant multiple of the previous term, then the sequence is called _____.

2. The constant multiplier is called the _____.

Find the following values for the sequence 2, 8, 32, 128, 512, ...

3. a_1 4. r 5. a_4 6. a_6

Find the following value for the sequence $-6, -12, -24, -48, -96, \ldots$

7. a_1 8. r 9. a_4 10. a_6

Write the first five terms of the following sequences.

11. $a_1 = 3; r = 2$ 12. $a_1 = -2; r = 3$ 13. $a_1 = 6; r = 4$ 14. $a_1 = -10; r = -3$

15. A(n) _____ formula specifies the step by which each term of the sequence is generated from the preceding step.

■ B. Exercises

Write the first five terms of the following recursively defined sequences.

16. $a_1 = 2; a_n = 4a_{n-1}$ 17. $a_1 = -1; a_n = -3a_{n-1}$ 18. $a_1 = -3; a_n = -2a_{n-1}$

19. $a_1 = 6; a_n = 5a_{n-1}$ 20. $a_1 = -20; a_n = 0.5a_{n-1}$ 21. $a_1 = -1; a_n = -5a_{n-1}$

22. $a_1 = 3; a_n = 6a_{n-1}$

Write the recursive formula for the following sequences.

23. 3, 6, 12, 24, 48, ...   24. −6, −18, −54, −162, −486, ...   25. −2, 8, −32, 128, −512, ...

26. 60, 30, 15, 7.5, 3.75, ...   27. −2, −10, −50, −250, −1,250, ...   28. 4, −8, 16, −32, 64, ...

State whether the following sequences are arithmetic, geometric, or neither. Give the value of *d* or *r*.

29. −1, −2, −4, −8, −16, ...   30. −3, −1, 1, 3, 5, ...   31. 20, 18, 14, 6, ...

32. −17, −7, 3, 13, 23, ...   33. 2, 5, 9, 14, 20, ...   34. 128, 64, 32, 16, 8, ...

■ C. Exercises

35. A ball bounces three-fourths the height of its fall. If the ball falls 12 ft., how high does it bounce on the first bounce? on the second bounce? on the third bounce?

36. In exercise 35, the height of the bounces forms a geometric sequence. Find the common ratio of this geometric sequence.

37. If the ball falls 12 ft. and begins bouncing, what is the total distance it has traveled when it hits the ground the third time?

38. When will the ball stop bouncing?

CUMULATIVE REVIEW

Write the following numbers in scientific notation. [1.8]

39. 38   40. 142,000   41. −0.00029   42. 8,450,000

Specify what the variable stands for, write an equation, and solve. [3.5]

43. Tickets to a baseball game are $11 for adults and $6 for children. If twenty more children's tickets are sold than adult tickets, how many of each type of ticket is sold if a total of $9,300 is taken in?

44. Mr. Johnson is in charge of buying two types of candy for the annual Christmas bags to be handed out to the children in his church. He wants to buy peppermints and lemon drops. Peppermints cost $3.50 per pound and lemon drops cost $4.00 per pound. If he has $22.50 to spend on the candy and he wants an equal number of pounds of each type, how many pounds of each should he buy?

State whether the given number is prime, composite, or neither. [4.1]

45. 2   46. 39   47. 52   48. 23

PROBLEM
SOLVING

Look for a Pattern

Patterns often occur in nature. The spiral shape is seen in a seashell and in the arrangement of the seeds in a sunflower. This same curve can be seen in the whorls of a pineapple and the seeds of a pinecone. God created the universe to follow mathematical patterns. Many problems can be solved by recognizing patterns in numbers and nature.

Fibonacci's sequence is observed in a sunflower seed pod.

Example Since his first birthday, Andre's uncle has given him a gift of money such that the number of dollars matched his age. Today is Andre's fourteenth birthday. How much money has he been given over the years by his uncle? If Andre's uncle continues giving him these gifts until Andre is 50, how much will he have received by then?

Answer

Think: Determine what you are trying to find.

You want to know the total amount of money Andre received from his uncle in 14 years and how much he will have received after 50 years.

Think: How could you find this sum? Is there an easier way than just adding the numbers from 1 to 14 and then adding the numbers from 1 to 50? Is there a pattern to this sum? Is there a rule based on the year number that can be used to find the sum in dollars?

Look at the first few years to try to determine a pattern in the sums. Making a table may help you organize this information.

Year	Sum in Dollars
1	1
2	1 + 2 = 3
3	1 + 2 + 3 = 6
4	1 + 2 + 3 + 4 = 10
5	1 + 2 + 3 + 4 + 5 = 15
6	1 + 2 + 3 + 4 + 5 + 6 = 21
7	1 + 2 + 3 + 4 + 5 + 6 + 7 = 28

There definitely is a pattern in the sums. The next number in the sequence can be found from the previous number.

Think: How can you find the sum of the numbers to 14 and to 50 without writing down the entire list of numbers?

Notice that the numbers that are added to get 28 in the table can be added in pairs that always give the same numerical result. That is, 1 + 7 = 8, 2 + 6 = 8, and 3 + 5 = 8. Since there are 7 numbers in the sum, there are 3 pairs of numbers and an unpaired middle number. The middle one is one half the sum of one of the pairs.

Think: What will be the sum of the first and last terms in 1 + 2 + 3 + … + 13 + 14? How many pairs will there be in the sum?

1 + 14 = 15, as does 2 + 13. There are 7 pairs with no remainder.

14 years: $7 \times 15 = \$105$

For 50 years, the sum of the first and last terms is 1 + 50 = 51. Since there are 50 terms, there would be $50 \div 2 = 25$ pairs to be added.

50 years: $25 \times 51 = \$1{,}275$

Another way to look at this same problem is to look at the sum of two sets of numbers from 1 to 7. The answer is obviously twice what is needed and requires you to divide by 2.

	1	2	3	4	5	6	7
	7	6	5	4	3	2	1
sum	8	8	8	8	8	8	8

$$1 + 2 + 3 + 4 + 5 + 6 + 7 = \frac{7(7+1)}{2} = \frac{7 \times 8}{2} = 28$$

Likewise, considering the sum of two sets of numbers from 1 to 50, there are twice what is needed in the product of (1 + 50) and 50. Thus the sum $1 + 2 + 3 + 4 + 5 + … + 50 = \frac{50(1+50)}{2} = 1{,}275$.

Think: How can this rule be generalized for a sum of the first *n* whole numbers?

Following the same pattern, the sum of the first *n* whole numbers, $1 + 2 + 3 + 4 + 5 + … + n$, can be found. Find the common sum (*n* + 1), multiply it by *n*, and, realizing that this is twice the needed sum, divide by 2 to get the correct answer.

$$1 + 2 + 3 + 4 + 5 + … + n = \frac{n(n+1)}{2}$$

Now try this out with some of your examples to convince yourself that it works.

$$1 + 2 + 3 + 4 + 5 + 6 = \frac{6(6+1)}{2} = 21$$

This answer matches the value of the sum of the first six whole numbers in the table at the beginning of the section.

Recognizing patterns will help you become a better problem solver.

■ Exercises

Devise a plan and use it to solve each of the following problems. Give a written explanation of your thought process for exercises 1–4.

1. Square numbers are numbers that can be displayed by a pattern of dots that form a square. Give the number of dots in each square shown. Draw the next square; then give the rule for finding the *n*th term of this sequence.

2. Look at the pattern of sums given below. Write the next four patterns and their sums. Write a rule for finding the sum based on the quantity of odd numbers n in the sum. Find the sum of the first 20 odd numbers by using your rule. Then use a calculator to check your sum by adding the first 20 odd numbers together.

$1 = 1$

$1 + 3 = 4$

$1 + 3 + 5 = 9$

$1 + 3 + 5 + 7 = 16$

$1 + 3 + 5 + 7 + 9 = 25$

3. An eccentric math teacher told his class that he would assign one problem on the first day of school, two problems on the second day, four problems on the third day, eight problems on the fourth day, and so on. At this rate, how many problems would he assign on the tenth day? Find a rule that can be used to determine the number of problems assigned on the nth day.

4. Triangular numbers are numbers that can be displayed by a pattern of dots that form a triangle. The first four triangular numbers are 1, 3, 6, and 10. What are the next four triangular numbers? What is the rule for finding the value of a triangular number based on the number of the term in the sequence?

5. Find the sum of the first eight positive multiples of 11. Write out this sum. If you add the first and last addends, then the second and next to last, and continue in this pattern, what is the common sum of each pair? How many pairs of addends are there in this sum? How does the number of pairs relate to the number of addends? What could you do with the common sum and the number of pairs to find the entire sum?

6. Find the sum of the first ten natural numbers and then the first one hundred natural numbers. Give a rule that can be used to find the sum of the first n natural numbers.

7. In exercises 5 and 6, the number of addends was always even. Verify that this same rule will work for finding the sum of the first five natural numbers. Do you think this rule works for all natural numbers?

8. The following pattern is called the *Fibonacci sequence*: 1, 1, 2, 3, 5, 8, 13, 21, … Describe how to find the next term in the pattern using the terms that already exist. Find the next three terms of the sequence.

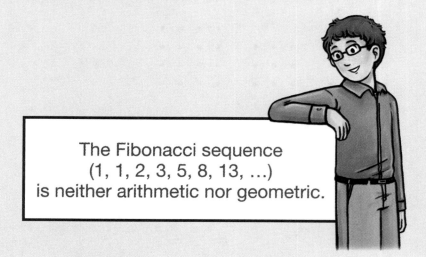

The Fibonacci sequence
(1, 1, 2, 3, 5, 8, 13, …)
is neither arithmetic nor geometric.

4.7 Bases

Our number system, the decimal system, is a base 10 system. It uses ten digits—0, 1, 2, 3, 4, 5, 6, 7, 8, 9. All numerals contain some arrangement of these digits. The value of the numeral depends on the placement of the digits in the number. Each digit has two meanings. It has a *face value*, or quantity assigned to it, and a *place value*, its position in the numeral based on a power of ten. Review the base 10 place-value table below.

Computers use number bases that are powers of two.

	Ten Thousands (10,000)	Thousands (1,000)	Hundreds (100)	Tens (10)	Ones (1)	Tenths (0.1)	Hundredths (0.01)	Thousandths (0.001)	Ten-Thousandths (0.0001)
Place value	10^4	10^3	10^2	10^1	10^0	10^{-1}	10^{-2}	10^{-3}	10^{-4}
Face value		4	8	9	2	6	7		

The numeral 4,892.67 has the following meaning:

$4,892.67 = 4,000 + 800 + 90 + 2 + 0.6 + 0.07$
$= 4(1,000) + 8(100) + 9(10) + 2(1) + 6(0.1) + 7(0.01)$
$= (4 \times 10^3) + (8 \times 10^2) + (9 \times 10^1) + (2 \times 10^0) + (6 \times 10^{-1}) + (7 \times 10^{-2}).$

Some ancient numeration systems used bases other than 10. The Babylonian system used base 60. Perhaps Daniel of the Bible learned this system. The ancient Mayan numeration system used a modified base 20 system. Even relatively modern cultures have used other bases. The Luo peoples of Kenya and the Yoruba of Nigeria used the *quinary* (or base 5) system until the twentieth century, when they changed to the base 10 system. In the base 5 system there are five digits—0, 1, 2, 3, 4. The place values are based on a power of five. Study the chart below.

	Place Values						
Decimal system	10^6	10^5	10^4	10^3	10^2	10^1	10^0
Base 5 system	5^6	5^5	5^4	5^3	5^2	5^1	5^0

Counting in base 5 is similar to counting in base 10. However, when you reach five, you must regroup and place a one in the 5^1 place and a zero in the 5^0 place. The base 10 number 5 is written 10_5 as a base 5 numeral. This number is read "one zero base five," not "ten base five."

Base 5	1_5	2_5	3_5	4_5	10_5	11_5	12_5	13_5	14_5	20_5
Base 10	1	2	3	4	5	6	7	8	9	10

Example 1 Write 134_5 in base 10.

Answer

Place value	5^2	5^1	5^0
Face value	1	3	4

1. Set up a place-value chart similar to the base 10 chart.
2. Write the face values of the numeral in their place-value positions.
3. Write the numeral in expanded form and simplify.

$(1 \cdot 5^2) + (3 \cdot 5^1) + (4 \cdot 5^0)$
$= 1(25) + 3(5) + 4(1)$
$= 25 + 15 + 4$
$= 44$
44 is equivalent to 134_5.

Even today, bases other than 10 are used frequently. Computers run on a *binary* (or base 2) system. A computer's electrical impulses are either off or on, and a computer program represents these two possibilities by a 0 and a 1. The binary system uses only these two digits.

Example 2 Write 101_2 in base 10.

Answer

Place value	2^2	2^1	2^0
Face value	1	0	1

1. Set up a place-value chart.
2. Write the face values of the numeral in their place-value positions.
3. Write the numeral in expanded form and simplify.

$(1 \times 2^2) + (0 \times 2^1) + (1 \times 2^0)$
$= 1(4) + 0 + 1(1)$
$= 4 + 1$
$= 5$
5 is equivalent to 101_2.

Base 2 numbers can become quite long. Even the number 9, which is one digit in base 10, requires four digits in base 2; it is written as 1001_2 ($9 = 2^3 + 2^0$). Larger base numbers are more convenient for expressing large numbers. To have commonality with the binary system and thus be useful in computer work, a system that is a power of two is needed. This means we could choose base 4, base 8, or base 16. Base 4 has the same limitations as the binary system—too many digits are required to express large numbers. Therefore, in the computer field base 8 (*octal* system) and base 16 (*hexadecimal* system) are used.

Since 16 is higher than 10, extra digits are needed in the hexadecimal system. The letters of the alphabet are used for additional digits.

Digit in Base 16	A	B	C	D	E	F
Face Value in Base 10	10	11	12	13	14	15

These same letters can be used for other bases above 10. If more digits are needed, keep going with G as 16, H as 17, and so on.

Example 3   Write $A53_{12}$ in base 10.

Answer

Place value	12^2	12^1	12^0
Face value	A	5	3

$(10 \cdot 12^2) + (5 \cdot 12^1) + (3 \cdot 12^0)$
$= 10(144) + 5(12) + 3(1)$
$= 1,440 + 60 + 3$
$= 1,503$
1,503 is equivalent to $A53_{12}$.

1. Set up a place-value chart.

2. Write the face values of the numeral in their place-value positions.

3. Write the numeral in expanded form and simplify. Remember that A = 10.

Skill Check 1

Write the following numbers in base 10.

1. 1331_4 2. 431_5 3. $B40_{16}$ 4. 1205_6

5. Write the first ten numbers in base 2.

You can also change base 10 numerals to other bases. The place values of the base you are changing to will be needed to do this conversion. The highest place value less than or equal to the base 10 number must be divided into the number to determine the number of times that power appears. Then the remainder is divided by the highest place value less than or equal to it. You continue this division process until the remainder is zero. Any power of the base that was not used as a divisor will have a zero as its face-value digit. Follow the examples below.

Example 4   Write 28 in base 2.

Answer

Place value	2^5	2^4	2^3	2^2	2^1	2^0
Base 10 value	32	16	8	4	2	1

$$16\overline{)28} \quad 8\overline{)12} \quad 4\overline{)4}$$
$$\underline{16} \quad \underline{8} \quad \underline{4}$$
$$12 \quad 4 \quad 0$$

quotients: 1, 1, 1

$$\frac{1}{2^4} \quad \frac{1}{2^3} \quad \frac{1}{2^2} \quad \frac{0}{2^1} \quad \frac{0}{2^0}$$

$28 = 11100_2$

1. Write the place values from base 2 and their base 10 values. Continue until you reach a value greater than the number being converted.

2. Divide the number by the largest base 10 power of two that is less than or equal to the number. Divide the remainder by the largest base 10 power of two less than or equal to the remainder. Continue dividing remainders until the final remainder is zero.

3. Establish the place value of each quotient. Fill in missing place values as zeros.

4. Write 28 as a base 2 numeral. (Notice the place holders for 2^1 and 2^0, since they were not needed in the division process.)

Example 5   Write 43 in base 5.

Answer

Place value	5^3	5^2	5^1	5^0
Base 10 value	125	25	5	1

$$
\begin{array}{r} 1 \\ 25\overline{)43} \\ \underline{25} \\ 18 \end{array}
\qquad
\begin{array}{r} 3 \\ 5\overline{)18} \\ \underline{15} \\ 3 \end{array}
\qquad
\begin{array}{r} 3 \\ 1\overline{)3} \\ \underline{3} \\ 0 \end{array}
$$

$$
\frac{1}{5^2} \; \frac{3}{5^1} \; \frac{3}{5^0}
$$

$$43 = 133_5$$

1. Write the place values from base 5 and their base 10 values.

2. Do the division process.

3. Place the quotients in the correct place values.
4. Write the number in base 5.

Example 6   Write 2,564 in base 16.

Answer

Place value	16^3	16^2	16^1	16^0
Base 10 value	4,096	256	16	1

$$
\begin{array}{r} 10 \\ 256\overline{)2,564} \\ \underline{2\;56} \\ 4 \end{array}
\qquad
\begin{array}{r} 4 \\ 1\overline{)4} \\ \underline{4} \\ 0 \end{array}
$$

$$
\frac{A}{16^2} \; \frac{0}{16^1} \; \frac{4}{16^0}
$$

$$2,564 = A04_{16}$$

1. Write the place values from base 16 and their base 10 values.

2. Do the division process.

3. Place the quotients in the correct place values. Fill in the missing place value as a zero.
4. Write the number in base 16.

Skill Check 2

Write the following base 10 numerals in the indicated base.

1. 29 in base 2   2. 87 in base 5   3. 650 in base 8

Numbers are part of God's creation. Whether the quantity of five items is represented by 5, V, or 101_2 makes no difference in the value of the number. However the value is represented, the concept represented is the same.

■ A. Exercises

Write the following numbers in base 10.

1. 34_5

2. 110_5

3. 13_5

4. 123_5

5. 2431_5

6. 11001_2

7. 1111_2

8. 1010_2

9. 110_2

10. 10011_2

11. 735_8

12. 24_9

13. 606_7

14. 213_4

15. 555_6

■ B. Exercises

Write the first sixteen numbers in the following bases. (You may omit the subscript.)

16. base 2

17. base 4

18. base 16

Write the following numbers in base 5.

19. 64

20. 103

21. 292

22. 417

23. 2,005

24. 7,123

Write the following numbers in base 2.

25. 16

26. 35

27. 8

28. 51

29. 103

30. 6

Write the following numbers in the indicated base.

31. 27 in base 3

32. 81 in base 6

33. 126 in base 7

34. 218 in base 8

35. 12 in base 4

36. 1,493 in base 8

■ C. Exercises

Write the following numbers in base 10.

37. $2A7_{12}$

38. 94_{12}

39. $BC5_{16}$

40. $1F8_{16}$

Write the following numbers in the indicated base.

41. 89 in base 12

42. 290 in base 12

43. 892 in base 16

44. 798 in base 16

▭ ■ CUMULATIVE REVIEW ■ ▭

Estimate the sum or difference by rounding to the highest place value. [2.7]

45. $678 + 214 + 278$

46. $3,909 + 9,214$

47. $892 + 638 + 572$

48. $3,967 - 892$

Solve. [3.4]

49. $9x - 6x = 24$

50. $36 = -9x + 8x$

51. $7x - 3x = 32$

52. $42x - (-x) = 86$

Daniel, Praying Prophet

Have you wondered why there are sixty minutes in an hour? Why not one hundred minutes? Timekeeping would be so much easier if 213 minutes equaled 2.13 hours instead of 3.55 hours. Our system of timekeeping originated in ancient Babylon, where timekeeping, as well as math, was based on the number sixty rather than the number ten.

When Daniel was captured by the Babylonians in 605 BC, he was forced to learn their system of math along with their language and other areas of knowledge. Rather than complain, he worked hard and became "ten times" smarter than all the other wise men of the kingdom (Dan. 1:20). Decades later King Darius made Daniel his chief governor.

During more than seventy years of service in the palace, Daniel won fame for his wisdom and courage. However, his greatest trait was his relationship with God, to Whom Daniel prayed every day.

One of the well-known prophecies in Scripture, the prophecy of the seventy weeks, was given to Daniel while he was praying. In this prophecy the word translated by the English word "week" is the Hebrew word for "period of seven." The events of history suggest that a "week" is best interpreted as a period of seven years. Thus, the prophecy of seventy weeks refers to seventy periods of seven years, or 490 years.

According to Daniel 9:25, a period of "seven weeks, and threescore and two weeks" (sixty-nine weeks, or 483 years) would pass between the command to rebuild the temple and the death of the Messiah. (A score is twenty years, so "seven weeks, and threescore and two weeks" is $7 + 3(20) + 2 = 69$ weeks.) This leaves a one-week period (seven years) of the prophecy of seventy weeks that remains to be fulfilled.

We are now in the period of time after the Messiah's death and before the final week of prophecy (Dan. 9:26). This final "week" is reserved for the Tribulation, when "the prince that shall come" (the Antichrist) will "confirm the covenant with many for one week" (Dan. 9:26–27). The terrible events of the last half of this final "week" are described in numerous other places in Scripture. (See Dan. 7:25; 12:7; Matt. 24:15–31; Rev. 11:2–3; 13:5–8.)

The angel Gabriel advised Daniel, who had confessed his sins and lived a righteous life, not to worry about the future: "Go thou thy way till the end be: for thou shalt rest" (Dan. 12:13). If you receive Christ as your Savior and serve the Lord faithfully, you will not have to worry about the future either. Are you following Daniel's example?

4.8 Operations in Bases

Adding, subtracting, multiplying, and dividing are the basic operations of arithmetic. The same operations can be done in other bases. If you understand how to perform these operations in different bases, then you will have a clear understanding of the concepts, not just a procedure for performing them. Understanding concepts allows you to apply knowledge, including biblical knowledge, to new and varied situations.

Performing addition depends on a thorough knowledge of the place-value system. Because you have been adding numbers for quite a few years, you probably do not consciously think about the step-by-step process. It is important that you understand those steps in order to apply them to other bases. Before adding in other bases, read through Example 1 to review the addition process in base 10. Although renaming when adding in base 10 can be done mentally, it will be shown here to emphasize the procedure. You will need to do this in other bases.

Computers represent base 2 numbers using electric circuits that are on (1) or off (0).

Example 1   Add $874 + 397$.

Answer

$$
\begin{array}{r}
{\scriptstyle 1} \\
874 \\
+397 \\
\hline
1
\end{array}
$$

1. Add the digits in the 10^0 place. The sum is 11, which is too large to be placed in the 10^0 place. Regroup the 11 ones as 1 group of ten and 1 one. The 1 stays in the 10^0 place, and the 1 group of ten is placed above the 7 in the 10^1 place.

$$
\begin{array}{r}
{\scriptstyle 1\,1} \\
874 \\
+397 \\
\hline
71
\end{array}
$$

2. Add the digits in the 10^1 place. The sum is 17. Since 17 is too large to be placed in the 10^1 place, regroup the 17 tens as 1 group of one hundred and 7 groups of ten. The 7 groups of ten stay in the 10^1 place, and the 1 group of one hundred is placed above the 8 in the 10^2 place.

$$
\begin{array}{r}
{\scriptstyle 1\,1\,1} \\
874 \\
+397 \\
\hline
1{,}271
\end{array}
$$

3. Add the digits in the 10^2 place. The sum is 12, which is too large to be placed in the 10^2 place. Regroup the 12 hundreds as 1 group of one thousand and 2 groups of one hundred. The 2 groups of one hundred are placed in the 10^2 place, and the 1 group of one thousand is placed in the 10^3 place in the answer.

The same concepts will be used to add in other bases.

Example 2 Add $342_5 + 144_5$.

Answer

$$\overset{1}{3}42_5$$
$$+144_5$$
$$\overline{\qquad 1}$$

1. Add the digits in the ones (5^0) place. The sum is 6, which is too large to be placed in the 5^0 place. Regroup the 6 ones as 1 group of five and 1 one. Place the 1 group of five above the 4 in the 5^1 place and the 1 one in the 5^0 place in the answer.

$$\overset{1\ 1}{3}42_5$$
$$+144_5$$
$$\overline{\qquad 41}$$

2. Add the digits in the 5^1 place to obtain 9 groups of five. Since 9 is too large to be placed in the 5^1 place, regroup the 9 fives as 1 group of twenty-five and 4 groups of five. Place the 1 group of twenty-five above the 3 in the 5^2 place and the 4 fives in the 5^1 place in the answer.

$$\overset{1\ 1\ 1}{3}42_5$$
$$+\ 144_5$$
$$\overline{1041_5}$$

3. Add the digits in the 5^2 place. The sum is 5, which is too large to be placed in the 5^2 place. Regroup the 5 groups of twenty-five as 1 group of 125 (5^3). Place a 0 in the 5^2 place and a 1 in the 5^3 place in the answer.

The following example gives a shortened version of the thinking process. Even if you do not write out all the steps, do not skip a step as you do the problems.

Example 3 Add $352_8 + 767_8$.

Answer

$$\overset{1}{3}52_8$$
$$+767_8$$
$$\overline{\qquad 1}$$

1. Add the digits in the ones (8^0) place. Regroup the 9 ones as 1 group of eight (8^1) and 1 one.

$$\overset{1\ 1}{3}52_8$$
$$+767_8$$
$$\overline{\qquad 41}$$

2. Add the digits in the 8^1 place. Regroup the 12 eights as 1 group of 8^2 and 4 groups of 8^1.

$$\overset{1\ 1\ 1}{3}52_8$$
$$+\ 767_8$$
$$\overline{1341_8}$$

3. Add the digits in the 8^2 place. Regroup the 11 sixty-fours (8^2) as 1 group of 8^3 and 3 groups of 8^2.

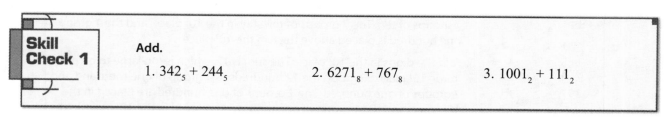

Skill Check 1 Add.

1. $342_5 + 244_5$ 2. $6271_8 + 767_8$ 3. $1001_2 + 111_2$

Subtraction in different bases is done exactly the same way as it is done in our base 10 system. Remember to rename when necessary to be able to subtract.

Example 4 Subtract $431_5 - 234_5$.

Answer

$$\overset{2\ 6}{4\ \cancel{3}\ 1}_5$$
$$-\ 2\ 3\ 4_5$$
$$\overline{2}$$

1. Subtract the digits in the ones (5^0) place. To do this, 1 group of five must be renamed from the 5^1 place, so change the 3 in the 5^1 place to 2. Rename the 1 group of five to 5 ones, which results in 6 ones in the ones place. Now subtract 4 ones from 6 ones and place 2 in the answer.

$$\overset{\ \ 7}{\overset{3\ \cancel{2}\ 6}{\cancel{4}\ \cancel{3}\ 1}}_5$$
$$-\ 2\ 3\ 4_5$$
$$\overline{4\ 2}$$

2. Subtract the digits in the 5^1 place. You cannot subtract 3 fives from the remaining 2 fives in the 5^1 place. Therefore, rename 1 group from the 5^2 (25) place as 5 groups of fives (leaving 3). This now gives 7 groups of five. Subtract 3 from 7 to obtain 4 groups of 5 in the answer.

$$\overset{\ \ 7}{\overset{3\ \cancel{2}\ 6}{\cancel{4}\ \cancel{3}\ 1}}_5$$
$$-\ 2\ 3\ 4_5$$
$$\overline{1\ 4\ 2}_5$$

3. Subtract 2 from 3 in the 5^2 place.

Example 5 Subtract $621_8 - 567_8$.

Answer

$$\overset{1\ 9}{6\ \cancel{2}\ 1}_8$$
$$-\ 5\ 6\ 7_8$$
$$\overline{2}$$

1. Begin with the ones (8^0) place. Rename 1 group from the 8^1 place as 8 ones and combine it with the 1 one. Subtract 7 from 9 in the ones place.

$$\overset{\ \ \ 9}{\overset{5\ \cancel{1}\ 9}{\cancel{6}\ \cancel{2}\ 1}}_8$$
$$-\ 5\ 6\ 7_8$$
$$\overline{3\ 2}_8$$

2. To subtract the 6 eights in the 8^1 place, rename 1 group from the 8^2 (64) place as 8 groups of eight (giving 9). Place 3 in the answer. Five subtracted from 5 in the 8^2 place is just 0, which we do not write as part of the answer.

Skill Check 2

Subtract.

1. $521_8 - 346_8$ 2. $4413_5 - 2434_5$ 3. $10011_2 - 1101_2$ 4. $2A6C_{16} - 795_{16}$

■ **A. Exercises**

Add or subtract in the indicated base.

1. $321_5 + 122_5$ 2. $4_5 + 2_5$ 3. $24_5 + 13_5$ 4. $41_5 + 24_5$

5. $201_5 + 302_5$ 6. $143_6 + 22_6$ 7. $14_7 - 10_7$ 8. $20_8 - 14_8$

9. $101_2 - 11_2$ 10. $443_5 - 414_5$ 11. $217_8 - 107_8$ 12. $315_6 - 243_6$

■ B. Exercises

Add or subtract in the indicated base.

13. $14_8 + 65_8$

14. $101_2 + 111_2$

15. $11101_2 + 101_2$

16. $1011_3 + 21_3$

17. $11001_2 + 10101_2$

18. $4611_7 + 1061_7$

19. $110_5 - 14_5$

20. $761_8 - 417_8$

21. $765_8 - 567_8$

22. $1110_5 - 344_5$

23. $1010_2 - 111_2$

24. $2141_6 - 1051_6$

■ C. Exercises

Add or subtract in the indicated base.

25. $B07_{15} + 653_{15}$

26. $ABC_{14} - 9FD_{14}$

27. $922_{12} + 81A_{12}$

28. $223_{11} - 132_{11}$

29. $97A_{12} + 4B5_{12}$

30. $456_{12} - 257_{12}$

31. $87A_{16} + C94_{16}$

32. $CBA_{16} - A97_{16}$

33. What procedure would you use to add two numbers in different bases, such as $321_5 + 101_2$?

Perform the indicated operations. Leave the answers in base 10.

34. $321_5 + 101_2$

35. $1022_4 + 372_8$

36. $896_{10} - 332_5$

37. $763_9 - 10001_2$

CUMULATIVE REVIEW

Write an inequality, solve it, and express the answer in words. [3.8]

38. Elisha has 35 lb. of tomatoes to sell for his grandmother. If he needs to receive at least $50, how much should he sell them for per pound?

39. Mrs. Richards has 550 antique wooden spools that she can give away. If she plans to make 20 packages of spools for her grandchildren, what is the maximum number of spools she should put in each?

40. Lance and Dale need to sell at least three boxes of candy bars to raise money for a school trip. There are a dozen candy bars in each box. If Lance sells six more than Dale, how many must each boy sell?

41. A merchant has 400 pairs of socks to sell. He wants to take in at least $525 for them. What should be the price of a pair of socks?

Write which of the following numbers are factors of the given number: 2, 3, 4, 5, 6, 8, 9, 10, or none. [4.1]

42. 76

43. 90

44. 122

45. 116

46. 61

47. 570

If 2 is raised to a prime number power and 1 is subtracted from this value, a special number called a *Mersenne prime* is the result. Since 2 is the first prime number, $2^2 - 1 = 4 - 1 = 3$ is the first Mersenne prime number. List the next three Mersenne prime numbers.

If a Mersenne prime number is used as p in the expression $2^{(p-1)}(2^p - 1)$, a perfect number results. A perfect number is a number that equals the sum of its divisors other than itself. For example, since 3 is a Mersenne prime, $2^{(3-1)}(2^3 - 1) = 2^2(8 - 1) = 4(7) = 28$. The divisors of 28, other than 28, are 1, 2, 4, 7, and 14. Notice that $1 + 2 + 4 + 7 + 14 = 28$. What number less than 28 is also a perfect number?

MATH & SCRIPTURE

Daniel's Seventy Weeks

In Daniel 9:20–23 the angelic messenger Gabriel appears to Daniel with an answer to his prayer for Israel's restoration. His prayer was based on Jeremiah's prophecy of seventy years of captivity for the wayward nation (Jer. 25:11). Gabriel's message dealt with Israel's restoration and set down the progression of time until the promised coming of the Messiah, the Christ. The message given in Daniel 9:24–27 established the time when the weeks would begin and the time when 69 of them would have transpired. Those who read Daniel's words may be troubled by the use of a week to stand for 7 years. The history of the Jewish nation strongly suggests that they have not yet grasped the certainty of Christ's coming as set down in the book of Daniel. The term *week* used by Daniel actually means a "unit of seven," which in this case is 70 units of 7 years each, or 490 years. From our perspective of looking back in history, the time frame is obviously not 490 ordinary weeks, which is less than 10 years.

Daniel prayed toward Jerusalem three times a day.

Read Daniel 9:20–27 and answer the following questions.

1. How many years do the 69 weeks represent?

2. In Daniel 9:25 what did the decree say was to be built?

3. A decree of Cyrus, given in Ezra 1:1–4, can be dated around 538 BC. What did this decree say was to be built?

4. In Ezra 6:6–12 what did Darius decree was to be built? This date is around 520 BC.

5. In Ezra 7:11–26 what was Ezra to do according to the decree of Artaxerxes? This date is around 458 BC.

6. In Nehemiah 2:1–8 what was Nehemiah allowed to do by the decree of Artaxerxes? This date is around 445 BC.

7. What event takes place at the end of Daniel's sixty-ninth week?

8. Establish the year (date) for the event in exercise 7 using your answer to exercise 1 and the date for exercise 6.

9. There are often difficulties with establishing ancient calendar dates, and many scholars have suggested that calendars relating to prophecy used a 360-day year. Convert your answer to exercise 1 from 360-day years to 365-day years and recalculate your answer to exercise 8.

10. Historians have placed Christ's birth around 4 BC and His death around AD 30. How well does your answer to exercise 9 agree with the date of the Crucifixion?

Infinite Truths

Seventy weeks are determined upon thy people and upon thy holy city, to finish the transgression, and to make an end of sins, and to make reconciliation for iniquity. *Daniel 9:24*a

Chapter 4 Review

Vocabulary

arithmetic sequence	greatest common factor (GCF)
common difference	least common multiple (LCM)
common ratio	multiple
composite number	prime number
explicit formula	recursive formula
factor	relatively prime
Fundamental Theorem of Arithmetic	sequence
geometric sequence	

List in order all the factors of the given number.

1. 12
2. 27
3. 56
4. 84

State whether the given number is prime, composite, or neither.

5. 89
6. 105
7. 117
8. 97

Write which of the following numbers are factors of the given number: 2, 3, 4, 5, 6, 8, 9, 10, or none.

9. 1,240
10. 462
11. 725
12. 239

13. State the Fundamental Theorem of Arithmetic.

Write the prime factorization of each number.

14. 58
15. 60
16. 252
17. 88

18. 975
19. 315

Find the greatest common factor of each pair of numbers.

20. 18, 70
21. 126, 90
22. 75, 270
23. 33, 70

Is each pair of numbers relatively prime?

24. 165, 54
25. 21, 130

Find the least common multiple of each pair of numbers.

26. 15, 33
27. 72, 123
28. 2, 18
29. 40, 75

30. Find the least common multiple and greatest common factor of 270 and 42. Find the product of 270 and 42 and the product of the LCM and the GCF. What do you notice about these two products?

31. State the definition of an arithmetic sequence.

32. State the definition of a geometric sequence.

33. State the difference between a recursive definition and an explicit definition.

Write the first five terms of the following sequences.

34. $a_1 = 6;\ d = 3$

35. $a_1 = -8;\ r = -2$

Write the first five terms of the following recursively defined sequences.

36. $a_1 = -4;\ a_n = a_{n-1} - 3$

37. $a_1 = 1;\ a_n = 2a_{n-1}$

Write the first five terms of the following explicitly defined sequences.

38. $a_n = 4n + 2$

39. $a_n = 2(-3)^{n-1}$

Write the recursive definition for the following sequences.

40. 2, 6, 10, 14, 18, …

41. 9, 18, 36, 72, 144, …

Write the simplified form of the explicit formula for the following sequences.

42. 4, 8, 12, 16, 20, …

43. 9, 18, 36, 72, 144, …

44. Write 13_5 in base 10.

45. Write 15 in base 2.

46. Write 2,776 in base 16.

Add or subtract in the indicated base.

47. $1111_2 + 1010_2$

48. $431_5 - 341_5$

49. $753_8 - 267_8$

50. State the mathematical significance of Daniel 9:24.

5 RATIONAL NUMBERS

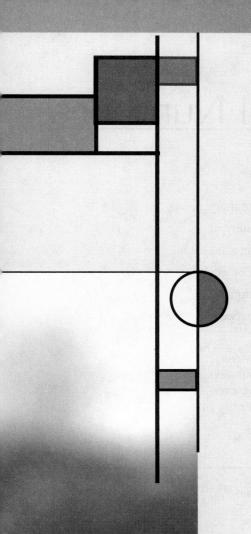

In the United States most people are focused on owning and driving automobiles rather than bicycles. In many countries, however, cars are too expensive, so large numbers of people travel by bicycle. Cycle racing is a prominent sport in many countries. The success of American competitors in the famous bicycle race *Tour de France* reveals that Americans are gaining a greater interest in cycling. These competitive races have inspired significant improvements to the modern racing bike. The frames are now made from strong, lightweight alloys or composites. The tires are more durable; the wheels are stronger and more precise. The gearing system of chain-rings and cogs provides a large number of ratios with a smooth progression between them, advancing the ability to go up steep hills and to go very fast on flat roads. These ratios, whether written using decimals such as 3.5 : 1 or as fractions such as $\frac{4}{1}$, are rational numbers.

After this chapter you should be able to

1. reduce fractions to lowest terms.

2. change mixed numbers to improper fractions and vice versa.

3. graph rational numbers on a number line.

4. order fractions using cross multiplication or a common denominator.

5. convert fractions and mixed numbers to decimals and vice versa.

6. express ratios as unit rates.

7. solve proportions containing a variable.

8. apply proportions to solve word problems.

9. classify numbers as natural, whole, integer, rational, or irrational.

5.1 Forms of Rational Numbers

The set of integers is expanded by including all of the fractions between the integers to form the set of *rational numbers*. Just as the set of integers extends infinitely in the positive and negative directions, so does the set of rational numbers. There are also an infinite number of rational numbers between each pair of integers. For example, take the rational numbers $\frac{1}{2}, \frac{1}{3}, \frac{1}{4}, \ldots$ and continue writing a new fraction with the next consecutive integer in the denominator. Each of these fractions is between 0 and 1, and there are an infinite number of them.

The concept of infinity is difficult for our finite minds to comprehend. However, infinity is part of God's plan. Our days on earth are finite (Ps. 90:10), but our days in eternity are infinite. God tells us in His Word that after death we will receive everlasting life or everlasting punishment (Matt. 25:46; John 3:36). To spend eternity in heaven, we must repent of our sins and trust Christ for salvation.

Definition

A **rational number** is any number that can be written in the form $\frac{a}{b}$, where a and b are integers and $b \neq 0$.

The following are examples of rational numbers.

$$\frac{2}{3}, \frac{19}{7}, -\frac{5}{7}, 4.25, 18, -3, 0.08\overline{3}, -0.\overline{27}, 3\frac{2}{3}$$

Every number in this list can be written in $\frac{a}{b}$ form. The first three are obviously in the proper form. However, all the other numbers can be changed to the form $\frac{a}{b}$. Consider the integers 18 and -3. By placing the integer in the numerator and one in the denominator, the numbers are written in rational form as $\frac{18}{1}$ and $\frac{-3}{1}$. In fact, every integer can be written in rational form by using a denominator of one.

> **Integers are rational numbers.**

Mixed numbers, such as $3\frac{2}{3}$, can be converted to the form $\frac{a}{b}$.

Also, all terminating and repeating decimals can be converted to rational form.

Mixed numbers will be discussed in more detail later in this section, and you will learn how to express decimals in rational form in Section 5.3.

Rational numbers are in simplest form when they are reduced to lowest terms.

Definition

A rational fraction $\frac{a}{b}$ is in **lowest terms** if the GCF of a and b is one.

To reduce a fraction to lowest terms, find the GCF of the numerator and the denominator. Canceling uses the principle that $\frac{n}{n} = 1$, where n is the GCF of the numerator and denominator. Since multiplying by one does not change the value of the rational number, the reduced form has equivalent value to the original rational number.

Example 1 Rename $\frac{12}{18}$ in lowest terms.

Answer

$12 = 2 \cdot 2 \cdot 3$ 　　1. Find the GCF of the numerator and denominator.
$18 = 2 \cdot 3 \cdot 3$
$GCF = 2 \cdot 3 = 6$

$\frac{12}{18} = \frac{2 \times \cancel{6}}{3 \times \cancel{6}}$ 　　2. Factor the numerator and denominator using the GCF. Cancel the GCF.

$\phantom{\frac{12}{18}} = \frac{2}{3}$

When the GCF of the numerator and denominator is not obvious, a fraction can be reduced to lowest terms by using the prime factorizations of the numerator and the denominator.

Example 2 Rename $\frac{24}{90}$ in lowest terms.

Answer

$\frac{24}{90} = \frac{2 \times 2 \times 2 \times 3}{2 \times 3 \times 3 \times 5}$ 　　1. Find the prime factorizations of 24 and 90.

$\phantom{\frac{24}{90}} = \frac{\cancel{2} \times 2 \times 2 \times \cancel{3}}{\cancel{2} \times \cancel{3} \times 3 \times 5}$ 　　2. Cancel common factors and multiply the remaining factors to find the reduced fraction.

$\phantom{\frac{24}{90}} = \frac{4}{15}$

Skill Check 1

Rename each fraction in lowest terms.

1. $\frac{21}{98}$　　　　2. $\frac{9}{24}$　　　　3. $\frac{57}{95}$　　　　4. $\frac{84}{144}$

A *proper fraction* is one whose numerator is less than its denominator. If the numerator is greater than or equal to the denominator, the fraction is greater than or equal to one and is called an *improper fraction*. The diagrams below illustrate the proper fraction $\frac{3}{4}$ and the improper fraction $\frac{4}{3}$.

Proper fraction:
$\frac{3}{4}$

Improper fraction:
$\frac{4}{3}$

A *mixed number* is actually the sum of a whole number and a fraction. For example, $1\frac{1}{3}$ means $1 + \frac{1}{3}$ and can be written in rational form as an improper fraction:

$1 + \frac{1}{3} = \frac{3}{3} + \frac{1}{3} = \frac{4}{3}$.

Likewise, the improper fraction $\frac{4}{3}$ is 1 whole and $\frac{1}{3}$ of a whole, so it is the same as the mixed number $1\frac{1}{3}$.

$$\text{improper fraction} \blacktriangleright \quad \frac{4}{3} = 1\frac{1}{3} \quad \blacktriangleleft \text{ mixed number}$$

To rename an improper fraction as a mixed number, follow these steps.

Renaming Improper Fractions as Mixed Numbers
1. Divide the numerator by the denominator.
2. Write the quotient as the whole number.
3. Write the remainder over the divisor as a fraction.
4. If possible, reduce the fraction to lowest terms.

Example 3   Rename each improper fraction as a mixed number.

a. $\frac{19}{7}$ b. $\frac{12}{8}$

Answer

a. $7\overline{)19}$ $\frac{19}{7} = 2\frac{5}{7}$

   $\begin{array}{r} 2 \\ 7\overline{)19} \\ 14 \\ \hline 5 \end{array}$

b. $8\overline{)12}$ $\frac{12}{8} = 1\frac{4}{8} = 1\frac{1}{2}$

   $\begin{array}{r} 1 \\ 8\overline{)12} \\ 8 \\ \hline 4 \end{array}$

Example 4   Evaluate the expression $\frac{y}{3z}$ when $y = 38$ and $z = 2$. Write the answer as a mixed number in lowest terms.

Answer

$\frac{38}{3(2)} = \frac{38}{6}$

$\frac{38}{6} = \frac{19 \times \cancel{2}}{3 \times \cancel{2}} = \frac{19}{3}$

$\begin{array}{r} 6 \\ 3\overline{)19} \\ 18 \\ \hline 1 \end{array}$ $6\frac{1}{3}$

1. Substitute the values for the variables and perform the indicated operations.

2. Reduce the improper fraction.

3. Divide the numerator by the denominator. Write the quotient as the whole number part and the remainder over the divisor as the fraction part of the mixed number.

Skill Check 2

Give an improper fraction and a mixed number for each diagram.

1.

2.

Rename each improper fraction as a mixed number or an integer.

3. $\frac{29}{6}$ 4. $-\frac{19}{3}$ 5. $\frac{65}{5}$

6. Evaluate $\frac{x}{7}$ when $x = 39$. Write the answer as a mixed number.

When multiplying or dividing mixed numbers, you will need to rename the mixed numbers as improper fractions. To do this, express the mixed number as the sum of the whole number and the fraction part. Then change the whole number to a fraction with a denominator equal to the denominator of the fraction part. Finally, add the two fractions.

$2\dfrac{4}{5}$ is equivalent to $2 + \dfrac{4}{5} = \dfrac{2}{1}\left(\dfrac{5}{5}\right) + \dfrac{4}{5} = \dfrac{10}{5} + \dfrac{4}{5} = \dfrac{14}{5}$.

The shortcut method can be expressed as $2\dfrac{4}{5} = \dfrac{5(2) + 4}{5} = \dfrac{14}{5}$.

Renaming Mixed Numbers as Improper Fractions
1. Multiply the whole number by the denominator.
2. Add the numerator to the product.
3. Write the sum over the denominator.
4. If possible, reduce the fraction to lowest terms.

Example 5 Rename each mixed number as an improper fraction in lowest terms.

a. $3\dfrac{1}{5}$

b. $7\dfrac{6}{8}$

Answer

a. $3\dfrac{1}{5} = \dfrac{5(3) + 1}{5} = \dfrac{15 + 1}{5} = \dfrac{16}{5}$

b. $7\dfrac{6}{8} = \dfrac{8(7) + 6}{8} = \dfrac{56 + 6}{8} = \dfrac{62}{8} = \dfrac{31 \times \cancel{2}}{4 \times \cancel{2}} = \dfrac{31}{4}$

In part *b* of Example 5, the given number contains an unreduced fraction. If the fractional part of the mixed number had been reduced before changing it to an improper fraction, the improper fraction would have been in lowest terms.

$$7\dfrac{6}{8} = 7\dfrac{3}{4} = \dfrac{4(7) + 3}{4} = \dfrac{31}{4}$$

In a negative mixed number both the whole number and the fraction are negative. It follows that $-3\dfrac{5}{7} = -\dfrac{3}{1} + \left(-\dfrac{5}{7}\right) = -\dfrac{21}{7} + \left(-\dfrac{5}{7}\right) = \dfrac{-21 + (-5)}{7} = -\dfrac{26}{7}$.

When using the shortcut method, change the positive mixed number $3\dfrac{5}{7}$ to the improper fraction $\dfrac{26}{7}$, and then affix the negative sign.

$$-3\dfrac{5}{7} = -\dfrac{7(3) + 5}{7} = -\dfrac{21 + 5}{7} = -\dfrac{26}{7}$$

Example 6 Rename $-6\frac{4}{5}$ as an improper fraction.

Answer

$$-6\frac{4}{5} = -\frac{5(6)+4}{5} = -\frac{30+4}{5} = -\frac{34}{5}$$

Skill Check 3

Rename each mixed number as an improper fraction.

1. $1\frac{2}{7}$ 2. $8\frac{2}{3}$ 3. $9\frac{5}{8}$

4. $33\frac{1}{3}$ 5. $-7\frac{2}{3}$ 6. $-17\frac{3}{4}$

■ A. Exercises

Rename each fraction in lowest terms.

1. $\frac{14}{16}$ 2. $\frac{21}{35}$ 3. $\frac{16}{40}$ 4. $\frac{36}{64}$ 5. $\frac{34}{64}$ 6. $\frac{14}{24}$

Reduce each fraction using prime factorizations of the numerator and denominator.

7. $\frac{18}{54}$ 8. $\frac{34}{51}$ 9. $\frac{26}{104}$ 10. $\frac{38}{95}$ 11. $\frac{24}{30}$ 12. $\frac{32}{84}$

Rename each mixed number as an improper fraction.

13. $2\frac{7}{8}$ 14. $3\frac{1}{4}$ 15. $6\frac{2}{3}$ 16. $-2\frac{1}{2}$ 17. $-3\frac{1}{3}$ 18. $14\frac{5}{6}$

19. $-3\frac{7}{10}$ 20. $11\frac{2}{7}$ 21. $-21\frac{4}{5}$

■ B. Exercises

Rename each improper fraction as a mixed number.

22. $\frac{78}{9}$ 23. $\frac{42}{16}$ 24. $-\frac{11}{9}$ 25. $\frac{37}{5}$ 26. $-\frac{26}{8}$ 27. $\frac{55}{18}$

28. $\frac{37}{16}$ 29. $-\frac{102}{8}$ 30. $\frac{77}{6}$

Evaluate the following expressions when $w = 15$, $x = -2$, $y = 3$, and $z = -4$.

31. $-\frac{6}{w}$ 32. $2y - \frac{w}{y}$ 33. $\frac{5x}{7y}$ 34. $100 - \frac{z}{x}$ 35. $-\frac{w}{xy}$ 36. $\frac{-3w}{xyz}$

37. $w + \frac{z^2}{2x}$ 38. $\frac{8xy}{z}$ 39. $\frac{x^3}{y^2}w$

■ C. Exercises

40. In your own words, explain when a rational fraction is in lowest terms.

41. Without using the shortcut technique, develop a formula to rename the mixed number $A\frac{c}{d}$ as an improper fraction. Use your formula to rename $6\frac{8}{9}$ as its equivalent improper fraction.

■ Dominion thru Math

The front sprocket on a bicycle, called the chain-ring, is driven by the pedals. A chain connects the front sprocket directly to one of the cogs (series of teeth on a wheel) on the rear sprocket. The ratio of the number of teeth on the chain-ring to the number of teeth on the rear cog is the number of times the rear sprocket turns for each revolution of the pedals. For example, if there are 39 teeth on the chain-ring and 12 teeth on the cog of the rear sprocket, the rear sprocket will turn $\frac{39}{12} = 3.25$ revolutions for every revolution of the pedals. When the rear sprocket completes a revolution, the rear tire also completes a revolution, causing the bike to move forward a distance equal to the circumference of the tire. The ratios are called gear ratios and can be used to find out how fast the bike will go with a certain speed of pedaling.

Multiple cogs on the front and rear sprockets allow many gear ratios.

42. Suppose your bicycle has two front rings with 39 and 53 teeth and eight rear cogs with 12, 13, 14, 15, 17, 19, 21, and 23 teeth. Make a chart and write the gear ratios associated with the 39-tooth front ring. Write the gear ratios as decimals by using a calculator to divide out the fractions.

	12	13	14	15	17	19	21	23
39								

43. Make a chart and write the gear ratios associated with the 53-tooth front ring.

	12	13	14	15	17	19	21	23
53								

44. Which combination of gears will make the bicycle go slowest, and which will make it go fastest? Explain why.

45. Which combination of gears will make it easiest to pedal, and which will make it hardest to pedal? Explain why.

CUMULATIVE REVIEW

Write an equation using *n* for the variable for each sentence below; then solve. [3.5]

46. A number divided by –9, decreased by 18, is –17.

47. Three times a number, increased by 8, is –19.

48. Ten times the sum of a number and 12 is 84.

49. The difference between a number and 7, divided by –8, is –56.

50. Nineteen is the quotient of a number and 6, increased by 9.

Write the prime factorization of each number. [4.2]

51. 62   52. 85   53. 231   54. 116   55. 72

5.2 Comparing Rational Numbers

Fractions can be used to describe the amount of shaded area in the circles below. In each of the circles, the same portion is shaded; so the fractions name the same rational number and are called *equivalent fractions*.

$\frac{1}{2}$ $\frac{2}{4}$ $\frac{3}{6}$

Definition

Equivalent fractions are fractions representing the same rational number; thus they are reducible to the same fraction.

To find equivalent fractions, multiply the numerator and denominator of a fraction by the same number. This is equivalent to multiplying the fraction by a number of the form $\frac{n}{n}$, which is equal to one. The Identity Property of Multiplication guarantees that the result is an equivalent value ($a \times 1 = a$). Likewise, dividing the numerator and denominator of a fraction by the same number is equivalent to dividing the fraction by one, so dividing also produces an equivalent fraction.

Consider the fraction $\frac{1}{3}$, which is in lowest terms. If you multiply the numerator and denominator by the natural numbers 2, 3, 4, …, all the resulting fractions, namely, $\frac{2}{6}, \frac{3}{9}, \frac{4}{12}, \ldots$, are equivalent to $\frac{1}{3}$. Taking a fraction such as $\frac{24}{48}$ and dividing the numerator and the denominator by the same number, such as 2, 3, and 4, produces $\frac{12}{24}, \frac{8}{16}$, and $\frac{6}{12}$, all equivalent fractions.

$$\frac{2}{3} = \frac{2(3)}{3(3)} = \frac{6}{9} \qquad \frac{30}{42} = \frac{30 \div 3}{42 \div 3} = \frac{10}{14}$$
$$\llcorner \text{ equivalent } \lrcorner \qquad\qquad \llcorner \text{ equivalent } \lrcorner$$

Example 1
Find a fraction equivalent to the one given by the means specified.

a. $\frac{5}{8}$ by multiplying the numerator and denominator by 3

b. $\frac{15}{20}$ by dividing the numerator and denominator by 5

Answer

a. $\frac{5}{8} = \frac{5(3)}{8(3)} = \frac{15}{24}$ Multiply the fraction by 1 in the form $\frac{3}{3}$.

b. $\frac{15}{20} = \frac{15 \div 5}{20 \div 5} = \frac{3}{4}$ Divide the fraction by 1 in the form $\frac{5}{5}$.

It is often necessary to compare two fractions to determine their relative size. This can be done by renaming the fractions as equivalent fractions having a common denominator. The least common denominator is the LCM of the two denominators.

Example 2 Determine the relative size of $\frac{5}{6}$ and $\frac{7}{8}$.

Answer

$6 = 2 \cdot 3$ and $8 = 2 \cdot 2 \cdot 2$ 1. Find the prime factorizations of the denominators.

$\text{LCM} = 2 \cdot 2 \cdot 2 \cdot 3 = 24$ 2. The LCM is 24 since 8 requires three 2s and 6 requires a 3.

$24 \div 6 = 4$ and $24 \div 8 = 3$ 3. Find the multiplier for each denominator by dividing 24 by each denominator.

$\frac{5}{6} = \frac{5(4)}{6(4)} = \frac{20}{24}$

$\frac{7}{8} = \frac{7(3)}{8(3)} = \frac{21}{24}$

    4. Find each equivalent fraction by multiplying each numerator and denominator by the multiplier.

$\frac{20}{24} < \frac{21}{24}$; therefore, $\frac{5}{6} < \frac{7}{8}$.   5. The fraction with the smaller numerator is smaller.

Example 3 Compare $\frac{5}{8}$ and $\frac{7}{12}$, using <, =, or >.

Answer

$8 = 2^3$ and $12 = 2^2 \cdot 3$ 1. Find the LCM of the denominators.

$\text{LCM} = 2^3 \cdot 3 = 24$

$\frac{5}{8} = \frac{5 \times 3}{8 \times 3} = \frac{15}{24}$

$\frac{7}{12} = \frac{7 \times 2}{12 \times 2} = \frac{14}{24}$

    2. Multiply $\frac{5}{8}$ by $\frac{3}{3}$, since $8 \cdot 3 = 24$. Multiply $\frac{7}{12}$ by $\frac{2}{2}$, since $12 \cdot 2 = 24$.

$\frac{15}{24} > \frac{14}{24}$; therefore, $\frac{5}{8} > \frac{7}{12}$.   3. The fraction with the larger numerator is larger.

Skill Check 1

If the fraction is not in lowest terms, find an equivalent fraction by reducing the fraction to lowest terms. If it is in lowest terms, use the smallest natural number multiplier to find an equivalent fraction.

1. $\frac{3}{8}$ 2. $\frac{36}{42}$ 3. $\frac{108}{198}$

Rename as fractions with common denominators and compare by using <, =, or >.

4. $\frac{5}{6} \,\square\, \frac{3}{4}$ 5. $-\frac{5}{8} \,\square\, -\frac{1}{2}$ 6. $\frac{2}{5} \,\square\, \frac{6}{15}$

Definition

Cross multiplication is multiplying the numerator of the first fraction times the denominator of the second and multiplying the denominator of the first times the numerator of the second.

Cross multiplication can be used to compare the relative size of two positive rational numbers. Consider the fractions $\frac{a}{b}$ and $\frac{c}{d}$. The cross products ad and bc will compare in the same order as the fractions compare, if the multiplications are performed in the order given in the above definition. If $ad < bc$, then $\frac{a}{b} < \frac{c}{d}$. This method works for comparing two rational numbers because the inequality sign reverses only when both sides are multiplied by the same negative number.

$$\frac{a}{b} < \frac{c}{d}$$

$$\cancel{b}d\left(\frac{a}{\cancel{b}}\right) < b\cancel{d}\left(\frac{c}{\cancel{d}}\right)$$ 1. Multiply both sides of the equation by the product of the denominators.

$$da < bc$$ 2. Simplify. This is true if $b > 0$ and $d > 0$.

$$ad < bc$$ 3. Apply the Commutative Property of Multiplication.

Comparing $\frac{1}{4}$ and $\frac{1}{2}$ by the cross-multiplication process, $1 \cdot 2 < 4 \cdot 1$, so we can conclude that $\frac{1}{4} < \frac{1}{2}$.

Example 4   Use cross multiplication to compare $\frac{5}{8}$ and $\frac{4}{7}$. Use <, =, or >.

Answer

$$\frac{5}{8} \;\bowtie\; \frac{4}{7}$$ 1. Perform cross multiplication, placing the products in the correct order.

$$5 \cdot 7 \;\boxed{}\; 8 \cdot 4$$

$$35 \;\boxed{>}\; 32$$ 2. Order the products. The correct sign is "is greater than."

$$\frac{5}{8} > \frac{4}{7}$$ 3. The fractions compare in the same order.

Cross multiplication also provides a convenient test to determine whether two fractions are equivalent. If the product of the numerator of the first fraction with the denominator of the second equals the product of the denominator of the first with the numerator of the second, then the fractions are equal. The proof of this property will be given in Section 5.5.

In essence, all you are doing is multiplying both fractions by the same amount. In the example below you are multiplying both fractions by 32 (i.e., the product of 4 and 8).

Consider the fractions $\frac{3}{4}$ and $\frac{6}{8}$.

$$\frac{3}{4} \;\overset{?}{\bowtie}\; \frac{6}{8}$$

$$3 \times 8 \overset{?}{=} 4 \times 6$$

$$24 = 24$$

Therefore, $\frac{3}{4} = \frac{6}{8}$.

Example 5   Are the fractions $\frac{13}{16}$ and $\frac{33}{40}$ equivalent?

Answer

$$\frac{13}{16} \overset{?}{=} \frac{33}{40}$$

$$13 \cdot 40 \overset{?}{=} 16 \cdot 33$$ 1. Perform cross multiplication.

$$520 \neq 528$$

$$\frac{13}{16} \neq \frac{33}{40}$$ 2. Because the products are not equal, the fractions are not equal.

Example 6 Are the fractions $\frac{6}{7}$ and $\frac{78}{91}$ equivalent?

Answer

$$\frac{6}{7} \overset{?}{=} \frac{78}{91}$$

$6 \cdot 91 \overset{?}{=} 7 \cdot 78$ 1. Perform cross multiplication.

$546 = 546$

$$\frac{6}{7} = \frac{78}{91}$$ 2. Because the products are equal, the fractions are equal.

Skill Check 2

Use cross multiplication to compare the given fractions. Use <, =, or >.

1. $\frac{7}{12} \ \square \ \frac{8}{13}$ 2. $\frac{5}{6} \ \square \ \frac{7}{11}$ 3. $\frac{9}{13} \ \square \ \frac{11}{15}$

Use cross multiplication to determine whether each pair of fractions is equivalent. Write *yes* or *no*.

4. $\frac{3}{5}, \frac{12}{20}$ 5. $\frac{2}{3}, \frac{5}{9}$ 6. $\frac{6}{8}, \frac{18}{24}$

Rational numbers, whether expressed as integers, fractions, mixed numbers, or decimals, can be graphed on a number line. The position for nonintegers must be estimated between integers. For instance, as indicated on the number line below, the number $\frac{1}{2}$ is located half of the way from 0 to 1. The number $\frac{3}{2} = 1\frac{1}{2}$ is located half of the way from 1 to 2. The number $-1\frac{1}{4}$ is located one-fourth of the way from -1 to -2. The number $-\frac{3}{8}$ is located three-eighths of the way from 0 to -1.

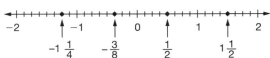

Example 7 Graph the following rational numbers on a single number line.

a. $\frac{1}{4}$ b. $-\frac{3}{4}$ c. $1\frac{3}{4}$ d. $-\frac{9}{4}$

Answer

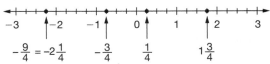

a. Place $\frac{1}{4}$ one-fourth of the way from 0 to 1.

b. Place $-\frac{3}{4}$ three-fourths of the way from 0 to -1.

c. Place $1\frac{3}{4}$ three-fourths of the way from 1 to 2.

d. $-\frac{9}{4} = -2\frac{1}{4}$; place it one-fourth of the way from -2 to -3.

A number line is a convenient way to compare rational numbers. As you move from left to right, rational numbers increase in size. The farther right you go, the larger the number. The farther left you go, the smaller the number. The following inequality statements illustrate this.

$-2 < -1$ $-1\frac{1}{4} < -\frac{3}{8}$ $\frac{1}{2} < 1\frac{1}{2}$

All of the numbers shown in the above statements of inequality are shown on the number line just above Example 7. Notice that the relative sizes are all expressed using the less than sign. This allows the numbers in the inequality to be in the same order as they appear on the number line reading left to right.

Example 8 Graph the following rational numbers on a single number line. Write an inequality using less than signs to compare all the numbers: $-4\frac{1}{4}$, $2\frac{1}{3}$, 0, and $-\frac{4}{5}$.

Answer

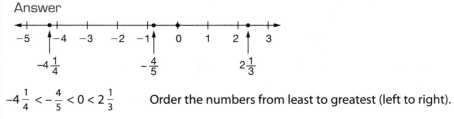

$$-4\frac{1}{4} < -\frac{4}{5} < 0 < 2\frac{1}{3}$$ Order the numbers from least to greatest (left to right).

Skill Check 3

Give the rational number form for each point.

```
        D   B              A           C
  ←+--+--+--+--+--+--+--+--+--+--+--+--+--+→
     -3    -2    -1     0     1     2     3
```

1. A   2. B   3. C   4. D

5. Graph the numbers $-2\frac{1}{4}$, $2\frac{2}{3}$, $1\frac{1}{2}$, and $-\frac{3}{4}$ on a single number line; then order them from least to greatest using the < symbol.

■ A. Exercises

Graph and label the following rational numbers on a single number line.

1. $2\frac{3}{8}$ 2. -3 3. $-3\frac{1}{2}$ 4. $\frac{3}{4}$ 5. $\frac{1}{3}$ 6. $2\frac{7}{8}$

7. Place the numbers in exercises 1–6 in order from least to greatest.

Use cross multiplication to test each pair of fractions for equality. Use = or ≠.

8. $\frac{4}{7}$, $\frac{17}{28}$ 9. $\frac{2}{3}$, $\frac{84}{124}$ 10. $\frac{6}{7}$, $\frac{78}{91}$

11. $\frac{4}{5}$, $\frac{52}{65}$ 12. $\frac{8}{17}$, $\frac{5}{11}$ 13. $\frac{8}{31}$, $\frac{31}{120}$

Use cross multiplication to compare the given fractions. Use <, =, or >.

14. $\frac{3}{5} \square \frac{7}{9}$ 15. $\frac{7}{8} \square \frac{5}{6}$ 16. $\frac{4}{7} \square \frac{24}{42}$

17. $\frac{6}{7} \square \frac{20}{21}$ 18. $\frac{8}{15} \square \frac{9}{16}$ 19. $\frac{17}{5} \square \frac{25}{8}$

20. $\frac{-3}{4} \square \frac{-7}{10}$ 21. $\frac{-5}{17} \square \frac{-6}{19}$ 22. $\frac{8}{17} \square \frac{4}{9}$

23. $\frac{3}{5} \square \frac{31}{49}$

■ B. Exercises

Rename as fractions with common denominators and compare by using < or >.

24. $\frac{5}{8} \,\square\, \frac{3}{4}$

25. $\frac{2}{3} \,\square\, \frac{5}{7}$

26. $\frac{1}{6} \,\square\, \frac{2}{13}$

27. $\frac{8}{3} \,\square\, \frac{5}{2}$

28. $-\frac{17}{3} \,\square\, -\frac{23}{4}$

29. $\frac{17}{3} \,\square\, \frac{23}{4}$

Graph the rational numbers for each exercise on a single number line; then order them from least to greatest using the < symbol.

30. $2\frac{7}{8}, 2\frac{2}{3}, 2\frac{5}{6}, 2\frac{1}{2}$

31. $\frac{4}{5}, \frac{1}{6}, \frac{1}{2}, \frac{7}{10}$

32. $-\frac{2}{3}, -\frac{1}{2}, -\frac{1}{4}, -\frac{5}{8}$

■ C. Exercises

Order the following lists of rational numbers from least to greatest using the < symbol.

33. $\frac{17}{9}, \frac{9}{17}, \frac{1}{2}, \frac{4}{3}, \frac{3}{8}$

34. $\frac{5}{9}, \frac{2}{3}, \frac{4}{5}, \frac{6}{5}, \frac{10}{9}$

35. When you compare rational numbers by the cross-multiplication process, $\frac{a}{b} < \frac{c}{d}$ when $ad < bc$, provided b and d are both positive. What happens when b is negative or d is negative? What happens if both b and d are negative?

■ Dominion thru Math

Use the tables completed in Section 5.1, Dominion thru Math, when answering the following questions. Remember that the gear ratio is the number of times the rear wheel turns for each revolution of the pedals.

36. Beginning cyclists often think that all the lowest gear ratios occur when using the smaller chain-ring and that all the higher gear ratios occur when using the larger chain-ring. Using the tables in Section 5.1, complete the chart ranking the gear ratios from hardest to pedal (16th) to easiest to pedal (1st).

	16th	15th	14th	13th	12th	11th	10th	9th
Ratio of chain-ring to rear sprocket								
Gear ratio								

	8th	7th	6th	5th	4th	3rd	2nd	1st
Ratio of chain-ring to rear sprocket								
Gear ratio								

37. Describe a general pattern of chain-ring to rear sprocket combinations that would simply describe high, low, and medium gears.

CUMULATIVE REVIEW

Solve. [3.7]

38. $-6y > 12$

39. $9y \neq 27$

40. $18z \leq 54$

41. $-4z \leq 44$

42. $8x \geq 208$

Find the GCF of each pair of numbers. [4.3]

43. 48, 15

44. 82, 105

45. 90, 132

46. Are 48 and 49 relatively prime? Why or why not? [4.3]

47. Are 112 and 104 relatively prime? Why or why not? [4.3]

PROBLEM SOLVING

Draw a Picture

Pictures are often helpful for solving word problems. Representing the data in a problem with a sketch or picture allows you to see relationships and visualize what is happening. Use the strategy "draw a picture" whenever possible.

Example 1 The three towns of Garden City, Scott City, and Oakley are located along a straight highway. The distance between Garden City and Oakley is 81 mi. Scott City is located between Garden City and Oakley and is 36 mi. from Garden City. How far is it from Scott City to Oakley?

Answer

Think: What is the relationship of these towns to each other? Use a picture to show the relationship.

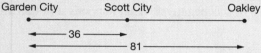

Think: What is being asked? What mathematical operation does the relationship suggest?

Represent the unknown with a variable: d = the distance from Scott City to Oakley.

Use the picture to select the operation of addition: $d + 36 = 81$.

Think: How is the equation solved?

Subtract 36 from both sides of the equation: $d + 36 - 36 = 81 - 36$; $d = 45$.

The distance from Scott City to Oakley is 45 mi.

Think: As you look back at the diagram, does 45 mi. seem reasonable considering the facts given in the problem?

Yes, the answer is correct, since $45 + 36 = 81$.

Example 2 There are eight friends at a party. If everyone at the party shakes hands with everyone else at the party exactly once, how many handshakes occur during the party?

Answer

Think: Use a diagram to help you visualize the handshaking at this party.

If person A shakes hands with everyone in the room, 7 handshakes will occur.

Think: What happens when person B starts to shake hands?

Notice that when person B shakes hands with everyone, his handshake with person A is not counted. It was counted in the handshakes for person A. There are 6 additional handshakes. Person C will have 5 additional handshakes, and so on down to person G, who will have one new handshake with person H.

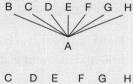

Think: How can the total of all handshakes be determined?

There are a total of $7 + 6 + 5 + 4 + 3 + 2 + 1 = 28$ different handshakes at this party.

Think: To check this answer, think back through the problem using the diagrams to make sure the answer is reasonable.

■ Exercises

Devise a plan for solving each of the following problems and write an explanation of your plan. Use pictures whenever possible. Solve and check that your answer is reasonable.

1. The three towns of Liberal, Dalhart, and Tucumcari are located in that order along a straight highway. The distance between Liberal and Dalhart is 114 mi. Tucumcari is located 93 mi. beyond Dalhart on the highway. How far is it from Liberal to Tucumcari?

2. A ball made of a special rubber compound was propelled 40 ft. into the air. Each time the ball hit the ground, it bounced half as high as its previous high point. How many times did the ball hit the ground before it bounced to a height of less than 2 ft.?

3. During a busy period of time in a 25-story office building, an elevator started at the first floor, rose 2 floors, rose 9 floors, descended 6 floors, rose 8 floors, descended 5 floors, rose 6 floors, and descended 8 floors. On which floor was the elevator at the end of the period of time? If it takes the elevator 20 sec. to go from one floor to the next, how long was the elevator in motion?

4. Twelve basketball teams will play in a tournament. Four will be given byes in the first round. They will be matched against the four first-round winners from the other eight teams. How many games will a team have to win in order to win the tournament?

5. A spinner has four equally sized spaces on it numbered 1 through 4. If the spinner is spun twice, what are the possible sums that can be obtained? Which sum occurs most often?

6. Kellen and Sean start walking at the same time on the track. If Kellen can complete a lap in 3 min. and Sean can complete a lap in 4 min., how often will they cross the starting line together if they both walk for 30 min.?

7. A picture frame is 2 in. wide and encloses a rectangular picture that has dimensions of 11 in. by 14 in. If the area of a rectangle is found by multiplying the length times the width, what is the area of the picture and frame together?

8. The town of Palaski is 29 mi. south of Bixler. Grantville is 22 mi. north of Palaski. Philo is 18.5 mi. north of Grantville. What is the order of the towns from north to south? What is the distance between each town and the total distance from the town that is the farthest south to the town that is the farthest north?

5.3 Decimal Equivalents

A rational number, when expressed as a decimal, is either terminating or repeating. In the first section of this chapter, $0.08\overline{3}$, $-0.\overline{27}$, and 4.25 were given as examples of rational numbers. The first two are repeating decimals, and the last one is a terminating decimal. In this section, rational numbers will be changed from fractions to decimals and from decimals to fractions.

To understand the meaning of the fraction $\frac{3}{4}$, consider four friends who have enough money to buy three candy bars. They have three candy bars to divide into four equal parts. This means that each will get three-fourths of a candy bar. The fraction $\frac{3}{4}$ indicates $3 \div 4$. By performing the division, you will convert the fraction to its decimal form.

This man is using a shop grinder, but machinists doing more precise work measure to thousandths of an inch.

Example 1 Convert $\frac{3}{4}$ to a decimal.

Answer

$$
\begin{array}{r}
0.75 \\
4\overline{)3.00} \\
\underline{2\,8} \\
20 \\
\underline{20} \\
0
\end{array}
$$

$\frac{3}{4} = 0.75$

1. Divide the numerator by the denominator. Stop when the remainder is zero.

2. The decimal is a terminating decimal.

Example 2 Convert $\frac{5}{12}$ to a decimal.

Answer

$$
\begin{array}{r}
0.416 \\
12\overline{)5.000} \\
\underline{4\,8} \\
20 \\
\underline{12} \\
80 \\
\underline{72} \\
8
\end{array}
$$

$\frac{5}{12} = 0.4166666...,$
which is written as
$0.41\overline{6}$.

1. Divide the numerator by the denominator. The appearance of the remainder 8 for the second time indicates that the decimal repeats. Since the remainder of 8 appeared in consecutive divisions, the repeating sequence is only one digit long.

2. The decimal is written with a line over the repeating portion.

Rational numbers as decimals terminate or repeat.

$0.275 \qquad 0.8\overline{3}$

Example 3 Convert $\frac{2}{11}$ to a decimal.

Answer

$$\begin{array}{r} 0.18 \\ 11\overline{)2.00} \\ \underline{11} \\ 90 \\ \underline{88} \\ 2 \end{array}$$

1. Divide the numerator by the denominator. The appearance of 2 as the remainder indicates that the decimal repeats, since 2 was the original numerator.

$\frac{2}{11} = 0.181818\ldots,$ which is written as $0.\overline{18}$.

2. The decimal is written with a line over the repeating portion.

Skill Check 1

Convert the following fractions to decimals.

1. $\frac{3}{8}$

2. $\frac{2}{9}$

3. $\frac{4}{25}$

Suppose you want to convert decimals to their rational form. To convert a terminating decimal, place the digits that follow the decimal point over the place value of the last digit. Be sure to reduce the fraction to lowest terms.

Example 4 Convert 0.175 to its reduced rational form using the GCF.

Answer

$$\frac{175}{1,000} = \frac{7 \times 25}{40 \times 25}$$

$$= \frac{7}{40}$$

The decimal ends in the thousandths place. Place the digits after the decimal point over 1,000. Reduce the fraction.

Converting repeating decimals to their rational form requires the use of algebra. Follow the steps used to convert $0.\overline{3}$ to its rational form.

Set the decimal equal to x.

$$x = 0.\overline{3}$$

Then write a second equation by multiplying both sides of the first equation by 10^n, where n is the number of repeating digits. Since $0.\overline{3}$ has only one repeating digit, multiply both sides by $10^1 = 10$.

$$10x = 3.\overline{3}$$

Subtract each side of the first equation from its corresponding side in the second equation.

$$\begin{array}{r} 10x = 3.33\ldots \\ \underline{-\ x = 0.33\ldots} \\ 9x = 3 \end{array}$$

Solve for x, reducing the fraction to lowest terms if possible.

$$\frac{9x}{9} = \frac{3}{9}$$

$$x = \frac{1}{3}$$

Example 5   Convert $0.\overline{45}$ to rational form.

Answer

$x = 0.\overline{45}$ 1. Write an equation, letting x equal the repeating decimal.

$\begin{array}{r} 100x = 45.4545... \\ - \quad x = \ \ 0.4545... \\ \hline 99x = 45 \end{array}$ 2. Multiply both sides of the equation by $10^2 = 100$ (move the decimal right two places). Then subtract the original equation from the new equation.

$\dfrac{99x}{99} = \dfrac{45}{99}$ 3. Divide both sides of the equation by 99.

$x = \dfrac{5}{11}$ 4. Reduce the fraction. Both the numerator and denominator are divisible by 9.

Many repeating decimals have a nonrepeating sequence of digits before the repeating sequence. In this case, multiply both sides of the original equation by two different powers of ten to make two new equations. The following example contains a single digit, 1, before the repeating sequence begins.

Example 6   Convert $0.1\overline{36}$ to rational form.

Answer

$x = 0.1\overline{36}$ 1. Write an equation, letting x equal the repeating decimal.

$\begin{array}{r} 1,000x = 136.3636... \\ - \quad 10x = \ \ \ \ 1.3636... \\ \hline 990x = 135 \end{array}$ 2. Move the decimal behind the first repeating sequence by multiplying both sides of the original equation by $10^3 = 1,000$. Move the decimal before the first repeating sequence by multiplying both sides of the original equation by $10^1 = 10$. Subtract both sides of the equation.

$\dfrac{990x}{990} = \dfrac{135}{990}$ 3. Divide both sides by 990.

$x = \dfrac{3}{22}$ 4. Reduce the fraction; the LCM of 135 and 990 is 45.

Skill Check 2   **Convert the following decimals to fractions.**

1. 0.8   2. 0.15   3. $0.\overline{36}$ 4. $0.1\overline{6}$

To understand repeating decimals better, try ordering a set of decimals of which some are repeating and some are not. Suppose you want to order the following set from least to greatest.

$\{0.57\overline{1},\ 0.579,\ 0.5\overline{7},\ 0.6,\ 0.\overline{571},\ 0.5714,\ 0.59\}$

The first digit after the decimal point is 5 in all the numbers except 0.6. It is the greatest. Among the other six, the second digit is 7 in all but 0.59, so it is the next greatest.

The remaining five numbers all have 57 as the first two decimal places. We must examine the third decimal place.

Number	Third Place	Fourth Place	Rank
0.57111...	1	1	1st
0.579	9		5th
0.5777...	7		4th
0.571571...	1	5	3rd
0.5714	1	4	2nd

It is easily seen from the table column listing the third decimal place that 0.579 and $0.5\overline{7}$ are the third and fourth largest. Three of the numbers have ones in the third decimal place. We go to the fourth decimal place to order these three. The number $0.57\overline{1}$ has a 1 in the fourth place, so it is the smallest. Then comes 0.5714, which has a 4 in the fourth place, followed by $0.\overline{571}$, which has a 5 in the fourth place.

Including 0.59 and 0.6, the correct order is $\{0.57\overline{1}, 0.5714, 0.\overline{571}, 0.5\overline{7}, 0.579, 0.59, 0.6\}$.

Three ways to compare rational numbers:
1. Get a common denominator.
2. Use cross multiplication.
3. Change to decimals.

■ A. Exercises

Convert the following fractions to decimals.

1. $\dfrac{3}{5}$
2. $\dfrac{1}{20}$
3. $-\dfrac{7}{25}$
4. $\dfrac{3}{8}$
5. $\dfrac{17}{5}$
6. $-\dfrac{7}{8}$

7. $\dfrac{55}{16}$
8. $\dfrac{5}{32}$
9. $\dfrac{9}{40}$

Convert the following decimals to fractions or mixed numbers in lowest terms.

10. 0.625
11. 0.52
12. −0.8
13. 0.375
14. 2.55
15. −4.7

■ B. Exercises

Convert the following decimals to fractions or mixed numbers in lowest terms.

16. 0.5625
17. 0.90625
18. 5.68

Convert the following fractions to decimals. Use a line over the repeating sequence.

19. $\dfrac{5}{6}$
20. $\dfrac{11}{9}$
21. $-\dfrac{4}{9}$
22. $\dfrac{7}{11}$
23. $\dfrac{7}{12}$
24. $\dfrac{8}{15}$

25. $\dfrac{5}{33}$
26. $\dfrac{61}{9}$
27. $-6\dfrac{7}{24}$
28. $\dfrac{3}{7}$
29. $\dfrac{529}{99}$
30. $\dfrac{83}{99}$

Place the following quantities in ascending order.

31. $0.3, 0.3\overline{2}, 0.31\overline{8}, 0.32, 0.3\overline{18}, 0.\overline{318}, 0.320\overline{8}$

32. $0.54, 0.45, 0.5\overline{4}, 0.\overline{45}, 0.\overline{405}, 0.45\overline{6}, 0.47$

Convert the following decimals to fractions in lowest terms.

33. $0.\overline{43}$
34. $0.1\overline{23}$
35. $0.\overline{9}$
36. $0.\overline{428571}$

■ C. Exercises

Convert the following decimals to fractions in lowest terms.

37. $0.12\overline{57}$
38. $0.12\overline{3}$
39. $0.1\overline{23}$

■ Dominion thru Math

The circumference of a rear tire can be calculated directly from its diameter using the formula $c = \pi d$. This can be combined with the gear ratio to determine the distance the bike moves with each rotation of the pedals. The following calculations determine the distance traveled for each revolution of the pedals by a bike with 26" diameter tires using the 39 : 12 chain-ring : rear sprocket (CR : RS) ratio.

$$\frac{39}{12} = 3.25 \; \frac{\text{RS rev.}}{\text{ped. rev.}}; \quad \frac{3.25 \; \text{RS rev.}}{\text{ped. rev.}}\left(\frac{26\pi \text{ in.}}{1 \; \text{RS rev.}}\right) \approx 265.33 \; \frac{\text{in.}}{\text{ped. rev.}}, \text{ or about 22.1 ft.}$$

If the bike was pedaled at 30 revolutions per minute (rpm), the speed of the bike can be determined.

$$\frac{30 \; \text{ped. rev.}}{\text{min.}}\left(\frac{22.1 \text{ ft.}}{\text{ped. rev.}}\right) \approx 663 \; \frac{\text{ft.}}{\text{min.}}$$

This speed should be converted to a more understandable rate.

$$663 \; \frac{\text{ft.}}{\text{min.}}\left(\frac{1 \text{ mi.}}{5,280 \text{ ft.}}\right)\left(\frac{60 \text{ min.}}{1 \text{ hr.}}\right) \approx 7.5 \text{ mi./hr.}$$

40. Determine the distance that a bike with 27 in. wheels will travel per rotation of the pedals when the bike is in its highest gear (CR : RS ratio of 53 : 12) and in its lowest gear (CR : RS ratio of 39 : 23).

41. Determine the speed of the bike in miles per hour if it is pedaled in highest gear at 25 rpm and in lowest gear at 35 rpm.

CUMULATIVE REVIEW

Solve. [3.4]

42. $-11x - (-x) = -45$

43. $-90 = -6y + 12y$

44. $2z - 8z = -138$

45. $-3x + 8(x + 4) + 9x = 144$

46. $-7y + 6y - 12 + 4 - y = 2$

Write the first five terms of the following arithmetic sequences. [4.5]

47. $a_1 = -9; d = 4$

48. $a_1 = \frac{1}{2}; d = \frac{1}{2}$

49. $a_1 = 8; d = -3$

50. $a_1 = 0.7; d = 0.4$

5.4 Ratio and Rate

At Calvary Christian School, there are 192 students and 12 teachers. Schools are often interested in their student-teacher ratio. They want to know the average number of students each teacher would have if the students were divided evenly among the teachers.

Definition
A **ratio** is a comparison of two numbers by division and is often written as a fraction.

There are three ways to write the ratio of students to teachers mentioned above.

$$\frac{192}{12} \qquad\qquad 192 \text{ to } 12 \qquad\qquad 192 : 12$$

When a ratio is written as a fraction, it can be reduced to lowest terms. The ratio of students to teachers in lowest terms is $\frac{192}{12} = \frac{16 \times \cancel{12}}{1 \times \cancel{12}} = \frac{16}{1}$. Even though the fraction reduces to a whole number, it remains in fraction form. It is read "16 to 1" regardless of which of the three forms it is written in.

Example 1 If Calvary Christian School, mentioned above, has 112 girls and 80 boys enrolled, what is the ratio of girls to boys? teachers to boys? boys to teachers?

Answer

$\frac{112}{80} = \frac{7 \times \cancel{16}}{5 \times \cancel{16}} = \frac{7}{5}$ — There are 7 girls for every 5 boys.

$\frac{12}{80} = \frac{3 \times \cancel{4}}{20 \times \cancel{4}} = \frac{3}{20}$ — There are 3 teachers for every 20 boys.

$\frac{80}{12} = \frac{20 \times \cancel{4}}{3 \times \cancel{4}} = \frac{20}{3}$ — There are 20 boys for every 3 teachers.

Example 2 A baseball team won eight games and lost ten. Write the ratio of games won to games played. Then write the ratio of games won to games lost.

Answer

The team played $8 + 10 = 18$ games.

$\frac{\text{games won}}{\text{games played}} = \frac{8}{18} = \frac{4 \times \cancel{2}}{9 \times \cancel{2}} = \frac{4}{9}$

$\frac{\text{games won}}{\text{games lost}} = \frac{8}{10} = \frac{4 \times \cancel{2}}{5 \times \cancel{2}} = \frac{4}{5}$

Skill Check 1

Use the trail mix formula to write the following ratios. Do not express in lowest terms. (Doing so would result in the wrong mixture of ingredients and less mix than the recipe is supposed to yield.) Write the answers in the form $a : b$.

Trail Mix Formula
4 parts peanuts
3 parts granola
2 parts raisins
1 part chocolate chips

1. chocolate chips to peanuts

2. granola to raisins

3. raisins to peanuts

4. peanuts to raisins and granola

A *rate* is a special type of ratio comparing different kinds of measures. A rate often expresses the numerator per one unit of the denominator. This is referred to as a *unit rate*. The denominator is often time, such as per second, although it need not be. Calvary Christian School, mentioned above, has a unit rate of 16 students per teacher.

A **rate** is a ratio comparing different kinds of measures.
A **unit rate** is a ratio that compares a quantity to one.

Example 3   A car traveled 210 mi. in 4 hr. What was its unit rate?

Answer

$$\frac{\text{miles}}{\text{hours}} = \frac{210}{4}$$

1. Write the desired ratio and supply the amounts given.

$$\frac{210 \div 4}{4 \div 4} = \frac{52.5}{1}$$

2. Divide the denominator by itself to obtain a denominator of 1. The numerator must be divided by the same amount.

52.5 mi./hr.

3. Express the ratio as a unit rate.

Example 4   A plumber charges $288 for 6 hr. of work. What is his unit rate?

Answer

$$\frac{\text{dollars}}{\text{hours}} = \frac{288}{6}$$

1. Write the ratio of dollars to hours.

$$\frac{288 \div 6}{6 \div 6} = \frac{48}{1}$$

2. Divide the denominator by 6 to obtain a unit rate. Divide the numerator by the same amount.

$48/hr.

3. Write the rate per hour.

Skill Check 2

State a situation where each rate might be used.

1. mi./hr.

2. words/min.

3. dollars/hr.

4. revolutions/min.

Find the unit rate.

5. 168 mi. in 3 hr.

6. 432 words in 9 min.

7. 300 mi. on 15 gal.

8. 5,400 revolutions in 18 min.

⊕ Invention

Probably no other single piece of machinery has ever been the focus of so many inventors as the *bicycle*. As far back as 1818, the German Baron Karl Drais von Sauerbronn patented his bicycle-like all-wood running machine and exhibited it in Paris. At one time the US Patent Office had a separate building just to house the bicycle patents. The nineteenth century was the proving ground for bicycle design innovation, with most of the resulting evolution of the frame, wheels, and drive train taking place. By 1885 the Starley family of Coventry, England, had produced a bicycle with almost all the basic elements of the modern bike. As ideas came and went, the best survived to give us the technologically advanced modern bicycle. The modern bicycle can be summed up in just a few words—very light, very strong, and very fast. For the professional cyclist, you can also add the words "very expensive."

■ A. Exercises

A dairy farm has the following cows: 12 Holstein, 6 Jersey, and 4 Brown Swiss. Find the ratio in lowest terms of each of the following.

1. Holsteins to Jerseys
2. Jerseys to Brown Swiss
3. Brown Swiss to Jerseys
4. Holsteins to non-Holsteins
5. Holsteins to Brown Swiss
6. non-Jerseys to Jerseys

Express the answers to the following questions in lowest terms using the word "to."

7. A school has 2,600 students and 104 teachers. What is the student-to-teacher ratio?

8. A store has 10 departments and 48 employees. What is the ratio of employees to departments?

9. A department store ordered 80 regular-length suits, 40 talls, and 20 shorts. What is the ratio of regular lengths to both other lengths combined? regular lengths to talls? regular lengths to shorts?

10. Some concrete was mixed using 550 lb. of cement and 1,650 lb. of sand. What was the ratio of cement to sand?

11. If concrete is mixed using 1,650 lb. of sand and 330 lb. of water, what is the ratio of sand to water?

12. Mr. and Mrs. Jackson have fourteen grandchildren. Find the ratio of girls to boys if there are four more girls than boys.

■ B. Exercises

Ike, Pedro, and Harry picked 10, 6, and 3 bushels of peaches, respectively. Find the following ratios of the quantities picked. Express answers as reduced rational numbers.

13. Pedro to Harry
14. Ike to Pedro
15. Ike to Harry
16. Harry to Pedro
17. Pedro to Ike and Harry
18. Ike to Pedro and Harry

Marie typed 60 words/min. with five errors. Jim typed 45 words/min. with eight errors. Find the following ratios and express answers using the word "to."

19. Marie's rate to Jim's rate
20. Marie's errors to Jim's errors
21. Jim's rate to Marie's rate
22. Jim's errors to Marie's errors

Find the unit rate.

23. 70 words in 2 min.
24. 270 acres in 3 days
25. 580 mi. on 29 gal.
26. 130 yd. on 25 carries
27. $2.95 for 5 cans
28. $75 for 30 lb.
29. 5 lawns for $90
30. $306 payment for 36 hr.

31. At the rate of 3 almonds per bar, how many candy bars could be made using 140 almonds?

32. At an average rate of 47 mi./hr., how far can you go in 5 hr.?

33. If you can travel 462 mi. using 22 gal. of gas, what is the mileage rate?

34. A running back made gains of 6 yd., 8 yd., and 1 yd. on three carries. What is his per carry rate?

35. A seamstress made five dresses using 8 yd. of trim. Find the rate of trim per dress.

36. A farmer took five loads of wheat to the elevator and was credited with 1,060 bu. What was the average number of bushels per load?

■ C. Exercises

37. Three partners in a business have ownership in the ratio 3 : 5 : 7. How much will each get from $387,000 profit if it is divided on the basis of the ratio of ownership?

38. During biblical times the firstborn son in a Jewish family traditionally got twice as much inheritance as the other sons. If there are four sons in the family and the inheritance to be divided totals $875,000, how much will each son inherit?

■ Dominion thru Math

39. If a bicyclist rides 100 mi. on a large, flat track, how many total revolutions of the pedals will it take for 27 in. wheels with the chain-ring : rear sprocket gearing set at 53 : 15 (to the nearest hundred)?

40. At 60 rpm, how long will it take the rider in exercise 39 to finish the 100 mi.?

CUMULATIVE REVIEW

List in order all the positive factors of the given number. [4.1]

41. 38   42. 126   43. 12

44. 28   45. 42

Do the following equations have solutions over the set of integers? If yes, solve. [3.6]

46. $x + 22 = 8$ 47. $4y = 12$ 48. $6x = 3$

49. $\dfrac{x}{8} = -5$ 50. $-3(x + 7) = 34$

5.5 Proportions

The ratio of boys to girls in Mrs. Smith's class is $\dfrac{6}{8}$. The ratio of boys to girls in Mr. Burke's class is $\dfrac{9}{12}$. Since both of the above ratios reduce to $\dfrac{3}{4}$, it is correct to say that the ratios are equal; that is, $\dfrac{6}{8} = \dfrac{9}{12}$. The equation formed is a *proportion*.

| Definition |

A **proportion** is a statement of equality between two ratios.

The proper way to read the proportion $\frac{6}{8} = \frac{9}{12}$ is "6 is to 8 as 9 is to 12." The terms of the proportion are numbered in the order in which they are pronounced when reading the proportion. In the proportion above, 6 is the first term, 8 is the second, 9 is the third, and 12 is the fourth. The first and fourth terms (6 and 12) are called the *extremes* of the proportion. The second and third terms (8 and 9) are called the *means*.

Notice that the product of the extremes and the product of the means are equal.

$$\frac{\text{first}}{\text{second}} \quad \frac{6}{8} \bowtie \frac{9}{12} \quad \frac{\text{third}}{\text{fourth}}$$

$$6(12) = 8(9)$$

$$72 = 72$$

This illustrates the important Property of Proportions.

Property of Proportions
The product of the extremes is equal to the product of the means.

To verify that this property always works, let $\frac{a}{b} = \frac{c}{d}$. Multiply both sides of the equation by the product of the denominators. Cancel where possible.

$$\not{b}d\left(\frac{a}{\not{b}}\right) = b\not{d}\left(\frac{c}{\not{d}}\right)$$

$$da = bc$$

By the Commutative Property of Multiplication, $ad = bc$.

Proportions are also true by inversion. This means that if both ratios are inverted (their reciprocals taken), a new proportion is produced. For example, consider the proportion $\frac{3}{4} = \frac{6}{8}$. Inversion of the ratios produces $\frac{4}{3} = \frac{8}{6}$.

Proportions are also true by alternation of the terms (the first is to the third as the second is to the fourth). Again, consider the proportion $\frac{3}{4} = \frac{6}{8}$. Alternation of terms produces $\frac{3}{6} = \frac{4}{8}$.

All of these alternate forms of a given ratio are true proportions because of the Property of Proportions. The product of the extremes and the means remains unchanged. $\frac{a}{b} = \frac{c}{d}$, $\frac{b}{a} = \frac{d}{c}$, $\frac{c}{a} = \frac{d}{b}$, and $\frac{a}{c} = \frac{b}{d}$ are all true because each gives the same cross product $ad = bc$.

Example 1 Given $\frac{3}{5} = \frac{12}{20}$, write a proportion by inversion of ratios and a proportion by alternation of terms.

Answer

$$\frac{3}{5} = \frac{12}{20}$$

$$\frac{5}{3} = \frac{20}{12} \qquad \text{1. Invert the ratios.}$$

$$\frac{3}{12} = \frac{5}{20} \qquad \text{2. Alternate terms of the original proportion (the first term is to the third as the second term is to the fourth).}$$

Skill Check 1

For each proportion given, write a proportion by inversion of ratios and a proportion by alternation of terms.

1. $\dfrac{5}{9} = \dfrac{15}{27}$
2. $\dfrac{x}{y} = \dfrac{6}{15}$

When a proportion contains a variable, you can use the Property of Proportions to solve for the variable.

Example 2 Solve $\dfrac{6}{15} = \dfrac{8}{n}$ for n.

Answer

$\dfrac{6}{15} = \dfrac{8}{n}$

$6n = 15 \cdot 8$ 1. Apply the Property of Proportions.

$6n = 120$ 2. Simplify.

$\dfrac{6n}{6} = \dfrac{120}{6}$ 3. Divide both sides of the equation by 6.

$n = 20$

Example 3 Solve $\dfrac{32}{x} = \dfrac{108}{27}$ for x.

Answer

$\dfrac{32}{x} = \dfrac{108}{27}$

$108x = 32(27)$ 1. Apply the Property of Proportions.

$108x = 864$ 2. Simplify.

$\dfrac{108x}{108} = \dfrac{864}{108}$ 3. Divide both sides by 108.

$x = 8$

Skill Check 2

Solve by using the Property of Proportions.

1. $\dfrac{2}{5} = \dfrac{4}{b}$
2. $\dfrac{6}{9} = \dfrac{n}{21}$
3. $\dfrac{s}{15} = \dfrac{9}{27}$
4. $\dfrac{9}{x} = \dfrac{4}{7}$

When writing proportions to solve word problems, be careful to set up the two ratios in the same order. If one ratio is comparing adults to students, then the other ratio must compare adults to students. If one ratio compares a larger group of adults to a smaller group of adults, the other ratio must compare a larger group of students to a smaller group of students.

| **Example 4** | The ratio of adults to students on a bus is 2 to 7. If there are 8 adults, how many students are on the bus? |

Answer

$$\frac{2}{7} = \frac{8}{n}$$

1. Let n = the number of students. The ratio 2 : 7 compares adults to students, so the other ratio must compare adults to students. There are 8 adults and n students.

$2n = 56$

$\frac{2n}{2} = \frac{56}{2}$

2. Apply the Property of Proportions and solve for n.

$n = 28$ students

| **Example 5** | Sam can paint 200 ft. of privacy fence in 3 hr. To the nearest foot, how many feet can he paint in 5 hr.? |

Answer

$$\frac{200 \text{ ft.}}{x \text{ ft.}} = \frac{3 \text{ hr.}}{5 \text{ hr.}}$$

1. The lesser amount of fence is to the greater amount of fence as the lesser amount of time is to the greater amount of time.

$3x = 200(5)$ 2. Apply the Property of Proportions.

$3x = 1,000$ 3. Simplify.

$\frac{3x}{3} = \frac{1,000}{3}$ 4. Divide both sides by 3.

$x \approx 333$ ft.   5. Round to the nearest foot.

Alternate Method

$$\frac{200 \text{ ft.}}{3 \text{ hr.}} = \frac{x \text{ ft.}}{5 \text{ hr.}}$$

1. The smaller amount of fence is to the shorter time as the larger amount of fence is to the longer time.

$3x = 200(5)$ 2. Apply the Property of Proportions.

$3x = 1,000$ 3. Simplify.

$\frac{3x}{3} = \frac{1,000}{3}$ 4. Divide both sides by 3.

$x \approx 333$ ft.   5. Round to the nearest foot.

Skill Check 3

Write a proportion and solve.

1. If two carrots cost $0.27, how many carrots can you buy for $1.35?

2. If seven of fifteen coins are dimes, then fourteen of how many coins will be dimes?

■ A. Exercises

1. An equation with two equal _____ is called a(n) _____.

2. How is the proportion $\frac{a}{b} = \frac{c}{d}$ read?

3. In exercise 2, which term is the second term of the proportion?

4. Which terms in exercise 2 are the extremes? What are the other two terms called?

Write a proportion for each of the following. Do not solve.

5. If two identical tasks can be accomplished in 5 hr., how many can be accomplished in 7 hr.?

6. If three grain augers can be assembled in 5 hr., how many can be assembled in an 8 hr. day?

7. If three pages were done in 5 min., how many could be completed in 1 hr.?

8. If two barrels weighed 300 lb. together, how many barrels would it take to weigh 7,000 lb.?

9. Logan gained 340 yd. in his first seven games. At that rate, how many games would it take him to reach a total of 1,000 yd. gained?

10. It took 40 lb. to reseed 5,000 yd.^{2}. How many yd.^{2} could be reseeded with 225 lb.?

11. If a recipe calls for $1\frac{1}{2}$ cups of flour and makes 24 cookies, how many cups of flour will be needed to make 72 cookies?

12. Five yards of 72 in. fabric is needed to make three pairs of curtains. If eight pairs of curtains are needed, how many yards of fabric should be purchased?

■ B. Exercises

Solve by using the Property of Proportions.

13. $\dfrac{x}{15} = \dfrac{12}{9}$

14. $\dfrac{91}{y} = \dfrac{13}{5}$

15. $\dfrac{4}{3} = \dfrac{z}{6}$

16. $6 : 5 = c : 4$

17. 4 is to 5 as 408 is to x.

18. $\dfrac{a}{13} = \dfrac{30}{78}$

19. $\dfrac{14}{b} = \dfrac{7}{2}$

20. $\dfrac{6}{7} = \dfrac{3}{n}$

21. $29 : 8 = 58 : d$

22. $a : 7 = 9 : 14$

23. $9 : b = 18 : 5$

24. 85 is to 9 as 34 is to y.

25. An automobile manufacturer paints cars, some silver and some red, in the ratio of $5 : 2$. If they plan to paint 75 silver, how many will they paint red?

26. A store stocks pine and spruce seedlings in approximately the ratio of $7 : 2$. If they order 24 pines, how many spruce seedlings should they order? Round to the nearest whole number.

27. Some rectangles are to be drawn with sides in the length-to-width ratio of $3 : 2$. How long should a rectangle be if its width is 7 in.?

28. If $\dfrac{a}{b} = \dfrac{3}{5}$, then $\dfrac{a}{3} = \dfrac{?}{?}$.

29. If $\dfrac{a}{b} = \dfrac{3}{5}$, then $\dfrac{b}{a} = \dfrac{?}{?}$.

30. If $\dfrac{a}{b} = \dfrac{3}{5}$, then $\dfrac{5}{b} = \dfrac{?}{?}$.

31. What is the ratio of the diameter of any circle to its radius?

32. A farmer produced 28 bu./acre on 400 acres. Another farmer has 800 acres. How many total bushels of wheat should be expected by the second farmer if the bushels per acre is in the same ratio?

33. A children's baseball park is being designed. The ratio of its dimensions to an adult field is to be 2 to 3. The bases on an adult field are 90 ft. apart. How far apart should they be on the smaller field? Write a proportion and solve.

■ C. Exercises

34. Given $\dfrac{a}{b} = \dfrac{7}{3}$, rewrite the proportion three times, using the three smallest ratios of natural numbers that are equivalent to $\dfrac{7}{3}$.

35. Do the numerator and denominator in a proportion need to have the same units? If yes, explain why. If not, why not?

36. Prove that if $\dfrac{a}{b} = \dfrac{c}{d}$, then $\dfrac{a+b}{b} = \dfrac{c+d}{d}$. (Hint: Add 1 to each side of the equation.)

37. What is the ratio of the circumference of a circle to its diameter? circumference to radius?

38. The ratio of the lengths of two rectangles is 4 : 5. The ratio of their widths is also 4 : 5. Will the ratio of their areas also be 4 : 5? Give an example to support your answer.

39. The ratio of the lengths of two rectangles is 4 : 5. The ratio of their widths is also 4 : 5. Will the ratio of their perimeters also be 4 : 5? Give an example to support your answer.

40. Draw a triangle with all three sides of different lengths. Draw a second triangle of the same shape inside the first one. If the smaller triangle has sides of a, b, and c listed in order of increasing size, and the short side of the larger triangle is $2a$, make a conjecture (educated guess) as to what the lengths of the other two sides of the larger triangle would be.

■ Dominion thru Math

41. At what speed in rpm would you have to pedal a bike with 27 in. wheels in order to go 30 mi./hr. in the highest gear (53 chain-ring : 12 rear sprocket)? Is your answer humanly possible? (Hint: Find the speed in inches per minute first; then convert it to revolutions of the pedals per minute.)

42. For a bicycle with 27 in. wheels, how many teeth are needed on a cog of the rear sprocket used in combination with the 39-tooth chain-ring if you want the bike to move at 3 mi./hr. in the lowest gear when pedaled at 25 rpm? (Hint: Use the ratio of rates of revolution for the pedals and the rear tire [and sprocket] to find the desired gear ratio.)

CUMULATIVE REVIEW

Estimate the product or quotient by rounding. [2.7]

43. 22×89

44. 620×189

45. $\dfrac{587}{31}$

46. $62(14)$

47. $3{,}921 \div 52$

Write the first five terms of the following recursively defined sequences, and name the type of sequence illustrated. [4.5–4.6]

48. $a_1 = 0.5;\ a_n = 3a_{n-1}$

49. $a_1 = -4;\ a_n = 6a_{n-1}$

50. $a_1 = 7;\ a_n = -0.2a_{n-1}$

51. $a_1 = 12;\ a_n = a_{n-1} + 5$

52. $a_1 = -2;\ a_n = a_{n-1} - 8$

53. $a_1 = -2;\ a_n = a_{n-1}$

Eleazar, Priest of Israel

Eleazar was the second high priest of Israel. He was a son of Aaron, the brother of Moses.

When Aaron's two oldest sons offered incense in the tabernacle contrary to God's command, they were consumed by fire from the Lord (Lev. 10:1–2). Although their brother Eleazar did not join in their sin, he later disobeyed the Lord's command when he failed to eat the sin offering. Only his father's intercession saved him from Moses' wrath (Lev. 10:16–20).

Later in life, Eleazar became an example of obedience. God entrusted him with many responsibilities, including making him chief of the Levites in charge of the sanctuary (Num. 3:32). After God's destruction by fire of Korah and his followers for their rebellion against Moses and Aaron, God commanded Eleazar to scatter the fire and collect their censers so that they could be hammered into plates for a covering of the altar (Num. 16:36–40).

Some of Eleazar's responsibilities required the use of fractions. When Israel conquered Midian, Moses and Eleazar were given instructions from the Lord on dividing the spoils taken from the Midianites. They were commanded to divide the spoils equally, half for the soldiers who fought in the battle and half for the rest of the people. Of the soldiers' spoils, one-five-hundredth was a tribute to the Lord; and the people were to give

Eleazar collected censers to be hammered into plates.

one-fiftieth of their spoils to the Levites in charge of the tabernacle. The account of the distribution of the spoils is recorded in Numbers 31. The results of Eleazar's calculations are summarized in the table at the bottom of the page.

In Numbers 31:31, the Bible notes that "Moses and Eleazar the priest did as the Lord commanded Moses." If you are a Christian, you should follow the example of Eleazar and be obedient to those in authority over you. You should also strive to be responsible in every area of your life—including your math assignments. Obedience is an evidence of our love for God and those He has placed in authority over us.

Spoils	Amount	$\frac{1}{2}$ of Amount	$\frac{1}{500}$ of the Soldiers' Amount	$\frac{1}{50}$ of the People's Amount
Sheep	675,000	337,500	675	6,750
Cattle	72,000	36,000	72	720
Donkeys	61,000	30,500	61	610
Virgins	32,000	16,000	32	320

5.6 Real Numbers

The real number system contains several sets of numbers within it. Therefore, before discussing the real number system, we will review the following information about sets. A *set* is a collection of objects, usually named by a capital letter. Each object contained within the set is called an *element* or *member* of the set. Set *A* contains four elements, all integers.

$$A = \{3, 6, 12, 24\}$$

The fact that a particular object is an element of a set is indicated by using the symbol $\in$. To state that a number is not an element of a set, the symbol $\notin$ is used.

$$6 \in A \text{ but } 8 \notin A$$

If a whole number can represent the number of elements in a set, then the set is a *finite set*. Set *A* above is finite; it has four elements.

Consider the following set.

$$B = \{2, 4, 6, 8, \ldots\}$$

The three dots are used to symbolize the fact that the pattern continues forever with no largest number. Since there is no last member, we cannot count the number of elements. Set *B* is not finite; it is referred to as an *infinite set*.

A set with no elements is the *empty set* (often called the *null set*) and is symbolized by $\varnothing$ or by { }.

Sets can have relationships to one another. Two sets with no common elements are *disjoint sets*. The Venn diagram to the right illustrates disjoint sets $C = \{6, 12\}$ and $D = \{1, 2, 3, 4, 5\}$.

If all of the elements of one set are contained in a second set, then the first set is a subset of the second. Set *C* is a *subset* of set *A*. This is symbolized by $C \subseteq A$ and is illustrated in the Venn diagram below.

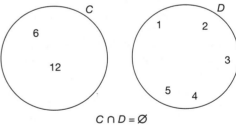

Disjoint sets

$C \cap D = \varnothing$

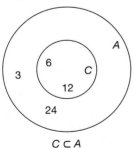

$C \subseteq A$

$\varnothing \subseteq$ every set
$A \subseteq A$

The definition of *subset* implies that every set has at least two subsets. The empty set is a subset of every set, and every set is a subset of itself.

Consider the sets $D = \{1, 2, 3, 4, 5\}$ and $E = \{2, 4, 6, 8, 10\}$. These two sets have the elements 2 and 4 in common. The set containing only the elements 2 and 4 is the intersection of sets D and E. This is written as $D \cap E$. The intersection of sets is illustrated in the Venn diagram to the right.

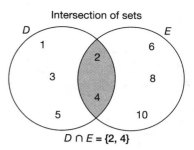

Intersection of sets

$D \cap E = \{2, 4\}$

The set formed by combining all the elements of two sets D and E is called the union of sets D and E, designated by $D \cup E$ and illustrated in the second Venn diagram to the right. Sets D and E themselves may be disjoint, or they may have common elements.

With this background, let's look at our number system.

The set of numbers that are used for counting are the natural numbers, designated by $\mathbb{N}$.

$$\mathbb{N} = \{1, 2, 3, \ldots\}$$

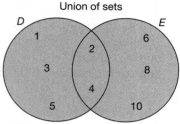

Union of sets

$D \cup E = \{1, 2, 3, 4, 5, 6, 8, 10\}$

One of the greatest advances in numbering systems occurred when a symbol was introduced to represent zero. Ancient numbering systems, such as Roman numerals, did not possess a symbol for zero. When zero is added to the set of natural numbers, the set of whole numbers is formed. Whole numbers are symbolized by $\mathbb{W}$.

$$\mathbb{W} = \{0, 1, 2, 3, \ldots\}$$

The need for numbers to represent quantities such as temperature below zero, overdrawn bank accounts, decreasing rates, and so on, required negative numbers. Negating the natural numbers and including them with the whole numbers and zero became known as the set of integers and is represented by $\mathbb{Z}$.

$$\mathbb{Z} = \{\ldots, -3, -2, -1, 0, 1, 2, 3, \ldots\}$$

In higher mathematics, the terms *natural numbers* and *whole numbers* are often replaced by the terms *positive integers* and *nonnegative integers*, respectively. The term *negative integers* is used when referring to integers less than zero.

Including fractions with the set of integers forms the set of rational numbers, symbolized by $\mathbb{Q}$. Listing this set of numbers is impossible since there is no easily established pattern. Therefore, they are often described as follows.

$$\mathbb{Q} = \left\{ \frac{a}{b} \,\middle|\, a \in \mathbb{Z}, b \in \mathbb{Z}, \text{ and } b \neq 0 \right\}$$

The vertical line within the braces is read "such that." The above notation is read "the set of all numbers a over b, such that a is an integer, b is an integer, and b is not equal to zero."

The restriction $b \neq 0$ must be included because division by zero is impossible. If $b = 1$, then $\frac{a}{b}$ equals the integer a. Therefore, all integers are included in the set of rational numbers. Recall from Section 5.3 that all rational numbers also have a decimal form that either terminates or repeats.

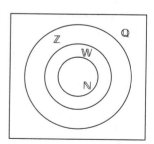

Rational numbers $\mathbb{Q}$

The sets of numbers discussed so far have the following relationships: $\mathbb{N} \subseteq \mathbb{W} \subseteq \mathbb{Z} \subseteq \mathbb{Q}$. The Venn diagram to the right illustrates their relationships as subsets of one another.

Skill Check 1

Classify the following numbers as natural, whole, integer, or rational. Give the most specific set.

1. -5.5
2. 0
3. $-1{,}903$
4. $\frac{15}{62}$
5. 59
6. $0.4\overline{12}$

The set of real numbers also includes *irrational numbers* (not rational). These numbers cannot be written in $\frac{a}{b}$ form. Irrational numbers include π (3.14159265...) and the square roots of numbers that are not perfect squares, such as $\sqrt{2}$ (1.41421356...). A *perfect square* is obtained by multiplying a number by itself. The square roots of perfect squares are rational. For instance, 49 is a perfect square, since $7 \cdot 7 = 49$. $\sqrt{49} = 7$, which is rational. Nonterminating, nonrepeating decimals are irrational numbers. For example, the number 0.12122122212222... is irrational.

The sets of rational and irrational numbers are disjoint. There is no rational number that is also irrational. The union of these two disjoint sets forms the set of real numbers, $\mathbb{R}$. This union is symbolized as $\mathbb{R} = \mathbb{Q} \cup$ Irrationals.

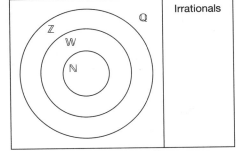

The Venn diagram to the right illustrates the relationship of the real numbers and their subsets.

The left side represents the set of rational numbers, and the right side represents the set of irrational numbers. The two sides, then, represent disjoint sets. The rectangle formed by joining the two sides is the union of the two sets formed by the sides, which is the set of real numbers.

Real numbers $\mathbb{R}$

Example 1   On the Venn diagram representing the real number system, place the given numbers within the innermost set to which they belong.

$$15, -\frac{5}{9}, -41, \sqrt{5}, 0.\overline{72}, 0, \sqrt{16}, \pi$$

Answer

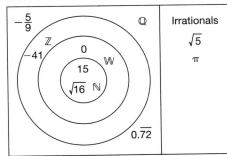

Real numbers $\mathbb{R}$

Skill Check 2

Copy the Venn diagram representing the real number system; then place the given numbers within the innermost set to which they belong.

1. $\frac{2}{9}$ 2. $\sqrt{15}$ 3. -99

4. $-\sqrt{16}$ 5. $\frac{24}{8}$ 6. $0.\overline{6}$

The properties of integers presented in Chapter 2 extend to the set of real numbers. Review the properties as listed in the tables below.

Property of Addition	Description	Example
Commutative $a + b = b + a$	Changing the order of the addends does not change the sum.	$-4 + 7 = 7 + (-4)$
Associative $(a + b) + c = a + (b + c)$	Changing the grouping of the addends does not change the sum.	$(5 + 4) + \frac{3}{4} = 5 + \left(4 + \frac{3}{4} \right)$
Identity $a + 0 = 0 + a = a$	Adding a zero does not change the number.	$\sqrt{7} + 0 = 0 + \sqrt{7} = \sqrt{7}$
Inverse $a + (-a) = -a + a = 0$	The sum of a number and its opposite is zero.	$\frac{6}{13} + \left(-\frac{6}{13} \right) = -\frac{6}{13} + \frac{6}{13} = 0$

Property of Multiplication	Description	Example
Commutative $ab = ba$	Changing the order of the factors does not change the product.	$4.3 \times 13.1 = 13.1 \times 4.3$
Associative $(ab)c = a(bc)$	Changing the grouping of the factors does not change the product.	$(-8 \times 6) \times (-3) = -8 \times [6 \times (-3)]$
Identity $a \times 1 = 1 \times a = a$	Multiplying by one does not change the number.	$\frac{9}{16} \times 1 = 1 \times \frac{9}{16} = \frac{9}{16}$
Zero $a \times 0 = 0 \times a = 0$	The product of zero and any number is zero.	$\sqrt{3} \times 0 = 0 \times \sqrt{3} = 0$

For the set of real numbers, multiplication also has an inverse property. The identity element for multiplication is one. The product of a number n and $\frac{1}{n}$ equals the identity element, one.

$$n \times \frac{1}{n} = 1$$

Therefore, $\frac{1}{n}$ is the *multiplicative inverse*, or *reciprocal*, of n.

> **Definition**
>
> Two nonzero numbers are **reciprocals**, or **multiplicative inverses**, of one another if their product is one.

> **Inverse Property of Multiplication**
>
> For any number $a \neq 0$, $a\left(\dfrac{1}{a}\right) = \dfrac{1}{a}(a) = 1$.

Recall that $\dfrac{1}{a} = a^{-1}$.

Example 2 Name the properties illustrated by each of the following.

a. $15.3(8 - 8) = 0$

b. $-\frac{1}{2}\left[\frac{1}{3}\left(-\frac{2}{5}\right)\right] = \left(-\frac{1}{2} \times \frac{1}{3}\right)\left(-\frac{2}{5}\right)$

c. $-\sqrt{17} + \sqrt{17} = 0$

d. $\frac{2}{7}\left(\frac{7}{2}\right) = 1$

Answer

a. $15.3(8 - 8) = 0$ — Inverse Property of Addition ($8 - 8 = 0$) and Zero Property of Multiplication (Zero times any number equals zero.)

b. $-\frac{1}{2}\left[\frac{1}{3}\left(-\frac{2}{5}\right)\right] = \left(-\frac{1}{2} \times \frac{1}{3}\right)\left(-\frac{2}{5}\right)$ — Associative Property of Multiplication (The factors were regrouped.)

c. $-\sqrt{17} + \sqrt{17} = 0$ — Inverse Property of Addition (The sum of a number and its opposite is zero.)

d. $\frac{2}{7}\left(\frac{7}{2}\right) = 1$ — Inverse Property of Multiplication (If the product of two numbers is one, they are multiplicative inverses.)

Skill Check 3

Name the property illustrated by each of the following.

1. $3 + \sqrt{5} = \sqrt{5} + 3$

2. $-3 \cdot 1 = -3$

3. $-\frac{2}{3} + \frac{2}{3} = 0$

4. $4.7 \times 0 = 0$

5. $\frac{2}{3} + \left(\frac{5}{6} + 4\right) = \left(\frac{2}{3} + \frac{5}{6}\right) + 4$

6. $2.5(0.4) = 1$

■ A. Exercises

True or false

1. Every natural number is an integer.

2. Every integer is a rational number.

3. There exists a whole number that is not a natural number.

4. Every square root is irrational.

5. Zero is neither rational nor irrational.

6. If a number is rational, then it is a real number.

7. Every real number is an integer.

8. A rational number is the ratio of any two integers.

9. $\sqrt{7}$ is an example of an irrational number.

10. $0 \cdot \sqrt{3}$ is a whole number.

Classify the following numbers as natural, whole, integer, rational, or irrational. Give the most specific set.

11. 2.56

12. $-\sqrt{100}$

13. 0

14. π

15. -3

16. $\sqrt{7}$

17. $5.2\overline{3}$

18. $-\frac{2}{3}$

19. 3.24

20. $\sqrt{8}$

21. 6

22. $\frac{4}{5}$

23. $0.5656656665\ldots$

■ B. Exercises

24. Copy the Venn diagram representing the real number system; then place the numbers in exercises 11–23 within the correct set.

Name the property of real numbers illustrated by each of the following.

25. $\sqrt{2} + \frac{1}{3} = \frac{1}{3} + \sqrt{2}$

26. $-5\left(2\sqrt{3}\right) = [-5(2)]\sqrt{3}$

27. $-\frac{5}{2}\left(3 + \sqrt{5}\right) = -\frac{15}{2} - \frac{5}{2}\sqrt{5}$

28. $1\left(-\frac{2}{3}\right) = -\frac{2}{3}$

29. $5\pi + 0 = 5\pi$

30. $7\left(\frac{1}{7}\right) = 1$

31. $-\sqrt{7} + \sqrt{7} = 0$

32. $\left(\frac{1}{2} + \sqrt{11}\right) + (-4) = \frac{1}{2} + [\sqrt{11} + (-4)]$

33. $\frac{2}{3}\left(\frac{4}{5}\right) = \frac{4}{5}\left(\frac{2}{3}\right)$

34. $\left(\sqrt{2} + \sqrt{3}\right) + \sqrt{5} = \sqrt{5} + \left(\sqrt{2} + \sqrt{3}\right)$

35. $\frac{-2}{3} \cdot \frac{3}{-2} = 1$

36. $8 \cdot 0 = 0 \cdot 8$

37. $-4 + 4 = 0$

■ C. Exercises

38. Write a word problem that would be impossible to solve if the whole numbers were the only set of numbers that you had available to use.

39. Can you always find a rational number between any two given rational numbers? Give an example. How many rational numbers are there?

CUMULATIVE REVIEW

Solve. [3.7]

40. $-7y + 9 < -19$

41. $6x - 12 > -24$

42. $23x \leq 40.25$

43. $-5(x - 6) > -60$

44. $0.5x + 9.5 \geq 13$

Write which of the following numbers are factors of the given number: 2, 3, 4, 5, 6, 8, 9, 10, or none. [4.1]

45. 918

46. 1,560

47. 368

48. 91

49. 90

MIND OVER MATH

The head of a dog is 5 in. long. The tail is as long as the head plus $\frac{1}{16}$ the length of the body. The body is as long as the head and the tail together. What is the total distance from the tip of the dog's nose to the tip of its tail?

MATH
& SCRIPTURE

Mathematics and the Priests

Through the Mosaic law God gave the priests very specific instructions for both their work and the religious duties of the people, as well as for practical everyday matters. Many of these word-for-word instructions required the use of mathematics, especially the arithmetic of fractions.

In Exodus 16 we are introduced to the *omer* and the *ephah*, which are units of dry measure for volume.

God gave the law to Moses at Mt. Sinai.

1. According to Exodus 16:15–16, how was an omer defined?

2. According to Exodus 16:36, how much was an ephah?

3. According to Ezekiel 45:11, what are two other measures of volume, and how are they related to an ephah?

4. If an omer is approximately 2 dry qt., or 2.2 L, state the customary and SI equivalents for the other three measures.

In Leviticus we find some ways the priests used the arithmetic of fractions.

5. If a poor Israelite could not afford two birds as a sin offering, he could offer fine flour. How much flour was required (Lev. 5:11)?

6. If an Israelite committed a trespass and sinned through ignorance in regard to the holy things, he could bring a ram and make restitution by adding what part of the value of the offering in silver (Lev. 5:15–16)?

7. If an Israelite had deceived or cheated a neighbor concerning some goods, he was to return the goods to his neighbor plus an additional part of those goods. How much was he to add (Lev. 6:2–5)?

8. How much fine flour were Aaron and his sons to offer regularly each morning and each night for a grain offering? How many omers was this (Lev. 6:20)?

9. If someone mistakenly ate of the priest's food, which was considered a holy thing, that person would add what part to it before making restitution to the priest (Lev. 22:14)?

10. If someone wanted to redeem (buy back) anything he had tithed, he would add what part in addition to its value (Lev. 27:31)?

11. The Israelites counted their flocks by having them pass under a rod. Once the flock was counted, what part was to be set apart as holy unto the Lord (Lev. 27:32)?

Infinite Truths

And concerning the tithe of the herd, or of the flock, even of whatsoever passeth under the rod, the tenth shall be holy unto the Lord. *Leviticus 27:32*

Chapter 5 Review

Vocabulary

cross multiplication	Property of Proportions	rational number
equivalent fractions	proportion	real number
Inverse Property of Multiplication	rate	reciprocal
lowest terms	ratio	unit rate
multiplicative inverse		

Rename each fraction in lowest terms.

1. $\dfrac{12}{18}$

2. $\dfrac{105}{270}$

Rename each mixed number as an improper fraction.

3. $-5\dfrac{3}{5}$

4. $2\dfrac{6}{11}$

Rename each improper fraction as a mixed number.

5. $\dfrac{19}{8}$

6. $\dfrac{-25}{4}$

Evaluate the following expressions when $x = -4$, $y = 3$, and $z = 7$.

7. $\dfrac{3x}{z}$

8. $\dfrac{yz}{5x}$

Compare the given fractions, using <, =, or >.

9. $\dfrac{5}{9} \square \dfrac{8}{11}$

10. $\dfrac{-9}{4} \square \dfrac{-7}{3}$

11. $\dfrac{-3}{10} \square \dfrac{-2}{7}$

12. $\dfrac{8}{15} \square \dfrac{7}{13}$

13. Graph the following rational numbers on a single number line; then order them from least to greatest using the < symbol: $\dfrac{5}{7}$, $\dfrac{2}{3}$, $\dfrac{7}{9}$, and $\dfrac{4}{5}$.

Find three equivalent fractions for each.

14. $\dfrac{-5}{7}$

15. $\dfrac{9}{2}$

Convert the following fractions to decimals.

16. $\dfrac{2}{5}$

17. $\dfrac{5}{8}$

18. $\dfrac{15}{8}$

19. $\dfrac{7}{3}$

20. $\dfrac{11}{12}$

21. $\dfrac{9}{16}$

Convert the following decimals to fractions or mixed numbers in lowest terms.

22. 0.52

23. −4.16

24. $-6.\overline{6}$

If there are 26 brown, 28 yellow, 26 red, 48 blue, 40 tan, and 32 green marbles in a bag, find the following ratios in lowest terms.

25. red to blue

26. green to brown

27. red to brown

28. A bag of grass seed blend contains 58 lb. of Kentucky bluegrass and 42 lb. of fine fescue. What is the ratio of bluegrass to fescue?

29. Twenty-four teachers teach six hundred students at Faith Christian Academy. What is the student-to-teacher ratio in this school?

30. Mrs. Benton graded an English test that she gave to her eighth-grade class. The results were 3 As, 8 Bs, 12 Cs, 2 Ds, and 2 Fs. What is the ratio of Bs to Ds in this class? As to Cs?

Find the unit rate.

31. 450 mi. on 15 gal.

32. $69 for 6 hr.

33. 240 calories in 5 oz.

34. $1.80 for 12 rolls

35. What are the extremes and the means in the proportion $\dfrac{m}{n} = \dfrac{x}{y}$?

Solve the following proportions.

36. $\dfrac{x}{9} = \dfrac{4}{15}$

37. $\dfrac{8}{a} = \dfrac{12}{33}$

38. $\dfrac{22}{9} = \dfrac{y}{3}$

39. $\dfrac{5}{7} = \dfrac{18}{z}$

40. $\dfrac{-5}{3} = \dfrac{x}{9}$

41. $\dfrac{3x}{7} = \dfrac{4}{5}$

42. Will makes three out of every five free throws he attempts. If he shot 65 free throws during the season, how many did he make?

43. A cookie recipe that makes three dozen cookies calls for 2 cups of flour. How many cups of flour will be needed to make only two dozen cookies?

Classify the following numbers as natural, whole, integer, rational, or irrational. Give the most specific set.

44. $\sqrt{5}$

45. -18

46. $\dfrac{5}{9}$

47. 29

Name the property of real numbers illustrated by each of the following.

48. $6 \cdot \dfrac{1}{6} = 1$

49. $-9(x + 2) = -9x - 18$

50. State the mathematical significance of Leviticus 27:32.

6 OPERATIONS ON RATIONAL NUMBERS

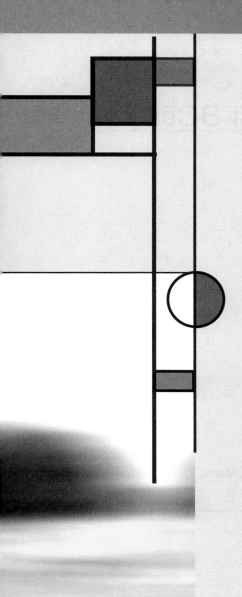

The African cheetah is capable of extremely fast bursts of speed for short periods of time, often maintaining a speed of 70 mi./hr. for several hundred yards. The pronghorn antelope of North America is by far the fastest animal on its continent, capable of maintaining speeds of 60 mi./hr. for a distance of about 2 mi. The special way God made the antelope allows it to run very fast for a long time, averaging 35 mi./hr. for 20–25 mi.

No animal running on the ground can match the speed of birds flying in the air. The fastest birds fly at over 100 mi./hr. The peregrine falcon regularly flies up to 60 mi./hr., but in a dive for prey it could get close to 200 mi./hr. Some species of swifts have been timed at 170 mi./hr. for short periods of time. The homing pigeon has been recorded at average speeds of 90 mi./hr. for 80 mi. All of these fast creatures have been designed by the Creator with special wings or legs, lungs that have extra capacity, and even blood that has more hemoglobin to carry more oxygen.

The fastest human runners, on the other hand, can manage just about 25 mi./hr. for a few seconds. In the 1996 Olympics, Michael Johnson ran the 200 m event in 19.3 sec. His average speed was 10.352 m/sec., or 23.1 mi./hr. In 1963 Bob Hayes managed to run 27.9 mi./hr. for 1.1 sec. in the course of a 100 yd. dash, but his average speed for the race was only 22.5 mi./hr. The numbers used to time runners in track events are rational numbers, the kind of numbers you will be studying in this chapter.

After this chapter you should be able to

1. add, subtract, multiply, and divide common fractions, mixed numbers, and decimals.

2. evaluate and simplify algebraic expressions.

3. use the properties of equality to solve equations containing rational numbers.

4. write equations from word problems and solve them.

5. convert numbers to scientific notation and add, subtract, multiply, or divide them.

6.1 Addition and Subtraction

The rectangles below illustrate the addition of rational numbers with like denominators.

$$\frac{1}{5} \quad + \quad \frac{3}{5} \quad = \quad \frac{4}{5}$$

The general procedure for adding and subtracting rational numbers with like denominators is stated below for all integers a, b, and c, where $c \neq 0$.

$$\frac{a}{c} + \frac{b}{c} = \frac{a+b}{c} \qquad \frac{a}{c} - \frac{b}{c} = \frac{a-b}{c}$$

Adding and Subtracting with Like Denominators
1. Add or subtract the numerators.
2. Write the sum or difference over the like denominator.
3. If necessary, rename the answer in lowest terms.
4. Improper fractions in a sum or difference can be renamed as mixed numbers.

Example 1

Add or subtract as indicated.

a. $\frac{4}{9} + \frac{7}{9}$

b. $\frac{11}{12} - \frac{3}{12}$

Answer

a. $\frac{4}{9} + \frac{7}{9} = \frac{4+7}{9}$

1. Add the numerators and place the sum over the like denominator.

$= \frac{11}{9}$

$= 1\frac{2}{9}$

2. Change the improper fraction to a mixed number.

b. $\frac{11}{12} - \frac{3}{12} = \frac{11-3}{12}$

1. Subtract the numerators and place the difference over the like denominator.

$= \frac{8}{12}$

$= \frac{2}{3}$

2. Reduce the fraction to lowest terms. Cancel the common factor of 4 from both the numerator and the denominator.

Skill Check 1

Use the diagrams to find the sum or difference. Rename answers in lowest terms.

1.

2.

Add or subtract. If necessary, rename in lowest terms.

3. $\frac{2}{7} + \frac{3}{7}$

4. $\frac{8}{9} - \frac{2}{9}$

5. $\frac{2}{15} + \frac{8}{15}$

6. $\frac{11}{12} - \frac{7}{12}$

To add or subtract fractions with unlike denominators, you first rename the fractions with a common denominator. The smallest common denominator is the least common multiple (LCM) of the denominators.

Adding and Subtracting with Unlike Denominators
1. Find the LCM of the denominators.
2. Rename the fractions as equivalent fractions using the LCM as the new denominator.
3. Add or subtract the fractions with like denominators.
4. If necessary, rename the answer in lowest terms or as a mixed number.

Example 2 Add $\frac{5}{8} + \frac{2}{3}$.

Answer

$8 = 2^3$ 1. Find the LCM of the denominators.

$3 = 3$

$LCM = 2^3 \cdot 3 = 24$

$\frac{5}{8} + \frac{2}{3} = \frac{5}{8}\left(\frac{3}{3}\right) + \frac{2}{3}\left(\frac{8}{8}\right)$ 2. Rename the fractions with the LCM as the denominators. Multiply $\frac{5}{8}$ by 1 in the form of $\frac{3}{3}$ and multiply $\frac{2}{3}$ by 1 in the form of $\frac{8}{8}$. Add the numerators, keeping the common denominator.

$= \frac{15}{24} + \frac{16}{24}$

$= \frac{31}{24}$

$= 1\frac{7}{24}$ 3. Express the improper fraction as a mixed number.

Example 3 Subtract $\frac{7}{10} - \frac{4}{15}$.

Answer

$10 = 2 \cdot 5$ 1. Find the LCM of the denominators.

$15 = 3 \cdot 5$

$LCM = 2 \cdot 3 \cdot 5 = 30$

$\frac{7}{10} - \frac{4}{15} = \frac{7}{10}\left(\frac{3}{3}\right) - \frac{4}{15}\left(\frac{2}{2}\right)$ 2. Rename the fractions with denominators of 30 and subtract.

$= \frac{21}{30} - \frac{8}{30}$

$= \frac{13}{30}$

Rational numbers can be negative as well as positive. A negative fraction can be expressed with the negative sign in front of the fraction or with the negative sign in the numerator or denominator.

$$-\frac{5}{6} = \frac{-5}{6} = \frac{5}{-6}$$

All three forms are equivalent. The form with the negative sign in the numerator is most useful for adding or subtracting rational numbers.

The rules for performing operations on rational numbers are the same as those used with integers.

1. The sum of two positive numbers is positive, and the sum of two negative numbers is negative.
2. To find the sum of two rational numbers with different signs, take the difference of their absolute values. The answer takes the sign of the rational number with the larger absolute value.
3. Subtract rational numbers by adding the opposite of the subtrahend.

Example 4   Add $-\frac{5}{8} + \frac{1}{5}$.

Answer

$8 = 2^3$

$5 = 5$

$LCM = 2^3 \cdot 5 = 40$

$-\frac{5}{8} + \frac{1}{5} = \frac{-5}{8}\left(\frac{5}{5}\right) + \frac{1}{5}\left(\frac{8}{8}\right)$

$\qquad = \frac{-25}{40} + \frac{8}{40}$

$\qquad = \frac{-25 + 8}{40}$

$\qquad = \frac{-17}{40}$

$\qquad = -\frac{17}{40}$

1. Find the LCM of the denominators.

2. Rename the fractions with the common denominator. Notice that $-\frac{5}{8}$ was changed to $\frac{-5}{8}$.

3. Add the numerators and place the sum over the common denominator.

4. Rename as a negative fraction.

Example 5   Subtract $-\frac{2}{3} - \frac{1}{9}$.

Answer

$3 = 3$

$9 = 3^2$

$LCM = 3^2 = 9$

$-\frac{2}{3} - \frac{1}{9} = \frac{-2}{3}\left(\frac{3}{3}\right) - \frac{1}{9}$

$\qquad = \frac{-6}{9} + \frac{-1}{9}$

$\qquad = \frac{-6 + (-1)}{9}$

$\qquad = \frac{-7}{9}$

$\qquad = -\frac{7}{9}$

1. Find the LCM of the denominators.

2. Rename the first fraction so that it has the common denominator. Notice that the negative sign was moved to the numerator.

3. Subtract by adding the opposite.

4. Add the numerators and place the sum over the common denominator.

5. Rename as a negative fraction.

Example 6   Add $-\frac{11}{12} + \frac{3}{4}$.

Answer

$12 = 3 \times 4$

$-\frac{11}{12} + \frac{3}{4} = \frac{-11}{12} + \frac{3}{4}\left(\frac{3}{3}\right)$

$\qquad = \frac{-11}{12} + \frac{9}{12}$

$\qquad = \frac{-11 + 9}{12}$

$\qquad = \frac{-2}{12}$

$\qquad = \frac{-1}{6}$

$\qquad = -\frac{1}{6}$

1. Find the LCM of the denominators. Since 12 is a multiple of 4, the LCM of 4 and 12 is 12.

2. Rename the second fraction so that it has the common denominator. Notice that the negative sign was moved to the numerator in the first fraction.

3. Add the numerators and place the sum over the common denominator.

4. Reduce the fraction by dividing the numerator and denominator by 2.

5. Rename as a negative fraction.

Add or subtract as indicated.

1. $\dfrac{7}{12} + \dfrac{2}{3}$ 2. $\dfrac{8}{15} - \dfrac{3}{5}$ 3. $-\dfrac{3}{4} - \dfrac{1}{6} + \dfrac{1}{3}$ 4. $\dfrac{9}{10} + \left(-\dfrac{7}{8}\right)$

To add mixed numbers, add the integer parts and then add the fraction parts. If necessary, simplify the result. If the sum contains an improper fraction, change it to its mixed number equivalent and add it to the integer part of the sum.

Example 7   Add $1\dfrac{5}{6} + 4\dfrac{4}{9}$.

Answer

$1\dfrac{5}{6} = 1\dfrac{15}{18}$ and $4\dfrac{4}{9} = 4\dfrac{8}{18}$

1. The LCM of the denominators is 18. Change the fraction parts to have the common denominator.

$$1\dfrac{15}{18}$$
$$+\,4\dfrac{8}{18}$$
$$\overline{5\dfrac{23}{18}} = 5 + 1\dfrac{5}{18} = 6\dfrac{5}{18}$$

2. Add the integers; then add the fractions. Be sure to simplify the mixed number.

To subtract mixed numbers, subtract the fraction parts and then subtract the integer parts. If the fraction in the minuend is less than the fraction in the subtrahend, rename one from the integer part of the minuend as a fraction. Add it to the fraction part.

Example 8   Subtract $5\dfrac{1}{4} - 2\dfrac{3}{8}$.

Answer

$5\dfrac{1}{4} = 5\dfrac{2}{8}$

1. Use the LCM for a common denominator.

$5\dfrac{2}{8} = 4\dfrac{8}{8} + \dfrac{2}{8} = 4\dfrac{10}{8}$

2. After the first number is renamed with the common denominator, its numerator is smaller than that of the fraction in the subtrahend. Rename one from the 5 as $\dfrac{8}{8}$ and add it to the $\dfrac{2}{8}$.

$$4\dfrac{10}{8}$$
$$-\,2\dfrac{3}{8}$$
$$\overline{2\dfrac{7}{8}}$$

3. Subtract the fractions; then subtract the integers.

Recall that both terminating and repeating decimals are rational numbers. The following examples show addition and subtraction with decimals. Remember that adding and subtracting decimals requires the alignment of the decimal point.

Example 9   Add or subtract as indicated.

a. $42.678 + 8.34 + 127.6$ b. $-0.25 - 0.375$ c. $13 - 8.4$

Answer

a.
$$\begin{array}{r} \overset{1\ 1\ 1}{42.678} \\ 8.34 \\ +\ 127.6 \\ \hline 178.618 \end{array}$$

b.
$$\begin{array}{r} \overset{1}{-0.25} \\ +\ -0.375 \\ \hline -0.625 \end{array}$$

c.
$$\begin{array}{r} \overset{2\ 10}{1\cancel{3}.0} \\ -\ 8.4 \\ \hline 4.6 \end{array}$$

Add or subtract as indicated.

1. $5\frac{4}{9} + \left(-2\frac{1}{3}\right)$ 2. $(8.95 + 17.4) - 13.465$

3. $12\frac{3}{8} - 5\frac{4}{5}$ 4. $-5.23 + 14.6$

■ A. Exercises

Add or subtract as indicated.

1. $\frac{1}{5} + \frac{2}{5}$ 2. $\frac{3}{8} + \frac{1}{8}$ 3. $\frac{5}{10} + \frac{3}{10}$ 4. $\frac{7}{15} - \frac{4}{15}$

5. $\frac{8}{9} - \frac{4}{9}$ 6. $\frac{11}{13} + \frac{2}{13}$ 7. $\frac{6}{5} + \frac{2}{5}$ 8. $\frac{1}{2} + \frac{1}{8}$

9. $\frac{3}{8} + \frac{1}{6}$ 10. $\frac{1}{12} + \frac{2}{3}$ 11. $\frac{1}{6} - \frac{3}{4}$ 12. $5\frac{1}{2} + 2\frac{1}{4}$

13. $9\frac{3}{10} + 4\frac{1}{2}$ 14. $7\frac{5}{6} - 2\frac{1}{2}$ 15. $7 - 3\frac{1}{3}$ 16. $3.04 + 2.881$

17. $14.9 - 6.18$ 18. $8.19 - 0.042$ 19. $73.24 + 12.623$

■ B. Exercises

Perform the indicated operations.

20. $19.63 - 200.8$ 21. $-4.22 + 80.2$ 22. $-5.28 - 9.97$

23. $2.35 - (-5.81)$ 24. $-7.13 - (-4.7)$ 25. $\frac{1}{2} + \frac{3}{4} + \frac{7}{8}$

26. $\frac{3}{5} + \frac{1}{2} + \frac{3}{4}$ 27. $\frac{5}{6} + \frac{3}{8} - \frac{1}{4}$ 28. $\frac{7}{8} - \frac{2}{5} - \frac{1}{4}$

29. $12\frac{1}{3} - 5\frac{3}{4} - 4\frac{1}{2}$ 30. $14 - 7\frac{5}{6} + 5\frac{2}{3}$ 31. $6\frac{3}{4} + \left(8\frac{3}{10} - 4\frac{1}{2}\right)$

32. $28 - \left(13\frac{3}{10} + 6\frac{3}{4}\right)$

■ C. Exercises

33. Jill spent $\frac{5}{6}$ hr. studying math and $\frac{3}{4}$ hr. studying science. How much time did she spend studying altogether?

34. On Wednesday the rainfall was $1\frac{7}{8}$ in. On Friday the rainfall was $\frac{1}{4}$ in. How much more did it rain on Wednesday?

35. If the temperature is 2.5°C and drops 3.4°C, what is the new temperature?

■ Dominion thru Math

36. The maximum speed of a horse is about 10 km/hr. less than twice the maximum speed of a man. If the maximum speed of a man is about 37 km/hr., what is the maximum speed of a horse?

37. The maximum speed of a lion is about one and one-third times as fast as a horse. Use your answer to exercise 36 to find the maximum speed of a lion.

38. A sparrow can fly $\frac{7}{12}$ the speed of a duck, and a crow can fly $\frac{2}{3}$ the speed of a duck. The speeds of the sparrow and crow combined would be 15 mi./hr. faster than the duck. What are the flying speeds of the three birds?

39. A pigeon flies twice as fast as a starling, and a starling flies 2.25 times as fast as a blue jay. A pigeon flies how many times as fast as a blue jay?

40. A jackrabbit can run 42 mi./hr. for 5 min., and then it must slow to 20 mi./hr. for the next 30 min. After 35 min. it must stop to rest. A coyote can run 36 mi./hr. for up to 20 min. How long will it take the coyote to overtake the rabbit? Assume they run the same path. (Hint: First find the distance the rabbit is ahead after 5 min.)

CUMULATIVE REVIEW

Estimate the sum or difference by rounding each fraction to the nearest whole number. [2.7]

41. $3\frac{5}{6} + 4\frac{3}{8}$

42. $8\frac{15}{22} + 6\frac{5}{11}$

43. $7\frac{2}{5} + 11\frac{3}{8}$

44. $6\frac{2}{3} - 8\frac{1}{5}$

45. $12\frac{8}{15} - 4\frac{3}{5}$

Specify what the variable stands for, write an equation, and solve. [3.5]

46. Jesse bought 2 gal. of milk costing $3.15 each and seven pumpkin muffins for a total bill of $12.53. How much did he pay for each muffin?

47. Hannah and Jen eat out at the pizza buffet. They each buy a buffet meal and a drink that costs $1.42, and their total bill is $14.74 before tax. What is the price of an individual pizza buffet dinner?

48. A craft project requires four skeins of yarn and $8.16 worth of notions. If the total bill is $18.88, how much does each skein of yarn cost?

49. Peter can spend no more than $175 for soccer equipment. If he buys new cleats for $129 and a new pair of shin guards for $30.50, how many pairs of socks can he buy? The cost of a pair of socks that he likes is $2.42.

50. Cassie makes $13/hr. for baby-sitting the three Gonzales children and $7/hr. for other work for the family such as housecleaning. If she baby-sits for 15 hr., how many hours will she need to do other work to make a total of $272?

6.2 Multiplication

The figure below models the fact that $\frac{1}{3}$ of $\frac{1}{2}$ equals $\frac{1}{6}$.

$\frac{1}{2}$ shaded $\quad$ $\frac{1}{3}$ of $\frac{1}{2}$ shaded $\quad$ $\frac{1}{6}$ shaded

Observe that the result is equal to the product found by multiplying the numerators and denominators of these two fractions.

$$\frac{1}{3} \times \frac{1}{2} = \frac{1 \times 1}{3 \times 2} = \frac{1}{6}$$

This illustrates the general rule for multiplying two rational numbers.

Multiplying Rational Numbers

To multiply two rational numbers, multiply the first numerator times the second numerator and the first denominator times the second denominator. Express the product in lowest terms.

For all rational numbers $\frac{a}{b}$ and $\frac{c}{d}$ $(b \neq 0, d \neq 0)$, $\frac{a}{b} \times \frac{c}{d} = \frac{a \times c}{b \times d}$.

Example 1 $\quad$ Multiply $\frac{4}{5} \times \frac{7}{9}$.

Answer

$\frac{4}{5} \times \frac{7}{9} = \frac{4 \times 7}{5 \times 9}$ $\qquad$ 1. Multiply the numerators and multiply the denominators.

$\qquad = \frac{28}{45}$ $\qquad$ 2. The fraction is in lowest terms.

Remember the rules for multiplying integers. The same rules apply to rational numbers.

1. If the factors have like signs (both positive or both negative), the product is positive.

2. If the factors have unlike signs, the product is negative.

Example 2 $\quad$ Multiply $-\frac{4}{7} \times \frac{2}{5}$.

Answer

$-\frac{4}{7} \times \frac{2}{5} = \frac{-4 \times 2}{7 \times 5}$ $\qquad$ 1. Multiply the numerators and multiply the denominators.

$\qquad = \frac{-8}{35}$ $\qquad$ 2. The product of a negative and positive factor is negative.

$\qquad = -\frac{8}{35}$ $\qquad$ 3. Rewrite the answer as a negative fraction.

Example 3 Evaluate $\left(\dfrac{2}{3}\right)^3$.

Answer

$$\left(\dfrac{2}{3}\right)^3 = \dfrac{2}{3} \times \dfrac{2}{3} \times \dfrac{2}{3}$$ 1. Express as a product of three identical factors.

$$= \dfrac{2 \times 2 \times 2}{3 \times 3 \times 3}$$ 2. Multiply the numerators and multiply the denominators.

$$= \dfrac{8}{27}$$

It is customary in algebra to accept improper fractions as answers rather than requiring that they be changed to mixed numbers. From this point on, give answers for computational practice problems in rational form. However, you will need to change answers for word problems to mixed numbers to help you understand the size of the answer.

Example 4 Evaluate each of the following.

a. $\left(-\dfrac{5}{3}\right)^2$ b. $\left(-\dfrac{5}{3}\right)^3$

Answer

a. $\left(-\dfrac{5}{3}\right)^2 = -\dfrac{5}{3}\left(-\dfrac{5}{3}\right)$ 1. Express as a product of two identical factors.

$$= \dfrac{-5(-5)}{3(3)}$$ 2. Multiply the numerators and multiply the denominators.

$$= \dfrac{25}{9}$$

b. $\left(-\dfrac{5}{3}\right)^3 = -\dfrac{5}{3}\left(-\dfrac{5}{3}\right)\left(-\dfrac{5}{3}\right)$ 1. Express as a product of three identical factors.

$$= \dfrac{25}{9}\left(-\dfrac{5}{3}\right)$$ 2. Multiply the numerators and denominators of the first two factors.

$$= -\dfrac{125}{27}$$ 3. Multiply the numerators and denominators of the result by the third factor.

Skill Check 1

Multiply.

1. $\dfrac{2}{3} \times \dfrac{5}{7}$

2. $-\dfrac{10}{3}\left(-\dfrac{2}{3}\right)$

3. $\dfrac{7}{11}\left(-\dfrac{3}{5}\right)$

4. $-\dfrac{3}{4}\left(\dfrac{3}{5}\right)\left(-\dfrac{7}{11}\right)$

5. $\left(\dfrac{5}{4}\right)^3$

6. $\left(-\dfrac{2}{7}\right)^3$

Canceling is simplifying the factors of a multiplication problem by dividing one of the numerators and one of the denominators by the same number. This is similar to reducing a fraction in which the numerator and denominator are parts of the same fraction. The result is division of the product by one. If the factors are canceled completely, the product will be in lowest terms. Failure to find all possible cancellations will result in having to reduce the product.

Note the product below.

$$\dfrac{3}{4} \times \dfrac{5}{9} = \dfrac{3 \times 5}{4 \times 9} = \dfrac{\cancel{3} \times 5}{4 \times 3 \times \cancel{3}} = \dfrac{5}{12}$$

The next example reworks the problem above by canceling before multiplying.

Example 5 Multiply $\frac{3}{4} \times \frac{5}{9}$.

Answer

$$\frac{3}{4} \times \frac{5}{9} = \frac{\overset{1}{\cancel{3}}}{4} \times \frac{5}{\underset{3}{\cancel{9}}}$$

1. The 3 in the numerator of the first fraction and the 9 in the denominator of the second fraction can be canceled. Divide both by 3.

$$= \frac{1 \times 5}{4 \times 3}$$

2. Multiply the new numerators and multiply the new denominators.

$$= \frac{5}{12}$$

Multiplying a series of rational numbers gives more opportunities to cancel and provides a better payoff in simplifying the work. All that is needed is to find one numerator and one denominator that contain a common factor.

Example 6 Multiply $-\frac{4}{9}\left(\frac{2}{5}\right)\left(-\frac{15}{16}\right)$.

Answer

$$\frac{-4}{9} \times \frac{2}{5} \times \frac{-15}{16} = \frac{\overset{-1}{\cancel{-4}}}{\underset{3}{\cancel{9}}} \times \frac{\overset{1}{\cancel{2}}}{\underset{1}{\cancel{5}}} \times \frac{\overset{-1}{\cancel{-15}}}{\underset{4}{\underset{2}{\cancel{16}}}}$$

1. Rewrite with negatives in the numerators. Cancel completely. The −4 and 16 are divided by 4; the 2 and 4 are divided by 2; the −15 and 5 are divided by 5; and, finally, the −3 and 9 are divided by 3.

$$= \frac{-1(1)(-1)}{3(1)(2)}$$

2. Multiply the numerators and multiply the denominators.

$$= \frac{1}{6}$$

3. Two negative factors in the numerator result in a positive product.

Whole numbers and mixed numbers should be expressed as improper fractions before being multiplied. For example, the whole number 9 is changed to $\frac{9}{1}$, and the mixed number $2\frac{1}{6}$ is changed to $\frac{13}{6}$ in the example below.

Example 7 Multiply $2\frac{1}{6} \times 9$.

Answer

$$2\frac{1}{6} \times 9 = \frac{13}{6} \times \frac{9}{1}$$

1. Express the mixed number and whole number as improper fractions.

$$= \frac{13}{\underset{2}{\cancel{6}}} \times \frac{\overset{3}{\cancel{9}}}{1}$$

2. Cancel by dividing the 6 and 9 by 3.

$$= \frac{13 \times 3}{2 \times 1}$$

3. Multiply the numerators and multiply the denominators.

$$= \frac{39}{2}$$

4. Leave the answer as an improper fraction.

Skill Check 2

Multiply. Write the products as rational numbers in lowest terms.

1. $\frac{1}{2} \times 4\frac{3}{5}$

2. $-\frac{2}{5} \times \frac{1}{6}$

3. $3\frac{3}{8} \times 1\frac{2}{3} \times 4$

4. $-\frac{8}{9} \times \left(-\frac{15}{16}\right) \times \frac{7}{25}$

Since terminating and repeating decimals are rational numbers, we will include multiplying decimals in this section. Decimals are multiplied like integers, though there are special rules for placing the decimal point in the product. If there are n decimal places in the first factor and m decimal places in the second factor, then there are $n + m$ decimal places in the product. This concept is explained by the following discussion.

Multiply 0.753×0.35.

Express each decimal as a fraction: $\dfrac{753}{1,000} \times \dfrac{35}{100}$.

Multiply the numerators and multiply the denominators.

$$\frac{753 \times 35}{1,000 \times 100} = \frac{26,355}{100,000}$$

Dividing by 100,000, or 10^5, requires moving the decimal point five places to the left, so there will be five digits after the decimal point in the product. Notice that five is the combined number of decimal places in the two factors, which is the usual way to determine the decimal placement.

$$0.753 \times 0.35 = 0.26355$$

Example 8   Multiply 0.0034×2.06.

Answer

$$\begin{array}{r} 2.06 \\ \times\ 0.0034 \\ \hline 824 \\ 618 \\ \hline 0.007004 \end{array}$$

1. Multiply the numbers without regard to the decimal point.

2. Add the decimal places in the factors: $2 + 4 = 6$ decimal places needed in the product. Annex two zeros and place them in front of the 7 before inserting the decimal point.

Skill Check 3

Multiply.

1. 0.45×2.1 2. -3.61×0.22 3. 0.014×0.05 4. $-2.6 \times (-11.453)$

■ A. Exercises

Multiply.

1. $\dfrac{1}{3} \times \dfrac{4}{7}$

2. $-\dfrac{4}{9} \times \dfrac{2}{3}$

3. $\dfrac{5}{6} \times \dfrac{1}{5}$

4. $\dfrac{4}{5} \cdot \left(-\dfrac{7}{12}\right)$

5. $\dfrac{2}{3} \times \dfrac{3}{8}$

6. $\dfrac{3}{10} \times 5$

7. $\dfrac{1}{2} \times 3\dfrac{5}{8}$

8. $1\dfrac{3}{4} \cdot (-4)$

9. $\dfrac{4}{5} \times 2\dfrac{1}{3}$

10. $1\dfrac{7}{8} \times 3\dfrac{2}{3}$

11. $4\dfrac{1}{5} \times 1\dfrac{2}{3}$

12. $2\dfrac{2}{3} \times 2\dfrac{3}{4}$

13. 7.5×0.9

14. $5.94(-8)$

15. 3.8×0.02

16. 0.96×0.43

17. 1.57×4.8

18. 32.4×27

19. -1.2×0.038

20. 0.063×52

21. 185.2×0.01

22. 63.78×0.09

23. 45.2×100

24. 328×0.46

■ B. Exercises

Perform the indicated operations.

25. $\dfrac{1}{2} \times \dfrac{3}{4} \times \dfrac{3}{8}$

26. $\dfrac{2}{3}\left(-\dfrac{3}{5}\right) \times \dfrac{1}{4}$

27. $\dfrac{3}{5} \times 12 \times 7\dfrac{1}{2}$

28. $3\dfrac{1}{8} \times 4 \times 2\dfrac{2}{5}$

29. $\left(\dfrac{5}{9}\right)^3$

30. $\left(-\dfrac{4}{7}\right)^3$

31. 0.09×1.005

32. 0.082×0.037

33. $6.2 \times 0.03 \times 8$

34. $-2.1(1.9 + 4.8)$

35. $4.2(7.6 - 6.7)$

36. $-2.5(3.7 - 9.07)$

37. $7.32(7.28)$

38. $3(-3.1)$

■ C. Exercises

Evaluate.

39. $\dfrac{1}{5}\left(\dfrac{3}{4}\right)^2\left(\dfrac{2}{3}\right)^4$

40. $\dfrac{8}{15}\left(\dfrac{3}{4} + \dfrac{1}{2}\right)^2$

41. $\left(\dfrac{5}{6} - \dfrac{3}{4}\right)\dfrac{8}{9}$

42. $\left(\dfrac{2}{5} - \dfrac{1}{3}\right)^2$

■ Dominion thru Math

Besides expressing the speeds of fast animals and birds, rational numbers can express a wide variety of other relationships in real-life problems. Measurements, rates, ratios, percents, and growth all have contexts where the fractional form of rational numbers is as useful as the decimal form.

43. The depreciation of an automobile expresses how much it declines in value over a period of time. The depreciation rate is the ratio of the amount of depreciation over a time interval to the value of the vehicle at the beginning of the interval. If a $20,000 automobile is valued at $12,800 after two years, what is the depreciation rate in dollars per year and as a percentage of the original price per year?

44. A cabinet maker is cutting drawer fronts from an oak board. Each drawer has a height that matches the width of the oak board. Each drawer front is $8\dfrac{3}{4}$ in. wide, and each saw cut uses up $\dfrac{1}{8}$ in. of the board. What is the minimum length of oak board needed for ten drawer fronts?

45. In exercise 44, how long is the piece of scrap lumber from making the ten drawer fronts if the oak board was 8 ft. long?

CUMULATIVE REVIEW

Find the LCM of each set of numbers. [4.4]

46. 6, 25

47. 45, 63

48. 24, 18, 6

49. 175, 10, 40

50. 165, 50, 99

Convert the following fractions to decimals. [5.3]

51. $\dfrac{9}{11}$

52. $\dfrac{3}{16}$

53. $-\dfrac{4}{15}$

54. $\dfrac{-18}{5}$

55. $\dfrac{5}{16}$

John Philip Sousa, Musician

John Philip Sousa was born in 1854 and lived until 1932. He showed great musical talent even as a boy growing up in Washington DC. By the age of thirteen, he was an accomplished musician who could sing and play the piano, the violin, and the flute.

In 1867 a traveling circus band offered the teenager a job as a musician. Although Sousa wanted to accept the offer, his father decided otherwise. Antonio Sousa made arrangements for his headstrong son to serve as an apprentice in the United States Marine Band instead.

Sousa stayed with the Marine Band for seven years. He left in 1874 to travel the country and play in theater orchestras. Just six years later, the twenty-six-year-old musician eagerly accepted an offer to return to Washington as conductor of the Marine Band. In 1892 Sousa left again to form his own musical group, the Sousa Band. For the next forty years, the Sousa Band played in big cities and small towns throughout the world.

As a composer, Sousa developed his own unique musical style. This style, noted for its mathematical rhythm and precision, became Sousa's hallmark throughout his life. A prolific composer, he wrote well over a hundred marches, seventy songs, fifteen operettas, and numerous other works.

Of all Sousa's compositions, the most well known and best loved were his marches. The stirring refrains of "El Capitan" and the "Washington Post March" echoed in concert halls throughout the country. The United States Marine Corps adopted "Semper Fidelis" as its official march.

Americans swelled with pride for their country whenever they heard the band begin to play "The Stars and Stripes Forever." This march proved to be Sousa's most popular composition. This flag-waving, patriotic march was composed on board a ship as Sousa returned from a tour of Europe. He once said, "Day after day as I walked, it persisted in crashing into my very soul." He considered this march, written on Christmas Day, 1896, as his gift to his country. And his country received it with open arms: audiences demanded that it be played at every performance of the Sousa Band.

His abilities extended beyond composing and conducting music. To improve the musical quality of his band for concert performances, Sousa suggested the design for a brass instrument similar to a tuba. The sousaphone, named for him by its first manufacturer, comprised a tube that snaked around the musician's body and ended in a large adjustable bell.

Sousa's reputation as America's March King flourished well into the twentieth century. He scorned retirement, saying that his retirement would not take place until his death. When death did call for the March King, it came as he would have wanted—immediately after a rehearsal of "The Stars and Stripes Forever."

Marches comprise a significant portion of a military band's repertoire.

6.3 Division

To divide rational numbers, you must be able to identify the reciprocal of the divisor. The divisor is the number you are dividing by. In the problem $a \div b$, b is the *divisor* and a is the *dividend*. Recall from Section 5.6 that multiplicative inverses (reciprocals) are numbers whose product is one.

To find the reciprocal of a rational number, interchange the numerator and the denominator. Doing so allows the terms to cancel when multiplied, resulting in a product of one.

$$\frac{\overset{1}{\cancel{a}}}{\underset{1}{\cancel{b}}} \times \frac{\overset{1}{\cancel{b}}}{\underset{1}{\cancel{a}}} = \frac{1 \times 1}{1 \times 1} = 1$$

If the rational number is an integer, place the integer in rational form with a denominator of one before writing the reciprocal. Change a mixed number to its equivalent improper fraction before finding the reciprocal.

Rational Number	Reciprocal (Multiplicative Inverse)	Product
$6 = \dfrac{6}{1}$	$\dfrac{1}{6}$	$\dfrac{6}{1} \times \dfrac{1}{6} = 1$
$\dfrac{2}{3}$	$\dfrac{3}{2}$	$\dfrac{2}{3} \times \dfrac{3}{2} = 1$
$-\dfrac{4}{9}$	$-\dfrac{9}{4}$	$-\dfrac{4}{9}\left(-\dfrac{9}{4}\right) = 1$
$4\dfrac{3}{5} = \dfrac{23}{5}$	$\dfrac{5}{23}$	$\dfrac{23}{5} \times \dfrac{5}{23} = 1$

Just as subtraction was defined as adding the opposite (or additive inverse), so division of rational numbers is defined as multiplying by the multiplicative inverse (or reciprocal).

Definition

The **division** of two numbers is the product of the dividend and the multiplicative inverse (reciprocal) of the divisor. In symbols, $a \div b = a \times \dfrac{1}{b}$ for any real numbers a and b, where $b \neq 0$.

Applying this definition to the division of integers, we see that $6 \div 2 = 6 \times \dfrac{1}{2} = 3$. Notice that $\dfrac{1}{2}$ is the multiplicative inverse of 2. Now consider the division of the rational numbers $\dfrac{2}{5}$ and $\dfrac{4}{9}$. The definition of division says that $\dfrac{2}{5} \div \dfrac{4}{9} = \dfrac{2}{5} \times \dfrac{9}{4}$. The steps on the next page show why these expressions must be equal.

$$\frac{2}{5} \div \frac{4}{9} = \frac{\frac{2}{5}}{\frac{4}{9}}$$ Division can be expressed as a fraction.

$$= \frac{\frac{2}{5} \times \frac{9}{4}}{\frac{4}{9} \times \frac{9}{4}}$$ Multiply by $\frac{9}{4} = 1$.

$$= \frac{\frac{2}{5} \times \frac{9}{4}}{\frac{\cancel{4}}{\cancel{9}} \times \frac{\cancel{9}}{\cancel{4}}}$$ Cancel in the denominator.

$$= \frac{\frac{2}{5} \times \frac{9}{4}}{1}$$

$$= \frac{2}{5} \times \frac{9}{4}$$ Remove the denominator of 1.

Example 1 Divide $\frac{3}{8}$ by $\frac{7}{16}$.

Answer

$$\frac{3}{8} \div \frac{7}{16} = \frac{3}{8} \times \frac{16}{7}$$ 1. Divide by multiplying by the reciprocal of the divisor.

$$= \frac{3}{\cancel{8}_1} \times \frac{\cancel{16}^2}{7}$$ 2. Cancel.

$$= \frac{3 \times 2}{1 \times 7}$$ 3. Multiply the numerators and multiply the denominators.

$$= \frac{6}{7}$$

Example 2 Divide $4\frac{7}{8}$ by -3.

Answer

$$4\frac{7}{8} \div (-3) = \frac{39}{8} \div \frac{-3}{1}$$ 1. Express the mixed number and integer as improper fractions.

$$= \frac{39}{8}\left(-\frac{1}{3}\right)$$ 2. Divide by multiplying by the reciprocal of the divisor.

$$= \frac{\cancel{39}^{13}}{8}\left(-\frac{1}{\cancel{3}_1}\right)$$ 3. Cancel.

$$= -\frac{13}{8}$$ 4. The product is negative because the factors have unlike signs. You can leave the answer as an improper fraction.

Skill Check 1

Divide.

1. $\frac{9}{15} \div 6$

2. $-3\frac{4}{7} \div \frac{5}{14}$

3. $4\frac{4}{5} \div 1\frac{1}{15}$

4. $-18 \div \left(-\frac{12}{25}\right)$

Dividing rational numbers in their decimal form is similar to dividing integers. However, you must be careful to place the decimal point at the correct place in the quotient. When the divisor is an integer, the decimal point is placed directly over the decimal point in the dividend.

| **Example 3** | Divide 51.5 by 25. |

Answer

$$
\begin{array}{r}
2.06 \\
25\overline{)51.50} \\
\underline{50} \\
150 \\
\underline{150} \\
0
\end{array}
$$

1. Place the decimal point in the quotient directly over the decimal point in the dividend.
2. Annex zeros and continue dividing until the remainder is zero or the digits repeat.

To divide rational numbers in which the divisor contains a decimal point, it is necessary to convert the divisor into an integer. This is done by multiplying by the power of ten required to move the decimal point to the right until the divisor becomes an integer. The dividend must be multiplied by the same amount. You are then actually multiplying by one in the form of $\dfrac{10^n}{10^n}$.

Suppose 68.4 is divided by 2.85. The divisor, 2.85, must be multiplied by 10^2 to move the decimal two places to the right to form the integer 285. Therefore, the dividend must be multiplied by the same power of ten.

$$
68.4 \div 2.85 = \frac{68.4}{2.85} = \frac{68.4 \times 10^2}{2.85 \times 10^2} = \frac{6{,}840}{285}
$$

| **Example 4** | Divide 7.3254 by 3.1. Round the answer to the nearest hundredth. |

Answer

$$
\frac{7.3254}{3.1} = \frac{7.3254 \times 10}{3.1 \times 10} = \frac{73.254}{31}
$$

$$
\begin{array}{r}
2.363 \\
31\overline{)73.254} \\
\underline{62} \\
112 \\
\underline{93} \\
195 \\
\underline{186} \\
94 \\
\underline{93} \\
1
\end{array}
$$

$7.3254 \div 3.1 \approx 2.36$

1. To change the divisor to an integer, multiply both the numerator and denominator by 10.
2. Divide, placing the decimal point directly above the decimal point in the dividend. Stop dividing after the thousandths place in order to round to the nearest hundredth.
3. Do not increase the digit in the hundredths place since it is followed by a 3.

When the dividend and divisor are both rational numbers, the quotient is also a rational number. This means the decimal quotient will either repeat or terminate. The decimal for the fraction $\dfrac{1}{7} = 0.\overline{142857}$. The repeating sequence is six digits long. This is because all the possible remainders, 1 through 6, occur before any appears a second time. When the same remainder occurs a second time, or matches the dividend, the quotient will repeat from that time on.

Example 5   Divide 39.15 by −7.25.

Answer

$$\frac{39.15}{7.25} = \frac{39.15 \times 100}{7.25 \times 100} = \frac{3,915}{725}$$

1. Ignore the negative sign until the long division is completed. Divide the absolute values. To change the divisor to an integer, multiply both the numerator and the denominator by 100.

$$\begin{array}{r} 5.4 \\ 725\overline{)3,915.0} \\ \underline{3\ 625} \\ 2900 \\ \underline{2900} \\ 0 \end{array}$$

2. Divide, placing the decimal point directly above the decimal point in the dividend.

$$39.15 \div (-7.25) = -5.4$$

3. Recall that the divisor was a negative number. A positive number divided by a negative number is negative.

Skill Check 2

Divide.

1. $89.65 \div 5.5$

2. $24.89 \div 4.125$

3. $0.25 \div 0.6$

4. $-9.345 \div 1.5$

■ A. Exercises

Divide.

1. $\frac{1}{2} \div \frac{2}{3}$

2. $\frac{1}{4} \div \frac{5}{8}$

3. $\frac{2}{3} \div \frac{2}{3}$

4. $5 \div \left(-\frac{1}{4}\right)$

5. $\frac{3}{8} \div \frac{5}{8}$

6. $\frac{2}{3} \div \frac{1}{2}$

7. $25 \div 8\frac{1}{3}$

8. $3\frac{2}{3} \div 1\frac{1}{2}$

9. $6\frac{1}{2} \div 1\frac{1}{6}$

10. $6\frac{7}{8} \div 1\frac{5}{6}$

11. $-2 \div \left(-2\frac{1}{4}\right)$

12. $4\frac{2}{3} \div 1\frac{7}{9}$

■ B. Exercises

Divide.

13. $47.2 \div 8$

14. $17.28 \div 4$

15. $16.32 \div 17$

16. $38.75 \div 31$

17. $0.192 \div 0.3$

18. $76.2 \div 0.06$

19. $0.378 \div (-1.4)$

20. $21.42 \div 0.63$

21. $0.225 \div 7.5$

22. $14.31 \div (-2.7)$

23. $-2.664 \div 3.6$

24. $27.37 \div 1.19$

Perform the indicated operations.

25. $\frac{3}{4} \div \left(\frac{1}{2} \div \frac{1}{4}\right)$

26. $\left(\frac{2}{3} \div \frac{5}{6}\right) \div \frac{1}{5}$

27. $10 \div \left(\frac{2}{3} \div \frac{1}{2}\right)$

28. $\left(\frac{9}{10} \div 3\right) \div \frac{2}{3}$

29. $\left(\frac{3}{5} \div \frac{4}{5}\right) \times \left(-\frac{2}{7}\right)$

30. $\frac{7}{8} \div \left(\frac{3}{4} \times 2\frac{1}{2}\right)$

31. $\frac{2}{3} \div \left(-\frac{3}{7} + \frac{4}{7}\right)$

32. $4\frac{2}{5} \div 3\frac{8}{15}$

Divide and round to the nearest hundredth.

33. $0.032 \div 0.07$

34. $-2.48 \div 0.9$

35. $0.675 \div 0.23$

36. $13.9 \div 0.8$

37. $7.47 \div 0.35$

38. $0.117 \div 0.059$

■ C. Exercises

39. What is the additive inverse of 6? What is the sum of a number and its additive inverse? What is this number called? What is the multiplicative inverse of 6? What is the product of a number and its multiplicative inverse? What is this number called? In your own words, give a definition of the additive inverse and the multiplicative inverse.

40. In the development of the division rule for fractions, the following step was given: $\dfrac{\frac{2}{5} \times \frac{9}{4}}{1} = \frac{2}{5} \times \frac{9}{4}$. What real number properties guarantee that this is true?

■ Dominion thru Math

41. A factory worker is paid time and a half for work exceeding 40 hr. per week and double time for work taking place on a holiday. If he makes \$14.50/hr., what was his gross weekly pay (before taxes were taken out) for working $44\frac{1}{2}$ hr.? What was his gross pay for working 40 hr. in a week if one of the 8 hr. days was a holiday?

42. If the worker in exercise 41 had gross pay of \$819.25 for a week with no holidays, how many hours did he work that week?

43. Another worker with a different pay scale worked $46\frac{3}{4}$ hr. and had gross pay of \$822.05. What is his hourly pay rate?

CUMULATIVE REVIEW

Write the following numbers in base 5. [4.7]

44. 52

45. 19

46. 231

47. 43

48. 682

Compare by using <, =, or >. [5.2]

49. $\dfrac{-1}{9} \ \square \ \dfrac{-6}{25}$

50. $\dfrac{5}{8} \ \square \ \dfrac{3}{4}$

51. $\dfrac{-2}{7} \ \square \ \dfrac{2}{7}$

52. $\dfrac{13}{12} \ \square \ \dfrac{8}{7}$

53. $\dfrac{-3}{7} \ \square \ \dfrac{-4}{5}$

6.4 Evaluating Algebraic Expressions

In Chapter 2 algebraic expressions were introduced and evaluated for particular values of the variable. The variables in an algebraic expression can represent other rational numbers besides integers.

Example 1 Evaluate $2xy$ when $x = \frac{1}{3}$ and $y = \frac{5}{7}$.

Answer

$2xy$

$2\left(\frac{1}{3}\right)\left(\frac{5}{7}\right)$ 1. Substitute the given values for the variables.

$\frac{2}{1}\left(\frac{1}{3}\right)\left(\frac{5}{7}\right)$ 2. Express 2 as a rational number.

$\frac{10}{21}$ 3. Multiply the numerators and multiply the denominators.

Example 2 Evaluate $\frac{x}{y} + \frac{3y}{z}$ when $x = -3$, $y = 4$, and $z = 7$.

Answer

$\frac{x}{y} + \frac{3y}{z}$

$\frac{-3}{4} + \frac{3(4)}{7}$ 1. Substitute the given values for the variables.

$\frac{-3}{4} + \frac{12}{7}$ 2. Simplify the numerator of the second fraction.

$\frac{-3(7)}{4(7)} + \frac{12(4)}{7(4)}$ 3. Find a common denominator. The LCM of 4 and 7 is $4 \cdot 7 = 28$.

$\frac{-21 + 48}{28}$ 4. Add the numerators and place them over the common denominator.

$\frac{27}{28}$

Example 3 Evaluate $5x - 12y$ when $x = 0.4$ and $y = -2.05$.

Answer

$5x - 12y$

$5(0.4) - 12(-2.05)$ 1. Substitute the given values for the variables.

$2 + 24.6$ 2. Multiplication is done before addition.

26.6 3. Add.

Skill Check 1

Evaluate.

1. $\frac{e}{f} + \frac{f}{e}$ when $e = 15$ and $f = 9$

2. $\frac{8a}{b} + ab$ when $a = 9$ and $b = -18$

3. $5x - 7y$ when $x = \frac{2}{3}$ and $y = -\frac{5}{9}$

4. $12a + 3b$ when $a = \frac{1}{3}$ and $b = -\frac{3}{4}$

Example 4   Evaluate $4x^2y$ when $x = 3$ and $y = -\dfrac{1}{6}$.

Answer

$4x^2y$

$4(3^2)\left(-\dfrac{1}{6}\right)$ 1. Substitute the given values for the variables.

$4(9)\left(-\dfrac{1}{6}\right)$ 2. Eliminate the exponent.

$\overset{2}{\cancel{4}}(\overset{3}{\cancel{9}})\left(-\dfrac{1}{\underset{3}{\underset{1}{\cancel{6}}}}\right)$ 3. Cancel.

-6 4. The single negative factor makes the product negative.

Example 5   Evaluate $-3x - 2xy + 9y$ when $x = \dfrac{1}{2}$ and $y = 9$.

Answer

$-3x - 2xy + 9y$

$-3\left(\dfrac{1}{2}\right) - 2\left(\dfrac{1}{2}\right)(9) + 9(9)$ 1. Substitute the given values for the variables.

$-\dfrac{3}{2} - 9 + 81$ 2. Multiplication comes before addition and subtraction.

$-1.5 - 9 + 81$ 3. Change the fraction to a decimal for ease of work.

$-10.5 + 81$ 4. Subtracting 9 is equivalent to adding a negative 9.

70.5 5. Add 81 to the result.

Example 6   Evaluate $\dfrac{2x}{3y^3} - (4y - 3x)$ when $x = 6$ and $y = 2$.

Answer

$\dfrac{2x}{3y^3} - (4y - 3x)$

$\dfrac{2(6)}{3(2)^3} - [4(2) - 3(6)]$ 1. Substitute the given values for the variables.

$\dfrac{12}{3(8)} - (8 - 18)$ 2. Simplify the numerator and eliminate the exponent from the denominator. Also do the multiplication inside the brackets.

$\dfrac{12}{24} - [8 + (-18)]$ 3. Simplify the denominator. Apply the definition of subtraction inside the parentheses.

$\dfrac{1}{2} - (-10)$ 4. Reduce the fraction. Add inside the brackets.

$10\dfrac{1}{2}$ 5. Apply the definition of subtraction: $\dfrac{1}{2} - (-10) = \dfrac{1}{2} + 10$.

Skill Check 2

Evaluate the following when $x = -3$, $y = \dfrac{5}{8}$, $z = 3.7$, and $w = 0.05$.

1. $x^2 + y^2$ 2. $\dfrac{1}{x} + 4y$ 3. $5z - 0.1w$

4. $\dfrac{z}{w} - x^2$ 5. $x(z + 2w)$

■ A. Exercises

Evaluate. Write fractional answers in lowest terms.

1. $b - \dfrac{4}{7}$ when $b = \dfrac{6}{7}$

2. $y + \dfrac{1}{8}$ when $y = \dfrac{3}{8}$

3. $a - \dfrac{7}{15}$ when $a = \dfrac{17}{15}$

4. $x + \dfrac{13}{3}$ when $x = \dfrac{5}{3}$

5. $a + \dfrac{3}{8}$ when $a = \dfrac{1}{2}$

6. $k - \dfrac{1}{4}$ when $k = \dfrac{2}{3}$

7. $\dfrac{3}{4}a$ when $a = 1\dfrac{3}{7}$

8. $\dfrac{5}{2}n$ when $n = 18$

9. $\dfrac{2}{3}r - 1\dfrac{7}{8}$ when $r = 9$

10. $\dfrac{5}{6}y + \dfrac{3}{8}$ when $y = \dfrac{-1}{2}$

11. $6.3a$ when $a = 0.008$

12. $15.7m$ when $m = 0.034$

13. $24.9s$ when $s = 0.265$

14. $1.48z$ when $z = 9.01$

15. $-8a + 3.71$ when $a = 0.16$

■ B. Exercises

Evaluate. Write fractional answers in lowest terms.

16. $\dfrac{a + b}{a}$ when $a = 7$ and $b = -4$

17. $\dfrac{3x - 3}{2y}$ when $x = 7$ and $y = 3$

18. $\dfrac{w + x}{y + z}$ when $w = 2$, $x = 7$, $y = -3$, and $z = 10$

19. $a + b$ when $a = \dfrac{9}{17}$ and $b = \dfrac{12}{17}$

20. $x - y$ when $x = \dfrac{17}{18}$ and $y = \dfrac{11}{18}$

21. b^2 when $b = 31.4$

22. $c^2 + 2$ when $c = 0.56$

23. ab when $a = 7.9$ and $b = 0.82$

24. $2x - y$ when $x = 1.738$ and $y = 1.25$

25. $a^2 + \dfrac{3}{8}$ when $a = \dfrac{1}{3}$

26. $2k^3 - \dfrac{1}{4}$ when $k = \dfrac{2}{3}$

27. $r + w$ when $r = 0.591$ and $w = -4.29$

28. $b - p$ when $b = \dfrac{7}{12}$ and $p = \dfrac{4}{9}$

29. $a^3 - 3a$ when $a = \dfrac{1}{2}$

30. $\dfrac{a}{2b}$ when $a = \dfrac{2}{5}$ and $b = \dfrac{-3}{10}$

■ C. Exercises

Evaluate. Write fractional answers in lowest terms.

31. $3a^2 - 5b^2$ when $a = \dfrac{2}{3}$ and $b = \dfrac{1}{4}$

32. $5x + \dfrac{2}{3}y^2$ when $x = \dfrac{-5}{4}$ and $y = 9$

33. $p \div q$ when $p = 0.36$ and $q = 37.5$

34. $\dfrac{x}{t}$ when $t = 5.7$ and $x = 471.39$

35. $\dfrac{a + b}{c}$ when $a = 5.7$, $b = 3.04$, and $c = 0.2$

36. $\dfrac{x - y}{z}$ when $x = 10$, $y = 2.69$, and $z = 3.4$

37. $-0.04w + \dfrac{a}{1.4} - b^2$ when $a = 0.56$, $b = -1.2$, and $w = -4.2$

■ **Dominion thru Math**

38. A certain bowling club uses a handicap system to enhance competition. Anyone with an average below 200 has three-fourths of the difference between his average and 200 added to his score for a given game. His average score is always calculated without the handicap added. What is the handicap bonus for a person with a 176 average?

39. What is the minimum score a bowler with a 192 average can bowl and still beat a bowler with a 176 average who bowls his average? (See exercise 38.)

CUMULATIVE REVIEW

State whether the given number is prime, composite, or neither. [4.1]

40. 0   41. 15   42. 17   43. 58   44. 129

Rename each fraction in lowest terms. [5.1]

45. $\frac{24}{16}$ 46. $\frac{36}{42}$ 47. $\frac{28}{14}$ 48. $\frac{125}{550}$ 49. $\frac{124}{38}$

MIND OVER MATH

In the local baseball league the Cardinals and Mets have reached the playoffs. The first team to win three out of five games will advance to the finals. Based on the order in which the games are won and by which team, how many different ways could this playoff series occur?

6.5 Simplifying Algebraic Expressions

In Section 2.5 algebraic expressions containing integer coefficients were simplified by combining like terms. In this section algebraic equations with rational coefficients will be simplified. Recall that like terms must contain the same variable(s) with the same exponent(s). The terms $3x$ and $3y$ are not like terms because they have different variables. The terms $3x^2$ and $3x$ are not like terms because they have different exponents. The following are examples of like terms: $3x^2$ and $8x^2$, $-7xy$ and $3xy$, and $-9xy^2$ and $2xy^2$.

240   CHAPTER 6   OPERATIONS ON RATIONAL NUMBERS

Like rational terms are added or subtracted using the Distributive Property.

$$\frac{7}{5}xy - \frac{4}{5}xy = \left(\frac{7}{5} - \frac{4}{5}\right)xy = \frac{3}{5}xy$$

$$\frac{5}{9}x^2 + \frac{2}{9}x^2 = \left(\frac{5}{9} + \frac{2}{9}\right)x^2 = \frac{7}{9}x^2$$

Example 1   Simplify $\frac{1}{6}x + \frac{2}{3}x$.

Answer

$\frac{1}{6}x + \frac{2}{3}x = \left(\frac{1}{6} + \frac{2}{3}\right)x$ 1. Apply the Distributive Property.

$\qquad = \left(\frac{1}{6} + \frac{4}{6}\right)x$ 2. Convert $\frac{2}{3}$ to the equivalent fraction with a common denominator of 6.

$\qquad = \frac{5}{6}x$ 3. Add the numerators over the common denominator.

Example 2   Simplify $7.2y + 5.29y$.

Answer

$7.2y + 5.29y = (7.2 + 5.29)y$ 1. Apply the Distributive Property.

$\qquad = 12.49y$ 2. Add the rational numbers.

Example 3   Simplify $\frac{2}{3}x + 9y + 5y + 8x$.

Answer

$\frac{2}{3}x + 9y + 5y + 8x = \left(\frac{2}{3} + 8\right)x + (9 + 5)y$ 1. Apply the Distributive Property to each pair of like terms.

$\qquad = \left(\frac{2}{3} + \frac{24}{3}\right)x + (9 + 5)y$ 2. Change 8 to $\frac{24}{3}$.

$\qquad = \frac{26}{3}x + 14y$ 3. Add each pair of rational numbers to get the coefficient of each variable.

Skill Check 1

Simplify.

1. $\frac{7}{5}x + \frac{1}{3} + 7x - 2$

2. $-4x + 3y + \frac{1}{3}x + 8y$

3. $2.82x^2 - 5x + 4.1x^2 - 4.4x$

4. $0.03a - b + 7a + 8.2b$

Example 4   Simplify $5x^2 - \frac{2}{3}x + 6 - \frac{1}{4}x + 8x^2$.

Answer

$(5x^2 + 8x^2) + \left(-\frac{2}{3}x - \frac{1}{4}x\right) + 6$ 1. Group like terms. Notice the plus sign separating the x^2 and x terms. The minus sign was kept with the term that followed it.

$(5 + 8)x^2 + \left(-\frac{2}{3} - \frac{1}{4}\right)x + 6$ 2. Apply the Distributive Property.

$13x^2 + \left[-\frac{8}{12} + \left(-\frac{3}{12}\right)\right]x + 6$ 3. Add the 5 and 8 to find the coefficient of x^2. To find the coefficient of x, obtain a common denominator and apply the definition of subtraction.

$13x^2 - \frac{11}{12}x + 6$ 4. The sum of the fractions is $-\frac{11}{12}$. Adding a negative is the same as subtracting; therefore, the plus sign is changed to a minus sign.

Example 5   Simplify $\frac{2x}{3y}(4y - 3xy)$.

Answer

$\frac{2x}{3y}(4y) - \frac{2x}{3y}(3xy)$ 1. Apply the Distributive Property.

$\frac{2x}{3y}\left(\frac{4y}{1}\right) - \frac{2x}{3y}\left(\frac{3xy}{1}\right)$ 2. Cancel.

$\frac{8x}{3} - 2x^2$ 3. Multiply the numerators and multiply the denominators.

$-2x^2 + \frac{8}{3}x$ 4. Write the terms in descending powers of the variable.

Example 6   Simplify $11.2x^2y + 7.54xy - 3.02x^2y - xy$.

Answer

$(11.2x^2y - 3.02x^2y) + (7.54xy - xy)$ 1. Group like terms.

$(11.2 - 3.02)x^2y + (7.54 - 1)xy$ 2. Apply the Distributive Property. Remember that xy is the same as $1xy$.

$8.18x^2y + 6.54xy$ 3. Simplify.

Skill Check 2

Simplify.

1. $7y + 4 - \frac{3}{5}y$ 2. $5.42x^2 + 3.4x - 7.3x^2 + 5$

3. $\frac{2}{3}x + \frac{5}{6}x^3 - \frac{2}{9}x$ 4. $2.6a^4 - 5a^2 - 0.85a^4 + 7a^2$

■ A. Exercises

Simplify.

1. $\frac{2}{5}x - \frac{8}{5}x$ 2. $2a + \frac{4}{5}a - 3a$ 3. $\frac{7}{5}x - \frac{2}{3}x$ 4. $-8w + \frac{1}{4}w - \frac{3}{4}w$

5. $-5x + \frac{7}{2}x$ 6. $-\frac{2}{5}y + \frac{8}{5}y$ 7. $9z - \frac{4}{3}z$ 8. $21a + \frac{9}{5}a$

9. $\frac{1}{2}x + \frac{1}{3}x + \frac{1}{6}x$ 10. $\frac{9}{11}a + \frac{2}{5}a - a$ 11. $-8x^2 + x - 5x + 6x$ 12. $428.9z - 3.69z + 62.5$

■ B. Exercises

Simplify.

13. $\frac{7}{9}y + \frac{2}{3}w - \frac{5}{9}y - \frac{4}{3}w$

14. $\frac{-2}{9}\left(y - \frac{3}{5}\right) + \frac{5}{9}y$

15. $\frac{5}{7}b + \frac{2}{3}\left(b + \frac{4}{3}\right) - 9$

16. $\frac{1}{3}x^2 + 9 + \frac{2}{3}x^2 - 23$

17. $7x + 6y - 5.5x + 3.4y$

18. $-6.8w - y + 0.69w + 8.24y - 2.9$

19. $-8.99h + h - 7.31g - 0.23 + 5.33g$

20. $\frac{7}{9}x + 8y - \frac{8}{3}x - \frac{1}{5}y$

21. $27a - \frac{5}{3}c + \frac{2}{5}c - 8a$

22. $\frac{8}{7}x^2 - 6x + x^2 - 7x$

23. $\frac{21}{5}x^2 - 3x^3 + 8x - \frac{4}{5}x^2$

24. $7b - \frac{2}{5}c + 4b - \frac{7}{10}c$

25. $\frac{2}{7}(3a - b) + \frac{1}{3}(7a + 2b)$

26. $2.8(x^2 - 3x + 8) - 1.7(x^2 + 5x - 2)$

27. $-0.5(a + b + c) - 2.1(a + c) + 3.5(b - c)$

28. $\frac{-3}{5}(5x^2 - 3x + 7) + \frac{2}{5}\left(x - \frac{2}{3}\right)$

29. $6\left(\frac{1}{5}r^2 + 5r - \frac{7}{3}\right) + 3\left(r^2 - \frac{5}{3}\right)$

■ C. Exercises

30. What property of real numbers is applied when combining like terms? Illustrate the use of this property in the simplification of an algebraic expression involving rational numbers.

31. Does $\frac{4}{5}x = \frac{4x}{5}$? Does $\frac{4}{5}x = \frac{4}{5x}$? Why or why not?

Simplify.

32. $\frac{2x}{9y}\left(\frac{3}{8}y - \frac{5}{4}x\right)$

33. $\frac{5a^2}{2b}\left(\frac{3}{5}a - \frac{4}{5}b + 7\right)$

34. $(3.9w^2 + 5.37y)5.39wy$

35. $(2.6x + 4.1y)5 - 4(6.9x - 1.3y)$

■ Dominion thru Math

36. A car rental company charges $35 per day plus $0.32 for every mile over 150 mi. Write an equation for the daily charges to rent a car from this company, where x is the number of miles in excess of 150 driven in a day.

37. What will the rental charges be if you drive the rental car 168 mi. on a given day?

When a car is rented for multiple days, the company charges mileage only for total miles driven in excess of an average of 150 mi. per day. This means they do not charge for extra mileage if the car was driven more than 150 mi. on a given day, as long as the total does not exceed 150 mi. per day.

38. Find the rental charge if the car is driven for 812 mi. over a five-day period.

39. Find the rental charge if the car is driven 452 mi. over a four-day period.

Solve. [3.3–3.4]

40. $-6(x + 12) = -120$

41. $\dfrac{x + 6}{7} = -9$

42. $15 = \dfrac{x - 7}{3}$

43. $\dfrac{s + 2}{8} = 21$

44. $-150 = -6(h + 29)$

45. $\dfrac{t - 8}{9} = 13$

Add or subtract in the indicated base. [4.8]

46. $101_2 + 1101_2$

47. $110_2 - 101_2$

48. $413_5 - 324_5$

49. $753_8 + 267_8$

6.6 Solving Equations with Rational Numbers

Use the properties of equality to solve equations containing rational numbers. Recall that subtracting is adding a negative, and dividing is multiplying by the reciprocal.

	Properties of Equality
Addition	If $a = b$ and c is any real number, then $a + c = b + c$.
Multiplication	If $a = b$ and c is any real number, then $ac = bc$.

Example 1 Solve $x + \dfrac{4}{9} = \dfrac{1}{3}$.

Answer

$$x + \frac{4}{9} = \frac{1}{3}$$

$$x + \frac{4}{9} - \frac{4}{9} = \frac{1}{3} - \frac{4}{9}$$ 1. Subtract $\dfrac{4}{9}$ from both sides.

$$x = \frac{3}{9} - \frac{4}{9}$$ 2. Change $\dfrac{1}{3}$ to an equivalent fraction with a denominator of 9.

$$x = -\frac{1}{9}$$ 3. Subtract the fractions.

Example 2 Solve $\dfrac{5}{6}x = 7$.

Answer

$$\frac{5}{6}x = 7$$

$$\frac{6}{5}\left(\frac{5}{6}x\right) = \frac{6}{5}(7)$$ 1. Multiply both sides by the reciprocal of $\dfrac{5}{6}$.

$$x = \frac{42}{5}$$ 2. Leave the answer as an improper fraction.

Example 3 Solve $x - 2.45 = 8.1$.

Answer

$x - 2.45 = 8.1$

$x - 2.45 + 2.45 = 8.1 + 2.45$ Add 2.45 to both sides.

$x = 10.55$

Example 4 Solve $0.15x = 52.5$.

Answer

$0.15x = 52.5$

$\dfrac{0.15x}{0.15} = \dfrac{52.5}{0.15}$ Divide both sides by 0.15.

$x = 350$

Alternate Method:
Use the LCM to clear fractions.

$$18\left(\frac{1}{2}x\right) + 18\left(\frac{2}{3}\right) = 18\left(\frac{1}{9}\right)$$

$$9x + 12 = 2$$

Skill Check 1

Solve.

1. $x + 0.25 = 7.4$

2. $\dfrac{x}{2} = \dfrac{7}{9}$

3. $5x = 7.2$

4. $x - \dfrac{9}{5} = -\dfrac{1}{10}$

If an equation contains a mixed number, it may be helpful to change it to an improper fraction. In the following example this is less complicated than subtracting with the mixed number.

Example 5 Solve $3y + \dfrac{5}{8} = 1\dfrac{3}{4}$.

Answer

$3y + \dfrac{5}{8} = \dfrac{7}{4}$ 1. Express the mixed number as an improper fraction.

$3y + \dfrac{5}{8} - \dfrac{5}{8} = \dfrac{7}{4} - \dfrac{5}{8}$ 2. Subtract $\dfrac{5}{8}$ from both sides of the equation.

$3y = \dfrac{14}{8} - \dfrac{5}{8}$ 3. Change $\dfrac{7}{4}$ to eighths: $\dfrac{2 \times 7}{2 \times 4} = \dfrac{14}{8}$.

$3y = \dfrac{9}{8}$

$\dfrac{3y}{3} = \dfrac{9}{8} \div 3$ 4. Divide both sides by 3.

$y = \dfrac{\overset{3}{\cancel{9}}}{8} \times \dfrac{1}{\cancel{3}}$ 5. Multiply by the reciprocal of 3. Cancel as shown.

$y = \dfrac{3}{8}$ 6. Multiply the numerators and multiply the denominators.

Example 6 Solve $\frac{2}{3}x = \frac{5}{7}$.

Answer

$$\frac{2}{3}x = \frac{5}{7}$$

$$\frac{3}{2} \cdot \frac{2}{3}x = \frac{3}{2} \cdot \frac{5}{7}$$ Multiply both sides by the reciprocal of $\frac{2}{3}$.

$$x = \frac{15}{14}$$

Example 7 Solve $2x - \frac{1}{4} = \frac{5}{6}$.

Answer

$$2x - \frac{1}{4} = \frac{5}{6}$$

$$2x - \frac{1}{4} + \frac{1}{4} = \frac{5}{6} + \frac{1}{4}$$ 1. Add $\frac{1}{4}$ to both sides.

$$2x = \frac{13}{12}$$ 2. Change the fractions so that they have a common denominator and then add. The LCM of 6 and 4 is 12: $\frac{10}{12} + \frac{3}{12} = \frac{13}{12}$.

$$\frac{1}{2}(2x) = \frac{1}{2}\left(\frac{13}{12}\right)$$ 3. Multiply both sides by the reciprocal of 2.

$$x = \frac{13}{24}$$

Notice that the following example contains a negative coefficient of x.

Example 8 Solve $-5x + 6.5 = 24.75$.

Answer

$$-5x + 6.5 = 24.75$$

$$-5x + 6.5 - 6.5 = 24.75 - 6.5$$ 1. Subtract 6.5 from both sides.

$$-5x = 18.25$$

$$\frac{-5x}{-5} = \frac{18.25}{-5}$$ 2. Divide both sides by −5.

$$x = -3.65$$

Skill Check 2

Solve.

1. $3x - \frac{4}{7} = 2$ 2. $0.45x + 2 = 4.7$ 3. $2y - 1\frac{4}{5} = 2\frac{3}{5}$ 4. $5x + 1.25 = 6.8$

■ **A. Exercises**

Solve. Answers may be left as improper fractions.

1. $x + \frac{1}{5} = \frac{4}{5}$ 2. $x - \frac{5}{9} = \frac{8}{9}$ 3. $x - \frac{3}{8} = \frac{7}{8}$ 4. $x + \frac{1}{6} = \frac{2}{3}$

5. $x + \frac{5}{12} = \frac{3}{4}$ 6. $x - \frac{3}{8} = \frac{1}{4}$ 7. $x + \frac{2}{3} = \frac{8}{9}$ 8. $x - \frac{7}{10} = \frac{1}{2}$

9. $x + \frac{1}{12} = \frac{3}{4}$ 10. $3a = \frac{5}{7}$ 11. $\frac{3}{5}b = 4$ 12. $6c = \frac{4}{5}$

Solve.

13. $a + 3.2 = 7.9$ 14. $m - 15.6 = 32.2$ 15. $z - 8.1 = 1.8$ 16. $d - 29.5 = 42.6$

17. $k - 7.35 = 8.27$ 18. $r + 0.57 = 3.65$ 19. $y + 1.47 = 9.61$ 20. $p - 3.28 = 6.74$

■ B. Exercises

Solve. Answers may be left as improper fractions.

21. $w - 8.48 = 4.36$ 22. $\dfrac{t}{2} = \dfrac{3}{7}$ 23. $x - \dfrac{1}{4} = \dfrac{5}{6}$

24. $1\dfrac{3}{4}s = \dfrac{2}{3}$ 25. $3\dfrac{1}{3}x = 1\dfrac{3}{5}$ 26. $2\dfrac{2}{9}y = 10$

27. $26.35 + c = 64.71$ 28. $0.7r = 6.3$ 29. $3.2a = 14.4$

30. $-0.18n = 0.288$ 31. $\dfrac{x}{2.8} = 4$ 32. $0.039 = 0.003v$

33. $\dfrac{z}{0.5} = 8.3$ 34. $0.39p = 1.092$ 35. $-x + 4 = 9\dfrac{3}{5}$

36. $x - \dfrac{5}{6} = 3\dfrac{1}{6}$ 37. $3\dfrac{5}{6} + x = 15\dfrac{2}{5}$ 38. $x - 2\dfrac{7}{10} = 5\dfrac{3}{8}$

39. $5\dfrac{1}{2} = x + \dfrac{11}{2}$

■ C. Exercises

Write an equation and solve.

40. A number is multiplied by 2.4, resulting in the product 324. What is the number?

41. $\dfrac{12}{7}$ of a number is $\dfrac{4}{3}$. Find the number.

42. Solve $\dfrac{3}{5}x + \dfrac{2}{3}(5x - 8) = \dfrac{4}{15}$ for x and give the justifying property for each step of the solution.

CUMULATIVE REVIEW

Use prime factorizations to find the LCM of each pair of numbers. [4.4]

43. 12, 26   44. 90, 21   45. 15, 27   46. 63, 12   47. 35, 70

Express the ratios in lowest terms using the word "to." [5.4]

48. A school has 713 students and 23 teachers. What is the student-to-teacher ratio?

49. Robert got 28 hits during the baseball season and 12 strikeouts. What was his ratio of hits to strikeouts?

50. In a box of chocolates there are 6 caramels and 32 buttercreams. What is the ratio of caramel to buttercream chocolates in the box?

51. If 120 lb. of bluegrass seed is mixed with 20 lb. of clover seed, what is the ratio of bluegrass seed to clover seed?

52. If concrete is mixed using 130 lb. of sand and 25 lb. of water, what is the ratio of sand to water?

PROBLEM SOLVING

Divide and Conquer

You can solve some complicated word problems by dividing them into several smaller problems. With the strategy "divide and conquer," you first solve the smaller problems and then combine the results to find the solution.

Example 1 | Before Mrs. McKee gave her coupons to the cashier, the total cost of her groceries was $62.04. She had the following manufacturer's coupons, which were worth twice their face value at the store where she shopped: three coupons for 25¢ off, two coupons for 30¢ off, and one coupon for 40¢ off. In addition, she had the following in-store coupons worth their face value: two coupons for 35¢ off and one coupon for 60¢ off. After the coupons were subtracted, how much was Mrs. McKee's grocery bill?

Answer

Think: What is the goal in this problem and what steps should be used to meet this goal?

The goal is to find the amount of Mrs. McKee's grocery bill after the value of the coupons has been subtracted from the subtotal.

Think: Divide the problem into smaller problems. First, find the total value of the manufacturer's coupons and double it.

$3(0.25) + 2(0.30) + 0.40 = 0.75 + 0.60 + 0.40 = \$1.75$
Double this amount: $2(1.75) = \$3.50$.

Think: Second, find the total value of the in-store coupons.

$2(0.35) + 0.60 = 0.70 + 0.60 = \$1.30$

Think: Add the two sums to find the total value of all the coupons.

$3.50 + 1.30 = \$4.80$

Think: Finally, subtract the total value of the coupons from the original total of the groceries.

$62.04 - 4.80 = \$57.24$

Think: Does this seem to be a reasonable answer? Recheck the calculations for accuracy.

This is a reasonable answer, and the calculations are correct.

Example 2 | Nina works at a plant and tree nursery during her summer break. Her main job each morning is to water the plants in the greenhouse. Five quarts of water are needed to water a 2 ft. × 5 ft. flat of plants. How many gallons of water are needed to water the plants in a greenhouse that contains 32 ft. × 20 ft. of flats?

Answer

Think: Determine what you are trying to find.

You want to find the number of gallons of water needed to water the plants in this greenhouse.

Think: How can the total number of gallons be found? What would be the best way to approach this problem? Could you divide the problem into parts to make it easier to solve?

The size of a rectangular flat is known. The size of the space that holds them is known.

Think: How can you find the number of flats in this space?

Find the area of one flat and the total area of all of them; then you can divide to find the number of flats.

Think: If I can find the number of flats, I can multiply by the amount of water needed per flat. The amount of water for one is known, so multiply by the number of flats.

Think: It may help to draw a picture of the space and see how the flats fit into it.
Each flat contains $2 \times 5 = 10$ ft.² There are $20 \times 32 = 640$ ft.² in all the flats combined.
$640 \div 10 = 64$ flats will fit into this space.

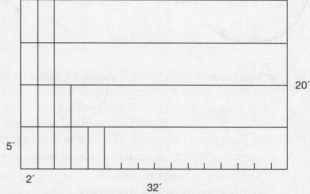

Think: How can the number of gallons of water be determined? First, find the number of quarts required to water the plants, and then convert this amount into gallons.
Each flat requires 5 qt. of water, and there are 64 flats.
$5(64) = 320$ qt.

Since there are 4 qt. in a gallon, divide the number of quarts by 4 to find the number of gallons of water needed.
$320 \div 4 = 80$ gal.

Think: How did solving several simpler problems make the problem-solving process easier? Is there some more efficient way to solve this problem?

Each sub-problem was easy to solve, and combining them led to a relatively easy solution. It was an efficient method.

■ Exercises

Solve. Write down the thinking process you used to work toward a solution for exercises 1 and 2.

1. Gordon mowed lawns to earn money last summer. He was paid $10 for each of three yards, $15 for each of eight yards, and $20 for each of five yards. Assuming he cuts each lawn once every week, how much did Gordon earn before expenses during the twelve weeks of summer?

2. Judy works some evenings as a babysitter. She charges $7.50/hr. for hours before 11 PM and $8/hr. for hours after 11 PM. If Judy baby-sits from 8 PM until 1 AM, how much does she earn?

3. A pharmaceutical company uses three ingredients in a prescription medicine. Each pill contains 3 mg of one ingredient, 4 mg of another, and 13 mg of a third. If the amount of the second ingredient is increased by 2 mg and the third ingredient is increased by 5 mg in each pill, what is the ratio of the three ingredients contained in the new pill?

4. How much do 3 gal. of strawberries cost if a quart costs $2.98?

5. Elwood must have an average of 92% to get an A in science class. He currently has 490 out of 550 points. He still has to take two more tests worth 80 points each, three quizzes worth 10 points each, and a final exam worth 150 points. How many of the remaining points must he earn to get an A in science? Round to the nearest whole number.

6. The cheerleaders want to toss red and white candies at the pep rally. They found a bag of candy that has red, white, and blue candies in the ratio of 4 : 3 : 3. If there are 120 pieces of candy in a bag and the squad needs 450 pieces of red or white candy, how many bags of candy must they buy?

7. Allison reads two books during the school week and five books on the weekend each week for an entire fourteen-week semester. How many books does she read during the semester?

8. Tyler started a pet boarding business and keeps dogs and cats. Dogs require more care than cats, so he charges $60/week or $10/day for dogs and $40/week or $7/day for cats. He keeps the following pets: Bob's dog for 12 days, Patricia's dog for 3 days, Beau's dog for 8 days, Martha's cat for 4 days, and Paul's cat for 14 days. How much money will he collect from keeping these pets?

6.7 Using Algebra

Algebra is a useful tool for solving word problems. The four-point checklist discussed in the Problem Solving feature of Chapter 1 also applies to solving word problems algebraically. After reading the problem to gain information, you must make a plan, which involves writing an equation that relates to the information. You then need only solve the equation using the properties of equality to answer the question. Finally, check to be sure your answer is reasonable.

You can solve many problems by writing and solving an equation. When you plan to use this strategy, follow these steps as a guide. The following table gives the details for step 3 of the four-point checklist.

Steps to Solving Problems with Equations
1. Represent an unknown quantity with a variable.
2. When necessary, represent other conditions in the problem in terms of the same variable.
3. Identify two equal quantities in the problem.
4. Write and solve an equation.

Example 1 Choose a variable for the unknown in the following problem. Then write an equation that could be used to solve the problem. **Do not solve.**

Coach Mahoney ran six times as far as he swam and cycled thirty times as far as he swam. If he covered a total of 37 mi. in the triathlon, how far did he swim?

Answer

Let x = length of swim.
$6x$ = length of run
$30x$ = length of bicycle ride

1. Choose a variable to represent an unknown. Express other unknowns in terms of that variable.

length of swim + length of run + length of bicycle ride = 37

2. Identify two equal quantities.

$x + 6x + 30x = 37$

3. Write the equation.

Example 2 Choose a variable for the unknown in the following problem. Then write an equation that could be used to solve the problem. **Do not solve.**

A soccer field has a perimeter of 380 yd., and its length is $40\frac{1}{3}$ yd. longer than its width. Find the dimensions of the field.

Answer

Let w = width.

$w + 40\frac{1}{3}$ = length

1. Represent the unknown quantities.

$2 \cdot \text{width} + 2 \cdot \text{length} = \text{perimeter}$

2. Identify two equal quantities.

$2w + 2\left(w + \frac{121}{3}\right) = 380$

3. Write the equation.

Skill Check 1

Choose a variable to represent the unknown. Then write an equation that could be used to solve the problem. **Do not solve.**

1. Add four to a number; then subtract five and a third from the sum. The result is forty-three. Find the number.

2. One number is one-third of another, and their sum is negative sixteen. Find the numbers.

3. A professional hockey team played eighty-four games. They lost one-fifth as many as they won. How many games did they win?

Example 3

A carpenter is nailing baseboard molding along a wall that is 88 in. long. He has nailed in place a piece of molding that is $32\frac{5}{8}$ in. long. What length of molding does he need to finish the job?

Answer

Let m = length of molding needed.   1. Choose a variable to represent the unknown.

molding needed + molding nailed   2. Identify two equal quantities.
= length of baseboard

$$m + 32\frac{5}{8} = 88$$ 3. Write the equation.

$$m + 32\frac{5}{8} - 32\frac{5}{8} = 88 - 32\frac{5}{8}$$ 4. Solve for m.

$$m = 55\frac{3}{8} \text{ in.}$$

$$55\frac{3}{8} + 32\frac{5}{8} = 87\frac{8}{8} = 88$$ 5. Check the solution by substituting into the original equation.

Example 4

The drama club performed the school play on Friday and Saturday nights. Attendance at the Saturday performance was $1\frac{1}{4}$ times the attendance on Friday. If there were 95 people in attendance on Saturday, what was the total attendance for both performances?

Answer

Let f = Friday's attendance.   1. Represent the unknown with a variable.

$1.25 \cdot$ Friday's attendance   2. Identify two equal quantities. Change the fraction to a
= Saturday's attendance   decimal for ease of work.

$1.25f = 95$ 3. Write the equation.

$$\frac{1.25f}{1.25} = \frac{95}{1.25}$$ 4. Solve for f.

$$f = 76$$

$76 + 95 = 171$ people for the two nights   5. Find the total attendance.

Skill Check 2

1. A math teacher discovered that five-eighths of his students made either an A or a B on the semester exam. There were 15 such students. How many students were in his class?

2. The offering received at the Sunday morning service was $55 less than 2.5 times the offering received Sunday evening. The offering Sunday morning was $6,895. What was the offering Sunday evening?

⊕ Invention

In 1884 the first reliable fountain pen was patented. But fountain pens still had many problems, so by the early twentieth century consumers desired a substitute for the fountain pen: one that wrote smoothly, would not leak, and had ink that would dry quickly without fading or clogging the pen. As early as 1888 John Loud created a different kind of pen, with a rolling ball in the tip, for writing on leather; but his pen was never commercially marketed. The first real work toward a *ballpoint pen* began in Hungary in 1938 with Laszlo and Georg Biro. They invented and patented a pen with a cylinder-shaped ink reservoir fitted on one end and a ball bearing that collected ink as it rolled, simultaneously marking the paper. Their design was mostly impractical, so their ballpoint pen was not a success. But further improvements continued, and by 1950 Patrick Frawley and Fran Seech had successfully marketed the Paper Mate ballpoint pen. Also in 1950, a French manufacturer, Marcel Bich, introduced the inexpensive but highly successful BIC pen, which basically adapted the Biros' design. Today the ballpoint pen has replaced the fountain pen as the popular choice for an everyday writing instrument.

■ A. Exercises

Choose a variable to represent the unknown. Then write an equation that could be used to solve the problem. Do not solve.

1. Two-thirds of a number is 46. Find the number.

2. Forty-five percent is written in decimal form as 0.45. If 45% of a number is 36, what is the number?

3. Jean decided to spend $104.76 on gift favors for a party. If each gift costs $5.82, how many gifts did she buy?

4. T.J. is wallpapering his bedroom. The room has 8 ft. high ceilings and is $12\frac{1}{2}$ ft. long. If the perimeter of the room is $48\frac{1}{2}$ ft., what is the width of the room?

Choose a variable to represent the unknown. Write an equation and solve.

5. After cutting $1\frac{5}{8}$ in. off the end of a piece of molding, a carpenter had the exact length that he needed, which was $32\frac{1}{8}$ in. What was the length of the original piece of molding?

6. Becky spent $\frac{2}{3}$ of her piano practice time on her recital piece. If she spent 25 min. on other pieces, how many hours did Becky spend practicing?

7. David worked in the library on Friday and Saturday. He worked a total of $7\frac{3}{4}$ hr. during those two days. If he worked $4\frac{1}{4}$ hr. on Friday, then how many hours did he work on Saturday?

8. The coach wants to spend three-eighths of basketball practice time on defense. He plans to spend 45 min. on this. How many hours will the team spend practicing?

9. Mrs. Bai spent twice as much money as Alice on their shopping trip. If they spent a total of $386.16, how much did each spend?

10. Mr. Jordan plans to leave the total of his savings to his four children. If they all are to receive the same amount of inheritance and the total savings that he has is $501,052.40, how much will each of them receive?

■ B. Exercises

Choose a variable to represent the unknown. Write an equation and solve.

11. A recipe calls for $2\frac{1}{2}$ cups of sugar. Maddie has only $1\frac{2}{3}$ cups of sugar. How much more sugar does she need?

12. A Christian university found that about 3% of its students came from a certain state. The university had 156 students from that state. What is the total enrollment in the university?

13. Bob worked $1\frac{3}{4}$ hr. longer on Tuesday than he did on Monday. He worked a total of $13\frac{1}{4}$ hr. for the two days. How many hours did he work on Monday? on Tuesday?

14. A music teacher needed 0.25 hr. per student to administer an oral test. If the teacher spent 3.75 hr. administering the test, how many students were tested?

15. The cost of a reserved seat is $1\frac{3}{4}$ times the cost of general admission. If a reserved seat is $14, what is the price of general admission?

16. Mrs. Harris made a quilt for her granddaughter. She used a total of $7\frac{7}{8}$ yd. of material. If she used $2\frac{3}{4}$ yd. of light blue material and $3\frac{5}{8}$ yd. of dark blue, and the remaining material was a red print, how many yards of red material did she use?

17. Ron is nailing three boards of the same thickness together. If the total thickness of the nailed boards is 4.5 in., what is the thickness of each board?

18. In one year, 144 of the students enrolled in a Christian school went on a soul-winning outreach during the school year. This was $\frac{4}{5}$ of the students enrolled in the school. How many of those enrolled in the school did not go on the outreach?

■ C. Exercises

Choose a variable to represent the unknown. Write an equation and solve.

19. The sum of two numbers is 18. If the larger number is four times the smaller number, what are the two numbers?

20. Mr. Johns has worked for the same company for ten years. He makes 2.5 times as much as Mr. Bradley per hour. If their combined hourly salary is $29.40, what does each man earn per hour?

21. The ratio of points scored by Jennie, Sarah, and Sadie in the basketball games played last week was 1 : 3 : 5. If Jennie scored 10 points last week, what was the total number of points scored by these three girls?

22. At a construction site two different machines can be used for an excavation. The BC machine can do the job in ten hours, so BC does $\frac{1}{10}$ of the job in one hour. The BH machine can do it in six hours, so it does $\frac{1}{6}$ of the job in one hour. How long will it take to do the job with both machines working together? Assume they will not get in each other's way.

23. If the BC machine costs $80/hr. to operate and the BH machine costs $150/hr. to operate, find the cost of doing the job using both machines.

24. What percent of the job does the BC machine complete, and what percent of the job does the BH machine complete?

CUMULATIVE REVIEW

Use prime factorizations to find the GCF of each pair of numbers. [4.3]

25. 42, 60   26. 315, 450   27. 60, 792   28. 75, 150   29. 585, 567

Solve the following proportions. [5.5]

30. $\frac{x}{8} = \frac{7}{12}$ 31. $\frac{-7}{y} = \frac{26}{15}$ 32. $\frac{5}{3} = \frac{z}{27}$

33. $7 : 9 = c : 2$ 34. 18 is to −8 as 12 is to x.

6.8 Operations with Scientific Notation

We are told to look up, but how about a heavenly view of the earth?

Extremely large or small rational numbers in decimal form are often written in scientific notation. Numbers written in scientific notation can be added and subtracted, but only if they have the same power of ten. The Distributive Property is used when performing operations on numbers in scientific notation. Review the Distributive Property below.

$$a(b + c) = ab + ac$$

Example 1   Add $(6.4 \times 10^5) + (3.79 \times 10^5)$.

Answer

$(6.4 \times 10^5) + (3.79 \times 10^5) = (6.4 + 3.79) \times 10^5$ 1. Apply the Distributive Property.

$= 10.19 \times 10^5$ 2. Simplify inside the parentheses. The first factor is not between 1 and 10.

$= (1.019 \times 10) \times 10^5$ 3. Write 10.19 in scientific notation.

$= 1.019 \times (10 \times 10^5)$ 4. Apply the Associative Property.

$= 1.019 \times 10^6$ 5. Add exponents when multiplying.

| Example 2 | Subtract $(5.6 \times 10^{-7}) - (2.9 \times 10^{-7})$. |

Answer

$(5.6 \times 10^{-7}) - (2.9 \times 10^{-7}) = (5.6 - 2.9) \times 10^{-7}$ 1. Apply the Distributive Property.

$\qquad\qquad\qquad\qquad\qquad\qquad = 2.7 \times 10^{-7}$ 2. Simplify inside the parentheses.

Skill Check 1

Add or subtract.

1. $(9.3 \times 10^7) + (1.86 \times 10^7)$ 2. $(6.67 \times 10^{14}) - (9.6 \times 10^{14})$

3. $(1.6 \times 10^{-5}) + (4.3 \times 10^{-5}) - (3.81 \times 10^{-5})$

If the numbers do not have the same power of ten, one of the numbers must be converted to an equivalent form so that the powers of ten match. For instance, in order to add 4.2×10^3 and 5.13×10^5, you must do one of the conversions in Examples 3 and 4.

Numbers can be converted to the lowest power of ten.

| Example 3 | Add 4.2×10^3 and 5.13×10^5 using a common factor of 10^3. |

Answer

$5.13 \times 10^5 = 5.13 \times (10^2 \times 10^3)$ 1. Rewrite the power of ten as a product having 10^3 as a factor.

$\qquad\qquad\quad = (5.13 \times 10^2) \times 10^3$ 2. Apply the Associative Property of Multiplication.

$\qquad\qquad\quad = 513 \times 10^3$ 3. Simplify.

$(4.2 \times 10^3) + (513 \times 10^3)$ 4. Restate the problem using a common power of ten.

$(4.2 + 513) \times 10^3$ 5. Apply the Distributive Property.

517.2×10^3 6. Simplify.

$(5.172 \times 10^2) \times 10^3$ 7. Rewrite the answer in scientific notation.

5.172×10^5

Adjusting numbers so they have the exponent of the number with the larger exponent often saves the last step of readjusting the power of ten at the end of the problem.

| Example 4 | Add 4.2×10^3 and 5.13×10^5 using a common factor of 10^5. |

Answer

$4.2 \times 10^3 = (0.042 \times 10^2) \times 10^3$ 1. To increase the exponent by 2, move the decimal two places to the left (dividing the number by 10^2), and multiply by 10^2 to keep the value equivalent.

$\qquad\qquad\quad = 0.042 \times (10^2 \times 10^3)$ 2. Apply the Associative Property of Multiplication.

$\qquad\qquad\quad = 0.042 \times 10^5$ 3. Simplify.

$(0.042 \times 10^5) + (5.13 \times 10^5)$ 4. Restate the problem using a common power of ten.

$(0.042 + 5.13) \times 10^5$ 5. Apply the Distributive Property.

5.172×10^5 6. Simplify.

Skill Check 2

Add or subtract.

1. $(6.2 \times 10^4) - (8.1 \times 10^3)$

2. $(1.58 \times 10^3) + (1.04 \times 10^5)$

Numbers written in scientific notation can be multiplied or divided. The numbers do not need to have the same power of ten for these operations.

To find the product of numbers in scientific notation, reordering and regrouping are necessary. The Associative and Commutative Properties allow you to group the numbers between 1 and 10 together and to group the powers of ten together. Study the example below.

Example 5 Multiply $(3.27 \times 10^4)(4.6 \times 10^3)$.

Answer

$(3.27 \times 10^4)(4.6 \times 10^3) = (3.27 \times 4.6)(10^4 \times 10^3)$ 1. Reorder and regroup.

$= 15.042 \times 10^7$ 2. Multiply the numbers and multiply the powers of ten.

$= (1.5042 \times 10^1) \times 10^7$ 3. Rewrite the answer in scientific notation.

$= 1.5042 \times (10^1 \times 10^7)$ 4. Apply the Associative Property.

$= 1.5042 \times 10^8$ 5. Add the exponents.

The general rule for multiplying rational numbers says that $\frac{a}{c} \times \frac{b}{d} = \frac{ab}{cd}$. For dividing numbers in scientific notation, this process is used in reverse. Suppose (8×10^7) is to be divided by (2×10^5). Write the division problem in fraction form; then express it as the product of two separate fractions.

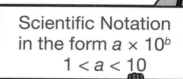

Scientific Notation in the form $a \times 10^b$
$1 < a < 10$

$$\frac{8 \times 10^7}{2 \times 10^5} = \frac{8}{2} \times \frac{10^7}{10^5} = 4 \times 10^{7-5} = 4 \times 10^2$$

Example 6 Divide (7.2×10^8) by (6×10^5).

Answer

$\dfrac{7.2 \times 10^8}{6 \times 10^5} = \dfrac{7.2}{6} \times \dfrac{10^8}{10^5}$ 1. Write the division problem in fraction form. Apply the reverse process of multiplying fractions.

$= 1.2 \times 10^{8-5}$ 2. Simplify each fraction.

$= 1.2 \times 10^3$

Example 7 Divide (6.9×10^{-6}) by (2.3×10^{-2}).

Answer

$\dfrac{6.9 \times 10^{-6}}{2.3 \times 10^{-2}} = \dfrac{6.9}{2.3} \times \dfrac{10^{-6}}{10^{-2}}$ 1. Write the division problem in fraction form. Apply the reverse process of multiplying fractions.

$= 3 \times 10^{-6-(-2)}$ 2. Divide the numbers. Divide the powers of ten by subtracting the exponents.

$= 3 \times 10^{-4}$ 3. Simplify the exponents: $-6 - (-2) = -6 + 2 = -4$.

Example 8   The wavelength of violet light in the visible spectrum is 400 nanometers, and a nanometer is one-billionth of a meter. Express this distance in meters using scientific notation.

Answer

One-billionth of a meter is written 0.000000001 m, so a nanometer is 1×10^{-9} m.

400 nanometers $= 400(1 \times 10^{-9})$ m	1. Change to scientific notation.
$= (400 \times 1) \times 10^{-9}$ m	2. Apply the Associative Property.
$= (4 \times 10^2) \times 10^{-9}$ m	3. Change to scientific notation.
$= 4 \times (10^2 \times 10^{-9})$ m	4. Apply the Associative Property.
$= 4 \times 10^{-7}$ m	5. Simplify.

Skill Check 3

Multiply or divide.

1. $(9.72 \times 10^8)(4.8 \times 10^{-20})$ 2. $(1.82 \times 10^5) \div (9.1 \times 10^{17})$

3. Light travels at 186,000 mi./sec., and sound travels at 0.283 mi./sec. Convert both numbers to scientific notation, and find the ratio of the speed of light to the speed of sound.

■ A. Exercises

Convert each number to scientific notation, and then add or subtract as indicated. Leave answers in scientific notation.

1. $530{,}000{,}000 + 610{,}000{,}000$ 2. $0.00000058 - 0.00000041$

3. $4{,}030{,}000 - 2{,}100{,}000$ 4. $0.000069 + 0.0000721$

Add or subtract as indicated. Leave answers in scientific notation.

5. $(2.89 \times 10^8) + (8.7 \times 10^8)$ 6. $(3.5 \times 10^{-4}) - (1.82 \times 10^{-4})$

7. $(9.32 \times 10^{-8}) + (1.3 \times 10^{-8})$ 8. $(6.4 \times 10^{19}) + (2.5 \times 10^{19})$

9. $(1.43 \times 10^{-4}) - (1.15 \times 10^{-4})$ 10. $(7.49 \times 10^6) - (3.88 \times 10^6)$

Multiply or divide as indicated. Leave answers in scientific notation.

11. $(6.2 \times 10^3)(1.8 \times 10^3)$ 12. $(2.8 \times 10^9)(6.33 \times 10^2)$

13. $(1.8 \times 10^{-6})(2.56 \times 10^6)$ 14. $(2.77 \times 10^{12})(2.57 \times 10^5)$

15. $(8.91 \times 10^7)(3.6 \times 10^{-4})$ 16. $(4.18 \times 10^{-6})(3.6 \times 10^{-8})$

17. $(2.85 \times 10^4) \div (1.9 \times 10^8)$ 18. $(5.98 \times 10^9) \div (2.6 \times 10^7)$

19. $(7.14 \times 10^9) \div (2.8 \times 10^{12})$ 20. $(3.05 \times 10^{-7}) \div (5 \times 10^8)$

21. $(6.72 \times 10^{21}) \div (4.2 \times 10^{11})$ 22. $(3.74 \times 10^{-8}) \div (8.5 \times 10^4)$

■ B. Exercises

Add or subtract as indicated. Leave answers in scientific notation.

23. $(5.3 \times 10^6) + (6.1 \times 10^4)$

24. $(8.2 \times 10^{-3}) + (1.6 \times 10^{-5})$

25. $(4.7 \times 10^8) + (3.08 \times 10^7)$

26. $(2.14 \times 10^{12}) - (1.6 \times 10^9)$

27. $(9.66 \times 10^6) - (3.82 \times 10^4)$

28. $(7.01 \times 10^{-5}) + (8.33 \times 10^{-7})$

29. $(8.94 \times 10^6) + (6.77 \times 10^8)$

30. $(7.94 \times 10^{-7}) - (3.65 \times 10^{-8})$

■ C. Exercises

Convert each number to scientific notation, and then perform the indicated operations.

31. $(320{,}000{,}000 + 148{,}000{,}000)(32{,}000{,}000)$

32. $(0.000006 - 0.000004)(0.00000007 + 0.000008)$

33. $\dfrac{89{,}000{,}000 + 123{,}000}{0.00000073}$

34. $\dfrac{0.0000043(38{,}900{,}000 + 61{,}000{,}000)}{52{,}000}$

Solve. Write answers in scientific notation if possible.

35. Light travels a mile in about 0.000005 sec. What is the approximate speed of light in miles per second? in miles per hour?

36. It is estimated that the influenza epidemic of 1918–19 caused approximately 22 million deaths worldwide. Of that number, close to 550,000 deaths occurred in the United States. Use scientific notation to find the percentage of the deaths that occurred in the United States during this flu epidemic.

37. In the most densely populated areas of China, approximately 115 million people live in a 47,000 km² area. What is the population density (people/km²) in this area? If the entire population of approximately 1.3 billion people were distributed evenly over the total land area of 9.6 million km², what would be the population density?

CUMULATIVE REVIEW

Solve. [3.1–3.2]

38. $x + 9 = -29$

39. $6c = 45$

40. $\dfrac{x}{9} = -14$

41. $\dfrac{-7}{z} = 12$

42. $21a = -42$

Write the prime factorization of each number. [4.2]

43. 36

44. 56

45. 128

46. 250

47. 116

The Wilderness Tabernacle

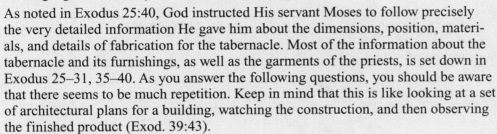

The wilderness tabernacle, Solomon's temple, and Ezekiel's temple provide an interesting context to observe the character of our God, as well as His gracious employment of frail humanity. Although these three structures are basically replications of the same place of worship, they display increasing degrees of splendor, size, and magnificence. Studying the details of these structures can be tedious and time consuming, so it makes sense to study what others with greater skill and knowledge of the language have already extracted from the Scriptures.

As noted in Exodus 25:40, God instructed His servant Moses to follow precisely the very detailed information He gave him about the dimensions, position, materials, and details of fabrication for the tabernacle. Most of the information about the tabernacle and its furnishings, as well as the garments of the priests, is set down in Exodus 25–31, 35–40. As you answer the following questions, you should be aware that there seems to be much repetition. Keep in mind that this is like looking at a set of architectural plans for a building, watching the construction, and then observing the finished product (Exod. 39:43).

1. State, in cubits, the length and width of the court surrounding the tabernacle (Exod. 27:9–13, 18).

2. Using the fact that 1 cubit is approximately 1.5 ft. or 18 in., determine the dimensions of the courtyard in feet and then calculate the square footage of the courtyard.

3. Determine the square footage of a regulation basketball court that is 84 ft. long and 50 ft. wide and use the result to see how many times larger the courtyard of the tabernacle was.

4. How many cubits high was the curtain around the court? How many feet high is this? Would anyone be able to see over it (Exod. 27:18)?

5. Give the overall dimensions, in cubits, of the tabernacle (tent) that contained the holy place and the holy of holies. Figure out these three dimensions using the information given about vertical side boards (Exod. 26:15–22).

6. State the dimensions of the tabernacle in feet.

7. In Exodus 25:10 the size of the ark of the covenant is given. What are its dimensions in feet?

8. If gold weighs 1,204 lb./ft.³ and the ark was covered inside and out with a layer $\frac{1}{32}$ in. thick, find the approximate weight of the gold on the ark.

9. Who were the skilled artisans, called of God and filled with His Spirit, to make all the beautiful designs, furniture, carvings, engravings, and metal work for the tabernacle (Exod. 35:30–35)?

10. What were at least three overall purposes of the tabernacle? Look up Exodus 25:8; 40:35; and Hebrews 8:5 (see also Heb. 9:1–28).

Infinite Truths

Thus was all the work of the tabernacle of the tent of the congregation finished: and the children of Israel did according to all that the Lord commanded Moses, so did they. *Exodus 39:32*

Chapter 6 Review

Vocabulary

Addition Property of Equality

dividend

division

divisor

Multiplication Property of Equality

Perform the indicated operations.

1. $\dfrac{7}{9} + \dfrac{4}{9}$

2. $8\dfrac{1}{5} - 2\dfrac{3}{4}$

3. $\dfrac{2}{5} - \dfrac{7}{5}$

4. $-4\dfrac{6}{7} + 3\dfrac{1}{4}$

5. $\dfrac{-4}{7} + \dfrac{6}{5}$

6. $-6.28 - 0.395$

7. $\dfrac{8}{15} - \dfrac{4}{5}$

8. $198.274 + 3.98 - 0.14$

Multiply.

9. $\dfrac{7}{3} \cdot \dfrac{5}{9}$

10. $3\dfrac{4}{7} \cdot \dfrac{3}{4}$

11. $\dfrac{-3}{5} \cdot \dfrac{5}{9}$

12. $-7.2(3.61)(-0.2)$

13. $6\dfrac{2}{3} \times \left(-3\dfrac{4}{5}\right)$

14. $11.9(-29.45)$

15. What is the multiplicative inverse of -7?

Divide.

16. $\dfrac{3}{7} \div \left(-\dfrac{9}{4}\right)$

17. $5\dfrac{3}{5} \div \dfrac{6}{15}$

18. $-\dfrac{6}{5} \div \left(-\dfrac{8}{9}\right)$

19. $5\dfrac{2}{3} \div 6$

20. $5.3 \div 0.6$

21. $-6.4 \div 0.2$

Evaluate.

22. $4x + 2y$ when $x = \dfrac{5}{8}$ and $y = \dfrac{3}{7}$

23. $xy - 5x + 4$ when $x = \dfrac{6}{5}$ and $y = \dfrac{2}{3}$

24. $-\dfrac{8}{3}(x + 2y)$ when $x = \dfrac{7}{3}$ and $y = \dfrac{4}{9}$

25. $x - y + z$ when $x = -4.5$, $y = 73.9$, and $z = 16.8$

26. $-5x + xy$ when $x = 3.1$ and $y = -58.6$

27. $187.3z - 34.87y$ when $y = 3.9$ and $z = 16.2$

Simplify.

28. $\dfrac{3}{7}x + 8 - \dfrac{4}{9} + \dfrac{2}{5}x$ ✓

29. $5x^2 - \dfrac{1}{8}x - \dfrac{4}{7} + \dfrac{7}{2}x^2 + \dfrac{2}{3}x - 6$

30. $x\left(\dfrac{3}{2}x - 2\right) + 6\left(\dfrac{5}{2}x - \dfrac{2}{3}\right)$

31. $\left(1\dfrac{1}{5}\right)\left(x + \dfrac{3}{2}\right) - \dfrac{9}{10}$

32. $(3.9x^2 - 0.05x - 6.2) + (0.7x^2 + 2.6x + 8.3)$

33. $-5.3(x + xy - 2.6y) + 3.8(x - 0.6xy - 2.1y)$

Solve.

34. $\dfrac{2}{9}x = \dfrac{2}{3}$

35. $\left(1\dfrac{2}{3}\right)\left(x - \dfrac{1}{9}\right) = \dfrac{2}{5}$

36. $7x + \dfrac{1}{7} = \dfrac{4}{7}$

37. $-0.4x - 2.7 = -6.8$

38. $\dfrac{1}{5}\left(x + \dfrac{3}{5}\right) - \dfrac{4}{5} = 5$

39. $64.8x - 4.2(x - 3.1) = 6.7$

40. Five-eighths of the young people in the youth group went on the ski trip. If 25 young people attended this activity, how many are in the youth group?

41. A football costs 1.5 times the amount of a basketball. If one of each is purchased and the total price is $37.70 before tax, what is the price of each ball?

42. The new playground at the elementary school is $15\frac{4}{5}$ ft. longer than it is wide. If the perimeter that requires fencing is $177\frac{1}{5}$ ft., what are the dimensions of the playground?

43. An apple in a dessert contributes one-thirtieth the number of fat grams that the cup of cottage cheese contributes. If the total number of fat grams in the dessert is 4.03 g, how many fat grams are in the apple and how many are in the cup of cottage cheese?

Perform the indicated operations. Leave answers in scientific notation.

44. $(3.52 \times 10^8) + (6.99 \times 10^8)$

45. $(1.9 \times 10^{-6}) - (1.2 \times 10^{-5})$

46. $(3.69 \times 10^{-8})(1.9 \times 10^{-6})$

47. $(8.7 \times 10^5) \div (2.1 \times 10^8)$

48. $(5.9 \times 10^6)(8.6 \times 10^8)$

49. $(9.2 \times 10^{-12}) + (3.6 \times 10^{-8})$

50. State the mathematical significance of Exodus 39:32.

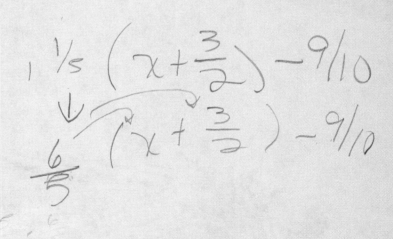

Proverbs 31:10–31 identifies the good business dealings of the virtuous woman. She is hardworking, diligent in the care of her affairs, willing to invest in raw materials and land, and consistent in providing quality merchandise. In other words, the woman of Proverbs 31 is an *entrepreneur*.

Entrepreneurship includes organizing, operating, and assuming the risk of starting a business. If an entrepreneur fails to consider all that is involved in operating a business, he will not be successful. A large amount of money is required for such things as renting a building, paying legal fees, providing office supplies, and paying salaries. Billions of dollars are lost annually due to the failure of small businesses. However, many small businesses do extremely well and return an excellent profit. Companies typically thrive because of careful planning, a conservative amount of debt, good management, and an excellent product or service.

One of the first considerations when starting a business is doing a market analysis. The owner must know the extent of the need for his product or service by defining his customer base. He also needs to know his competitors and whether there is a large enough market for a similar business. After determining that there is a market for his product or service, an entrepreneur must determine what he can charge the customer. If cost exceeds income, the business is doomed. A clear understanding of percents—their forms and uses—is essential to a successful business venture.

After this chapter you should be able to
1. change percents to fractions or decimals and vice versa.

2. use the percent formula (percent × whole = part) to set up and solve problems for any of the three quantities.

3. write proportions and use them to solve percent problems.

4. use proportions to solve problems relating scale drawing lengths to actual lengths and map distances to actual mileage.

5. use percents to calculate the size of enlargements and reductions.

6. use percents to compute the amount of discount, the percent of discount, and the sale price for discounted items.

7. compute markup and sale price for store items.

8. solve percent problems involving commissions, tips, and interest.

9. calculate percent change.

7.1 Forms of Percents

A percent is a ratio. It compares a given number to one hundred. The word *percent* comes from the Latin phrase *per centum*, which means "per hundred."

Definition

A **percent** is a ratio of a number to one hundred. The symbol for percent is %.

% is a ratio.

Seventy-five percent is written 75%, and it means the same as the ratio 75 : 100. Since a ratio can be expressed as a fraction, $75\% = \frac{75}{100}$. When expressing a percent as a fraction, reduce the fraction to lowest terms.

$$75\% = \frac{75}{100} = \frac{3 \times 25}{4 \times 25} = \frac{3}{4}$$

Converting a Percent to a Fraction

1. Express the percent as a fraction with the number over 100.
2. Reduce the fraction to lowest terms.

Example 1 Express 88% as a fraction in lowest terms.

Answer

$88\% = \frac{88}{100} = \frac{22 \times 4}{25 \times 4} = \frac{22}{25}$ Write the percent as a fraction and reduce to lowest terms.

Example 2 Express $37\frac{1}{2}\%$ as a fraction in lowest terms.

Answer

$37\frac{1}{2}\% = 37.5\%$

$= \frac{37.5}{100}$

$= \frac{37.5 \times 10}{100 \times 10}$

$= \frac{375}{1{,}000}$

$= \frac{375 \div 125}{1{,}000 \div 125}$

$= \frac{3}{8}$

1. Express one-half percent as a decimal.

2. Change the percent to a ratio expressed per hundred.

3. Multiply the numerator and denominator by 10 to remove the decimal in the numerator.

4. Reduce the fraction to lowest terms.

Example 3   Express $13\frac{1}{3}\%$ as a fraction in lowest terms.

Answer

$$13\frac{1}{3}\% = \frac{13\frac{1}{3}}{100} = 13\frac{1}{3} \div 100$$

1. Express the percent as a ratio per hundred. A fraction indicates division.

$$= \frac{\overset{2}{\cancel{40}}}{3} \times \frac{1}{\underset{5}{\cancel{100}}}$$

2. Change the mixed number to an improper fraction; then multiply by the reciprocal of 100.

$$= \frac{2}{15}$$

A percent can also be expressed as a decimal. Since percent means "per hundred," or divided by 100, the decimal equivalent is found by removing the percent symbol and moving the decimal point two places to the left.

$$75\% = 75 \div 100 = 0.75$$

Converting a Percent to a Decimal
1. Replace the percent sign with ÷ 100 (per hundred).
2. Move the decimal two places to the left to divide by 100.

Example 4   Express 8% as a decimal.

Answer

$8\% = 8 \div 100 = 0.08$ Replace the percent sign with ÷ 100. Move the decimal point two places to the left.

Example 5   Express $32\frac{1}{4}\%$ as a decimal.

Answer

$$32\frac{1}{4}\% = 32.25\%$$

1. Change the fraction to a decimal: $\frac{1}{4} = 0.25$.

$$= 32.25 \div 100$$

2. Replace the percent sign with ÷ 100.

$$= 0.3225$$

3. Move the decimal point two places to the left.l.

Skill Check 1

Write each percent as a fraction or mixed number in lowest terms.

1. 8%
2. $12\frac{1}{2}\%$
3. 365%
4. $\frac{2}{3}\%$

True or false

5. $41\% = 0.41$
6. $0.67 = 6.7\%$
7. $5\% = 0.5$

Write each percent as a decimal.

8. 60%
9. $13\frac{1}{4}\%$
10. 153%

Converting decimals to percents requires multiplying the percent by one in the form of 100%. This moves the decimal point two places to the right and affixes the % symbol.

$$0.83 \times 1 = 0.83 \times 100\% = 83\%$$

Converting a Decimal to a Percent
1. Multiply by one in the form 100%.
2. Move the decimal point two places to the right. Affix the percent symbol.

Example 6 Express 2.4 as a percent.

Answer

$2.4 = 2.4(100\%) = 240\%$ Move the decimal point two places to the right and affix the percent symbol.

Skill Check 2 Write each decimal as a percent.

1. 0.54   2. 0.009   3. 2.3

4. 0.535   5. 1.07   6. 11.3

The conversion of fractions and decimals to percents illustrates the general relationship among fractions, decimals, and percents. If the denominator of a fraction is 100, you can use the percent symbol instead of dividing by 100.

$$\frac{43}{100} = 43\%$$

If the denominator is a factor of 100, it is easy to rename the fraction as an equivalent fraction with a denominator of 100.

$$\frac{4}{5} = \frac{4 \times 20}{5 \times 20} = \frac{80}{100} = 80\%$$

Example 7 Express $\frac{3}{20}$ as a percent.

Answer

$\frac{3}{20} = \frac{3 \times 5}{20 \times 5} = \frac{15}{100}$ 1. Multiply the numerator and denominator by 5 to make an equivalent fraction with a denominator of 100.

$\frac{15}{100} = 15\%$ 2. Write the fraction in its equivalent percent form.

You can also convert fractions to percents by first changing them to their decimal form. This is especially helpful if the denominator is not a factor of 100.

Example 8 Express $\frac{7}{8}$ as a percent.

Answer

$$\begin{array}{r} 0.875 \\ 8)\overline{7.000} \\ \underline{6\,4} \\ 60 \\ \underline{56} \\ 40 \\ \underline{40} \\ 0 \end{array}$$

1. Find the decimal equivalent.

$0.875 = 87.5\%$ 2. Move the decimal point two places to the right and affix the percent symbol.

Example 9 Express $\frac{5}{2}$ as a percent.

Answer

$$\begin{array}{r} 2.5 \\ 2)\overline{5.0} \\ \underline{4} \\ 10 \\ \underline{10} \\ 0 \end{array}$$

1. Find the decimal equivalent.

$2.5 = 250\%$ 2. Move the decimal point two places to the right and affix the percent symbol.

Example 10 Express $\frac{5}{12}$ as a percent.

Answer

$$\begin{array}{r} 0.41 \\ 12)\overline{5.00} \\ \underline{4\,8} \\ 20 \\ \underline{12} \\ 8 \end{array} \quad ; 0.41\frac{8}{12} = 0.41\frac{2}{3}$$

1. Divide to find the decimal equivalent. Express any remainder after the hundredths place as a reduced fraction.

$0.41\frac{2}{3} = 41\frac{2}{3}\%$ 2. Move the decimal point two places to the right and affix the percent symbol.

You can also use a proportion to rename a fraction as a percent. The first ratio of the proportion is the given fraction. The second ratio is an unknown number to 100. Solve the proportion for the unknown numerator, which is the percent. Study the following example.

Example 11 Use a proportion to express $\frac{5}{8}$ as a percent.

Answer

$\dfrac{5}{8} = \dfrac{n}{100}$ 1. Write a proportion with the given fraction as one ratio and an unknown number to 100 as the other ratio.

$8n = 5(100)$ 2. Use cross multiplication to solve.

$8n = 500$

$\dfrac{8n}{8} = \dfrac{500}{8}$ 3. Divide both sides by 8.

$n = 62\frac{1}{2}$

$\dfrac{5}{8} = 62\frac{1}{2}\%$, or 62.5%

Skill Check 3

Write each fraction as a percent.

1. $\frac{4}{5}$ 2. $\frac{3}{25}$ 3. $\frac{43}{50}$

Use a proportion to write each fraction as a percent.

4. $\frac{15}{10}$ 5. $\frac{12}{3}$ 6. $\frac{1}{200}$ 7. $\frac{2}{3}$

■ A. Exercises

Write each percent as a fraction.

1. 28% 2. 45% 3. 96% 4. 18% 5. 70% 6. 95%

Write each percent as a decimal.

7. 19% 8. 452% 9. 6% 10. 1.7% 11. 0.2% 12. 137%

Write each fraction as a percent.

13. $\frac{2}{5}$ 14. $2\frac{3}{5}$ 15. $\frac{21}{25}$ 16. $\frac{3}{50}$ 17. $\frac{3}{10}$ 18. $\frac{11}{20}$

Write each decimal as a percent.

19. 0.67 20. 0.075 21. 3.5 22. 0.005 23. 235.6 24. 4.05

■ B. Exercises

Write each fraction as a decimal and a percent.

25. $\frac{4}{5}$ 26. $7\frac{1}{2}$ 27. $\frac{17}{25}$ 28. $\frac{13}{50}$ 29. $\frac{9}{16}$ 30. $1\frac{5}{6}$

Write a proportion to change each fraction to a percent. Solve the proportion to find the percent equivalent of the fraction. Round to the nearest tenth of a percent.

31. $\frac{17}{40}$ 32. $\frac{19}{30}$ 33. $\frac{8}{11}$

34. $\frac{3}{16}$ 35. $\frac{3}{64}$ 36. $\frac{5}{7}$

■ C. Exercises

Write each percent as a fraction.

37. $47\frac{1}{4}\%$ 38. $2\frac{1}{2}\%$ 39. $\frac{5}{8}\%$ 40. $\frac{3}{10}\%$

Write each fraction as a percent.

41. $\frac{3}{8}$ 42. $\frac{5}{16}$ 43. $\frac{7}{9}$ 44. $\frac{7}{12}$

■ Dominion thru Math

Three partners are starting a health and fitness company to serve the employees of corporations in large urban areas. From personal funds, each partner contributed one-third of the startup cost of $300,000. Projections show the ongoing monthly operating costs to be $150,000. Before the opening date, charter memberships were available for $200 for the initiation fee plus $80/mo. Regular memberships are $100 for the initiation fee plus $100/mo.

45. After how many months will the accumulated cost of a charter membership be less than the accumulated cost of a regular membership?

46. The company sold 200 charter memberships before opening the business. Assuming that only monthly fees are used to meet the $150,000 monthly operating costs, how many regular memberships will the company need to sell to meet these monthly operating costs?

47. Assume that, along with the 200 charter memberships, the company is able to sell the needed number of regular memberships to meet its monthly operating costs. If all the initiation fees are put into a reserve fund, how much will be in this fund?

Exercise is one of the keys to good health.

CUMULATIVE REVIEW

Write the first five terms of the following recursively defined geometric sequences. [4.6]

48. $a_1 = -6; a_n = 0.5a_{n-1}$

49. $a_1 = 2; a_n = 4a_{n-1}$

50. $a_1 = -5; a_n = -3a_{n-1}$

51. $a_1 = -8; a_n = 0.25a_{n-1}$

52. $a_1 = 100; a_n = 0.8a_{n-1}$

Find the unit rate. [5.4]

53. 200 words in 4 min.

54. 256 mi. on 8 gal.

55. $330 for 40 hr.

56. $38.40 for 6 yd.

57. 780 calories in three candy bars

7.2 Solving Percent Equations

There are three basic types of percent problems:
1. finding a percent of a number (part);
2. finding what percent one number is of another;
3. finding the whole amount.

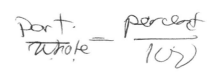

There are two methods used in setting up an equation to solve percent problems:

1. by formula;
2. by proportion.

By converting the percent to a decimal, you can solve the problem by using a basic equation.

Percent Formula
The percent of the whole is equal to the part: *percent* × *whole* = *part*.

To use this formula, express the percent as a decimal. When the percent is greater than 100%, the "part" will actually be larger than the "whole."

Proportion Method
The part is to the whole as the percent is to 100: $\dfrac{part}{whole} = \dfrac{percent}{100}$.

Once the proportion is set up, use cross multiplication to solve for the missing quantity. The first three examples find a part of a number.

Example 1 Find 5% of $115 by the formula method.

Answer

5% = 0.05   1. Express the percent as a decimal.
percent × whole = part
0.05(115) = part   2. Substitute the known percent and the whole amount in the formula.
$5.75 = part   3. Multiply.

The percent could be expressed as a fraction rather than as a decimal. Some fraction equivalents are well known, such as $25\% = \dfrac{1}{4}$, $50\% = \dfrac{1}{2}$, and $75\% = \dfrac{3}{4}$. Substituting the fraction equivalent for the percent may be easier if the whole is a multiple of the denominator of the fraction. For example, 25% of 480 could be solved more easily by taking $\dfrac{1}{4} \times 480$.

Example 2 Find 104% of 250 by the proportion method.

Answer

$\dfrac{part}{whole} = \dfrac{percent}{100}$

$\dfrac{part}{250} = \dfrac{104}{100}$ 1. Set up a proportion.

100(part) = 250(104)   2. Cross-multiply.

100(part) = 26,000

part = 260   3. Divide by 100.

Example 3   Mr. Ward decided that he would give an additional $2\frac{1}{2}$% above his tithe, or $12\frac{1}{2}$% total. Find $12\frac{1}{2}$% of $4,500.

Answer

$12\frac{1}{2}\% = 12.5\% = 0.125$ 1. Rename the fraction as a decimal percent; then convert it to decimal form.

percent × whole = part

$0.125 \times 4,500 = \text{part}$ 2. Substitute the given values into the formula.

$\$562.50 = \text{part}$ 3. Multiply.

Skill Check 1

Solve the following by using the formula method with decimal values for percents.

1. Find 6% of $170.   2. Find 10.5% of 400.   3. Find 110% of 80.

Solve the following by using the formula method with equivalent fractions for percents.

4. If 160 is increased by 25%, how much is it increased?

5. If 200 is decreased by 10%, how much is it decreased?

Solve the following by using a proportion.

6. Find 32% of 75.   7. Find 220% of 400.

The following two examples are of the second type listed at the beginning of this section, finding what percent one number is of another.

$$\frac{Part}{whole} = \frac{percent}{100}$$

Example 4   What percent of 12 is 16?

Answer

percent × whole = part

$p \times 12 = 16$ 1. Write an equation using p for percent. 16 is compared to 12, so 16 is the part and 12 is the whole.

$$\frac{12p}{12} = \frac{16}{12}$$ 2. Divide both sides by 12, going two places beyond the decimal point.

$$\frac{?}{170} = \frac{6}{100}$$

$$100p = 1020$$

$$\begin{array}{r} 1.33 \\ 12\overline{)16.00} \\ \underline{12} \\ 40 \\ \underline{36} \\ 40 \\ \underline{36} \\ 4 \end{array}$$

$$\frac{percent \times whole = part}{12} = 16$$

$p = 1.33\frac{1}{3}$ 3. Express the remainder as a reduced fraction: $\frac{4}{12} = \frac{1}{3}$.

$p = 133\frac{1}{3}\%$ 4. Change the decimal to a percent.

Note: If the quotient does not terminate when you divide to find the percent, carry out the division to two decimal places. Then write the remainder as a fraction or round to the nearest thousandth, expressing the answer to the nearest tenth of a percent.

Example 5   108 is what percent of 150? Solve by using a proportion. Round to the nearest tenth.

Answer

$$\frac{\text{part}}{\text{whole}} = \frac{\text{percent}}{100}$$

$$\frac{108}{150} = \frac{p}{100}$$

1. Substitute the known values—the part and the whole amount. Use the variable p for percent.

$$150p = 10{,}800$$

2. Cross-multiply.

$$\frac{150p}{150} = \frac{10{,}800}{150}$$

3. Divide both sides by 150.

$$p = 72$$

108 is 72% of 150.

Skill Check 2

Find the following percents by using the formula. Round to the nearest tenth of a percent if necessary.

1. 14 is what percent of 70?

2. What percent of 144 is 24?

Find the following percents by using a proportion. Round to the nearest tenth of a percent if necessary.

3. 245 is what percent of 98?

4. What percent of 60 is 2.7?

The following two examples are of the third type listed at the beginning of this section, finding the whole amount.

Example 6   Eight is 16% of a number. Find the number by using the formula.

Answer

percent × whole = part

$$0.16 \times w = 8$$

1. Determine the unknown and assign the variable w to the whole amount. Substitute the given values, converting the percent to a decimal.

$$\frac{0.16w}{0.16} = \frac{8}{0.16}$$

2. Divide both sides by 0.16.

$$w = 50$$

The whole amount is 50.

Example 7   28% of what number is 182? Solve by using a proportion.

Answer

$$\frac{\text{part}}{\text{whole}} = \frac{\text{percent}}{100}$$

$$\frac{182}{w} = \frac{28}{100}$$

1. Write a proportion. Let w represent the unknown number.

$$28w = 18{,}200$$

2. Cross-multiply.

$$\frac{28w}{28} = \frac{18{,}200}{28}$$

3. Divide both sides by 28.

$$w = 650$$

The whole amount is 650.

Forms of the % equation:

percent × whole = **part**

$$\text{percent} = \frac{\text{part}}{\text{whole}}$$

$$\text{whole} = \frac{\text{part}}{\text{percent}}$$

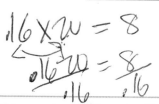

Find the whole amount in the following problems.

1. 35% of a number is 17.5.

2. 12 is 8% of a number.

3. 250% of a number is 18.

4. 11 is 550% of a number.

■ A. Exercises

Find the following amounts.

1. 62% of 40

2. 3.5% of 90

3. 140% of 80

4. 2.5% of 4,000

5. 3% of 260

6. 4.65% of $800

Find the following percents.

7. _18_ is what percent of 9?

8. 8 is what percent of 400?

9. What percent of 60 is 21?

10. 20 is what percent of 80?

11. 88 is what percent of 40?

12. 73.8 is what percent of 90?

Find the following amounts.

13. 70 is 40% of what number?

14. 28 is 110% of what number?

15. What number is 200% of 80?

16. 75 is 300% of what number?

17. What is 150% of 90?

18. 15.8 is 40% of what number?

■ B. Exercises

Write the fraction corresponding to the given percent in lowest terms. Use the fraction to find the following amounts.

19. 30% of 80

20. 25% of $124

21. 15% of 190

22. 70% of 840

23. $12\frac{1}{2}$% of 404

24. $66\frac{2}{3}$% of $96

Write a proportion that can be used to solve each of the following percent problems. Use the proportion to solve the problem.

25. Find 82% of 900.

26. 46 is what percent of 160?

27. 32 is 40% of what number?

28. 400 is what percent of 750?

29. $75 is 80% of what?

30. Find 30% of 140.

■ C. Exercises

Solve.

31. A Christian school had 25 students in the senior class. A total of 80% of these students went to college. How many students went to college?

32. A math test had a total of 80 points. What percent correct is 76 points?

33. The band at Calvary Christian Academy has 24 members. This is 15% of all the students in the school. What is the total enrollment at the school?

34. A town has an adult population of 45,000. If 8% of the adults in the town are unemployed, how many adults in the town are employed?

35. There are 20 students on the honor roll at the high school. This number is 125% of the students on the honor roll last semester. How many students were on the honor roll last semester?

36. A tennis class is limited to 20 people. If 25 people have signed up, what percent of the limited class size is the number of people who have signed up?

■ Dominion thru Math

Continue working on business analyses for the three partners in the health and fitness corporation. Initiation fees are placed in the reserve fund and are not considered to be profit since they cannot be distributed.

37. For the second month the partners want monthly fees to make 1.5% profit on their $300,000 investment. How many more regular memberships must they sell (in addition to your answer to exercise 46 in Section 7.1, Dominion thru Math)?

38. What percent increase would this be in their total membership?

39. If the same increase in the number of members (exercise 37) continues for ten more months, how much profit in monthly fees will they make in the twelfth month after starting the business?

40. How much will be in the reserve fund after twelve months? (Hint: Use your answer to exercise 47 in Section 7.1, Dominion thru Math, as a starting point.)

CUMULATIVE REVIEW

Write the following numbers in the indicated base. [4.7]

41. 42 in base 3

42. 512 in base 6

43. 89 in base 7

44. 341 in base 8

45. 76 in base 4

Use cross multiplication to compare the given fractions. Use <, =, or >. [5.2]

46. $\dfrac{9}{11}, \dfrac{15}{17}$

47. $\dfrac{4}{9}, \dfrac{52}{117}$

48. $\dfrac{-4}{5}, \dfrac{-7}{8}$

49. $\dfrac{12}{5}, \dfrac{216}{90}$

50. $\dfrac{-8}{3}, \dfrac{-9}{4}$

PROBLEM SOLVING

Mixed Review

In the previous chapters you have used several problem-solving strategies. Any of these strategies could be used to solve the following problems. Carefully read each problem and try to figure out whether it is like any of the problems you have solved in previous chapters. Try to determine which strategy would be the most efficient to use. Remember that there may be different problem-solving strategies that will lead you to the correct solution, but often there is a most efficient strategy.

Problem-Solving Strategies		
Select the operations	Look for a pattern	Divide and conquer
Guess and check	Draw a picture	

■ Exercises

Solve each of the following by using one of the problem-solving strategies above. Write a general explanation of the plan you will use to solve the problem.

1. An auditorium has 22 rows with 40 seats in each row. The admission charge for a concert is $15 for adults and $7.50 for children. At a recent sold-out performance there were 616 adults in attendance. The remaining seats were filled with children. What was the total amount collected for admission?

2. A department store buyer ordered 430 shirts. He ordered twice as many red as white and 50 more blue than white. How many of each color did he order?

3. Dave's phone bill included a 71 min. long-distance phone call that cost $6.08. The rate was $2 for the first 3 min. and a set rate per minute for each additional minute. What was the rate charged per additional minute?

4. A bookstore has 92 Bibles in stock. The store has 30 more study Bibles than pocket Bibles and 10 fewer large-print Bibles than pocket Bibles. How many Bibles of each type are there?

5. A bookstore ordered 114 greeting cards. The manager ordered twice as many birthday cards as sympathy cards and 18 more anniversary cards than sympathy cards. How many cards of each type were ordered?

6. A man is planning to make a 1,200 mi. round trip by automobile. In order to determine the cost of the trip, he needs to know how many tanks of gas he will need. His car gets 18 mi./gal., and his tank holds 15 gal. Round to the next whole tank.

7. Billy proposed the following plan to his parents for his weekly allowance. Billy would receive $1 the first week. On each successive week, his allowance would be doubled. Under these conditions, what would Billy's allowance be on the tenth week? Do you think his parents will agree to this arrangement?

8. Mr. Kane was stacking twenty-one bales of hay. Each row had one bale fewer than the row below it. If there was only one bale on the top row, how many rows were there in all? How many bales were on the bottom row?

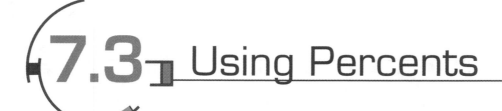

7.3 Using Percents

This section contains word problems involving the three types of percent problems introduced in the previous section. Recall that the basic percent formula is

$$percent \times whole = part.$$

Recall the following guidelines from Section 6.7 that will help you solve word problems using algebra.

1. Represent an unknown quantity with a variable.

2. When necessary, represent other conditions in the problem in terms of the same variable.

3. Identify two equal quantities in the problem.

4. Write and solve an equation.

When word problems involve percents, remember to convert them to their decimal or fraction form before placing them in an equation.

Example 1 Of the 430 delegates, only 350 showed up due to the bad weather. What percent were able to attend? Round to the nearest tenth of a percent.

Answer

Let p = the percent.   1. Assign a variable for the unknown.

percent × whole = part   2. Use the percent formula to find the **percent**.

$p(430) = 350$ 3. A percent of the delegates (whole) were able to attend.

$\dfrac{430p}{430} = \dfrac{350}{430}$ 4. Divide both sides of the equation by 430. Carry out to four decimal places.

$p = 0.8139...$

$p \approx 81.4\%$ 5. Convert to a percent and round to one decimal place.

81.4% of the delegates were able to attend.

Example 2 There are 200 kg of a metal alloy known to be 60% zinc. How much zinc does the alloy contain?

Answer

Let z = the amount of zinc present in the alloy.

1. Assign a variable for the unknown.

percent × whole = part

2. Use the percent formula to find the **part**.

$0.6(200) = z$

3. Convert the percent to a decimal when substituting known values.

$z = 120$

4. Multiply.

The alloy contains 120 kg of zinc.

Metal will liquefy if heated to a high enough temperature.

Example 3 Find the monthly income of the Oliver family if their monthly mortgage payment of $840 represents 21% of their monthly income.

Answer

Let m = the monthly income.

percent × whole = part

$0.21m = 840$

$\dfrac{0.21m}{0.21} = \dfrac{840}{0.21}$

$m = 4,000$

The Olivers' monthly income is $4,000.

1. Assign a variable for the unknown.
2. Use the percent formula to find the **whole**.
3. Convert the percent to a decimal when substituting known values.
4. Solve by dividing both sides by 0.21.

Skill Check 1

Write an equation and solve.

1. A company sells mixed nuts. They advertise that 15% of their mixed nuts are cashews. If they have only 12 lb. of cashews on hand, how many pounds of mixed nuts can they make?

2. A basketball player took 20 shots from the court during a game and made 35% of them. How many shots did he make?

3. Justine correctly answered 69 of the 75 questions on the test. What percent of the questions did she answer correctly?

Percentages less than 100% separate the whole into two parts: the described percent and the rest of the whole. If 60% of 200 tickets are sold, the other 40% are not sold. The number of unsold tickets can be determined by calculating the number of sold tickets and then subtracting this amount from the total number of tickets. But using the other percentage allows you to calculate the number directly: 0.40(200) = 80 unsold tickets.

Example 4 Only 24% of the registered voters participated in the last election. How many of the 33,000 registered voters did not cast a vote?

Answer

Let n = the number of non-voters.

$n = 0.76(33,000)$

$n = 25,080$

25,080 did not vote.

1. Assign a variable for the unknown.
2. If 24% voted, the other (100 – 24)%, or 76%, of the registered voters did not.
3. Multiply.

Use this approach when the total amount is not given.

Example 5 The 2,256 in attendance left 6% of the seats in the auditorium vacant. Determine the seating capacity of the auditorium.

Answer

Let s = the number of seats.

$0.94s = 2,256$

$s = \dfrac{2,256}{0.94} = 2,400$

There are 2,400 seats in the auditorium.

1. Assign a variable for the unknown.
2. If 6% of the seats were vacant, (100 – 6)%, or 94%, of the seats were occupied.
3. Solve the equation.

In other situations, a percentage is added to the original amount. If Alexander was 65" tall before growing 5% during the last year, we can calculate that he grew 3.25" during the last year and then add the amount of increase to his original height. He is now 65 + 3.25 = 68.25" tall. Alternatively, we know that his height at the end of the year is (100 + 5)% = 105% of his original height, so we can calculate his new height directly: 1.05(65) = 68.25".

| **Example 6** | The cost of a large beverage is 40% more than the cost of a small beverage. Determine the price of the large drink if the small costs $0.95. |

Answer

Let l = the cost of a large beverage.

$l = 1.4(0.95)$

$l = \$1.33$

The large beverage costs $1.33.

1. Assign a variable to represent the large beverage.
2. The cost of the large beverage is (100 + 40)%, or 140%, of the cost of the small beverage.
3. Multiply.

Skill Check 2

Solve.

1. The box says to use 3 oz. of a powdered drink mix and add enough water to make 16 oz. How much water is used? What percent of the drink is water?

2. If a jetliner was filled to 85% of its capacity, how many of the 240 seats were empty?

3. What is the total cost of a used car after an 8% sales tax is added to the $5,000 price of the vehicle?

■ A. Exercises

Specify what the variable stands for, write an equation, and solve.

1. A used car dealer estimates that 40% of his customers buy sedans. If he sells 26 sedans, about how many total cars would he expect to sell?

2. Only 35 people out of the 250 to whom the offer was made refused it. What percent refused it?

3. Twelve of the fifty dogs in the show were some breed of terrier. What percent is this?

4. Ten years ago, a company survey indicated that 2.5% of its work force possessed an advanced college degree. If the company had 110 employees with an advanced degree at that time, how many employees did the company have?

5. A school's student body is about 35% Asian. If there are 72 Asian students, how many students are enrolled in the school? Round to the nearest whole number.

6. A soccer player took fifteen shots on goal and made two. What percent of his shots resulted in a goal? Round to the nearest percent.

7. Mr. Broun paid $3.30 in tax on a $55 motel bill. What percent of $55 was the tax?

8. How many respondents prefer Sparkle toothpaste if 62% of the 300 people surveyed indicated that this was their preference?

9. How many questions did Don get right on the sixty-question Bible test if his score was 85%?

■ B. Exercises

Specify what the variable stands for, write an equation, and solve.

10. It was conjectured that at least 20% of the families in a particular region owned two or more cars. A random survey of 500 people found 80 such families. Find out whether the survey supports the conjecture.

11. How many pounds of butterfat are in one gallon of whole milk that weighs approximately 8.6 lb. and contains about 4% butterfat?

12. Measurable precipitation occurred in a city on 20% of the days of last year. On how many days did no measurable precipitation fall?

13. The temperature in a city fell below 0°F on twelve days last winter. On what percent of winter days did the temperature stay above zero? (Use ninety-one days as the length of winter.) Round to the nearest percent.

14. Mr. Keeler was promoted from a job paying $45,000/yr. to one where his salary increased by $10,000. His increase is what percent of his previous salary? Round to the nearest percent.

15. The church offering last Sunday was $6,500. One year ago it was $4,800. Last Sunday's offering is what percent of the one a year ago? Round to the nearest percent.

16. A church building fund has $3.2 million in it, which is 60% of the amount necessary for the project. What is the total amount needed for the building? Round to the next higher tenth of a million.

17. A city received 17 in. of rain last year, which is only 37% of the normal amount. How many inches does it normally get? Round to the nearest inch.

18. Of a football team's season touchdowns, about 43% came by passing. If the team scored 28 touchdowns, how many were by other means?

19. Research indicates that the leading brand of laundry detergent accounted for 35% of the 400,000 total sales in the marketplace. How many sales were made by all the other brands combined?

20. The size of a computer class is limited to fifteen people. If three seats are still available, to what percent of its capacity is the class full?

21. The price of a loaf of bakery bread was recently raised 5% to a retail price of $3.57. What was the original price?

22. The total cost of the airline ticket was $432, including an 8% tax. What was the cost of the ticket before the tax was added?

23. The concert center sold 11,900 tickets this year, which was 40% more than last year. How many tickets were sold last year?

24. There are 108 seniors in a high school of 450 students. What percent of the student body are not seniors?

25. Out of a shipment of 12,000 bolts, 3% were defective. How many of the bolts could be used?

■ C. Exercises

Solve.

26. A twelve-slice pizza is to be divided proportionally between two teens based on the amount that each contributed toward the total cost of $13. One contributed $8 and the other $5. To the nearest percent, what percent of the pizza should the larger contributor get? To the nearest half-slice, how much is this?

27. One day 10% of the students enrolled in the school were absent. There were 1,620 students present on that day. How many students were absent?

28. A car gets 30 mi./gal. on the open road and 22 mi./gal. in the city. If 60% of the driven mileage is on the open road, and the car was driven 20,000 mi., how many gallons of gas were used for traveling in the city? Round to the nearest gallon.

29. A farmer planted 320 acres of one variety of wheat and 160 acres of a second variety. He also planted 40 acres of milo, and he has 440 acres that will lie fallow (not be planted) this year. What percent of his land did he plant in wheat? Round to the nearest percent.

30. An automobile tire with an original tread of $\frac{11}{32}$ in. failed when the tread measured $\frac{5}{32}$ in. The owner's warranty says that the cost of the tire is to be reimbursed based on the percent of tread left when the tire fails. What percent of the purchase price should be refunded? Round to the nearest tenth of a percent.

31. A store discounted an article of clothing by 25% and then by an additional 40%. The item was sold for $18. Find the original list price. (Hint: Find the first sale price; then use it to find the original price.)

32. The cost of a child's ticket is 40% of the cost of an adult ticket. The total cost of one adult and one child ticket is $10.50. What is the cost of an adult ticket?

33. The difference between the prices of a first-class airline ticket and a coach ticket is $135. The cost of a first-class ticket is 175% of the cost of a coach ticket. What is the cost of a coach ticket?

CUMULATIVE REVIEW

Solve the following proportions by using the Property of Proportions. Round to the nearest tenth. [5.5]

34. $\frac{x}{8} = \frac{20}{7}$

35. $\frac{-29}{y} = \frac{8}{3}$

36. $\frac{9}{7} = \frac{z}{4}$

37. $9 : 14 = c : 42$

38. 6 is to 17 as −54 is to x.

Add or subtract as indicated. [6.1]

39. $\frac{-4}{5} + \frac{3}{10} + \frac{11}{2}$

40. $\frac{6}{7} + \frac{-3}{2} + \frac{-9}{14}$

41. $\frac{2}{9} + \frac{7}{6} - \frac{3}{4}$

42. $5.89 - 2.645 - 8.66$

43. $0.033 + 2.87 - 14.991$

MIND OVER MATH

You are given four cubes. The two-dimensional diagram of each cube after it is flattened is given here.

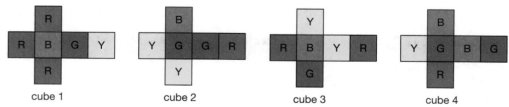

cube 1   cube 2   cube 3   cube 4

Can you stack the cubes in such a way that each of the four colors appears only once on each side of the stack? (Hint: It may help you to make actual models of these cubes.)

7.4 Scales

Maps, diagrams of mechanical parts, and house plans are examples of scale drawings. All the lengths on a drawing must produce an equal ratio when compared to the actual lengths represented by the drawing. This ratio is called the *scale*.

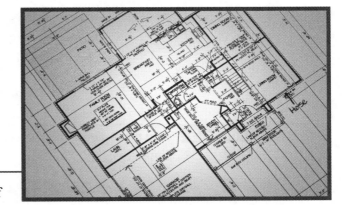

Definitions

The **scale** for a drawing or map is the ratio of the drawing's length to the actual length.

A **scale drawing** is a drawing in which all the lengths are at the same scale, or ratio, to the actual lengths of the object.

In the scale drawing below, the scale is 1 cm : 5 m. This means that 1 cm in the drawing represents 5 m of actual length. You can set up a proportion and use the Property of Proportions—the product of the extremes equals the product of the means—to find the length of the bridge in the drawing when the actual length is 27 m.

A scale is a ratio.

$$\frac{1 \text{ in.}}{10 \text{ ft.}} = \frac{1 \text{ in.}}{120 \text{ in.}} = \frac{1}{120}$$

$\frac{1}{120}$ of actual size

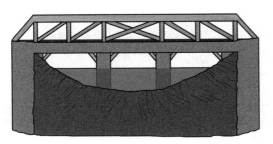

Example 1   Find the length of the bridge in the drawing above.

Answer

Let b = the length of the bridge in the drawing.

$\dfrac{1}{5} = \dfrac{b}{27}$ 1. Set up an appropriate proportion. The ratios should compare drawing lengths to actual lengths: $\frac{\text{cm}}{\text{m}}$.

$27 = 5b$ 2. Apply the Property of Proportions.

$5b = 27$ 3. Use the Symmetric Property of Equality to reverse the equation.

$\dfrac{5b}{5} = \dfrac{27}{5}$ 4. Divide both sides of the equation by 5.

$b = 5.4 \text{ cm}$

Example 2   The distance between two towns on a map is 3.6 cm. The scale on the map is 2 cm : 15 km. What is the actual distance between the towns?

Answer

Let n = the actual distance between the two towns.

$\dfrac{2}{15} = \dfrac{3.6}{n}$ 1. Write a proportion comparing the distance on the map to the actual distance.

$2n = 54$ 2. Apply the Property of Proportions.

$\dfrac{2n}{2} = \dfrac{54}{2}$ 3. Divide both sides of the equation by 2.

$n = 27$ km

Example 3   Find the distance from Carville to Danville.

Answer

$\dfrac{2}{25} = \dfrac{5}{n}$ 1. Write a proportion comparing the distance on the map to the actual distance.

$2n = 125$ 2. Apply the Property of Proportions.

$\dfrac{2n}{2} = \dfrac{125}{2}$ 3. Divide both sides of the equation by 2.

$n = 62.5$ km

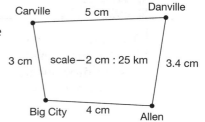

Skill Check 1

Find the distance between towns with the given map distance. Use the scale 1 cm : 15 km.

1. 3 cm   2. 5.2 cm   3. 12.7 cm

Use the map and scale in Example 3 to find the distances between the following cities.

4. Big City and Allen   5. Danville and Allen

Example 4   A map is to be made with a scale of 1 in. to 40 mi. How far apart will two cities appear on the map if they are actually 55 mi. from each other?

Answer

Let n = the map distance.   1. Assign a variable for the unknown.

$\dfrac{1}{40} = \dfrac{n}{55}$ 2. Write a proportion comparing the distance on the map to the actual distance.

$40n = 55$ 3. Apply the Property of Proportions.

$\dfrac{40n}{40} = \dfrac{55}{40}$ 4. Divide both sides of the equation by 40.

$n = 1\dfrac{15}{40} = 1\dfrac{3}{8}$ in.   5. Reduce to lowest terms.

Example 5   Find the scale used if two cities that are 60 mi. apart appear on a map at a distance of $\frac{3}{4}$ in.

Answer

$\dfrac{\frac{3}{4}\text{ in.}}{60\text{ mi.}}$

1. Write a proportion comparing the distance on the map to the actual distance.

$\dfrac{3}{4} \div 60 = \dfrac{\cancel{3}}{4} \times \dfrac{1}{\underset{20}{\cancel{60}}} = \dfrac{1}{80}$

2. Express the fraction as a division problem and simplify.

The scale is 1 in. : 80 mi.

3. Write the scale as a ratio of map distance to actual distance.

Skill Check 2

What distances would be represented on a map with a scale of 1 in. to 30 mi. if two towns are the following distances apart?

1. 75 mi.   2. 7.5 mi.

3. Find the blueprint scale if a 26 ft. room is shown as $6\frac{1}{2}$ in. on the blueprint.

Photocopiers list enlargements and reductions as percents of the original size. For instance, a reduction made at 50% would have a length and width one-half the size of the original, and an enlargement of 125% would have dimensions $1\frac{1}{4}$ times that of the original. These types of problems are another application of the basic percent formula: original dimension × percent reduction/enlargement = new dimension.

Example 6   If a 2.5 in. × 3.5 in. photo is to be enlarged to 5 in. × 7 in., what enlargement setting would be used?

Answer

Let p = the percent enlargement.

$2.5p = 5$

1. Write an equation, choosing one side of the original photo and a corresponding side of the enlarged photo.

$\dfrac{2.5p}{2.5} = \dfrac{5}{2.5}$

2. Solve the equation.

$p = 2$, or 200% enlargement

3. Change the value for p to a percent.

Note: Using the equation $3.5p = 7$ gives the same enlargement setting.

Example 7   A 10 cm × 16 cm table of data is reduced using a copier setting of 67%. What are the dimensions of the new table? Round to the nearest tenth if necessary.

Answer

$10(0.67) = 6.7$ cm

$16(0.67) \approx 10.7$ cm

Multiply the original dimensions by the percent reduction. Express the percent as a decimal.

6.7 cm × 10.7 cm

A scale may also be expressed as a ratio with no units. For example, a picture of an animal in a reference book may say 1 : 80 or a model airplane might say 1 : 32 scale. Such a ratio means the numbers can be viewed as having the same units. The picture of the animal would be one-eightieth the typical size of the real-life animal. The model plane would be one thirty-second the size of the real plane. If the model plane is 1 ft. long, the real plane would be 32 ft. long. If the model is 18 in. = 1.5 ft. long, the real plane would be 1.5 × 32 = 48 ft. long.

Example 8 If a picture in a book is labeled $\frac{1}{30}$ and an object in the photo is 5 in. wide, how wide is the real object?

Answer

30 × 5 in. = 150 in. = $\frac{150}{12}$ ft. = 12.5 ft. wide

Note: 150 in. is correct, but one does not usually give so large a dimension in inches.

Skill Check 3

Solve.

1. What setting would be used to make a table appear $4\frac{1}{2}$ in. wide from a picture in which it appears 3 in. × 4 in.?

2. What is the length of the new table in the problem above?

3. Give the dimensions of the table in exercise 1 if the photocopier setting was 75% instead.

4. A 1 : 72 scale model of the F-18 jet used by the Blue Angels is $9\frac{1}{3}$ in. long. How many feet long is the actual plane?

✥ Invention

Have you ever tried to copy a long document by hand? Perhaps you have tried to read carbon copies of a signature on a form, but the person did not press down hard enough for the signature to go onto the bottom copy. In 1937 these problems led a New Yorker named Chester Carlson to invent a document-copying process that was easily readable and not as tedious as hand-copying. He laid the document on a cylinder that would copy it using static electricity. Because of an electrostatic charge on a specially coated drum (cylinder), a negatively charged dry ink, called toner, would be attracted to only the positively charged image on the drum. A paper was placed where the toner was, so the image was created on the paper. The toner was then heated so that it melted and stuck to the paper as a copy of the original document. Carlson called the process *electrophotography* or *xerography* (a term coined from Greek words meaning "dry writing"). His machine required special electrostatic paper. In 1959 the first push-button automatic office *photocopier* that took regular office paper was introduced. Today, with the advent of digital technology, many electrostatic machines are obsolete; but the principle is still the same: transferring from one paper onto another with no hand-copying.

■ A. Exercises

Find the distance represented by points separated by the following distances on a map. The scale is 1 cm : 20 km.

1. 3 cm
2. 8 cm
3. 2.6 cm
4. 10.4 cm

Find the distance represented by points separated by the following distances on a map. The scale is 2 cm : 35 km.

5. 6 cm
6. 4.8 cm
7. 9.2 cm
8. 12.4 cm

Find the distance represented by points separated by the following distances on a map. The scale is 1 in. : 50 mi. Round to the nearest mile.

9. $5\frac{3}{4}$ in.
10. $4\frac{7}{8}$ in.

Using a scale of 1 cm : 30 km, find the distance between the following locations on the diagram.

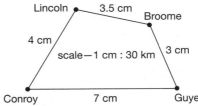

11. Lincoln and Conroy

12. Broome and Guyer

13. Guyer and Conroy

14. Broome and Lincoln

Find the size of the picture produced if a 60 mm × 90 mm picture is copied using the following settings.

15. 150%
16. 60%
17. 15%
18. 250%

■ B. Exercises

Measure the distances between the points on the map to the nearest eighth of an inch. Using the scale 1 in. : 50 mi., find the actual distance between the represented locations. Round to the nearest mile.

19. A to B

20. C to D

21. A to C

22. D to B

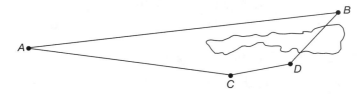

If a road map has a scale of 3 in. : 100 mi., find the following distances.

23. How far is it between Cardwell and Claremont if they are 4.5 in. apart on the map?

24. How far is it between Kingston and Goldsboro if they are 2 in. apart? Round to the nearest mile.

25. If Dodge City and Pine Bluff are 500 mi. apart, what is the distance between them on the map?

26. If Stenson and South Fork are 175 mi. apart, what is the distance between them on the map?

Solve.

27. A historical diorama (3D scene) is being built using a 1 : 24 scale. Determine the correct height in inches of the model of a 6 ft. tall individual.

28. A 1 : 24 model of a car is $7\frac{1}{4}$ in. long. How long is the car?

29. Model trains often use the HO scale, which is approximately 1 : 87. What is the actual length in feet of a locomotive whose model is 8 in. long?

30. Determine the length, to the nearest inch, of a 1 : 265 scale model of the *Titanic*, which was 883 ft. 9 in. long.

Find the percent setting needed to copy a $2\frac{1}{2}$ in. × $3\frac{1}{2}$ in. photo to the given dimensions.

31. 10 in. × 14 in.

32. $1\frac{7}{8}$ in. × $2\frac{5}{8}$ in.

33. $1\frac{1}{4}$ in. × $1\frac{3}{4}$ in.

34. 3 in. × 4.2 in.

■ C. Exercises

Solve.

35. Two points are $3\frac{5}{8}$ in. apart on a map. If the map scale is 1 in. : 45 mi., what is the actual distance between the cities? Round to the nearest mile.

36. Find the distance, to the nearest $\frac{1}{8}$ in., between two cities on a map that are 85 mi. apart. The scale of the map is 1 in. : 60 mi.

37. Two cities that are actually 55 mi. apart appear $1\frac{5}{8}$ in. apart on a map. What is the map's scale? Round the scale mileage to the nearest 5 mi.

■ Dominion thru Math

Architects and engineers use scale drawings to represent the design of their buildings and structures. Construction contractors use these drawings to build the actual structures and lay out the site.

38. A D-size drawing sheet is 24" × 36". Find the dimensions of the drawing of a building measuring 56' × 64' if the architect draws the floor plan at a scale of 1" : 4'. If a 3" outer boundary is desired, will this drawing fit on this sheet?

39. Can the architect of the building in the previous question fit two floor plans onto a D-size sheet if he maintains the 3" outer boundary and allows 2" between floor plans?

40. Using the same scale, find the dimensions of the floor plan of a 72' × 120' building and determine whether it will fit on a D-size drawing sheet with a 3" outer boundary.

CUMULATIVE REVIEW

Convert the following fractions to decimals. Use a line over the repeating sequence. [5.3]

41. $\frac{8}{9}$

42. $-\frac{3}{8}$

43. $\frac{14}{15}$

44. $-\frac{8}{3}$

45. $\frac{3}{5}$

Divide. Round decimals to the nearest hundredth. [6.3]

46. $\frac{5}{27} \div \frac{-7}{3}$

47. $\frac{-8}{15} \div \frac{-2}{5}$

48. $12 \div \frac{4}{3}$

49. $3.5 \div (-0.06)$

50. $428.7 \div 21.9$

Julia Morgan, Architect

Julia Morgan was known for her character and devotion to her work. Even as a child, she worked diligently on every project that she attempted. Julia was born in 1872 and grew up in Oakland, California. Charles and Eliza Morgan, her upper middle-class parents, believed in promoting higher education for all of their children. The family frequently took walks together through building and construction sites in the community. Julia became interested in mechanical objects and was fascinated with the idea of designing and constructing buildings. In school she took the most difficult subjects available and excelled in them. She especially enjoyed the logical thinking process used in solving difficult math problems.

Upon graduating from high school, Julia had no interest in social gatherings and parties like other young girls of her day. After discussing her desires with her mother, she gained her mother's full support to pursue the study of architecture. She graduated from the University of California at Berkeley as one of the first women to earn a degree in civil engineering.

One of her geometry professors, Bernard Maybeck, encouraged her to continue pursuing her interest in architecture by going to École Nationale Supérieure des Beaux-Arts, a school in Paris. With the support of her family, Julia arrived in Paris in 1896 but was refused admission to the school because of her gender. After two years of waiting, studying, and taking entrance exams, she was finally admitted and became the first woman to receive a certificate in architecture.

After completing her studies in Paris, she returned to the University of California at Berkeley. Through her work on such buildings as the Hearst Mining Building and the Hearst Greek Theater, she became associated with the multi-millionaire William Randolph Hearst.

Morgan began her own architectural business in 1904 and secured a number of residential commissions. Her philosophy was to never turn down a job because it was small, since she did not know where it might lead. Consequently, she designed some eight hundred buildings in California and Hawaii, more than were designed by Frank Lloyd Wright. She designed several buildings for the YWCA as well as the Berkeley Baptist Divinity School, the Methodist Chinese Mission School in San Francisco, and the Bell Tower and Carnegie Library at Mills College. The buildings at Mills College survived the devastating earthquake of 1906 with little or no damage.

Morgan's acquaintance with the Hearst family developed into a twenty-eight-year commission of building many extravagant homes and ranches. The buildings she designed for the Hearst family's estate in San Simeon covered 90,000 square feet and contained fifty-six bedrooms, sixty-one bathrooms, and indoor and outdoor pools.

After retiring in the early 1950s, Julia Morgan led a quiet life until her death in 1957.

Merrill Hall at Asilomar Conference Center in Pacific Grove, California, was designed by Julia Morgan in 1928.

7.5 Discount and Markup

The Outdoor Store is selling camping equipment for 20% off the regular or *retail price*. A tent is priced at $95. What is the discount? What is the sale price?

The *discount* is the amount by which the price of the item is reduced. The *discount rate* is the percent of the retail price by which the retail price is reduced. Finding the discount is an application of the basic percent formula: percent × whole = part. To find the discount (the part), multiply the retail price (the whole) by the discount rate (the percent).

$$\begin{aligned}
\text{discount} &= \text{discount rate} \times \text{retail price} \\
&= 0.2(95) \\
&= \$19 \text{ discount}
\end{aligned}$$

The *sale price* is the difference of the retail price and the discount.

$$\begin{aligned}
\text{sale price} &= \text{retail price} - \text{discount} \\
&= 95 - 19 \\
&= \$76 \text{ sale price}
\end{aligned}$$

Example 1 Find the discount and sale price if the retail price is $27.80 and the discount rate is 15%.

Answer

discount = discount rate × 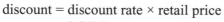 retail price   1. Write the appropriate formula.

discount = 0.15(27.80)   2. Substitute the known values.

$\qquad$ = $4.17

sale price = retail price − discount   3. Write the appropriate formula.

sale price = 27.80 − 4.17   4. Substitute the known values.

$\qquad$ = $23.63

The sale price can also be found by multiplying the percent paid times the original cost. If an item is discounted 15%, then 100% − 15% = 85% of the retail price is paid by the consumer. The sale price in Example 1 could be found by multiplying 0.85 × $27.80 = $23.63.

The basic percent formula, percent × whole = part, is used to find the discount rate. Remember that the discount rate is the percent.

A 20% discount means you pay 80%.

Example 2 An item originally priced at $45 sold for $32.85. What was the discount rate?

Answer

45 − 32.85 = $12.15   1. Find the amount of discount.

discount rate × retail price = discount

$p \times 45 = 12.15$ 2. Substitute the known values into the equation.

$45p = 12.15$ 3. Simplify.

$\dfrac{45p}{45} = \dfrac{12.15}{45}$ 4. Divide both sides by 45.

$p = 0.27 = 27\%$

The discount rate is 27%.

Skill Check 1

Find the discount and sale price for the following items.

1. retail price: $9
   discount rate: 10%

2. retail price: $25.80
   discount rate: 25%

3. retail price: $3,450
   discount rate: 20%

4. retail price: $590
   discount rate: 12.5%

Find the discount rate for the following items.

5. retail price: $50
   discount: $12

6. retail price: $80
   sale price: $60

A store owner buys merchandise from a manufacturer at a set price (his *cost*). He then increases his cost by some amount to arrive at the retail price he will ask of his customers. This increase above his cost is called *markup* and is expressed as a dollar amount. It can also be expressed as a percent of his cost, the *markup rate*. This is another application of the basic percent formula, where the part is the markup and the whole is the cost.

markup = markup rate × cost

Suppose a merchant buys a shirt for $18 from the manufacturer, marks it up 20%, which is $3.60, and sells it for $21.60. He has added $3.60, the markup amount, to his cost to obtain the retail price. The markup amount must be high enough to generate profit after covering the expenses of running the business. These expenses include such things as renting or buying a building, paying employees, and the cost of goods and utilities.

retail price = cost + markup

Definitions

Cost is the amount a merchant pays for the merchandise he will sell.
Retail price is the regular amount a merchant asks his customer to pay for merchandise.
Markup is the amount the merchant adds to his cost to arrive at the retail price.
Markup rate is the amount of markup on an item as a percent of its cost.

Example 3 A merchant buys shirts at $28 each and uses a 25% markup rate. Find the markup amount and retail price.

$28 \times .25 = $7

Answer

markup = markup rate × cost
$$= 0.25(28)$$
$$= \$7$$
retail price = cost + markup
$$= 28 + 7$$
$$= \$35$$

1. Substitute the known values into the equation.
2. Multiply to find the markup amount.
3. Substitute the known values into the equation.
4. Add to find the retail price.

Example 4 A merchant buys ties for $15 and sells them for $18. Find the markup and markup rate.

Answer

cost + markup = retail price
$$15 + m = 18$$
$$15 + m - 15 = 18 - 15$$
$$m = 3$$
The markup is $3.
markup rate × cost = markup
$$p \times 15 = 3$$
$$\frac{15p}{15} = \frac{3}{15}$$
$$p = 0.2 = 20\%$$
The markup rate is 20%.

1. Substitute the known values into the equation.
2. Solve to find the markup amount.

cost + markup
= real price
15 + m ? = 18

3. Substitute the known values into the equation.
4. Divide both sides by 15.
5. Change the decimal to a percent.

Skill Check 2

Find the markup and retail price for the following items.

1. cost: $25
   markup rate: 20%

2. cost: $100
   markup rate: 35%

Find the markup and markup rate for the following items.

3. cost: $20
   retail price: $30

4. cost: $15
   retail price: $17.70

■ A. Exercises

40

Find the discount and sale price for the following items.

1. retail price: $40; discount rate: 40% $16

2. retail price: $120; discount rate: 20%

3. retail price: $350; discount rate: 30%

4. retail price: $1,200; discount rate: 25%

5. retail price: $18; discount rate: 33.33%

6. retail price: $180; discount rate: 75%

7. retail price: $25; discount rate: 20%

8. retail price: $750; discount rate: 50%

9. retail price: $6; discount rate: 15%

10. retail price: $875; discount rate: 24%

Find the discount rate for the following merchandise.

11. retail price: $80; discount: $16

12. retail price: $7.50; discount: $2.50

13. retail price: $250; discount: $100

14. retail price: $365; discount: $73

15. retail price: $400; discount: $60

16. retail price: $30,000; discount: $1,950

Find the markup and retail price for the following items.

17. cost: $15; markup rate: 25%

18. cost: $155; markup rate: 18%

19. cost: $25.50; markup rate: 30%

20. cost: $650; markup rate: 40%

21. cost: $5; markup rate: 5%

22. cost: $1,200; markup rate: 17%

■ B. Exercises

Find the markup rate for the following store items.

23. cost: $50; markup: $12.50

24. cost: $125; markup: $23.75

25. cost: $17.50; retail price: $35

26. cost: $30; retail price: $40

27. cost: $2.50; retail price: $4

28. cost: $1,800; retail price: $2,340

[handwritten annotation:]
markup rate × cost = markup
?x 50 = 12.50
x
50x = 12.50
12.5   12.50

Find the sale price for the following items. Round to the nearest cent.

29. retail price: $8.95; discount rate: 6%

30. retail price: $24.50; discount rate: 15%

31. retail price: $175.95; discount rate: 10%

32. retail price: $12.98; discount rate: 30%

33. retail price: $295; discount rate: 6.5%

34. retail price: $745; discount rate: 12.5%

■ C. Exercises

Jody wants to buy a road bike for racing. The manager of OutBike bicycle shop just got in a new shipment of road bikes, and the one that Jody is interested in costs the store $1,480. The manager marks the bike up 40%.

35. What is the retail price of the road bike that Jody is interested in?

36. After three months the manager advertises a 20% off sale on all bikes in the store. How much would the bike that Jody wants cost during this sale?

37. Three months after the first sale the manager takes an additional 20% off the sale bikes. How much would the bike cost at this point?

38. Jody talked to the manager about the bike, and he told her she could have the bike for either 40% off the original price or the price after both 20% discounts are taken off. Which should she choose?

39. Why is the price after two 20% discounts are taken off different from the price when a 40% discount is taken off?

40. How does the 40% discount compare to the cost of the bike before the markup? Why are these amounts different?

■ Dominion thru Math

Use a calculator to find the answers to the following problems.

41. Karyn and Meagan have permission to set up a lemonade stand at the little league games for four Saturdays. Their competition is the soft drink machine, which charges $1.00 for a 20 oz. drink. What should they charge for a 16 oz. glass of lemonade to match the price of the competition?

42. If Karyn and Meagan decide to charge $0.75 per glass for their lemonade, what will they take in from the sale of 10 gal. of lemonade on a Saturday (1 gal. = 128 oz.)?

43. The girls have a delicious lemonade recipe and have priced the cost of lemons, lemon juice, sugar, ice, and disposable glasses. They know it will cost them $5.25/gal. to make their lemonade. At $0.75 per glass, what will their profit be per 10 gal., and what percent is their markup rate (to the nearest tenth of a percent)?

44. Meagan's dad suggests that they use 20 oz. cups, put 16 oz. of lemonade in each cup, fill the rest with ice, and charge $1.00. This will increase their cost by only $0.15/gal. Under this proposal, find their total cost, their total income, their profit, and their markup rate (to the nearest percent) to make and sell 10 gal. of lemonade.

45. At the price of $1.00 per glass, how much of their 10 gal. of lemonade will they need to sell to break even? This means that their income is the same as their expenses.

46. During the four Saturdays that they ran their lemonade stand, Karyn and Meagan made and sold 10 gal., made and sold 15 gal., sold 12 of 15 gal. made, and sold 10 of 12 gal. made. Find their total cost, total income, profit, and markup rate (to the nearest percent) for the four weeks they ran the K&M Lemonade Stand.

CUMULATIVE REVIEW

Perform the indicated operations. [6.1–6.3]

47. $2\frac{1}{2} + 3\frac{2}{3}$

48. $2\frac{1}{2} - 3\frac{2}{3}$

49. $2\frac{1}{2} \times 3\frac{2}{3}$

50. $2\frac{1}{2} \div 3\frac{2}{3}$

Classify the following numbers as natural, whole, integer, rational, or irrational. Give the most specific set. [5.6]

51. –3.4

52. 0

53. $-\sqrt{72}$

54. $-\sqrt{36}$

55. $\frac{4}{9}$

56. 17

7.6 Commissions and Tips

All or part of a salesperson's salary is often calculated as a percent of his sales. This dollar amount is sometimes referred to as a commission. In this text, however, we will use the term *commission* to refer to the percent and the term *earnings* to refer to the dollar amount. Commission problems are another application of the basic percent formula. In commission problems the amount of earnings is the part, and the amount of sales is the whole.

Example 1

Find the earnings if the commission is 7% and the amount of sales is $3,750.

Answer

earnings = commission × sales

$= 0.07(3{,}750)$ 1. Substitute the known values into the equation.

$= 262.50$ 2. Multiply.

The earnings on the sales are $262.50.

Commission refers to a %.
percent × whole = part
commission × sales = earnings

Example 2

Find the commission if $3,000 in sales earns a salesperson $270.

Answer

commission × sales = earnings

$c \times 3{,}000 = 270$ 1. Substitute the known values into the equation.

$3{,}000c = 270$ 2. Use the Commutative Property to reorder the factors.

$\dfrac{3{,}000c}{3{,}000} = \dfrac{270}{3{,}000}$ 3. Divide both sides of the equation by 3,000.

$c = 0.09$

The commission is 9%.   4. Change the decimal to a percent.

Example 3

Miss Kay receives a 6% commission for selling houses. If she earned $8,340 for the sale of a house, how much did the house sell for?

Answer

commission × sales = earnings

$0.06s = 8{,}340$ 1. Substitute the known values into the equation.

$\dfrac{0.06s}{0.06} = \dfrac{8{,}340}{0.06}$ 2. Divide both sides of the equation by 0.06.

$s = 139{,}000$

The house sold for $139,000.

Skill Check 1

Find the earnings.

1. sales: $850
   commission: 25%

2. sales: $9,600
   commission: 12.5%

Find the commission.

3. sales: $8,500
   earnings: $1,275

4. sales: $12,500
   earnings: $2,125

Find the amount of the sales.

5. earnings: $1,665
   commission: 9%

6. earnings: $322.50
   commission: 15%

Income paid for a personal service is called a *tip*. Some workers receive all or a portion of their income in tips. These workers include waiters and waitresses, bellhops, hairdressers, and taxi drivers. Billions of dollars are exchanged annually in America by tipping. This custom was originally held in disfavor in America and was even banned in several states. However, it gradually gained favor over the years and is commonly done today. A customary tip for restaurant service is considered to be about 15–18% of the bill. Since wait staff earn much of their pay from tips, it is important for Christians to be generous representatives of Christ's love and tip correctly.

Calculating the approximate tip to leave is an application of the basic percent formula. In this case, the tip is the part and the bill is the whole.

$$\text{percent} \times \text{total bill} = \text{tip}$$

Tip amounts are usually rounded to a convenient denomination of money. In this text, unless instructed otherwise, round all tips to the nearest five cents. For example, a $7.58 tip will be rounded to $7.60.

15–18% of the bill is an appropriate tip.

Example 4 How much of a tip should you leave at a restaurant if your bill is $34.75 and you want to leave a 15% tip? Round to the nearest nickel.

Answer

tip = percent × total bill

$\quad$ = 0.15(34.75) $\qquad$ 1. Substitute the known values into the equation.

$\quad$ = 5.2125 $\qquad\qquad$ 2. Multiply.

$\quad$ ≈ $5.20 $\qquad\qquad$ 3. Round to the nearest five cents.

Example 5 A hairdresser gave a $55 perm and received a $10 tip. What percent of the bill did she receive? Round to the nearest percent.

Answer

percent × total bill = tip

$\qquad p \times 55 = 10$ $\qquad\qquad$ 1. Substitute the known values into the equation.

$\qquad \dfrac{55p}{55} = \dfrac{10}{55}$ $\qquad\qquad$ 2. Divide both sides by 55.

$\qquad p = 0.\overline{18} \approx 0.18$ $\qquad$ 3. To obtain the nearest percent, round the decimal to the nearest hundredth.

The hairdresser received about an 18% tip.

Skill Check 2

Find the tip if the percent used is 15%. Round to the nearest nickel.

1. bill total: $48.39 $\qquad\qquad\qquad$ 2. bill total: $132

Find the percent used for the following tips. Round to the nearest whole percent.

3. bill total: $64.92 $\qquad\qquad\qquad$ 4. bill total: $87.50
$\quad$ tip: $8 $\qquad\qquad\qquad\qquad\qquad$ tip: $16

■ A. Exercises

Find the earnings for the following sales and commissions.

1. sales: $4,300; commission: 7%

2. sales: $25,500; commission: 12%

3. sales: $6,780; commission: 35%

4. sales: $1,750; commission: 12%

5. sales: $10,009; commission: 20%

6. sales: $13,000; commission: 17.5%

Find the appropriate tip for the following services at the rate of 15% of the cost. If the answer is not a multiple of twenty-five cents, round to the next higher quarter.

7. haircut: $15

8. dinner out: $35

9. taxi ride: $18.90

10. perm: $62

11. shoe shine: $5

12. clothing pressed: $7.50

■ B. Exercises

Find the commission for the following sales and earnings.

13. sales: $10,800; earnings: $864

14. sales: $30,500; earnings: $3,660

15. sales: $140,000; earnings: $21,000

16. sales: $17,500; earnings: $1,837.50

17. sales: $42,500; earnings: $7,225

18. sales: $102,000; earnings: $21,420

Find the amount of sales that generated the following earnings.

19. earnings: $2,425; commission: 25%

20. earnings: $40,000; commission: 20%

21. earnings: $18,500; commission: 8%

22. earnings: $4,620; commission: 25%

23. earnings: $2,200; commission: 12.5%

24. earnings: $5.85; commission: 9%

The following amounts represent restaurant bills followed by the tip left. Find, to the nearest percent, what percentage of the bill was left as a tip.

25. bill: $35.60; tip: $4

26. bill: $26.45; tip: $5

27. bill: $15.90; tip: $3.50

28. bill: $52.75; tip: $6.75

29. bill: $63.20; tip: $10

30. bill: $32.40; tip: $5.80

31. Find the appropriate 15% tip for a restaurant bill of $17.85. Round to the nearest quarter.

32. Find the range of an appropriate tip for a permanent costing $75, assuming 15% to 18% is typical.

33. Find the commission when a salesperson received a $52 payment for a sale of $650.

34. Find the amount earned by a salesperson who sold a $250 dress if she gets a 12.5% commission.

35. A salesperson who is paid a 15% commission received $402.75 for a sale. Find the amount sold.

■ C. Exercises

36. Complete the following chart by writing the basic percent equations using words in the columns under each of the three parts of the percent equation. Notice the similarities of the five equations.

Percent equation	percent	×	whole	=	part
Discount equation		×		=	
Markup equation		×		=	
Commission equation		×		=	
Tip equation		×		=	

37. Why is it important for you to know these basic equations involving percents?

38. A value-added tax is a tax that is assessed at each point of sale. For example, a 5% value-added tax would charge a wholesaler 5% on the price he pays when he purchases from a manufacturer. A storekeeper would then have to pay 5% on the price he pays when he purchases from a wholesaler. The consumer would have to pay 5% on the price he pays when he purchases from the storekeeper. If it costs the manufacturer $10 to make a pair of shoes, what will the consumer have to pay if there is a 5% value-added tax and everybody (manufacturer, wholesaler, and storekeeper) wants to make a 20% profit?

■ Dominion thru Math

Karyn and Meagan are analyzing how their lemonade business turned out. They want a good understanding of what happened so they can improve their overall sales and profits should they decide to run this business again. Review the information in Section 7.5, Dominion thru Math, to answer the following questions.

39. What percent of the first week's sales was the increase in sales from week one to week two?

40. What percent of the second week's sales was the decrease in sales from week two to week three?

41. What percent of the lemonade inventory sold during the four weeks? Round to the nearest percent.

42. Suppose Karyn and Meagan had sold their remaining lemonade at the end of each day at 25% off ($0.75 per glass). If they had disposed of their inventory this way on weeks three and four, what would their profit and markup rate have been?

43. Karyn and Meagan think that selling pre-packaged chips for $0.50 each would increase their lemonade sales by 25% due to the "thirst factor." If the bags of chips cost them $0.25 each and they had sold chips to one-third of their customers, what would their third-week sales, profit, and markup rate have been?

Save or invest about 10% of your take-home pay. You will be glad you did.

CUMULATIVE REVIEW

Write an equation and solve. [3.5]

44. A number divided by −8, increased by 12, is 34.

45. Eleven times a number, decreased by 4, is 62.

46. Nine times the sum of a number and 19 is −18.

47. The product of a number and 7, divided by 8, is 49.

48. Twenty-three is 8 times a number, decreased by 21.

Write the following numbers in base 2. [4.7]

49. 17   50. 6   51. 21   52. 10   53. 87

7.7 Interest

Interest is the amount of money paid for the use of money. If you invest money, you earn interest on your investment; but if you borrow money, you must pay interest on your loan. There are two common types of interest, simple and compound. *Simple interest* means that at the end of a specified period of time, the borrower pays the lender the full amount borrowed, plus the interest due, as a single payment.

In some situations you may be the borrower, in others the lender. Although it is sometimes necessary to borrow in order to produce wealth, it is better to be the lender. Proverbs 22:7 tells us that "the borrower is servant to the lender." So if you must borrow money, remember that you are a servant—under obligation—to the one you borrowed from.

It is necessary to understand how simple interest works before studying other types of interest calculations.

Simple Interest Formula
$I = Prt$, where $I =$ interest, $P =$ principal, $r =$ annual rate of interest, and $t =$ time in years.

Example 1   Find the simple interest earned from a one-time investment of $3,000 at 8% interest if the account is closed at the end of two years.

Answer

$I = Prt$

  $= 3,000(0.08)(2)$

  $= \$480$

Example 2   Aaron borrowed $465 for one year to buy an eighteen-speed touring bicycle. His bank gave him a simple interest loan at 12% annual interest for one year. How much interest will Aaron pay?

Answer

$I = Prt$

  $= 465(0.12)(1)$

  $= 55.80$

Aaron owes $55.80 simple interest on this loan.

To find the amount that Aaron will have to repay at the end of the year, add the interest to the principal. Aaron will have to repay $465 + $55.80 = $520.80.

Amount Formula
$A = P + I$, where $A =$ amount due, $P =$ principal, and $I =$ interest.

Example 3   Find the interest and the total value of an investment of $1,500 at 5% simple interest for 9 mo.

Answer

$t = \dfrac{9}{12} = \dfrac{3}{4} = 0.75$

1. Since time is in terms of years, determine the part of a year that 9 mo. represents by dividing by 12.

$I = Prt$

$= 1,500(0.05)(0.75)$

$= \$56.25$

2. Substitute the known values into the simple interest formula.

$A = P + I$

$= 1,500 + 56.25$

$= \$1,556.25$

3. Use the amount formula to find the total value of the investment.

Skill Check 1

Find the interest earned from the following savings accounts. Each account was started with a one-time deposit, and no additional deposits or withdrawals were made.

1. $2,500 deposited at 4% simple interest for 3 yr.

2. $8,000 deposited at 4.5% simple interest for 9 mo.

Find the interest and the amount to pay back on the following loans.

3. $5,000 loan at 10% simple interest for 18 mo.

4. $3,000 loan at 9% simple interest for 8 mo. (Hint: Express the months in fraction form.)

Most savings accounts pay *compound interest*, which means interest is calculated at set intervals on the sum of the principal and any previous interest earned. Because the interest is added to the principal at the end of the interval, the principal for the next period is slightly larger, resulting in a slightly larger interest payment for that period. Common intervals used are given below.

Compounding Interval	Meaning	Payments per Year
annually	every year	1
semiannually	every six months	2
quarterly	every three months	4
monthly	every month	12

A compound interest account will yield more interest than a simple interest account. If $4,000 is invested for a year at 3% interest, the simple interest earned would be

$$4,000(0.03)(1) = \$120.$$

Suppose the $4,000 is deposited in an account that offers 3% annual interest compounded quarterly (every three months). Since the interest is compounded four times per year, the time for each compounding period is $\dfrac{1}{4}$ of a year, or in decimal form $t = 0.25$. The simple interest formula, $I = Prt$, is used to find the interest for the first quarter.

$$4,000(0.03)(0.25) = \$30$$

The interest is added to the original principal to obtain the principal for the second quarter.

$$4{,}000 + 30 = \$4{,}030$$

The interest for the second quarter is calculated using the new principal. The interest amount is rounded to the nearest cent.

$$4{,}030(0.03)(0.25) = \$30.23$$

Continue this process to find the balance at the end of the first year.

$4{,}030 + 30.23 = \$4{,}060.23$	Balance at the end of the second quarter
$4{,}060.23(0.03)(0.25) = \$30.45$	Simple interest for the third quarter
$4{,}060.23 + 30.45 = \$4{,}090.68$	Balance at the end of the third quarter
$4{,}090.68(0.03)(0.25) = \$30.68$	Simple interest for the fourth quarter
$4{,}090.68 + 30.68 = \$4{,}121.36$	Balance at the end of the first year

The amount of interest accumulated for the year is

$$4{,}121.36 - 4{,}000 = \$121.36.$$

This is a simple example of how compound interest helps your money grow faster than it would with simple interest. $1.36 additional interest may not seem like a big difference, but compounding over a long period of time increases the difference. Also, other factors being equal, an account that compounds monthly will earn even more interest than an account that compounds quarterly.

Example 4 A savings account offers 4% interest compounded monthly. Find the amount in the account at the end of 3 mo. if the initial deposit is $10,000. How much interest was earned during the first 3 mo.?

Answer

Since the interest is compounded monthly, let $t = \frac{1}{12}$. Use a calculator to multiply the principal times 0.04; then divide the product by 12. Remember to round to the nearest cent.

Period	Principal	Interest	New Principal
1	$10,000	$10{,}000(0.04)\left(\frac{1}{12}\right) \approx \$33.33$	$10,000 + 33.33 = \$10,033.33$
2	$10,033.33	$10{,}033.33(0.04)\left(\frac{1}{12}\right) \approx \$33.44$	$10,033.33 + 33.44 = \$10,066.77$
3	$10,066.77	$10{,}066.77(0.04)\left(\frac{1}{12}\right) \approx \$33.56$	$10,066.77 + 33.56 = \$10,100.33$

The amount of interest earned was 10,100.33 – 10,000 = $100.33.

Skill Check 2

Find the amount on deposit in the following savings accounts after two interest periods. How much interest was earned during this time?

1. $6,000 deposit for 4% interest, compounded semiannually

2. $9,500 deposit for 5% interest, compounded quarterly

Calculating compound interest can be much more involved than calculating simple interest. Compounding interest monthly over a period of two years could involve twenty-four separate calculations. However, there is a compound interest formula that allows the calculations to be done more quickly.

The formula that will be used in this text is for interest compounded annually. There is a more general formula for compounding at other intervals, but it is somewhat more involved. It can be found in CONSUMER MATH (BJU Press).

Annual Compound Interest Formula

$S = P(1 + i)^n$, where S = amount in the savings account, P = principal, i = annual interest rate, and n = number of annual interest payments.

Example 5 Use a calculator to find the amount in a savings account at the end of 5 yr. if $5,200 is invested at 3.5% interest compounded annually. Also find the amount of interest earned.

Answer

$P = \$5,200$	1. Identify the values for P, i, and n.
$i = 3.5\% = 0.035$	
$n = 5$	
$S = P(1 + i)^n$	
$S = 5{,}200(1 + 0.035)^5$	2. Substitute the values into the compound interest formula.
$S = 5{,}200(1.035)^5$	3. Add the amount inside the parentheses.
$S = 5{,}200(1.187686306)$	4. Eliminate the exponent. (See the note below.)
$S \approx \$6{,}175.97$	5. Multiply to get the total amount in the account.
$6{,}175.97 - 5{,}200 = \$975.97$	6. Subtract to find the total interest earned in 5 yr.

Note: The exponent can be eliminated by multiplying:
$$1.035 \times 1.035 \times 1.035 \times 1.035 \times 1.035.$$

A calculator with an exponential function key will allow you to find the value of $(1.035)^5$ without doing the repeated multiplication. This key appears as $\boxed{y^x}$ on some calculators and as $\boxed{\wedge}$ on graphing calculators.

Skill Check 3

Find the amount in each savings account at the end of the designated time. Also find the amount of interest earned. Round to the nearest cent.

1. $7,000 at 5.5% interest compounded annually for 4 yr.

2. $1,500 at 6% interest compounded annually for 5 yr.

■ A. Exercises

Find the amount of interest due on the following simple interest loans.

1. $4,200 at 12% for 2 yr.

2. $850 at 9% for 6 mo.

3. $4,000 at 15% for 3 yr.

4. $6,250 at 10% for 18 mo.

5. $10,000 at 8.5% for 4 yr.

6. $5,000 at 9% for 2 yr.

Find the interest and the amount to pay back on the following simple interest loans.

7. $750 at 12% for 9 mo.

8. $1,500 at 14% for 2 yr.

9. $2,500 at 11% for 18 mo.

10. $12,500 at 10.5% for 3 yr.

11. $4,500 at 8% for 2 yr.

12. $1,850 at 9.5% for 18 mo.

13. $7,000 at 6.25% for 2 yr.

14. $300 at 18% for 2 mo.

15. $960 at 6.05% for 5 yr.

State the number of times per year the following accounts are compounded.

16. quarterly

17. semiannually

18. monthly

19. daily

■ B. Exercises

The following are one-time deposits into accounts where interest is compounded annually. Find the amount of interest earned the first year, the amount earned the second year, and the total on deposit at the end of the second year.

20. $2,000 at 4%

21. $3,500 at 3%

22. $10,000 at 4.5%

23. $6,300 at 5%

24. $20,000 at 5.2%

25. $100 at 3.25%

The following are one-time deposits into accounts where interest is compounded annually. Using the annual compound interest formula, find the amount in the account at the end of the given time period. Then find the total interest earned over the time period. Round to the nearest cent. Use a calculator to do these problems.

26. $8,000 at 5% for 3 yr.

27. $10,000 at 4.5% for 10 yr.

28. $5,250 at 5% for 20 yr.

29. $12,145 at 4.2% for 12 yr.

30. $6,745 at 6% for 7 yr.

31. $4,800 at 4.75% for 18 yr.

32. $1,800 at 18% for 3 yr.

33. $100,000 at 8% for 30 yr.

Solve.

34. Mr. Anderson borrowed $4,600. The loan was for 3 yr. at a simple interest rate of 15%. What is the total amount he must repay?

35. The Robbins family borrowed $1,050 at a simple interest rate of 18% for 3 mo. to purchase a new washer and dryer. What is the total amount that they must repay?

36. Stan has $800 in an account earning 4% simple interest. How much interest will he earn in one and one-half years?

■ C. Exercises

Find the total amount in the following accounts after two compounding periods. Notice that the compounding period is not annual in these problems. The annual rate given in the problem must be divided by the number of times the account is compounded per year to find i, the interest rate per compounding period that is used in the compound interest formula.

37. $5,000 at 5% compounded semiannually

38. $3,200 at 4% compounded quarterly

39. $12,000 at 10% compounded quarterly

40. $9,450 at 6% compounded monthly

Use a calculator to find the total amount in the following compound interest accounts and the total interest earned. In the formula $S = P(1 + i)^n$, the exponent n represents the number of compounding periods.

41. $10,000 at 4% compounded quarterly for 6 mo.

42. $6,500 at 4.5% compounded quarterly for 6 mo.

43. $4,500 at 4% compounded monthly for 10 yr.

44. $7,000 at 4.5% compounded quarterly for 12 yr.

45. $10,000 at 5% compounded monthly for 20 yr.

■ Dominion thru Math

46. If Karyn and Meagan will invest their $376 income from their lemonade business, their fathers each promise to match the amount. They found a federal credit union that pays 5% compounded quarterly and invested the total amount. How much will be in their account in ten years?

CUMULATIVE REVIEW

Name the inverse operation, including the quantity, that would be used to solve each equation. [3.1–3.2]

47. $x + 7 = -82$ 48. $8z = 24$ 49. $s + 4 = 9$

50. $-48 = c - 26$ 51. $a - 49 = -17$

Multiply. [6.2]

52. $6\frac{4}{7} \times 4\frac{3}{4}$ 53. $-6\frac{2}{5} \times \left(-1\frac{1}{4}\right)$ 54. 3.29×0.3 55. -2.7×4.1

7.8 Percent Change

Analyzing change is very important in business. A business owner is interested in knowing if there has been an increase or a decrease in his profits over a period of time. Recall that the new amount can be calculated directly when the percent increase or decrease from an original amount is given. An increase in sales of 25% implies that the new amount is 125% of the original amount, while a decrease of 25% means that the new amount is 75% of the original amount. This idea can be generalized in the following statements. An increase of x% implies the new amount is $(100 + x)$% of the original, and a decrease of x% means that the new amount is $(100 - x)$% of the original.

> **Example 1**   Determine next year's sales goal, N, if the company wants to increase this year's sales of $250,000 by 15%.
>
> **Answer**
>
> The goal is 115% of last year's sales. 1. The new amount is $(100 + x)\%$ of the original.
>
> $N = 1.15(250,000)$ 2. Translate into the general percent formula.
>
> $N = \$287,500$ 3. Simplify.

Knowing the percent change is often more valuable than knowing the actual amount that a quantity has changed. The percent increase or decrease is the ratio of the amount of change to the original amount, expressed as a percent. Many business decisions are made as a result of these calculations. The percent change formula is a form of the general percent formula that has been solved for the percent.

Percent Change Formula
$\text{percent change} = \dfrac{\text{amount of change}}{\text{original amount}} \times 100\%$

The following steps are used to find the percent change.

Finding the Percent Change
1. Subtract to find the amount of change.
2. Divide the amount of change by the original amount.
3. Convert the quotient to a percent and indicate whether it is an increase or a decrease.

> **Example 2**   What is the percent change from 75 to 100?
>
> **Answer**
>
> $100 - 75 = 25$ 1. Find the amount of change.
>
> $\dfrac{\text{change}}{\text{original}} = \dfrac{25}{75} = 0.\overline{3}$ 2. Write the ratio of the amount of change to the original amount. Divide.
>
> The percent change is a $33.\overline{3}\%$ increase. 3. Change the quotient to a percent.

If 100 is decreased to 75, will the percent decrease also be $33.\overline{3}\%$? No, because the ratio is now comparing the change (25) to a different original amount (100). The ratios are not equal;

$$\frac{25}{100} \neq \frac{25}{75}.$$

The percent decrease from 100 to 75 is

$$\frac{25}{100} = 0.25 = 25\%.$$

> **Example 3**   Find the percent change, to the nearest whole percent, from 19 to 16. Indicate whether it is an increase or a decrease.
>
> **Answer**
>
> $19 - 16 = 3$ 1. Find the amount of change.
>
> $\dfrac{3}{19} \approx 0.16 = 16\%$ decrease 2. Write the ratio $\dfrac{\text{change}}{\text{original}}$ and divide. Change the quotient to a percent.

Calculate the new amount.

1. increase 20 by 30%   2. decrease 40 by 15%

Find the percent change. Indicate whether it is an increase or a decrease.

3. original amount: 10   4. original amount: 25
   new amount: 13   new amount: 6

5. original amount: 40   6. original amount: 50
   new amount: 42   new amount: 46

Example 4   Last year Mrs. Rutherford's homeroom sold 56 cartons of candy bars. This year her home-room sold 80 cartons. What was the percent change? Give the answer to the nearest tenth of a percent.

Answer

$80 - 56 = 24$ 1. Find the amount of change.

$\frac{24}{56} \approx 0.429 = 42.9\%$ increase   2. Write the ratio $\frac{\text{change}}{\text{original}}$. Divide and round the quotient to the nearest thousandth. Change the quotient to a percent.

Example 5   Dillon has 65 baseball cards and Joseph has 50. Dillon has what percent more than Joseph? Joseph has what percent less than Dillon?

Answer

$65 - 50 = 15$ 1. Find the difference.

$\frac{15}{50} = \frac{30}{100} = 30\%$ 2. More than what? Compare to Joseph's 50.

$\frac{15}{65} \approx 0.23 = 23\%$ 3. Less than what? Compare to Dillon's 65.

Dillon has 30% more cards than Joseph. Joseph has 23% less than Dillon.

Find the percent change. Indicate whether it is an increase or a decrease. Round to the nearest whole percent.

1. Marcus earned an average of $25 per week mowing lawns last summer. This summer, he estimates he will make about $40 per week. What is the percent increase?

2. A $400 guitar is reduced to $340. Find the percent decrease in the price.

3. Marjorie raised her score from 41 correct out of 50 on her first test to 49 out of 50 correct on the next test. What was the percent increase in her score?

4. Rajeesh's new method allowed the job to be accomplished in 3.5 hr. instead of the 6 hr. that it would normally take. What is the percent change in the time required to complete the job?

■ A. Exercises

Calculate the new amount.

1. increase 40 by 20%

2. decrease 37 by 10%

3. increase 14 by 50%

4. decrease 105 by 8%

5. decrease 35 by 20%

6. increase 210 by 130%

Find the percent change. Round to the nearest percent.

7. original: 60; change: 12

8. original: 45; change: 10

9. original: 100; change: 19

10. original: 600; change: 90

11. original: 54; change: 60

12. original: 24; change: 30

Find the percent change. Indicate whether it is an increase or a decrease.

13. original amount: 30; new amount: 36

14. original amount: 20; new amount: 21

15. original amount: 28; new amount: 42

16. original amount: 36; new amount: 27

17. original amount: 80; new amount: 24

■ B. Exercises

Write the amount of change; then find the percent change. Indicate whether it is an increase or a decrease. Round to the nearest percent.

18. from 18 to 36

19. from 25 to 20

20. from 15 to 18

21. from 40 to 30

22. from 120 to 90

23. from 75 to 175

Find the percent change. Indicate whether it is an increase or a decrease. Round to the nearest percent.

24. Katelyn got an increase in pay of $0.40/hr. Her old rate was $7.50/hr.

25. Cindy bought a sweater for $40 that was priced the week before at $50.

26. The attendance at this year's festival was estimated at 20,000. Last year the attendance was estimated at 15,000.

27. The factory hired seven new workers, bringing its total to sixty-two.

28. After the fire, the company had to lay off four workers, leaving it with twenty-five.

29. The new car sells for $46,000. A comparably equipped one sold for $39,000 five years ago.

30. When sugar was replaced with a sugar substitute, sales dropped to 20,000 units per week. This was 3,000 fewer than when sugar was used.

31. The university added 20,500 new seats to the existing stadium's 45,000 seats.

32. When plastic was used for some of the parts instead of metal, the cost of the finished product dropped $10 to a new price of $72.

33. When the new machine was introduced, the output went from 24 to 80 units per day.

■ C. Exercises

Calculate both the percent more and the percent less for the following exercises. Round to the nearest percent, and state the results in two sentences (as was done in Example 5).

34. The price of a reserved seat is $20, but the price of general admission is $12.

35. The Grizzlies beat the Bulldogs 67 to 45.

36. The list price of the sedan is $35,600. The list price of the sports car is $50,200.

37. The larger truck will hold about 350 bushels. The smaller one will hold about 220 bushels.

38. Explain why a change from 8 to 9 is not the same percent change as a change from 9 to 8.

39. Express the percent change as a ratio.

■ Dominion thru Math

40. Find the percent decrease in Karyn and Meagan's profit from week two to week three. They made 15 gal. of lemonade both weeks, but they sold only 12 gal. on week three. (Hint: Recall from previous Dominion thru Math exercises that their cost is $5.40/gal. and their total income is $8/gal.)

41. If Karyn and Meagan had decided to sell potato chips with their lemonade, they could have increased their sales to 15 gal. of lemonade on week three instead of 12 gal. Using the information from Section 7.6, Dominion thru Math, what would the expected percent increase in their profit be?

CUMULATIVE REVIEW

Rename each mixed number as an improper fraction. [5.1]

42. $-3\frac{2}{9}$ 43. $8\frac{1}{5}$ 44. $-9\frac{5}{7}$ 45. $-4\frac{2}{3}$ 46. $7\frac{1}{8}$

Evaluate. Write fractional answers in lowest terms. [6.4]

47. $\frac{-9}{11}a$ when $a = \frac{4}{7}$

48. $\frac{3}{5}n + 7$ when $n = 55$

49. $\frac{1}{4}r - 2\frac{5}{8}$ when $r = -7$

50. $\frac{2}{7}y + \frac{1}{14}$ when $y = \frac{-1}{2}$

51. $-0.7a$ when $a = 8.9$

52. $32.08m + 5.2$ when $m = 0.06$

MATH & SCRIPTURE

Solomon's Temple

In 1 Chronicles 28 King David shares his heart about his vision to build a permanent home for the ark of the covenant. God did not allow him to build the temple because he was a man of war. God gave that task to his son Solomon. Just as God gave Moses very specific details for constructing the wilderness tabernacle, God also gave David instructions for the temple. David then put these plans in writing for Solomon (1 Chron. 28:11–12, 19). In addition to the plans, God gave special wisdom to Solomon (1 Kings 4:29–34), who sought out skilled artisans to carry out the plans. One of the most important of these skilled craftsman was Hiram of Tyre (also called Huram, and not to be confused with King Hiram), who fashioned all the works of brass, including the pillars, the sea, and the ten basins (1 Kings 7:13–14).

1. What were the dimensions in feet of the main house of the temple that contained the holy place and the holy of holies (1 Kings 6:2)?

2. What were the dimensions in feet of the porch (1 Kings 6:3)?

3. What was the height, including the capitals (called "chapiters" in the KJV), and diameter of its pillars in feet (1 Kings 7:15–16)? (Recall that the formula for the circumference of a circle is $c = \pi d$.) Round to the nearest tenth.

4. How many feet was the widest dimension of the chambers that surrounded the house (1 Kings 6:5–6)?

5. How were the upper two levels of chambers accessed (1 Kings 6:8)?

6. What were the shape and dimensions of the holy of holies in feet (1 Kings 6:20)?

7. What were the dimensions of the holy place in feet (1 Kings 6:2, 17)?

8. How long did it take Solomon to build the house of God (1 Kings 6:38)?

9. How did Solomon describe the house he had built for the ark of the covenant (1 Kings 8:13, 27, 43)?

10. How did Solomon know that God had chosen to inhabit the beautiful house (2 Chron. 7:1–3)?

Infinite Truths

In the fourth year was the foundation of the house of the Lord laid, in the month Zif: and in the eleventh year, in the month Bul, which is the eighth month, was the house finished throughout all the parts thereof. *1 Kings 6:37–38a*

Chapter 7 Review

Vocabulary

amount formula	earnings	percent formula
commission	interest	proportion method
compound interest	markup	retail price
compound interest formula	markup rate	scale
cost	percent	scale drawing
discount	percent change	simple interest
discount rate	percent change formula	simple interest formula

Write each percent as a fraction.

1. 60%   2. 34%   3. 18%

Write each percent as a decimal.

4. 53.5%   5. 78%   6. 0.4%

Write each fraction as a percent.

7. $\dfrac{18}{5}$ 8. $\dfrac{3}{4}$ 9. $\dfrac{1}{16}$

Write each decimal as a percent.

10. 5.9   11. 0.795

12. Eighteen is what percent of 36?   13. What is 52% of 98?

14. Sixteen is 80% of what number?

15. If 38% of the church budget is designated for missions and the church's quarterly income is $52,000, how much goes to missionary support each quarter?

16. Joey made 33 out of 60 free throws this season. What was his free throw percentage for the year?

17. Jillian sold 12% of the candy bars the class sold to raise money for a new water cooler in the school. If she sold 36 candy bars, what was the total number of candy bars sold by the class?

18. The total cost of a dress, including tax, was $121.37. If 6% tax was added to the sale price, what was the sale price before taxes?

Find the distance between two cities on a map if the scale is $\dfrac{1}{4}$ in. : 60 mi.

19. 1 in.   20. 2.5 in.

How far apart should the following distances be located on a map if the scale is 1 cm : 4 km?

21. 150 km   22. 60 km

23. What size picture will result when a 5 in. × 7 in. picture is reduced using an 80% setting?

24. Find the percent setting needed to copy a 3 in. × 4 in. photo to $8\dfrac{1}{4}$ in. × 11 in.

Find the discount and sale price for the following discounted items.

25. retail price: $892; discount rate: 12%   26. retail price: $87.50; discount rate: 70%

Find the discount rate for the following merchandise. Round to the nearest tenth of a percent.

27. retail price: $15.80; sale price: $12.90

28. retail price: $1,898; sale price: $1,518.40

Find the markup and retail price for the following items.

29. cost: $42.50; markup rate: 60%

30. cost: $2,857; markup rate: 34%

Find the commission for the following sales and earnings.

31. sales: $4,935; earnings: $444.15

32. sales: $145,000; earnings: $17,400

Find the amount of sales that generated the following earnings.

33. earnings: $6,054.30; commission: 7%

34. earnings: $36,720; commission: 24%

Find the appropriate tip for the following services at the rate of 15% of the cost. If the answer is not a multiple of twenty-five cents, round to the next higher quarter.

35. restaurant: $45

36. haircut: $38

Find the amount to pay back on the following simple interest loans.

37. $2,900 at 8.5% for 4 yr.

38. $52,900 at 9.3% for 6 mo.

Find the interest and the amount to pay back on the following simple interest loans.

39. $380 at 12.5% for 2 yr.

40. $875 at 8.7% for 10 yr.

41. A typical credit card charges 18.99%. Find the interest owed on a credit card with a balance of $372 for one month.

The following are one-time deposits into accounts where interest is compounded annually. Using the compound interest formula, find the amount in the account at the end of the given time period. Then find the total interest earned over the time period. Round to the nearest cent.

42. $2,600 at 5.3% for 4 yr.

43. $12,500 at 4.8% for 10 yr.

44. $350 at 5.2% for 2 yr.

Write the amount of change; then find the percent change. Indicate whether it is an increase or a decrease. Round to the nearest percent.

45. from 138 to 92

46. from 26 to 81

47. Mrs. Starnes had 24 students in her class last year and 31 in her class this year. What is the percent change?

48. Leigh got a thirty-cent raise after her first anniversary at work. If her starting salary was $7.50/hr., what percent change did she experience in her raise?

49. Jay's weight increased 12% during his high-school years. If he weighed 158 lb. when he graduated, how much did he weigh when he began high school?

50. State the mathematical significance of 1 Kings 6:37–38a.

8

APPLYING EQUATIONS AND INEQUALITIES

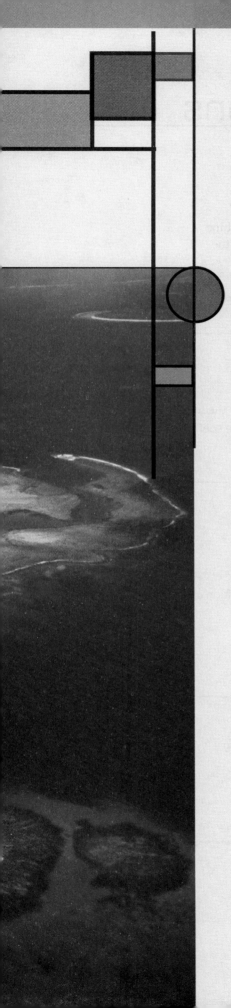

The science that studies weather is called meteorology, but it has nothing to do with meteors. Meteor showers and rain showers both occur in the atmosphere above the earth. The former are streaks of light emitted by a meteor burning up as it enters the earth's atmosphere. Rain showers are water from clouds that help to sustain life over much of the earth.

Even though people often complain about rain or snow, all animal and plant life depends on sufficient amounts of water to prosper. Even destructive storms, such as hurricanes, provide certain benefits. Hurricanes are just the regular hydrological cycle gone overboard.

God designed our earth with a certain amount of water. About 97% of the water is in the earth's oceans. Water evaporates from the oceans and rises into the atmosphere, where it unites into drops to form clouds. The wind and atmospheric currents carry these clouds over the land, where the water is discharged in the form of rain. The oceans lose more to evaporation than they gain by rainfall, while the land masses lose less to evaporation than they gain by rainfall. This imbalance is corrected by the return of water to the seas by the rivers of the world. The hydrological cycle is another beautiful example of God's handiwork on the earth (Ps. 19:1).

After this chapter you should be able to

1. solve equations containing parentheses.

2. solve equations with variables on both sides.

3. write equations from word sentences and solve them.

4. solve two-step inequalities and graph their solutions.

5. write two-step inequalities for word problems and solve them.

8.1 Simplifying Equations

In Chapter 3 you learned that the Commutative and Associative Properties allow us to group like terms together. The Distributive Property then permits us to combine the like terms. The result is a simplified equation that can easily be solved for the variable. The Distributive Property is restated below in its usual written form.

Distributive Property: $a(b + c) = ab + ac$

The following examples review the use of the Distributive Property.

Example 1 Simplify $5y + 2 - 6y + 14$.

Answer

$5y + 2 - 6y + 14$

$(5y - 6y) + (2 + 14)$ 1. Group the like terms. Keep the minus sign with the term that follows it.

$-y + 16$ 2. Subtract the coefficients of y. $5 - 6 = -1$, but the coefficient is not written since $-1y = -y$. Add 2 and 14.

Example 2 Solve $8x - 4x + 6 = -86$.

Answer

$8x - 4x + 6 = -86$

$(8x - 4x) + 6 = -86$ 1. Group the like terms.

$4x + 6 = -86$ 2. Simplify by subtracting the coefficients of x.

$4x + 6 - 6 = -86 - 6$ 3. Subtract 6 from both sides. Use the definition of subtraction: $-86 - 6 = -86 + (-6)$.

$4x = -92$

$\dfrac{4x}{4} = \dfrac{-92}{4}$ 4. Divide both sides by 4.

$x = -23$

Skill Check 1

Simplify.

1. $3b + 5 - 14b - 8$

2. $18r - 6r + 9 - 2r$

Solve.

3. $3x + 5x = 104$

4. $9x - 2x + 2 = -12$

5. $4 - 7x = 18$

6. $2x + 8 - 5x = 74$

Before combining like terms in an algebraic equation such as $7(x + 3) + 5x = 69$, you must remove the parentheses by applying the Distributive Property. Once the parentheses are removed, the Commutative and Associative Properties allow you to combine like terms, simplifying the expression.

Example 3 Solve $7(x + 3) + 5x = 69$.

Answer

$7(x + 3) + 5x = 69$

$7x + 21 + 5x = 69$ 1. Apply the Distributive Property.

$12x + 21 = 69$ 2. Combine like terms on the left side.

$12x + 21 - 21 = 69 - 21$ 3. Subtract 21 from both sides.

$12x = 48$

$\dfrac{12x}{12} = \dfrac{48}{12}$ 4. Divide both sides by 12.

$x = 4$

Example 4 Solve $20 - 9(y + 4) = 2$.

Answer

$20 - 9(y + 4) = 2$

$20 - 9y - 36 = 2$ 1. Apply the Distributive Property.

$-16 - 9y = 2$ 2. Combine like terms on the left side.

$-16 - 9y + 16 = 2 + 16$ 3. Add 16 to both sides.

$-9y = 18$

$\dfrac{-9y}{-9} = \dfrac{18}{-9}$ 4. Divide both sides by -9.

$y = -2$

You will often see a quantity in parentheses immediately preceded by a plus or minus sign but with no multiplier shown before it. If the quantity is preceded by a plus sign, you need only remove the parentheses; every sign remains as it was within the parentheses.

$$9x + (3x - 2) = 9x + 3x + (-2)$$
$$= 9x + 3x - 2$$

Once this is understood, you need not write the intermediate form when solving an equation.

If a parenthesis is preceded by a minus sign with no multiplier, it will change the sign of every term within the parentheses. This fact follows from the definition of subtraction. Subtraction is equivalent to adding the opposite. Study the following example.

Example 5 Simplify $18x - (4x - 9)$.

Answer

$18x - (4x - 9) = 18x + (-4x + 9)$ 1. Definition of subtraction: $4x - 9$ and $-4x + 9$ are opposites since their sum is zero.

$= 18x + (-4x) + 9$ 2. Remove the parentheses (for a sum, the signs remain the same as inside the parentheses in the right side of step 1).

$= 18x - 4x + 9$ 3. Simplify by using the definition of subtraction.

$= 14x + 9$ 4. Combine like terms.

When this process is understood, the intermediate steps need not be written. Rather, we can immediately say that $18x - (4x - 9) = 18x - 4x + 9$. The following examples show how these ideas are used in solving equations.

Example 6   Solve $9 - (x + 8) = 20$.

Answer

$9 - (x + 8) = 20$

$9 - x - 8 = 20$ 1. Subtract the quantity in parentheses; both signs change.

$1 - x = 20$ 2. Combine the constants on the left side.

$1 - x - 1 = 20 - 1$ 3. Subtract 1 from both sides.

$-x = 19$

$-1(-x) = -1(19)$ 4. Multiply (or divide) both sides by -1.

$x = -19$

Example 7   Solve $5x + (3x + 4) = 40$.

Answer

$5x + (3x + 4) = 40$

$5x + 3x + 4 = 40$ 1. Remove the parentheses; the signs remain the same.

$8x + 4 = 40$ 2. Combine like terms.

$8x + 4 - 4 = 40 - 4$ 3. Subtract 4 from both sides.

$8x = 36$

$\dfrac{8x}{8} = \dfrac{36}{8}$ 4. Divide both sides by 8.

$x = 4.5$

$$-(x + 7) \neq -x + 7$$
$$-(x + 7) = -x - 7$$

Skill Check 2

Solve.

1. $7x - 2(x + 4) = 27$ 2. $9 - 3(2x - 7) = 42$

3. $5(x + 1) - (2x - 3) = 53$ 4. $7x - 2 - (4x + 1) = -2$

Invention

Like many inventions, the digital *compact disc* solved a problem in the existing sound-recording technology. Because plastic phonograph records wore out from the pickup needles riding in the plastic grooves, in the late 1960s engineer and inventor James Russell developed a way to play and record audio without actual contact between the "record" and the pickup. In 1970 he patented the first digital-to-optical recording and playback system. On the photosensitive surface of a plastic disc, tiny bits of dark and light are recorded on a continuous spiral track; a laser reads this binary data so a computer can convert it to an electrical signal. This system kept the disc from wearing out. It also added storage space; whereas the 3.5 in. floppy disk could hold only about 1.44 megabytes of information, the CD can hold more than 700 megabytes. This increase in information meant more music on each disc (and thus fewer discs). The goal of the first marketers of the CD was to fit all of Beethoven's Ninth Symphony onto one CD (instead of two records). As a result, the first CDs could hold 74 minutes of music—the time for the longest recording available of Beethoven's Ninth.

■ A. Exercises

Simplify.

1. $-5x + 19 - 8x$

2. $18 + 17x - 9x$

3. $12(n - 4) + n$

4. $-4(z - 11) + 9$

5. $17 - 2(x - 14)$

6. $3(y - 8) + 3(2y)$

7. $18 - 3(2y + 6)$

8. $3(-7 + 2) - 5(3y)$

Solve.

9. $4(2x - 3) = 92$

10. $5(2x + 1) = 20$

11. $3(-y + 12) - 4y = 85$

12. $12 - 2(x + 4) = 2$

13. $9n + 4(2n) = 68$

14. $2(3m) + 5m - 6 = 27$

15. $4n - 6n + 7 - 4 = 25$

16. $-6x + 3 - 12x - 8 = 31$

■ B. Exercises

Solve.

17. $7(x + 3) = 21$

18. $-4(x - 2) = 30$

19. $3(y + 8) = 39$

20. $4(3 - 2z) = -84$

21. $3(2x - 5) - 4x = 10$

22. $7(17 - x) = 28$

23. $7(6y) - 3(2y) = 108$

24. $4(x - 23) + 3(-2) = 2$

25. $3(x - 5) + 2(x - 1) = 8$

26. $-6(14 + 2x) = 48$

27. $20 - 3(x + 5) = 8$

28. $5x - 2(x + 1) = 10$

29. $13x + 4(x + 9) = 104$

30. $4z - 8(z + 1) = 38$

31. $(x + 3) + 2(x + 3) = 3$

32. $8x + 2(7 + x) = 16$

33. $3(2y) - (y + 1) = 6$

34. $6 - (y - 1) = 8$

■ C. Exercises

Solve.

35. $-2.5k + 3(k - 6) = 7$

36. $4.4(n - 5) + (-3n) = 20$

37. $\frac{2}{3}w - \frac{1}{4}(w + 10) = 6$

38. $\frac{6}{7}p - \frac{5}{7}p - 17 = 18$

39. $\frac{2}{5}r + 9 + \frac{1}{5}r = 21$

■ Dominion thru Math

Relative humidity provides a means to describe the water vapor content of the air. In an intuitive sense, relative humidity is the ratio (as a percent) of the amount of water vapor in the air to the maximum amount of water vapor the air can hold at a given temperature. Actually, however, the water content of air is measured using vapor pressure since it is directly proportional to the water vapor concentration. If the relative humidity is 100%, then the air is saturated and water will start to condense. The following is the formula for relative humidity (*RH*).

Weather prediction provides advanced warning of most major storms.

$$RH = \frac{\text{actual vapor pressure}}{\text{saturation vapor pressure}} \times 100\%$$

Vapor pressure is measured in millibars (mb). 1,000 millibars = 1 bar $\approx \dfrac{14.5 \text{ lb.}}{\text{in.}^2}$. This means that, at sea level, the weight of the air above every square inch of area is about 14.5 lb. Atmospheric pressure is measured with an instrument called a barometer and is often referred to as barometric pressure.

Use a calculator to find answers to the following weather-related problems.

40. What is the relative humidity at 50°F if the saturation vapor pressure is 9.21 mb and the actual vapor pressure is 3.6 mb?

41. What is the relative humidity at 85°F if the saturation vapor pressure is 3,004 pascals (Pa) and the actual vapor pressure is 751 Pa? (*Note:* 1 mb = 100 Pa. Pascals are the SI unit for measuring vapor pressure.)

42. The saturation vapor pressure increases about 6% for every degree Celsius the air temperature increases. This increase can be seen from the following model for the saturation vapor pressure between 0°C and 55°C: $V = 5.227(1.0605)^x$, where x is the temperature in °C and V is the vapor pressure in mb. What is the saturation vapor pressure at 15°C?

43. What is the saturation vapor pressure at 25°C?

44. If the relative humidity is 30% at 15°C, what will it be if the air temperature increases to 25°C? (Hint: Use your answers from exercises 42 and 43 along with the relative humidity formula).

CUMULATIVE REVIEW

Solve. [3.7]

45. $x - 12 \le 28$

46. $x + 9 < 4$

47. $32 > x + 15$

48. $2y - 7 < 19$

49. $-4y > -72$

Order the following lists of rational numbers from smallest to largest using the < symbol. [5.2–5.3]

50. $\dfrac{9}{5}, \dfrac{7}{6}, \dfrac{3}{2}, \dfrac{11}{10}$

51. $-5\dfrac{7}{8}, -5\dfrac{2}{3}, -5\dfrac{1}{2}, -5\dfrac{5}{6}$

52. $-\dfrac{4}{5}, -\dfrac{7}{9}, -\dfrac{3}{4}, -\dfrac{9}{10}$

53. $4.345, 4.3\overline{4}, 4.\overline{34}, 4.\overline{345}$

54. $-35.7, -35\dfrac{3}{5}, -35.6\overline{5}, -35.\overline{65}$

Moses, Leader of Israel

Moses helped to establish Israel as a nation—redeeming God's people from Egypt, giving them the law, and judging them for forty years. What was the secret of his success?

As a prince in the pharaoh's court, Moses was well educated. "Moses was learned in all the wisdom of the Egyptians, and was mighty in words and in deeds" (Acts 7:22). Moses found many opportunities to use his math skills after he became ruler over Israel. As an example, consider when God commanded Moses to number the people (take a census).

The Lord commanded Moses, "Take ye the sum of all the congregation of the children of Israel, . . . from twenty years old and upward, all that are able to go forth to war in Israel" (Num. 1:2–3). After Moses found the number in each tribe, he combined the results to find that "all they that were numbered were six hundred thousand and three thousand and five hundred and fifty" (Num. 1:46). So the grand total of all the fighting men of Israel was 603,550.

Although Moses was a learned man, his learning was not the key to his success. Before he could lead God's people, Moses needed to learn about meekness. While attempting to deliver Israel at the age of forty, Moses killed an Egyptian, was rejected by his people, and was forced to flee for his life (Exod. 2:11–15; Acts 7:23–29). He spent forty years as a shepherd in the wilderness. There, living in obscurity, he learned to let God use his skills in His way and in His time. When God eventually did call him to deliver Israel, Moses replied, "Who am I, that I should go unto Pharaoh, and that I should bring forth the children of Israel out of Egypt?" (Exod. 3:11). Moses had learned true meekness: "Now the man Moses was very meek, above all the men which were upon the face of the earth" (Num. 12:3).

In this chapter, you will use some of the same addition and subtraction skills that Moses used years ago. Although these skills are necessary to your success in math, your success in life requires much more than a knowledge of math skills. You too need to learn meekness. Ask God to help you develop your pre-algebra skills. Admitting your dependence on Him will help you grow in meekness, and the Lord will reward you for your humble spirit—just as He rewarded Moses!

8.2 Variables on Both Sides

Some equations contain a variable on both sides of the equal sign. To solve an equation like this, you will apply the properties of equality to eliminate the variable from one side of the equation. You can eliminate the variable from either side of the equation to arrive at the correct solution, though the steps you use to obtain the solution will vary. If you eliminate the variable from the side that has the smaller coefficient, the variable will have a positive coefficient. Another approach is to always eliminate the variable on the right. This method has the advantage of giving an answer of the form $x = 6$ instead of $6 = x$.

Example 1 Solve and check $7x = 16 + 5x$.

Answer

$7x = 16 + 5x$

$7x - 5x = 16 + 5x - 5x$ 1. Eliminate the x-term from the right side by subtracting $5x$. Subtract $5x$ from the left side also.

$2x = 16$

$\dfrac{2x}{2} = \dfrac{16}{2}$ 2. Divide both sides of the equation by 2.

$x = 8$

$7(8) = 16 + 5(8)$ 3. **Check**: Substitute 8 for x.

$56 = 16 + 40$

$56 = 56$ 4. The solution is verified.

Example 2 Solve and check $8x + 5 = x$.

Answer

$8x + 5 = x$

$8x + 5 - 8x = x - 8x$ 1. Eliminating the x-term from the side containing a constant will shorten the process of solving the equation.

$5 = -7x$

$\dfrac{5}{-7} = \dfrac{-7x}{-7}$ 2. Divide both sides of the equation by -7.

$x = -\dfrac{5}{7}$

$8\left(-\dfrac{5}{7}\right) + 5 = -\dfrac{5}{7}$ 3. **Check**: Substitute $-\dfrac{5}{7}$ for x.

$-\dfrac{40}{7} + \dfrac{35}{7} = -\dfrac{5}{7}$

$-\dfrac{5}{7} = -\dfrac{5}{7}$ 4. The solution is verified.

What would you do to both sides of the equation to get the variable only on the left?

1. $7c = 16 + 4c$

2. $4x = 12 - 2x$

What would you do to both sides of the equation to get the variable only on the right?

3. $3n + 5 = -8n$

4. $5y - 24 = 9y$

Solve and check.

5. $3x + 18 = 5x$

6. $6r = 27 - 3r$

The equation $2x + 9 = 5x - 3$ (in Example 3 below) contains not only a variable on both sides, but also a constant on both sides. To solve this equation, it is necessary to get the variable on one side of the equation and the constant on the other side. You may prefer to get the variable on the left side, or you may prefer instead to get it on whichever side makes the coefficient of the variable positive.

Example 3 Solve and check $2x + 9 = 5x - 3$.

Answer

$2x + 9 = 5x - 3$

$2x - 2x + 9 = 5x - 2x - 3$ 1. Eliminate $2x$ from the left side of the equation. Subtract $2x$ from the right side also.

$9 = 3x - 3$

$9 + 3 = 3x - 3 + 3$ 2. Eliminate -3 from the right side by adding 3. Add 3 to the left side also.

$12 = 3x$

$\dfrac{12}{3} = \dfrac{3x}{3}$ 3. Divide both sides of the equation by 3.

$x = 4$

$2(4) + 9 = 5(4) - 3$ 4. **Check**: Substitute 4 for x.

$8 + 9 = 20 - 3$

$17 = 17$ 5. The solution is verified.

Study the following solution of Example 3. It demonstrates that the solution is the same regardless of which side contains the variable.

$2x + 9 = 5x - 3$

$2x - 5x + 9 = 5x - 5x - 3$

$-3x + 9 = -3$

$-3x + 9 - 9 = -3 - 9$

$-3x = -12$

$\dfrac{-3x}{-3} = \dfrac{-12}{-3}$

$x = 4$

Example 4 Solve and check $7x - 5 = 3x + 10$.

Answer

$$7x - 5 = 3x + 10$$

$7x - 5 - 3x = 3x + 10 - 3x$ 1. Subtract $3x$ from both sides.

$$4x - 5 = 10$$

$4x - 5 + 5 = 10 + 5$ 2. Add 5 to both sides.

$$4x = 15$$

$\dfrac{4x}{4} = \dfrac{15}{4}$ 3. Divide both sides by 4.

$$x = \dfrac{15}{4}$$

$7\left(\dfrac{15}{4}\right) - 5 = 3\left(\dfrac{15}{4}\right) + 10$ 4. **Check**: Substitute $\dfrac{15}{4}$ for x in the original equation.

$\dfrac{105}{4} - \dfrac{20}{4} = \dfrac{45}{4} + \dfrac{40}{4}$

$\dfrac{85}{4} = \dfrac{85}{4}$ 5. The solution is verified.

Example 5 Solve and check $4(x - 3) = -2(3x + 11)$.

Answer

$$4(x - 3) = -2(3x + 11)$$

$4x - 12 = -6x - 22$ 1. Eliminate the parentheses from both sides of the equation.

$4x + 6x - 12 = -6x + 6x - 22$ 2. Add $6x$ to both sides to eliminate the variable from the right side.

$$10x - 12 = -22$$

$10x - 12 + 12 = -22 + 12$ 3. Add 12 to both sides to eliminate the constant from the left side.

$$10x = -10$$

$\dfrac{10x}{10} = \dfrac{-10}{10}$ 4. Divide both sides by 10.

$$x = -1$$

$4(-1 - 3) = -2[3(-1) + 11]$ 5. **Check**: Substitute -1 for x in the original equation.

$$4(-4) = -2(-3 + 11)$$

$$-16 = -2(8)$$

$-16 = -16$ 6. The solution is verified.

The steps used in solving equations are summarized below and illustrated in Example 6.

Steps in Solving an Equation
1. Eliminate parentheses by distributing.
2. Simplify each side by adding like terms.
3. Isolate the variable on one (either) side.
4. "Undo" additions to or subtractions from the variable term.
5. "Undo" multiplications or divisions of the variable.

Example 6   Solve $-3(x + 4) - 8 = 3x + 4$.

Answer

$-3(x + 4) - 8 = 3x + 4$

$-3x - 12 - 8 = 3x + 4$ 1. Distribute -3 (step 1).

$-3x - 20 = 3x + 4$ 2. Combine like terms (step 2).

$-3x - 20 - 3x = 3x + 4 - 3x$ 3. Subtract $3x$ from both sides (step 3).

$-6x - 20 = 4$

$-6x - 20 + 20 = 4 + 20$ 4. Add 20 to both sides (step 4).

$-6x = 24$

$\dfrac{-6x}{-6} = \dfrac{24}{-6}$ 5. Divide both sides by -6 (step 5).

$x = -4$

Skill Check 2

Solve and check.

1. $2m + 12 = 5m - 6$

2. $-6s + 5 = 2s - 3$

3. $5(x - 6) = 2x$

4. $3(2y + 4) = -2(y - 4)$

■ A. Exercises

What would you do to both sides of the equation to get the variable only on the left?

1. $-3x = 8x - 5$

2. $7x = -2x + 14$

3. $8n - 5 = 17n$

4. $4 - 9x = -6x$

Solve.

5. $5x = 28 - 2x$

6. $2x = 40 - 6x$

7. $-8z = 6z + 42$

8. $2a = -6a - 64$

9. $7b - 20 = 8b$

10. $5(x - 6) = 3x$

11. $3(x + 4) = -7x$

12. $2x = 5x - 6$

13. $8y + 4 = 3y + 19$

14. $8p - 13 = 5p + 8$

15. $2z + 8 = 6z - 12$

■ B. Exercises

Solve. Express noninteger answers as fractions in lowest terms or decimals rounded to the nearest tenth.

16. $12x = 6(x - 2)$

17. $7x - 4 = 2x + 5$

18. $3y - 8 = 5y + 4$

19. $12x - 7 = 2x + 5$

20. $17 - 7x = 2x - 1$

21. $5 - 10x = 8x + 5$

22. $3(2x - 5) = x$

23. $7x = 4(x - 3)$

24. $13x - 8 = 2x - 15$

25. $4 - 7x = 2 + 6x$

26. $3(x - 6) = 2(x + 4)$

27. $2(x + 4) = 3(x - 2)$

28. $7(x - 8) = 2(x + 1)$

29. $-4(2x - 3) = 7(x + 8)$

30. $6(x + 3) - 6 = 24$

31. $4(x + 2) + 6 = 34$

32. $2(s + 1) = 6s - 6$

33. $6(y + 1) = 3(y + 3)$

34. $7(x + 4) = 5(x + 8)$

35. $5(b - 2) = 3(b - 6)$

36. $4(f - 3) = 2(f - 7)$

■ C. Exercises

Solve.

37. $\dfrac{5}{7}k + 4 = \dfrac{2}{7}k + 13$

38. $\dfrac{7}{9}v - 2 = \dfrac{2}{9}v + 8$

39. $4\left(\dfrac{1}{5}y - 1\right) = \dfrac{2}{3}y + 17$

■ **Dominion thru Math**

The following relative humidity problems are continued from Section 8.1, Dominion thru Math. You may need to copy the formulas from that section on your paper before trying these problems. Use the following formula for conversions between degrees Fahrenheit and degrees Celsius: $C = \frac{5}{9}(F - 32)$.

40. If the relative humidity is 45% at 30°C, what will it be at 20°C? (Hint: Use the model from Section 8.1.)

41. Find the relative humidity at 41°F if the vapor pressure is 316 Pa. (Hint: Be sure to convert the temperature scale and the vapor pressure units.)

42. Find the relative humidity at 95°F if the vapor pressure is 3,678 Pa.

43. What is the percent increase in saturation vapor pressure as the temperature goes from 15°C to 35°C?

CUMULATIVE REVIEW

Write the recursive definition for the following sequences. [4.5–4.6]

44. 6, 8, 10, 12, 14, …

45. −1, 7, 15, 23, 31, …

46. 3, 3.5, 4, 4.5, 5, …

47. 32, 16, 8, 4, 2, …

48. $\frac{1}{81}, -\frac{1}{27}, \frac{1}{9}, -\frac{1}{3}, 1, \ldots$

Choose a variable to represent the unknown. Write an equation and solve. [6.7]

49. Five-eighths of a number is 30. Find the number.

50. If 20% of a number is 9, what is the number?

51. Jeremiah buys a dozen doughnuts for $9.84. How much does each doughnut cost?

52. A recipe calls for $\frac{3}{4}$ cup of flour. Gloria has 5 cups of flour. How many batches of the recipe can she make?

53. Mr. Crittenden found that 30% of his students made either an A or a B in his classes. If there were 12 As and Bs, how many students were in his classes?

MIND OVER MATH

In the Smith family there are three children. The youngest is 7 years younger than the oldest, and the oldest is 2 years older than the middle child. In 12 years the sum of their ages will be 57. What are their ages now?

8.3 Applying Equations

An algebraic equation is a useful tool for solving a word problem. When you are expressing a word sentence as an algebraic equation, it is often helpful to identify the verb of the word sentence. The verb usually indicates the placement of the equal sign in the equation. The phrase that precedes the verb should be translated into symbols and placed on the left side of the equation. The phrase that follows the verb should be translated into symbols and placed on the right side of the equation.

Word sentence: The sum of three times a number and seven is one less than twice the same number.

Verb: "Is" indicates the location of the equal sign.

Phrase 1: "The sum of three times a number and seven" translates to $3n + 7$.

Phrase 2: "One less than twice the same number" translates to $2n - 1$.

Equation: $3n + 7 = 2n - 1$.

Example 1   Find a number such that five times the sum of that number and –3 is three less than the opposite of the number.

Answer

$5(n - 3) = -n - 3$	1. Write the equation.
$5n - 15 = -n - 3$	2. Eliminate the parentheses by distributing.
$5n + n - 15 = -n + n - 3$	3. Add n to both sides to eliminate the variable from the right side.
$6n - 15 = -3$	
$6n - 15 + 15 = -3 + 15$	4. "Undo" the subtraction.
$6n = 12$	
$\frac{6n}{6} = \frac{12}{6}$	5. "Undo" the multiplication.
$n = 2$	

$5n + 3 = 2n - 6$

Skill Check 1

Write an equation and solve.

1. The sum of two times a number and three is half the number.

2. Five times the sum of a number and three is six less than twice the number.

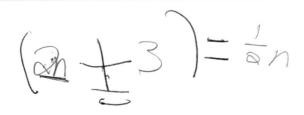

$(2n + 3) = \frac{1}{2}n$

In Section 6.7 you were given the following set of guidelines for using equations to solve problems. Review these four steps, along with a new fifth step, and apply them to the following examples.

Steps in Solving a Word Problem
1. Represent an unknown quantity with a variable.
2. When necessary, represent other conditions in the problem in terms of the variable.
3. Identify two equal quantities in the problem.
4. Write and solve an equation.
5. Check the answer.

One type of problem involving *consecutive integers* is often used in algebra to give students practice in setting up equations and solving them. Begin by letting a variable x represent one of the numbers. If you choose to let x represent the smaller integer, then the next larger integer is one greater than x, or $x + 1$.

Example 2 The sum of two consecutive integers is 173. Find the integers.

Answer

Let x = the smaller integer.

Let $x + 1$ = the larger integer.

$x + (x + 1) = 173$	1. Write the equation.
$(x + x) + 1 = 173$	2. Apply the Associative Property of Addition.
$2x + 1 = 173$	3. Combine like terms.
$2x + 1 - 1 = 173 - 1$	4. Subtract 1 from both sides.
$2x = 172$	
$\dfrac{2x}{2} = \dfrac{172}{2}$	5. Divide both sides by 2.
$x = 86$	
$x + 1 = 87$	

Problems involving integers often specify consecutive *odd integers* or consecutive *even integers*. A look at the first few odd integers reveals that they always differ by 2.

$$1, 3, 5, 7, 9, 11, 13, \ldots$$

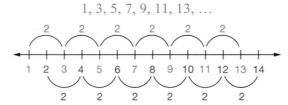

Consecutive even integers also differ by 2.

$$2, 4, 6, 8, 10, 12, 14, \ldots$$

Therefore, x, $x + 2$, $x + 4$, and so on can be used to represent either consecutive even or consecutive odd integers.

Example 3 Find three consecutive odd integers such that three times the third is 2 more than five times the first.

Answer

Let x = the smallest integer.

Let $x + 2$ = the next consecutive odd integer.

Let $x + 4$ = the largest odd integer.

$3(x + 4) = 5x + 2$	1. Write the equation.
$3x + 12 = 5x + 2$	2. Distribute to remove the parentheses.
$3x - 3x + 12 = 5x - 3x + 2$	3. Subtract $3x$ from both sides.
$12 = 2x + 2$	
$12 - 2 = 2x + 2 - 2$	4. Subtract 2 from both sides.
$10 = 2x$	
$\dfrac{10}{2} = \dfrac{2x}{2}$	5. Divide both sides by 2.
$x = 5$	
$x + 2 = 7$	
$x + 4 = 9$	

Skill Check 2

Write an equation and solve to find the integers.

1. Find two consecutive integers whose sum is 91.

2. Find two consecutive even integers whose sum is 94.

3. Find three consecutive odd integers such that twice the first is 7 more than the third.

The basic equation for solving motion problems is distance = rate × time, or $d = rt$.

Example 4 If a ship is traveling at 20 knots (nautical miles per hour), how long will it take to travel 55 nautical miles?

Answer

$rt = d$	
$20t = 55$	1. Substitute the known rate and distance.
$\dfrac{20t}{20} = \dfrac{55}{20}$	2. Divide both sides by 20.
$t = 2.75$ hr.	

The rate of a boat in a river is affected by the current, c, in the same way that the rate of an airplane is affected by the wind. A 2 mi./hr. current would cause a boat capable of 25 mi./hr. in still water to travel at a rate of 27 mi./hr. downstream and a rate of only 23 mi./hr. upstream. Similarly, the wind speed, w, should be added to a plane's air speed, r, when it is traveling with the wind to determine the plane's ground speed, $r + w$. When the plane is flying into a headwind, the wind speed is subtracted from the plane's air speed for a ground speed of $r - w$.

Example 5   What is the speed of the wind if a plane capable of flying 400 mi./hr. takes 3 hr. to travel 1,050 mi. into a headwind?

Answer

$(r - w)t = d$	1. The plane's rate must be adjusted due to the headwind.
$(400 - w)3 = 1,050$	2. Substitute the known values.
$1,200 - 3w = 1,050$	3. Eliminate the parentheses by distributing.
$1,200 - 1,200 - 3w = 1,050 - 1,200$	4. "Undo" the addition.
$-3w = -150$	
$\dfrac{-3w}{-3} = \dfrac{-150}{-3}$	5. "Undo" the multiplication.
$w = 50$ mi./hr.	

Example 6   Luke and Andrew paddled their canoe 22 mi. down the river in 4 hr. If the river's current averages 1.5 mi./hr., what is their average rate in still water?

Answer

$(r + c)t = d$	1. Their rate must be adjusted due to the current.
$(r + 1.5)4 = 22$	2. Substitute the known values.
$4r + 6 = 22$	3. Eliminate the parentheses by distributing.
$4r + 6 - 6 = 22 - 6$	4. "Undo" the addition.
$4r = 16$	
$\dfrac{4r}{4} = \dfrac{16}{4}$	5. "Undo" the multiplication.
$r = 4$ mi./hr.	

Skill Check 3

Write an equation and solve.

1. If an Olympic sprinter runs 100 m in 9.80 sec., what is his average speed?

2. A boat capable of traveling 25 mi./hr. in still water travels 110 mi. up the river in 5 hr. What is the average speed of the river's current?

3. A jet takes 2 hr. to complete a flight of 680 mi. when flying into a headwind of 65 mi./hr. Determine the air speed of the plane.

■ **A. Exercises**

Write an equation and solve to find the numbers.

1. The sum of two consecutive integers is 471.

2. The sum of two consecutive integers is 65.

3. The sum of two consecutive even integers is 74.

4. The sum of two consecutive odd integers is 116.

5. Find three consecutive integers whose sum is 132.

6. Find three consecutive even integers whose sum is 84.

7. Twice the sum of a number and three is 88.

8. When the sum of twice a number and 4 is tripled, the result is 72.

9. Doubling the difference between a number and 4 is 6 more than the number.

10. Five less than the opposite of a number is three times the sum of the number and –7.

Write an equation using *d* for distance, *r* for rate, or *t* for time. Solve.

11. A man drove 450 mi. at an average rate of 45 mi./hr. How long did it take him?

12. A plane flew 390 nautical miles in 45 min. Find its average speed in knots (nautical miles per hour).

13. A biker rode for 2.5 hr. at an average rate of 12 mi./hr. Find the distance traveled.

14. Kathryn leaves her home and travels at an average speed of 45 mi./hr. until she reaches her grandmother's home 180 mi. away. How long does it take her to reach her grandmother's house?

■ B. Exercises

Write an equation and solve to find the numbers.

15. Four times the larger of two consecutive integers is 94 more than three times the smaller.

16. Two times the smaller of two consecutive even integers is 18 more than the larger.

17. Three times the largest of three consecutive even integers is equal to the sum of the other two.

18. Find two consecutive integers such that five times the smaller is four times the larger.

19. Find two consecutive odd integers such that twenty more than the first is three times the second.

20. Find three consecutive even integers such that 50 times the smallest is 88 less than 46 times the largest.

21. Eighteen times a number, increased by five times one more than the number, is 97.

22. Five times the sum of –2 and a number is 91 more than the sum of the opposite of the number and 1.

23. Twelve times a number is 3 more than twice the sum of the number and 1.

24. One-fifth of the sum of a number and –3 is twice the number.

25. Determine the speed of a boat in still water if it takes 3 hr. to travel 27 mi. down a river with a current of 2 mi./hr.

26. A commercial flight from New York to Los Angeles allows 6 hr. for the plane to travel the 2,850 mi. while cruising at an average air speed of 500 mi./hr. What is the average headwind speed that is expected during the flight?

27. If a speedboat capable of traveling 35 mi./hr. in still water went 84 mi. up the river in 3 hr., what was the average speed of the river's current?

Airline travel has seemingly reduced the size of our world.

28. What is the speed of an airport's moving sidewalk if a person is conveyed one-eighth of a mile through the airport in one and a half minutes while walking at his normal pace of 300 ft./min. on the moving sidewalk? (1 mi. = 5,280 ft.)

29. A transcontinental supersonic plane flies the 3,510 mi. from New York to London in 2 hr. 36 min. If the plane had an average air speed of 1,200 mi./hr., determine the average wind speed and state whether it was a headwind or a tailwind.

30. It takes Carlos and Hattie 45 min. to paddle their canoe 3 mi. against a 2 mi./hr. current. How fast can they paddle their canoe in still water?

■ C. Exercises

Write an equation and solve.

31. Find two consecutive even integers such that twice the larger is four more than twice the smaller.

32. Find two consecutive integers such that five times the smaller equals three times the larger.

33. After rowing down the stream in 4 hr., the students were able to row back up the stream in 6 hr. If the stream flows at 1 mi./hr., how fast can the students row their boat in still water?

34. Solve the formula $d = rt$ for the variable t and then for the variable r.

■ Dominion thru Math

Our bodies regulate our temperature when it is hot by the cooling process of evaporation. We perspire (sweat) through the pores of our skin, and this moisture evaporates. However, the higher the relative humidity, the less evaporation takes place and, consequently, the more uncomfortable we become. The effect of high humidity and high heat can be very dangerous. Scientists have devised a heat index that gives the apparent temperature we experience due to heat and humidity. For example, on a hot, humid summer day with a temperature (T) of 95°F and relative humidity (RH) of 60%, we experience an apparent temperature of 115°F. Any time the heat index is above 90°F, we should exercise caution in our physical activity. Since the heat index formula is very long and messy, we will substitute the following summer simmer index (SSI), which gives results that are close to the heat index numbers:

$$SSI = 1.98[T - (0.55 - 0.0055RH)(T - 58)] - 56.83,$$

where the value of RH is expressed as a percent (not as a decimal) and T is measured in degrees Fahrenheit.

You can use a calculator to do the calculation in one long string of steps following the order of operations. For example, if the temperature is 95°F with relative humidity of 60%, then the calculation can be done as follows:

$$.55\boxed{-}\boxed{(}\boxed{(}.0055\boxed{\times}60\boxed{)}\boxed{=}\boxed{\times}\boxed{(}95\boxed{-}58\boxed{)}\boxed{=}\boxed{-}95\boxed{=}\boxed{\pm}\boxed{\times}1.98\boxed{=}\boxed{-}56.83\boxed{=}.$$

Alternatively, you can enter the calculation from left to right:

$$1.98\boxed{(}95\boxed{-}\boxed{(}.55\boxed{-}.0055\boxed{\times}60\boxed{)}\boxed{\times}\boxed{(}95\boxed{-}58\boxed{)}\boxed{)}\boxed{-}56.83\boxed{=}.$$

Use a calculator to find the summer simmer indexes (*SSI*) to the nearest tenth of a degree, given the following temperatures and relative humidities.

35. $T = 85°F$ and $RH = 50\%$ 36. $T = 98°F$ and $RH = 80\%$ 37. $T = 105°F$ and $RH = 15\%$

Use a calculator to find the relative humidity (*RH*) to the nearest percent, given the following temperatures and summer simmer indexes.

38. $T = 78°F$ and $SSI = 95.4°F$ 39. $T = 90°F$ and $SSI = 116.1°F$

■ CUMULATIVE REVIEW ■

Solve by using the Property of Proportions. [5.5]

40. $\dfrac{6}{b} = \dfrac{-4}{7}$

41. $\dfrac{10}{7} = \dfrac{28}{n}$

42. $-8 : 15 = 21 : d$

43. $a : 42 = 16 : 12$

44. $\dfrac{x + 2}{8} = \dfrac{3}{4}$

Solve. [3.1–3.3]

45. $-9c = \dfrac{8}{13}$

46. $\dfrac{4}{5}x = 2\dfrac{2}{7}$

47. $a + 0.95 = -6.8$

48. $2m - 3.92 = 54.3$

49. $z - 71.05 = -83.42$

PROBLEM SOLVING

Write an Equation

You can use the strategy "write an equation" to solve some word problems.

When you plan to use this strategy, follow the steps given in the previous section.

Example 1 The price of a sports coat is reduced by $25.80. The new price is $103.20. What was the original price of the coat?

Answer

Think: What is the unknown in this problem? Let a variable represent this unknown value.

Let p = the original price.

Think: Identify two equal quantities. The original price reduced by $25.80 equals the sale price of $103.20. Write the equation; then solve it.

$$p - 25.8 = 103.2$$
$$p - 25.8 + 25.8 = 103.2 + 25.8$$
$$p = \$129$$

The original price of the sports coat was $129.

Think: Does this answer seem to be a reasonable price for a sports coat? Does this answer fit the conditions of the problem?

This is a reasonable answer, and it fits the conditions of the problem since $129 – $25.80 = $103.20. It is the correct answer.

Example 2 The teacher says, "Take any number and add 4 to it. Now multiply the sum by 6. Next, subtract 12 from the product. Divide the difference by 6 and subtract 3 from the quotient. Now tell me the answer, and I will tell you the original number." He always gives the correct number. How is he able to do this? Write the series of steps in the problem, using n for the original number. Why does this work?

Answer

Think: Determine what you are trying to find.

You want to know what the number is and how the teacher always knows the correct answer.

Think: The answer depends on the original number. How does the teacher know the original number after the answer to the calculation is found? Is there a constant relationship between the original number and the final answer?

Try several original numbers and see if there is a constant relationship between the original number and the answer.

If the original number is 2, then $2 + 4 = 6$; $6(6) = 36$; $36 - 12 = 24$; $24 \div 6 = 4$; $4 - 3 = 1$.

If the original number is 5, then $5 + 4 = 9$; $9(6) = 54$; $54 - 12 = 42$; $42 \div 6 = 7$; $7 - 3 = 4$.

If the original number is 8, then $8 + 4 = 12$; $12(6) = 72$; $72 - 12 = 60$; $60 \div 6 = 10$; $10 - 3 = 7$.

Think: What is the relationship between the original number and the final calculation?

The final calculation is always 1 less than the original number. So the teacher knows that if he adds 1 to the final calculation, he will have the original number.

Think: Why does this work? Let the original number be n, and find the algebraic expression that represents the arithmetic calculations.

$n + 4$

$6(n + 4)$

$6(n + 4) - 12$

$\dfrac{6(n + 4) - 12}{6}$

$\dfrac{6(n + 4) - 12}{6} - 3$

Think: What happens if this expression is simplified?

$$\dfrac{6(n + 4) - 12}{6} - 3 = \dfrac{6n + 24 - 12}{6} - 3 \qquad \text{Distribute the 6.}$$

$$= \dfrac{6n + 12}{6} - 3 \qquad \text{Combine like terms.}$$

$$= \dfrac{6n}{6} + \dfrac{12}{6} - 3 \qquad \text{Reverse the method of adding fractions.}$$

$$= n + 2 - 3$$

$$= n - 1$$

This shows that no matter the value of n, the final result of the calculation will be 1 less than the original number. So if you add 1 to the final result, you will obtain the original number.

■ Exercises

Write an equation and solve.

1. Five people went together to buy pizza costing $18.95. How much did each person pay?

2. The amount that the boys collected for the mission trip was four times the amount that the girls collected. Together they collected $124.25. How much did the girls collect?

3. You tell your friend, "Choose any number, subtract 8 from it, multiply the difference by 6, add 48, and then divide the result by 2." How can you always give the original number? Give an algebraic reason as to why your answer is always correct.

This young lady is witnessing for her Lord, as every Christian should.

4. The soccer players were required to run 6 more laps per day than the tennis players for five straight days. If the soccer players ran 45 laps total during these days, how many laps did the tennis players run each day?

5. Bodie scored 94%, 82%, and 85% on his first three math tests. What score must he make on the next test to have an overall average of 90%?

6. Miss Sneed has nine more boys than girls in her class. If she has a total of 37 students in her class, how many boys and girls does she have in her class?

7. Stefan collects baseball cards. He has three times as many National League players' cards as American League players' cards. If he has 212 cards in his collection, how many of each league does he have?

8. Taylor consumed a total of 580 calories in dessert (cupcakes and cookies). Each cupcake had 140 calories and each cookie had 80 calories. If he ate one more cupcake than cookie, how many of each did he eat?

8.4 Solving Inequalities

Simple one-step inequalities were introduced in Chapter 3. Use the table below to review the properties used to solve them. Inequalities with more than one operation use the same properties and simplifying procedures as used for solving equations. Additionally, you must remember to reverse the inequality symbol when either multiplying or dividing both sides by a negative number.

Properties of Inequalities		
	Properties	**Examples**
Addition	If $a < b$, then $a + c < b + c$.	$6 < 7$ and $6 + 3 < 7 + 3$; i.e., $9 < 10$
	If $a < b$, then $a - c < b - c$.	$-4 < -2$ and $-4 - 5 < -2 - 5$; i.e., $-9 < -7$
Multiplication	If $a < b$ and $c > 0$, then $ac < bc$.	$2 < 5$ and $2(3) < 5(3)$; i.e., $6 < 15$
	If $a < b$ and $c < 0$, then $ac > bc$.	$2 < 5$ and $2(-3) > 5(-3)$; i.e., $-6 > -15$
	If $a < b$ and $c > 0$, then $\dfrac{a}{c} < \dfrac{b}{c}$.	$4 < 8$ and $\dfrac{4}{2} < \dfrac{8}{2}$; i.e., $2 < 4$
	If $a < b$ and $c < 0$, then $\dfrac{a}{c} > \dfrac{b}{c}$.	$4 < 8$ and $\dfrac{4}{-2} > \dfrac{8}{-2}$; i.e., $-2 > -4$

Example 1 Solve $-4x + 3 > 23$, and graph the solution.

Answer

$-4x + 3 > 23$

$-4x + 3 - 3 > 23 - 3$ 1. Subtract 3 from both sides of the inequality.

$-4x > 20$

$\dfrac{-4x}{-4} < \dfrac{20}{-4}$ 2. Divide both sides of the inequality by –4, and reverse the inequality symbol.

$x < -5$

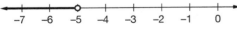

3. Graph the inequality on a number line. Recall that the < symbol does not include the boundary number, so use a circle.

Reverse signs if:
- multiplying by a negative
  $-\dfrac{x}{4} > 10 \rightarrow x < -40$
- dividing by a negative
  $-3x < 6 \rightarrow x > -2$

Example 2 Solve $-\frac{3}{4}x + 8 \leq 23$, and graph the solution.

Answer

$-\frac{3}{4}x + 8 \leq 23$

$-\frac{3}{4}x + 8 - 8 \leq 23 - 8$ 1. Subtract 8 from both sides of the inequality.

$-\frac{3}{4}x \leq 15$

$-\frac{4}{3}\left(-\frac{3}{4}x\right) \geq -\frac{4}{3}(\overset{5}{\cancel{15}})$ 2. Multiply both sides of the inequality by the reciprocal of $-\frac{3}{4}$,

$x \geq -20$ which is $-\frac{4}{3}$, and reverse the inequality symbol.

3. Graph the solution. The inequality includes the boundary number, so use a dot rather than a circle.

```
<----+------●------+------+------+---->
    -30   -20   -10    0    10
```

Note: Step 2 above could have been done in two steps by multiplying both sides by 4 and then dividing both sides by -3.

Example 3 Solve $-2(r + 4) > 19$, and graph the solution.

Answer

$-2(r + 4) > 19$

$-2r - 8 > 19$ 1. Remove the parentheses by applying the Distributive Property.

$-2r - 8 + 8 > 19 + 8$ 2. Add 8 to both sides of the inequality.

$-2r > 27$

$\frac{-2r}{-2} < \frac{27}{-2}$ 3. Divide both sides of the inequality by -2, and reverse the inequality symbol.

$r < -13.5$ 4. Graph the solution.

```
<----+------+------+--○--+------+---->
   -16   -15   -14   -13   -12
```

Skill Check 1

Solve and graph the solutions.

1. $5x - 7 > 3$ 2. $\frac{2}{3}n + 8 \leq 12$

3. $-4a - 9 \geq 7$ 4. $6(x - 2) > 18$

When variables appear on both sides of the inequality, isolate the variable on one side just as you would with equations. The Addition Property of Inequality allows you to do the required manipulations. Study the following examples.

Example 4 Solve $2x \geq -2x + 8$.

Answer

$2x \geq -2x + 8$

$2x + 2x \geq -2x + 2x + 8$ 1. Add $2x$ to both sides to eliminate the variable from the right side.

$4x \geq 8$

$\frac{4x}{4} \geq \frac{4}{4}$ 2. Divide both sides by 4.

$x \geq 1$

Example 5 Solve $3x - 1 < x + 9$.

Answer

$3x - 1 < x + 9$

$3x - 1 - x < x + 9 - x$ 1. Subtract x from both sides. This places the variable on the left side only.

$2x - 1 < 9$

$2x - 1 + 1 < 9 + 1$ 2. Add 1 to both sides to eliminate the constant from the left side.

$2x < 10$

$\dfrac{2x}{2} < \dfrac{10}{2}$ 3. Divide both sides by 2.

$x < 5$

Example 6 Solve $5x - 8 \le 9x + 2$.

Answer

$5x - 8 \le 9x + 2$

$5x - 8 - 9x \le 9x + 2 - 9x$ 1. Subtract $9x$ from both sides to eliminate the variable from the right side.

$-4x - 8 \le 2$

$-4x - 8 + 8 \le 2 + 8$ 2. Add 8 to both sides to eliminate the constant from the left side.

$-4x \le 10$

$\dfrac{-4x}{-4} \ge \dfrac{10}{-4}$ 3. Divide both sides by –4, and reverse the inequality symbol.

$x \ge -2.5$

Skill Check 2

Solve the following inequalities.

1. $5x \le 2x - 9$

2. $-2x < x + 27$

3. $4x + 3 < 2x - 1$

4. $16 - 8y \ge y - 20$

[handwritten: $-16 \quad -16$; $-8 \ge y - 36$; $-y \; \underline{-1}$; $9y \ge -36$; $\div 9 \quad \div 9$; $y \le 4$]

■ A. Exercises

Solve and graph the solutions.

1. $2x - 4 > 8$

2. $\dfrac{a}{6} + 28 \le 30$

3. $\dfrac{b}{2} - 9 \ge -7$

4. $400 - 32x \ge 720$

5. $7.5x + 10 > 100$

6. $115 + 45x \ge 340$

7. $\dfrac{9}{5}y \le 18$

8. $-\dfrac{1}{3}c + 4 < 7$

Solve the following inequalities. Do not graph the solutions.

9. $45 < 2x - 21$

10. $-33x + 37 > 70$

11. $4x + 3 < 15$

12. $5x - 4 > 21$

13. $\dfrac{p}{2} - 6 > 21$

14. $\dfrac{w}{-3} + 7 > 16$

15. $2x - 10 > 18$

16. $3x + 6 \ge 24$

17. $7 - 2x \le 16$

18. $\dfrac{y}{-5} + 8 \le 15$

19. $\dfrac{x}{2} - 8 \le 10$

20. $-5 > x - 2$

■ B. Exercises

Solve the following inequalities.

21. $-6b + 2b < 72$

22. $-13n + 5n > 56$

23. $3(x + 5) < 45$

24. $2n - 4n > 6$

25. $5x - 2 < 3x + 4$

26. $6x - 8 \geq x - 9$

27. $3(x - 4) > 2x + 1$

28. $4(x - 9) < x + 3$

29. $-\frac{3}{4}x > 9$

30. $\frac{1}{3}x + 4 < 7$

31. $2.5x + 5 < 18$

32. $2x - 178 \leq 20$

33. $42 - \frac{2}{7}z \geq 23$

34. $\frac{2}{5}x - 13 < 27$

35. $18 - \frac{4}{3}y \geq 15$

36. $-2(c - 8) < 100$

37. $-2x + 1 > \frac{x}{2} + 4$

38. $3(x - 5) \leq 2(x + 5)$

39. $\frac{x}{3} > \frac{x}{6} + 1$

40. $3(5 - y) > 12$

■ C. Exercises

41. Using the inequality $ax - b \leq c$, and assuming that a, b, and c are real numbers with $a \neq 0$, solve the inequality for x. Be careful to account for all possible values of a, b, and c.

42. Using the inequality $\frac{x}{r} + s > t$, and assuming that r, s, and t are real numbers, solve the inequality for x. Be careful to account for all possible values of r, s, and t.

Solve the following inequalities. Check to see if the answers agree with your answers to exercises 41 and 42 respectively.

43. $-5x - 8 \leq 17$

44. $\frac{x}{-9} + 12 > 8$

■ Dominion thru Math

Have you ever noticed how much colder it seems in the winter if the wind is blowing? This extra sense of cold is called the *wind-chill factor*. Temperatures above 45°F are not of great concern; but temperatures below 0°F and winds above 20 mi./hr. can be life threatening, and frostbite can occur very quickly. For example, a temperature of −40°F and a wind of 40 mi./hr. create a wind-chill factor of −84°F. At this temperature frostbite occurs within five minutes on any exposed skin.

The following formula is used to calculate the wind-chill factor:

$$WC = 35.74 + 0.6215T - 35.75W^{0.16} + 0.4275TW^{0.16},$$

where T = air temperature (°F) and W = wind speed (mi./hr.).

The following calculator steps will calculate the wind-chill factor if the air temperature is 15°F and the wind speed is 30 mi./hr. Notice that the memory of the calculator is used to store the value of $W^{0.16}$ for use throughout the calculation. Study how this is done with the following series of calculator steps. The answer is −5.5°F.

Glacier National Park is located in Montana near the Canadian border.

1. $30 \boxed{y^x} .16 \boxed{=} \boxed{\text{STO}} \boxed{1} \boxed{\text{CE/C}}$

2. $35.74 \boxed{+} \boxed{(} \boxed{(} .6215 \boxed{\times} 15 \boxed{)} \boxed{=} \boxed{-} \boxed{(} 35.75 \boxed{\times} \boxed{\text{RCL}} \boxed{1} \boxed{)} \boxed{=} \boxed{+} \boxed{(} .4275 \boxed{\times} 15 \boxed{\times} \boxed{\text{RCL}} \boxed{1} \boxed{)} \boxed{=}$

Alternatively, many calculators perform calculations according to the order of operations, which allows simple left-to-right entry of complicated expressions like those above.

Use a calculator to find the answers to the following problems. Round answers to the nearest degree.

45. Find the wind-chill factor if the air temperature is 20°F and the wind speed is 20 mi./hr.

46. Find the wind-chill factor if the air temperature is –20°F and the wind speed is 20 mi./hr. (Remember to use the ⊞ key to change the sign of a number.)

47. The McCloud family visited Glacier National Park last summer. At the top of Logan Pass, the air temperature was 35°F and the wind was blowing at 30 mi./hr. What was the wind-chill factor on that sunny summer day high in the mountains of Montana?

48. When the McCloud family got to Lake Mary near the east entrance to Glacier National Park, the temperature was up to 68°F, but the wind was still blowing at 30 mi./hr. Use the wind-chill factor to decide whether they need to wear coats when outside the car.

CUMULATIVE REVIEW

State whether the given number is prime, composite, or neither. [4.1]

49. 0   50. 61   51. 38   52. 15   53. 29

Write each percent as a decimal. [7.1]

54. 87%   55. 160%   56. $\frac{1}{4}$%   57. 6.9%   58. 0.04%

8.5 Applying Inequalities

Inequalities can be written and solved for real-life problems. When a quantity is said to be more or less than another quantity, an inequality can be written using > or <. The inequality can be solved to give a range of solutions.

Example 1 Mr. Tobin wants to buy four new tires and spend less than $250. What is the range of prices he can spend per tire?

Answer

Let n = cost per tire.   1. Assign a variable to represent the unknown value.

$4n < 250$ 2. Write an inequality.

$\dfrac{4n}{4} < \dfrac{250}{4}$ 3. Divide both sides of the inequality by 4.

$n < 62.50$

Mr. Tobin must spend less than $62.50 per tire.

Recall that consecutive integers can be represented by the expressions n, $n + 1$, $n + 2$, and so on.

Example 2 The sum of three consecutive integers is more than 20. What are the smallest possible values for the integers?

Answer

Let n = the first integer.
$n + 1$ = the second integer.
$n + 2$ = the third integer.

1. Represent the unknowns. Consecutive integers differ by 1.

$n + (n + 1) + (n + 2) > 20$ 2. Write the inequality.

$3n + 3 > 20$ 3. Simplify.

$3n + 3 - 3 > 20 - 3$ 4. Subtract 3 from both sides.

$3n > 17$

$\dfrac{3n}{3} > \dfrac{17}{3}$ 5. Divide both sides by 3.

$n > 5\dfrac{2}{3}$

The smallest possible integer value for n is 6.
The three consecutive integers are 6, 7, and 8.
Check: $6 + 7 + 8 > 20$
$21 > 20$

> **Consecutive Integers**
> integers: $n, n + 1, n + 2$, etc.
> even integers: $n, n + 2, n + 4$, etc.
> odd integers: $n, n + 2, n + 4$, etc.

Both consecutive even integers and consecutive odd integers differ by two. For this reason, n, $n + 2$, $n + 4$, and so on can be used to represent either consecutive even or consecutive odd integers.

Example 3 Four times the smaller of two consecutive odd integers is less than three times the larger. What are the largest possible values for the integers?

Answer

Let n = the first odd integer.
$n + 2$ = the second odd integer.

1. Represent the unknowns. Consecutive odd integers differ by two.

$4n < 3(n + 2)$ 2. Write the inequality.

$4n < 3n + 6$ 3. Remove the parentheses by distributing the 3.

$4n - 3n < 3n - 3n + 6$ 4. Subtract $3n$ from both sides to eliminate the variable from the right side.

$n < 6$ 5. n must be an odd integer less than 6.

The largest odd integer for n is 5. The second integer would be $5 + 2 = 7$.
Check: $4(5) < 3(7)$
$20 < 21$

Skill Check 1

Write an inequality and solve.

1. Asher delivers a daily newspaper in his hometown. He makes $0.70 per week for each newspaper he delivers. He spends $1.50 per week on rubber bands. If Asher wants to make more than $42 profit per week, how many customers must he maintain on his route?

2. Three times the larger of two consecutive integers is greater than 70. Find the range of values for the integers.

When two real numbers, a and b, are compared, there are only three possible outcomes: $a > b$, $a < b$, or $a = b$. This idea is formally stated by the trichotomy axiom.

Trichotomy Axiom
For all real numbers a and b, $a > b$, $a < b$, or $a = b$.

When we are told that two of the three possibilities are not true, the third must be true. Therefore, the phrase "not greater than or equal to" is equivalent to "less than."

If $a \not\geq b$, then $a < b$.

If $a \not\leq b$, then $a > b$.

If one of the three choices is not true, we must allow for the other two possibilities.

If $a \not> b$, then $a \leq b$.

If $a \not< b$, then $a \geq b$.

Always rewrite a negated inequality using the equivalent inequality before solving.

Example 4 Solve $-5x + 7 \not\leq 22$.

Answer

$$-5x + 7 > 22$$ 1. Replace the negated inequality with the equivalent inequality.

$$-5x + 7 - 7 > 22 - 7$$ 2. Subtract 7 from both sides.

$$-5x > 15$$

$$\frac{-5x}{-5} < \frac{15}{-5}$$ 3. Divide both sides by –5, and reverse the inequality symbol.

$$x < -3$$

Carefully examine the chart below to understand some of the various ways of stating an inequality.

Common Wording	Negated Inequality	Meaning	Equivalent Inequality
"is at most" or "is not more than" or "is the maximum amount"	$\not>$	is less than or equal to	$\leq$
"is at least" or "is not less than" or "is the minimum amount"	$\not<$	is greater than or equal to	$\geq$

at most $\leq$
at least $\geq$

Example 5 Write the corresponding inequality for the following statements.

a. Four more than a number is at most 84.

b. Twice a number decreased by 7 is at least 90.

c. Forty less than a number is not less than 95.

d. Six more than a number is not equal to 63.

Answer

For each of the sentences, identify the verb phrase and place the inequality symbol in the sentence. Translate the word phrases before and after the verb phrase into symbols.

a. $n + 4 \leq 84$ Four more than a number **is at most** 84.

b. $2x - 7 \geq 90$ Twice a number decreased by 7 **is at least** 90.

c. $y - 40 \geq 95$ Forty less than a number **is not less than** 95.

d. $x + 6 \neq 63$ Six more than a number **is not equal** to 63.

Example 6   Noah and Kim are planning to attend the state fair. They will pay $5 to park the car and $2.50 per event ticket. What is the range of the number of event tickets that they can purchase if they cannot spend more than $36 at the fair?

Answer

Let n = the number of event tickets.
$$5 + 2.5n \le 36$$
$$5 - 5 + 2.5n \le 36 - 5$$
$$2.5n \le 31$$
$$\frac{2.5n}{2.5} \le \frac{31}{2.5}$$
$$n \le 12.4$$

1. Assign a variable for the unknown quantity.
2. Write an inequality.
3. Eliminate the constant from the left side by subtracting 5 from both sides.
4. Divide both sides by 2.5.

Since the number of tickets must be a whole number, they can purchase up to 12 tickets.

Skill Check 2

Write an inequality and solve.

1. Six times the smaller of two consecutive integers is at most 35 more than five times the larger. What is the range of values for the integers?

2. Five times the smaller of two consecutive odd integers is at least 50 more than the larger.

3. The measure of $\angle A$ is twice the measure of $\angle B$. The measure of $\angle C$ is one degree more than the measure of $\angle A$. If the sum of the three angles is at least 61°, what is the range of possible measurements for $\angle B$?

■ **A. Exercises**

Replace the negated inequality with the equivalent inequality and solve.

1. $x + 7 \not< 15$
2. $x - 5 \not> 8$
3. $-3x \not\le 12$
4. $4x \not\le -24$
5. $2x - 7 \not\le 3$
6. $3x - 5 \not\ge 4$
7. $3x - 7 \not< 20$
8. $-5x + 4 \not> -6$

Write an inequality and solve.

9. Find the largest two consecutive integers whose sum is less than 46.

10. Find the largest two consecutive odd integers whose sum is not greater than 46.

11. Johannes wants to earn at least $350 per week. If his work week will be 40 hr., what is the minimum hourly wage he must make?

12. In order to receive at least $55,000 in sales from 250 suits, what is the minimum average price at which Mr. Cortes needs to sell the suits?

13. The total bill for a lawnmower and fifteen drawer pulls was within the family's $400 budget. If the lawn-mower cost $325, what was the maximum cost of each drawer pull?

14. Mr. Graham's business expenses exceeded the company's allowance of $100 when he spent $15 for dinner and $10 for breakfast and paid to stay in a motel overnight. What was the cost of the motel room?

■ B. Exercises

Write an inequality and solve.

15. Find the smallest two consecutive integers such that five times the smaller is at least eight more than three times the larger.

16. Find the smallest two consecutive even integers such that three times the smaller is at least 19 more than the sum of the two integers.

17. Find the largest two consecutive odd integers such that four times the larger reduced by the smaller is less than 100.

18. Patrick purchased a few pairs of socks at $7.50 each and a $15 belt for less than $40 total. What is the maximum number of pairs of socks that he purchased?

19. Sara can spend at most $150 for books at the used book store. Paperback books cost $4 and hardcover books cost $7. If she buys twelve more paperbacks than hardcovers, how many of each type of book can she buy?

20. If there were five times as many children as adults at the picnic and there were at least 120 people at the picnic, how many adults and children were at the picnic?

21. An automobile salesman makes $100 plus a 2% commission when he sells a car. In order to make at least $800 on a sale, what would the sale price of a car have to be?

22. Nils is going to buy a new suit, two shirts, and some ties. He found a suit for $200, shirts for $30, and ties for $20. There is a 5% sales tax. How many ties can he buy if he stays within his budget of $325?

23. What is the minimum price for a dozen eggs if the cost of four dozen eggs and a half gallon of milk costing $2.97 exceeded the $10 Chase had in his pocket?

24. Jim would like to earn more than $100 in a day. He can work for eight hours at his regular pay rate of $7.90/hr. and is paid time-and-a-half for overtime above the eight hours. What is the least number of full hours of overtime he must work to meet his goal?

25. A merchant bought several blazers at $85 each and 100 ties at $13 each. His cost exceeded $2,000. How many blazers did he purchase?

26. The steak dinner was $3 more than the chicken dinner, and the bill was less than $30. Find the cost of the two dinners.

27. A child's ticket is $40 less than an adult ticket. Find the price range for each type of ticket if the total cost for one adult and two children's tickets was more than $250.

28. What is the minimum average speed required if a cyclist wants to complete more than 150 mi. of his trip in 8 hr.?

29. How much money must be invested at 6% simple interest to generate at least $500 of interest in 3 yr.?

30. Rowan had scores of 85, 95, 91, and 87 points on his first four tests. What is the lowest score he can receive on the final test for his test average to be at least 90 points?

■ C. Exercises

Solve.

31. Edwin, his brother Edward, and their cousin P.J. are on the same basketball team. Edwin scored 10 more points than his brother and the same number as P.J. The rest of the team had 8 points, and the team total exceeded 70. How many points did each of the three boys get?

32. The dead man's will stated that his three heirs would inherit his money in the ratio of 3 : 2 : 1. The estate was worth more than $1,500,000. How much would each one get?

33. Find three consecutive integers such that the sum of twice the middle integer and the other two integers is more than −8.

34. The average of four consecutive even integers is at least 15. What possible even consecutive integers could they be?

■ Dominion thru Math

35. Using the formula from Section 8.4, Dominion thru Math, complete the chart recording the wind-chill factors (to the nearest tenth of a degree) when the air temperature is 0°F for each of the listed wind speeds.

Wind speed (mi./hr.)	5	10	15	20	25	30	35
Wind-chill factor at 0°F							

36. In your chart of wind-chill factors, what was the greatest drop, and which change in wind speed created this drop?

37. In your chart of wind-chill factors, what was the least drop, and which change in wind speed created this drop?

38. What observation can you make about the change in wind-chill factor with every 5 mi./hr. increase in the wind speed?

39. Find a temperature and wind speed that gives a wind-chill factor of −100°F.

CUMULATIVE REVIEW

Write the first five terms of the following sequences. [4.5–4.6]

40. $a_1 = -6; r = 4$

41. $a_1 = 81; r = \dfrac{1}{3}$

42. $a_1 = 1; d = -2$

43. $a_1 = -1; d = 0.5$

44. $a_1 = 15; d = 6$

Add or subtract as indicated. Leave answers in scientific notation. [6.8]

45. $(3.91 \times 10^{12}) + (7.1 \times 10^{12})$

46. $(7.88 \times 10^8) - (3.1 \times 10^8)$

47. $(4.92 \times 10^{-91}) + (6.77 \times 10^{-91})$

48. $(1.04 \times 10^{-7}) + (3.69 \times 10^{-7})$

49. $(5.734 \times 10^{-4}) - (2.84 \times 10^{-4})$

$(3.91 + 7.1) \times 10^{21}$

MATH
& SCRIPTURE

Ezekiel's Temple Vision

In Ezekiel 40–43 the Lord gives the prophet a vision of a magnificent temple, similar to Solomon's temple but built on a grander scale. The prophet records in careful detail the dimensions of this overpowering structure, which at first appears like a city (Ezek. 40:2). The measurements and descriptions in these chapters make for tedious and difficult reading, and Bible scholars have devoted years to studying the temple's layout.

This temple proclaims the holiness and glory of God and is meant to inspire worship and praise from His people. We have in this passage a beautiful example of mathematics and artistic beauty serving as an inspiration for God's people to worship Him Who is holy beyond all possible human imagination.

1. According to Ezekiel 40:1–4 and Ezekiel 43:10–11, why did the Lord give Ezekiel this vision?

2. According to Ezekiel 41:13–14, what is the length and width of the temple?

3. Ezekiel 40:5 states that the cubit used in these measurements was the long cubit—a normal cubit plus a handbreadth (3 in.). Using 1 cubit ≈ 21 in., determine the area of the temple in square feet.

4. If 1 acre = 43,560 ft.^{2}, this area is approximately what fraction of an acre?

5. Bible commentaries suggest that the dimensions of the temple complex are 500 cubits × 500 cubits. Convert these dimensions to the nearest acre.

6. According to Ezekiel 41:4, what are the dimensions of the most holy place?

7. The height of the most holy place is not given, but based on your study of Solomon's temple, what would you expect the height to be?

Over the last three chapters we have seen wonderfully detailed presentations with significant mathematical issues in both dimensions and implied use of mathematics in actual construction. We have also seen how God uses people's artistic ability to produce works of magnificence and beauty. Yet in the final analysis, it is about the glory of the Lord and not the instruments He chooses to use. Skilled workers simply use mathematics and art to render praise to God and display His majesty.

Infinite Truths

And, behold, the glory of the God of Israel came from the way of the east: and his voice was like a noise of many waters: and the earth shined with his glory. . . . And the glory of the Lord came into the house. *Ezekiel 43:2, 4*a

Chapter 8 Review

Vocabulary

at least	even integers	odd integers
at most	not less than	trichotomy axiom
consecutive integers	not more than	

Simplify.

1. $6x - 9x + 8$

2. $-4x - 3y + 2 - 9x - 5$

3. $2x + 6z - 14 + 3z - 8 + 6x$

Solve.

4. $6x + 2 - 4x = -6$

5. $9y + 7 - 8y - 17 = 14$

6. $4z - (9z + 7) = -22$

7. $8x + 2(3x - 12) = -122$

8. $-6 - 4(a + 9) = -26$

9. $5(3x + 7) - 7(2x - 8) = 105$

What would you do to both sides of the equation to get the variable only on the left?

10. $x + 8 = 4x - 7$

11. $9z - 14 = -6z - 12$

Solve. Express noninteger answers as fractions in lowest terms or decimals rounded to the nearest tenth.

12. $4x + 7 = 12x + 9$

13. $-8y - 11 = y + 7$

14. $6(z + 9) + 4z = 8 - (z + 2)$

15. $4(x - 7) = 2(3x + 6)$

16. $-6a - 12 = 8(a - 9)$

17. $\frac{2}{3}x + 5 = \frac{5}{3}x + 12$

18. $8.9y + 2.65 = 3.8(2y - 7)$

19. $-4.7m - 9(8.2m - 6.1) = 9.7m - (1.9m + 6)$

20. $6n - 4(3n + 9) = 5n - 12$

Write an equation. Do not solve.

21. Six more than eight times a number is 21.

22. Four times the sum of a number and 9 is 16.

23. The product of seven and the difference of three times a number and eight is –9.

24. The sum of half of a number and six is 18.

Write an equation and solve to find the numbers.

25. Six times the difference of a number and three is –42.

26. One-tenth of a number, decreased by four, is eight.

27. Nine less than 14 times a number is equal to the sum of the number and 17.

28. The product of a number and 23 is equal to 11 less than the number.

29. The sum of two consecutive numbers is –37. Find the numbers.

30. Find two consecutive even numbers such that three times the smaller is 30 more than the larger.

31. The sum of Sasha's and Natalya's ages is 31. Twice Natalya's age is eleven years more than Sasha's age. Find each of their ages.

Solve the following inequalities. Express noninteger answers as fractions in lowest terms or decimals rounded to the nearest tenth.

32. $\frac{3}{5}x \le -9$

33. $-6m + 9 < 18$

34. $7x - 12 > 25$

35. $4(y + 2) - 16 \le -3(6y - 8)$

36. $3x + 7 > 28$

37. $-6n < 3 + 4n + 27$

38. $6a + 4(3a - 7) \le a - (2a - 5)$

39. $6.5n + 3(4.8n - 2) < 4n - (2.8n - 7.3)$

40. $-\frac{4}{5}y - \frac{2}{3}(y - 9) \ge \frac{3}{5}(y + 15)$

Write an inequality. Do not solve.

41. The sum of a number and 19 is greater than –7.

42. Twice the difference of a number and 12 is at least 38.

43. The quotient of a number and 6 is not greater than 21.

44. Mrs. Svinski needs to buy as many calculators as possible for her math class. She has $50 to spend, and each calculator costs $6.75. If sales tax is 6%, how many calculators can she buy?

Write an inequality and solve. Round decimal answers to the nearest hundredth.

45. Cashews cost $6.75/lb., and Jeanna can spend at most $30 for them. How many pounds can she buy?

46. Benjamin wants an average of at least 92% in his science class. The tests in the class are each worth 100 points, and the sum of his scores on the first three tests is 273. What range of scores on the last test will guarantee that he gets the average that he desires in the class?

47. Mr. Ashburn is a car salesman. He earns a $250 commission for each car that he sells and a guaranteed monthly salary of $1,000. If he needs to earn at least $4,500 to pay his bills each month, how many cars must he sell each month?

48. The bill at the craft store for six picture frames and six pieces of matting is more than the $100 that Ginny has in her purse for this purchase. If the picture frames cost $12.45 each, how much does each piece of matting cost?

49. Find the three smallest consecutive odd integers whose sum is more than 100.

50. State the mathematical significance of Ezekiel 43:2, 4a.

9 RELATIONS AND FUNCTIONS

When one quantity changes in proportion to another quantity so that they both get larger or smaller simultaneously at a constant rate, we say they are *directly proportional*. This relationship can be expressed with variables. When two quantities are directly proportional, their ordered pairs graph in the coordinate plane as a straight line through the origin. If you do not know the relationship of two quantities, you can plot corresponding pairs of points on a graph to see if the points are located on a line.

The equation $y = 12x$ represents the relationship between feet and inches, where x is the number of feet and y is the number of inches. In this example, as the number of feet increases, the number of inches increases by a factor of 12. The number of feet and the number of inches are said to be directly proportional. The constant, 12 inches per foot, is called the *constant of proportionality.*

Many quantities are directly proportional. Electricity costs depend on the kilowatts of electricity used. The constant of proportionality for electrical charges might be something like 7.256¢/kilowatt-hour. Water bills depend on the number of gallons or cubic feet of water used by the customer. A typical rate for city water might be $1.88/1,000 gallons used, or approximately 0.2¢/gal.

After this chapter you should be able to

1. graph points and lines in the coordinate plane.

2. identify the domain and the range of a relation.

3. determine, from a set of ordered pairs, a circle mapping, or a coordinate graph, whether a relation is a function.

4. find the slope of a line from its graph, from its equation, and by using the slope formula.

5. find the x- and y-intercepts of a line from its equation.

6. use $f(x)$ notation to designate a function and its value at individual points.

7. determine whether a function is a direct variation.

8. find the constant of proportionality and additional ordered pairs for a direct variation, given one ordered pair.

9. graph linear inequalities in the coordinate plane.

9.1 The Coordinate Plane

A coordinate plane is used to record each artifact's position.

A number line and the set of real numbers have a unique relationship called a *one-to-one correspondence*. For every point on the number line there is a real number that corresponds to it. Also, for every real number there is a corresponding point on the number line.

Definition

Two sets have a **one-to-one correspondence** if every element in one set is paired with one and only one element in the other set and no elements in either remain unpaired.

The grid shown to the right is called the *Cartesian coordinate plane*, the *rectangular coordinate plane*, or just the *coordinate plane* for short. The coordinate plane contains a horizontal number line and a vertical number line called axes, which intersect at right angles. The point of intersection of the number lines is given the coordinates (0, 0).

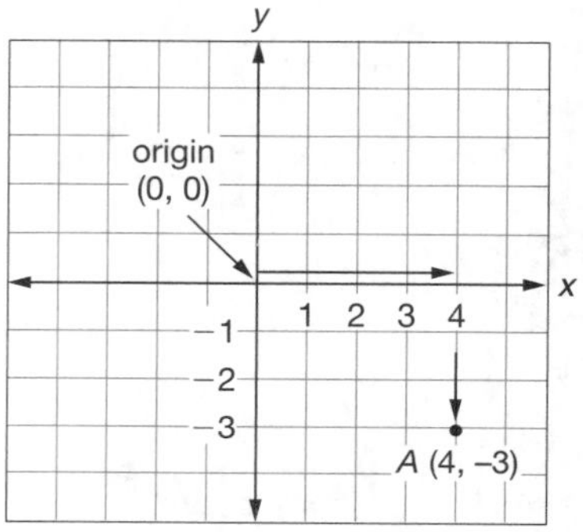

Definitions

The **x-axis** is the horizontal number line in a plane.
The **y-axis** is the vertical number line in a plane.
The **origin** is the point at which the x-axis and y-axis intersect.

Observe that point A in the coordinate plane is four units to the right of the origin and three units below the x-axis. Its location is described by the pair of numbers (4, −3). This pair of numbers is called an *ordered pair*. The order of the numbers is important; (−3, 4) locates a different point.

Definition

An **ordered pair** is a pair of numbers written in parentheses used to locate a particular point in the coordinate plane.

The first number of an ordered pair references the x-axis distance and is called the *x-coordinate*. Point A is located four units to the right of the origin; thus the x-coordinate is 4. The second number of an ordered pair references the distance parallel to the y-axis and is called the *y-coordinate*. Point A lies three units below the x-axis; thus the y-coordinate is −3.

$$A\ (4, -3)$$

x-coordinate   y-coordinate

Definitions

The **x-coordinate** is the first coordinate of an ordered pair.
The **y-coordinate** is the second coordinate of an ordered pair.

The ordered pair for the origin is (0, 0). A point located on the x-axis has an ordered pair (x, 0). A point located on the y-axis has an ordered pair (0, y).

The x- and y-axes separate the coordinate plane into four regions called *quadrants*. These quadrants are numbered counterclockwise, beginning with the upper right region, as I, II, III, and IV.

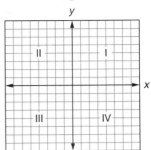

Ordered Pairs
(3, 2) ↔ (x, y)

Example 1   Give the coordinates and quadrant location of each point.

a. *P*
b. *Q*
c. *R*
d. *S*

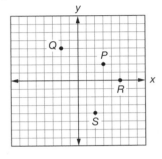

Answer

a. *P* is located at (3, 2). It is in quadrant I.

Point *P* lies three units right of the origin and two units above the x-axis.

b. *Q* is located at (−2, 4). It is in quadrant II.

Point *Q* lies two units left of the origin and four units above the x-axis.

c. *R* is located at (5, 0). It is on the x-axis.

Point *R* lies five units right of the origin on the x-axis.

d. *S* is located at (2, −4). It is in quadrant IV.

Point *S* lies two units right of the origin and four units below the x-axis.

Skill Check 1

Name the quadrant or the axis on which the following points lie.

1. (−3, 10) 2. (−8, 0) 3. (7, 1) 4. (−2, 4)

5. (7, −5) 6. (−3, 9) 7. (0, −4) 8. (−3, −4)

To graph a point, start at the origin and move horizontally according to the value of the x-coordinate. Then move vertically according to the value of the y-coordinate.

The four descriptions below indicate the signs of both coordinates in each quadrant. Below the signs are directions for plotting a point in each quadrant. Directions begin at the origin.

I	II	III	IV
(+, +)	(−, +)	(−, −)	(+, −)
right, then up	left, then up	left, then down	right, then down

Example 2 Graph each point.

a. *J* (2, 4)   b. *K* (–1, –2)   c. *L* (–3, 3)   d. *M* (0, –5)

Answer

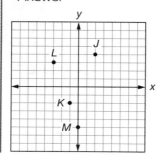

a. From the origin, move two units to the right, then four units up. Label the point *J*.

b. From the origin, move one unit to the left, then two units down. Label the point *K*.

c. From the origin, move three units to the left, then three units up. Label the point *L*.

d. From the origin, move five units down. Label the point *M*.

Skill Check 2

Graph each point.

1. *G* (–3, 2)   2. *H* (4, –1)   3. *I* (0, 3)   4. *J* (–2, –4)

■ A. Exercises

Give the coordinates of each point.

1. *I*   2. *J*

3. *K*   4. *L*

5. *M*   6. *N*

7. *X*   8. *Y*

9. *Z*

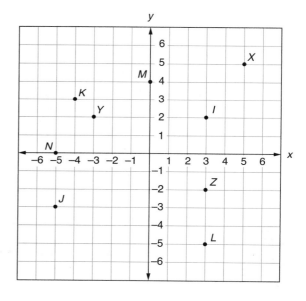

Name the quadrant or the axis on which the following points lie.

10. (6, 0)   11. (–4, 7)

12. (–3, –9)   13. (0, –7)

14. (6, 4)   15. (0, 0)

16. (12, –2)   17. (–3, 2)

■ B. Exercises

Graph each point in the same coordinate plane.

18. *A* (4, –2)   19. *P* (–3, –5)   20. *Q* (–5, 2)   21. *R* (5, 4)

22. *S* (6, –3)   23. *T* (–6, –4)   24. *U* (–2, 5)   25. *V* (3, 6)

26. *W* (–2, –2)   27. *B* (0, 6)   28. *C* (–4, 0)   29. *D* (–3, 5)

■ C. Exercises

Using the coordinate plane to the right, name the point located by each ordered pair.

30. $(2.5, 5)$

31. $\left(2, -1\frac{1}{2}\right)$

32. $(0, 3)$

33. $(-3, 4.5)$

34. $(4, -5)$

35. $\left(-3, -4\frac{1}{2}\right)$

36. $(-2, -3)$

37. $(4, 4)$

38. $(-3.5, 2.5)$

39. $\left(-2\frac{1}{2}, 0\right)$

40. $(5, -2.5)$

41. $(0, -4)$

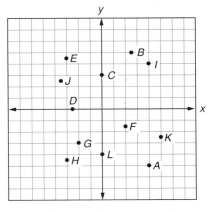

42. Locate several points on the y-axis and write their coordinates. Make a conjecture about the x value in every ordered pair coordinate located on the y-axis.

43. Locate several points on the x-axis and write their coordinates. Make a conjecture about the y value in every ordered pair coordinate located on the x-axis.

■ Dominion thru Math

Use a calculator to solve the following problems that require numerical answers.

44. In 2006 US first-class mail cost 39¢ for one ounce or less and 24¢ for each additional ounce or fractional part of an ounce. Find what it cost in 2006 to mail a first-class letter that weighed 3.3 oz.

45. Write an equation that gives the cost of first-class postage in 2006 as a function of the weight, w, of the parcel in ounces.

46. The US Postal Service first-class mail prices go up every two or three years or so. Write a general equation that expresses the cost (C, in cents) of a letter exceeding one ounce, given its weight (w, in ounces), if it costs a¢ for the first ounce and b¢ for each additional ounce or fractional part of an ounce. (Note: Parts of an ounce are always rounded up to the next ounce.)

47. Do some research and find the cost to mail the letter in exercise 44 in February of 1963.

48. What would it cost to mail the first-class letter in exercise 44 at current rates?

CUMULATIVE REVIEW

Solve. Round decimals to the nearest tenth. [6.6]

49. $x - \dfrac{7}{9} = \dfrac{5}{3}$

50. $6x + \dfrac{3}{7} = \dfrac{4}{7}$

51. $\dfrac{1}{8}y + \dfrac{5}{4} = \dfrac{7}{24}$

52. $z - 16.3 = -9.2$

53. $7d + 56.39 = -28.4$

Write the prime factorization of each number. [4.2]

54. 135

55. 48

56. 126

57. 175

58. 891

9.2 Relations

Which one is Jimmy?

In a family, a relation is an association between two people connected by blood or marriage. Your parents, grandparents, and any siblings, cousins, uncles, and aunts you might have are all related to you. They are your relatives, or relations. The most important relationship a person can have is with God the Father and Jesus Christ, His Son. Through the shed blood of Jesus Christ we can have forgiveness of sins and be made children of God. John 1:12 declares, "But as many as received him [Jesus], to them gave he power to become the sons of God, even to them that believe on his name." What a wonderful relationship we can have with God. Do you have this relationship with God?

In mathematics, points are located in a plane by an ordered pair of numbers. The term "ordered pair" means that (2, 3) and (3, 2) do not represent the same point. Mathematics has borrowed the term "relation" to mean a set of such points. The graph of these points illustrates their "relationship." Sometimes they form a straight line (which you will study in this text) or a curve or even a circle.

Definition

A **relation** is a set of ordered pairs.

A relation is often written in set form and named with a capital letter. Consider relation A listed below. It consists of just four points.

$$A = \{(2, 3), (-3, 2), (-4, -3), (4, -3)\}$$

The set of all the x-coordinates of the ordered pairs is the *domain* of the relation. The set of all the y-coordinates is the *range* of the relation. The domain and range of A are listed below.

$$\text{domain: } D = \{-4, -3, 2, 4\}$$
$$\text{range: } R = \{-3, 2, 3\}$$

Observe that, although −3 occurs twice as a y-coordinate, it is listed only once in the range. Also, the domain and range numbers are usually listed in ascending order to make them easier to read.

Example 1   Give the domain and range of relation C.

$C = \{(-1, 3), (2, 0), (2, 3), (3, -2), (-2, -4)\}$

Answer

domain: $D = \{-2, -1, 2, 3\}$

range: $R = \{-4, -2, 0, 3\}$

Skill Check 1

Give the domain and range of the following relations.

1. $A = \{(1, 10), (-3, 9), (2, 5), (4, -3)\}$

2. $B = \{(-6, 8), (-7, 7), (3, -1), (-4, 8)\}$

3. $C = \{(-3, 5), (-4, 6), (-3, 10), (8, -6)\}$

4. $D = \{(-3, 8), (2, 8), (0, 8), (-6, 8), (3, 8)\}$

Example 2   Write the set of ordered pairs for the relation shown. Name the relation C.

Answer

$C = \{(-2, 5), (-5, -2), (3, 2), (1, 6), (3, -6), (0, -5)\}$

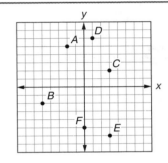

A relation is not always written as a set of ordered pairs. Instead, sometimes a relation is defined by an equation that the ordered pairs must satisfy. Example 3 below is such an instance.

Example 3   Write the set of ordered pairs for relation G if $y = 2x$ for each ordered pair and the domain of the relation is $\{-2, 0, 1, 3\}$.

Answer

$y = 2x$

$x = -2$ $y = 2(-2) = -4$

$x = 0$ $y = 2(0) = 0$

$x = 1$ $y = 2(1) = 2$

$x = 3$ $y = 2(3) = 6$

$G = \{(-2, -4), (0, 0), (1, 2), (3, 6)\}$

1. Find the y-coordinates that will pair with each of the given x-coordinates.

2. Write the relation.

Skill Check 2

Write the set form of the relations from the graphs shown.

1.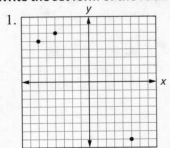

2.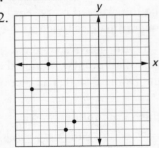

3. If the domain of relation H is $\{-3, 1, 5\}$, find the ordered pairs (x, y) for relation H when $y = x - 1$.

Example 4   Graph the relation $G = \{(-2, 3), (-4, -1), (0, 6), (3, 6), (5, 7)\}$.

Answer

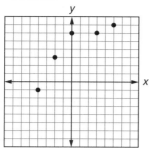

Example 5   Graph relation J if $y = x + 3$ for each ordered pair and the domain of the relation is $\{-4, 0, 3\}$.

Answer

$y = x + 3$

$x = -4$ $y = -4 + 3 = -1$

$x = 0$ $y = 0 + 3 = 3$

$x = 3$ $y = 3 + 3 = 6$

$J = \{(-4, -1), (0, 3), (3, 6)\}$

1. Substitute the given domain values into the equation to find the corresponding range values.

2. Write the ordered pairs of the relation.

3. Graph the relation.

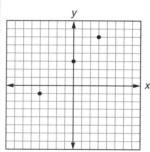

The relations you have seen up to this point have all consisted of a finite number of ordered pairs. However, a relation can have an infinite number of ordered pairs. For example, suppose a relation contains all the ordered pairs that lie on a line in the coordinate plane. Every line or segment contains an infinite number of points, so the relation contains an infinite number of ordered pairs. Since all of the ordered pairs of such a relation could not be written, an equation or rule is used to describe the ordered pairs. For example, $y = 2x$ describes all ordered pairs in which the y-coordinate is twice its x-coordinate.

The graph at the right shows a segment with endpoints $(-2, 2)$ and $(0, -1)$. The segment consists of all points contained on it. The x-coordinate ranges across all the real numbers from -2 to 0. The y-coordinate ranges across all the real numbers from -1 to 2.

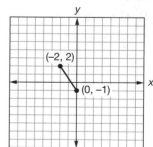

We can write this in the following way.

$$D = -2 \leq x \leq 0 \text{ and } R = -1 \leq y \leq 2$$

Skill Check 3

Graph each relation.

1. $A = \{(-3, 6), (-2, 4), (0, 0), (2, -4), (4, -6)\}$

2. $B = \{(-8, -4), (-6, -3), (2, 4), (5, 10)\}$

3. Graph relation C if its domain is $\{-1, 1, 2\}$ and $y = 2x + 1$.

4. Graph the segment with endpoints $(-7, 5)$ and $(3, 2)$. State the domain and range of the segment.

■ A. Exercises

Give the domain and range of the following relations.

1. $\{(-6, 5), (-2, 5), (1, -3), (5, 6)\}$

2. $\{(4, 7), (-6, 2), (0, -3), (-6, 6)\}$

3. $\{(0, 5), (1, -7), (3, -7), (5, 0)\}$

4. $\{(3, 5), (-2, 5), (8, 17), (9, 5)\}$

5. $\{(2, 6), (3, 6), (18, 6), (20, 6)\}$

6. $\{(1, -9), (1, -6), (1, 5), (-1, 8)\}$

Give the domain and range of the following segments.

7.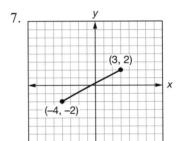

8.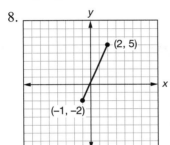

9.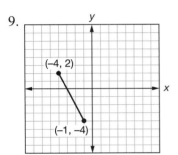

Write the set form of the relations from the graphs shown.

10.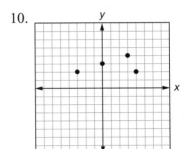

11.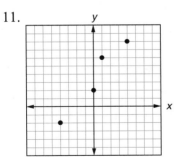

12.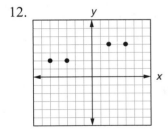

13.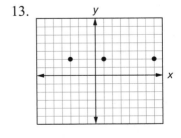

14.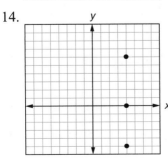

15.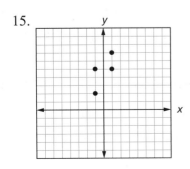

Graph each relation.

16. $A = \{(-3, -1), (0, 1), (2, 4)\}$

17. $B = \{(-5, 2), (-2, 1), (0, -2)\}$

18. $C = \{(-4, 0), (-3, 1), (-1, 3), (2, 1)\}$

19. $D = \{(-2, -1), (-2, 2), (3, 1), (3, 4)\}$

20. $E = \{(-1, 0), (0, 5), (4, 5), (6, 8)\}$

21. $F = \{(-2, 3), (2, 4), (3, 6), (7, -2)\}$

■ B. Exercises

Determine the ordered pairs from the given equation and domain.

22. $y = x + 2$; $D = \{-3, -2, 1\}$

23. $y = x - 5$; $D = \{-2, 4, 6, 8\}$

24. $y = -3x$; $D = \{-3, 0, 3, 6\}$

25. $y = 0.5x$; $D = \{4, 6, 8, 10\}$

26. $y = \frac{2}{3}x$; $D = \{-6, 0, 3, 9\}$

27. $y = 2x - 3$; $D = \{-4, -2, 3, 6\}$

Determine the ordered pairs from the given equation and domain. Graph each relation.

28. $y = 2x$; $D = \{-2, 0, 2\}$

29. $y = x - 2$; $D = \{-1, 3, 5\}$

30. $y = -x + 3$; $D = \{-2, 1, 3\}$

31. $y = -\frac{3}{2}x$; $D = \{-2, 0, 2\}$

32. $y = 2x + 1$; $D = \{-3, -1, 1\}$

33. $y = x - 0.5$; $D = \{-4, 0, 4\}$

■ C. Exercises

Give the domain and range of the following relations, and determine the equation that describes each relation.

34. $\{(3, 3), (5, 5), (-2, -2), (-4, -4), (0, 0)\}$

35. $\{(1, -4), (2, -8), (3, -12), (4, -16)\}$

36. $\{(-9, -3), (-6, -2), (-3, -1), (0, 0)\}$

■ Dominion thru Math

37. An electric utility company has a fixed monthly charge of $8.50 plus 6.8¢/kWh (kilowatt-hour) for the first 375 kWh and 7.15¢/kWh for usage above 375 kWh. Find the monthly charge for a home that used 792 kWh during a given month.

38. If the cost in exercise 37 was based on a meter reading spanning 29 days, find the cost per day.

39. Write an equation that gives the cost of electric service as a function of the kWh used in a given month for usage exceeding 375 kWh per month. Check your equation against your answer for exercise 37.

■ CUMULATIVE REVIEW

Convert the following fractions to decimals. [5.3]

40. $\frac{7}{8}$

41. $\frac{1}{25}$

42. $-\frac{9}{50}$

43. $\frac{2}{5}$

44. $\frac{13}{20}$

Solve the following percent problems. [7.2]

45. 18% of 92 is what?

46. 16 is what percent of 80?

47. 120 is 30% of what number?

48. 90% of what number is 19.8?

49. What percent of 45 is 36?

PROBLEM SOLVING

Make a Table

The problem-solving strategy "make a table" is often useful for organizing the information given in word problems. After you construct the table, you can discover additional information by expanding the table.

How long will it take the car to catch up?

Example

A motorcycle and a car start from the same point and travel in the same direction along the same road. The motorcycle starts first and travels 20 mi. before the car starts. The motorcycle averages 53 mi./hr. and the car averages 58 mi./hr. How many hours will it take the car to catch up with the motorcycle?

Answer

Think: What are you trying to find?

We are finding the time it takes for the car to catch up with the motorcycle.

Think: What formula have you seen in the past that relates rate, time, and distance?

Use the basic formula for distance, $d = rt$, where d = distance traveled, r = rate (or the speed of the vehicle), and t = time spent traveling.

Think: How could you organize the information to find out when the two vehicles have traveled the same distance? How far ahead is the motorcycle when the car begins to travel?

Since you are trying to find the time that the car travels, let the time (t) start when the car begins to travel. The motorcycle has a 20 mi. head start, so at time 0 the motorcycle has traveled 20 mi. The calculation for d after one hour for the motorcycle is $20 + 53(1) = 73$ mi. The distance that the car has traveled after one hour is $58(1) = 58$ mi. Make a table to track these distances as the hours increase. Continue the table until both vehicles have traveled the same distance.

Motorcycle			Car		
r	t	$d = 20 + rt$	r	t	$d = rt$
53	1	$20 + 53(1) = 20 + 53 = 73$	58	1	$58(1) = 58$
53	2	$20 + 53(2) = 20 + 106 = 126$	58	2	$58(2) = 116$
53	3	$20 + 53(3) = 20 + 159 = 179$	58	3	$58(3) = 174$
53	4	$20 + 53(4) = 20 + 212 = 232$	58	4	$58(4) = 232$

According to the table, the car traveled the same distance as the motorcycle after 4 hr. Therefore, it will take the car 4 hr. to catch up with the motorcycle.

Think: Does this answer seem reasonable? Is there any other way this problem could be solved?

This is a reasonable answer, and when checked it is correct. This is an acceptable strategy to use for this problem; however, there are other ways to approach the problem. For example, notice that the car gains $58 - 53 = 5$ mi./hr. Since the car started 20 mi. behind the motorcycle, divide 20 by 5 to get the 4 hr. needed for the car to catch up to the motorcycle. Algebraic methods could also be used (e.g., solve for t in $20 + 53t = 58t$).

■ Exercises

For each of the following exercises, devise a plan for finding the solution. Explain the steps of your plan, and use the plan to solve the problem.

1. Two cars start from the same point and travel in the same direction along the same road. One car starts first and travels 35 mi. before the other car starts. The first car travels at an average rate of 55 mi./hr., and the second car travels at an average rate of 62 mi./hr. How many hours will it take the second car to catch up to the first?

2. One car travels north at a constant rate of 59 mi./hr. A second car starts at the same time at the same point and travels south at a constant rate of 66 mi./hr. How many hours will it be before they are 625 mi. apart?

3. List all the different three-digit numbers that you can write using the digits 2, 3, and 4, once each.

4. A baseball coach decided that his first four batters would be Ames, Bailey, Cox, and Davis. The coach does not want Ames to bat first or second. How many different batting orders can the coach make?

5. A bag contains tickets numbered 9, 2, 1, 4, and 0. Suppose you draw three tickets at random without replacing those previously drawn and add the numbers together. How many different totals are possible? What are they?

6. Amy, Beth, Carol, and Dottie are to sit in one row of desks, one behind the other. Their teacher does not want Beth and Carol to be seated one behind the other. How many different ways can the four students be arranged?

7. Josie wants to make change for a half dollar. How many different ways can she do so if pennies cannot be used in the change?

8. Two cars leave towns that are 459 mi. apart at the same time and travel toward each other along the same road. The first car travels at an average rate of 48 mi./hr., and the second car travels at an average rate of 54 mi./hr. How long will it take until the two cars pass each other?

9.3 Functions

A *function* is a special type of relation. When each ordered pair of a relation has a unique x-coordinate, the relation is a function. The relation $A = \{(-4, 0), (-3, 2), (1, -3), (2, 5)\}$ is an example of a function, since each ordered pair has a different x-coordinate.

Definition

A **function** is a relation in which no two ordered pairs have the same first coordinate.

$$\{functions\} \subseteq \{relations\}$$

Another way to express the property of a function is to say that for each domain element there is exactly one range value corresponding to it. A *circle mapping* is useful in determining whether a relation is a function. Consider the relation $B = \{(-2, 1), (0, 7), (3, 5), (4, 3)\}$. Place the elements of the domain in one circle and the elements of the range in a second circle. For the sake of better organization, list the numbers in the circles vertically in ascending order. Draw arrows connecting the domain elements to their corresponding range elements. Since only one arrow comes from each element in the domain, this relation is a function. If two or more arrows come from any element of the domain, that element is paired with more than one y-coordinate, and the relation is not a function.

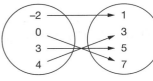

Example 1 Make a circle mapping of relation C, and give the domain and range. Is the relation a function?

$C = \{(-3, -2), (-2, 3), (1, -3), (3, 4), (4, 3)\}$

Answer

$D = \{-3, -2, 1, 3, 4\}$

$R = \{-3, -2, 3, 4\}$

Yes, relation C is a function. No two ordered pairs have the same x-coordinate.

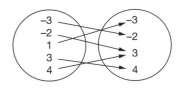

Example 2 Determine whether each relation is a function. Explain your answer.

a. $M = \{(-2, 5), (-1, 4), (2, 3), (3, 3)\}$

b. $N = \{(-1, 4), (2, 5), (3, -3), (3, 5)\}$

Answer

a. Yes, relation M is a function. No two ordered pairs have the same x-coordinate.

b. No, relation N is not a function. Two points have the x-coordinate 3.

Example 3   Is $P = \{(-3, 6), (1, 6), (2, 6)\}$ a function?

Answer

Yes; no two points have the same first coordinate. The fact that they all have the same second coordinate does not matter. The three points lie on a horizontal line.

Skill Check 1

Make a circle mapping of each relation, and determine whether it is a function.

1. $\{(-2, 4), (7, -1), (0, -1)\}$

2. $\{(5, 3), (4, 2.5), (-4, -3), (4, 5)\}$

3. $\{(5, 1), (0, 9), (4, -2)\}$

Functions are often named with lowercase letters, particularly f and g. Consider the following function.

$$f = \{(-3, 4), (0, 3), (3, -2)\}$$

The domain of f is $\{-3, 0, 3\}$, and the range of f is $\{-2, 3, 4\}$. Each element of the range is called a *value* of the function at a particular point. Because the ordered pair $(0, 3)$ is contained in the function, we say the value of the function f at 0 is 3. You can abbreviate this in *standard function notation* as demonstrated below.

$$f(0) = 3 \text{ (Read, "} f \text{ of zero equals three.")}$$

For any function f and ordered pair (x, y) contained in it, the value of f at x is y. This is denoted by the equation

$$f(x) = y.$$

Example 4   Find each of the following values for function $g = \{(-1, 1), (0, 2), (1, 3)\}$.

a. $g(1)$

b. $g(0)$

c. $g(-1)$

Answer

a. $g(1) = 3$, since 1 is paired with 3.

b. $g(0) = 2$, since 0 is paired with 2.

c. $g(-1) = 1$, since -1 is paired with 1.

Rather than list the ordered pairs of a function, you can describe them using an equation, or *function rule*. Remember that $f(x) = y$, so $f(x)$ is the y-coordinate that pairs with the given x-coordinate. For example, the equation $f(x) = x + 1$ describes all ordered pairs in which the y-coordinate is one more than the x-coordinate.

For the above function rule, $f(3) = 3 + 1 = 4$, indicating that the ordered pair $(3, 4)$ is part of the function.

Example 5   Find each of the following values for $f(x) = 2x + 4$.

a. $f(3)$ b. $f(-3)$

Answer

a. $f(x) = 2x + 4$

$f(3) = 2(3) + 4$ Substitute 3 for x and evaluate.

$= 6 + 4$

$= 10$

b. $f(x) = 2x + 4$

$f(-3) = 2(-3) + 4$ Substitute -3 for x and evaluate.

$= -6 + 4$

$= -2$

Skill Check 2

If $f(x) = 3x - 4$, find the following.

1. $f(0)$ 2. $f(-2)$ 3. $f(2)$ 4. $f(4)$

Example 6   Find the range of function $g(x) = 3x - 2$ for the domain $\{-3, 0, 2\}$. Then write the function as a set of ordered pairs.

Answer

Find $g(x)$ for each value of the domain.

$g(-3) = 3(-3) - 2$ $g(0) = 3(0) - 2$ $g(2) = 3(2) - 2$

$= -9 - 2$ $= 0 - 2$ $= 6 - 2$

$= -11$ $= -2$ $= 4$

The range of $g(x)$ is $\{-11, -2, 4\}$.

The function is $g = \{(-3, -11), (0, -2), (2, 4)\}$.

A graph of a relation can also be used to determine whether a relation is a function. If ordered pairs have the same x-coordinate, they will lie on the same vertical line when graphed. If two or more points lie on the same vertical line, the relation is not a function. This test is called the *vertical line test*. Examine the graphs of the relations below. Relation A is not a function. There are two points on the same vertical line, $(-1, 4)$ and $(-1, -3)$. Relation B is a function. No two points lie on the same vertical line. Since it fails the vertical line test, Relation C is not a function. Relation D is a function since any vertical line intersects only one point of the graph.

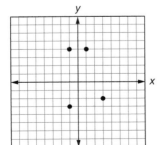

Relation A

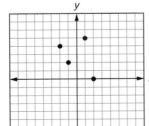

Relation B

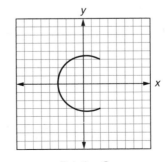

Relation C

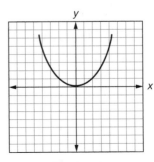

Relation D

Skill Check 3

1. Find the range of the function $f(x) = \dfrac{x}{2} + 4$ if the domain is $\{-2, 4, 6, 9\}$.

Determine from the graphs whether the relations are functions.

2.

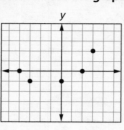

3.

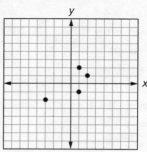

4.

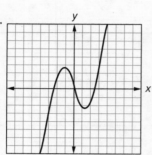

5.

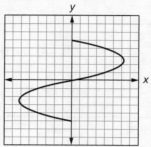

■ A. Exercises

Determine from the sets of ordered pairs whether the relations are functions.

1. $\{(-3, 4), (2, 6), (5, 9)\}$

2. $\{(-6, 2), (-4, 5), (3, -5)\}$

3. $\{(-5, -7), (-2, -4), (1, -6)\}$

4. $\{(-3, 6), (3, 1), (3, 4), (5, -2)\}$

5. $\{(2, 1), (4, 1), (6, 1), (10, 1)\}$

6. $\{(-1, 8), (-1, 5), (-1, 3), (-1, 1)\}$

Determine from the circle mappings whether the relations are functions.

7.

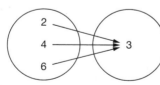

8.

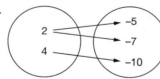

9.

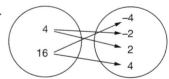

10.

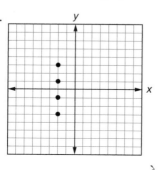

11.

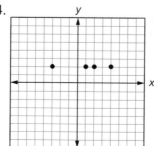

12.

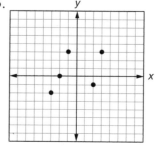

Determine from the graphs whether the relations are functions.

13.

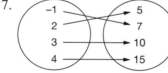

14.

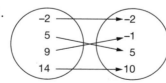

15.

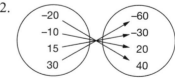

16.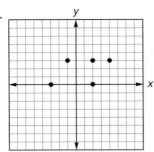

17.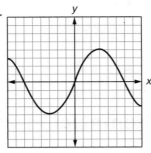

18.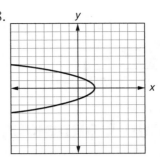

■ B. Exercises

If $f(x) = -3x + 2$, find the following.

19. $f(-5)$ 20. $f(-2)$ 21. $f(0)$ 22. $f(4)$ 23. $f(10)$ 24. $f(12)$

If $g(x) = \dfrac{x}{2} - 3$, find the following.

25. $g(-6)$ 26. $g(-2)$ 27. $g(0)$ 28. $g(2)$ 29. $g(4)$ 30. $g(8)$

Make a circle mapping with the domain elements in ascending order from smallest to largest. Then determine whether the relation is a function.

31. $\{(-3, 6), (0, 9), (12, 7)\}$ 32. $\{(-6, 2), (-4, 8), (8, -5)\}$

33. $\{(-5, -6), (-5, 7), (1, 4)\}$ 34. $\{(-3, 6), (2, -2), (3, -1), (3, 1)\}$

35. $\{(-1, 1), (2, 0), (4, -3), (6, 0)\}$ 36. $\{(-1, 8), (-1, 1), (2, 3), (6, 5)\}$

Find the range of the following functions if their domain is $\{-3, 2, 5\}$.

37. $f(x) = 2x + 7$ 38. $g(x) = -x - 1$ 39. $h(x) = \dfrac{x}{4} + 1$

40. $f(x) = -4x + 1$ 41. $g(x) = 6x - 2$ 42. $h(x) = \dfrac{5}{2}x$

■ C. Exercises

Find the indicated values for $f = \{(-6, -7), (-3, -6), (0, 5), (3, -4), (6, -3), (9, -6)\}$.

43. $f(0)$ 44. $f(3)$ 45. $f(-6)$ 46. $f(9)$

47. Is the following relation a function: $\{(3, 8), (4, 8), (5, 8)\}$? Why or why not?

48. Create a graph that represents a relation that is not a function. Identify the points that cause the relation to not be a function. What type of line connects these dots?

CUMULATIVE REVIEW

Classify the following numbers as natural, whole, integer, rational, or irrational. Give the most specific set. [5.6]

49. -72.8 50. $-\sqrt{18}$ 51. 29 52. $\sqrt{64}$ 53. $\dfrac{4}{9}$

Write each fraction as a percent. [7.1]

54. $\dfrac{3}{2}$ 55. 6 56. $\dfrac{8}{25}$ 57. $\dfrac{7}{50}$ 58. $\dfrac{9}{100}$

Benjamin Banneker, Mathematician and Astronomer

Benjamin Banneker, America's first black scientist and mathematician, was a free black man whose parents farmed in Maryland, not far from modern-day Baltimore. He was born in 1731 and died in 1806.

Benjamin's grandmother used the Bible to teach him how to read. In 1744 a young Quaker by the name of Peter Heinrich started a school near the Banneker farm. Recognizing the genius of young Benjamin, Heinrich persuaded his parents to allow the boy to attend school in the winter when he was not needed on the farm. Benjamin flourished under Heinrich's teaching and demonstrated an instinctive skill in mathematics. For enjoyment he would sit up at night creating and solving his own mathematical puzzles.

Banneker's fascination with mathematics went hand-in-hand with his extraordinary mechanical genius. In his early twenties, he constructed a clock by carving each part from pieces of wood. The amazing thing about this accomplishment is that Banneker had never seen a clock, though he had once taken a watch apart and studied the movement of its gears. His clock was a larger version of the watch, fashioned from memory. It took two years to complete and kept accurate time for more than twenty years.

Banneker later turned his interest in mathematics upward toward the night sky. He had studied astronomy as a boy, and now he began to study the heavens in an effort to determine the effects of astronomy on farming. Banneker compiled tables that listed the position of celestial bodies for each day of the year. In 1789 he correctly predicted a solar eclipse.

Three years later, Banneker published his calculations in an almanac bearing his name. This book, which contained weather predictions along with snippets of literary works and historical facts, was cherished by farmers in the states of Pennsylvania, Delaware, Maryland, and Virginia.

Banneker was active in championing the abilities of other members of his race. He strongly believed that if black men and women were given their freedom and access to quality education, they would become vital

Benjamin Banneker

Black Heritage USA 15c

© The Granger Collection, New York

assets to the intellectual development of America. He corresponded with President Thomas Jefferson about his ideas, and Jefferson sent a copy of Banneker's popular almanac to the prestigious French Academy of Sciences as an example of African-American scholarship.

In 1791 Banneker worked with surveyors Andrew and George Ellicott in laying out the plan for Washington DC, the new federal city. Throughout his life, Benjamin Banneker served as a brilliant example of what can be accomplished with dedication, persistence, and hard work.

9.4 Graphing Linear Functions

Graphing a function in the coordinate plane helps us to understand some of its characteristics. One type of function contains an infinite number of points and graphs as a line; thus it is called a linear function.

Definition

A **linear function** is a function whose graph is a line. Such an equation contains not more than two variables expressed only to the first power.

Because it is impossible to list all of the ordered pairs of a linear function, it is described by a function rule, or equation. The function rule $y = 2x + 3$ represents a linear function. This function can also be expressed as $f(x) = 2x + 3$ since $f(x) = y$. An ordered pair that makes the equation true when the x and y values are substituted into the equation is a *solution* to the equation and represents a point on the line.

Example 1   Is $(-1, 2)$ a solution to the equation $y = 2x + 3$?

Answer

$y = 2x + 3$

$2 = 2(-1) + 3$ 1. To determine whether $(-1, 2)$ is a solution, substitute $x = -1$ and $y = 2$ into the equation.

$2 = -2 + 3$ 2. Simplify the right side to see if the equation is true for these values.

$2 \neq 1$ 3. Since the equation is not true, the ordered pair $(-1, 2)$ is not a solution.

Example 2   Is $(2, 7)$ a solution to the equation $y = 2x + 3$?

Answer

$y = 2x + 3$

$7 = 2(2) + 3$ 1. To determine whether $(2, 7)$ is a solution, substitute $x = 2$ and $y = 7$ into the equation.

$7 = 4 + 3$ 2. Simplify the right side to see if the equation is true for these values.

$7 = 7$ 3. Since the equation is true, the ordered pair $(2, 7)$ is a solution.

Skill Check 1

Is the given ordered pair a solution to the equation $y = 3x + 4$?

1. $(-2, -1)$ 2. $(0, 4)$ 3. $(-4, -8)$ 4. $(3, 14)$

A line is often used to measure. A plumb line is mentioned in Amos 7:7–8. A plumb line is a cord with a pointed weight (plumb bob) on it that, when suspended in the air, points directly to the center of the earth. Carpenters use plumb lines to determine vertical and perpendicular lines. In Amos 7 God pronounced judgment on Israel because they did not measure up to His expectations. Just as a builder exercises care in building a structure, so God measures us against His expectations as spelled out in His Word.

To graph the linear function $y = 2x - 1$, you must know at least two ordered pairs that satisfy the equation. Two such ordered pairs are $(-1, -3)$ and $(2, 3)$. By graphing these ordered pairs and drawing a line through the points on the graph, you have graphed the entire function. Be sure to place arrows on the ends of the line to show that the function continues in both directions.

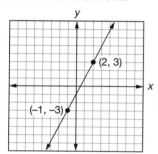

A table is useful for finding ordered pairs that satisfy a linear function. Even though only two points are needed to determine a line, find at least three ordered pairs as a check for accuracy. To find the desired ordered pairs, choose any three real numbers for x and substitute those values into the equation to find the corresponding y values.

Example 3   Find three ordered pairs that satisfy the equation $f(x) = x - 4$.

Answer

x	$x - 4$	$f(x)$
-2	$-2 - 4$	-6
0	$0 - 4$	-4
2	$2 - 4$	-2

$(-2, -6), (0, -4), (2, -2)$

1. Make a table. Choose three values for x and find the corresponding values for y. Any real numbers can be chosen for x; choosing 0, 2, and -2 makes the calculations simple and keeps the values of y smaller for graphing. However, choosing points too close together reduces the accuracy of the graph.

2. Write the ordered pairs.

Example 4　Graph the function $y = x + 2$.

Answer

x	$x + 2$	y
−2	−2 + 2	0
0	0 + 2	2
2	2 + 2	4

(−2, 0), (0, 2), (2, 4)

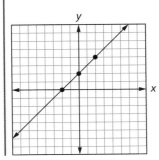

1. Make a table. Choose three values for x and find the corresponding values for y.

2. Write the ordered pairs.

3. Plot the points on the coordinate plane. Draw a line connecting the points to picture the entire function.

Example 5　Graph the function $f(x) = -2x - 5$.

Answer

x	$-2x - 5$	$f(x)$
−2	−2(−2) − 5	−1
−1	−2(−1) − 5	−3
0	−2(0) − 5	−5

(−2, −1), (−1, −3), (0, −5)

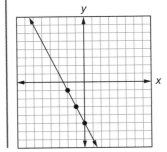

1. Make a table. Choose three values for x and find the corresponding values for y.

2. Write the ordered pairs.

3. Graph the points and connect them with a line.

Example 6 Graph the function $f(x) = \frac{x}{3} + 1$.

Answer

x	$\frac{x}{3} + 1$	$f(x)$
-3	$\frac{-3}{3} + 1$	0
0	$\frac{0}{3} + 1$	1
3	$\frac{3}{3} + 1$	2

1. Make a table. Choose three values for x and find the corresponding values for y. Choose x-coordinates divisible by 3 so that the y-coordinates will be integers.

$(-3, 0), (0, 1), (3, 2)$

2. Write the ordered pairs.

3. Graph the points and connect them with a line.

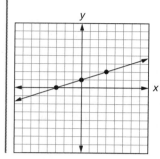

Skill Check 3

Graph each linear function.

1. $y = -x + 7$

2. $y = 3x + 1$

■ A. Exercises

Is the given ordered pair a solution to the equation $y = 2x - 9$?

1. $(4, -1)$
2. $(8, -2)$
3. $\left(\frac{7}{2}, -2\right)$
4. $\left(\frac{1}{2}, -8\right)$
5. $(-2, 13)$
6. $(2, -5)$

Is the given ordered pair a solution to the equation $y = -x + 8$?

7. $(5, -13)$
8. $(14, -6)$
9. $(3, 5)$
10. $(-4, -4)$
11. $(-2, 10)$
12. $(1, 7)$

For each equation, make a table of ordered pair solutions for $x = \{-2, -1, 0, 1, 2\}$.

13. $y = x + 8$
14. $y = -2x + 7$
15. $y = 3x - 6$
16. $y = -4x - 1$

■ B. Exercises

Using a table, find three ordered pairs that satisfy the given function rules. Graph each linear equation.

17. $y = x + 5$
18. $f(x) = x - 3$
19. $y = -2x + 5$
20. $y = 3x - 2$
21. $f(x) = 2x$
22. $y = 3x - 1$
23. $y = \frac{x}{6}$
24. $f(x) = 4 - x$
25. $y = 2x + 8$
26. $y = \frac{9}{2}x - 7$
27. $y = -\frac{2}{3}x - 3$
28. $y = 3(x + 1)$
29. $y = \frac{2}{5}x$
30. $f(x) = 3.5x$
31. $y = -2.5x + 2$
32. $y = \frac{3}{4}x + 2$

■ C. Exercises

33. What do the graphs of exercises 21, 23, 29, and 30 have in common? Look at their equations. What do the equations have in common? Make a conjecture about what you discovered. Make up three other equations similar to these equations and graph them to test your conjecture.

34. In exercises 22, 24, and 25, find the point where the line crosses the *y*-axis. Write the *y*-coordinate of each of these points. Look at the equation that is associated with each line. Make a conjecture about the relationship between the point where the line crosses the *y*-axis and the equation. Make up three other equations of this form and graph them to test your conjecture.

■ Dominion thru Math

The NexDay package delivery company offers overnight delivery on parcels up to and including 50 lb. to the surrounding eight states under the following rates: $12 for the first pound, $1.25 for each additional pound up to 25, and $1.00 for each pound above 25.

35. Find the shipping charges for an 18 lb. package sent via NexDay.

36. Find the shipping charges for a 43 lb. package sent via NexDay.

37. Write a simplified equation that gives the NexDay shipping charges for parcels weighing 25 lb. or less.

38. Write a simplified equation that gives the NexDay shipping charges for parcels weighing over 25 lb.

CUMULATIVE REVIEW

Convert each number to scientific notation, and then perform the operations. Leave answers in scientific notation. [6.8]

39. $7,300,000 + 1,800,000$

40. $0.000041 + 0.00003$

41. $840,000,000 - 360,000,000$

42. 0.00032×0.0000049

43. $3,400,000 \times 2,940$

Specify what the variable stands for, write an equation, and solve. [7.3]

44. The total cost of Amanda's groceries came to $160.50, including 7% sales tax. What was the cost of the groceries before the tax was added?

45. The freshman class at a Christian university grew from 1,200 to 1,308 in one year. What was the percent of increase in the freshman class that year?

46. Twenty percent of Mr. Datski's students made As in his classes. If 14 students made As, what was the total number of students in his classes?

47. This year the Candy Cane Creations store had a 30% increase in sales over last year. If they had a total of $62,000 in sales last year, how much in sales did they have this year?

48. Brandon was on vacation and bought some souvenirs to give to his friends at home. Before tax the total bill was $21.50, but after tax the bill came to $23.22. What was the tax rate at the souvenir shop?

Skiers are concerned with the slope of the trail they are skiing. Of course, this varies from one stretch of the trail to another, so the average top-to-bottom percent grade is often discussed when the merits of particular trails come up. The percent grade is the steepness of the hill. A 20% grade means that for every 100 ft. you travel horizontally, the trail descends 20 ft. The maximum ski slope even for short stretches is about 35% and is for only the very expert skier.

In mathematics the steepness of a line is called its slope. Unlike a ski trail, it does not curve or change slope. The slope of a line is constant at any point on it. The slope of a line is the ratio of vertical change to horizontal change from one point on the line to another point.

Skiing is one of the most popular winter sports.

Definitions

The **rise** is the vertical change from point P_1 to point P_2 on a line.
The **run** is the horizontal change from point P_1 to point P_2 on a line.
The **slope** of a line is the ratio of the rise to the run. The variable m is often used for slope.

Rise is considered positive if measured upward and negative if measured downward. Run is considered positive if measured to the right and negative if measured to the left. These conventions match the positive directions and negative directions of the y-axis and x-axis respectively. They also are in agreement with the division of positive and negative numbers. If the rise and run are both positive, or both negative, the slope will be positive. Such a line will slope upward to the right.

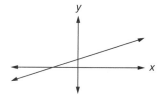

If either the rise or run is positive and the other negative, the slope will be negative. Such a line will slope downward to the right.

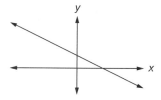

Slope
up to right → positive
down to right → negative
horizontal → zero
vertical → undefined

Consider the graph of $\overrightarrow{AB}$. Observe that it has a vertical *rise* of 4 units for a horizontal *run* of 3 units as you move from A to B. The slope of $\overrightarrow{AB}$ is the ratio of the rise to the run.

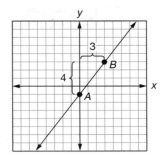

$$\text{slope of } \overrightarrow{AB} = m = \frac{\text{rise}}{\text{run}} = \frac{4}{3}$$

Example 1 Find the slope of the given line.

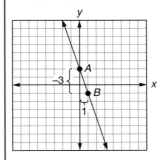

Answer

The line passes through (0, 2) and (1, −1).

rise = −3

run = 1

$m = \frac{-3}{1} = -3$

1. Locate two points on the graph of the line.
2. Move down three units (−3) from A to (0, −1).
3. Move right one unit (1) from (0, −1) to B.
4. Write the slope as a ratio and simplify.

Skill Check 1

Find the slope of the given lines.

1.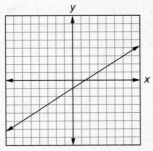

2.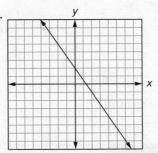

If you know the coordinates of two points on a line, $P_1(x_1, y_1)$ and $P_2(x_2, y_2)$, you can find the slope of the line without its graph. Examine the graph shown here. The rise, or vertical change, is the difference of the y-coordinates of the two points: $y_2 - y_1$. The run, or horizontal change, is the difference of the x-coordinates of the given points: $x_2 - x_1$.

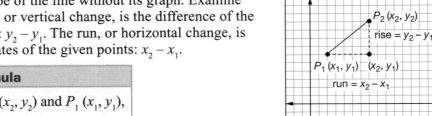

Slope Formula
If a line contains the points $P_2(x_2, y_2)$ and $P_1(x_1, y_1)$, then $m = \dfrac{\text{vertical change}}{\text{horizontal change}} = \dfrac{y_2 - y_1}{x_2 - x_1}$.

If you know the coordinates of any two points on a line, you can graph the line and find its slope from the graph, or you can use the slope formula. The slope formula is much quicker and yields more accurate results.

Example 2 Find the slope of the line that contains the points (1, 2) and (7, 5).

Answer

$$m = \frac{y_2 - y_1}{x_2 - x_1} = \frac{5 - 2}{7 - 1}$$

1. Choose (1, 2) as P_1, whose coordinates are (x_1, y_1), and (7, 5) as P_2, whose coordinates are (x_2, y_2). Substitute the values of the subscripted variables into the slope formula.

$$= \frac{3}{6}$$

2. Simplify.

$$= \frac{1}{2}$$

What would happen to the slope if we let (7, 5) be P_1 and (1, 2) be P_2? Examine the steps below to discover how this change affects the slope.

$$m = \frac{y_2 - y_1}{x_2 - x_1} = \frac{2 - 5}{1 - 7}$$

1. Choose (7, 5) as P_1 (x_1, y_1) and (1, 2) as P_2 (x_2, y_2). Substitute the values of the subscripted variables into the slope formula.

$$= \frac{-3}{-6}$$

2. Simplify.

$$= \frac{1}{2}$$

3. Even though the rise and run both had additive inverses from their values in Example 2, the slope was not affected. The slope of a line is constant.

It makes no difference which point is chosen as P_1 and which is chosen as P_2; the answer is the same.

Example 3 Find the slope of $\overleftrightarrow{CD}$ passing through (5, 3) and (2, 5).

Answer

$$m = \frac{y_2 - y_1}{x_2 - x_1} = \frac{5 - 3}{2 - 5}$$

1. Choose (5, 3) as P_1 and (2, 5) as P_2. Substitute the values of the subscripted variables into the slope formula.

$$= \frac{2}{-3}$$

2. Simplify. A positive divided by a negative gives a negative quotient.

$$= -\frac{2}{3}$$

The slope of $\overleftrightarrow{CD}$ is $-\frac{2}{3}$.

Example 4 Find the slope of $\overleftrightarrow{EF}$ passing through (3, 2) and (–1, 2).

Answer

$$m = \frac{y_2 - y_1}{x_2 - x_1} = \frac{2 - 2}{-1 - 3}$$

1. Choose (3, 2) as P_1 and (–1, 2) as P_2. Substitute the values of the subscripted variables into the slope formula.

$$= \frac{0}{-4}$$

2. Simplify.

$$= 0$$

The slope of $\overleftrightarrow{EF}$ is 0.

Notice that the y-coordinate of each point of line $\overleftrightarrow{EF}$ is 2. If you graph the line, it is parallel to the x-axis and two units above it. This line is horizontal. Every horizontal line has a slope of 0.

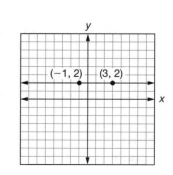

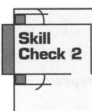

Example 5 Find the slope of the line passing through points (2, 1) and (2, 5).

Answer

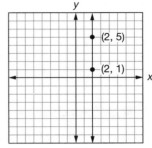

$$m = \frac{y_2 - y_1}{x_2 - x_1} = \frac{5 - 1}{2 - 2}$$ 1. Use the slope formula with (2, 1) as P_1 and (2, 5) as P_2.

$$= \frac{4}{0}$$ 2. Simplify.

Since we cannot divide by zero, the slope of the line through (2, 1) and (2, 5) is undefined.

The *x*-coordinate of each point is 2, which means (2, 5) is directly above (2, 1) in the plane. This line is a vertical line. Since we cannot divide by zero, we say that the slope of any vertical line is undefined.

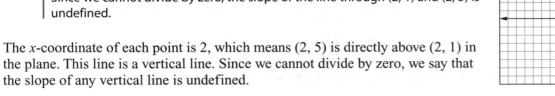

Skill Check 2

Using the slope formula, find the slope of the line through the two given points.

1. (6, 4), (2, –3)

2. (–5, 8), (–7, –3)

3. (2, 9), (–6, 9)

4. (–2, 5), (7, –2)

5. (5, –2), (5, 6)

6. (–2, 4), (–3, 8)

■ A. Exercises

Find the slope of the given lines by counting the rise and run from the graphs.

1.
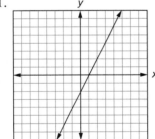

2.
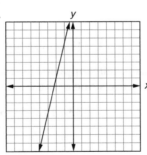

3.
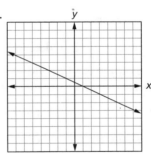

4.
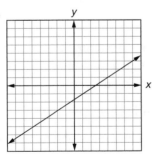

5.
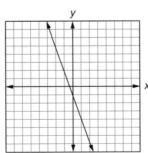

6.
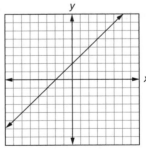

7.
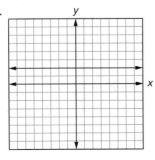

8.
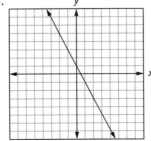

9.
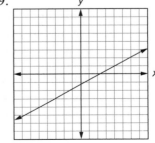

10. 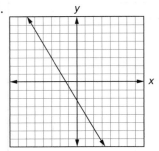 11. 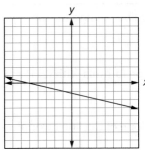 12.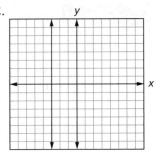

■ B. Exercises

Using the slope formula, find the slope of the line through the two given points.

13. (3, 5), (4, 7)

14. (0, 5), (2, 4)

15. (–2, 6), (3, –8)

16. (–4, 5), (–6, 8)

17. (4, 0), (–3, 10)

18. (2, –8), (2, –1)

19. (4, 2), (6, 4)

20. (7, –2), (–1, 9)

21. (6, 2), (4, –7)

22. (–4, 3), (5, 2)

23. (3, 8), (–5, 6)

24. (4, 1), (–6, 1)

From the given points, determine whether $\overleftrightarrow{AB}$ is parallel to $\overleftrightarrow{CD}$. (Hint: Lines that have the same slope are parallel.)

25. A (2, 5), B (3, 7), C (3, 4), D (5, 8)

26. A (2, –1), B (–2, 2), C (–2, –6), D (2, –3)

27. A (2, –5), B (–6, 7), C (5, 1), D (3, 4)

28. A (–4, 7), B (–6, –1), C (–3, 4), D (–6, –8)

29. A (3, –1), B (2, 9), C (7, –2), D (0, 8)

30. A (–5, –8), B (5, 9), C (3, 7), D (9, 14)

■ C. Exercises

31. Without graphing, determine whether (1, 5), (3, 11), and (4, 14) lie on the same line.

A parallelogram is a four-sided figure that has parallel opposite sides. Determine whether the figure whose vertices are given is a parallelogram by finding the slope of the opposite sides.

32. A (4, 8), B (–6, 8), C (–10, 0), D (0, 0)

33. A (2, 3), B (7, 8), C (10, 4), D (5, –1)

34. A (–4, 7), B (2, 8), C (0, 6), D (–2, 5)

■ Dominion thru Math

35. In 1990 the population of Montana was 799,065; and in 2000 it was 902,195. Assuming the rate of growth is proportional to the time elapsed in years, write a linear equation that approximates the population of Montana from 1990 to 2000. (Round the rate of change to the nearest hundred.)

36. Using your equation from exercise 35, calculate the expected population of Montana in 2010.

37. Based on your equation from exercise 35, when would you expect the population of Montana to have reached 1,000,000?

38. In 1950 the population of West Virginia was 2,005,552; and in 1990 it had decreased to 1,793,477. Write a linear equation that approximates the population of West Virginia from 1950 to 1990. (Round the rate of change to the nearest hundred.)

39. Using your equation from exercise 38, calculate the expected population of West Virginia in 2000. According to the US Census Bureau, the population of West Virginia was 1,808,344. How did the actual population compare to that predicted by the equation?

Find the percent change. Round to the nearest percent. [7.8]

40. original: 8; increase: 36

41. original: 150; decrease: 30

42. original: 85; final: 91

43. original: 210; final: 195

44. original: 270; final: 240

Find the amount of interest due on the following simple interest loans. [7.7]

45. $8,345 at 18% for 2 yr.

46. $380 at 6% for 4 mo.

47. $100,000 at 8% for 30 yr.

48. $7,900 at 9% for 18 mo.

49. $25,000 at 6.75% for 15 yr.

In a list of 27 English words, what is the least number of words that begin with the same letter? What is the most number of words in this list that begin with the same letter?

9.6 Slope-Intercept Form

There are several forms of linear equations. The *standard form* for a linear equation is $ax + by = c$, where a, b, and c are real numbers. You can graph equations in standard form quite easily by determining the x- and y-intercepts of the line they describe.

Good brakes are essential.

> **Definitions**
>
> The **y-intercept** is the point where a line crosses the y-axis.
> The **x-intercept** is the point where a line crosses the x-axis.

Every point on the y-axis has an x-coordinate of zero. Therefore, the y-intercept can be found by substituting zero for x in the equation of the line and solving for the corresponding y-coordinate. Similarly, the x-intercept is found by substituting zero for y and solving for the corresponding x-coordinate.

The two points $(x, 0)$ and $(0, y)$ determine the graph of a linear equation. Check the graph by choosing another convenient point on the line and verifying that it is a solution to the equation.

Example 1   Find the *x*- and *y*-intercepts of the line $2x + 3y = 6$ and use them to graph the line.

Answer

$2(0) + 3y = 6$ 1. Substitute zero for *x*.

$3y = 6$ 2. Solve for *y*.

$\dfrac{3y}{3} = \dfrac{6}{3}$

$y = 2$ 3. The *y*-intercept is (0, 2).

$2x + 3(0) = 6$ 4. Substitute zero for *y*.

$2x = 6$ 5. Solve for *x*.

$\dfrac{2x}{2} = \dfrac{6}{2}$

$x = 3$ 6. The *x*-intercept is (3, 0).

         7. Plot the points and draw the line through them.

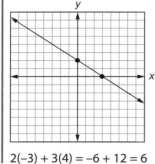

$2(-3) + 3(4) = -6 + 12 = 6$ 8. (-3, 4) appears to be on the line. Use it to check the graph.

Horizontal and vertical lines of the form $y = k$ or $x = k$, $k \neq 0$, have only one intercept since they are parallel to an axis.

Skill Check 1

Find the *x*- and *y*-intercepts of the following lines.

1. $3x - 2y = 12$ 2. $x - 4y = 10$

Find the *x*- and *y*-intercepts of the following linear equations and graph the lines.

3. $3x + 5y = 15$ 4. $2x + 5y = -10$

Graphing using both intercepts works well in some cases, such as when the constant *c* is divisible by both the coefficient of *x* and the coefficient of *y*. Otherwise, one or both of the intercepts will be mixed numbers or fractions. An accurate graph will be difficult to draw when the intercepts are close together, such as (1, 0) and (0, 1).

The form of an equation that is most useful is the *slope-intercept form*.

Definition

The **slope-intercept form** of a linear equation is $y = mx + b$. The slope of the line is *m*, and the *y*-intercept is at (0, *b*).

The line in the graph crosses the y-axis at (0, –2), so $b = -2$. By counting the rise (4) and the run (1) from (0, –2) on the graph, you can easily see that the line has a slope of $\frac{4}{1} = 4$, so $m = 4$. Substituting 4 for m and –2 for b in $y = mx + b$ gives $y = 4x - 2$, the equation of the line in slope-intercept form.

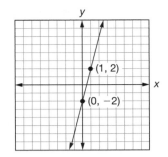

Example 2 Find the slope and y-intercept of the line $y = 3x - 2$.

Answer

The equation is in slope-intercept form, $y = mx + b$.

The slope is $m = 3$.

Since $b = -2$, the y-intercept is (0, –2).

If an equation is not in slope-intercept form, you can change it to slope-intercept form by solving for y. Use the properties of equality, and be sure to write the term with the x variable before the constant term on the right side of the transformed equation.

Example 3 Change $2x - y = 10$ to slope-intercept form.

Answer

$2x - y = 10$

$2x - 2x - y = -2x + 10$ 1. Subtract $2x$ from both sides of the equation. Place the $-2x$ before the

$-y = -2x + 10$ constant term.

$\frac{-y}{-1} = \frac{-2x}{-1} + \frac{10}{-1}$ 2. Divide (or multiply) both sides by -1 to solve for y.

$y = 2x - 10$

Skill Check 2

Change the following equations to slope-intercept form and find the slope and y-intercept.

1. $x + y = 7$

2. $3x - y = -2$

3. $y - x = 2$

4. $4x - 2y = 8$

Linear equations are easily graphed once they are stated in slope-intercept form. The y-intercept is used to locate the point at which the graph intersects the y-axis. Other points are determined using the rise and run from the slope. Only two points are needed to draw the line, but at least one other point should be used to check for accuracy.

Consider the equation $y = 2x + 3$. The y-intercept is at (0, 3). Place this point in the coordinate plane. The slope of the line is $m = 2 = \frac{2}{1} = \frac{rise}{run}$. Starting from the point (0, 3), move up two units and right one unit to locate a second point. This point is (1, 5). Graph the equation by drawing a line through the points (0, 3) and (1, 5). The $\frac{rise}{run}$ ratio of $\frac{-2}{-1}$ also describes the slope of 2. From the y-intercept (0, 3), move down two units and left one unit to the point (–1, 1), another point located on the graph of the equation. This third point can be used to check your graph.

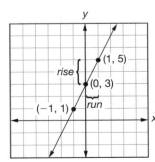

Example 4 Use the slope-intercept form to graph the line $y = 3x - 2$.

Answer

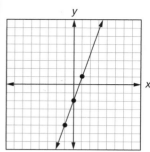

1. Identify the y-intercept as $(0, -2)$ and plot it on the graph.
2. Express the slope as a ratio to find rise and run:
$$m = 3 = \frac{3}{1} = \frac{rise}{run}.$$
The rise is 3 (up three), and the run is 1 (right one).
3. From $(0, -2)$, move up three and right one to plot a second point on the line, $(1, 1)$.
4. Draw a line through the two points.
5. Use $m = 3 = \frac{-3}{-1} = \frac{rise}{run}$ to check your graph.
From $(0, -2)$, move down three and left one to plot a third point on the line, $(-1, -5)$.

Example 5 Graph the line $2x + 3y = 3$.

Answer

$$2x + 3y = 3$$
$$2x - 2x + 3y = -2x + 3$$
$$3y = -2x + 3$$
$$\frac{3y}{3} = \frac{-2x}{3} + \frac{3}{3}$$
$$y = -\frac{2}{3}x + 1$$

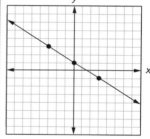

1. State the equation in slope-intercept form.

2. Plot the y-intercept: $(0, 1)$.
3. Use the rise and run to locate several more points on the graph.
   a. Using $m = \frac{-2}{3}$, from $(0, 1)$ move down two and right three to $(3, -1)$.
   b. Using $m = \frac{2}{-3}$, from $(0, 1)$ move up two and left three to $(-3, 3)$.
4. Draw a line through the points to graph the linear equation.

Graphing an Equation Using the Slope-Intercept Form
1. Solve the equation for y to put it in slope-intercept form.
2. Plot the y-intercept at $(0, b)$.
3. Express the slope as a ratio to find the rise and run.
4. From the y-intercept, use the rise and run to graph two other points.
5. Draw a line through the points.

Skill Check 3

Use the slope-intercept form to graph the following lines.

1. $y = -2x + 1$

2. $y = \frac{1}{3}x + 4$

Change the following equations to slope-intercept form; then use the y-intercept and slope to graph the lines.

3. $4x - y = 5$

4. $-2x + 3y = 6$

■ A. Exercises

Find the *x*- and *y*-intercepts of the following lines.

1. $2x + 3y = 24$

2. $3x - 5y = 30$

3. $7x - 4y = 84$

4. $x + y = 8$

5. $x = 5$

6. $3y = 66$

Find the slope and *y*-intercept of the following lines.

7. $y = 3x - 5$

8. $y = 2x + 4$

9. $y = \frac{1}{2}x + 5$

10. $y = -\frac{3}{2}x + 8$

Change the following equations to slope-intercept form and find the slope and *y*-intercept.

11. $7x - y = 14$

12. $3x - 8y = 16$

13. $x + 8y = 0$

14. $7x - 2y = 14$

■ B. Exercises

Find the *x*- and *y*-intercepts of the following linear equations and graph the lines.

15. $-2x + 8y = 16$

16. $2x + y = -4$

17. $x - 2y = 6$

18. $-4x - 3y = 12$

Use the slope-intercept form to graph the following lines.

19. $y = -2x + 1$

20. $y = \frac{1}{2}x - 1$

21. $y = 3x$

22. $y = x - 4$

23. $y = -\frac{3}{5}x + 2$

24. $y = -3x$

Change the following equations to slope-intercept form; then use the *y*-intercept and slope to graph the lines.

25. $2x + 5y = 10$

26. $x - 3y = 9$

27. $x + 4y = -8$

28. $2x + y = 5$

29. $2x + 3y = 6$

30. $x - 5y = 15$

31. $6x - 3y = 0$

32. $-4x + y = 1$

33. $x + 3y = 6$

34. $-5x + 2y = 0$

35. $5x + 2y = -10$

■ C. Exercises

Write an equation for a line with the following characteristics.

36. slope of 4 and *y*-intercept (0, 12)

37. slope of 0 and *y*-intercept (0, –9)

38. undefined slope and *x*-intercept (5, 0)

39. *x*-intercept (3, 0) and *y*-intercept (0, 6)

■ Dominion thru Math

40. A water utility company serving an urban area charges $15.75 per quarter for the first 5,000 gal. and $2.85 per 1,000 gal. above 5,000. Find the quarterly charges for a residence that used 8,500 gal. in a given quarter.

41. Write a simplified equation that gives the quarterly cost for water usage greater than 5,000 gal. as a function of each 1,000 gal. used. Check your equation with your answer for exercise 40.

42. In many communities the sewer bill is coupled with the water bill since some part of the water usage eventually winds up at the sewage treatment facility. If the sewer charges are based on 75% of the metered water usage and are rated at $2.25 per 1,000 gal., what would the household in exercise 40 pay for their water/sewer bill if they used 15,600 gal. of water in a given quarter?

Add or subtract as indicated. [6.1]

43. $\frac{2}{7} + \frac{3}{5} - 4$

44. $\frac{5}{9} + \frac{2}{3} - \frac{5}{6}$

45. $6\frac{2}{3} + 3\frac{7}{8}$

46. $7.03 - 8.99 + 6.1$

47. $-0.38 - 4.89 + 0.77$

48. $-60.4 + 20.08 - 45.2$

Find the distance represented by points separated by the following distances on a map. The scale is 3 cm : 62 km. [7.4]

49. 9 cm

50. 15 cm

What distances would be represented on the same map if two towns are the following distances apart? Round to the nearest tenth. [7.4]

51. 93 km

52. 300 km

9.7 ⊓ Direct Variations

Definitions

The variables x and y form a **direct variation** if the ratio $\frac{y}{x}$ always equals a constant k, where k is a positive number. The variable y is said to *vary directly* with x, or x and y are said to be **directly proportional**. The constant k is the **constant of variation**, or the **constant of proportionality**.

Consider the following table, which shows the number of miles traveled, y, in a certain number of hours, x, at a constant rate of 30 mi./hr.

x hours	y miles	$\dfrac{y}{x}$
1	30	$\dfrac{30}{1} = 30$
2	60	$\dfrac{60}{2} = 30$
3	90	$\dfrac{90}{3} = 30$
4	120	$\dfrac{120}{4} = 30$

Since the ratio $\frac{y}{x}$ always equals a constant in the general form of the equation for a direct proportion, we represent it with the letter k. That is, $\frac{y}{x} = k$. By multiplying both sides of the equation by x, an equivalent form of the equation is obtained: $y = kx$. This form of the equation for the table above would be $y = 30x$. This form is most commonly used.

Example 1

Does y vary directly with x in the following table? If so, find the constant of variation and write an equation for the direct variation.

x	y
1	3
3	9
5	15
7	21

Answer

$\dfrac{y}{x} = \dfrac{3}{1} = 3$ 1. Determine whether the ratio $\dfrac{y}{x}$ is equal to a constant.
Yes, y varies directly with x.

$\dfrac{y}{x} = \dfrac{9}{3} = 3$

$\dfrac{y}{x} = \dfrac{15}{5} = 3$

$\dfrac{y}{x} = \dfrac{21}{7} = 3$

$\dfrac{y}{x} = 3 = k$ 2. The ratio is 3 for all ordered pairs, so the constant of variation is $k = 3$.

$y = kx$ 3. Write the equation for a direct variation and substitute the value for k into it.

$y = 3x$

Skill Check 1

Determine whether each table of values represents a direct variation. If it does, find the constant of variation and write an equation for the variation.

1.

x	1	2	3	3
y	5	10	12	20

2.

x	1	2	3	4
y	6	12	18	24

The term *constant of variation* is interesting, since the two main words, *constant* and *variation*, are contradictory. Yet they are used together to describe a type of change. There is variation, but that variation is at a constant, predictable rate. Many characteristics of God's created universe vary, but in a consistent way. The seasons, for example, are constantly changing but are consistent in their change. Genesis 8:22 says, "While the earth remaineth, seedtime and harvest, and cold and heat, and summer and winter, and day and night shall not cease." Analyzing change helps you better understand the universe that God created.

Example 2

Indicate which equations represent a direct variation. If an equation describes a direct variation, give the constant of variation.

a. $f(x) = 2.2x$

b. $y = 4x - 1$

c. $d = 45t$

d. $y = -2x$

Answer

a. $f(x) = 2.2x$ is a direct variation; $k = 2.2$.

b. $y = 4x - 1$ is not a direct variation because of the -1. The variable y must be a multiple of x.

c. $d = 45t$ is a direct variation; $k = 45$.

d. $y = -2x$ is not a direct variation; the coefficient of x (the constant of variation) must be positive.

Skill Check 2

Indicate which equations represent a direct variation. If an equation describes a direct variation, give the constant of variation.

1. $y = 3.5x$

2. $c = \pi d$

3. $y = 2x + 7$

4. $xy = 100$

Notice the similarity between the forms of the equations for a straight line and for a direct variation.

$$y = mx + b$$
$$y = kx$$

A direct variation is an equation of the form $y = mx + b$, where $b = 0$ and $m > 0$. Therefore, its graph is a line with a y-intercept of $(0, 0)$, the origin, and a slope of k, the positive constant of variation.

Example 3   Graph the direct variation $y = 4x$.

Answer

x	y
−1	−4
0	0
1	4

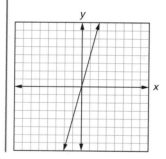

1. Make a table to find ordered pairs that satisfy the equation. You could also use the slope of 4 and the y-intercept $(0, 0)$ to graph the line.

2. Graph the line.

Skill Check 3

Graph the following direct variations.

1. $y = 3x$

2. $y = \dfrac{1}{2}x$

Example 4   Find k if y varies directly with x and $y = 12$ when $x = \dfrac{1}{2}$. Write an equation for the direct variation.

Answer

$y = kx$ 1. Use the general form for a direct variation.

$12 = k\left(\dfrac{1}{2}\right)$ 2. Substitute the given values for x and y.

$2(12) = k\left(\dfrac{1}{2}\right)(2)$ 3. Multiply both sides of the equation by 2.

$k = 24$

$y = 24x$ 4. Substitute the value of k into the equation of a direct variation, $y = kx$.

Example 5 If y varies directly with x and $y = 6$ when $x = 2$, find y when $x = \frac{2}{3}$.

Answer

$y = kx$ 1. Use the general form for a direct variation.

$6 = k(2)$ 2. Substitute the given values for x and y.

$\dfrac{6}{2} = \dfrac{k(2)}{2}$ 3. Solve for k.

$k = 3$

$y = kx$ 4. Rewrite the general form of the equation and substitute the value of $\frac{2}{3}$ for x and

$y = \cancel{3}\left(\dfrac{2}{\cancel{3}}\right) = 2$ 3 for k into it.

Skill Check 4

1. Find k if y varies directly with x and $y = 18$ when $x = 4$.

2. Find k if y varies directly with x and $y = 32$ when $x = 4$.

3. If y varies directly with x, and $y = 5$ when $x = 10$, find y when $x = 22$.

4. If y varies directly with x, and $y = 2$ when $x = 5$, find y when $x = 22$.

⊕ Invention

It seems amazing that such a key invention as the *zipper* would take over thirty years to be totally accepted by the clothing industry and its customers. In 1893 Whitcomb Judson received a patent for a zipper-like shoe closer that he called the "clasp locker"; it was not very successful. In 1905 he called the next generation of the invention the "Judson C-curity Fastener," but it too had a number of failures. Finally, in 1914 one of his employees, Gideon Sundback, came up with the right design for the "separable fastener," and the modern zipper was on its way up.

The name "zipper" was actually given to the fastener in 1923 by an important customer, B. F. Goodrich, who bought 150,000 of them for rubber boots and thought the sound they made was "zip." But clothing manufacturers were reluctant to use zippers until well into the 1930s, when they were promoted as a self-help item for children's clothing. After this nothing else would come close as the mainstay of clothing closure until the late 1950s, when hook and loop fasteners caught the fancy of so many. Even today, the much-refined modern zipper stands well ahead of buttons and the hook and loop system.

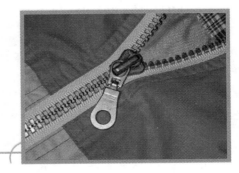

■ A. Exercises

Indicate which equations represent a direct variation. If an equation describes a direct variation, give the constant of variation.

1. $y = 2.7x$

2. $y = 3x + 1$

3. $y = \frac{5}{2}x$

4. $y = 8x$

5. $y = \pi x$

6. $y = \frac{\pi x}{2}$

Determine whether each table of values represents a direct variation. If it does, find the constant of variation and write an equation for the variation.

7.

x	y
5	10
10	20
15	30
20	50

8.

x	y
4	24
7	42
8	48
12	72

9.

x	y
2	18
6	54
9	81
20	180

10.

x	y
1	2
2	4
3	6
4	8

11.	x	y
	3	12
	6	9
	9	6
	12	3

12.	x	y
	2	8
	4	16
	6	24
	8	32

13.	x	y
	1	2
	2	−4
	3	6
	4	−8

14.	x	y
	2	1
	6	3
	7	3.5
	10	5

Do the following graphs show direct variation?

15.

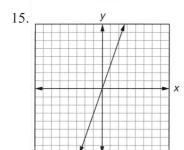

16.

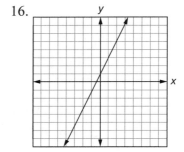

17.

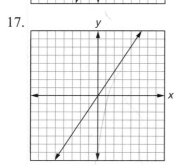

18.

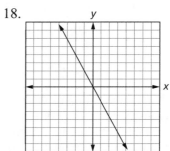

■ B. Exercises

Find k if y varies directly with x.

19. $y = 18$ when $x = 4$　　20. $y = 6$ when $x = 24$　　21. $y = 100$ when $x = 20$

22. $y = 20$ when $x = \frac{1}{2}$　　23. $y = 10$ when $x = \frac{1}{3}$　　24. $y = \frac{1}{2}$ when $x = 45$

Find y if y varies directly with x.

25. If $y = 15$ when $x = 10$, find y when $x = 32$.　　26. If $y = 3$ when $x = 20$, find y when $x = 40$.

27. If $y = 8$ when $x = 16$, find y when $x = 24$.　　28. If $y = 30$ when $x = 42$, find y when $x = 140$.

29. If $y = 12$ when $x = 20$, find y when $x = 8$.　　30. If $y = 8$ when $x = 10$, find y when $x = 22$.

Graph the following direct variations.

31. $y = 2x$　　32. $y = \frac{1}{3}x$　　33. $y = \frac{1}{2}x$　　34. $y = 2.5x$

■ C. Exercises

Fill in the blanks in the following tables of direct variations and give the constant of variation.

35.	x	y
	3	6
	5	
		18
	12	

36.	x	y
	10	25
	−4	
	3	
		17.5

37.	x	y
	2	12
		24
		36
		48

38.	x	y
	12	3
	−4	
	8	
		4

CUMULATIVE REVIEW

Rename each fraction in lowest terms. [5.1]

39. $\dfrac{22}{38}$ 　　　 40. $\dfrac{30}{42}$ 　　　 41. $\dfrac{245}{63}$ 　　　 42. $\dfrac{825}{1,617}$ 　　　 43. $\dfrac{60}{150}$

Find the discount and sale price for the following items. [7.5]

44. retail price: \$135; discount rate: 75%

45. retail price: \$42; discount rate: 35%

46. retail price: \$250; discount rate: 50%

47. retail price: \$2,450; discount rate: 15%

48. retail price: \$23,000; discount rate: 30%

9.8 Graphing Linear Inequalities in the Plane

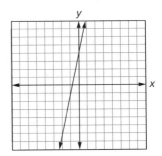

> ### Definition
>
> A **linear inequality** is any inequality of the form $ax + by \neq c$, where the $\neq$ can be replaced by $>$, $<$, $\geq$, or $\leq$.

The solution to a linear equation in two variables is a set containing an infinite number of ordered pairs, all of which lie on the same line. Consider the linear function $y = 5x + 4$. We know its graph is a line with y-intercept $(0, 4)$ and slope $m = 5$.

The line $y = 5x + 4$ divides the plane into three sets of points—the set of points above the line, the set of points on the line, and the set of points below the line.

Consider any point on the line. If you proceed vertically downward from that point, the value of y decreases as indicated by the numbers on the y-axis. Therefore, the set of points below the line are those such that $y < 5x + 4$. If you proceed vertically upward from any point on the line, the value of y increases. Thus the set of points above the line are those such that $y > 5x + 4$.

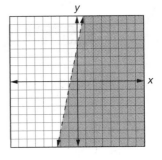

Consider the inequality $y < 5x + 4$. The solution is the region of the plane below the graph of the line $y = 5x + 4$, not including the line. To show that the line is not part of the solution, draw the boundary as a dashed line. Shade the portion of the plane below the boundary line.

The inequalities $\geq$ and $\leq$ signify that the line is also part of the solution. Therefore, the line in the graph of $y \geq 5x + 4$ is solid rather than dashed.

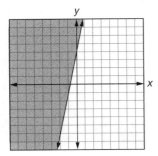

$y \geq ax + b \rightarrow$ solid line
$y > ax + b \rightarrow$ dashed line

For each function, is the solution the region above the line or below it, and should the line be solid or dashed?

1. $y \leq x + 1$

2. $y > \dfrac{1}{3}x - 2$

3. $y > 2x$

4. $y \geq -\dfrac{5}{3}x + 2$

Example 1 Graph the solutions to $y \geq -2x + 3$.

Answer

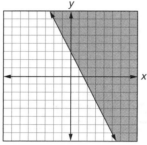

Plot at least two points on the graph that satisfy the equation.

Draw a solid line through the points.

Shade the region that is vertically above any point on the line.

1. Use the y-intercept $(0, 3)$ and the slope $m = -2 = \dfrac{-2}{1}$ (down two, right one).

2. The inequality includes "equal to."

3. The inequality includes "greater than."

Another way to find the region containing the solutions is to check a convenient point above or below the line to see if it is a solution. If the chosen point satisfies the inequality, all points on that side of the line are solutions. If the point does not satisfy the inequality, all points on the opposite side of the boundary are solutions. The point $(0, 0)$ is often used to test a region of points to see if it is part of the solution. In Example 1 $(0, 0)$ is below the line. It does not satisfy the inequality since $0 \not\geq -2(0) + 3$. Since the test point is not part of the solution, shade all points above the line.

Example 2 Check the points $(0, 0)$ and $(3, -2)$ to see if they are solutions to the inequality $2x - 3y > 6$.

Answer

$2x - 3y > 6$

$2(0) - 3(0) ? 6$

$0 \not> 6$

$2x - 3y > 6$

$2(3) - 3(-2) ? 6$

$6 + 6 ? 6$

$12 > 6$

1. Substitute the values $x = 0$ and $y = 0$ in the inequality.

2. The inequality is not true; therefore, $(0, 0)$ and all points on the same side of the line as $(0, 0)$ are not solutions.

3. Substitute the values $x = 3$ and $y = -2$ in the inequality.

4. The inequality is true; therefore, $(3, -2)$ and all points on the same side of the line as $(3, -2)$ are solutions.

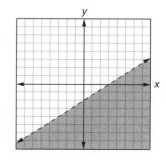

Changing the equation $2x - 3y > 6$ to slope-intercept form produces $y < \dfrac{2}{3}x - 2$. This form clearly indicates that the region below the line contains solutions to the inequality.

Example 3 Graph the solutions to $y < 4x - 5$.

Answer

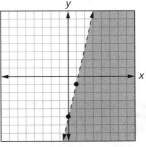

Plot at least two points on the graph that satisfy the equation.

1. Use the y-intercept $(0, -5)$ and the slope $m = 4 = \frac{4}{1}$ (up four, right one).

Draw a dashed line through the points. It is only a boundary; points on it are not part of the solution.

2. The inequality does not include "equal to."

Shade the region that is vertically below any point on the line.

3. The inequality is "less than."

$0 \not< 4(0) - 5$, so $(0, 0)$ is not part of the solution.

4. Use the test point $(0, 0)$ to check the solution.

Skill Check 2

Graph the solutions to the following inequalities.

1. $y > x + 1$ 2. $y \leq 0.5x + 3$ 3. $x + y \geq 2$ 4. $x - 3y > 12$

■ A. Exercises

Determine whether the line on the graph of the solution should be dashed or solid.

1. $y \leq 3x - 5$ 2. $y > 5x$ 3. $y < -4x + 6$ 4. $y \geq \frac{2}{5}x - 8$

5. $3x + y \leq 9$ 6. $7x - 2y < 12$ 7. $x + 3y > 9$ 8. $5x + y \leq 4$

State whether the given ordered pair is a solution to $y < 4x + 6$. ~~true/false~~

9. $(0, 0)$ 10. $(1, -6)$ 11. $(-8, 4)$ 12. $(6, 10)$ 13. $(-4, -2)$

State whether $(0, 0)$ is a solution to the given equation.

14. $y \geq \frac{8}{5}x - 7$ 15. $y \leq -8x + 3$ 16. $y > -2x + 1$

17. $y < 5x$ 18. $3x + y > 12$ 19. $-6x + 9y > -9$

■ B. Exercises

Graph the solutions to the following inequalities.

20. $y \leq -\frac{1}{5}x + 2$ 21. $y > x - 8$ 22. $y < -3x + 2$ 23. $y \geq 4x - 5$

24. $y \leq \frac{3}{7}x - 6$ 25. $y < 5x$ 26. $6x - 2y > 12$ 27. $7x + 4y \leq 16$

28. $x - 3y \leq 9$ 29. $4x + y > -2$ 30. $5x - 2y \geq 10$ 31. $-4x + 6y < 12$

32. $3x - y \leq -4$

■ **C. Exercises**

Graph both of the inequalities in each problem on the same set of axes. Shade the area where the regions overlap darker than the regions where only one of the inequalities is true.

33. $y > 2x - 3$ and $y < -x + 4$

34. $y \le \frac{4}{5}x + 2$ and $y > -3x - 1$

35. $y < \frac{-1}{4}x + 3$ and $y \le 2x + 1$

36. $3x + y \ge 5$ and $-2x - 3y \le 9$

37. $-x - 6y > 18$ and $y \le \frac{2}{3}x + 4$

■ **Dominion thru Math**

The earned run average (ERA) for a professional base-ball pitcher is defined as the number of earned runs he allows the hitters to make for every nine innings pitched. This means the total number of innings pitched will have to be divided into blocks of nine innings. Earned run averages are customarily expressed to the nearest hundredth.

38. Write a simplified equation to express a pitcher's ERA in terms of earned runs (E) and innings pitched (I).

39. In 1978 Ron Guidry of the New York Yankees pitched 273.7 innings and allowed 53 earned runs. What was his ERA?

40. In 1994 Greg Maddux of the Atlanta Braves pitched 202 innings and allowed 35 earned runs. What was his ERA?

41. In 2000 Pedro Martinez of the Boston Red Sox pitched 217 innings and allowed 42 earned runs. What was his ERA?

CUMULATIVE REVIEW

Find the appropriate tip for the following services at the rate of 15% of the cost. If the answer is not a multiple of twenty-five cents, round to the next higher quarter. **[7.6]**

42. hair permanent: $75

43. luggage handler: $8

44. paper delivery: $24

Find the commission for the following sales and earnings. **[7.6]**

45. sales: $8,400; earnings: $924

46. sales: $120; earnings: $7.20

47. sales: $250,000; earnings: $22,500

Solve. **[8.1]**

48. $-6(2x + 5) = -78$

49. $7(-2x + 8) = 19$

50. $9(-y + 4) + 7y = 128$

51. $17 + 2(x + 6) = 53$

MATH & SCRIPTURE

Stewardship of Wealth

A steward is an overseer of someone's property, much like a manager of a store that is owned by someone else. A steward has considerable freedom to make decisions—but within the long-range goal of making his master prosper and his master's wealth increase. First Peter 4:10 urges believers to be "good stewards of the manifold grace of God." Believers have a two-fold stewardship: they are overseers of the money and resources entrusted to them by God and, more importantly, overseers of spiritual wealth. Christians are to make God's resources increase and abound to His glory.

Read the parable of the talents in Matthew 25:14–28, and answer the following questions.

1. What was the basis for the number of talents given to each servant (steward)?

2. What percent increase did the stewards given five and two talents each realize?

3. We are not told how long the master was gone, only that it was a long time. You can use a growth of 10% per year (typical for investors in our age) and use the compound interest formula $S = P(1 + i)^n$ to make a few guesses to find n, the least number of years needed for an investment to grow like that of the first two stewards. To do this, first represent P and S in numbers of talents. What did you find n to be?

4. If the third steward who hid the money had invested it in a bank like the master suggested, what percent growth would it have realized while the master was away, assuming that the length of absence was that from the previous problem and that the bank paid 4% per year?

5. If a family's average annual income over forty-five working years is about $50,000, what total amount will they have contributed to the Lord's work if they give just 10%?

6. If the same family in exercise 5 faithfully saves just 5% per year for retirement, how much will they have contributed into a retirement fund over the forty-five years?

7. What is the average amount per year they put into their retirement fund?

8. What is the average amount per week they put into their retirement fund?

9. If the money they invest in their retirement fund earns 8% interest over the 45 yr. period, the compound interest earned will cause their retirement fund to increase their total contribution by 759%. What amount will actually be in their retirement fund?

10. Because the family we have considered was a faithful steward of the resources that came to them from God's good hand, they have more than adequate resources during retirement to serve the Lord any place in the world He wants them to go. They can certainly continue to be good stewards of the manifold grace of God. Suppose that after they retire, they invest the entire amount (see answer to exercise 9) at 6%. What will their annual interest income be?

Infinite Truths

Moreover it is required in stewards, that a man be found faithful. *1 Corinthians 4:2*

Chapter 9 Review

Vocabulary

circle mapping

constant of proportionality*

coordinate plane**

directly proportional

direct variation

domain

function

function notation

function rule

linear function

linear inequality

one-to-one correspondence

ordered pair

origin

quadrant

range

relation

rise

run

slope

slope-intercept form

vertical line test

x-axis

x-coordinate

x-intercept

y-axis

y-coordinate

y-intercept

*or constant of variation

**also called Cartesian coordinate plane or rectangular coordinate plane

Graph each point in the same coordinate plane.

1. A (–6, 2)

2. B (9, 3)

3. C (–5, –6)

4. D (0, 4)

Give the domain and range of the following relations.

5. {(5, 8), (0, –3), (9, 2), (4, 7)}

6. {(–4, 2), (–3, 8), (0, 2), (1, 3), (5, 8)}

Use the given equation to write ordered pairs of the relation with the domain {–2, 0, 1, 4}.

7. $y = 5x + 1$

8. $8x + y = 7$

Graph each relation.

9. {(5, 3), (–4, 2), (0, 6), (7, –3)}

10. {(6, –6), (5, –5), (4, –4), (3, –3)}

Determine from the sets of ordered pairs whether the relations are functions.

11. {(0, 4), (0, 2), (0, 5)}

12. {(–4, 3), (5, 3), (8, 4), (–2, 4)}

Determine from the graphs and diagrams whether the relations are functions.

13.

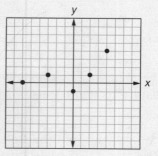

14.

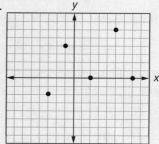

15.

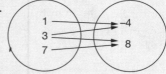

16.

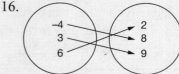

If $f(x) = 3x - 1$, find the following.

17. $f(5)$ 18. $f(0)$ 19. $f(-2)$ 20. $f(3)$

Find the range of the following functions if their domain is {–6, 1, 4}.

21. $f(x) = 7x + 2$ 22. $g(x) = -2x - 1$

Is the given ordered pair a solution to the equation $y = -2x + 1$?

23. $(2, -5)$ 24. $(3, -5)$

Using a table, find three ordered pairs that satisfy the given function rules. Graph each linear equation.

25. $y = 3x - 5$ 26. $y = -x + 8$

Using the slope formula, find the slope of the line through the two given points.

27. $(3, 9), (-1, 4)$ 28. $(-5, -7), (6, -1)$ 29. $(0, 4), (5, -2)$ 30. $(8, -4), (6, 3)$

Find the x- and y-intercepts of the following lines.

31. $3x - y = 9$ 32. $8x + y = 10$

33. $-4x - 2y = 8$ 34. $x + 5y = 6$

Change the following equations to slope-intercept form, find the slope and y-intercept, and graph.

35. $4x + y = -12$ 36. $x - 5y = 20$

37. $5x - 2y = 12$ 38. $-3x + y = -4$

Determine whether each table of values represents a direct variation. If it does, find the constant of variation and write an equation for the variation.

39.

x	y
2	4
3	6
4	8
5	10

40.

x	y
3	6
4	12
5	15
6	18

Find k if y varies directly with x.

41. $y = 6$ when $x = 3$ 42. $y = 150$ when $x = 8$

43. $y = 45$ when $x = 9$ 44. $y = \dfrac{9}{5}$ when $x = 27$

Graph the solutions to the following inequalities.

45. $y < 2x + 5$ 46. $y \geq \dfrac{1}{5}x - 2$ 47. $3x + y \leq 6$

48. $x + 4y > -12$ 49. $-3x - y < 6$

50. State the mathematical significance of 1 Corinthians 4:2.

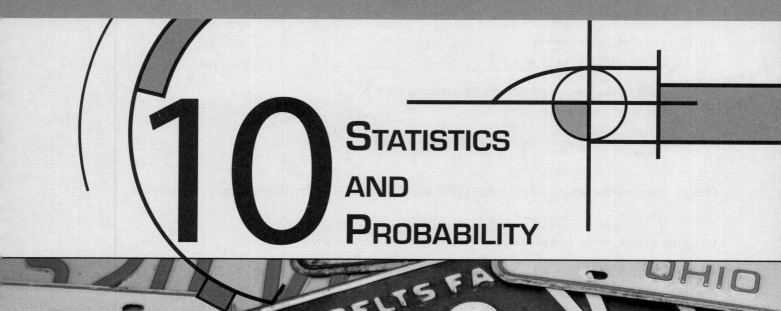

10 STATISTICS AND PROBABILITY

Probability and statistics are found many places in the world around us. Perhaps you have heard someone say, "You had better drive more carefully or you'll be another statistic!" Or maybe you have heard a weather forecaster say, "There is a 60% chance of rain today."

In one way or another, we all can be placed under the category "statistic." As participants in our country's census, we are part of statistical information such as population, age intervals (e.g., 12–18), or income brackets. The government wants information about the populace in order to judge factors such as growth trends or population shifts. The Creation Mandate implies that humans will make use of statistics and probability. These mathematical tools enable people to manage the world around them by organizing what they know about the world in useful ways.

Most decisions are made from incomplete information, rather than the mass of information found in a census. The science of statistics draws reasonable conclusions from incomplete information. Statisticians obtain smaller samples from a larger population and use mathematics to make reasonable conclusions about the entire population based on those samples. Pollsters who predict the outcomes of elections use information from samples to make predictions about which candidate the voters will choose. The predictions depend on probability distribution models and methods to generate conclusions. Insurance companies use probability and statistics to predict the frequency of accidents involving drivers of different ages and genders. They know which ages and gender have a higher probability of having an accident, and they set the insurance premiums for those individuals higher to cover the cost. Professionals who do this type of work are called *actuaries*.

After this chapter you should be able to

1. differentiate between a statistical sample and a population.

2. differentiate among the various types of sampling.

3. calculate the range, mean, median, mode, and quartiles for a given set of data.

4. construct a box-and-whisker diagram, a stem-and-leaf diagram, and a scatterplot for a data set.

5. make a frequency distribution table or an interval frequency table for a set of data and construct a histogram from it.

6. create bar graphs, line graphs, and pie charts from a given set of data.

7. use the Fundamental Principle of Counting to find the number of ways in which two consecutive, independent tasks can be completed.

8. for n objects taken r at a time, evaluate the number of permutations $(_nP_r)$ and combinations $(_nC_r)$.

9. find the probability of occurrence of a single event and of two independent events.

10.1 ⌐ Statistical Measures

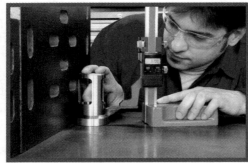

The branch of mathematics that deals with collecting, organizing, analyzing, and reporting quantitative information is called *statistics*. The recorded observations that can be measured or counted are called *data*. Statisticians are interested in information they can obtain using the data.

Definitions

A **population** is an entire set of objects sharing similar characteristics, such as human beings, automobiles, or measurements, from which data can be collected and analyzed.

A **sample** is a portion of a population from which data is collected to estimate the characteristics of the entire population.

A **statistic** is a measure calculated from a sample of data.

A **parameter** is a measure calculated from data for an entire population.

Example 1   Identify each of the following as a sample or a population.

a. the snacks dispensed from a vending machine during its existence

b. 100 freshmen from among those enrolled at a local college for the fall of 2010

c. the automobiles built by General Motors in the 1990s

Answer

a. population—all snacks are being considered

b. sample—a small number of students is being considered

c. population—all of the automobiles produced by the company are being considered

Populations are often large and immeasurable. Therefore, calculating parameters for these types of populations is impossible. The purpose of calculating statistics is to estimate parameters of large populations.

Suppose a statistician wants to know the average height of the adults in a city of about 200,000 people. It would be impractical in terms of time and money to determine each person's height. Instead, a sample is chosen, and the heights of those people are determined. Then the sample heights are used to draw conclusions about the heights of the population. One of the most important steps in obtaining good statistical measures is choosing an appropriate sample. The following points are very important.

1. Make sure that the sample size is large enough to obtain valid statistical measures. If the sample is too small, the results are invalid and the estimated parameters are useless.

2. If measurements are needed, take the measurements yourself rather than asking for them (e.g., weight or height of a person).

3. Choose your method of data collection carefully (e.g., mail, phone, or interview).

4. Make certain the samples are representative of the population.

Skill Check 1

Identify each of the following as a sample or a population.

1. a few junior-high math teachers of the Christian schools in Virginia

2. thirty of the eighth-grade students who attend a large public school

3. all the people who have eaten a hamburger at the Grill Zone

4. A company wants to obtain information about what its customers think of a new product in order to determine whether it should continue producing the product. Which method of choosing a sample would be most appropriate?
   a. stand in a mall and ask survey questions of anyone who happens to pass by
   b. call friends and relatives and ask their opinions
   c. mail a survey to former purchasers and include a postage-paid response envelope

Four types of sampling are listed below. For the discussion of each type, suppose a phone book is used to obtain the sample.

1. Random—A random number generator is used to determine page number, column, and row of each person in the sample.

2. Systematic—Every thirtieth person listed in the phone book is included in the sample.

3. Convenience—A questionnaire with a return envelope is mailed out with the phone bill.

4. Cluster—Everyone whose address indicates that he lives in a particular section of town is included in the sample.

Example 2 Identify the following samples as random, systematic, convenience, or cluster.
a. math teachers who attended a workshop at the regional conference
b. every fifth person on the class roster
c. 500 people who voted in the 2008 election, based on phone numbers chosen by computer-generated selection of page number and column in the local phone book

Answer
a. convenience
b. systematic
c. random

Skill Check 2

Identify the following samples as random, systematic, convenience, or cluster.

1. young people in the church youth group

2. Fifty Christian school principals are chosen from a list of principals whose schools are members of a large organization. Every tenth name is selected until fifty principals are chosen.

3. All the students in a large school are given a unique number. Students' numbers are then chosen by drawing from a rotating drum containing pieces of paper, each with one of the numbers on it.

4. One of several eighth-grade homerooms is polled about the school's concession stand menu.

The following statistical measures are among those used to describe a set of data collected from a sample or a population.

Definition

The **range** is the difference between the largest and smallest numbers in a set of data.

In many sets of data there is a tendency for the numbers in the middle of the set to appear more frequently. This characteristic of sets of data is particularly true when the data is measuring some human characteristic, such as height, weight, or intelligence. For example, there are usually more Cs on a test in school than there are As or Fs. If one number is needed to represent the entire set of data, the middle number is a good choice. There are several ways to choose the representative number for a set of data. The most common of these numbers, called *measures of central tendency*, are the mean, the median, and the mode.

Definitions

The **mean** is the arithmetic average of a set of numbers (sum of data divided by the number of data).
The **median** is the middle number in a set of data arranged in numerical order. If there is an even number of data, the median is the average of the two middle numbers.
The **mode** is the number or numbers that occur most frequently in a set of data. If no number occurs more than once, there is no mode. Data sets in which two values occur most frequently are called bimodal, while other data sets may have no mode.

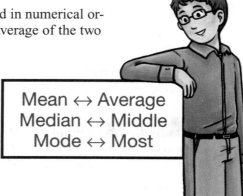

Mean ↔ Average
Median ↔ Middle
Mode ↔ Most

When you are finding the range and measures of central tendency, it is helpful to arrange the data in order of size (either ascending or descending).

Example 3	Find the range, mean, median, and mode of the following set of data: {6, 9, 7, 3, 6, 7, 10, 5}.

Answer

10, 9, 7, 7, 6, 6, 5, 3   1. Arrange the data in descending order.

range: $10 - 3 = 7$ 2. Subtract the smallest value from the largest to find the range.

mean: sum of data = 53
average = $53 \div 8 \approx 6.6$ 3. Find the sum of the data. Then divide the sum by the number of data values. Round the answer to the nearest tenth.

median: 10, 9, 7, 7, 6, 6, 5, 3
$\frac{7 + 6}{2} = \frac{13}{2} = 6.5$ 4. There is an even number of data values, so average the two middle numbers to find the median.

mode: 6 and 7   5. There are two modes since both numbers are used twice.

Example 4   Find the range, mean, median, and mode of the following set of data: {58, 38, 60, 44, 45, 42, 49, 50, 41}.

Answer

38, 41, 42, 44, 45, 49, 50, 58, 60

range: 60 − 38 = 22

mean: sum of data = 427
average = 427 ÷ 9 ≈ 47.4

median: 38, 41, 42, 44, 45, 49, 50, 58, 60

mode: none

1. Arrange the data in ascending order.
2. Subtract the smallest value from the largest to find the range.
3. Find the sum of the data. Then divide the sum by the number of data values. Round the answer to the nearest tenth.
4. There is an odd number of data values; the median is in the middle, the fifth of the nine numbers.
5. All data values are different.

Example 5   The following are daily low temperatures from the preceding week. Find the range, mean, median, and mode of the temperatures.

Day	Monday	Tuesday	Wednesday	Thursday	Friday	Saturday	Sunday
Temperature (°F)	25°	21°	20°	29°	25°	22°	19°

Answer

29, 25, 25, 22, 21, 20, 19

range: 29 − 19 = 10°

mean: sum of data = 161
average = 161 ÷ 7 = 23°

median: 29, 25, 25, 22, 21, 20, 19

mode: 25°

1. Arrange the data in descending order.
2. Subtract the lowest temperature from the highest.
3. Find the sum of the data. Then divide the sum by the number of data values.
4. There is an odd number of data values; the median is the fourth of the seven numbers.
5. The temperature that occurs most often (twice) is 25°.

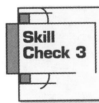

Skill Check 3

Calculate the following statistics for this set of data: {10, 31, 12, 25, 31, 35, 6, 36, 30, 40}.

1. range   2. mean   3. median   4. mode

■ A. Exercises

Identify each of the following as most likely a sample or a population.

1. the governors of the fifty states

2. thirty boys of various ages from a high school containing 3,000 students

3. a hundred identical manufactured parts off of an assembly line

4. all the math teachers in a state

5. all the boys in a particular high school who are at least 6 ft. tall

6. every tenth customer who patronized a particular store

Identify the following samples as random, systematic, convenience, or cluster.

7. everyone who lives on Elm Street in Valley Falls

8. all the customers who buy pastry at the Big Sky Bakery on November 18

9. every fourth person on the alphabetic list of the church membership

10. the last person to pass through a toll gate each day for a month

11. Twenty people are chosen from a rotating drum containing names of those who attended an annual meeting.

12. Two grades are randomly chosen from among grades 1–12 in a school, and all the people in those grades are given a standardized test appropriate for their grade level.

13. A random number generator is used to choose fifty people by their driver's license number.

14. every third person listed in the teacher's grade book

■ B. Exercises

Find the range, mean, median, and mode of each set of data. Round answers to the nearest tenth.

{7, 9, 7, 4, 7, 8, 10, 5, 5}

15. range   16. mean   17. median   18. mode

{45, 90, 86, 78, 91, 88, 79}

19. range   20. mean   21. median   22. mode

{25, 40, 19, 39, 18, 26}

23. range   24. mean   25. median   26. mode

{3, 20, 22, 22, 34, 36, 40, 90, 120}

27. range   28. mean   29. median   30. mode

Find the value of x so that the mean of the list of numbers will be equal to the given number.

31. 24, 29, x; mean: 26   32. 19, 36, x; mean: 27

33. 7, 11, 15, x; mean: 12   34. 12, 18, 20, x; mean: 17

■ C. Exercises

Notice in exercises 27–30 that the three measures of central tendency are not particularly close to one another. Two of the numbers in the data set are over twice as large as any of the other seven numbers. Also, the smallest number is only 15% of the next smallest number. Take the same set of data without the numbers 3, 90, and 120 and calculate the following statistics.

35. range   36. mean   37. median   38. mode

39. How do the statistics in exercises 27–30 compare with those found in exercises 35–38?

Find the mean, median, and mode of the following set of data: {1, 2, 4, 5, 2, 8, 6}. If 4 were changed to 11, which of the following measures would change? Write *yes* or *no* beside each measure to indicate whether it would change.

40. mean   41. median   42. mode

43. If each number in a list of data is increased by 3, how is the mode affected? the mean affected?

■ Dominion thru Math

When someone says that his car averages 32 mi./gal., he is probably referring to the mean. When a company reports that the salary of an average employee is $42,000 per year, it is often referring to the median salary. The gas mileage for a person's family vehicle can be found by dividing the total gallons used by the miles traveled, which is the mean of gas consumption for a window of time (such as a vacation). A corporation typically uses the median salary because the mean salary will include compensation for some highly paid executives who earn five to ten times what the typical worker earns. Extreme values affect the mean significantly but have little effect on the median. A calculator or computer is usually used to find statistics for large sets of data. Use a calculator to find the answers to the following problems.

44. Javier surveyed his neighbors and found the gas mileage for each family's vehicle. His findings are given in the following set of data: {30, 17, 29, 12, 18, 24, 19, 24, 25, 27, 20, 28}. He reported in class that the average mileage for the cars of his twelve neighbors was 22.75 mi./gal. Was he using the mean or the median?

45. What is the mode of the mileage figures given in exercise 44?

46. What is the range of the mileage figures given in exercise 44?

47. From your personal experience, what type of vehicle would you say probably had the lowest mileage, and what type had the highest mileage?

CUMULATIVE REVIEW

Use cross multiplication to compare the given fractions. Use <, =, or >. [5.2]

48. $\frac{7}{9} \square \frac{5}{8}$ 49. $\frac{12}{17} \square \frac{3}{5}$ 50. $\frac{-4}{5} \square \frac{-9}{11}$ 51. $\frac{-13}{15} \square \frac{-7}{9}$ 52. $\frac{8}{3} \square \frac{7}{4}$

Solve. [8.2]

53. $4x + 2 = x - 7$

54. $-6x - 4 = 7x + 8$

55. $7(x + 5) = 9x - 7$

56. $10x - 4(x - 3) = 8(2x - 6)$

57. $-7x + 8x - 4 = 2(3x + 9) + 4(x - 2)$

10.2 ⌐ Diagramming Data

Looking at lists of data is not always the best way to examine the data values and how they relate to one another. The range, mean, median, and mode of the data give considerably more information. Diagramming data is another useful tool in observing data relationships.

The box-and-whisker diagram uses five important numbers to describe the data set—the largest number, the smallest number, the median, the lower quartile, and the upper quartile. Arrange the numbers in ascending or descending order before finding these important statistics.

A **quartile** is any one of three values that divide the data into four equally sized groups.
The **lower quartile** is the median for the lower half of the data.
The **middle quartile** is the median for all of the data.
The **upper quartile** is the median for the upper half of the data.

Example 1 The following numbers represent the pages read yesterday by the twelve students in the class. Find the lower, middle, and upper quartiles: {16, 51, 29, 35, 70, 29, 40, 44, 39, 30, 50, 46}.

Answer

16, 29, 29, 30, 35, 39, 40, 44, 46, 50, 51, 70   1. Arrange the data in ascending order.

middle quartile: $\frac{39 + 40}{2} = 39.5$ 2. The middle quartile (median) is the middle number or the average of the two middle numbers.

lower quartile: $\frac{29 + 30}{2} = 29.5$ 3. The lower quartile is the middle number or the average of the two middle numbers of the lower half.

upper quartile: $\frac{46 + 50}{2} = 48$ 4. The upper quartile is the middle number or the average of the two middle numbers of the upper half.

Note: When the number of data is even, include the lower of the middle two numbers in the calculation of the lower quartile and the higher of the middle two numbers in the calculation of the upper quartile.

A *box-and-whisker-diagram* is a line segment showing the highest and lowest values, the upper and lower quartiles, and the median of a set of data. It can be either horizontal or vertical and includes a line. The line's endpoints, representing the lowest and highest numbers, are called the whiskers. A narrow rectangle (box) is drawn between the lower and upper quartile, and a hash mark is placed at the median.

Example 2 Construct a box-and-whisker diagram for the data in Example 1.

Answer

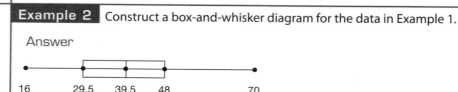

Range is a measure of the spread of the data. Its disadvantage is that one extreme value increases the range dramatically. The solution to this problem is the interquartile range: a statistical measure of the spread that can be used to minimize the influence of extreme values.

The *interquartile range* is the difference between the upper and lower quartile. The interquartile range for Example 1 is 48 − 29.5 = 18.5. Compare this to the range, which is 70 − 16 = 54. The disparity between the two is due to extreme values at both ends of the data set. The data values are clumped fairly tightly in the middle, with ten data points from 29 to 51; but the low is 16 (13 less than the next value), and the high is 70 (19 more than the previous value).

Example 3 Construct a box-and-whisker diagram for the following set of data, and calculate the interquartile range: {12, 32, 29, 35, 33, 17, 28, 24, 22, 25, 31}.

Answer

12, 17, 22, 24, 25, 28, 29, 31, 32, 33, 35

median: 28

lower quartile: 22

upper quartile: 32

interquartile range: 32 – 22 = 10

  12   22   28 32 35

1. Arrange the data in ascending order.
2. The median (middle quartile) is the middle number.
3. The lower quartile is the middle number of the lower half.
4. The upper quartile is the middle number of the upper half.
5. Subtract the lower from the upper quartile.
6. Construct a box-and-whisker diagram. Place the lowest number at the left of the number line and the highest number at the right.

Note: When there is an odd number of data, do not include the median in the calculation of either the lower quartile or the upper quartile.

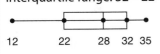

Skill Check 1

Find the lower quartile, median (middle quartile), and upper quartile for the following sets of data. Then calculate the interquartile range.

1. {10, 12, 13, 13, 21, 21, 29, 32}

2. {181, 199, 220, 220, 225, 233, 240}

Construct box-and-whisker diagrams for the following sets of data.

3. lowest: 18, highest: 90, lower quartile: 45, median: 55, upper quartile: 75

4. lowest: 45, highest: 77, lower quartile: 52, median: 64, upper quartile: 70

A *stem-and-leaf diagram* is a type of bar graph in which the data points in each interval are listed in order to illustrate statistical data. Each number is separated into two parts—a "stem" and a "leaf." In this text, the leaf is the last digit of the number, and the stem is all other digits of the number. The stems and leaves are separated from each other by a vertical segment. All numbers with the same stem are written on the same horizontal line. If a stem has two leaves that are the same, both leaves are entered on the stem-and-leaf diagram.

Example 4 Make a stem-and-leaf diagram for the following set of data, which represents the number of pages read by twelve students: {16, 29, 29, 30, 35, 39, 40, 44, 46, 50, 51, 70}.

Answer

Number of Pages Read

1	6		
2	9	9	
3	0	5	9
4	0	4	6
5	0	1	
7	0		

Key: 1|6 means 16.

Since the numbers are all two digits, the stem will be the tens digit and the leaves will be the ones digit.

| **Example 5** | Make a stem-and-leaf diagram for the following set of data: |

{120, 125, 129, 129, 134, 138, 143, 143, 149, 149, 156, 159, 161}.

Answer

```
12 | 0  5  9  9        Use the first two digits as the stem and the last digit as the leaf.
13 | 4  8
14 | 3  3  9  9
15 | 6  9
16 | 1
```

Key: 12|0 means 120.

Skill Check 2

Make stem-and-leaf diagrams for the following sets of data.

1. {10, 12, 13, 13, 21, 21, 29, 32}
2. {181, 199, 220, 220, 225, 233, 240}

If a set of data involves a relationship between two variables, then the data can be graphed as a set of ordered pairs in a coordinate plane. The resulting picture is known as a *scatterplot*. The scatterplot can be used to derive a linear function or a curve that best approximates the relationship of the two variables. This method works well with a large number of points that are not spread out too much.

The following data represent eighteen people whose height (*h*) is given in inches and whose weight (*w*) is given in pounds.

h	65	63	72	64	70	70	64	70	76	71	73	63	61	66	66	70	66	68
w	160	145	180	150	220	180	130	170	180	200	210	150	120	145	155	175	160	170

In the scatterplot the horizontal axis is *h* for height (instead of *x*), and the vertical axis is *w* for weight (instead of *y*). Since all of the values for *h* and *w* are positive, the entire scatterplot is in the first quadrant. To eliminate empty space, you can reposition the origin at the ordered pair (61, 120) since it represents the lowest height and weight. Plot the points for the ordered pairs (*h*, *w*) from the above table. The graph then shows weight as a function of height.

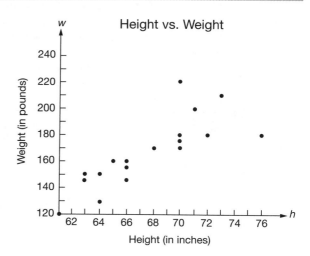

The scatterplot indicates that, in general, as the height *h* increases, the weight *w* increases. Therefore, from the scatterplot we can conclude that the taller a person is, the more likely it is that he weighs more. This relationship is referred to as a *correlation*. In this case, as the variable *h* increases, *w* also increases. This is called a *positive correlation* and relates to the fact that a line sloping upward to the right has a positive slope.

Comparing students' grade point averages (GPA) to hours spent watching TV would most likely reveal that more hours per week watching TV corresponds to a lower grade point average. That is, as one variable increases, the other decreases. Graphing the ordered pairs (hours/week of TV, GPA) from the following table results in a scatterplot that slopes downward to the right. This is called a *negative correlation* and relates to the fact that a line sloping downward to the right has a negative slope.

Hours/Week of TV	GPA
4	3.7
8	3.5
11	3.0
10	2.8
15	2.7
12	2.6
20	2.6
18	2.4
25	1.9
20	1.5
15	1.3
25	1.1

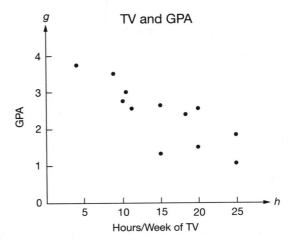

Example 6 Construct a scatterplot for the following data, which relates the number of exercise minutes per day (*m*) to a person's heart rate (*r*). What does the graph show? State whether the correlation seems to be positive or negative.

m	5	30	15	10	45	12	40	60	35	20	8	25
r	92	75	78	90	70	88	74	68	76	76	78	76

Answer

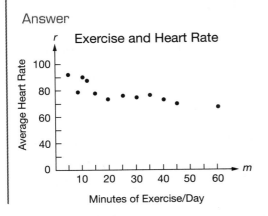

The scatterplot shows that the heart rate *r* decreases as one exercises more. The correlation is negative.

1. Construct a scatterplot for the following data and determine whether there is a positive or negative correlation.

Study Minutes	5	25	0	65	35	45	40	120	15	20	70	100
Test Grade	58	78	54	90	82	80	72	94	62	72	89	92

Doing scatterplots is one way we can obey God's command to "subdue" and "have dominion over" the earth (Gen. 1:28). The world God has called us to manage is filled with complicated data. By constructing scatterplots, we learn to arrange data and see patterns that help us understand the world and—to some extent—make predictions about the future. Often scatterplots are the first step in managing God's world rather than being managed by it.

■ A. Exercises

Calculate the following four statistics for each set of data; then construct the corresponding box-and-whisker diagram.

{10, 10, 9, 8, 7, 7, 6, 5, 4, 4, 4, 3}

1. middle quartile
2. lower quartile
3. upper quartile
4. interquartile range

5. Construct a box-and-whisker diagram for the above data.

{33, 40, 98, 80, 84, 86, 79}

6. middle quartile
7. lower quartile
8. upper quartile
9. interquartile range

10. Construct a box-and-whisker diagram for the above data.

{60, 68, 75, 89, 98, 100, 100, 105}

11. middle quartile
12. lower quartile
13. upper quartile
14. interquartile range

15. Construct a box-and-whisker diagram for the above data.

{2, 8, 10, 10, 10, 9, 5, 4, 9}

16. middle quartile
17. lower quartile
18. upper quartile
19. interquartile range

20. Construct a box-and-whisker diagram for the above data.

■ B. Exercises

For the following sets of data, list the numbers in ascending order and make stem-and-leaf diagrams.

21. {8, 12, 20, 17, 12, 15, 13, 29, 15, 29, 6}
22. {60, 58, 51, 51, 54, 47, 47, 44, 63, 65, 33}
23. {29, 34, 23, 55, 44, 44, 31, 52, 52, 61}
24. {61, 72, 66, 65, 66, 71, 56, 57, 69, 68, 68, 73}

For the following sets of data, make stem-and-leaf diagrams with the whole number part as the stem and the decimal part as the leaf.

25. {5.7, 5.1, 4.9, 6.3, 5.6, 6.4, 6.3, 6.3, 7.4, 8.1, 7.6, 4.7}

26. {2.3, 1.9, 2.1, 3.6, 2.4, 1.8, 3.2, 2.6, 4.0, 0.7, 2.9, 3.7, 2.8, 3.6}

Since the data in the following sets is very compact, make stem-and-leaf diagrams with two-digit stems and single-digit leaves.

27. {201, 219, 221, 217, 215, 217, 222, 224, 219, 208, 225, 228, 216}

28. {672, 681, 674, 679, 682, 691, 683, 695, 673, 661, 673, 679, 677, 688, 693}

29. Construct a scatterplot for the following data on the life of twenty-five light bulbs. What conclusion can you draw from the graph?

Wattage	Life (in hours)
25	1,500; 1,200; 1,750; 1,450; 1,600
40	1,200; 1,000; 1,100; 1,350; 1,250
60	1,000; 950; 1,050; 1,200; 900
75	800; 700; 750; 850; 900
100	700; 750; 800; 650; 900

A new, more economical light bulb may replace the old standard shape.

30. Construct a scatterplot for the following data on the value of a particular make, model, and year of a car as compared to its mileage.

Mileage (to the nearest thousand)	70	65	15	27	80	40	33	90	10	29	11	20	32	80	26	55
Value (in thousands)	13	12	26	17	10	17	14	8	24	20	25	25	16	11	21	15

31. Construct a scatterplot for the following data comparing the final grades of ten students in Algebra 1 with their grades in Geometry.

Algebra 1	70	95	82	85	79	76	84	89	75	90
Geometry	81	87	83	80	82	74	79	89	80	86

■ C. Exercises

Examine each of the following scatterplots and determine whether it describes a positive correlation, a negative correlation, or neither. Then write a sentence interpreting the scatterplot regarding the relationship of the variables described on the horizontal and vertical axes.

32.

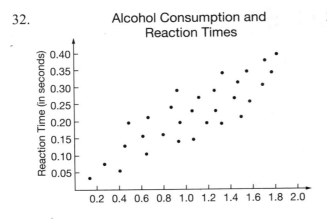

33.

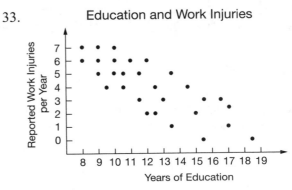

34.

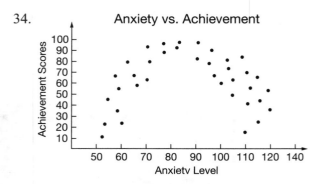

Anxiety vs. Achievement

■ Dominion thru Math

The ReTech Corporation has the following annual wages for its employees (in dollars): {35,000; 32,500; 30,800; 34,400; 28,500; 38,200; 42,500; 65,400; 92,300}.

35. What is the range of the salaries for the ReTech Corporation?

36. Find the median and mean salaries for this corporation.

37. Is the median or the mean the better measure of central tendency for the data?

38. After adding $200,000 to the highest salary, find the new mean. Does the median change?

CUMULATIVE REVIEW

Find the unit rate. [5.4]

39. 126 words in 2 min.   40. 870 bu. from 6 acres   41. 434 mi. in 7 hr.

42. 840 calls in 20 min.   43. 30 oz. can for $2.40

Calculate the new amount. [7.8]

44. increase 350 by 35%   45. decrease 49 by 16%   46. increase 3,280 by 60%

47. increase 12 by 40%   48. decrease 68 by 25%

10.3 Histograms

Mrs. Koontz gave a test to the twenty-four students in her class. Each student's percent score is given below.

92	88	96	100	76	88	96	72
84	80	68	76	88	88	86	76
100	80	72	92	88	96	80	84

When a set becomes fairly large and contains repeated elements, a *frequency distribution table* is used. Such a table is shown below for this set. The first column is the data, followed by a column for tallies to count the number of times each entry appears. The number of tallies is then placed in the frequency column. The product column is the data multiplied by the frequency for that data. The purpose of this column is to get the sum of all the data by using multiplication.

Frequency Distribution Table			
Data (D)	**Tally**	**Frequency (f)**	**Product (Df)**
68	|	1	68
72	||	2	144
76	|||	3	228
80	|||	3	240
84	||	2	168
86	|	1	86
88	﹀﹀|	5	440
92	||	2	184
96	|||	3	288
100	||	2	200
Total		24	2,046

Definitions

The **data column** of the frequency distribution table contains the data arranged in numerical order.

The **frequency column** of the frequency distribution table represents the number of times each number occurs (number of tallies). The number at the bottom of the column is the total number of data.

The **product column** of the frequency distribution table is the product of the numbers in the data column (D) and the frequency column (f). The number at the bottom of the column is the sum of all the data. The calculation of the range, mean, median, and mode is facilitated by this organization of the data.

Example

Find the range, mean, median, and mode for Mrs. Koontz's students' test scores. Use the frequency distribution table above.

Answer

range: $100 - 68 = 32$

mean: $\dfrac{\text{product total}}{\text{frequency total}} = \dfrac{2{,}046}{24} \approx 85.3$

median: twelfth score: 86
    thirteenth score: 88
    $\dfrac{86 + 88}{2} = \dfrac{174}{2} = 87$

mode: 88

1. Subtract the first data value from the last.

2. The mean is found by dividing the sum of all the data (product total) by the number of data (frequency total). Round to the nearest tenth.

3. Count tallies or add frequencies until you reach the twelfth and thirteenth score, and average the scores.

4. The greatest frequency is 5, so the mode is 88.

Skill Check 1

1. Make a frequency distribution table for the following set of data:
   {12, 10, 14, 17, 15, 15, 14, 14, 16, 10, 20, 19, 12, 13, 18, 17, 17, 11, 13}.

2. Calculate the range, mean, median, and mode for the data.

An *interval frequency table* can also be used to organize data. Although not as precise as a frequency distribution table, it is valuable when the amount of data is extremely large. A *histogram*, another way to picture data, can be constructed from the information found on an interval frequency table. The histogram is made of vertical bars that represent the frequency of data in each particular interval. The bars in a histogram touch each other to indicate that all numbers in the data are accounted for in the intervals.

An interval frequency table and its corresponding histogram are shown below.

Interval Frequency Table	
Age (interval)	Frequency (*f*)
10–19	14
20–29	10
30–39	17
40–49	8
50–59	15
60–69	12
70–79	5
80–89	2
Total	83

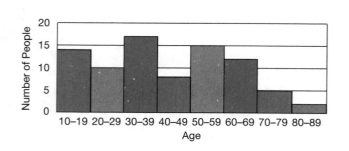

Only an approximation for the range can be made from interval data because the actual data values are unknown. The approximate range for the data pictured in an interval frequency table is found by subtracting the smallest value of the lowest interval from the largest value of the highest interval. For the ages represented by the above interval frequency table, the range is $89 - 10 = 79$.

Finding the mean is more involved than finding the mean from a frequency distribution table. Since the data is organized in intervals, you must find the midpoint of each interval and multiply that number times the frequency of the interval to find the product for the interval. Then divide the sum of the products by the sum of the frequencies to find the mean. Examine the table below. The midpoint of each interval is the sum of the beginning and ending values divided by two. For example, the midpoint of the first interval is $\dfrac{10 + 19}{2} = \dfrac{29}{2} = 14.5$.

Age (interval)	Midpoint (*m*)	Frequency (*f*)	Product (*mf*)
10–19	14.5	14	203
20–29	24.5	10	245
30–39	34.5	17	586.5
40–49	44.5	8	356
50–59	54.5	15	817.5
60–69	64.5	12	774
70–79	74.5	5	372.5
80–89	84.5	2	169
Total		83	3,523.5

mean: $\dfrac{\text{product total}}{\text{frequency total}} = \dfrac{3{,}523.5}{83} \approx 42.5$ (rounded to the nearest tenth)

The median is an interval rather than a single data value—the interval that contains the middle number. The interval that contains the middle number is found by first finding the position of the middle value. It is $\frac{f+1}{2}$ when f is odd. Since there are 83 values in the table, the position of the middle value is $\frac{f+1}{2} = \frac{83+1}{2} = \frac{84}{2} = 42$, that is, the forty-second one. The first three intervals have $14 + 10 + 17 = 41$ values. The forty-second data value will lie in the next interval, 40–49.

The modal interval is the interval with the largest frequency. In this case, the modal interval is 30–39 with a frequency of 17.

Skill Check 2

1. Fill in the rest of the interval frequency table and calculate the range, mean, median interval, and modal interval.

Interval	Midpoint (*m*)	Frequency (*f*)	Product (*mf*)
10–14		6	
15–19		15	
20–24		20	
25–29		10	
30–34		3	
Total		54	

2. Construct a histogram to picture the data.

■ A. Exercises

Make frequency distribution tables for the following sets of data.

1. {10, 10, 11, 12, 12, 12, 14, 15, 15, 15, 15, 17, 18, 18, 19, 20, 20, 20}

2. {6, 5, 7, 10, 9, 10, 10, 8, 4, 6, 7, 7, 3, 10, 9, 9, 7, 5, 9, 8}

3. {85, 80, 75, 100, 90, 75, 90, 100, 100, 95, 60, 75, 80, 85, 85, 80, 80}

4. {200, 250, 200, 225, 275, 275, 200, 200, 225, 225, 250, 250, 200, 200, 275}

5. {8, 9, 5, 7, 8, 9, 10, 8, 8, 6, 9, 10, 10, 9, 7, 9, 4, 5, 10, 9, 7, 6, 6}

Find the range, mean, median, and mode from the following frequency distribution tables. Round answers to the nearest tenth.

6.

Data (*D*)	Tally	Frequency (*f*)	Product (*Df*)
100	I	1	100
96	II	2	192
92	II	2	184
88	III	3	264
84	IIII	4	336
80	III	3	240
76	IIIII	5	380
72	I	1	72
Total		21	1,768

7.

Data (*D*)	Tally	Frequency (*f*)	Product (*Df*)
70	IIII	4	280
68	IIIII	5	340
66	III	3	198
64	II	2	128
62	II	2	124
60	III	3	180
58	I	1	58
Total		20	1,308

8.

Data (D)	Tally	Frequency (f)	Product (Df)
40	|	1	40
50	||	2	100
60	|||	3	180
70	||||	4	280
80	|||	3	240
90	||||	4	360
100	||	2	200
Total		19	1,400

9.

Data (D)	Tally	Frequency (f)	Product (Df)
31	|	1	31
32	||	2	64
33	|	1	33
34	|||	3	102
35	||	2	70
36	|||	3	108
37	|||||	5	185
38	||	2	76
39	|||	3	117
40	||	2	80
Total		24	866

10.

Data (D)	Tally	Frequency (f)	Product (Df)
210	||	2	420
200	||	2	400
195	|||	3	585
185	|||	3	555
170	||	2	340
160	|||||	5	800
Total		17	3,100

11.

Data (D)	Tally	Frequency (f)	Product (Df)
21	|	1	21
18	|||	3	54
16	|	1	16
15	|	1	15
12	||	2	24
9	||||	4	36
8	||	2	16
Total		14	182

■ **B. Exercises**

Use the histogram to answer exercises 12–16.

12. How many students does each mark on the vertical scale represent?

13. What is the frequency of the 91–95 interval?

14. How many students are represented in this histogram?

15. What is the modal interval of the histogram?

16. What is the median interval of the histogram?

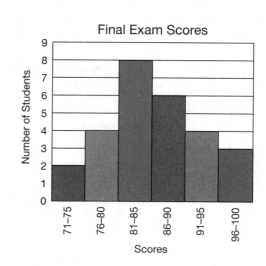

Final Exam Scores

Make interval frequency tables for the following sets of data. Use grouping intervals of 10, such as 0–9, 10–19, 20–29, and so on. Use the interval frequency to calculate the mean to the nearest tenth.

17. {0, 5, 5, 5, 6, 6, 7, 11, 15, 18, 18, 18, 18, 19, 19, 20, 26, 28, 29}

18. {41, 45, 49, 51, 60, 64, 64, 67, 72, 79, 79, 83, 85, 89, 90, 95}

19. {12, 15, 30, 48, 49, 41, 17, 25, 26, 45, 48, 32, 36, 24}

Make interval frequency tables for the following sets of data. Use grouping intervals of 20, such as 0–19, 20–39, and so on. Use the interval frequency to calculate the mean to the nearest tenth.

20. {20, 29, 51, 39, 43, 64, 23, 34, 28, 72, 42, 44, 18}

21. {62, 48, 63, 74, 28, 31, 27, 17, 19, 12, 10, 28, 37}

Make an interval frequency table for the following set of data. Use grouping intervals of 100, such as 0–99, 100–199, and so on. Use the interval frequency to calculate the mean to the nearest tenth.

22. {180, 201, 348, 302, 195, 190, 175, 160, 310, 379, 420, 490}

Find the range, mean, median interval, and modal interval from the following interval frequency tables.

23.

Interval	Frequency
10–14	5
15–19	12
20–24	19
25–29	8
30–34	4
Total	48

24.

Interval	Frequency
10–14	2
15–19	12
20–24	21
25–29	30
30–34	4
35–39	2
Total	71

25.

Interval	Frequency
0–9	5
10–19	15
20–29	20
30–39	10
40–49	3
Total	53

26.

Interval	Frequency
100–199	4
200–299	15
300–399	20
400–499	30
500–599	6
Total	75

Construct a histogram for the data in each exercise referenced.

27. exercise 23   28. exercise 24   29. exercise 25   30. exercise 26

31. Make a frequency distribution table for the following data. Find the range, mean, median, and mode for the data.

Daily High Temperatures				
89	85	84	89	92
91	90	89	92	95
88	84	85	86	91
91	87	83	82	81
80	82	85	81	82
85	82	84	81	84

32. Construct a histogram for the data in the interval frequency table.

Weight of Students in Seventh Grade	
Weight (lb.)	Students
80–89	5
90–99	8
100–109	10
110–19	9
120–29	4

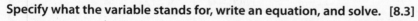

CUMULATIVE REVIEW

Specify what the variable stands for, write an equation, and solve. [8.3]

33. An answering machine costs $2.50 more than an alarm clock. If the total bill before taxes to purchase both of them is $51.50, how much does each item cost?

34. Millie reads five times as many fiction books as biographies. If she read a total of 108 books one summer, how many of each type did she read?

35. Jacob pays three cents a minute to use his phone, plus a monthly fee of $12.35. If his total bill before taxes and fees one month was $25.85, how many minutes did he talk?

36. Keisha sold three more than twice as many candy bars as Aimee. If they sold 81 bars total, how many did each girl sell?

37. Immediately after a thunderstorm the temperature decreases. If the temperature dropped at a constant rate from its high point to its low point for the day after the storm with a difference of 30°, and the average temperature for the day was 77°, what were the high and low temperatures for the day?

Determine the ordered pairs from the given equation and finite domain. [9.2]

38. $y = 4x + 5$; $D = \{0, 6, 9\}$

39. $y = -2x - 8$; $D = \{-2, -1, 3, 5\}$

40. $y = 8x$; $D = \{-2, -1, 0, 2\}$

41. $y = -3.2x + 4.1$; $D = \{-3, -1, 0, 1, 4\}$

42. $y = \frac{2}{3}x - 1$; $D = \{-9, -6, 0, 3\}$

10.4 Graphing Data

Box-and-whisker diagrams, stem-and-leaf diagrams, scatterplots, and histograms are all ways of using pictures, or graphs, to represent data. Numerical data can also be presented in picture form via bar graphs, line graphs, or pie charts. *Bar graphs* and *line graphs* are good at comparing a quantity over different time intervals, or showing the rise and fall of a quantity over the passage of time.

Consider the numerical data regarding automobile sales displayed in the table. These data are pictured below by a bar graph and by a line graph.

Year	Autos Sold (nearest 100,000)
2006	8,800,000
2007	8,400,000
2008	8,100,000
2009	7,600,000
2010	7,500,000

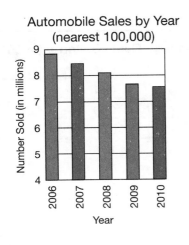

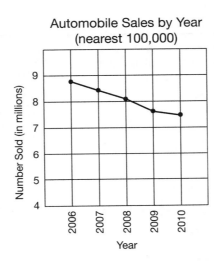

Making a Bar Graph or a Line Graph

1. Draw and label the horizontal and vertical axes of the graph.
2. Choose a scale to fit the data for each axis. Then mark intervals along each axis.
3. Draw a bar for each data interval, or plot points representing the data and connect them from left to right.
4. Title the graph.

A bar graph is very similar to a histogram except that there are no gaps between the bars in a histogram, whereas the bars in a bar graph have a space between them. The data pictured in a bar graph are not continuous like those in a histogram. A line graph can be made from a histogram by connecting the midpoints of each bar with a line segment.

Example 1 Make a bar graph of the following data for a college runner. The times, given in minutes, are his best times in the
1,500 m race for each of four consecutive years.

Year	Time
freshman	5:10
sophomore	4:58
junior	4:42
senior	4:37

Answer

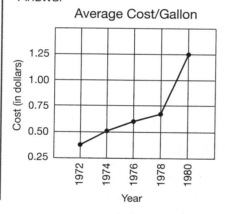

Example 2 Make a line graph of the average
price of a gallon of gasoline from
1972 through 1980. Prices are for
every other year.

Year x	Average Cost/Gallon y (in $)
1972	0.38
1974	0.51
1976	0.60
1978	0.67
1980	1.25

Answer

Average Cost/Gallon

Skill Check 1

1. Make a bar graph and a line graph to represent the following data.

South Australia Red Kangaroo Population	
Year	**Population (in millions)**
1985	1.14
1990	1.95
1995	1.70
2000	1.37
2005	0.71

A kangaroo can jump 25 ft. in a single bound.

Pie charts are used to compare how a whole is divided into parts. For example, what part of each tax dollar goes to support the police department versus how much is used to maintain city parks? The answer to such questions can be seen quickly on a pie chart.

Making a Pie Chart

1. Express each quantity to be shown as a percent.

2. Since a circle contains 360°, multiply 360 by each percent to get the number of degrees needed for each category.

3. Draw a circle with the desired radius, and use a protractor to measure the correct number of degrees for each category.

4. Label each pie-shaped piece in words and percents.

5. Title the graph.

To draw an angle measuring greater than 180°, draw a line beneath your protractor and mark a vertex on it. Then rotate your protractor until it can be fitted against the line on the opposite side. Subtract 180° from the angle you intend to draw, and mark that amount of degrees. Draw an arc on the larger of the two angles you see.

30 out of 50 = $\frac{30}{50}$ = 0.6 = 60%

0.6 × 360 = 216°

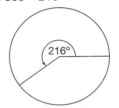

Example 3 In one city in 2000 the US Census Bureau found that there were about 21,000 Hispanics, 133,000 non-Hispanic whites, 20,500 blacks, and 7,500 Asians over the age of 25 with at least a high-school education. Make a pie chart of this data.

Answer

21,000 + 133,000 + 20,500 + 7,500 = 182,000   1. Total the populations.

$\frac{21,000}{182,000}$ ≈ 0.12 = 12%   2. Find the percent of the circle that represents each of the categories.

$\frac{133,000}{182,000}$ ≈ 0.73 = 73%

$\frac{20,500}{182,000}$ ≈ 0.11 = 11%

$\frac{7,500}{182,000}$ ≈ 0.04 = 4%

12% × 360° = 0.12(360) ≈ 43°   3. Find the number of degrees represented by each percent.

73% × 360° = 0.73(360) ≈ 263°

11% × 360° = 0.11(360) ≈ 40°

4% × 360° = 0.04(360) ≈ 14°

4. Draw and label the pie chart.

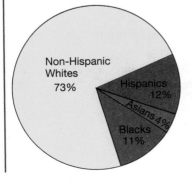

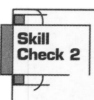
1. Make a pie chart of the results of the following survey conducted at Lighthouse Christian School.

Cookie Preferences	
Type	Number
peanut butter	38
chocolate chip	82
vanilla cream	17
gingersnap	41
oatmeal	29
Total	207

One of the most challenging aspects of reporting statistical data is choosing the appropriate type of graph that best communicates the information. There are advantages and disadvantages to the different types of diagrams or graphs presented in this chapter. Use the following table as a guide when you are deciding which type of graph will best represent your data.

Graph	When to Use	When Not to Use
Box-and-whisker diagram	• To illustrate the five-point summary • To quickly compare two or more data sets • When the data set is large	• When the exact values in the data set are important
Stem-and-leaf diagram	• To visually represent the range, mode, and data inconsistencies • To keep exact values of the data set visible • When the data set is large	• When central tendency information is to be conveyed by the representation
Scatterplot	• To illustrate the relationship between two characteristics of the data	• When the data set is large
Histogram	• To clearly illustrate large amounts of data when central tendency values are fairly apparent • When the data set is large	• When the exact values in the data set are important • When two or more sets of data are to be compared
Bar graph	• To illustrate data reported as frequency in groups • To compare two or more data sets	• When data is not organized by groups
Line graph	• To illustrate changes over a period of time • To compare two or more data sets	
Pie chart	• To display how the entire whole is separated into parts • When data is reported as percentages or frequencies in groups	• When two or more sets of data are to be compared • When there are many categories given in the data set

■ A. Exercises

1. Which type of graph should be used when exact data values are to be visible?

2. Which type of graph would best represent a large set of data if the mean, median, and mode are fairly apparent?

3. Which type of graph illustrates the five-point summary of a set of data?

4. Which type of graph would be best to compare two data sets that are reported as frequency by groups?

5. Which type of graph is used to compare two characteristics of a sample?

Use the line graph to answer exercises 6–10.

6. How many books were checked out in April?

7. In what month were the fewest books checked out?

8. Between what months did the number of books checked out decrease?

9. In what month were exactly fifty books checked out?

10. Between what months did the number of books checked out increase the most?

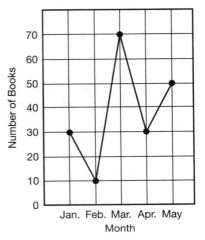

Library Books Checked Out

■ B. Exercises

Make bar graphs of the following data.

11. Use increments of 10.

Distances Students Travel to School	
Distance to School	**Number of Students**
less than 1 mi.	32
1 mi. to 5 mi.	75
5 mi. to 10 mi.	34
over 10 mi.	20

12. Use increments of 50.

Vehicles Sold by Type	
Vehicle Type	**Number Sold**
cars	300
vans	175
light trucks	90

13. Use increments of 50.

Distribution of Tickets Sold	
Classification	**Number Sold**
adults	175
students	120
children	90

14. Use increments of 5.

Enrollment by Classification	
Class	**Enrollment**
freshmen	45
sophomores	37
juniors	32
seniors	34

15. Number of people saved at a revival service: Monday, 3; Tuesday, 7; Wednesday, 4; Thursday, 6; Friday, 11. Use increments of 2.

16. Normal January temperatures (in degrees Fahrenheit): Albany, 21; Asheville, 37; Jackson, 46; Houston, 51; Miami, 67. Use increments of 10.

Make line graphs of the following data.

17. Use increments of 10 with the origin at (2004, 60).

XYZ Stock High by Year	
Year x	Price y (in $)
2005	63
2006	65
2007	60
2008	90
2009	100

18. Use increments of 5 with the origin at (0, 30).

Attendance by Games	
Home Game x	Attendance y (in thousands)
1	45
2	38
3	50
4	55
5	60

19. Use increments of 0.5 million with the origin at (2004, 2.0).

Company Sales by Year	
Year x	Sales y (in millions)
2005	3.0
2006	4.0
2007	4.2
2008	4.7

20. Use increments of 25 with the origin at (2006, 0).

Item Catalog Price by Year	
Year x	Low Price y (in $)
2007	150
2008	125
2009	90
2010	75

21. Cattle on farms in the United States (in millions): 1985, 109.5; 1990, 95.8; 1995, 102.8; 2000, 98.2; 2005, 95.4. Use increments of 5 million.

22. US National Debt (in billions of dollars): 1975, 533; 1980, 908; 1985, 1,946; 1990, 3,233; 1995, 4,974; 2000, 5,674; 2005, 7,933. Use increments of 1 trillion.

Calculate the number of degrees for each slice of a pie chart for the following data.

23. Tax distribution: 40% for local schools, 20% for police, 15% for fire department, 15% for parks, and 10% for indebtedness.

24. Grade distribution: 20% As, 25% Bs, 40% Cs, 10% Ds, and 5% Fs.

25. Middle-school enrollment: 40 sixth graders, 35 seventh graders, and 25 eighth graders.

26. Grade distribution: 3 As, 8 Bs, 17 Cs, 5 Ds, and 1 F.

Make a pie chart using the data from the indicated exercise.

27. exercise 23   28. exercise 24   29. exercise 25   30. exercise 26

31. Which type of graph would best show the relative sizes of categories of expenses in a budget?

32. Which type of graph should be used to illustrate the relationship between the ages and heights of students?

33. Which type of graph is best for comparing the achievement test scores of a student over a period of ten years?

34. Which type of graph should be used to summarize the scores of all students in a state on an achievement test?

Use the double bar graph to answer exercises 35–39.

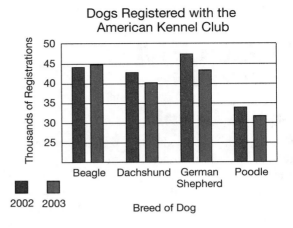

Dogs Registered with the American Kennel Club

35. Which breed had the largest number of dogs registered in 2002? The least registered in 2002?

36. Rank the breeds registered in 2003 in order from the least to the greatest number.

37. Was the number of beagles registered in 2002 above or below 45,000?

38. Which breed(s) increased in the number of registrations from 2002 to 2003?

39. Which two breeds showed the largest decrease in the number of registrations from 2002 to 2003?

■ C. Exercises

40. Make a double bar graph of the data in the following table. Use increments of 20.

July 15 High and Low Temperatures (in °F)		
City	Low	High
Cold Springs	47	64
Breezeville	53	71
Gulf City	76	89
Riverton	65	85

41. Take a survey of at least thirty people's favorite candy bar. Make a pie chart to illustrate your data.

■ Dominion thru Math

42. If a student has a mean of 78 on five tests in algebra, what will the student's new average be if he scores a 92 on the next test? Round to the nearest whole percent.

43. The median price of fourteen houses sold in a certain community during the first twenty-four days of the month of June was $164,000. What will the median price be for the whole month if four more houses sell at the following prices: $145,600; $189,400; $149,800; and $368,200?

44. The fourteen houses that were sold during the first twenty-four days of June sold with a mean price of $171,000. Using the prices in the previous problem, determine the new mean price for all eighteen houses sold during the entire month of June. Round to the nearest hundred dollars.

CUMULATIVE REVIEW

Evaluate. Write fractional answers in lowest terms. [6.4]

45. $a + \dfrac{5}{18}$ when $a = \dfrac{4}{9}$

46. $2y - \dfrac{7}{8}$ when $y = \dfrac{4}{5}$

47. $a + 3b$ when $a = -3.72$ and $b = 4.91$

48. $\dfrac{x + 5y}{4x}$ when $x = -6$ and $y = 3$

49. $b^2 - 9b + 4$ when $b = -2$

Solve the following inequalities. Round decimal answers to the nearest hundredth. [8.4]

50. $-9y + 41 < 89$

51. $9.1x + 8.6 < 12.4$

52. $7y - 51 > -8$

53. $-8.2x - 6.7 > 1.87$

54. $\dfrac{7}{5}x + \dfrac{9}{10} \le \dfrac{2}{3}$

PROBLEM SOLVING

Make a Graph

Previously, you have used diagrams to determine efficient solutions to problems. Problems that can be modeled or pictured as a function can often be solved using the "make a graph" strategy. When using graphing as a strategy, you must determine the shape of the graph and make sure that it is consistent throughout the range of values encountered in the problem. Sometimes graphs apply to only a limited range of values. This process is called *modeling*. Study the following example to see how a graph can help you understand and solve a problem.

| Example | Jeannie's candle was originally 20 cm long, but it measured 18 cm after burning for 30 min. and 16 cm after burning for 1 hr. How long would it take for the candle to burn completely? If she lit the candle at 6:00 PM and blew it out at 8:20 PM, how long is the candle? |

Answer

Think: Determine what you are trying to find.

You want to know how long the candle will burn and how long it will be at 8:20 PM.

Think: How can the data in the problem be organized?

Make a set of ordered pairs in which the first number represents the burning time in minutes (t) and the second number represents the length of the candle in centimeters (l).

t	l
0	20
30	18
60	16

Think: Can these ordered pairs be graphed to help you see the relationship more clearly?

Construct a graph in which the horizontal axis represents time, t, and the vertical axis represents the length of the candle, l. Plot the three ordered pairs from the table on the graph.

Think: Do these points form a particular shape? Do you think this shape will remain constant throughout the problem?

The ordered pairs form a line. This shape will remain constant as long as the candle burns at a constant rate.

Think: How could you find out what the length of the candle will be over an extended period of time?

Connect the points and extend the line until it reaches the horizontal axis.

Think: From this graph, how can you tell the total burning time of the candle?

The candle has completely burned when the line reaches the horizontal axis (the candle has no length). Find the value of t at this point on the graph; the total burning time of the candle is 5 hr.

Think: How does this information help you solve the problem? If Jeannie blows the candle out at 8:20 PM, how can you tell how much candle remains?

The candle has burned for 2 hr. 20 min. Locate this time on the horizontal axis of the graph, move up to the point on the line, and then move left to the vertical axis. The candle is approximately 11 cm at 8:20 PM.

Think: Was the graph helpful in solving this problem? Do you think there are any more efficient ways to solve it?

The graph was helpful, giving a useful estimate. A more precise graph, an extended table, or an algebraic equation could have also been used.

■ Exercises

1. It is found that for every five homework problems you do before an exam, your math grade will go up 1%. Assuming this is true and that your grade is currently 82%, graph this relationship. Use the point (0, 80) for the origin, and mark off the x-axis in units of five problems worked and the y-axis in units of 1%. From the given information, plot two points and draw a line graph. Use the graph to determine how many problems you should do before the next exam to get a 90%. What percentage would you predict if you worked fifty homework problems before the final exam?

A manufacturer estimates that he spends $2.50 for labor per model airplane plus the fixed costs of $900 per week to keep his plant open. The plant normally produces 3,000 models per week.

2. Using the information above, find the cost to produce the normal output of 3,000 model airplanes per week.

3. Assume the manufacturer keeps the plant open but produces no models. Use the point determined by this assumption and the one determined by your calculation in exercise 2 to graph a line. Use the point (0, 0) for the origin, increments of 500 models for the x-axis, and increments of $3,000 for the y-axis.

4. From the graph, find the cost of producing (a) only 2,000 planes in a week and (b) only 1,000 planes in a week.

5. Assume that the model planes net $9 each after the expenses of selling them are paid. Use this information and the costs calculated in exercises 2 and 4 to calculate the profit from producing and selling (a) 3,000 planes, (b) 2,000 planes, and (c) 1,000 planes.

The E-Z Fit center charges an initial fee of $50 and a monthly fee of $30. The Basic Fitness club has a monthly fee of $40 with no initial membership fee. On the same set of axes, produce a line graph of the cost for membership in each fitness club. Label the x-axis as length of membership in months, using one-month increments. Label the y-axis as cumulative cost, using $40 increments.

6. If you stay a member for three months, which fitness center would be more economical to join? How much cheaper is it?

7. If you use the fitness center for a year, which one would be more economical? How much would you save over the year by joining the center that is more economical?

8. At what point will the total cost of the fees for the two fitness centers be the same?

10.5 Fundamental Principle of Counting

Counting is certainly basic to mathematics. Who did the first counting? Counting is seen in the first chapters of the Bible. Genesis 1:5, 8, 13, 19, 23, and 31 reveal that God counted the days of His creation. Men have counted things ever since.

Calvary Christian Academy is having an election of student officers. Three students are running for president—Juan, Pam, and Jeff. There are two candidates for vice president—Doyle and Julianne. How many different ways are there to fill the offices?

A *tree diagram* can be used to find all of the possible outcomes for this election.

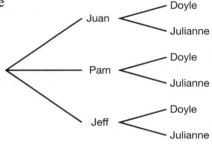

The possible election results are Juan and Doyle, Juan and Julianne, Pam and Doyle, Pam and Julianne, Jeff and Doyle, or Jeff and Julianne. The offices can be filled in six different ways.

Example 1   Find the number of ways that a student can select a two-digit number if the first digit must be odd and the second digit must be less than five.

Answer

possible first digit—1, 3, 5, 7, 9

possible second digit—0, 1, 2, 3, 4

1. Identify the possible first and second digits.

2. Draw a tree diagram.

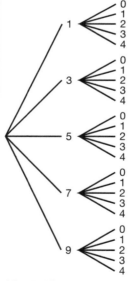

10, 11, 12, 13, 14

30, 31, 32, 33, 34

50, 51, 52, 53, 54

70, 71, 72, 73, 74

90, 91, 92, 93, 94

3. List the two-digit numbers.

There are 25 different two-digit numbers.

Skill Check 1

Make tree diagrams for the following and list all possible outcomes.

1. Find the number of combinations of a sport and a musical instrument. The sports to choose from are baseball, soccer, and tennis. The instruments to choose from are piano and trumpet.

2. Find the number of ways to form a two-digit number if the first digit is greater than five and the second digit is even.

The total number of possible outcomes for the election at Calvary Christian Academy (see the previous page) can also be determined using multiplication. There are three ways to choose a president—Juan, Pam, or Jeff. For each of these ways, there are two ways to choose a vice president—Doyle or Julianne. Therefore, there are $3 \times 2 = 6$ possible outcomes. This example illustrates the Fundamental Principle of Counting.

Fundamental Principle of Counting
If there are p ways that a first choice can be made and q ways that a second choice can be made, then there are $p \times q$ ways to make the first choice followed by the second choice.

Example 2 Reid has five dress shirts and four ties. How many different shirt-and-tie combinations are possible?

Answer

$5 \times 4 = 20$ Use the Fundamental Principle of Counting to multiply the number of shirts times the number of ties.

Example 3 How many different two-digit counting numbers can be formed if the first digit must be a nonzero even digit and the second digit must be less than seven but greater than zero?

Answer

There are four choices (2, 4, 6, 8) for the first digit and six choices (1, 2, 3, 4, 5, 6) for the second digit. By the Fundamental Principle of Counting, there are $4 \times 6 = 24$ such numbers.

Example 4 Mr. Dillard is buying a new car. He has the options given in the following table to choose from. How many different combinations of options does he have? If he chooses a white exterior, how many combinations does he have on the remaining options?

Exterior	Interior	Entertainment Package	Transmission
red	black	AM/FM	automatic
white	blue	AM/FM/CD	manual
black	gray	AM/FM/CD/DVD	
silver			

Answer

$4 \times 3 \times 3 \times 2 = 72$ 1. Use the Fundamental Principle of Counting. There are four choices for the exterior, three choices for the interior, three choices for the entertainment package, and two choices for the transmission.

$1 \times 3 \times 3 \times 2 = 18$ 2. The exterior is white, so there is only one choice for the exterior. There are still three choices for the interior, three choices for the entertainment package, and two choices for the transmission.

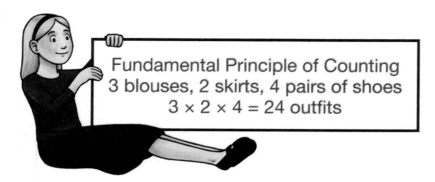

Fundamental Principle of Counting
3 blouses, 2 skirts, 4 pairs of shoes
3 × 2 × 4 = 24 outfits

Skill Check 2

Use the Fundamental Principle of Counting to find the number of possible outcomes.

1. How many different combinations of one flavor of ice cream and one topping are possible (ice cream flavors—vanilla and chocolate; toppings—nuts, cherries, and hot fudge)?

2. How many different combinations of one main dish and one vegetable are possible (main dishes—turkey, chicken, and ham; vegetables—potatoes, carrots, beans, and squash)?

■ A. Exercises

Make tree diagrams for the following and find the number of possible outcomes.

1. Jonathan has four dress shirts—white, blue, ecru, and striped. He has three ties—red, navy, and black. How many different shirt-and-tie combinations can he choose?

2. There are three candidates running for mayor and five running for a vacant county council seat. How many different ways can these seats be filled?

3. A deli has four kinds of soup, three kinds of sandwiches, and two kinds of desserts. How many combinations of one soup, one sandwich, and one dessert are possible?

4. There is apple, cherry, blueberry, and peach pie to choose from. There is vanilla and cinnamon ice cream to choose from. How many ways can you choose pie à la mode?

5. There are two choices for president, two choices for senator, and three choices for representative. How many ways can one vote for these three offices?

6. How many ways can you choose between five colors of socks and three pairs of shoes?

7. How many ways can you choose between three routes from Big City to Ruralville, followed by three routes from Ruralville to Beachtown?

Find the number of possible outcomes.

8. Select one fruit and one vegetable (fruits—apple, banana, and pear; vegetables—corn, beans, and potatoes).

9. Select one blouse and one skirt (blouses—white, yellow, and blue; skirts—navy and tan).

10. Select a two-digit number whose first digit is 0, 1, 2, 3, or 4, and whose second digit is 5, 6, 7, 8, or 9.

11. Select a two-digit number whose first digit is 1, 3, or 5, and whose second digit is any digit from 0 to 9.

12. Tickets for the five performances of a play are sold at three different prices. How many different choices are possible?

13. A ladder company makes three different grades of ladders. Each grade is made in seven different lengths. How many different types of ladders does the company make?

■ B. Exercises

Use the Fundamental Principle of Counting to find the number of possible outcomes.

14. Choose a number from one to ten (inclusive) followed by a flip of a coin.

15. Choose a number from one to six (inclusive); then spin a spinner with four spaces numbered 1 to 4 with each one equally likely.

16. Flip a coin three times in succession.

17. An event can be scheduled in the morning, afternoon, or evening of any day of the week.

18. Choose an hour during the week for an event that can occur during any hour of the day, any day of the week.

19. Choose an odd number between zero and ten and a letter of the alphabet.

20. There are ten names in a hat. How many ways are there to draw three names for first, second, and third prizes from the hat, assuming each person can win only one prize?

21. There are ten names in a hat. How many ways are there to draw three names for first, second, and third prizes if drawn names are replaced before the next drawing?

22. There are five choices of sandwiches, two choices of chips, and three choices of drinks. There is a limit of one sandwich, one bag of chips, and one drink.

23. Roll a die three times in succession; then form a three-digit number using the successive rolls as the hundreds, tens, and ones places respectively.

24. Draw three tickets from among one hundred for three different door prizes (drawn tickets are not replaced).

25. How many different outfits can be chosen from among six shirts, five ties, and four sport coats?

26. Choose five students for roles in a class play from among twenty-four in one class.

27. Elect four of six people to the offices of president, vice president, secretary, and treasurer.

28. There are four choices of meat, eight choices of vegetables, and two choices of dessert. How many different meals consisting of one meat, one vegetable, and one dessert could be ordered?

29. Nadia is choosing a cell phone from among three styles, each of which comes in five colors with either basic or expanded features. How many different choices are possible?

■ C. Exercises

At a certain company there are two managers, five office clerks, seven stock boys, three foremen, six secretaries, and four shipping clerks. How many different ways can the following personnel be selected?

30. a manager and a foreman

31. an office clerk and a shipping clerk

32. a stock boy and a secretary

33. a secretary and a foreman

34. a manager, office clerk, and stock boy

35. a secretary, shipping clerk, and stock boy

Mrs. Davies is buying a new car. She must choose from the following options.

Exterior	Interior	Entertainment Package	Transmission
blue	black	AM/FM	automatic
cream	blue	AM/FM/CD	manual
green	burgundy	AM/FM/CD/DVD	
red	charcoal		
white			

36. If she chooses a blue car with a black interior and an automatic transmission, how many combinations does she have on the remaining options?

37. If she chooses a white car with a burgundy interior, how many combinations does she have on the remaining options?

38. If she chooses a red exterior, how many combinations does she have on the remaining options?

39. If she chooses a manual transmission, how many combinations does she have on the remaining options?

40. How many different combinations of options does Mrs. Davies have to choose from?

CUMULATIVE REVIEW

Multiply. Round decimal answers to the nearest hundredth. [6.2]

41. $\dfrac{-7}{3} \times \dfrac{9}{5}$

42. $5{:}31 \times 0.25$

43. $-4.92 \times (-9.2)$

44. $\dfrac{3}{5} \times 15$

45. $\dfrac{8}{15} \times \dfrac{5}{3}$

Solve the following inequalities. Round decimal answers to the nearest hundredth. [8.4]

46. $-6y + 92 < 74$

47. $-6.9x + 2.7 < 0.18$

48. $12y - 5 > 9$

49. $15.8x - 26.4 > -8.1$

50. $-\dfrac{2}{7}a \le 142$

10.6 Permutations

A *permutation* is an arrangement of a group of objects in a particular order. To find how many different ways three letters can be arranged, you can make a list of the permutations. All possible permutations of the letters A, B, and C are shown below. Notice that the arrangements begin with A first, then with B first, and finally with C first.

ABC	BAC	CAB
ACB	BCA	CBA

There are six possible permutations of the letters A, B, and C.

How many different numbers can be dialed on this old-fashioned (but loud) residential phone?

> **Definition**
>
> A **permutation** is a way of arranging r out of n objects (if $r \leq n$).

You can find the number of permutations of three letters by using the Fundamental Principle of Counting. There are three ways to pick the first letter, two ways to pick the second letter, and one way to pick the third letter.

$$3 \times 2 \times 1 = 6 \text{ permutations}$$

$3 \times 2 \times 1$ can be represented by 3!, read "three factorial." In general, the number of permutations of a group of n different distinct objects is $n(n - 1)(n - 2)\ldots(3)(2)(1)$. This expression is written as $n!$, read "n factorial." The word *distinct* means all of the items can be distinguished from each other. If we had two As and one B, the As would not be distinguishable from one another.

> **Definition**
>
> The product of n natural numbers from n down to one is called *n factorial*. The symbol for "factorial" is an exclamation mark, and $n! = n(n - 1)\ldots(1)$. ($0! = 1$ by definition.)

Example 1 Evaluate 6!

Answer

$6(5)(4)(3)(2)(1) = 720$

Skill Check 1

Express each of the following as a factorial.

1. $5 \cdot 4 \cdot 3 \cdot 2 \cdot 1$
2. $8 \cdot 7 \cdot 6 \cdot 5 \cdot 4 \cdot 3 \cdot 2 \cdot 1$

Find the numerical value of each of the following.

3. $4!$
4. $7!$
5. $3(5!)$
6. $3! \times 6!$

The number of permutations of a group of n distinct objects, when using all n objects, is $_nP_n$, which is read "the number of permutations of n objects taken n at a time."

> **Formula for the Permutation of n Objects Taken n at a Time—$_nP_n$**
>
> To find the number of permutations of n distinct objects taken n at a time, find the product of the positive integers n down through one: $_nP_n = n(n - 1)(n - 2)\ldots(3)(2)(1) = n!$

Example 2 Find the number of permutations of the letters in the word *saved*.

Answer

There are five letters, and we are arranging all of them.

Use the formula $_5P_5 = 5! = 5(4)(3)(2)(1) = 120$.

There are 120 permutations of the letters s, a, v, e, and d.

The Fundamental Principle of Counting could also be used to find the number of permutations. There are five ways to choose the first letter, four ways to choose the second, three ways to choose the third, two ways to choose the fourth, and one way to choose the fifth.

$$5 \times 4 \times 3 \times 2 \times 1 = 120 \text{ permutations}$$

If you were asked to determine the number of permutations of the letters s, a, v, e, and d taken two at a time instead of using all five, you could list them as follows.

sa, sv, se, sd,

av, ae, ad, as,

ve, vd, vs, va,

ed, es, ea, ev,

ds, da, dv, de

There are twenty different arrangements of these five letters taken two at a time. Notice that *sa* and *as* are both in the list, as are *sv* and *vs*. Order matters when you are counting permutations; therefore, *sa* and *as* are not the same permutation, and each must be counted. The notation to indicate the permutation of five objects taken two at a time is $_5P_2$.

We could have gotten the twenty different arrangements by the counting principle: $20 = 5 \times 4$. Because many calculators have factorial buttons, it is helpful to use factorials to find permutations. Note that $\dfrac{5!}{3!} = \dfrac{5 \times 4 \times 3 \times 2 \times 1}{3 \times 2 \times 1} = 5 \times 4$. The formula for finding the number of permutations of n objects taken r at a time is given below. It will be particularly helpful for large values of n.

Formula for the Permutation of n Objects Taken r at a Time—$_nP_r$

To find the number of permutations of n distinct objects taken r at a time, use the formula $_nP_r = \dfrac{n!}{(n-r)!}$.

Applying this formula to the permutation of the letters s, a, v, e, and d taken two at a time gives

$$_5P_2 = \frac{5!}{(5-2)!} = \frac{5!}{3!} = \frac{5 \times 4 \times \not{3} \times \not{2} \times \not{1}}{\not{3} \times \not{2} \times \not{1}} = 5 \times 4 = 20.$$

There are twenty permutations of five objects taken two at a time.

Example 3 Find the number of permutations of the five letters s, a, v, e, and d taken three at a time.

Answer
$$_5P_3 = \frac{5!}{(5-3)!} = \frac{5!}{2!} = \frac{5 \times 4 \times 3 \times \not{2} \times \not{1}}{\not{2} \times \not{1}} = 5 \times 4 \times 3 = 60$$

Example 4 Find the number of permutations of eight distinct things taken three at a time.

Answer
$$_8P_3 = \frac{8!}{(8-3)!} = \frac{8!}{5!} = \frac{8(7)(6)\,\not{(5)(4)(3)(2)(1)}}{\not{5(4)(3)(2)(1)}} = 8(7)(6) = 336$$

Permutations

$$_nP_n = n!$$

$$_nP_r = \frac{n!}{(n-r)!}$$

Skill Check 2

1. There are six runners in a race. How many possible ways can a gold, a silver, and a bronze medal be awarded to the runners?

2. Geoffrey has eight books. How many different ways can he arrange these books on a shelf?

■ A. Exercises

Evaluate the following factorials.

1. $6!$ 2. $9!$ 3. $4!$ 4. $7!$ 5. $0!$ 6. $8!$

Evaluate the following products.

7. $2(3!)$ 8. $4(5!)$ 9. $3!(4!)$ 10. $5!(6!)$ 11. $16(0!)$ 12. $2!(5!)$

Evaluate the following permutations.

13. $_6P_6$ 14. $_4P_4$ 15. $_3P_3$ 16. $_7P_7$ 17. $_8P_8$ 18. $_5P_5$

■ B. Exercises

Evaluate the following permutations.

19. $_4P_2$ 20. $_6P_3$ 21. $_5P_4$ 22. $_6P_2$ 23. $_6P_4$ 24. $_8P_4$

25. $_7P_3$ 26. $_9P_5$ 27. $_4P_3$ 28. $_8P_2$ 29. $_7P_4$ 30. $_{15}P_3$

Find the number of different arrangements of the following.

31. three of eight different books on a shelf

32. Three different positions are to be filled from among six employees.

33. Three different offices are to be filled from among four students.

34. An organization with thirty people in it must choose two people for different jobs.

35. Two runners are to be chosen from among six for the first and last positions on a relay team.

36. A decorator is to arrange three potted plants chosen from a set of seven.

■ C. Exercises

Write an expression in the form $_nP_r$ to represent the number of permutations in the following situations.

37. Select first, second, and third place out of 500 contestants.

38. Elect a president, vice president, secretary, and treasurer from a class of twenty-eight students.

39. How many different two-digit whole numbers can you make from the digits 2, 4, 6, and 8 if no digit appears more than once in each number?

40. How many different three-letter arrangements are there of the letters of the alphabet?

■ Dominion thru Math

The table gives the 2005 baseball team earned run averages (ERA) in each major league. A lower ERA indicates a better pitching record.

41. Construct a box-and-whisker diagram for each league. Place one diagram above the other with the scales aligned so that they can be compared.

42. Calculate the mean ERA for each league.

43. Use statistics to argue that the National League had better pitching.

44. Use statistics to argue that the American League had better pitching.

American League		National League	
Chicago	3.52	St. Louis	3.34
Minnesota	3.70	Atlanta	3.78
Los Angeles	3.73	Houston	3.84
Cleveland	3.83	Washington	3.86
Detroit	3.92	Milwaukee	3.88
Oakland	3.93	New York	4.01
Toronto	4.15	San Diego	4.04
Seattle	4.23	Florida	4.12
Baltimore	4.37	Chicago	4.42
New York	4.68	Pittsburgh	4.43
Texas	4.82	Los Angeles	4.49
Boston	4.85	Philadelphia	4.55
Kansas City	5.31	Arizona	4.76
Tampa Bay	5.82	San Francisco	4.87
		Colorado	5.47
		Cincinnati	5.56

CUMULATIVE REVIEW

Which numbers are members of the solution sets for the given inequalities? [3.6]

45. $x - 20 < 15$; 10, 20, 30, 40

46. $-6x > 43$; $-4, -8, -10, -11$

47. $12x \neq 72$; $-8, 0, 6, 16$

48. $\frac{8x}{9} \geq 4$; $-7, 4, 10, 15$

49. $-8x + 19 \geq -4$; $-1, 0, 2, 3$

Write an inequality and solve. [8.5]

50. The sum of two consecutive integers is less than 87. Find the maximum values of the integers.

51. Three times the first of two consecutive integers is at least twelve more than four times the second. Find the greatest possible integers.

52. Find the least possible consecutive odd integers such that eight times the smaller one is at least 25 more than the difference of the two integers.

53. The total cost of a laptop computer and high-quality printer is at least $2,250. If the computer costs $200 more than the printer, what is the least each piece of equipment can cost?

54. The cost of several ties at $13.50 each and a package of socks costing $8.25 was less than $64. At most, how many ties were purchased?

10.7 Combinations

Suppose Amos buys seven used books and decides to take three of them with him on vacation. If he chooses *Sackett*, *Her Majesty's Rancho*, and *The Virginian*, does it matter whether *The Virginian* is chosen first or last? No, it matters only whether it is one of the chosen three. The order in which the three books are chosen does not matter. The selection of *r* items from *n* distinct items without regard to order is called a *combination*.

Definition

A **combination** is a selection of a subset of objects from a set without regard to the order in which they are selected. The notation for the number of combinations of *n* distinct objects taken *r* at a time is $_nC_r$.

The letters *a*, *b*, and *c* can be arranged in six different ways—*abc*, *acb*, *bac*, *bca*, *cab*, and *cba*. In other words, there are six permutations for the three letters *a*, *b*, and *c*.

However, there is only one combination of the letters *a*, *b*, and *c*. All of the permutations above have the same group of letters, so when order is not important they represent different ways of naming the same set of objects. If you are interested only in the set of three letters without regard to order (a combination), then *abc* and *acb* are the same set of objects.

If order is important, you are finding a permutation. If order is not important, you are finding a combination.

Example 1 | Identify each of the following as a permutation or a combination.

a. the number of ways to place five pictures in a line on a wall

b. the number of ways to fill four eighth-grade class offices from the seven nominees

c. the number of ways to choose a five-person class party committee from the twelve volunteers

Answer

a. permutation (the order of the pictures is important)

b. permutation (the office each person fills is important)

c. combination (the committee is the same regardless of the order in which students are chosen)

Skill Check 1

Identify each of the following as a permutation or a combination.

1. the number of ways to place three letters and three numbers on a license plate

2. the number of ways to choose the girls on the volleyball team

3. the number of ways to choose four pairs of shoes to pack for your trip

4. the number of ways to seat the students in the front row of the classroom

There would be $_7P_3 = \dfrac{7!}{4!} = 210$ ways for Amos to choose three books out of seven if order mattered. However, each set of three books would be counted $3! = 6$ times. So we can group the 210 permutations into $\dfrac{210}{6} = 35$ groups, where each group is the six different permutations of the same three books. Thus there are 35 ways of choosing three books from seven when order doesn't matter. Note that $35 = \dfrac{_7P_3}{3!} = \dfrac{7!}{4!3!}$. In general, we have the following formula.

Formula for Combinations

To find the number of combinations of n distinct objects taken r at a time, use the formula
$$_nC_r = \frac{n!}{r!(n - r)!}.$$

Example 2   Use the formula to find the number of combinations of three books that Amos could choose from the seven new books that he bought.

Answer
$$_7C_3 = \frac{7!}{3!(7 - 3)!} = \frac{7!}{3!4!} = \frac{7 \times 6 \times 5 \times 4!}{3 \times 2 \times 1 \times 4!} = 7 \times 5 = 35 \text{ different combinations}$$

Notice that 7! is written as the product of 7, 6, 5, and 4! The factors of 4! are not written out in detail because it can be canceled with the 4! in the denominator.

Combinations

$$_nC_n = 1$$
$$_nC_r = \frac{n!}{r!(n - r)!}$$

Example 3   There are ten girls in Mrs. Hernando's class, and six are to be selected for a volleyball team. How many different teams can be chosen?

Answer
$$_{10}C_6 = \frac{10!}{6!(10 - 6)!} = \frac{10!}{6!4!} = \frac{\overset{5}{\cancel{10}} \times \overset{3}{\cancel{9}} \times \overset{2}{\cancel{8}} \times 7 \times \cancel{6!}}{\cancel{6!} \times \cancel{4} \times \cancel{3} \times \cancel{2} \times 1} = 5 \times 3 \times 2 \times 7 = 210 \text{ teams}$$

Skill Check 2

1. The principal needs a four-person committee made from the eleven faculty members of the school. How many different committees are possible?

2. There are thirteen girls trying out for the cheerleading squad. If the squad consists of six girls, how many different squads are possible?

■ A. Exercises

Identify each of the following as a permutation or a combination.

1. choosing three books from among ten to take on vacation

2. choosing five starters for a basketball team

3. choosing officers for a club from among the membership

4. arranging three books from a set of six on a shelf

5. picking a committee of six people from an organization

6. picking a sequence of digits for a license plate number

7. choosing a batting order for a baseball game

8. choosing three friends from your class to accompany you on a shopping trip

9. finding the different arrangements of the letters of the alphabet to make "words"

10. choosing five candy bars from a sack of ten different kinds to take on a picnic

■ B. Exercises

Evaluate.

11. $_5C_3$

12. $_6C_3$

13. $_7C_5$

14. $_4C_3$

15. $_8C_6$

16. $_8C_2$

17. $_4C_2$

18. $_5C_5$

19. $_{12}C_8$

20. $_5C_2$

Label each exercise *C* for combination or *P* for permutation; then find the number of different ways each can be accomplished. Use a calculator for large computations.

21. picking nine people from among twelve

22. lining up nine people from among twelve from left to right

23. choosing four dogs from a litter of seven

24. assigning partners from among four people for a game

25. order of finish of first three runners in a race with four entrants

26. choosing three kinds of sandwiches, from among seven kinds, for a party

27. picking two neckties from among nine

28. arranging different centerpieces, from among ten different choices, on four different tables

29. choosing three vegetables to plant in a garden from among corn, peas, beans, peppers, and tomatoes

30. hiring two out of three candidates for identical jobs

31. hiring two out of three candidates for different jobs

32. different orders of finish of the first six cars in a NASCAR race

■ C. Exercises

The school principal wants to form a committee of five teachers. Twelve of the teachers in the school are women and six are men. Use a calculator for large computations.

33. How many different committees can be formed?

34. How many different all-women committees can be formed?

35. How many different all-men committees can be formed?

36. If there were three women on the committee, then two men would have to be chosen to fill the remaining positions on the committee. How many ways can three women be chosen for the committee? How many ways can two men be chosen for the committee? Using the Fundamental Principle of Counting, find how many ways a committee of three women and two men can be formed.

37. How many ways can a committee of four women and one man be formed?

Write each fraction as a decimal and a percent. Round to the nearest tenth of a percent. [7.1]

38. $\frac{8}{5}$ 39. $\frac{4}{7}$ 40. $\frac{6}{25}$ 41. $\frac{17}{28}$ 42. $\frac{13}{16}$

Using the slope formula, find the slope of the line through the two given points. [9.5]

43. $(-5, 4), (-3, 17)$ 44. $(0, -8), (6, 9)$ 45. $(-12, 1), (11, -4)$

46. $(-7, -3), (-9, -4)$ 47. $(12, 0), (0, 10)$

10.8 ⌐ Probability

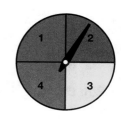

The spinner on the right has four possible outcomes: 1, 2, 3, or 4. Each outcome is equally likely, since there is one chance in four of getting a specific number.

Spinning the spinner is an example of an *experiment*. The set of all possible outcomes, {1, 2, 3, 4}, is this experiment's *sample space*, and any spin is a *trial*. A possible result or *outcome* of a single trial (i.e., spinning an odd number) is called an *event*. The *probability* of an event, $P(E)$, is a ratio that describes the likelihood that the event will occur.

Definitions

An **experiment** is an occurrence, leading to one of several specified outcomes, whose result cannot be known ahead of time.
A **sample space** is the set of all possible outcomes of an experiment.
A **trial** is a single observation.
An **outcome** is the result of a single trial.
An **event** is a possible outcome of a trial.

On the above spinner, the probability of the event "spinning a 4," $P(4)$, is $\frac{1}{4}$ since one of the four wedges has a 4 and all the wedges are the same size. To find the probability of an event E, find the ratio of favorable outcomes to possible outcomes. Probability can also be expressed as a decimal: $P(4) = \frac{1}{4} = 0.25$.

Probability Formula
The probability of an event E is $P(E) = \dfrac{\text{number of favorable outcomes}}{\text{number of possible outcomes}}$.

Example 1 For one spin, find each of the following probabilities (the number in parentheses is the number on which the spinner stops). Express the probability ratio as both a fraction in lowest terms and a decimal.

a. $P(3)$

b. $P(2)$

c. $P(1)$

Answer

a. There is one 3 on the spinner, so the number of favorable outcomes is one. The number of possible outcomes is six. The probability of the spinner stopping at 3 is $P(3) = \frac{1}{6} \approx 0.17$.

b. There are three 2s on the spinner, so the number of favorable outcomes is three. The number of possible outcomes is six. The probability of the spinner stopping at 2 is $P(2) = \frac{3}{6} = \frac{1}{2} = 0.5$.

c. There are two 1s on the spinner, so the number of favorable outcomes is two. The number of possible outcomes is six. The probability of the spinner stopping at 1 is $P(1) = \frac{2}{6} = \frac{1}{3} \approx 0.33$.

If a jar is filled with ten red marbles, then the probability of drawing a red marble is $\frac{10}{10} = 1$. The probability of drawing a black marble is $\frac{0}{10} = 0$. The probability of any event that is certain to occur is one, and the probability of an impossible event is zero.

Example 2 For one spin, find each of the following probabilities (x is the number on which the spinner stops).

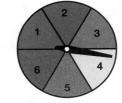

a. $P(x < 4)$

b. $P(x < 7)$

c. $P(x \geq 3)$

Answer

a. The numbers less than four are 1, 2, and 3. There are three favorable outcomes out of the six possible outcomes. $P(x < 4) = \frac{3}{6} = \frac{1}{2} = 0.5$.

b. All the numbers are less than seven, so the event is certain. $P(x < 7) = 1$.

c. The numbers greater than or equal to three are 3, 4, 5, and 6. There are four favorable outcomes out of six possible outcomes. $P(x \geq 3) = \frac{4}{6} = \frac{2}{3} \approx 0.67$.

Skill Check 1

State the possible outcomes for the following experiments.

1. a coin flip

2. a spin

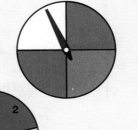

For one spin, find each of the following probabilities.

3. $P(5)$

4. $P(x > 6)$

5. $P(\text{odd})$

Consider the spinner shown. On a single spin, the pointer cannot stop on both a red wedge and a blue wedge. If two events cannot occur at the same time, they are *mutually exclusive*.

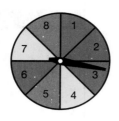

Five of the eight wedges on the spinner are either red or blue. Therefore, P(red or blue) $= \frac{5}{8} = 0.625$. To find the probability that one or the other of two mutually exclusive events will occur, add their probabilities.

Probability of Mutually Exclusive Events
If A and B are mutually exclusive events, then $P(A \text{ or } B) = P(A) + P(B)$.

Example 3 For one spin, find each of the following probabilities (x is the number on which the spinner stops, and the color denotes the color of the wedge on which the spinner stops).

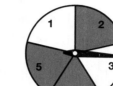

a. P(white or $x > 4$)
b. P(white or even)

Answer

a. E_1 = spinner stopping on a white wedge
E_2 = spinner stopping on a number greater than 4
They are mutually exclusive.
$P(\text{white}) = \frac{2}{5} = 0.4$; $P(x > 4) = \frac{1}{5} = 0.2$
$P(\text{white or } x > 4) = P(\text{white}) + P(x > 4)$
$= \frac{2}{5} + \frac{1}{5} = \frac{3}{5} = 0.6$

1. Determine the events and decide whether they are mutually exclusive.

2. Find the probabilities for the two events.
3. Use the formula for mutually exclusive events.

b. E_1 = spinner stopping on a white wedge
E_2 = spinner stopping on an even number
They are mutually exclusive.
$P(\text{white}) = \frac{2}{5} = 0.4$; $P(\text{even}) = \frac{2}{5} = 0.4$
$P(\text{white or even}) = P(\text{white}) + P(\text{even})$
$= \frac{2}{5} + \frac{2}{5} = \frac{4}{5} = 0.8$

1. Determine the events and decide whether they are mutually exclusive.

2. Find the probabilities for the two events.
3. Use the formula for mutually exclusive events.

Example 4 If one of the number squares pictured is drawn at random, find each of the following probabilities.

a. P(white or blue)
b. P(multiple of five or white)

Answer

a. Drawing a white square and drawing a blue square are mutually exclusive events; therefore,
$P(\text{white or blue}) = P(\text{white}) + P(\text{blue}) = \frac{4}{12} + \frac{4}{12} = \frac{8}{12} = \frac{2}{3} \approx 0.67.$
b. Drawing a multiple of five and drawing a white square are mutually exclusive events; therefore,
$P(\text{multiple of five or white}) = P(\text{multiple of five}) + P(\text{white}) = \frac{5}{12} + \frac{4}{12} = \frac{9}{12} = \frac{3}{4} = 0.75.$

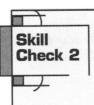

Skill Check 2

For one spin, find each of the following probabilities. Express your answer as both a fraction and a decimal rounded to the nearest hundredth.

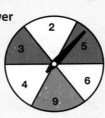

1. P(red)

2. P(red or white)

3. P(blue or white)

4. P(even number or blue)

5. P(odd number or white)

6. $P(x > 6$ or red)

■ A. Exercises

Six red marbles, five yellow marbles, and four green marbles are placed in a container, and one is drawn. Find each of the following probabilities. Express your answer as both a fraction and a decimal rounded to the nearest hundredth.

1. P(green)

2. P(red)

3. P(yellow)

A class contains ten boys and six girls. Their names are put into a hat, and one name is drawn. Find each of the following probabilities. Express your answer as both a fraction and a decimal rounded to the nearest hundredth.

4. P(boy)

5. P(girl)

6. P(boy or girl)

For one spin, find each of the following probabilities. Express your answer as both a fraction and a decimal rounded to the nearest hundredth.

7. P(3)

8. P(even number)

9. $P(x > 4)$

10. $P(x < 6)$

11. $P(x > 8)$

If one square is drawn, find each of the following probabilities. Express your answer as both a fraction and a decimal rounded to the nearest hundredth.

12. P(A)

13. P(B)

14. P(C)

15. P(D)

A track contains six lanes numbered 1–6, and runners draw for lanes before a race. Find each of the following probabilities for the first runner who draws a lane (x represents the number of the lane drawn). Express your answer as both a fraction and a decimal rounded to the nearest hundredth.

16. $P(x = 5)$

17. $P(x$ is odd)

18. $P(x > 2)$

19. $P(x \leq 3)$

Each of the names of these states is written on a separate index card: {Arizona, Florida, Kansas, Iowa, Ohio, Georgia}. The cards are placed in a hat and mixed, and one card is drawn. Find each of the following probabilities. Express your answer as both a fraction and a decimal rounded to the nearest hundredth.

20. P(state whose name ends in the letter a)

21. P(state whose name begins and ends with the same letter)

22. P(state located in the continental United States)

23. P(state whose name has four syllables)

24. P(state whose name has a y in it)

■ B. Exercises

Three white stones, five black stones, and twelve red stones are placed in a container, and one is drawn. Find each of the following probabilities. Express your answer as both a fraction and a decimal rounded to the nearest hundredth.

25. P(green)

26. P(red or black)

27. P(not red)

28. P(red, black, or white)

29. P(white or red)

30. P(white or black)

For one spin, find each of the following probabilities. Express your answer as both a fraction and a decimal rounded to the nearest hundredth.

31. P(red)

32. P(white or blue)

33. P(red or white)

34. P(odd number or blue)

35. P(even number or red)

36. P(multiple of four or $x < 4$)

■ C. Exercises

Each time a customer spent money at a store, his name was entered in a drawing proportional to the number of whole dollars he had spent. For instance, a customer who spent $508.79 was credited 508 points. When the contest was over, a total of 240,000 points were credited to customers. The store then held a drawing for one grand prize only. The following customers had accumulated the given point totals: Morris, 2,900; Norton, 120; Stone, 3,100; and Williams, 10,700. What are the probabilities that each of the following will win the drawing? Express your answer as a fraction, a decimal rounded to the nearest hundredth, and a percent.

37. P(Morris)

38. P(Morris or Stone)

39. P(one of the four)

40. P(none of the four)

Use the definition of probability, the Fundamental Principle of Counting, and the idea of combinations to answer exercises 41–43. Leave answers in symbol form.

41. If a committee of five students is selected from a class of thirteen boys and fifteen girls, what is the probability that the committee will have three girls on it?

42. What is the probability that the committee will have no boys on it?

43. What is the probability that the committee will have four boys on it?

■ Dominion thru Math

44. In the 2005 baseball season in the American League, Boston had the highest team batting average with .281, and Seattle had the lowest with .256. In the National League, Florida had the highest with .272, and Washington had the lowest with .252. Find the range of batting averages for the two leagues.

45. A player's batting average can be used as the probability of his getting a hit when he comes to bat. A batting average of .305 indicates a probability of 305 hits out of 1,000 at bats. About how many hits would a player with a .305 batting average expect to get in his next 24 times at bat?

46. In 2005 Derek Lee of the Chicago Cubs had 199 hits in 594 at bats. What was his batting average?

47. Based on your answer to exercise 46, about how many hits would Lee expect to make during his next 54 times at bat?

Write an inequality, solve it, and express the answer in words. [3.8]

48. Cayley wants to save at least $400 over the next two years to apply to the cost of a new computer for college. How much must she save monthly to achieve her goal? Round to the next higher dollar.

49. A college basketball coach has set a goal of keeping opposing teams to an average of fewer than 70 points per game. After five games, the team has given up a total of 340 points. How many points can they give up in the next game to stay within the coach's goal?

50. An advertisement says that during a sale, dresses originally priced "from $135" can be purchased for 40% off. How much will it cost for a dress at the sale?

51. Becca was allotted $150 to purchases supplies for the missionary closet at church. She wants to buy two sets of sheets at $22.50/set and several sets of bath towels that cost $8.50/set. How many sets of towels will she be able to purchase with the allotted funds?

52. Mrs. Sasser is planning to stay at a motel for two nights at $90 per night and has to buy six meals. She has budgeted $250 for the room and meals. How much can she spend on average per meal?

Simplify. [6.5]

53. $8x^2 - 3x + 9x^2 - 14x$

54. $\frac{6}{7}x^2 - 12x^3 + 5x - 8x^2$

55. $-11b - 12.7c + 9b - 18.6c$

56. $\frac{-9}{16}(7a - 4b) + \frac{3}{4}(-6a + b)$

57. $74.9(2x^2 - 6x + 1) - 6.9(x^2 + 8x - 4)$

MIND OVER MATH

Jenica's little sister, Susan, had a beautiful necklace made of colorful beads. Two successive beads in the necklace shared a common color at their meeting point. The figure below shows a possible segment of the necklace (each letter stands for the color pictured).

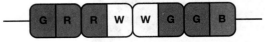

One day, the necklace broke and the beads were scattered all over the floor. Susan did her best to collect all the beads from the floor, but she is not sure whether she found all of them. Now she has come to Jenica for help. She wants to know whether it is possible to make a necklace using all the beads she has in the same way her original necklace was made and, if so, in which order the beads must be placed. If the following ordered pairs represent the bead colors, how could they go together to form the necklace?
(W, R) (G, B) (R, B) (G, W) (W, W) (B, G) (R, R) (W, G) (B, W)

Gideon, Judge of Israel

When Gideon is introduced in the book of Judges, he is threshing wheat in hiding so that the invading Midianites will not see him and steal his wheat. After the Lord revealed Himself to Gideon and commanded him to deliver Israel from the Midianites, Gideon replied, "Wherewith shall I save Israel? behold, my family is poor in Manasseh, and I am the least in my father's house" (Judg. 6:15). However, Gideon did accept his calling when the Lord confirmed it with signs.

In spite of his initial doubt, Gideon later exhibited a willingness to trust God in the face of overwhelming odds. When the Midianites invaded Israel again, Gideon gathered an army and advanced to meet the enemy. The army of the Midianites (including some Amalekites and other eastern peoples) numbered 135,000, while Gideon's army consisted of only 32,000 untrained men. For every man Gideon had assembled, the Midianites had more than four men. God wanted Israel to have no doubt as to Who had won the victory.

At God's instruction, Gideon told all who were fearful to leave, and 22,000 men went home. Since the Lord still considered the number of men to be too many, He told Gideon to test the men by having them drink from a brook. All who knelt were sent home. After this test, only 300 men remained. Now the odds were just right for God—300 against 135,000.

Gideon depended on the Lord to win the victory. At God's direction, he divided his army of 300 men into three parts and surrounded the enemy. They blew their trumpets and shouted together, "The sword of the Lord, and of Gideon" (Judg. 7:20). The surprised Midianites turned to flee and, in the confusion, started killing each other. At this time Gideon's men, including the ones who did not participate in the initial fight, joined in the slaughter. A remnant of only 15,000 Midianites fled and were pursued. The Bible records that two Midianite princes and two Midianite kings were caught and put to death. From that time on the Midianites ceased to be a people of any significance biblically.

10.9 Independent and Dependent Events

Suppose you have fifteen marbles of various colors in a bag and are told to randomly select two marbles. If you replace the first marble before drawing the second, the events are independent because the result of the first draw does not affect the second draw. If you do not replace the first marble before drawing the second, the events are dependent because the result of the first draw affects the second draw.

Definitions

Independent events are two events in which the occurrence of one has no effect on the probability of the other.

Dependent events are two events in which the occurrence of one changes the probability of the other.

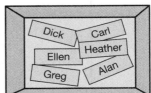

Consider the following events.

Event A: Draw one name from the box and do not replace it.

Event B: Draw a second name from the box.

What is the probability of drawing Ellen's name first and then Greg's name? The probability of choosing Ellen's name from the box on the first draw is $\frac{1}{6}$. If the name drawn is not placed back in the box, then there are only five names in the box for the second draw. The probability of choosing Greg's name on the second draw is $\frac{1}{5}$. You can see that the probability of a particular name being drawn on the second draw (Event B) has changed because of the occurrence of the first draw (Event A).

Events A and B are dependent.

A new notation, $P(B|A)$, is used for the second draw. It is read as "probability of B given A." To find the probability of two dependent events occurring one after the other, use the following formula.

Probability of Dependent Events
If A and B are dependent events, then $P(A \text{ and } B) = P(A) \times P(B|A)$.

Example 1

Select a name from the box on the previous page, and then select a second name without replacing the first. Find the probability of drawing a boy's name followed by a girl's name.

Answer

B = select a boy's name
$G|B$ = select a girl's name, given that a boy's name was selected on the first draw

$P(B) = \dfrac{4}{6} = \dfrac{2}{3}$

$P(G|B) = \dfrac{2}{5}$

$P(B \text{ and } G) = P(B) \times P(G|B)$

$\qquad\qquad = \dfrac{2}{3} \times \dfrac{2}{5}$

$\qquad\qquad = \dfrac{4}{15} \approx 0.27$

1. The probability of the second selection is affected by the occurrence of the first. The events are dependent.

2. Find the probability of the first event.

3. Find the probability of the second event, assuming that the first event has occurred.

4. Use the formula for the probability of dependent events.

Example 2

A bag of chocolate candies contains ten brown, eight orange, three yellow, and four green candies. What is the probability that the first two candies drawn from the bag without replacement will be brown?

Answer

B = select a brown candy
$B|B$ = select a brown candy, given that a brown was already selected

$P(B) = \dfrac{10}{25} = \dfrac{2}{5}$

$P(B|B) = \dfrac{9}{24} = \dfrac{3}{8}$

$P(B \text{ and } B) = P(B) \times P(B|B)$

$\qquad\qquad = \dfrac{2}{5} \times \dfrac{3}{8}$

$\qquad\qquad = \dfrac{3}{20} = 0.15$

1. The probability of the second selection is affected by the occurrence of the first. The events are dependent.

2. Find the probability of the first event.

3. Find the probability of the second event, assuming that the first event has occurred.

4. Use the formula for the probability of dependent events.

Skill Check 1

Suppose you select two marbles from a bag containing fifteen red marbles and five black ones without replacement. Find each of the following probabilities. Express your answer as both a fraction and a decimal rounded to the nearest hundredth.

1. $P(\text{red and black})$

2. $P(\text{black and red})$

3. $P(\text{red and red})$

4. $P(\text{black and black})$

Consider the spinner and the coin shown. Suppose you spin and then flip the coin. Since the outcome of the spin does not influence the outcome of the coin flip, these events are independent.

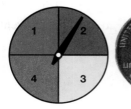

The probability of getting both a 4 on the spinner and heads on the coin flip is $P(4 \text{ and } H)$.

Below is a list of all eight possible combinations of spins and coin flips.

$$1H, \ 1T, \ 2H, \ 2T, \ 3H, \ 3T, \ 4H, \ 4T$$

The probability of getting a 4 and heads is $\dfrac{1}{8} \approx 0.13$.

Since event A and event B are independent, the occurrence of event A has no effect on event B. Therefore, the probability of B occurring, given that A has occurred, is just $P(B)$. That is,

$$P(B|A) = P(B).$$

In this case, $P(4) = \frac{2}{8} = \frac{1}{4}$ and $P(H|4) = P(H) = \frac{4}{8} = \frac{1}{2}$, and

$$P(4 \text{ and } H) = P(4) \times P(H|4) = P(4) \times P(H) = \frac{1}{4} \times \frac{1}{2} = \frac{1}{8} \approx 0.13, \text{ as before.}$$

Probability of Independent Events
If A and B are independent events, then $P(A \text{ and } B) = P(A) \times P(B)$.

Example 3   Using the given spinner, find $P(4 \text{ and tails})$.

Answer

$P(4) = \frac{2}{6} = \frac{1}{3}$; $P(T) = \frac{1}{2}$

$P(4 \text{ and } T) = P(4) \times P(T)$

$\qquad = \frac{1}{3}\left(\frac{1}{2}\right)$

$\qquad = \frac{1}{6} \approx 0.17$

Example 4   A three-digit number is to be formed by drawing one of four slips of paper with the digits 1, 2, 3, and 4 from a hat. The first draw determines the first digit of the number to be formed, and so on. Digits can be used more than once, so the digit drawn is replaced in the hat before the next draw. What is the probability that the three-digit number formed is 123?

Answer

$P(1 \text{ and } 2 \text{ and } 3) = P(1) \times P(2) \times P(3)$

$\qquad = \frac{1}{4} \times \frac{1}{4} \times \frac{1}{4}$

$\qquad = \frac{1}{64} \approx 0.016$

If this drawing was done 1,000 times, the number 123 would be formed about 16 times.

Skill Check 2

For one spin of each spinner, find each of the following probabilities. Express your answer as both a fraction and a decimal rounded to the nearest hundredth.

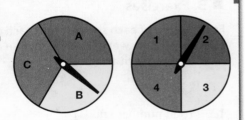

1. $P(A \text{ and } 4)$

2. $P(\text{consonant and odd number})$

A hat contains the names of three boys and five girls. Two names are drawn from the hat with replacement. Find each of the following probabilities. Express your answer as both a fraction and a decimal rounded to the nearest hundredth.

3. $P(\text{boy and boy})$ 4. $P(\text{girl and boy})$ 5. $P(\text{boy and girl})$

⊕ Invention

Leonardo da Vinci was blessed by God with a creative mind. He often conceived intriguing ideas for inventions that are commonplace today but that were dependent on technology that would not exist until centuries after his time. In the early sixteenth century he made sketches and illustrations of *contact lenses*, but even the first crude lenses were not made until three hundred years later. Several inventors worked on the construction of contacts during the nineteenth and early twentieth centuries, but the real breakthrough came in 1948 when optician Kevin Tuohy and later optometrist George Butterfield manufactured lenses made entirely of thin plastic. Another big step for contact lenses came in 1971 when Bausch & Lomb made soft contacts commercially available. Contact lenses not only provide vision correction and enhancement of appearance but can significantly slow the deteriorating effects of nearsightedness (myopia).

■ A. Exercises

State whether the following events are independent or dependent.

1. flipping a coin twice in a row

2. spinning a spinner twice in a row

3. using a spinner number to determine the number of times to flip a coin

4. choosing two letters for an ID code if the same letter cannot be chosen twice

5. choosing two letters for an ID code if the same letter can be chosen twice

6. choosing a class president and then choosing a class vice president

7. choosing a seventh-grade class president and then choosing an eighth-grade class president

8. selecting three members of the class to form a committee

9. selecting two marbles from a hat without replacing the first marble

10. selecting a marble from a hat twice with replacement between draws

■ B. Exercises

For one spin of each spinner, find each of the following probabilities. Express your answer as both a fraction and a decimal rounded to the nearest thousandth.

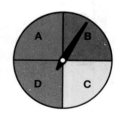

11. P(1 and A)

12. P(odd number and B)

13. P(even number and consonant)

14. P(multiple of 3 and C)

15. P(number < 5 and vowel)

16. P(number < 6 and [A, B, or C])

17. P(number > 6 and A)

18. P(number < 7 and C)

For two spins, find each of the following probabilities. Express your answer as both a fraction and a decimal rounded to the nearest thousandth.

19. P(6 and even number)

20. P(2 and 4)

21. P(multiple of 2 and odd number)

22. P(number > 3 and number < 3)

23. P(odd number and even number)

24. P(odd number and odd number)

Two number cards (at right) are drawn at random. The first draw is not replaced. Find each of the following probabilities. Express your answer as both a fraction and a decimal rounded to the nearest thousandth.

| 1 | 2 | 3 |
| 4 | 5 | 6 |

25. P(2 and 5)

26. P(even number and 1)

27. P(prime number and 4)

28. P(odd number and even number)

29. P(6 and number > 3)

30. P(odd number and 6)

Two letter squares (at right) are drawn at random. The first draw is not replaced. Find each of the following probabilities. Express your answer as both a fraction and a decimal rounded to the nearest thousandth.

| A | B | C | D |
| E | F | G | H |

31. P(A and D)

32. P(vowel and H)

33. P(I and H)

34. P([E or F] and [G or H])

35. P(B and [F or G])

■ C. Exercises

In a Christian high school of 250 students, 92 play only the piano, 12 play only the trumpet, and 8 play both. Use a Venn diagram to help you find the probability that each of the following will occur. Express your answer as both a fraction and a decimal rounded to the nearest thousandth.

36. a student drawn at random plays the trumpet

37. a student drawn at random plays the piano

38. a student drawn at random plays the piano and the trumpet

39. a student drawn at random plays the piano, given that he plays the trumpet

40. Does P(plays the piano and the trumpet) = P(plays the piano, given that he plays the trumpet)? Are these events independent?

CUMULATIVE REVIEW

Divide. [6.3]

41. $\frac{3}{8} \div \frac{6}{8}$

42. $\frac{-8}{15} \div \frac{4}{9}$

43. $7\frac{5}{9} \div 17$

44. $82.4 \div (-0.5)$

45. $0.63 \div 0.2$

Graph each point in the same coordinate plane. [9.1]

46. $B\ (-6, 2)$

47. $C\ (0, -4)$

48. $D\ (9, 7)$

49. $E\ (6, 0)$

50. $F\ (-3, -1)$

Gideon's Big Task

You are probably very familiar with the story of Gideon, especially his use of a fleece as a test for God's will. It is interesting that God does not seem to criticize him for the apparent lack of faith shown by his test with the fleece. Instead, God on four occasions gave Gideon special revelation to calm his fears concerning the seemingly impossible task that he was to undertake. Nevertheless, when God promised to deliver the Midianites into Gideon's hand, Gideon believed that He would do it. Regardless of what God calls you to do, He will help you to succeed if you depend on Him.

God had a very special reason for reducing Gideon's army to a mere 300 soldiers to face an enemy of over 135,000 (Judg. 7:2). You can use your knowledge of probability to find the chances that a man would be part of Gideon's final army, but remember that there are no probabilities with God—He is the blessed controller of all things.

Read Judges 6 through 8 before answering the following questions about Gideon's army.

1. What reason did God give for reducing Gideon's army?

2. Gideon called for soldiers out of four of the northern tribes of Israel. What is the total number that responded before the first reduction in size (Judg. 7:1–3)?

3. How many were left in the army after the "fear" test?

4. How many were left in the army after the "drinking water" test?

5. How many of the Midianites did Gideon pursue with his small army?

6. What is the probability that a soldier would have made it into the second roster of Gideon's army, given that he was among the original roster that volunteered from the four tribes?

7. What is the probability that a soldier would have made it into the final roster of Gideon's army, given that he was a part of the second roster?

8. What is the probability that a soldier would have made it into the final roster of Gideon's army, given that he was a part of the original roster?

9. As you meditate on God's deliverance of Israel from the Midianites, what important principles do you see that relate to how God uses people who trust Him?

Infinite Truths

The lot is cast into the lap; but the whole disposing thereof is of the Lord. *Proverbs 16:33*

Chapter 10 Review

Vocabulary

bar graph	interval frequency table	probability
box-and-whisker diagram	line graph	product column
combination	lower quartile	quartile
correlation	mean	range
data	measures of central tendency	sample
data column	median	sample space
dependent events	middle quartile	scatterplot
event	mode	statistic
experiment	mutually exclusive events	statistics
frequency column	*n* factorial	stem-and-leaf diagram
frequency distribution table	outcome	tree diagram
Fundamental Principle of Counting	parameter	trial
histogram	permutation	upper quartile
independent events	pie chart	
interquartile range	population	

Calculate the following statistics for this set of math scores: 79, 86, 95, 72, 88.

1. mean
2. median
3. mode
4. range

Identify each of the following as most likely a sample or a population.

5. all twelve-year-old boys in Kansas

6. forty-five twelve-year-old boys randomly selected from Kansas

Calculate the following statistics for this set of data: {58, 64, 71, 64, 61, 73, 75, 71, 68}.

7. median
8. lower quartile
9. upper quartile
10. interquartile range

11. Construct a box-and-whisker diagram for the above data.

12. Make a stem-and-leaf diagram for the following set of data. Use the tens digit as the stem and the ones digit as the leaf. Diastolic blood pressure readings: 82, 75, 66, 81, 79, 92, 64, 76, 85, 79, 89, 91.

13. Construct a scatterplot for the following data.

Daily Calorie Intake	Body Mass Index (BMI)	Daily Calorie Intake	Body Mass Index (BMI)	Daily Calorie Intake	Body Mass Index (BMI)
1,800	20	2,200	24	2,400	23
2,400	26	2,600	29	2,400	25
1,850	22	3,000	27	2,850	28
3,400	31	2,700	27	3,200	30
1,850	19	2,500	27	3,350	26
2,740	31	2,500	25	3,200	29
2,860	30	3,400	28	2,100	22

14. Find the range, mean, median, and mode from the following frequency distribution table.

Frequency Distribution Table			
Data (D)	Tally	Frequency (f)	Product (Df)
42	III	3	126
41	IIII	4	164
40	II	2	80
39	IIII	4	156
38	IIII	4	152
37	III	3	111
36	IIII II	7	252
35	III	3	105
Total		30	1,146

15. Make an interval frequency table for the following test scores: {58, 87, 73, 92, 71, 69, 92, 87, 76, 59, 76, 79, 70, 92, 99, 72, 79, 91, 80, 72}. Use grouping intervals of 10.

16. Use the interval frequency table from exercise 15 to find the range, mean, median interval, and modal interval for the data.

17. Construct a histogram for the data in exercise 15.

18. Make a bar graph of the data in the following table.

Percentage of US Population That Is Foreign Born	
Year	Percentage
1900	14
1920	13
1940	9
1960	5
1980	6
2000	10

19. Make a pie chart of the following data about the use of LaMont's weekly budget: tithe, $14; savings, $20; clothing, $50; entertainment, $24; gifts, $25; snacks, $7.

20. Make a line graph of the following data. Use increments of 1,000. Monthly offerings at Calvary Bible Church were as follows: January, $3,680; February, $4,920; March, $2,590; April, $5,640.

21. Julia has six blouses—green, ivory, lavender, pink, blue, and white. She has four skirts—tan, gray, navy, and black. Make a tree diagram of her wardrobe and find the number of different combinations of skirts and blouses she can choose.

22. There are sixteen flavors of ice cream at the parlor. If a triple-decker cone is constructed of three different flavors, determine how many different triple-decker cones are possible if the order of the scoops on the cone is important and if the order of the scoops is not important.

23. How many different two-digit numbers are possible if the first digit must be 1, 3, 5, or 7 and the second digit can be any number 0 through 7?

Evaluate.

24. 5!   25. 7!   26. 0!   27. $_3P_3$

28. $_6P_4$ 29. $_5C_3$ 30. $_7C_3$

31. On a nine-man baseball team, how many different batting orders are possible?

32. Rita has eight dolls that she likes to play with. If she can take only two on vacation, how many different pairs of dolls could she possibly take?

33. Suzanne has seven books on her bookshelf. In how many different orders could she read three of the books?

34. Mr. Dunn sells cars and is designing his new car display. He has twenty-eight cars to choose from and wants to put ten of them close to the road. How many different combinations of cars could he pick for the ten front cars? (Leave the answer in symbol form.)

For one spin, find each of the following probabilities.

35. P(even number)   36. P(number > 2)

37. P(prime number)   38. P(number < 6)

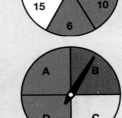

For one spin, find each of the following probabilities. Express your answer as both a fraction and a decimal rounded to the nearest hundredth.

39. P(red or white)   40. P(blue or number < 10)

41. P(odd number or blue)   42. P(red or odd number)

For one spin of each spinner, find each of the following probabilities. Express your answer as both a fraction and a decimal rounded to the nearest thousandth.

43. P(2 and B)

44. P(odd number and consonant)

45. P(number < 4 and vowel)

46. P(prime number and consonant)

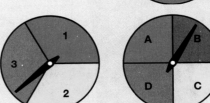

Two names (at right) are drawn at random. The first draw is not replaced. Find each of the following probabilities.

| Amy | Bob | Carol |
| Doug | Ellen |

47. P(Bob and Ellen)   48. P(boy and girl)

49. P(girl and girl)

50. State the mathematical significance of Proverbs 16:33 as related to the story of Gideon.

11 RADICALS

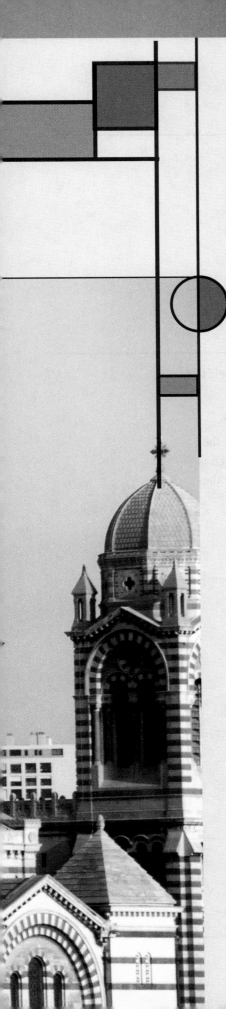

Would you like to be an architect, engineer, or scientist? These three professions depend on a number of mathematical tools for their advancement and effectiveness. Architectural design embodies a great many geometric relationships that give beauty and symmetry to buildings, bridges, and landscapes. Determining the stresses on and the strength of materials needed in these structures requires engineers to use vital mathematics and physics principles. Even before the development of calculus spawned the great industrial revolution, classical Greek and Roman designers and Renaissance architects such as Leon Battista Alberti were developing certain "laws of beauty" to guarantee their structures were pleasing to the eye. Alberti was the key figure who formulated the rules for architecture in fifteenth-century Italy. He observed the geometric beauty in God's creation and made extensive use of geometry and proportion in his work. Many of the great cathedrals of Europe were designed from the principles set down in his text *De Re Aedificatoria*.

Using geometry, proportion, symmetry, and repeated patterns within the principles of design allowed the Renaissance architects to produce some of the most beautiful structures ever built. In modern times the advancement in materials and construction equipment, along with the power of mathematics, allows architects and engineers to produce beautiful buildings and bridges. Tall skyscrapers and cable-supported bridges give testimony to the Creator's image in Adam's race. "So God created man in his own image, in the image of God created he him; male and female created he them" (Gen. 1:27).

After this chapter you should be able to

1. simplify square roots, cube roots, and radical expressions.

2. estimate square roots and cube roots.

3. solve radical equations.

4. solve equations of the form $ax^2 + b = c$.

5. apply the Pythagorean theorem.

6. add and subtract like radicals.

7. multiply and divide radicals.

11.1 ⌐ Square Roots

Recall that squaring a number means multiplying the number by itself. Consider the square of the number 9.

$$9^2 = 9(9) \qquad \text{read as "9 squared"}$$
$$= 81$$

Squaring a number and taking its *square root* are similar to the inverse operations of adding and subtracting.

Definition

The **square root** of x is a number whose product when multiplied by itself is x.

Every positive real number has two square roots, one positive and one negative. Since $9^2 = 9(9) = 81$ and $(-9)^2 = -9(-9) = 81$, the square roots of 81 are 9 and –9.

The notation $\sqrt{x}$ is used to indicate the positive square root, which is also called the *principal root*. $\sqrt{}$ is the *radical sign*, and the number contained in the radical sign is the *radicand*. To indicate a negative square root, place a negative sign in front of the radical sign: $-\sqrt{x}$. To give both square roots, use the notation $\pm\sqrt{x}$.

$\sqrt{81} = 9$ the positive square root

$-\sqrt{81} = -9$ the negative square root (additive inverse of the positive root)

Example 1 Find the following square roots.

a. $\sqrt{25}$ b. $-\sqrt{49}$

Answer

a. $\sqrt{25} = 5$ The positive square root of 25 is 5, since 5(5) = 25.

b. $-\sqrt{49} = -7$ The positive square root of 49 is 7; its opposite is –7.

Square roots of negative numbers do not exist in the real number system. Consider $\sqrt{-16}$. This symbol is asking for the number whose square is –16. No real number squared equals –16.

$$4^2 = 16, \text{ and } (-4)^2 = 16.$$

The only way to get a negative product is to multiply 4 and –4, but these are different numbers. $\sqrt{-16}$ is not a real number.

Skill Check 1

Simplify the following. If no answer exists, state "not real."

1. $\sqrt{25}$ 2. $\sqrt{-4}$ 3. $\sqrt{36}$

4. $-\sqrt{64}$ 5. $-\sqrt{-100}$ 6. $-\sqrt{100}$

An integer that is the square of another integer is a *perfect square*. The perfect squares obtained from squaring 1 to 20 are listed below and should be memorized.

$1^2 = 1$	$5^2 = 25$	$9^2 = 81$	$13^2 = 169$	$17^2 = 289$
$2^2 = 4$	$6^2 = 36$	$10^2 = 100$	$14^2 = 196$	$18^2 = 324$
$3^2 = 9$	$7^2 = 49$	$11^2 = 121$	$15^2 = 225$	$19^2 = 361$
$4^2 = 16$	$8^2 = 64$	$12^2 = 144$	$16^2 = 256$	$20^2 = 400$

If x is a perfect square, then $\sqrt{x}$ is a rational number.

$$\sqrt{16} = 4 = \frac{4}{1} \quad \text{rational}$$

If x is a positive integer, but not a perfect square, then $\sqrt{x}$ is an *irrational number*. For example, $\sqrt{5}$ is irrational. Recall that an irrational number is a nonterminating, nonrepeating decimal. A calculator will give the decimal equivalent for $\sqrt{5}$ to several decimal places (such as 2.236067977), but this is a rounded approximation. There is no exact decimal expression for $\sqrt{5}$.

A generous estimate!

The ability to estimate square roots without a calculator is a valuable mathematical tool. When x is not a perfect square, you can estimate $\sqrt{x}$ by finding the two perfect squares between which x lies. Then you can take the square roots of those perfect squares to find the integers that the square root lies between.

Example 2 Between what consecutive positive integers does $\sqrt{32}$ lie?

Answer

$25 < 32 < 36$ 1. 32 lies between the perfect squares 25 and 36.
$\sqrt{25} < \sqrt{32} < \sqrt{36}$ 2. Take the square root of all three numbers.
$5 < \sqrt{32} < 6$ 3. Change the perfect squares to their integer form.

$\sqrt{32}$ is greater than 5 but less than 6.

Skill Check 2

Find the consecutive integers between which the following square roots lie.

1. $\sqrt{69}$ 2. $\sqrt{130}$

3. $-\sqrt{18}$ 4. $-\sqrt{95}$

A guess and check method can be used to approximate irrational roots to the nearest tenth. To approximate $\sqrt{19}$, begin by determining the two integers between which the root lies.

$$16 < 19 < 25$$
$$\sqrt{16} < \sqrt{19} < \sqrt{25}$$
$$4 < \sqrt{19} < 5$$

Then estimate the root to the nearest tenth and compare the square of the estimate to the radicand.

Since 19 is closer to 16 than 25, estimate $\sqrt{19} \approx 4.2$.

$4.2^2 = 17.64$, which is 1.36 less than 19.

Adjust the estimate.

Estimate $\sqrt{19} \approx 4.3$.

$4.3^2 = 18.49$, which is still 0.51 less than 19.

Estimate $\sqrt{19} \approx 4.4$.

$4.4^2 = 19.36$, which is 0.36 greater than 19.

Therefore, $4.3 < \sqrt{19} < 4.4$ and $\sqrt{19} \approx 4.4$.

Example 3 Estimate $\sqrt{47}$ to the nearest tenth.

Answer

$36 < 47 < 49$ 1. Determine the two integers between which the root lies.

$\sqrt{36} < \sqrt{47} < \sqrt{49}$

$6 < \sqrt{47} < 7$

$6.9^2 = 47.61$; 2. Since 47 is closer to 49, estimate $\sqrt{47} \approx 6.9$ and compare 6.9^2 to 47.

0.61 greater than 47

$6.8^2 = 46.24$; 3. Lower the estimate to 6.8 and compare 6.8^2 to 47.

0.76 less than 47

$\sqrt{47} \approx 6.9$ 4. 6.9^2 is closer to 47 than 6.8^2.

Skill Check 3

Estimate the following square roots to the nearest tenth.

1. $\sqrt{7}$ 2. $\sqrt{23}$ 3. $-\sqrt{11}$

When working with radicals, you will often need to perform arithmetic operations on expressions with two radicals or on the radicand itself.

To add $\sqrt{16} + \sqrt{9}$, take the individual roots before adding.

$$\sqrt{16} + \sqrt{9} = 4 + 3 = 7$$

To simplify $\sqrt{16+9}$, add the two numbers first and then take the root. The order is essential because the radical symbol is a grouping symbol. Remember that, by the order of operations, you always do what is within grouping symbols first.

$$\sqrt{16+9} = \sqrt{25} = 5$$

Therefore, $\sqrt{16} + \sqrt{9} \neq \sqrt{16+9}$.

Example 4 Simplify the following.

a. $\sqrt{64} + \sqrt{25}$ b. $\sqrt{72 - 23}$

Answer

a. $\sqrt{64} + \sqrt{25} = 8 + 5$ 1. Take the individual square roots.

$= 13$ 2. Add.

b. $\sqrt{72 - 23} = \sqrt{49}$ 1. Subtract.

$= 7$ 2. Take the square root.

Review the order of operations as given in Section 1.7. Since taking square roots is similar to an inverse operation of squaring, radicals are performed in step 2 of the order of operations along with exponents.

Order of Operations
1. Symbols of grouping—evaluate quantities within symbols of grouping first.
2. Exponents and radicals—evaluate a term with an exponent or square root before performing other operations.
3. Multiplication and division—perform these operations in order from left to right.
4. Addition and subtraction—perform these operations last, in order from left to right.

Just as 3 times x is written as $3x$ with no operational sign, the product of 3 and $\sqrt{5}$ is written as $3\sqrt{5}$ with no operational sign. Likewise, $\sqrt{3}\sqrt{5}$ means $\sqrt{3}$ times $\sqrt{5}$.

Example 5 Simplify $-4\sqrt{116-35}$.

Answer

$$-4\sqrt{116-35} = -4\sqrt{81}$$ 1. Simplify under the radical sign.

$$= -4(9)$$ 2. Take the square root.

$$= -36$$ 3. Multiply.

Skill Check 4

Simplify the following.

1. $\sqrt{64} - \sqrt{25}$ 2. $\dfrac{\sqrt{9 \times 16}}{\sqrt{81-45}}$ 3. $\dfrac{-\sqrt{144}}{2\left(\sqrt{25}-\sqrt{9}\right)}$ 4. $3\sqrt{120+24}$

■ A. Exercises

Simplify the following. If no answer exists, state "not real."

1. $\sqrt{121}$ 2. $\sqrt{400}$ 3. $-\sqrt{144}$ 4. $\sqrt{-81}$

5. $-\sqrt{225}$ 6. $\sqrt{256}$ 7. $\sqrt{-1}$ 8. $-\sqrt{-196}$

Find the consecutive integers between which the following square roots lie.

9. $\sqrt{10}$ 10. $\sqrt{17}$ 11. $\sqrt{125}$ 12. $\sqrt{141}$ 13. $\sqrt{270}$ 14. $\sqrt{92}$

■ B. Exercises

Estimate the following square roots to the nearest tenth.

15. $\sqrt{13}$ 16. $\sqrt{53}$ 17. $\sqrt{89}$ 18. $\sqrt{94}$ 19. $\sqrt{143}$ 20. $\sqrt{279}$

Simplify the following.

21. $\sqrt{16+33}$ 22. $\sqrt{240-176}$ 23. $\sqrt{9(25)}$ 24. $\sqrt{6(24)}$

25. $3\sqrt{120+49} - \sqrt{36}$ 26. $\sqrt{400} - 2\sqrt{324}$ 27. $5\sqrt{98 \div 2} + 4\sqrt{25}$ 28. $\sqrt{81} - 2\sqrt{36}$

29. $\dfrac{4\sqrt{169}}{\sqrt{144}}$ 30. $\sqrt{81}\sqrt{9}$ 31. $3\left(\sqrt{81} - \sqrt{36}\right)$ 32. $\dfrac{4}{\sqrt{36}}$

33. $2\sqrt{196}$ 34. $\dfrac{\sqrt{64}}{\sqrt{4}}$ 35. $\dfrac{2\sqrt{9}}{\sqrt{25}}$ 36. $\dfrac{2\sqrt{169}}{\sqrt{81}}$

■ C. Exercises

37. Simplify $\dfrac{\sqrt{729 \times 4}}{\sqrt{81} - \sqrt{4}}$.

38. Find the value of $\sqrt{9 + 16}$. Find the value of $\sqrt{9} + \sqrt{16}$. Are they equal? Write a generalization of this principle in symbol form.

39. Estimate $\sqrt{517}$ to the nearest tenth.

40. Estimate $\sqrt{67}$ to the nearest hundredth.

■ Dominion thru Math

One goal of an architect is to design a structure that is pleasing to the eye. A common shape seen in God's creation and copied in many buildings and paintings is the length-by-width ratio called the golden ratio. The golden ratio is symbolized by the Greek letter φ (phi) and is equal to $\frac{1}{2}\left(1 + \sqrt{5}\right)$. The decimal approximation of the golden ratio can be found on your calculator and then stored in memory.

Use a calculator to solve the following problems.

41. An architect wants the width-to-height ratio of the rectangular front of a building to have the same proportion as the golden ratio. If the building will be 50 ft. wide (the long dimension), how high will it be?

42. The building will have windows and doors based on the golden ratio, but their long dimension will be vertical (height-to-width ratio). If the entryway for the building in exercise 41 will be 8 ft. wide, how high will it be?

43. There are three stories of rectangular windows for the building, and each window will be 5 ft. wide. If the width of the windows is the short dimension and the golden ratio is used, how high will the windows be?

CUMULATIVE REVIEW

Solve. [8.2]

44. $12y - 29 = 8y + 23$

45. $56 - 3x = 2(x - 12)$

Solve. Answers may be left as improper fractions. [6.6]

46. $x + \dfrac{6}{11} = \dfrac{8}{11}$

47. $x - \dfrac{4}{7} = \dfrac{3}{5}$

48. $-8\dfrac{5}{8}x = \dfrac{7}{24}$

Find the slope and y-intercept of the following lines. [9.6]

49. $-16x + 8y = 24$

50. $8x + 2y = 15$

51. $5y = -4x$

Graph the solutions to the following inequalities. [9.8]

52. $y \le -\dfrac{3}{2}x + 1$

53. $y > 3x - 4$

PROBLEM SOLVING

Work Backwards

You can solve some problems by working backwards from a given result. The problem-solving strategy "work backwards" enables you to solve the problem by using inverse operations in reverse order.

Sometimes the next step is to back up.

Example The manager of an appliance store multiplied the cost of a kitchen range by 1.3 to get the selling price, added $35.69 for sales tax, and then added $40 for delivery and installation. The resultant selling price to the customer was $789.39. What was the dealer's cost?

Answer

Think: What are we supposed to find in this problem, and what information do we know?

We are to find the dealer's cost. We know the final cost and a series of steps that the dealer used to determine the final cost.

Think: A diagram might help show the steps that were used to determine the total cost to the buyer.

The diagram illustrates the order of the operations as stated in the problem.

Think: The total cost to the buyer is known after the series of calculations. If we take the total cost to the buyer and "undo" the calculations in reverse order, then the cost to the dealer will be the result.

| Cost of range | → | × 1.3 | → | + 35.69 | → | + 40 | → | 789.39 |

Work backwards using inverse operations to solve the problem.

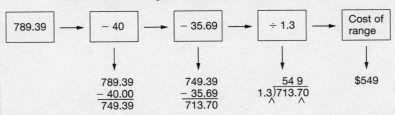

The diagram illustrates the working backward process. The inverse operations are used in reverse order.

Think: Does the answer of $549 seem to be a reasonable answer for this problem? Using $549, check the forward series of calculations and see if the final result is the total cost to the buyer.

549(1.3) = 713.70   Multiply by 1.3.

713.70 + 35.69 = 749.39   Add sales tax.

749.39 + 40 = 789.39   Add the delivery fee.

The answer of $549 is correct.

■ Exercises

For exercises 1–5 draw a diagram similar to the one in the example. Then draw a second diagram of the steps for working backwards to find the answer. Carry out the plan to find the answer to the question.

1. The manager of an electronics store multiplied the cost of a new TV by 1.5 to get his selling price. He then deducted $50 for a minor scratch, added $41.25 sales tax, and added $49.99 for an extended service plan. The resulting cost to the consumer was $1,278.74. What was the merchant's cost for the TV?

2. From 1970 to 1980 a city's population increased by 1,450. From 1980 to 1990 its population doubled. From 1990 to 2000 its population decreased by 798 to a population of 16,468. What was the population in 1970?

3. Two less than one-fourth of the soccer team came down with a virus before the big game and were unable to play. If 3 players were unable to play, how many players are on the team?

4. Shanda climbed a set of stairs and stopped on the middle step. She then walked down 8 steps, up 6 steps, and down 10 steps. She was at the bottom of the stairs again. How many steps are in the set of stairs?

5. Start with the variable x and perform the following operations on it in the order given. Subtract 9; multiply by 4; add 8; and divide by 12. What would the value of x be if the result is is 2?

The method is left up to you as to how to calculate the answers to exercises 6–8.

6. Uncle Larry left half of his estate to be split three ways between you and your two brothers. After this division, half of what was left went to the college he graduated from, and the remaining $100,000 was left to his church. What was the total value of his estate? How much did you and each of your two brothers get?

7. Lincoln Middle School is planning an old-fashioned carnival. The students have to budget their purchases wisely. They decide to spend a third of their budgeted allowance on prizes, a fourth on costumes, and two-fifths on booth construction. If they have $5 of petty cash left after their purchases, what was the budget allotted to them?

8. James spent his birthday money at four different places. He spent half of his money on CDs, a fourth of what was left playing paintball, a third of what was left after paintball at the video store, and a sixth of the rest on candy. If he had $10 left from his birthday money, what was the total amount that he got for his birthday?

11.2 ᴛ Radical Equations

A *radical equation* is an equation that contains a variable in a radicand. $\sqrt{x} = 5$ is a radical equation. To solve for x, the radical must be eliminated from the equation.

Remember that addition and subtraction are inverse operations. Therefore, to undo the addition of 5 in the equation $x + 5 = 8$, you must subtract 5. You subtract 5 from both sides of the equation to keep it equivalent.

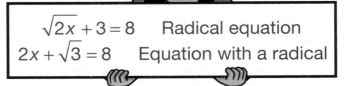

$$\sqrt{2x} + 3 = 8 \quad \text{Radical equation}$$
$$2x + \sqrt{3} = 8 \quad \text{Equation with a radical}$$

$$x + 5 = 8$$
$$x + 5 - 5 = 8 - 5$$
$$x = 3$$

Squaring a quantity and taking the square root are similar to inverse operations.

$$6^2 = 36, \text{ and } \sqrt{36} = 6.$$
$$9^2 = 81, \text{ and } \sqrt{81} = 9.$$

If the radicand is positive, you can "undo" square roots by squaring the radical term. (Recall that square roots of a negative quantity are not real numbers.)

$$\left(\sqrt{x}\right)^2 = x$$

$$\left(\sqrt{x+3}\right)^2 = x + 3$$

When solving a radical equation, you must square both sides of the equation to keep them equal.

Sometimes the answer produced by this process is not a solution of the radical equation. When substituted into the original equation, it does not make the statement true. Checking the solution is necessary when solving radical equations.

Example 1   Solve $\sqrt{x} = 5$.

Answer

$\sqrt{x} = 5$

$\left(\sqrt{x}\right)^2 = 5^2$ 1. Square both sides of the equation.

$x = 25$

$\sqrt{x} = 5$ 2. Write the original equation.

$\sqrt{25} = 5$ 3. Substitute 25 in the original equation to check the answer.

Example 2   Solve and check $\sqrt{x} = -8$.

Answer

$\sqrt{x} = -8$

$\left(\sqrt{x}\right)^2 = (-8)^2$ 1. Square both sides of the equation.

$x = 64$

$\sqrt{x} = -8$ 2. Check the answer in the original equation.

$\sqrt{64} = -8$ 3. The square root symbol indicates the principal square root, which is

$8 = -8$: false   always positive. Therefore, 64 is not a solution to this equation.

There is no number that makes this equation true.

Skill Check 1

Solve and check the following equations. If no answer exists, state "no real solution."

1. $\sqrt{x} = 7$ 2. $\sqrt{x} = 50$

3. $\sqrt{x} = -4$ 4. $\sqrt{x} = 12$

Some radical equations require manipulation before squaring both sides. The radical must first be isolated on one side of the equation. Here are the general steps to solve any radical equation.

Solving Radical Equations
1. Isolate the radical on one side of the equation.
2. Square both sides of the equation.
3. Solve the resulting equation, if necessary.
4. Check the solution.

If step 1 is necessary, it will require adding, subtracting, multiplying, or dividing both sides of the equation by a constant term. Examples 3–5 demonstrate this step.

Example 3   Solve and check $\sqrt{3x} + 2 = 8$.

Answer

$\sqrt{3x} + 2 = 8$

$\sqrt{3x} + 2 - 2 = 8 - 2$ 1. Subtract 2 from both sides of the equation to isolate the radical.

$\sqrt{3x} = 6$

$\left(\sqrt{3x}\right)^2 = 6^2$ 2. Square both sides to remove the radical sign.

$3x = 36$

$\dfrac{3x}{3} = \dfrac{36}{3}$ 3. Divide both sides by 3.

$x = 12$

$\sqrt{3(12)} + 2 = 8$ 4. Check the answer 12 in the original equation.

$\sqrt{36} + 2 = 8$

$6 + 2 = 8$

$8 = 8$ 5. Since 12 makes the original equation true, it is a solution.

Example 4 Solve and check $\sqrt{10+x}+6=7$.

Answer

$\sqrt{10+x}+6=7$

$\sqrt{10+x}+6-6=7-6$ 1. Isolate the radical on one side by subtracting 7 from both sides of the equation.

$\sqrt{10+x}=1$

$\left(\sqrt{10+x}\right)^2=1^2$ 2. Square both sides of the equation to eliminate the square root.

$10+x=1$

$10+x-10=1-10$ 3. Subtract 10 from both sides of the equation.

$x=-9$

$\sqrt{10+(-9)}+6=7$ 4. Check the answer -9 in the original equation.

$\sqrt{1}+6=7$

$1+6=7$

$7=7$ 5. Since -9 makes the original equation true, it is a solution.

Example 5 Solve $-4\sqrt{x}=28$.

Answer

$-4\sqrt{x}=28$

$\dfrac{-4\sqrt{x}}{-4}=\dfrac{28}{-4}$ 1. Isolate the radical on one side by dividing both sides of the equation by -4.

$\sqrt{x}=-7$ 2. This indicates that the principle, or positive, square root is to be a negative number, which is not possible.

The equation has no real solution.

Skill Check 2

Solve and check the following equations. If no answer exists, state "no real solution."

1. $\sqrt{3x}+18=27$

2. $\sqrt{x}+4=1$

3. $\sqrt{2x}-5=-3$

4. $\sqrt{68+x}=8$

5. $9\sqrt{x+1}=-108$

6. $4\sqrt{2x+1}=24$

Just as there can be false solutions to radical equations, so there are so-called Christians and preachers who are not true followers of Christ. Jesus speaks of them in Matthew 7:15–16: "Beware of false prophets, which come to you in sheep's clothing, but inwardly they are ravening wolves. Ye shall know them by their fruits." To determine whether a person is a true Christian, one must look at the results of his life (fruit) to see if it is what the life of a person living for Christ should produce.

■ A. Exercises

Solve and check the following equations. If no answer exists, state "no real solution."

1. $\sqrt{x}=4$

2. $\sqrt{x}=20$

3. $\sqrt{x}=15$

4. $\sqrt{x}=2.5$

5. $2\sqrt{x}=36$

6. $\sqrt{x}+16=13$

7. $-3\sqrt{x}=-18$

8. $8\sqrt{x}=40$

9. $\sqrt{x}-7=-3$

10. $5\sqrt{x}=-30$

■ B. Exercises

Solve and check the following equations. If no answer exists, state "no real solution."

11. $3 + \sqrt{x} = 19$

12. $\sqrt{x} + 17 = 12$

13. $5\sqrt{x-2} = -15$

14. $\sqrt{4x} - 2 = 20$

15. $\sqrt{3x} = 30$

16. $\sqrt{2x} - 14 = 17$

17. $3\sqrt{x} + 7 = 43$

18. $\sqrt{x+8} = 2$

19. $2\sqrt{3x} - 4 = 0$

20. $5\sqrt{2x+1} - 3 = 22$

21. $\sqrt{x+2} - 8 = 12$

22. $\sqrt{5x-4} + 3 = 8$

23. $4\sqrt{x-8} + 9 = 2$

24. $\sqrt{6x+1} + 4 = 19$

25. $\sqrt{10-3x} = 8$

Solve and check the following equations. If no answer exists, state "no real solution."

26. $-7 + \sqrt{5-x} = 18$

27. $12\sqrt{2x-3} = 96$

28. $-2\sqrt{x+7} = 16$

29. $\dfrac{\sqrt{3x}}{4} = -6$

30. $\sqrt{x+5} = \sqrt{2x-3}$

■ C. Exercises

Write an equation and solve.

31. The square root of a number, decreased by 2, is 4. Find the number.

32. The square root of the result of decreasing a number by 2 is 4. Find the number.

33. Seven more than the square root of a number is 12. Find the number.

34. The square root of 7 more than a number is 12. Find the number.

35. Explain one way to determine that there will be no real solution to a radical equation before completely solving it and checking the solution.

■ Dominion thru Math

A great number of practical formulas have been developed by engineers and physicists to provide answers to design questions. Some of these formulas came into use by applying calculus and physics principles to physical problems, while others result from the properties of a structure or system. Still other formulas emerge from extensive testing and experimentation and are called empirical formulas. Several formulas are given in the exercises below.

Use a calculator and the given formulas to solve the problems.

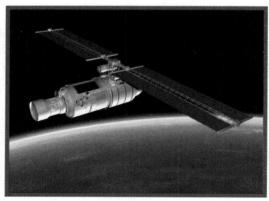

Another type of projectile is an orbiting satellite.

36. A projectile shot vertically into the air will go only so high before it stops and falls back to the earth. Ignoring air resistance, the height attained above the point of release is a function of time, gravity, and the initial velocity. The function is given by the following formula: $h = -16t^2 + v_0 t$, where v_0 is the initial velocity in feet per second, h is the height in feet, and t is the time in seconds. How high will an arrow shot vertically with an initial velocity of 270 ft./sec. rise during the first 5 sec. of flight?

37. Sketch a graph of the function by plotting the heights for the first 10 sec. Use the graph to determine the approximate time when the arrow reaches maximum height, and find that approximate height.

38. How far does the arrow travel before returning to its point of release, and how much time does the shooter have to get out of the way?

Find the markup and retail price for the following items. [7.5]

39. cost: $450; markup rate: 16%

40. cost: $12,900; markup rate: 23%

41. cost: $4.59; markup rate: 40%

42. cost: $890; markup rate: 31%

43. cost: $24.50; markup rate: 35%

54 54,59,63,63,68,71,72

Calculate the following statistics for this set of data: {54, 63, 59, 72, 68, 54, 63, 71}. [10.1]

44. range
45. mean
46. median
47. mode

Find the value of x so that the mean of the list of numbers will be equal to the given number. [10.1]

48. 92, 84, x; mean: 84

MIND OVER MATH

Trace the diagram of the miniature golf course hole on your paper and determine the exact point where Joel should hit the side to get a hole-in-one and avoid the obstacle. (Hint: The ball bounces off the wall at the same angle that it strikes the wall.)

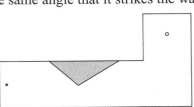

11.3 Equations with Exponents

To solve an equation that contains a squared variable, such as $x^2 = 100$, you must take the square root of both sides of the equation. This will "undo" the operation of squaring. Since you do not know whether the quantity being squared is positive or negative, you must take both roots—they are both solutions to the equation. The symbol ±, read "plus or minus," is used to show both roots. (The alternative would be to write x or $-x$.)

$$\sqrt{x^2} = \pm x$$

Be accurate. Measure twice; cut once.

Example 1   Solve $x^2 = 16$.

Answer

$x^2 = 16$

$\sqrt{x^2} = \pm\sqrt{16}$ 1. Take the square root of both sides of the equation. Both square roots are solutions.

$x = \pm 4$ 2. Simplify the result.

Solving Equations of the Form $x^2 = a$

If $x^2 = a$ and $a > 0$, then $x = \pm\sqrt{a}$.

Example 2   Solve $x^2 = 49$.

Answer

$x^2 = 49$

$\sqrt{x^2} = \pm\sqrt{49}$ 1. Take the square root of both sides of the equation. Include the positive and negative root.

$x = \pm 7$ 2. Simplify the result.

Example 3   Solve $x^2 - 4 = -3$.

Answer

$x^2 - 4 = -3$

$x^2 - 4 + 4 = -3 + 4$ 1. Add 4 to both sides of the equation.

$x^2 = 1$

$\sqrt{x^2} = \pm\sqrt{1}$ 2. Take the square root of both sides. Include both roots.

$x = \pm 1$ 3. Simplify the result.

Skill Check 1

Solve.

1. $x^2 = 81$ 2. $x^2 + 6 = 42$

3. $x^2 - 3 = 22$ 4. $15 = x^2 + 6$

If the solution is the square root of a number that is not a perfect square, leave the answer in radical form.

Example 4   Solve $3x^2 - 12 = 18$.

Answer

$3x^2 - 12 = 18$

$3x^2 - 12 + 12 = 18 + 12$ 1. Isolate the squared term.

$3x^2 = 30$

$\dfrac{3x^2}{3} = \dfrac{30}{3}$

$x^2 = 10$

$\sqrt{x^2} = \pm\sqrt{10}$ 2. Take the square root of both sides.

$x = \pm\sqrt{10}$ 3. Because 10 is not a perfect square, leave the answer in radical form.

If the solution is the square root of a negative number, there is no real number solution to the equation.

Example 5 Solve $x^2 + 21 = 12$.

Answer

$x^2 + 21 = 12$
$x^2 + 21 - 21 = 12 - 21$ 1. Isolate the squared term.
$x^2 = -9$
$\sqrt{x^2} = \pm\sqrt{-9}$ 2. Take the square root of both sides.
no real solution 3. There is no real square root of a negative number.

Skill Check 2

Solve. If no answer exists, state "no real solution."

1. $x^2 - 14 = 29$ 2. $6x^2 + 41 = 17$

3. $5x^2 - 17 = 28$ 4. $7x^2 + 3 = 80$

■ A. Exercises

Solve. If no answer exists, state "no real solution."

1. $x^2 = 144$ 2. $x^2 = 169$ 3. $x^2 = -49$ 4. $x^2 - 31 = 90$

5. $x^2 + 29 = 93$ 6. $x^2 + 107 = -37$ 7. $x^2 - 19 = 81$ 8. $x^2 - 91 = 105$

■ B. Exercises

Solve. Leave answers in radical form if the radicand is not a perfect square. If no answer exists, state "no real solution."

9. $x^2 = 66$ 10. $x^2 = 37$ 11. $-7x^2 = 28$ 12. $6x^2 = 96$

13. $3x^2 = 33$ 14. $-5x^2 = 30$ 15. $x^2 + 9 = 22$ 16. $2x^2 - 12 = 18$

17. $3x^2 - 10 = 29$ 18. $x^2 - 24 = 35$ 19. $x^2 + 61 = 39$ 20. $x^2 - 41 = 20$

21. $x^2 - 12 = 23$ 22. $3x^2 - 31 = 17$ 23. $2x^2 - 5 = 67$ 24. $3x^2 + 32 = -4$

25. $2.4x^2 + 1 = 25$ 26. $x^2 - 3.4 = 7.5$ 27. $4x^2 - 19 = -7$ 28. $\dfrac{x^2}{5} = 30$

29. $\dfrac{x^2}{4} + 1 = 10$ 30. $\dfrac{x^2}{12} - 8 = 4$

■ C. Exercises

Solve.

31. $(x + 4)^2 = 16$ 32. $(2x - 5)^2 = 49$ 33. $(6x - 7)^2 = 4$

34. $\dfrac{2x^2}{5} - 8 = 12$ 35. $\dfrac{2x^2}{3} = 40$

■ Dominion thru Math

36. The depth of an open well can be determined by dropping an object and recording the time between release and when the splash is heard. The depth of the well in feet (s) and the time when one hears the splash in seconds (T) are related by the following formula: $T = \dfrac{\sqrt{s}}{4} + \dfrac{s}{1{,}100}$. How long will it take to hear the splash for a 64 ft. deep well?

37. How deep is a well if it takes 5.15 sec. to hear the splash? Use your answer to exercise 36 to estimate the answer, and then use your calculator and the guess and check problem-solving method to find the answer.

38. The speed of an automobile can be determined by the length of the skid marks when the brakes are applied hard enough to lock up the wheels. The empirical formula for the velocity (speed) is $v(x) = 7.08\sqrt{x}$, where x is the length of the skid marks in feet, and $4 < x < 144$. How fast was a car going if the lockup skid marks are 100 ft.?

39. A empirical formula related to the one in the previous exercise gives the feet (N) needed to stop a car going v mi./hr. $N(v) = -0.015v^2 + 3v$, where $0 < v < 90$. How many feet will it take a car to stop if it is going 70 mi./hr.?

40. Compare the results from exercises 38 and 39. First determine the distance traveled while the driver reacts (before the skid marks begin). Then find the number of feet per second a car is moving at 70 mi./hr. Finally, use the results to convert the reaction distance to a reaction time.

▬ CUMULATIVE REVIEW ▬

Write an equation and solve. [6.7]

41. After cutting $1\dfrac{7}{8}$ yd. off the end of a piece of fabric, Molly had the exact length that she needed for the pattern she was making: $4\dfrac{2}{3}$ yd. What was the length of the original piece of fabric?

42. Jeremy spent $3\dfrac{3}{4}$ hr. working in the yard. He spent $\dfrac{3}{4}$ of that time mowing and the rest of the time trimming shrubs. How much time did he spend trimming shrubs?

43. Eva worked at the ice cream parlor for the same number of hours on Monday and Tuesday evening. If she worked $6\dfrac{1}{2}$ hr. on Wednesday and a total of 20 hr. that week, how many hours did she work on Monday and Tuesday?

44. A bag of oranges costs a third as much as a bag of apples. If the two bags together cost $7.56, how much does each bag of fruit cost?

45. Mrs. Swingle buys extra school supplies for the students in her class. At the beginning of the year she bought pens, pencils, and erasers. She bought half as many pens as pencils and one-fourth as many erasers as pencils. If she bought 98 items altogether, how many of each did she buy?

A caterer offers the following options on his menu: six entrees, eighteen side dishes, four beverages, and six desserts. Use a calculator for large computations. [10.5–10.7]

46. How many different meals could be made of an entree, a side dish, a beverage, and a dessert?

47. How many different meals could be made of an entree, a side dish, and a beverage?

48. How many different ways are there to choose three of the six entrees?

49. How many different ways are there to choose four of the eighteen side dishes?

50. How many different banquet buffet menus are possible if the buffet includes three entrees, four side dishes, two beverages, and one dessert?

11.4 The Pythagorean Theorem

The longest side of any triangle is always opposite the largest angle. Therefore, in any right triangle, the side opposite the right angle is the longest side. It is called the *hypotenuse*. The other two sides are called the *legs*. A unique relationship exists between the lengths of the sides of a right triangle. This relationship is known as the Pythagorean theorem, even though it was known and used long before this famous Greek mathematician's time.

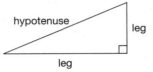

Building a house requires use of the Pythagorean theorem.

In the figure to the right, observe that the area of the square constructed on the hypotenuse is equal to the sum of the areas of the two squares constructed on the legs.

$$4^2 + 3^2 = 5^2$$

$$16 + 9 = 25$$

The Pythagorean theorem generalizes the relationship between the hypotenuse and the legs of a right triangle.

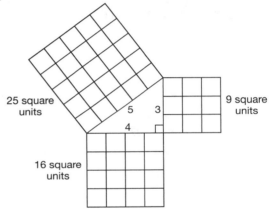

The Pythagorean Theorem	
If the hypotenuse of a right triangle has length c, and the legs have lengths a and b, then $a^2 + b^2 = c^2$.	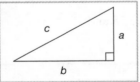

Example 1   Find the hypotenuse of a right triangle with legs of 8 and 15.

Answer

$c^2 = a^2 + b^2$

$c^2 = 8^2 + 15^2$ 1. Substitute the given values into the formula.

$c^2 = 64 + 225$

$c^2 = 289$

$\sqrt{c^2} = \sqrt{289}$ 2. Find the positive square root of both sides of the equation.

$c = 17$

Notice in Example 1 that only the positive root was taken (rather than both roots). This is because of the context. The variable c represents the length of the side of a triangle, which is always a positive distance.

Example 2 Find the hypotenuse of a right triangle with legs of 6 and 7.

Answer

$c^2 = a^2 + b^2$

$c^2 = 6^2 + 7^2$ 1. Substitute the given values into the formula.

$c^2 = 36 + 49$

$c^2 = 85$

$\sqrt{c^2} = \sqrt{85}$ 2. Find the square root of both sides.

$c = \sqrt{85} \approx 9.2$ 3. Since the radicand is not a perfect square, you can leave the radical answer or approximate the square root.

Skill Check 1

Given the lengths of the legs, find the hypotenuse.

1. 5 and 12   2. 10 and 24   3. 7 and 10

Example 3 Find the length of a leg of a right triangle whose hypotenuse is 16 and whose other leg is 7.

Answer

$a^2 + b^2 = c^2$

$a^2 + 7^2 = 16^2$ 1. Substitute the given values into the formula.

$a^2 + 49 = 256$ 2. Eliminate the exponents by squaring 16 and 7.

$a^2 + 49 - 49 = 256 - 49$ 3. Subtract 49 from both sides.

$a^2 = 207$

$a = \sqrt{207} \approx 14.4$ 4. Find the square root of both sides, recalling that lengths are always positive.

Skill Check 2

Given the hypotenuse and one leg, find the missing leg.

1. 25 and 20   2. 7 and 5   3. 61 and 60

The Pythagorean theorem says that if a triangle is a right triangle, then $a^2 + b^2 = c^2$, where a and b are legs of the right triangle and c is the hypotenuse. Reversing the "if" part and the "then" part of a theorem gives the *converse* of the theorem. The converse of a theorem may or may not be true. In the case of the Pythagorean theorem, it is true. The converse of the Pythagorean theorem is stated below.

Converse of the Pythagorean Theorem
If a triangle has sides a, b, and c, such that $a^2 + b^2 = c^2$, then the triangle is a right triangle.

If you verify that $a^2 + b^2 = c^2$ for the lengths of the sides of a triangle, then it is a right triangle. If $a^2 + b^2 \neq c^2$, the triangle is not a right triangle.

Example 4   Determine whether a triangle with sides of 12, 35, and 37 is a right triangle.

Answer

$a^2 + b^2 = c^2$

$12^2 + 35^2 = 37^2$ 1. Substitute the two shorter sides for the legs and the longest side for the hypotenuse.

$144 + 1{,}225 = 1{,}369$ 2. Simplify each side of the equation.

$1{,}369 = 1{,}369$ 3. Since $a^2 + b^2 = c^2$, the triangle is a right triangle.

Example 5   Determine whether a triangle with sides of 8, 12, and 14 is a right triangle.

Answer

$a^2 + b^2 = c^2$

$8^2 + 12^2 = 14^2$ 1. Substitute the two shorter sides for the legs and the longest side for the hypotenuse.

$64 + 144 = 196$ 2. Simplify each side of the equation.

$208 \neq 196$ 3. The equation is not true, so the triangle is not a right triangle.

Skill Check 3

Given the three side lengths, determine whether the following triangles are right triangles.

1. 15, 36, and 39   2. 10, 20, and 22   3. 14, 48, and 50

■ A. Exercises

Given the lengths of the legs, find the hypotenuse of the following right triangles. Round answers to the nearest tenth.

1. 12 and 16   2. 20 and 48   3. 4 and 5   4. 6 and 9

5. 10 and 10   6. 20 and 21   7. 10 and 24   8. 7 and 11

■ B. Exercises

Given the hypotenuse and one leg, find the missing leg. Round answers to the nearest tenth.

9. 30 and 24   10. 52 and 20   11. 10 and 8   12. 7 and 4

13. 9 and 5   14. 8 and 2   15. 74 and 24   16. 25 and 7

Given the three side lengths, determine whether the following triangles are right triangles.

17. 12, 16, and 19   18. 8, 15, and 17   19. 20, 48, and 51   20. 9, 40, and 41

21. 14, 48, and 50   22. 20, 99, and 101   23. 50, 120, and 130   24. 28, 45, and 52

■ C. Exercises

For each of the following exercises, draw a sketch of the situation and then write and solve an equation. Round answers to the nearest tenth.

25. A 16 ft. ladder leans against the side of a building. If the base of the ladder is 4 ft. from the base of the building, how high up on the side of the building will the ladder reach?

26. A 200 ft. tower is braced to the ground by a cable, from a point 150 ft. above the ground to a point 87 ft. from the base of the tower. How long is the cable?

27. The distance between bases on a baseball diamond is 90 ft. How far is it from home plate to second base?

28. An opening for a window is 23" wide, 54" tall, and 60" diagonally. Is the opening "square"; that is, do the height and width form a right angle?

■ Dominion thru Math

29. The design of some rectangular decorative panels requires that they have diagonals that are $18\frac{7}{8}$ ft. with an aspect ratio of 8 : 5. (The aspect ratio is the horizontal : vertical ratio.) What should the dimensions of the panels be?

30. The foundation of one rectangular part of a house measures 32 ft. × 56 ft. What length must the diagonal measure in order for the foundation to be square?

31. A round top window is actually a rectangle with a semicircle on top. What is the overall height of a round top window that is 36 in. wide with straight vertical sides measuring 6 ft. 2 in.?

CUMULATIVE REVIEW

The following is a list of runs scored by baseball teams on a given day: {5, 4, 8, 3, 16, 0, 6, 2, 6, 0, 13, 2, 5, 4, 9, 1, 3, 1, 7, 6}. [10.1–10.2]

32. Find the lower quartile, median, and upper quartile for the data.

33. Construct a box-and-whisker diagram for the data.

34. Find the mean and the mode of the data.

35. Find the range and the interquartile range of the data.

Find the number of ways the following can be done. [10.5–10.7]

36. travel from Chicago to New York with a layover in Cincinnati, if there are three flights to Cincinnati that will all connect with five flights to New York

37. select an outfit if there are five skirts, seven blouses, and three pairs of shoes available

38. fill the offices of president, vice president, secretary, and treasurer of a class of twenty-four students

39. select a committee of four students from a class of twenty-four students

40. choose six girls who will start for the volleyball team if there are twelve players on the team

41. choose the serving order for the six starters of the volleyball team

Nathaniel Bowditch, Marine Navigator

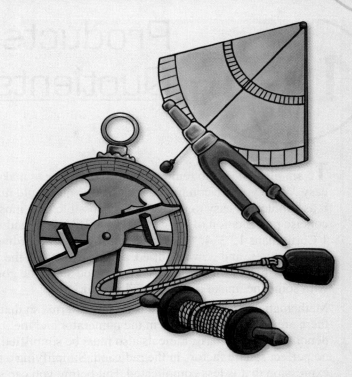

Nathaniel Bowditch lived from 1773 to 1838. At the age of fourteen, he received a gift that would change the course of his life. The gift was an algebra book that helped him discover his aptitude for mathematics. In the late eighteenth century, books were considered a treasure—especially for an avid reader like Nathaniel. Delighted with his present, he stayed up late at night learning the basic principles of algebra. He quickly fell in love with the study of mathematics.

Small and frail, Bowditch was completely unsuited for the rough, physically demanding life of a sailor. Yet in the bustling port of Salem, Massachusetts, the sea provided a profitable means of making a living. Before Bowditch could marry his high-school sweetheart, he had to be able to earn enough money to support a family. Thus motivated, Bowditch signed on board the *Henry*, a ship captained by his old school friend Henry Price.

After a few days at sea, Bowditch felt certain that he could improve upon the methods of navigation that the sailors were using. At the time, sailors navigated their ships mainly by intuition and experience. Bowditch proposed using mathematical formulas to calculate the ship's longitude and latitude so that sea captains could pinpoint their exact location on any given day.

The veteran sailors on board the *Henry* scoffed at Bowditch's proposal. However, Captain Price agreed to allow him to try out his theory once they reached the open seas. Using Bowditch's new methods of navigation, the *Henry* reached its destination in the Indian Ocean and returned to Salem in record time. Bowditch had piloted the vessel across the ocean in a straight line!

Impressed, Captain Price asked Bowditch to accompany him on voyages to the Philippines and to Spain. Just before the ship left for Spain, Edmund M. Blunt, a publisher, asked Bowditch to correct a set of navigational figures devised by English mathematician John Hamilton Moore. Although the tables were the most advanced navigational aid of their time, sailors insisted that they were full of miscalculations. While at sea, Bowditch discovered that Moore's unreliable formula for determining longitude had resulted in more than 8,000 calculation errors.

Bowditch learned upon returning home that his wife had died. Heartbroken, he agreed to sail to Manila with his friend Captain Price. On this voyage he began working on a book that would contain his own navigational calculations and formulas. As he wrote, Bowditch realized that his book would be used by sailors who had little formal education. Wondering if they would be able to grasp the mathematical principles necessary for navigation, he began to teach the crew both mathematical and navigational skills. When he was finished, the age of mathematical navigation had dawned.

Bowditch's book, *The New American Practical Navigator*, was published in England and the United States in 1802. More than just a navigational aid, the book was a valuable reference tool for sailors. Chapters covered a variety of topics such as marine terminology, currents, and geography. The book also instructed readers in the principles of mathematics, from basic decimals to advanced trigonometry and calculus.

This book soon became required reading for sailors throughout the world. The United States Navy continued to use it until technological advances made the book obsolete just prior to the start of World War II. However, to this day, *The New American Practical Navigator* is still considered a basic reference textbook on mathematical navigation.

11.5 Products and Quotients of Radicals

Camera memory card versus film: simplification by technology.

To simplify means to remove complications, or to make easy. When you are communicating truth, you should make it as simple and easy to understand as possible. The most concise presentation of the gospel in the Bible is found in 1 Corinthians 15:3–4, "Christ died for our sins according to the scriptures; and … was buried, and … rose again the third day according to the scriptures." When you share the gospel with someone, make it easy to understand.

Mathematicians change fractions to lowest terms so that there are no common factors in the numerator and the denominator. Similarly, radicals also must be simplified. *Simplified radicals* have no perfect square factors in the radicand. Simplifying a radical makes an equivalent expression that is less complicated. But before you can simplify radicals, you need to know how to multiply and divide radicals.

Consider the product $\sqrt{4} \cdot \sqrt{9}$.

We know $\sqrt{4} = 2$ and $\sqrt{9} = 3$. Therefore, $\sqrt{4} \cdot \sqrt{9} = 2 \cdot 3 = 6$.

It is also true that $\sqrt{4} \cdot \sqrt{9} = \sqrt{4 \cdot 9} = \sqrt{36} = 6$.

This example illustrates the product law for square roots.

Product Law for Square Roots
For all $a \geq 0$ and $b \geq 0$, $\sqrt{a} \cdot \sqrt{b} = \sqrt{ab}$.

The product law can be used to simplify radicals. You can find the square root of a number by expressing the number as a product of perfect square factors.

Example 1 Find $\sqrt{900}$.

Answer

$$\sqrt{900} = \sqrt{9 \times 100}$$ 1. Write 900 as the product of two perfect squares.
$$= \sqrt{9}\ \sqrt{100}$$ 2. Apply the product law for square roots.
$$= 3 \times 10$$ 3. Take the square roots of the perfect squares.
$$= 30$$ 4. Multiply.

Skill Check 1

Find the following square roots.

1. $\sqrt{1,600}$ 2. $\sqrt{8,100}$ 3. $\sqrt{12,100}$

Radicals can be simplified even if only one factor is a perfect square. Consider $\sqrt{40}$. Express 40 as a product of 4×10, since 4 is a perfect square. Use the product law to separate the radical into the product of two radicals, one of which is a perfect square. Then simplify the square root of the perfect square.

$$\sqrt{40} = \sqrt{4} \cdot \sqrt{10} = 2\sqrt{10}$$

$2\sqrt{10}$ is considered a simpler form than $\sqrt{40}$. Whenever the radicand contains a perfect square factor, the radical should be simplified.

Example 2   Simplify $\sqrt{48}$.

Answer

$\sqrt{48} = \sqrt{16 \times 3}$ 1. 16 is the largest perfect square that is a factor of 48.
$\phantom{\sqrt{48}} = \sqrt{16}\sqrt{3}$ 2. Use the product law to separate the radical into two radicals.
$\phantom{\sqrt{48}} = 4\sqrt{3}$ 3. Simplify $\sqrt{16}$ to 4.

If you had chosen $\sqrt{4 \times 12}$ in the first step, you would have gotten $2\sqrt{12}$ and would have needed to simplify the $\sqrt{12}$.

When the number under the radical sign is larger, it may take you more time to look for a perfect square factor than it would to change the original number into a product of primes.

Suppose you want to simplify $\sqrt{180}$. You can perform the following calculations: $\frac{180}{2} = 90$, $\frac{90}{2} = 45$, $\frac{45}{3} = 15$, and $\frac{15}{3} = 5$. So $\sqrt{180} = \sqrt{2 \cdot 2 \cdot 3 \cdot 3 \cdot 5}$. The square root of $2 \cdot 2$ is 2, and the square root of $3 \cdot 3$ is 3, so

$$\sqrt{180} = \sqrt{2 \cdot 2 \cdot 3 \cdot 3 \cdot 5} = \sqrt{2 \cdot 2} \cdot \sqrt{3 \cdot 3} \cdot \sqrt{5} = 2 \cdot 3 \cdot \sqrt{5} = 6\sqrt{5}.$$

Example 3   Simplify $\sqrt{162}$.

Answer

$\sqrt{162} = \sqrt{2 \cdot 3 \cdot 3 \cdot 3 \cdot 3}$ 1. Rewrite the radicand as a product of prime factors.
$\phantom{\sqrt{162}} = \sqrt{2}\sqrt{3 \cdot 3}\sqrt{3 \cdot 3}$ 2. Use the product law to separate radicals of perfect squares.
$\phantom{\sqrt{162}} = \sqrt{2} \cdot 3 \cdot 3$ 3. Simplify the radicals of perfect squares.
$\phantom{\sqrt{162}} = 9\sqrt{2}$ 4. Simplify the product.

Example 4   Simplify $\sqrt{675}$.

Answer

$\sqrt{675} = \sqrt{3 \cdot 3 \cdot 3 \cdot 5 \cdot 5}$ 1. Rewrite the radicand as a product of prime factors.
$\phantom{\sqrt{675}} = \sqrt{3 \cdot 3}\sqrt{5 \cdot 5}\sqrt{3}$ 2. Use the product law to separate radicals of perfect squares.
$\phantom{\sqrt{675}} = 3 \cdot 5\sqrt{3}$ 3. Simplify the radicals of perfect squares.
$\phantom{\sqrt{675}} = 15\sqrt{3}$ 4. Simplify the product.

Skill Check 2

Simplify the following radicals.

1. $\sqrt{12}$ 2. $\sqrt{125}$ 3. $\sqrt{242}$ 4. $\sqrt{63}$

Now consider the product rule used in the opposite direction. Suppose we have the product of two roots, such as $\sqrt{2}\sqrt{5}$. We can multiply them, getting

$$\sqrt{2}\sqrt{5} = \sqrt{2\cdot5} = \sqrt{10}.$$

This is certainly simpler than writing the product of two roots.

But suppose each root shares a common prime factor. Suppose we want to simplify $\sqrt{6}\sqrt{15}$. Neither root by itself contains a perfect square factor, but the product does.

$$\sqrt{6}\sqrt{15} = \sqrt{2\cdot3}\sqrt{3\cdot5} = \sqrt{2\cdot3^2\cdot5} = 3\sqrt{2\cdot5} = 3\sqrt{10}$$

Of course you can choose to multiply first, getting $\sqrt{90}$, and then simplify it. Doing so is desirable if the product is small like this one. However, if the product is large, you may have difficulty finding the prime factors. In that case, it is quicker to find the prime factors as shown above. The choice is yours.

Example 5   Simplify $\sqrt{7}\sqrt{3}$.

Answer

$\sqrt{7}\sqrt{3} = \sqrt{7\cdot3} = \sqrt{21}$ Apply the product rule.

Example 6   Simplify $\sqrt{14}\sqrt{21}$.

Answer

$\begin{aligned}
\sqrt{14}\sqrt{21} &= \sqrt{2\cdot7}\sqrt{3\cdot7} && \text{1. Simplify each radical.} \\
&= \sqrt{2\cdot3\cdot7^2} && \text{2. Multiply.} \\
&= \sqrt{7^2}\sqrt{2\cdot3} && \text{3. Apply the product rule.} \\
&= 7\sqrt{6} && \text{4. Take the square root of } 7^2, \text{ and simplify under the other radical.}
\end{aligned}$

By the Associative and Commutative Properties,
$a\sqrt{b}\cdot c\sqrt{d} = ac\sqrt{bd}$.

You can also multiply terms like $2\sqrt{3}\times5\sqrt{2}$.

Example 7   Simplify $2\sqrt{54}\cdot3\sqrt{15}$.

Answer

$\begin{aligned}
2\sqrt{54}\cdot3\sqrt{15} &= 6\sqrt{54\cdot15} && \text{1. Multiply the coefficients and radicands.} \\
&= 6\sqrt{2\cdot3\cdot3\cdot3\cdot3\cdot5} && \text{2. Rewrite the radicand as a product of prime factors.} \\
&= 6\cdot3\cdot3\sqrt{2\cdot5} && \text{3. Apply the product rule.} \\
&= 54\sqrt{10} && \text{4. Simplify the product.}
\end{aligned}$

Skill Check 3

Simplify the following radical expressions.

1. $\sqrt{5}\sqrt{10}$

2. $\sqrt{6}\sqrt{42}$

Examine the relationship that exists between $\dfrac{\sqrt{a}}{\sqrt{b}}$ and $\sqrt{\dfrac{a}{b}}$ (assuming that $a > 0$ and $b > 0$). For example, consider the quotients $\dfrac{\sqrt{36}}{\sqrt{9}}$ and $\sqrt{\dfrac{36}{9}}$.

$$\frac{\sqrt{36}}{\sqrt{9}} = \frac{6}{3} = 2, \text{ and } \sqrt{\frac{36}{9}} = \sqrt{4} = 2.$$

This illustrates the quotient law for square roots, which states that these two expressions are always equal.

Quotient Law for Square Roots

If a and b are positive real numbers, $\dfrac{\sqrt{a}}{\sqrt{b}} = \sqrt{\dfrac{a}{b}}$.

When a quotient contains perfect squares in both the numerator and the denominator, take the square root of each and simplify the resulting rational number.

Example 8 Simplify $\sqrt{\dfrac{25}{4}}$.

Answer

$\sqrt{\dfrac{25}{4}} = \dfrac{\sqrt{25}}{\sqrt{4}} = \dfrac{5}{2}$

When the radicand of the denominator divides the radicand of the numerator, change the expression to $\sqrt{\dfrac{a}{b}}$ form and divide. If possible, simplify the result.

Example 9 Simplify $\dfrac{\sqrt{45}}{\sqrt{5}}$.

Answer

$\dfrac{\sqrt{45}}{\sqrt{5}} = \sqrt{\dfrac{45}{5}} = \sqrt{9} = 3$

Example 10 Simplify $\dfrac{\sqrt{18}}{\sqrt{9}}$.

Answer

$\dfrac{\sqrt{18}}{\sqrt{9}} = \sqrt{\dfrac{18}{9}} = \sqrt{2}$ 9 is a perfect square. But since 9 divides into 18, reduce the fraction first.

Skill Check 4

Simplify the following radical quotients.

1. $\dfrac{\sqrt{8}}{\sqrt{2}}$ 2. $\dfrac{\sqrt{98}}{\sqrt{2}}$ 3. $\dfrac{\sqrt{81}}{\sqrt{16}}$ 4. $\dfrac{\sqrt{6}}{\sqrt{2}}$

■ A. Exercises

Find the following square roots.

1. $\sqrt{4,900}$ 2. $\sqrt{6,400}$ 3. $\sqrt{10,000}$ 4. $\sqrt{40,000}$ 5. $\sqrt{19,600}$ 6. $\sqrt{22,500}$

Simplify the following radicals.

7. $\sqrt{75}$ 8. $\sqrt{45}$ 9. $\sqrt{216}$ 10. $\sqrt{98}$ 11. $\sqrt{294}$ 12. $\sqrt{84}$

■ B. Exercises

Simplify the following radical expressions.

13. $\sqrt{2}\,\sqrt{3}$ 14. $\sqrt{7}\,\sqrt{5}$ 15. $\sqrt{6}\,\sqrt{3}$ 16. $\sqrt{3}\,\sqrt{15}$ 17. $\sqrt{29}\,\sqrt{58}$

18. $\sqrt{34}\,\sqrt{2}$ 19. $\sqrt{21}\,\sqrt{30}$ 20. $\sqrt{18}\,\sqrt{12}$ 21. $5\sqrt{6}\left(2\sqrt{14}\right)$ 22. $3\sqrt{20}\left(2\sqrt{5}\right)$

Simplify the following radical expressions.

23. $\dfrac{\sqrt{30}}{\sqrt{3}}$

24. $\dfrac{\sqrt{58}}{\sqrt{2}}$

25. $\dfrac{\sqrt{9}}{\sqrt{81}}$

26. $\dfrac{\sqrt{400}}{\sqrt{25}}$

27. $\dfrac{5\sqrt{10}}{\sqrt{2}}$

28. $\dfrac{\sqrt{20}}{2}$

29. $\dfrac{\sqrt{360}}{\sqrt{72}}$

30. $\dfrac{\sqrt{400}}{\sqrt{100}}$

31. $\dfrac{2\sqrt{80}}{8}$

32. $\sqrt{\dfrac{36}{81}}$

■ C. Exercises

Simplify the following radicals. Assume that $x \geq 0$ and $y \geq 0$.

33. $\sqrt{x^2 y^2}$

34. $\sqrt{x^3 y^4}$

Under what circumstances are the following true?

35. $\sqrt{x^2} = x$

36. $\sqrt{x^2} \neq x$

■ Dominion thru Math

37. The pitch of a gable roof for a building is given by a ratio of vertical rise to horizontal run. The horizontal number is always given as 12, so roof pitches would look like 6 : 12, 8 : 12, or 12 : 12. To determine the height of a gable, an architect divides the building width in half and adds the horizontal overhang at the eaves to give the measurement for the ratio proportion calculation. What is the height of a gable on a 64 ft. wide building with a 1 ft. overhang and a 7 : 12 pitch?

38. An architect will use the Pythagorean theorem to calculate the length of the rafters for a gable roof. The rafters are actually the hypotenuse of a right triangle with the height at the gable as one leg and half the width of the building plus the overhang as the other leg. Find the length of the rafters for the roof in exercise 37.

■ CUMULATIVE REVIEW

39. Construct a scatterplot for the following data, which illustrates how many runs were scored by major-league baseball teams in first place, second place, and so on in their respective divisions on a particular day. Notice that on this day four of the six division leaders played, five of the six second-place teams played, and so on. [10.2]

Place	Runs Scored
1st	8, 6, 2, 1
2nd	16, 0, 1, 9, 3
3rd	3, 6, 13, 5
4th	2, 1
5th	5, 4, 7, 3, 6

40. Determine whether the correlation is positive, negative, or not significant. [10.2]

In a class of twenty-four students, seven of the eleven boys play basketball and five of the thirteen girls play basketball. Express each of the following probabilities as both a fraction and a decimal rounded to the nearest hundredth. [10.8–10.9]

41. a student chosen at random does not play basketball

42. a student chosen at random is a female basketball player

A teacher wants to assign a two-character identifier to each of the students in his class. The identifier consists of a letter followed by a nonzero digit. [10.8–10.9]

43. How many identifiers are possible?

44. What is the probability that a randomly chosen student's identifier consists of a vowel followed by an even number?

45. What is the probability that a student's identifier contains a consonant and an odd number?

Add or subtract in the indicated base. [4.8]

46. $23_5 + 42_5$

47. $42_5 - 23_5$

11.6 Sums and Differences of Radicals

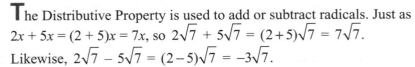 

The Distributive Property is used to add or subtract radicals. Just as $2x + 5x = (2 + 5)x = 7x$, so $2\sqrt{7} + 5\sqrt{7} = (2+5)\sqrt{7} = 7\sqrt{7}$. Likewise, $2\sqrt{7} - 5\sqrt{7} = (2-5)\sqrt{7} = -3\sqrt{7}$.

Square roots with the same radicand are like radicals. As shown above, like radicals can be added or subtracted. The expression $2\sqrt{3} + 5\sqrt{7}$ cannot be further simplified. The addition or subtraction of unlike radicals can be done only with rounded decimal approximations of the radicals.

$$\sqrt{a}\,\sqrt{b} = \sqrt{ab}$$
but
$$\sqrt{a} + \sqrt{b} \neq \sqrt{a+b}$$

Example 1   Simplify $6\sqrt{7} + 3\sqrt{2} - 2\sqrt{7}$.

Answer

$$\begin{aligned} 6\sqrt{7} + 3\sqrt{2} - 2\sqrt{7} &= 6\sqrt{7} - 2\sqrt{7} + 3\sqrt{2} \\ &= (6-2)\sqrt{7} + 3\sqrt{2} \\ &= 4\sqrt{7} + 3\sqrt{2} \end{aligned}$$

1. Group the like terms together.
2. Apply the Distributive Property to like radicals.

Example 2   Simplify $4\sqrt{2} - 3\sqrt{5} + 2\sqrt{7}$.

Answer

No simplification is possible. Unlike terms cannot be simplified further.

By the Distributive Property,
$$a\sqrt{d} + b\sqrt{d} - c\sqrt{d} = (a+b-c)\sqrt{d}.$$

Skill Check 1

Simplify the following radical expressions.

1. $5\sqrt{3} + \sqrt{3}$
2. $5\sqrt{6} - 2\sqrt{6}$
3. $5\sqrt{2} + 4\sqrt{3}$
4. $2\sqrt{2} + 3\sqrt{5} - 5\sqrt{2}$

Some radical expressions with different radicands can be simplified so their radicands are the same. For example,

$$\begin{aligned} 2\sqrt{12} + 8\sqrt{3} &= 2\sqrt{4 \cdot 3} + 8\sqrt{3} \\ &= 2 \cdot 2\sqrt{3} + 8\sqrt{3} \\ &= 4\sqrt{3} + 8\sqrt{3} \\ &= 12\sqrt{3} \end{aligned}$$

When adding or subtracting radical expressions, simplify each radical first. Then use the Distributive Property to combine like radicals.

Example 3   Simplify $\sqrt{27} + \sqrt{12}$.

Answer
$$\begin{aligned}
\sqrt{27} + \sqrt{12} &= \sqrt{3 \times 3 \times 3} + \sqrt{2 \times 2 \times 3} \\
&= 3\sqrt{3} + 2\sqrt{3} \\
&= (3+2)\sqrt{3} \\
&= 5\sqrt{3}
\end{aligned}$$

1. Factor the radicands.
2. Simplify each radical.
3. Combine like terms using the Distributive Property.

Example 4   Simplify $3\sqrt{8} - 2\sqrt{18} - \sqrt{12} + 4\sqrt{50}$.

Answer
$$\begin{aligned}
3\sqrt{8} - 2\sqrt{18} &- \sqrt{12} + 4\sqrt{50} \\
&= 3\sqrt{2 \times 2 \times 2} - 2\sqrt{2 \times 3 \times 3} - \sqrt{2 \times 2 \times 3} + 4\sqrt{2 \times 5 \times 5} \\
&= 6\sqrt{2} - 6\sqrt{2} - 2\sqrt{3} + 20\sqrt{2} \\
&= (6 - 6 + 20)\sqrt{2} - 2\sqrt{3} \\
&= 20\sqrt{2} - 2\sqrt{3}
\end{aligned}$$

1. Factor the radicands.
2. Simplify each radical.
3. Combine like terms using the Distributive Property.

Skill Check 2

Simplify the following radical expressions.

1. $\sqrt{8} - \sqrt{72}$

2. $4\sqrt{24} + \sqrt{54}$

3. $6\sqrt{50} - 5\sqrt{72} + \sqrt{300}$

4. $3\sqrt{12} - 2\sqrt{8} + 3\sqrt{32}$

⊕ Invention

Since a sphere has the largest volume for a given surface area, any building that approximates a sphere would be quite cost-effective in terms of price per cubic foot. A polyhedron-shaped building with lots of small surface polygons (and thus close to being a sphere) became known in 1954 as a *geodesic dome*. In that year R. Buckminster Fuller introduced the modern world to geodesic domes that were practical and economical. If you have ever visited Disney World's Epcot Center in Orlando, Florida, you were greeted at the gates by a huge "Bucky Ball." The polyhedral shape itself has been around for centuries, and Zeiss Optics in Germany was one of the first to display a geodesic dome in 1922. What Bucky Fuller actually invented was a clever way to build these structures so that they were strong, light, and economical.

Spaceship Earth Pavilion at Disney World's Epcot Center is one of the most recognizable geodesic domes.

■ A. Exercises

Simplify the following radical expressions.

1. $5\sqrt{17} + 8\sqrt{17}$

2. $3\sqrt{11} - 5\sqrt{11}$

3. $2\sqrt{6} + 8\sqrt{6}$

4. $19\sqrt{5} - 11\sqrt{5}$

5. $7\sqrt{6} - 2\sqrt{6} + 18\sqrt{6}$

6. $2\sqrt{3} - \sqrt{3} - 4\sqrt{3}$

7. $7\sqrt{3} - 3\sqrt{2} + 8\sqrt{3}$

8. $9\sqrt{7} + \sqrt{5} - 6\sqrt{5}$

9. $6\sqrt{6} + 2\sqrt{3} + 5\sqrt{3} - 5\sqrt{6}$

10. $4\sqrt{13} - 8\sqrt{7} - 5\sqrt{13} + 15\sqrt{7}$

■ B. Exercises

Simplify the following radical expressions.

11. $2 + 8\sqrt{4}$

12. $4 - 2\sqrt{9}$

13. $3\sqrt{5} - \sqrt{45}$

14. $\sqrt{27} - 10\sqrt{3}$

15. $5\sqrt{2} - 4\sqrt{8} - \sqrt{2}$

16. $7\sqrt{5} + 4\sqrt{20} - 2\sqrt{5}$

17. $5\sqrt{8} + 8\sqrt{18} + 3\sqrt{32}$

18. $6\sqrt{12} - 3\sqrt{75} + 2\sqrt{27}$

19. $2\sqrt{45} - 6\sqrt{12} + 9\sqrt{80}$

20. $9\sqrt{40} + \sqrt{90} + 8\sqrt{100}$

21. $7\sqrt{8} - 5\sqrt{80} + 2\sqrt{180} + \sqrt{50}$

22. $3\sqrt{63} + 4\sqrt{48} + 2\sqrt{28} + 3\sqrt{147}$

23. $3\sqrt{24} - \sqrt{150} + 2\sqrt{48} - \sqrt{54}$

24. $\sqrt{108} + \sqrt{80} - \sqrt{180} - \sqrt{18}$

25. $\sqrt{50} + \sqrt{27} + \sqrt{45} + \sqrt{54}$

26. $2\sqrt{112} - 3\sqrt{125} + 5\sqrt{63} - 5\sqrt{12}$

■ C. Exercises

Simplify the following radical expressions.

27. $3\sqrt{2}\left(2\sqrt{3} + 4\sqrt{2}\right)$

28. $\sqrt{6}\left(3\sqrt{7} - 5\sqrt{3}\right)$

29. $\sqrt{24}\left(\sqrt{30} + \sqrt{6}\right)$

30. $4\sqrt{12}\left(3\sqrt{32} + 5\sqrt{18}\right)$

31. $\dfrac{7\sqrt{15} - 2\sqrt{15}}{\sqrt{15}}$

32. $\dfrac{10\sqrt{26} - 5\sqrt{39}}{5\sqrt{13}}$

■ Dominion thru Math

33. The distance you can see to the horizon on the ocean is a function of the height of your eyes above the water and the curvature of the earth. The following formula gives the distance d in nautical miles the observer can see when his eyes are h feet above the water: $d = 1.17\sqrt{h}$. How far can a sailor see if he is in the crow's nest of a sailing ship with his eyes 120 ft. above the water? If a nautical mile (M) is about 1.15 statute miles (mi.), the mile that we use to measure on land, how many statute miles is this?

34. The period T of a pendulum is the time it takes to make a complete swing from one side to the other and back to where it began. The following formula shows that the period is a function of gravity and the length of the pendulum. $T = 2\pi\sqrt{\dfrac{L}{32}}$, where L is the length of the pendulum in feet and T is the time in seconds. Find the period for an 8 ft. pendulum and for a 4 ft. pendulum (assume $\pi = 3.14$).

35. A pendulum with a 2 sec. period can provide a nice control for a grandfather clock since each extreme of the swing can mark one second. How long would a pendulum need to be to have a period of 2 sec.?

36. Make a stem-and-leaf diagram for the following set of data, which represents the number of wins for each of the sixteen teams in a baseball league during the 2009 season: {76, 79, 66, 80, 76, 78, 82, 88, 75, 97, 85, 67, 88, 76, 83, 71}.   [10.2]

37. Construct a histogram to illustrate the data in the stem-and-leaf diagram.   [10.3]

Add or subtract in the indicated base. [4.8]

38. $101_2 + 110_2$

39. $11_2 + 110_2$

40. $10001_2 - 101_2$

41. $1011_2 + 111_2$

Simplify. [6.5]

42. $3b + \frac{3}{4}b - 4b$

43. $\frac{2}{7}y - \frac{8}{7}y$

44. $\frac{6}{5}z - \frac{4}{3}z$

45. $-7v + \frac{v}{6} - \frac{7}{8}v$

11.7 ⌐ Cube Roots

A positive real number has two square roots, one positive and one negative. For example, the square roots of 36 are ±6. We say that 36 is a perfect square. (The square root of a negative number has no solution in the set of real numbers.)

A number is a *perfect cube* if it is the result of cubing an integer. Eight is a perfect cube since $2^3 = 2 \cdot 2 \cdot 2 = 8$.

The *cube root* of 8 is 2. A cube root is indicated by placing a 3 in the upper left side of the radical sign. The 3 is called the *index* of the radical. It would be perfectly correct to write an index of 2 for square roots, but instead it is understood that the index is 2.

$$\text{index} \searrow \quad \overset{\text{radical sign}}{\nearrow}$$
$$\sqrt[3]{8} = 2$$
$$\underset{\text{radicand}}{\nwarrow}$$

There are two main differences between cube roots and square roots of real numbers.

1. Any real number has exactly one real cube root.

2. The cube root of a negative real number is a negative real number.

Two is the only real number that can be used as a factor in multiplication three times to obtain a perfect cube of 8. If −2 is used as a factor in multiplication three times, the result is −8.

$$(-2)^3 = -2(-2)(-2) = 4(-2) = -8. \text{ Therefore, } \sqrt[3]{-8} = -2.$$

The cube root of a negative number is negative, and the cube root of a positive number is positive.

$\sqrt{-64}$	0 real roots	$\sqrt{64}$	2 real roots
$\sqrt[3]{-64}$	1 real root	$\sqrt[3]{64}$	1 real root

Example 1 Find the following cube roots.

a. $\sqrt[3]{125}$

b. $\sqrt[3]{-216}$

Answer

a. Since $5^3 = 125$, the radical $\sqrt[3]{125} = 5$.

b. Since $(-6)^3 = -216$, the radical $\sqrt[3]{-216} = -6$.

When x is not a perfect cube, you can estimate $\sqrt[3]{x}$ by finding the two perfect cubes between which x lies. Then take the cube roots of those perfect cubes to find the integers that the cube root lies between.

Example 2 Find the consecutive integers between which the following cube roots lie. Use the < symbol to express your answers.

a. $\sqrt[3]{70}$

b. $\sqrt[3]{-5}$

Answer

a. $4^3 = 64$ and $5^3 = 125$. Since 70 lies between 64 and 125, $4 < \sqrt[3]{70} < 5$.

b. $(-1)^3 = -1$ and $(-2)^3 = -8$. Since -5 lies between -8 and -1, $-2 < \sqrt[3]{-5} < -1$.

Skill Check 1

Find the following perfect cubes.

1. 12^3

2. $(-7)^3$

Find the following cube roots.

3. $\sqrt[3]{-1,728}$

4. $\sqrt[3]{512}$

Find the consecutive integers between which the following cube roots lie.

5. $\sqrt[3]{30}$

6. $\sqrt[3]{-70}$

If the cube root is not an integer, you can find a decimal approximation of it by doing a series of estimates.

Example 3 Estimate $\sqrt[3]{17}$ to the nearest tenth.

Answer

$8 < 17 < 27$

$\sqrt[3]{8} < \sqrt[3]{17} < \sqrt[3]{27}$

$2 < \sqrt[3]{17} < 3$

$2.5^3 = 15.625;$

1.375 less than 17

$2.6^3 = 17.576;$

0.576 greater than 17

$\sqrt[3]{17} \approx 2.6$

1. Determine the two perfect cubes between which the root lies.

2. Seventeen is 9 more than 8 and 10 less than 27. It is slightly closer to 8. Estimate $\sqrt[3]{17} \approx 2.5$.

3. Raise the estimate to 2.6 and compare 2.6^3 to 17.

4. 2.6^3 is closer to 17 than 2.5^3.

If both guesses were too small, additional guesses would be needed until the result was higher than the radicand to ensure the closest estimate.

The product law for square roots can be generalized for any order of roots.

> ### Product Law for Roots
>
> For all $a \geq 0$ and $b \geq 0$ with $n > 0$, $\sqrt[n]{a} \cdot \sqrt[n]{b} = \sqrt[n]{ab}$.

This product law is used to simplify radicals of any order. After finding the prime factors of the radicand, you can easily simplify the cube root of any factor cubed.

Example 4 Simplify $\sqrt[3]{2,700}$.

Answer

$$\sqrt[3]{2,700} = \sqrt[3]{2 \cdot 2 \cdot 3 \cdot 3 \cdot 3 \cdot 5 \cdot 5}$$
$$= \sqrt[3]{3^3} \cdot \sqrt[3]{2 \cdot 2 \cdot 5 \cdot 5}$$
$$= 3\sqrt[3]{2 \cdot 2 \cdot 5 \cdot 5}$$
$$= 3\sqrt[3]{100}$$

1. Write the radicand as a product of prime factors.
2. Apply the product law for factors that are cubed.
3. Take the cube root of the perfect cube.
4. Simplify.

Example 5 Simplify $7\sqrt[3]{1,080}$.

Answer

$$7\sqrt[3]{1,080} = 7\sqrt[3]{2 \cdot 2 \cdot 2 \cdot 3 \cdot 3 \cdot 3 \cdot 5}$$
$$= 7\sqrt[3]{2^3} \cdot \sqrt[3]{3^3} \cdot \sqrt[3]{5}$$
$$= 7 \cdot 2 \cdot 3\sqrt[3]{5}$$
$$= 42\sqrt[3]{5}$$

1. Write the radicand as a product of prime factors.
2. Apply the product law for factors that are cubed.
3. Take the cube roots of the perfect cubes.
4. Simplify.

Skill Check 2

Estimate the following cube roots to the nearest tenth.

1. $\sqrt[3]{10}$

2. $\sqrt[3]{5}$

Simplify the following cube roots.

3. $\sqrt[3]{200}$

4. $\sqrt[3]{3,000}$

■ A. Exercises

1. True or false: There is always one cube root of any real number.

2. Copy and complete the chart of perfect cubes.

x	1	2	3	4	5	6	7	8	9	10
x^3										

Evaluate.

3. $(-3)^3$ 4. -3^3 5. -3^2 6. $(-3)^2$

Find the following perfect cubes.

7. 7^3 8. 11^3 9. $(-9)^3$ 10. $(-6)^3$ 11. 8^3 12. $(-40)^3$

Find the consecutive integers between which the following cube roots lie.

13. $\sqrt[3]{21}$ 14. $\sqrt[3]{89}$ 15. $\sqrt[3]{150}$ 16. $\sqrt[3]{71}$ 17. $\sqrt[3]{9}$ 18. $\sqrt[3]{190}$

■ B. Exercises

Find the following cube roots.

19. $\sqrt[3]{-27}$ 20. $\sqrt[3]{343}$ 21. $\sqrt[3]{64}$ 22. $\sqrt[3]{512}$ 23. $\sqrt[3]{1,000}$ 24. $\sqrt[3]{-1}$

25. $\sqrt[3]{-8}$ 26. $\sqrt[3]{1,728}$ 27. $\sqrt[3]{2,197}$

Estimate the following cube roots to the nearest tenth.

28. $\sqrt[3]{41}$ 29. $\sqrt[3]{15}$ 30. $\sqrt[3]{-9}$ 31. $\sqrt[3]{57}$ 32. $\sqrt[3]{99}$ 33. $\sqrt[3]{-2}$

Simplify the following cube roots.

34. $\sqrt[3]{270}$ 35. $\sqrt[3]{375}$ 36. $\sqrt[3]{-16}$ 37. $\sqrt[3]{800}$ 38. $\sqrt[3]{5,488}$ 39. $\sqrt[3]{-1,296}$

■ C. Exercises

Simplify the following radical expressions.

40. $\sqrt[3]{12} \sqrt[3]{18}$ 41. $\sqrt[3]{-140} \sqrt[3]{150}$ 42. $\sqrt[3]{24} + \sqrt[3]{81}$

43. $3\sqrt[3]{16} + 5\sqrt[3]{40} - \sqrt[3]{54}$ 44. Which is larger, $\sqrt{11}$ or $\sqrt[3]{11}$?

CUMULATIVE REVIEW

This bar graph illustrates the results of a survey of students' favorite sports at their school. [10.4]

45. How many students responded to the survey?

46. Calculate the number of degrees for each slice of a pie chart for the same set of data.

47. Make a pie chart of the data. Label each slice with its percentage.

Write an equation and solve. [8.3]

48. Find three consecutive integers such that twice the first is four more than the third.

49. How fast is the current if Johnny and Paulo can paddle a canoe in still water at 4 mi./hr. but it takes them 8 hr. to travel 24 mi. up the river?

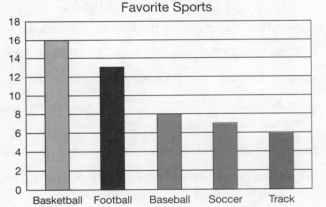

50. The force (F) that will cause an acceleration (a) when applied to a mass (m) can be determined using the formula $F = ma$. How quickly is a 6 kg mass accelerated by a 48 Newton (kg·m/s^2) force?

Solve and graph the solutions. [8.4]

51. $5x + 7 \geq 12$ 52. $9 - 3x < 15$ 53. $4(x - 3) > 3x - 8$ 54. $5 - 3x \geq 7 - x$

The New Jerusalem

Writing under inspiration, the apostle John describes what he calls "that great city, the holy Jerusalem" in Revelation 21:10. It descends out of heaven from God. Not only does he give the layout and dimensions, but he describes the breathtaking materials from which it is built. The height of the wall is measured in cubits (each cubit is about 1.5 ft.). The dimensions of the city, however, are stated in furlongs, the Greek term *stadion*. The stadion of the Roman empire was between 607 and 625 ft. Although seldom used today, the modern length of the furlong is set at $\frac{1}{8}$ mi. = 660 ft.

At the close of his description of the great city, John makes two very significant statements about it. Read these statements for yourself in verses 22 and 27.

Read Revelation 21 and answer the following questions.

1. In verse 9, what does the angel say he will show John?

2. In verse 10, what does John actually see from the high mountain?

3. Read Revelation 19:7–9; 21:2, 27 and give an explanation for the difference between what John was told in verse 9 and what he saw in verse 10.

4. How many gates did the great city have, and how were they placed?

5. What were the measurements of the city? Give a range of values in miles, using 607 and 660 ft. per furlong. What was its geometric shape?

6. What was the height of the walls around the city in cubits and feet?

7. If skyscrapers are 12 ft. per story (floor), how many stories tall would the wall be?

8. Calculate the volume of the city in cubic miles, using the longer approximation for the length of a side.

9. What do the size and costly beauty of the New Jerusalem proclaim about the Lord our God?

Infinite Truths

And the city lieth foursquare, and the length is as large as the breadth: and he measured the city with the reed, twelve thousand furlongs. The length and the breadth and the height of it are equal.
Revelation 21:16

Chapter 11 Review

Vocabulary

converse	legs of a right triangle	product
cube root	perfect cube	Pytha
hypotenuse	perfect square	quo
index of a radical	principal root	roots
		radical eq

Simplify the following. If no answer exists, state "not real."

1. $\sqrt{196}$

2. $-\sqrt{-36}$

3. $\sqrt{-25}$

Simplify the following.

5. $\sqrt{25+144}$

6. $\dfrac{4\sqrt{121}}{\sqrt{36}}$

7. $2\sqrt{25-16} + \sqrt{81}$

8.

Find the consecutive integers between which the following roots lie.

9. $\sqrt{11}$

10. $-\sqrt{147}$

11. $\sqrt[3]{36}$

12. $\sqrt[3]{-70}$

Estimate the following square roots to the nearest tenth.

13. $\sqrt{21}$

14. $\sqrt{116}$

Solve and check the following equations. If no answer exists, state "no real solution."

15. $\sqrt{x} - 5 = -2$

16. $\sqrt{x} = 1.7$

17. $3\sqrt{2x} + 9 = 0$

18. $2\sqrt{4x-3} = 6$

Solve. Leave answers in simplified radical form if the radicand is not a perfect square. If no answer exists, state "no real solution."

19. $x^2 + 31 = 112$

20. $7x^2 = 56$

21. $\dfrac{x^2}{3} - 1 = 11$

22. $4x^2 + 12 = 8$

Given the lengths of the legs, find the hypotenuse of the following right triangles. Simplify irrational roots or round to the nearest tenth.

23. 15 and 8

24. 5 and 5

Given the hypotenuse and one leg, find the missing leg. Simplify irrational roots or round to the nearest tenth.

25. 34 and 30

26. 6 and 3

Given the three side lengths, determine whether the following triangles are right triangles.

27. 10, 25, and 27

28. 16, 30, and 34

Simplify the following radicals.

29. $\sqrt{8,100}$

30. $\sqrt{250,000}$

31. $\sqrt{252}$

32. $\sqrt{80}$

Simplify the following radical expressions.

33. $\sqrt{6}\sqrt{30}$

34. $3\sqrt{10}\left(2\sqrt{15}\right)$

35. $\dfrac{\sqrt{36}}{\sqrt{2}}$

36. $\sqrt{\dfrac{25}{121}}$

37. $\dfrac{3\sqrt{8}}{6}$

38. $7\sqrt{3} - 3\sqrt{3} + \sqrt{3}$

39. $9\sqrt{5} + \sqrt{5} - 6\sqrt{7}$

40. $2\sqrt{50} - \sqrt{72}$

41. $3\sqrt{27} - \sqrt{125} + 2\sqrt{75} + \sqrt{45}$

Find the following perfect cubes or cube roots.

42. $(-4)^3$

43. 5^3

44. $\sqrt[3]{-1}$

45. $\sqrt[3]{216}$

46. $\sqrt[3]{1,331}$

47. Give the mathematical significance of Revelation 21:16.

12 GEOMETRY

$\mathbf{E}$ver since Noah built the first cargo ship, men have used ships to transport vast quantities of material between countries and continents. Yet compared to modern cargo ships, those of the ancient world appear small and frail. Modern cargo ships are specialized, such as tankers that transport oil and liquid gas and container ships that transport dry cargo such as grain or fertilizer.

World shipping transports about 100 million containers per year. These steel containers look like the trailer part of a tractor-trailer, but without wheels. They are called twenty-foot equivalent units (TEUs) because they are approximately 20 ft. long by 8 ft. wide by 8.5 ft. high, with a capacity of about 1,200 ft.[3]. A double TEU container (FEU) is roughly 40 ft. long, and a high cube container is a foot higher (9.5 ft.). Container ships are classified by how many TEU containers they can transport. For example, a ship with a 4,000 to 5,000 TEU capacity is about 900 ft. long by 125 ft. wide, has a draft (keel distance below the surface) when fully loaded of about 40 ft., and moves at a speed of 20 to 24 knots (27 mi./hr.). Can you imagine three football fields zipping along at 27 mi./hr.?

Even though these ships are impressive, consider Noah's amazing wooden ship with its diverse cargo of animals, food, and water. The ark was 450 ft. long, 75 ft. wide, and 45 ft. high, with a capacity of nearly 1,100 TEUs and a payload of at least 16,000 tn. (Gen. 6:14–16). This was the means of protection for Noah and his family during the Flood because they believed and obeyed God. The New Testament says of Noah, "By faith Noah, being warned of God of things not seen as yet, moved with fear, prepared an ark to the saving of his house" (Heb. 11:7).

After this chapter you should be able to

1. name, describe, and use the three basic terms of geometry.

2. draw and measure angles using a protractor.

3. find the complement and supplement of given angles.

4. identify by name pairs of angles formed when two parallel lines are intersected by a transversal, and give their measures when one angle is known.

5. identify polygons by the number of their sides and find the sum of their interior angles.

6. classify triangles according to the lengths of their sides and the measures of their angles.

7. find the perimeter of polygons and the circumference of circles.

8. identify corresponding parts of congruent polygons and write statements of congruence.

9. identify corresponding parts of similar figures and use proportions to find missing lengths.

10. use proportions to compute the length of two unknown sides in 30-60 and 45-45 right triangles.

11. find the distance between two points in a coordinate plane and the midpoint of the segment joining them.

12. distinguish line symmetry, point symmetry, and rotational symmetry.

13. reflect, translate, and rotate figures.

12.1 Basic Geometric Figures

Geometry is the study of points, lines, planes, and the figures they form. The table below lists the three basic geometric figures.

The plumb bob forms a vertical line that is used to keep the walls of a building vertical.

Figure	Name	Symbol	Description
• A	point A	A	A *point* shows an exact location in space and is represented by a dot.
B — C (line)	line BC	$\overleftrightarrow{BC}$	A *line* is a set of points that extends infinitely in opposite directions.
A C B (plane)	plane ABC	plane ABC	A *plane* is a flat surface that extends infinitely in all directions.

In the symbol $\overleftrightarrow{BC}$, the arrowheads indicate that the line continues without end in both directions. The table below lists two basic geometric figures that are part of a line.

Figure	Name	Symbol	Definition
G •———• H	segment GH	$\overline{GH}$	A *segment* is part of a line consisting of two endpoints and all the points between them.
J K (ray)	ray JK	$\overrightarrow{JK}$	A *ray* is part of a line consisting of one endpoint and extending infinitely in one direction through a second named point.

Example 1   Name all the possible points, lines, planes, segments, and rays in the figure using the letters X, Y, and Z.

Answer
Points: X, Y, and Z
Lines: $\overleftrightarrow{XY}$, $\overleftrightarrow{YZ}$, and $\overleftrightarrow{XZ}$
Planes: plane XYZ
Segments: $\overline{XY}$, $\overline{YZ}$, and $\overline{XZ}$
Rays: $\overrightarrow{XY}$, $\overrightarrow{YX}$, $\overrightarrow{YZ}$, $\overrightarrow{ZY}$, $\overrightarrow{XZ}$, and $\overrightarrow{ZX}$

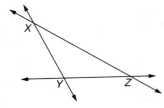

Skill Check 1

Draw and label the following geometric figures.

1. $\overline{AB}$ 2. $\overrightarrow{MN}$ 3. $\overrightarrow{XY}$

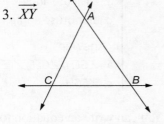

Use the figure at the right for exercises 4–6.

4. Name a line that passes through point A.

5. Name a segment with endpoint B.

6. Name two rays with endpoint C.

Definition

An **angle** is a geometric figure made up of two rays that have a common endpoint. The common endpoint is the *vertex*. Each of the rays is a *side* of the angle.

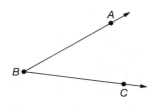

Using the symbol $\angle$ for angle, you can name the angle in the figure three different ways: $\angle ABC$, $\angle CBA$, or $\angle B$.

Notice the location of the vertex B in each of the names. When three letters are given in the name of an angle, the letter for the vertex is always the middle one. The sides of the angle are the rays $\overrightarrow{BA}$ and $\overrightarrow{BC}$.

Angles are usually measured in degrees. To measure an angle with a protractor, follow these steps.

Measuring an Angle

1. Position the center point of the protractor on the vertex of the angle to be measured.
2. Align the zero degree mark on the protractor with one side of the angle.
3. Read the number of degrees to the other side of the angle on the protractor.

In the figure at the right, the measure of the angle is 30°. To abbreviate this statement, write $m\angle XYZ = 30°$.

You can classify angles into four groups according to their measures.

acute angle	right angle	obtuse angle	straight angle
$m\angle X < 90°$	$m\angle Y = 90°$	$90° < m\angle Z < 180°$	$m\angle W = 180°$

As shown in the figure above, a right angle is symbolized by a small square.

Example 2 Find the measure of the following angles.

a. $\angle DAE$ b. $\angle CAE$
c. $\angle BAC$ d. $\angle BAE$

Answer

a. $m\angle DAE = 50°$ b. $m\angle CAE = 125°$
c. $m\angle BAC = 55°$ d. $m\angle BAE = 180°$

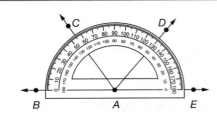

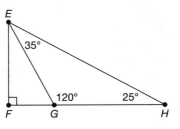

Example 3   Name the following angles in the figure.

a. all acute angles   b. a right angle
c. an obtuse angle   d. a straight angle

Answer

a. ∠GEH, ∠GEF, ∠FEH, ∠H, and ∠FGE   b. ∠F
c. ∠EGH   d. ∠FGH

You can write an equation to find the missing angle measure in the following example.

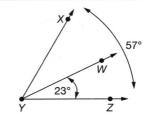

Example 4   If $m\angle WYZ = 23°$, write and solve an equation to find $m\angle XYW$.

Answer

$$m\angle XYW + 23 = 57$$
$$m\angle XYW + 23 - 23 = 57 - 23 \quad \text{Apply the Addition Property of Equality.}$$
$$m\angle XYW = 34°$$

Skill Check 2

Find the measure of the following angles and classify each as acute, right, obtuse, or straight.

1.   2.   3.

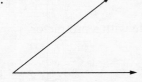

Write an equation similar to the one in Example 4 and use it to find the missing angle measure in the following figures.

4. $m\angle ABD$ 5. $m\angle PQS$

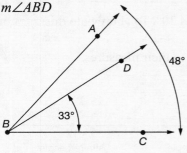

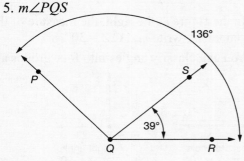

■ A. Exercises

Name all of the following found in the figure using the letters *D*, *E*, and *F*.

1. points   2. lines

3. planes   4. segments

5. rays

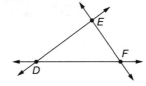

Draw and label the following geometric figures.

6. $\overline{LM}$ 7. $\overleftrightarrow{FG}$ 8. $\overrightarrow{YZ}$

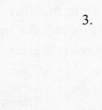

Use the figure at the right for exercises 9–11.

9. Name a line that passes through point C.

10. Name a segment with endpoint C.

11. Name two rays with endpoint B.

Use the figure at the right for exercises 12–13.

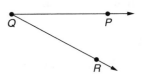

12. Name the sides and vertex of the angle.

13. Name the angle in three ways.

■ B. Exercises

Find the measure of the following angles and classify each according to its angle measure. Express each angle's measure in proper notation.

14.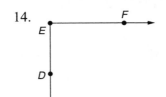

15.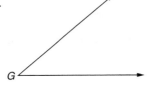

16.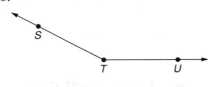

Draw an angle of each of the following types. Express each angle's measure in proper notation.

17. acute angle   18. right angle   19. straight angle   20. obtuse angle

Find the measure of the following angles using a protractor.

21. ∠*DAE*   22. ∠*CAE*

23. ∠*BAC*   24. ∠*BAE*

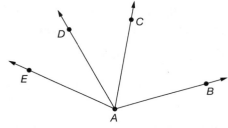

Write an equation to find the missing angle measure in the following figure. Classify each according to its angle measure.

25. $m\angle DPA$

26. $m\angle BPC$

27. $m\angle CPD$

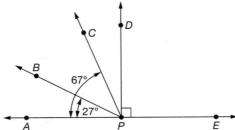

How many lines can be drawn to connect the following?

28. two different points

29. any two of three points that are not on the same line

30. any two of four points, no three of which are on the same line

31. any two of five points, no three of which are on the same line

32. any two of six points, no three of which are on the same line

■ C. Exercises

33. If we know that x lines can be drawn between k points, write an expression for the number of lines that can be drawn between $k + 1$ points, assuming that no three points lie on the same line.

34. Write a general expression for the number of lines that can be drawn to connect n different points, no three of which are on the same line.

■ Dominion thru Math

Use a calculator to solve the following problems.

35. Find the interior volume of a TEU if it is 19' 4$\frac{1}{4}$" long, 7' 8$\frac{5}{8}$" wide, and 7' 10" tall. Round to the nearest cubic foot.

36. Most of the containers used in international trade are now forty-foot equivalent units (FEUs). If the interior of a FEU has the same width and height but is 20' 1$\frac{1}{8}$" longer than the interior of a TEU, what is the interior volume of a FEU? Round to the nearest cubic foot.

37. If the interior of a FEU high cube is just one foot higher than a regular FEU, what is the interior volume of a high cube? Round to the nearest cubic foot.

■ CUMULATIVE REVIEW

Write an equation and solve. [7.5–7.6]

38. A clothing store purchased a suit jacket for $64 and marked it up to a retail price of $160. Find the markup and markup rate for the jacket.

39. The jacket with an original retail price of $160 was purchased during a clearance sale, when it was discounted by 75%. Find the discount and sale price.

40. Find the markup and retail price of a pair of shoes that cost the merchant $25 and were marked up 250%.

41. A salesman sold $2,400 of clothing and was paid a 15% commission. How much did the salesman make?

42. If a salesman earning 12.5% commission wants to make $1,000 a week, how much does he need to sell each week?

43. Write the set of ordered pairs for relation H if $y = -2x + 3$ for each ordered pair and the domain of the relation is $\{-2, -1, 0, 1, 2\}$. [9.2]

44. Give the range of the relation in exercise 43. [9.2]

45. Is the relation in exercise 43 a function? Why or why not? [9.3]

46. Every point on the x-axis has a(n) ____-coordinate of ____. [9.1]

Name the quadrant or the axis on which the following points lie. [9.1]

47. (6, –4)   48. (–7, 3)   49. (–9, 0)   50. (–7, –7)

12.2 Pairs of Angles

The two sets of figures below illustrate complementary and supplementary angles.

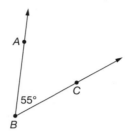

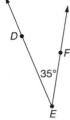

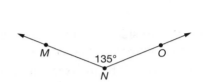

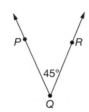

$m\angle ABC = 55°$ and $m\angle DEF = 35°$.
$55 + 35 = 90$, so $\angle ABC$ and $\angle DEF$ are complementary angles.

$m\angle MNO = 135°$ and $m\angle PQR = 45°$.
$135 + 45 = 180$, so $\angle MNO$ and $\angle PQR$ are supplementary angles.

Definitions

Two angles whose measures add up to 90° are **complementary**.
Two angles whose measures add up to 180° are **supplementary**.

Example 1   Write and solve an equation to find the supplement of 38°.

Answer

Let s = the supplement.

$s + 38 = 180$ 1. Apply the definition of supplementary angles.

$s + 38 - 38 = 180 - 38$ 2. Apply the Addition Property of Equality.

$s = 142°$

The supplement of a 38° angle is a 142° angle.

Skill Check 1

Find the measure of the following angles. If the given angle is acute, give its complement and supplement. If it is obtuse, give its supplement.

1. $\angle USV$

2. $\angle RST$

3. $\angle RSU$

4. If $m\angle WYZ = 22°$, write and solve an equation to find its supplement, $m\angle XYW$.

5. Write and solve an equation to find the complement of a 17° angle.

Angles that have a common vertex and a common ray between them are *adjacent angles*.

In the figure shown, $\angle BAC$ and $\angle CAD$ are adjacent angles. Notice that $\overrightarrow{AC}$ forms one side of each angle and is between the other rays. It is the common ray in the above definition.

$\angle BAD$ and $\angle CAD$ have a common ray, $\overrightarrow{AD}$, but it is not between them. These angles are not adjacent angles; instead, they overlap one another.

Lines that share a common point are *intersecting lines*. In the figure at the right, A is the point of intersection.

Two intersecting lines form four angles, as shown in the figure. These angles can be grouped into four pairs of adjacent angles, as indicated below.

$\angle 1$ and $\angle 2$ $\angle 3$ and $\angle 4$

$\angle 2$ and $\angle 3$ $\angle 1$ and $\angle 4$

Adjacent angles whose exterior sides lie on the same straight line are supplementary. All the pairs of angles listed above are supplementary.

Pairs of nonadjacent angles formed by intersecting lines are called *vertical angles*. There are two pairs of vertical angles in the above figure.

$\angle 1$ and $\angle 3$ $\angle 2$ and $\angle 4$

$\angle 1$ and $\angle 2$ are supplementary; therefore, $m\angle 1 + m\angle 2 = 180$.

$\angle 1$ and $\angle 4$ are supplementary; therefore, $m\angle 1 + m\angle 4 = 180$.

Therefore, $m\angle 1 + m\angle 2 = m\angle 1 + m\angle 4$. From this equation, we see that $m\angle 2 = m\angle 4$. Vertical angles always have the same measure. If $\angle 2$ is a 37° angle, then $\angle 4$ is also a 37° angle.

Example 2   Without measuring, find the measure of $\angle 3$, $\angle 4$, and $\angle 5$.

Answer

$m\angle 3 = 130°$ 1. $\angle 3$ and $\angle 6$ are supplementary; their sum is 180°.

$m\angle 4 = 130°$ 2. $\angle 4$ and $\angle 6$ are supplementary; their sum is 180°.

$m\angle 5 = 50°$ 3. $\angle 5$ and $\angle 6$ are vertical angles; they have the same measure.

Lines that intersect to form right angles are called *perpendicular lines*. In the figure at the right, $\overleftrightarrow{AB}$ is perpendicular to $\overleftrightarrow{CD}$. In symbols, this is written as $\overleftrightarrow{AB} \perp \overleftrightarrow{CD}$.

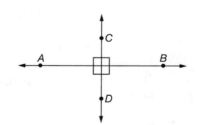

When lines intersect, you can use the relationships between the angles formed to find the measure of unknown angles.

Example 3 Without measuring, find $m\angle1$, $m\angle2$, and $m\angle3$.

Answer

$m\angle1 = 36°$ 1. $\angle1$ is vertical to a 36° angle.

$m\angle2 = 90°$ 2. $\angle2$ is supplementary to a right angle.

$m\angle3 = 54°$ 3. $\angle3$ is complementary to a 36° angle.

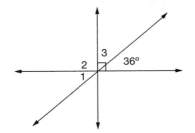

Skill Check 2

Fill in the blank to make a true statement.

1. $\angle9$ and $\angle$___ are vertical angles.

2. $\angle8$ and $\angle$___ are adjacent angles.

3. $\angle7$ and $\angle$___ are supplementary angles.

Without measuring, find the following angle measures.

4. $m\angle7$ 5. $m\angle8$ 6. $m\angle9$

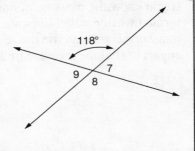

Definition

Parallel lines are lines in the same plane that do not intersect.

In the figure at the right, $\overleftrightarrow{AB}$ and $\overleftrightarrow{CD}$ are parallel, written in symbols as $\overleftrightarrow{AB} \parallel \overleftrightarrow{CD}$. A *transversal* is a line that intersects two or more lines; $\overleftrightarrow{EF}$ is a transversal.

When a transversal intersects two lines, several pairs of related angles are formed. When the intersected lines are parallel, these related angles have the same measure. The special related angles are shown in the table below.

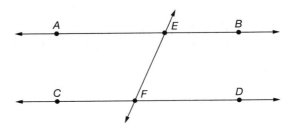

Alternate Interior Angles	Alternate Exterior Angles	Corresponding Angles
$m\angle3 = m\angle6$ $m\angle4 = m\angle5$	$m\angle1 = m\angle8$ $m\angle2 = m\angle7$	$m\angle1 = m\angle5$ $m\angle2 = m\angle6$ $m\angle3 = m\angle7$ $m\angle4 = m\angle8$
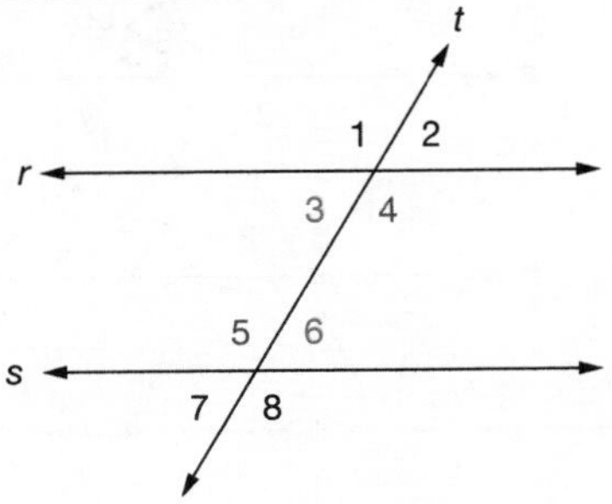 (diagram)	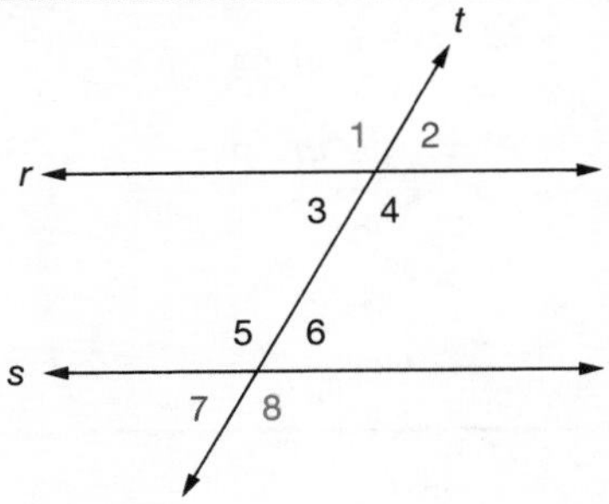 (diagram)	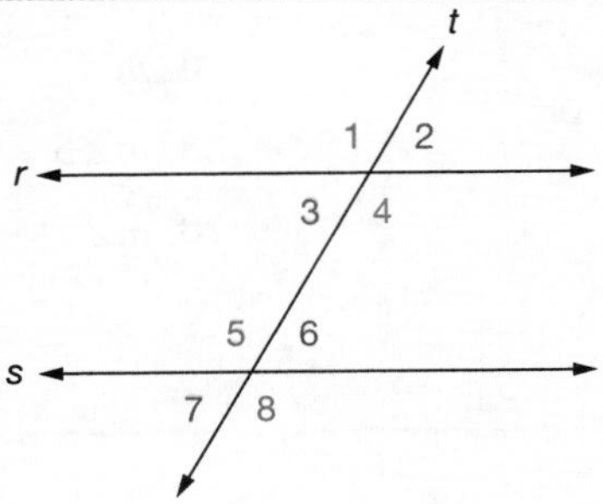 (diagram)

Example 4 Line *a* is parallel to line *b*. Use the figure to identify the following angles.

a. ∠9 and ∠___ are alternate interior angles.

b. ∠7 and ∠___ are alternate exterior angles.

c. ∠10 and ∠___ are corresponding angles.

d. ∠3 and ∠___ are corresponding angles.

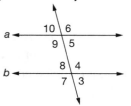

Answer

a. 4   b. 6   c. 8   d. 5

If you know the measure of one of the eight angles formed when parallel lines are intersected by a transversal, you can use the relationships between the angles to find the measure of the other seven angles.

This photo can be deceiving. If you do not see parallel boards cut by perpendicular transversals, look again.

Example 5 Assuming the two lines are parallel and cut by a transversal, find the measure of ∠1, ∠2, ∠3, and ∠4.

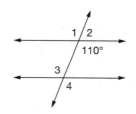

Answer

$m\angle 1 = 110°$ ∠1 and the 110° angle are vertical angles.

$m\angle 2 = 70°$ ∠2 and the 110° angle are supplementary angles.

$m\angle 3 = 110°$ ∠3 and the 110° angle are alternate interior angles.

$m\angle 4 = 110°$ ∠4 and the 110° angle are corresponding angles.

Skill Check 3

List two pairs of the following kinds of angles from the figure below.

1. alternate interior
2. alternate exterior
3. corresponding

In the figure, *a* ∥ *b* and *m*∠8 = 65°. Find the measure of the following angles.

4. $m\angle 1$ 5. $m\angle 2$

6. $m\angle 3$ 7. $m\angle 4$

8. $m\angle 5$ 9. $m\angle 6$

10. $m\angle 7$

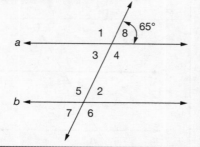

■ A. Exercises

Find the complement of the following angles.

1. 70°   2. 82°   3. 29°   4. 63°   5. 77°   6. 9°

Find the supplement of the following angles.

7. 75°   8. 118°   9. 26°   10. 4°   11. 98°   12. 149°

13. If two angles are both congruent and complementary, what is their measure?

14. If two angles are both congruent and supplementary, what is their measure?

15. Angles with a common vertex and a common ray between them are ___.

16. Draw two angles that have a common vertex and a common ray that is not between them.

17. When two lines intersect, how many pairs of adjacent angles are formed?

18. When two lines intersect, how many pairs of vertical angles are formed?

19. When two intersecting lines are perpendicular, how many right angles are formed?

■ B. Exercises

Without measuring, find the following angle measures.

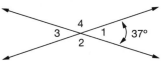

20. $m\angle 2$ 21. $m\angle 3$ 22. $m\angle 4$

23. A line that intersects two or more lines is called a ___ of those two lines.

24. Lines in the same plane that never intersect are called ___.

Suppose two parallel lines are intersected by a transversal. Describe the position of each of the following.

25. alternate angles

26. interior angles

27. alternate exterior angles

28. corresponding angles

Given lines *l* and *m* are parallel, fill in the blanks from the figure at the right.

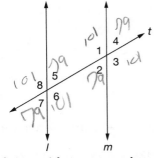

29. $\angle 2$ and $\angle 7$ are ___ angles.

30. $\angle 2$ and $\angle 5$ are ___ angles.

31. $\angle 3$ and $\angle 8$ are ___ angles.

Given $m\angle 1 = 101°$, find the measure of the following angles from the previous figure without measuring. Also give a reason for your answer.

32. $m\angle 4$ 33. $m\angle 2$

34. $m\angle 8$ 35. $m\angle 5$

36. $m\angle 6$ 37. $m\angle 7$

38. $m\angle 3$

Find the measure of the following angles. If the given angle is acute, give its complement and supplement. If it is obtuse, give its supplement.

39.

40.

41.

42.

■ **C. Exercises**

Given parallel lines *a* and *b* are cut by transversal *t* and $m\angle 1 = 143°$, find the measure of the following angles without measuring.

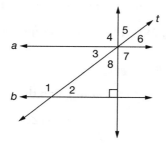

43. $m\angle 6$ 44. $m\angle 8$ 45. $m\angle 5$ 46. $m\angle 3$

CUMULATIVE REVIEW

Determine whether the relations are functions. [9.3]

47. {(–3, –5), (3, 7), (–3, 4), (5, –2)}

48. {(–3, 7), (3, 7), (–7, 7), (6, –1)}

49.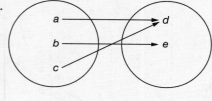

50.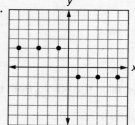

If $g(x) = \dfrac{x}{3} + 2$, find the following. [9.3]

51. $g(6)$ 52. $g(–9)$

A college football team is composed of students with the following classifications. [10.4]

53. Calculate each classification's percentage of the team.

54. Calculate the size of each slice of a pie chart for the data.

55. Make a pie chart for the data in the table. Label each slice with its classification and percentage.

56. Make a bar graph that illustrates the number of players of each classification.

Classification	Players
freshman	11
sophomore	16
junior	14
senior	9

PROBLEM
SOLVING

Organize Data with Diagrams

Some problems cannot be solved using the operations of arithmetic. Logic puzzles, such as the example below, are such problems. The strategy "organize data with diagrams" enables you to find the solution by using known facts and relationships between those facts to draw reasonable conclusions.

| Example 1 | Allen, Joel, Lisa, and Michelle each have a favorite sport. The sports are basketball, cycling, soccer, and tennis. Lisa's favorite sport does not use a ball. Joel once made a three-point shot in his favorite sport. Allen does not have a tennis racquet. Find each person's favorite sport. |

Answer

Think: What do I need to find in this problem, and what information is given to help me determine the answer?

I need to find the favorite sport for each person. I know that there are four people and four sports to pair up with the people.

Think: Make a table to help organize the known information.

	Allen	Joel	Lisa	Michelle
Basketball			X	
Cycling	X	X	yes	X
Soccer			X	
Tennis			X	

Since Lisa's favorite sport does not use a ball, it cannot be basketball, soccer, or tennis, so it must be cycling. Mark those boxes on the table. Since Lisa is the one who likes cycling, you can mark out cycling for all the other people.

Think: To help make the rest of the choices clear, put in the other given information. What other information will help to determine each person's favorite sport?

	Allen	Joel	Lisa	Michelle
Basketball	X	yes	X	X
Cycling	X	X	yes	X
Soccer		X	X	
Tennis		X	X	

Joel is the basketball player since he made a "three-point shot." Mark out basketball for all the other people, and mark out all the other sports for Joel.

Think: Find another piece of information that may help you decide who likes which sport.

	Allen	Joel	Lisa	Michelle
Basketball	X	yes	X	X
Cycling	X	X	yes	X
Soccer	yes	X	X	X
Tennis	X	X	X	

Allen is the soccer player because he does not have a tennis racquet. Mark out tennis for Allen, and mark out Michelle for soccer.

You can see from the table that Michelle must be the one who likes tennis.

Conclusion: Allen prefers soccer, Joel likes basketball, Lisa enjoys cycling, and Michelle favors tennis.

Example 2

A school contains 79 boys who are in one or more of three activities: 41 are out for football (F), 31 play in the band (B), and 20 are in the school play (P). Only two participate in all three activities. One member of the football team is in the play but not in the band. Five members of the football team play in the band. How many are in the play but not in the band or on the football team?

Answer

Think: I can draw three intersecting sets to represent the three activities. I can fill in the categories given in the problem.

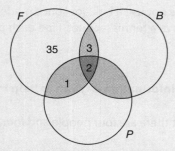

Think: There are 31 band members, and 5 are accounted for. This leaves 26. There are 20 students in the play. Three are accounted for, leaving 17.

Place 26 temporarily in the "band only" compartment and 17 temporarily in the "play only" compartment.

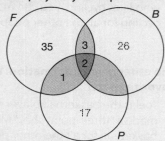

Think: I can add all the numbers. If the total exceeds 79, then the excess is the number of people who are in both the band and the play.

41 (4 football compartments) + 26 + 17 = 84. The excess is 84 − 79 = 5. Subtract 5 from the "band only" and 5 from the "play only" compartments. Place 5 in the "band and play" compartment.

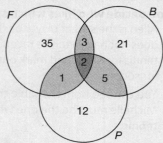

Think: I can verify that the total in band is 31 and the total in the play is 20.

Band: 21 + 3 + 2 + 5 = 31. Play: 12 + 1 + 2 + 5 = 20. The totals check.
Twelve boys are in the play but not in the band or on the football team.

■ Exercises

To help you solve each of the following exercises, devise a plan and make a table or list.

1. Anne, Doug, and Roy each play one of the following instruments in the band: clarinet, flute, and trumpet. The trumpet player is a boy. Roy bought a new reed for his instrument. Which instrument does each person play?

2. Chris, Frank, Orin, and Paresh drive cars made by Chevrolet, Ford, Buick, and Plymouth. Neither Chris nor Paresh drives a car that has the same first letter as his name. Frank has always driven a Mustang. Orin has never owned a General Motors car. Which person drives which car? (Hint: Chevrolets and Buicks are General Motors cars.)

3. Everyone at a youth activity was wearing navy or red. There were a total of ten people wearing navy, eight people wearing red, and three people wearing both navy and red. How many people were at the youth activity?

4. Miss Tipton surveyed the twenty-six students in her music class. She determined that seventeen students liked Chopin while five liked both Chopin and Vivaldi. The remaining students liked only Vivaldi. How many of her students liked only Vivaldi?

5. The song leader, youth pastor, and pastor at Trinity Bible Church are Mr. Carter, Mr. Peek, and Mr. López. Mr. Carter lives next door to the song leader. The youth pastor is Mr. Carter's son-in-law. Mr. Carter and Mr. Peek were on the debate team together in high school. Which job does each person have?

6. The Calvary youth group periodically goes on mission trips. Of the thirty-two young people in the group, sixteen have been to Mexico, fifteen have been to Canada, and seventeen have been to Puerto Rico on mission trips. Two went on all three trips. Five went to both Mexico and Canada, eight went to Canada and Puerto Rico, and six went to Mexico and Puerto Rico. How many of the group have not been on one of these mission trips?

7. Aiden, Jeffrey, Lori, and Nancy live in the towns of Athens, Jackson, Liberty, and Newark. Aiden has spent all of his life in Jackson. Neither Lori nor Nancy has ever been to Athens. Nancy lives in a town whose name has two syllables. Which person lives in which town?

8. Determine each girl's favorite among three drinks, and note any relationships among the girls. One girl's name is Sabina, and one of the drinks is cola. Two sisters have the same favorite drink. Belinda prefers a drink that all the other girls hate. Haley does not like root beer. Ashleigh is one of the two who likes lemonade, and Haley is Ashleigh's cousin.

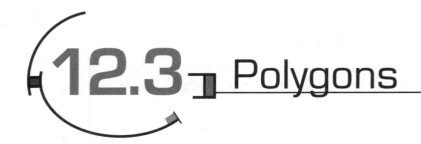

12.3 Polygons

A continuous set of points is called a *curve*. Lines and segments are continuous sets of points and are included in the family of all curves. Two-dimensional curves (curves contained in a plane) are *simple* if they do not intersect themselves. The shapes of the numerals 8 and 6 are examples of curves that are not simple. Two-dimensional curves in a plane are *closed* if they start and stop at the same point. The alphabetic letter C is an example of a simple curve that is not closed.

Two figures that are simple closed curves, and two that are not, are shown below.

simple	simple	simple,	closed,
closed	closed	not closed	not simple

Two simple closed curves that are studied in geometry are the polygon and the circle.

Definition

A **polygon** is a simple closed plane figure made up of line segments.

Polygons can be *convex* or *concave*. Every interior angle of a convex polygon has a measure less than 180°. A concave polygon has at least one interior angle with a measure greater than 180°. The concave polygon shown has such an angle marked. We will be concerned only with convex polygons in this text.

Each segment making up the polygon is a *side*. Any two adjacent sides of a polygon meet in a *vertex*. Polygons are named according to the number of their sides.

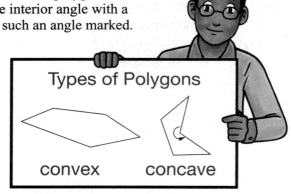

Types of Polygons

convex   concave

Number of Sides	Name	Number of Sides	Name
3	triangle	8	octagon
4	quadrilateral	9	nonagon
5	pentagon	10	decagon
6	hexagon	12	dodecagon
7	heptagon	n	n-gon

In a *regular polygon*, all sides have the same length and all angles have the same measure. Slash marks and arcs are often used to indicate which sides and angles have equal measures.

Example 1   Name each polygon and indicate whether it is regular.

a.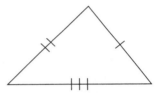

b.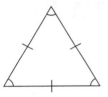

A honeycomb is composed of congruent hexagons.

Answer

a. *ABCD* is a quadrilateral.   It is a four-sided polygon.

b. *EFGHIJ* is a regular hexagon.   It is a six-sided polygon with all sides the same length and all angles equal in measure.

The polygon with the fewest possible number of sides is the triangle. Triangles are classified by the lengths of their sides.

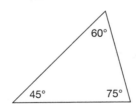

scalene triangle: no two sides have the same length

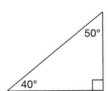

isosceles triangle: at least two sides have the same length

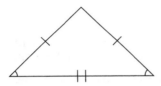

equilateral triangle: all sides have the same length

In an isosceles triangle, the angles opposite the sides of equal length are called the base angles and are also equal in measure. Notice that an equilateral triangle is also isosceles. This further implies that an equilateral triangle is also *equiangular*: All its angles have the same measure.

Triangles are also classified by the measures of their angles.

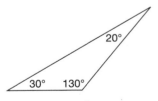

acute triangle:
three acute angles

right triangle:
one right angle

obtuse triangle:
one obtuse angle

A triangle is named by listing its three vertices after the △ symbol. For example, △*ABC* is read "triangle ABC."

Example 2 Classify △ABC, △DEF, and △GHI according to the measures of their angles and the lengths of their sides.

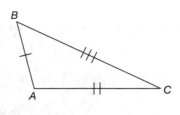
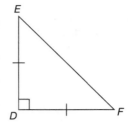
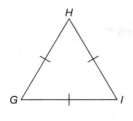

Answer

△ABC is obtuse scalene. ∠A is an obtuse angle; no two sides have the same length.

△DEF is right isosceles. ∠D is a right angle; two sides have the same length.

△GHI is acute equilateral. All the angles are acute; all the sides have the same length.

| Theorem |

In any triangle, the sum of the measures of the angles is 180°: in △ABC m∠A + m∠B + m∠C = 180°.

Example 3 Write and solve an equation to find m∠X.

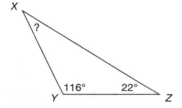

Answer

$$m\angle X + m\angle Y + m\angle Z = 180$$

$$m\angle X + 116 + 22 = 180$$
1. In any triangle, the sum of the measures of the angles is 180°.

$$m\angle X + 138 = 180$$
2. Subtract 138 from both sides.

$$m\angle X = 42°$$

Skill Check 1

Classify the following triangles according to the lengths of their sides.

1.

2.
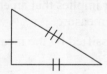

Classify the following triangles according to the measures of their angles.

3.
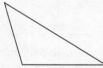

4.

Write and solve an equation to find m∠X.

5.
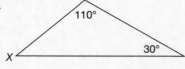

6.
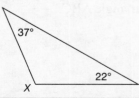

Definition

A **quadrilateral** is a four-sided polygon.

There are five special types of quadrilaterals. These are defined and listed below, beginning with the most general type.

Definitions

A **trapezoid** is a quadrilateral with at least one pair of parallel sides.

A **parallelogram** is a quadrilateral with two pairs of parallel sides.

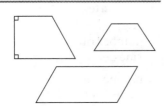

Notice from the definitions that parallelograms are special types of trapezoids; namely, they are trapezoids with two pairs of parallel sides.

Definitions

A **rectangle** is a parallelogram with four right angles.

A **rhombus** is a parallelogram with four congruent sides.

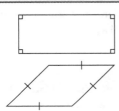

These two definitions indicate that rectangles and rhombi (plural of "rhombus") are special types of parallelograms.

Definition

A **square** is a rectangle with four congruent sides.

This definition shows that a square is a rectangle, but changing the definition to "a rhombus with four right angles" shows that a square can also be viewed as a special type of rhombus.

The relationships between the types of quadrilaterals are shown in the Venn diagram at the right.

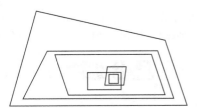

Definition

A **diagonal** is a line segment joining any two nonadjacent vertices of a polygon.

The fact that the sum of the angles of any triangle is 180° can be used to find the sum of the angles of any convex polygon. This is done by drawing all possible diagonals from one vertex of a polygon.

	Triangle	Quadrilateral	Pentagon	Hexagon
number of diagonals from one vertex				
number of sides, n	3	4	5	6
number of triangles formed	1	2	3	4
sum of angle measures	180°	2(180) = 360°	3(180) = 540°	4(180) = 720°

Notice that the number of triangles that can be formed by drawing all possible diagonals from one vertex is two less than the number of sides. Therefore, for any polygon of n sides, the sum of its angle measures is $(n - 2)180°$.

$n - 3$ diagonals from one vertex form $n - 2$ triangles.

Example 4 Find the following.
a. the sum of the measures of the angles in a regular octagon
b. the measure of each angle

Answer
a. Draw all possible diagonals from one vertex of the octagon to form six triangles. The sum of the angles of the octagon is the sum of the angles of the six triangles.
  $6(180) = 1,080°$

b. Since a regular octagon has eight angles, all equal in measure, each angle has a measure of $\frac{1,080}{8} = 135°$.
  A regular octagon contains eight 135° angles.

When you know the measures of all the angles of a polygon except one, you can write and solve an equation to find the missing angle.

Example 5 Write and solve an equation to find $m\angle A$.

Answer
$m\angle A + 80 + 55 + 120 = 360$
$m\angle A + 255 = 360$
$m\angle A + 255 - 255 = 360 - 255$
$m\angle A = 105°$

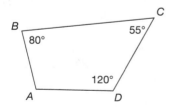

1. Name the polygon and find the sum of the measures of its angles.

2. Find the measure of each angle in the regular polygon.

3. Write and solve an equation to find $m\angle A$.

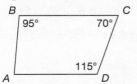

⊕ Invention

Even though the kaleidoscope is essentially a toy that displays beautiful patterns, it works because of some significant geometrical principles. It looks like a small telescope with an eyepiece at one end and a translucent lens at the other. Light enters the lens to illuminate some small colored stones or beads lying between two or three mirrors that meet at 60°. As the viewer slowly turns the tube, he actually sees reflections of reflections, so the entire field of view is divided into six sectors of beautiful colored symmetry. Sir David Brewster of Scotland invented the kaleidoscope in 1816 as a result of his keen interest in optics. Its popularity has come and gone a number of times over the years, but when first introduced to the public, it became a sensation and was widely enjoyed by all kinds of people.

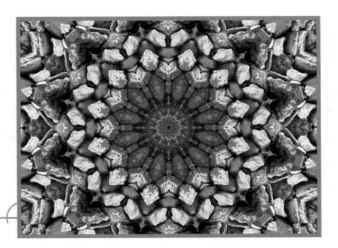

■ A. Exercises

1. Which of the figures are simple?

2. Which of the figures are closed?

3. Which of the figures are polygons? Which are convex?

    a   b   c   d

4. Which of the polygons appear to be regular?

    a   b   c   d

5. A pentagon has ___ sides and ___ vertices.

6. A polygon must have at least ___ sides.

7. The sum of the measures of the angles in any triangle is ___.

Classify the following triangles according to the lengths of their sides.

8.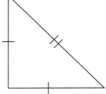
9.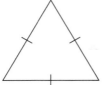
10.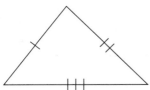

Classify the following triangles according to the measures of their angles.

11.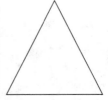
12.
13.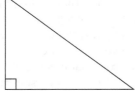

14. Draw an isosceles right triangle.

15. Draw a scalene obtuse triangle.

16. Write an equation to find $m\angle A$ in $\triangle ABC$ and solve it when $m\angle B = 41°$ and $m\angle C = 112°$.

True or false

17. Every square is a rectangle.

18. No quadrilateral is a rectangle.

19. Every rectangle is a trapezoid.

20. A rhombus and a square are the same thing.

21. Every rectangle is a parallelogram.

■ B. Exercises

Find the sum of the measures of the angles in the following polygons.

22. quadrilateral
23. pentagon
24. nonagon

Find the measure of each angle in the following regular polygons.

25. hexagon
26. twenty-sided polygon
27. decagon

Find the number of diagonals from one vertex and the total number of diagonals in each polygon.

28. nonagon
29. dodecagon
30. pentagon

Write an equation and use it to find the missing angle measure in the following polygons.

31. quadrilateral with $m\angle A = 72°$, $m\angle B = 80°$, and $m\angle C = 150°$

32. hexagon with $m\angle A = 140°$, $m\angle B = 150°$, $m\angle C = 84°$, $m\angle D = 100°$, and $m\angle E = 102°$

■ C. Exercises

33. Develop a formula for the measure of each interior angle in a regular n-gon.

34. Write an expression for the number of diagonals drawn from any one vertex of a convex n-gon.

35. Develop a formula for the total number of diagonals in a convex n-gon.

■ Dominion thru Math

36. If the load capacity of the TEU in Section 12.1, Dominion thru Math, is restricted to 19.25 tn., what is the acceptable weight per cubic foot of the container's contents? Round your answer to the nearest tenth of a pound per cubic foot.

37. If the maximum load capacity for the FEU in Section 12.1, Dominion thru Math, is 26.4 tn., what is the acceptable weight per cubic foot of the container's contents?

 CUMULATIVE REVIEW

Determine whether the ordered pairs are solutions to the given equation. [9.4]

38. $y = 2x - 1$

   a. (7, 15)

   b. (−4, −9)

39. $y = -\dfrac{1}{3}x + 2$

   a. $\left(1, \dfrac{5}{3}\right)$

   b. (0, 6)

Using a table, find three ordered pairs that satisfy the given function rules. Graph each linear equation. [9.4]

40. $y = 3x - 1$

41. $y = -\dfrac{1}{3}x + 2$

An investor has $10,000 to invest in a bank that is offering 5% simple interest. [7.7]

42. Find the amount in the savings account after 1 yr.

Use the following formula to find the amount in a savings account resulting from an investment of $10,000 compounded annually at 5%. [7.7]

$S = P(1 + i)^n$, where S = amount in the savings account, P = principal, i = interest rate, and n = number of interest payments.

43. Find the amount in the savings account after 20 yr.

44. Find the amount in the savings account after 40 yr.

Perform the indicated operations. Leave answers in scientific notation. [6.8]

45. $(6.4 \times 10^{19}) - (2.5 \times 10^{19})$

46. $(5.3 \times 10^{6}) + (6.1 \times 10^{5})$

47. $(4.5 \times 10^{6})(3.6 \times 10^{-3})$

48. $(8.84 \times 10^{17}) \div (3.4 \times 10^{12})$

12.4 Perimeter and Circumference

The distance around a polygon is its *perimeter*. The following perimeter formulas summarize the methods for finding this distance.

Perimeter Formulas for Polygons				
Triangle	**Rectangle**	**Square**	**Parallelogram**	**Trapezoid**
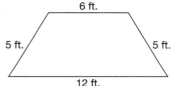				
$p = a + b + c$	$p = 2l + 2w$	$p = 4s$	$p = 2a + 2b$	$p = a + b + c + d$

Example 1   Find the perimeter of the following polygons.

a.
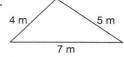
4 m   5 m
7 m

b.
6 ft.
5 ft.   5 ft.
12 ft.

Answer

a. $p = 4 + 5 + 7 = 16$ m

b. $p = 5 + 12 + 5 + 6 = 28$ ft.

Example 2   A parallelogram has a perimeter of 30 in. and a side of 6.5 in. Find the length of the other parallel sides.

Answer

$2a + 2b = p$

$2(6.5) + 2b = 30$ 1. Substitute the given values into the formula for the perimeter of a parallelogram.

$13 + 2b = 30$

$13 + 2b - 13 = 30 - 13$ 2. Apply the Addition Property of Equality.

$2b = 17$

$\dfrac{2b}{2} = \dfrac{17}{2}$ 3. Apply the Multiplication Property of Equality.

$b = 8.5$

The lengths of the other parallel sides of the parallelogram are 8.5 in.

Skill Check 1

Find the perimeter of the following polygons.

1. a square 8 m on a side

2. an isosceles triangle with one side of 9 m and two sides of 10 m

Find the following dimensions.

3. the length of a side of a square whose perimeter is 12.4 in.

4. the dimensions of a rectangle whose length is twice its width and whose perimeter is 42 cm

The other major two-dimensional figure studied in geometry is the circle.

Definitions

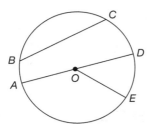

A **circle** is the set of points in a plane that are equidistant from a fixed point called the **center**.

A **chord** is a line segment with both endpoints on a circle. $\overline{BC}$ and $\overline{AD}$ are chords.

A **diameter** (d) is a chord passing through the center of a circle. The chord $\overline{AD}$ is a diameter of circle O.

A **radius** is a line segment from the center of a circle to a point on the circle. $\overline{OA}$, $\overline{OD}$, and $\overline{OE}$ are radii of circle O.

The distance around a circle is called its *circumference* (c). Circumference is similar to the concept of perimeter in a polygon. In the geometry of God's creation, circles have a unique characteristic. In every circle, the ratio of the circumference to the diameter is the special irrational number π, where $\frac{c}{d} = \pi \approx 3.14$.

By multiplying both sides of the equation by d, we can derive the formula for the circumference of a circle.

$$\frac{c}{d} = \pi$$

$$\cancel{d}\left(\frac{c}{\cancel{d}}\right) = \pi d$$

$$c = \pi d$$

This circular bin is used to store grain such as wheat.

Circumference Formulas for Circles	
$c = \pi d$	The circumference is equal to π times the diameter.
$c = 2\pi r$	The circumference is equal to two times π times the radius.

Example 3 Find the circumference of the following circles. Round to the nearest tenth.

a. radius of 5.3 cm   b. diameter of 8 ft.

Answer

a. $c = 2\pi r$
$\quad = 2\pi(5.3) = 10.6\pi$
$\quad = 10.6(3.14)$
$\quad = 33.284$
$\quad \approx 33.3$ cm

b. $c = \pi d$
$\quad = \pi(8) = 8\pi$
$\quad = 8(3.14)$
$\quad = 25.12$
$\quad \approx 25.1$ ft.

Example 4 Find the diameter and radius of a circle with a circumference of 30 in. Round to the nearest tenth of an inch.

Answer

$\pi d = c$
$3.14d = 30$
$\dfrac{3.14d}{3.14} = \dfrac{30}{3.14}$
$d \approx 9.6$ in.
$r = \dfrac{d}{2} = 4.8$ in.

Skill Check 2

Find the circumference of the following circles.

1. a circle with a radius of 10 in.

2. a circle with a diameter of 100 yd.

Find the following dimensions.

3. the diameter of a circle whose circumference is 9.42 ft.

4. the radius of a circle whose circumference is 2π m

■ A. Exercises

True or false

1. Every diameter is a chord.

2. A radius is twice the length of a diameter.

3. All radii of a circle are of equal length.

4. All chords of a circle are of equal length.

Find the circumference of the following circles. Round answers to the nearest hundredth.

5. radius of 8 ft.   6. diameter of 18 in.   7. diameter of $\dfrac{1}{2}$ in.

Find the diameter and radius of circles with the given circumference. Round answers to the nearest tenth.

8. 40 ft.   9. 2 mi.   10. 23.5 ft.

Find the perimeter of the following polygons.

11. 17 ft. by 9 ft. rectangle

12. a pentagon with two sides of 8.5 in., two sides of 12 in., and one side of 17 in.

13. a regular hexagon with sides of 9.5 cm

14. a regular octagon with sides of 12.4 cm

Find the perimeter of the following figures.

15.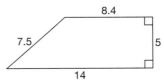

16.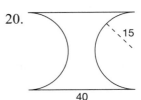

17.

18.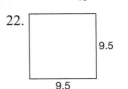

19.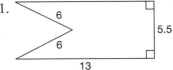

20.

21.

22.

Find the following dimensions.

23. the length of a side of a square whose perimeter is 22 ft.

24. the length of a side of a regular hexagon whose perimeter is 49.8 ft.

25. the dimensions of a rectangle whose length is four times its width and whose perimeter is 94 m

■ B. Exercises

What kind of triangle appears to be formed in the following circumstances?

26. A triangle is formed with one vertex at the center of a circle. Two sides are radii of the circle that meet to form a 60° angle, and the third side is a chord.

27. A triangle is formed within a circle. One side is a diameter, and the third vertex is on the circle.

28. What appears to be true of two chords that are equidistant from the center of a circle?

29. Consider a circle with a square of sides a inside of it, with all four vertices on the circle. Now suppose that the circle is in turn contained in a square of sides b, in such a way that the circle touches each side of the outer square at exactly one point. Compare the relative lengths of the circumference of the circle to the perimeters of the squares.

30. If one of two circles has a radius twice as long as the other, how do their circumferences compare?

31. If one of two squares has sides three times as long as the other, how do their perimeters compare?

32. If one of two squares has sides three times as long as the other, how do their areas compare?

33. A room is 12 ft. by 10 ft. with a door that is 30 in. wide. How many feet of baseboard are needed to go around the room?

34. A bicycle tire has a diameter of 28 in. How many full revolutions will it make while traveling a mile?

35. A clock's minute hand is 8 in. long. How many feet will the tip of the hand travel in one day?

■ C. Exercises

36. Find the perimeter of the shaded figure.

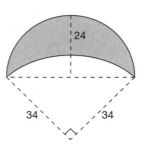

37. A running track is to have straightaways that are 100 m long. How far apart will the straightaways have to be for the track to be 400 m long? How far for an 800 m track with 200 m straightaways? Round to the nearest tenth of a meter.

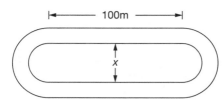

■ Dominion thru Math

Placing cargo in a container requires careful planning in order to most effectively use the available space and get the greatest quantity of boxes in a TEU. Many cartons require transport in an upright position, and the total weight of the load cannot exceed the payload capacity of the TEU. The basic packing process involves placing the cartons on the rectangular floor of the container to get the most cartons per layer. Then the number of layers is determined by the vertical dimension of the cartons and the available height of the container. Once the maximum number of cartons is determined, their gross weight must be checked against the maximum payload of the TEU or FEU. The following example will use the interior dimensions of a TEU from Section 12.1, Dominion thru Math.

Example: Find the best packing scheme for getting the maximum number of cartons in three TEUs, if the cartons weigh 55 lb., measure length-width-height as 1.5' × 1.25' × 1', and must be kept upright.

Solution: Method A places the cartons with their long side parallel to the length of the container. Method B places the cartons with their long side parallel to the width of the container.

Container Dimension	Method A	Method B
19.35 ft. length	12 rows	15 rows
7.72 ft. width	6 rows	5 rows
7.83 ft. height	7 layers	7 layers
Totals	504 cartons	525 cartons

Use a calculator and make a table of possible methods to determine the answers to the following exercises.

38. An overseas shipment of 2,000 PC monitors is to be transported in FEUs. The cartons are 2 ft. long by 1.8 ft. wide by 1.75 ft. high and must be kept upright. How many FEUs will be needed? If each carton weighs 65 lb., is there any restriction due to the weight?

39. Automobile transmissions are shipped in wooden crates measuring 3 ft. long by 2 ft. wide by 2.5 ft. high. These 270 lb. crates must be kept upright. What is the least number of FEUs needed to ship 5,495 crates?

Find the percent change. [7.8]

40. A worker's performance rating rose from 68 to 85 for the current month.

41. The worker's performance rating fell from 85 one year to 68 the following year.

42. Glen went on a special diet and engaged in weight training in preparation for football season. His weight increased by 15 lb. If he originally weighed 180 lb., what was the percent increase in his weight?

43. If Hye Ree paid $42 for a jacket that was originally priced at $60, what percent was the jacket discounted?

Solve. Express noninteger answers as fractions in lowest terms or decimals rounded to the nearest tenth. [8.1–8.2]

44. $14x = 4(x - 2)$

45. $3(2x - 5) = 4x - 10$

46. $(x + 2) + 2(x + 3) = 8x + 2(7 - x)$

Find the slope of the line through the two given points. [9.5]

47. $(6, -3)$ and $(2, 1)$

48. $(5, 4)$ and $(-7, 4)$

49. Find the slope of the graphed line.

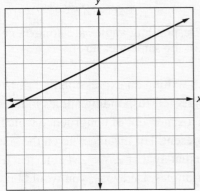

12.5 Congruence and Similarity

Definition

Congruent polygons are polygons with the same size and shape.

$\triangle ABC$ and $\triangle DEF$, pictured below, are congruent. This statement is represented symbolically as $\triangle ABC \cong \triangle DEF$, where the symbol $\cong$ is read "is congruent to."

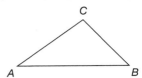
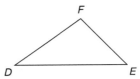

If you could lift $\triangle ABC$ and place it on top of $\triangle DEF$, the angles and the sides would coincide because $m\angle A = m\angle D$, $m\angle B = m\angle E$, $m\angle C = m\angle F$, $AB = DE$, $BC = EF$, and $AC = DF$. The matching angles are called *corresponding angles*, and the matching sides are called *corresponding sides*.

Congruent angles are angles with the same measure.
Congruent segments are segments with the same length.

The table below lists the congruent parts of the previous congruent triangles. To indicate that the corresponding angles and sides of two figures are congruent, the corresponding parts are marked with the congruence symbol (≅).

Corresponding Angles	Corresponding Sides
∠A ≅ ∠D ∠B ≅ ∠E ∠C ≅ ∠F	$\overline{AC} \cong \overline{DF}$ $\overline{AB} \cong \overline{DE}$ $\overline{BC} \cong \overline{EF}$
Corresponding angles are congruent (have the same measure).	Corresponding sides are congruent (have the same length).

When writing an expression like △ABC ≅ △DEF, you must list the vertices of each triangle's corresponding angles in the same order. This way you will be able to tell from a statement of congruence which parts are congruent, even when no figures are present. For instance, given the statement △PNR ≅ △WAQ, you would know immediately that ∠N ≅ ∠A since each is the second vertex in the names given for the triangles. Likewise, you would know that $\overline{NR} \cong \overline{AQ}$, since they are the last two letters in the names of the triangles containing them.

Example 1 △RST ≅ △XYZ. Complete each statement.

∠R ≅ _?_ $\overline{RT} \cong$ _?_

∠S ≅ _?_ $\overline{RS} \cong$ _?_

∠T ≅ _?_ $\overline{ST} \cong$ _?_

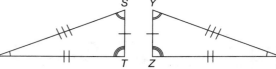

Answer

∠R ≅ ∠X   In the statement of congruence, R is written first in one triangle's name and X is written
∠S ≅ ∠Y   first in the other; therefore, ∠R ≅ ∠X, and so on for the other angles.
∠T ≅ ∠Z

$\overline{RT} \cong \overline{XZ}$ The first two letters in one triangle's name are RS, and the first two letters in the other

$\overline{RS} \cong \overline{XY}$ are XY; therefore, $\overline{RS} \cong \overline{XY}$, and so on for the other sides.

$\overline{ST} \cong \overline{YZ}$

Skill Check 1

△QRS ≅ △TUV. **Complete each statement.**

1. ∠Q ≅ ___   2. $\overline{RS} \cong$ ___   3. $m\angle S =$ ___

4. QR = ___   5. ∠U ≅ ___   6. $\overline{TV} \cong$ ___

Just as two triangles can be congruent, so can two quadrilaterals or any other pair of polygons with the same number of sides.

Congruent means having exactly the same size and shape, whereas *similar* means having the same shape but not necessarily the same size.

Christians are to be as similar to Jesus Christ as possible. It is impossible for a person here on earth to be sinless like Jesus, but the Christian must follow His example as closely as possible. First Peter 2:21 admonishes the Christian, "For even hereunto were ye called: because Christ also suffered for us, leaving us an example, that ye should follow his steps."

Figures other than polygons can be similar figures too.

> ### Definition
>
> **Similar polygons** are polygons that have the same shape but not necessarily the same size. The symbol ~ means "is similar to."

The corresponding angles of similar polygons are congruent. However, the corresponding sides are proportional, not necessarily congruent.

Suppose two triangles are similar, and a side of the larger triangle is three times as long as the corresponding side of the smaller triangle. The same will be true for the other two pairs of corresponding sides.

> ### Theorem
>
> If two polygons are similar, then the corresponding angles are congruent and the lengths of the corresponding sides are proportional.

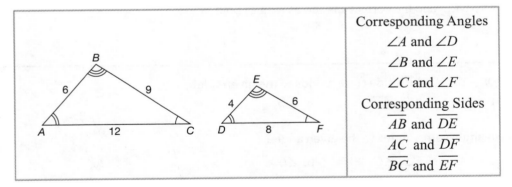

	Corresponding Angles
	$\angle A$ and $\angle D$
	$\angle B$ and $\angle E$
	$\angle C$ and $\angle F$
	Corresponding Sides
	$\overline{AB}$ and $\overline{DE}$
	$\overline{AC}$ and $\overline{DF}$
	$\overline{BC}$ and $\overline{EF}$

When stating that two triangles are similar, list the vertices of each triangle's corresponding angles in the same order. In the above figure, $\triangle ABC \sim \triangle DEF$. This means that $\angle A \cong \angle D$, $\angle B \cong \angle E$, $\angle C \cong \angle F$, $\frac{AB}{DE} = \frac{6}{4} = \frac{3}{2}$, $\frac{AC}{DF} = \frac{12}{8} = \frac{3}{2}$, and $\frac{BC}{EF} = \frac{9}{6} = \frac{3}{2}$.

Notice that the ratio of the corresponding sides is a constant $\frac{3}{2}$ for these similar triangles. This ratio is called the *scale factor*.

If you know the lengths of the sides in one of two similar triangles and the length of one side in the second triangle, you can use proportions to find the remaining two sides of the second triangle.

Example 2 $\triangle RST \sim \triangle XYZ$. Use a proportion to find XY.

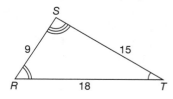 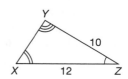

Answer

$\dfrac{XY}{RS} = \dfrac{XZ}{RT}$ 1. The lengths of corresponding sides are proportional.

$\dfrac{XY}{9} = \dfrac{2}{3}$ 2. Substitute the ratio of the lengths of two corresponding sides: $\dfrac{12}{18} = \dfrac{2}{3}$.

$3(XY) = 18$ 3. Apply the Property of Proportions.

$\dfrac{3(XY)}{3} = \dfrac{18}{3}$ 4. Solve for XY.

$XY = 6$

The proportion was set up with both ratios in the order $\dfrac{\text{side of smaller } \triangle}{\text{corresponding side of larger } \triangle}$. The reduced ratio of corresponding sides was $\dfrac{2}{3}$. If the proportion had been set up with ratios in the order $\dfrac{\text{side of larger } \triangle}{\text{corresponding side of smaller } \triangle}$, the reduced ratio of corresponding sides would have been $\dfrac{3}{2}$, and XY would have been in the denominator of the other ratio. Either way will yield the correct answer, as long as both ratios are in the same order.

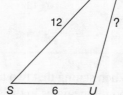

$\cong \triangle$s are $\sim \triangle$s

Skill Check 2

If $\triangle PQR \sim \triangle STU$, which side corresponds to the given side?

1. $\overline{PQ}$ 2. $\overline{SU}$ 3. $\overline{QR}$

Which angle corresponds to the given angle?

4. $\angle S$ 5. $\angle Q$ 6. $\angle U$

Use proportions to find the missing lengths.

7. PR 8. TU

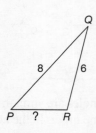 

■ A. Exercises

Given triangle congruence statements, complete the following statements of congruence of corresponding parts.

1. If $\triangle TXC \cong \triangle CDW$, then $\overline{TC} \cong$ ___.

2. If $\triangle TAC \cong \triangle EDV$, then $\angle C \cong$ ___.

3. If $\triangle ABC \cong \triangle QPB$, then $\overline{BC} \cong$ ___.

4. If $\triangle NML \cong \triangle AXK$, then $\angle M \cong$ ___.

5. If $\triangle TWC \cong \triangle CEM$, then $\angle T \cong$ ___.

6. If $\triangle RPQ \cong \triangle HCL$, then $\overline{RP} \cong$ ___.

Given triangle similarity statements, complete the following statements of congruence of corresponding parts.

7. If $\triangle ADJ \sim \triangle WTN$, then $\angle J \cong$ ___.

8. If $\triangle DXP \sim \triangle MFZ$, then $\dfrac{DX}{MF} = \dfrac{DP}{?}$.

9. If $\triangle YAP \sim \triangle MCW$, then $\angle A \cong$ ___.

10. If $\triangle PBC \sim \triangle DEF$, then $\angle B \cong$ ___.

11. If $\triangle MNP \sim \triangle XYZ$, then $\dfrac{NP}{YZ} = \dfrac{?}{XY}$.

■ B. Exercises

Find the corresponding parts for the following.

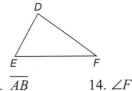 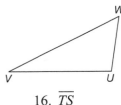

12. $\angle C$ 13. $\overline{AB}$ 14. $\angle F$ 15. $\angle R$ 16. $\overline{TS}$ 17. $\overline{TR}$

Write the statements showing the relationships of the pairs of triangles above.

18. congruence   19. similarity

Use proportions to find the missing lengths. Round answers to the nearest tenth.

20.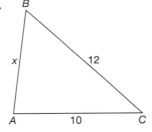

21.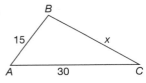

22.

23.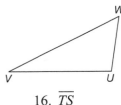

24.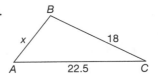

25.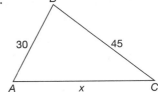

26.

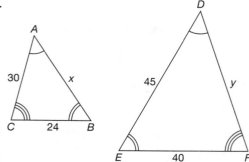

27.

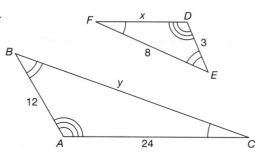

28.

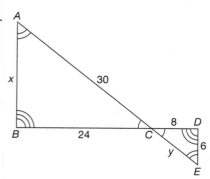

29.

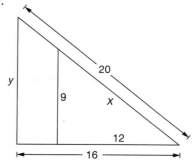

Are the following pairs of triangles similar? Write yes or no.

30.

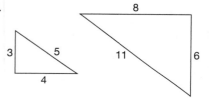

31.

■ C. Exercises

32. Suppose the sides of a quadrilateral are 3, 7, 9, and 13. The smallest side of a similar quadrilateral is 15. What are the other sides of the second quadrilateral?

33. Two regular hexagons have sides of 3 and 5.2 respectively. Are they similar?

34. Two rectangles are similar. One has sides of 5 and 8 units. If one side of the other rectangle is x, what is the length of a side adjacent to it?

■ Dominion thru Math

35. Cartons for shipping power tools are 18" long by 16" wide by 15" tall and must be kept upright. What is the least number of TEUs it will take to ship 6,000 cartons? Is anything gained by using high cubes?

36. A certain type of apparel is packaged in 3' × 2' × 2.5' high cartons that must be kept upright. Find the maximum number of cartons that can be packed per layer in a FEU by orienting some cartons one way and some another. Does a high cube provide a larger carton count per FEU? How many FEUs are needed to ship 8,000 cartons?

Write an inequality and solve. [8.5]

37. The sum of three consecutive integers is less than 45. Find the greatest possible value for the integers.

38. The sofa was $150 more than the loveseat, and together they cost at most $1,300. Find the maximum price for each piece of furniture.

39. The difference in the price of a large drink and a small drink was $0.80, and the cost of two large drinks and four small drinks was at least $8.20. Find the price range for each size of drink.

40. Change $3x + 8y = 24$ to slope-intercept form. [9.6]

41. Find the x- and y-intercepts of the line $5x - 3y = 15$ and use them to graph the line. [9.6]

42. Find the slope and y-intercept of the line $4x - 5y = 20$ and use them to graph the line. [9.6]

Simplify the following. If no answer exists, state "not real." [11.1]

43. $\sqrt{-81}$

44. $\sqrt{289}$

45. $3\sqrt{169 - 25} - \sqrt{49}$

46. $\sqrt{225} + 2\sqrt{-16}$

MIND OVER MATH

Fractals are interesting geometric figures. One of the most famous fractals is the *Sierpinski triangle*. To form a Sierpinski triangle, draw an equilateral triangle with side lengths of 2 units. Then form other equilateral triangles by connecting the midpoints of each side, as shown in the diagram. Notice that there are now four smaller triangles. Lightly shade the center triangle. How many unshaded triangles are there? What is the length of each side of these triangles? What is the sum of the perimeters of the unshaded triangles?

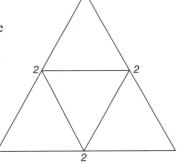

Find the midpoint of each side again and form equilateral triangles inside the unshaded triangles. Shade all the new center triangles. How many unshaded triangles are there? What is the length of each side now? What is the sum of the perimeters of the unshaded triangles now?

Do the same thing again. How many unshaded triangles are there? What is the length of each side now? What is the sum of the perimeters of the unshaded triangles now?

Is there a pattern in the number of unshaded triangles and perimeter values? Could this process go on forever? What would happen to the sum of the perimeters?

12.6 Special Right Triangles

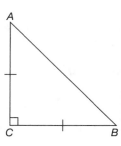

$\triangle ABC$ is an isosceles right triangle. The angles opposite the equal sides are equal; that is, $m\angle A = m\angle B$. The sum of the angles of any triangle is 180°; therefore, the two acute angles are each 45° angles.

In the figure below, each leg is one unit, and the hypotenuse is represented as c. According to the Pythagorean theorem, the length of c equals $\sqrt{2}$.

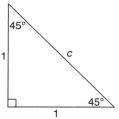

$$c^2 = a^2 + b^2$$
$$= 1^2 + 1^2$$
$$= 1 + 1$$
$$= 2$$
$$c = \sqrt{2}$$

Every isosceles right triangle, also called a 45-45 right triangle, is similar to the one above. The sides of similar triangles are proportional, so if you know the length of one side of such a triangle, you can find the missing lengths of the other two sides. If a is the length of a leg and c is the length of the hypotenuse, then the following proportion is true.

$\dfrac{a}{1} = \dfrac{c}{\sqrt{2}}$ 1. The length of a leg of one triangle is to the length of the corresponding leg in the other as the length of the hypotenuse in the first triangle is to the length of the hypotenuse in the second.

$1 \cdot c = a \cdot \sqrt{2}$ 2. Take the product of the extremes and means to solve for c.

$c = a\sqrt{2}$ 3. Simplify.

45-45 Right Triangle	
If each leg of a 45-45 right triangle is a units long, then the hypotenuse is $a\sqrt{2}$ units long.	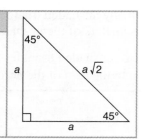

Example 1   Find the length of the hypotenuse in the 45-45 right triangle.

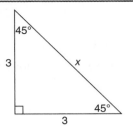

Answer

In a 45-45 right triangle, the length of the hypotenuse is $\sqrt{2}$ times the length of either leg.

Therefore, $x = 3\sqrt{2}$.

The length of the hypotenuse is $3\sqrt{2}$ units.

Example 2   Find the lengths of the legs in the 45-45 right triangle.

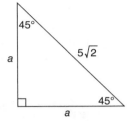

Answer

In a 45-45 right triangle, the length of the hypotenuse is $a\sqrt{2} = 5\sqrt{2}$.

Therefore, $a = 5$.

The length of each leg is 5 units.

Skill Check 1

Find the lengths of the legs in the following 45-45 right triangles.

1. hypotenuse of $10\sqrt{2}$ 2. hypotenuse of $3\sqrt{2}$

Find the length of the hypotenuse in the following 45-45 right triangles.

3. legs of 8   4. legs of 12

Another special triangle is an equilateral triangle. All its sides are equal in length, so the measures of the angles opposite the sides are all equal. Since the sum of the angle measures in any triangle is 180°, each angle measure is $\frac{180°}{3} = 60°$.

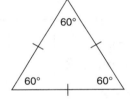

If you drop a perpendicular from one vertex of an equilateral triangle, the perpendicular will bisect both the opposite side and the angle at its vertex. Thus two congruent right triangles are formed, each with acute angles of 30° and 60°. Such triangles are called 30-60 right triangles.

In 30-60 right triangles, the side opposite the 30° angle is one-half the length of the hypotenuse. Notice that the leg and the hypotenuse are represented in the figure below as a and $2a$ respectively.

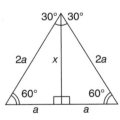

Applying the Pythagorean theorem, you can find the length of the long leg, x, in a 30-60 right triangle.

$$a^2 + b^2 = c^2$$
$$a^2 + x^2 = (2a)^2$$
$$a^2 + x^2 = 4a^2$$
$$x^2 = 3a^2$$
$$x = \sqrt{3a^2}$$
$$= a\sqrt{3}$$

The length of the long leg is $a\sqrt{3}$.

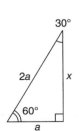

All 45-45 right triangles are ~.
All 30-60 right triangles are ~.

30-60 Right Triangle	
If the short leg of a 30-60 right triangle is a units long, then the long leg is $a\sqrt{3}$ units long and the hypotenuse is $2a$ units long.	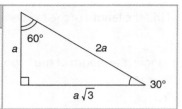

Example 3 Find the missing lengths x and y in the triangle.

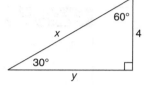

Answer
In a 30-60 right triangle, the length of the long leg is $a\sqrt{3}$, and the length of the hypotenuse is $2a$.
Since $a = 4$, the long leg is $4\sqrt{3}$ units, and the hypotenuse is $2(4) = 8$ units.

Example 4 Find the short leg and hypotenuse of a 30-60 right triangle whose long leg is $6\sqrt{3}$.

Answer
Since the long leg of a 30-60 right triangle is $a\sqrt{3} = 6\sqrt{3}$, it follows that the short leg is $a = 6$. Then the hypotenuse is $2a = 2(6) = 12$.

Example 5 Find the long leg and short leg of a 30-60 right triangle whose hypotenuse is 9.

Answer
The hypotenuse is $2a = 9$, so the short leg is $a = \dfrac{9}{2} = 4.5$. The long leg is $a\sqrt{3} = 4.5\sqrt{3}$ or $\dfrac{9\sqrt{3}}{2}$.

Skill Check 2

Find the other two sides in the following 30-60 right triangles.

1.
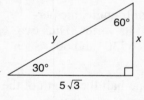

2.
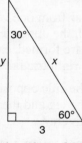

3.
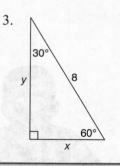

4. short leg of 9

5. hypotenuse of 15

6. long leg of $14\sqrt{3}$

◼ A. Exercises

Find the unknown lengths in the following special right triangles.

1.
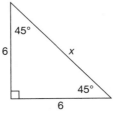

2.
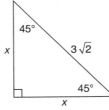

3.
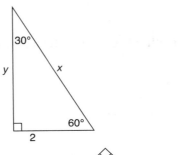

4.
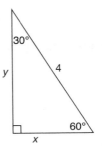

5.
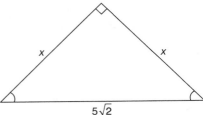

6.
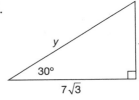

Draw a 45-45 right triangle and use the drawing for exercises 7–8.

7. Find the length of the hypotenuse if the length of each leg is 7.

8. Find the length of each leg if the length of the hypotenuse is $\sqrt{2}$.

Draw a 30-60 right triangle and use the drawing for exercises 9–10.

9. Find the lengths of the long leg and hypotenuse if the length of the short leg is 5.

10. Find the lengths of the legs if the length of the hypotenuse is 3.

Find the lengths of the legs in the following 45-45 right triangles.

11. hypotenuse of $8\sqrt{2}$

12. hypotenuse of $5.5\sqrt{2}$

Find the length of the hypotenuse in the following 45-45 right triangles.

13. legs of 9

14. legs of 12

15. legs of $3\sqrt{2}$

16. legs of $17\sqrt{2}$

Find the other two sides in the following 30-60 right triangles.

17. short leg of 9

18. short leg of 7

19. short leg of 5.6

20. short leg of $\sqrt{3}$

21. hypotenuse of 19

22. hypotenuse of 6

23. hypotenuse of 20.4

24. hypotenuse of $7\sqrt{3}$

25. long leg of $16\sqrt{3}$

26. long leg of $7\sqrt{3}$

■ B. Exercises

Find the other two sides in the following special right triangles. Express answers in radical form, and then use a calculator to calculate them to the nearest tenth.

27. 45-45 with a leg of 12

28. 45-45 with hypotenuse of 19

29. 30-60 with short leg of 7

30. 30-60 with long leg of 20

31. 30-60 with hypotenuse of 32

Use a calculator to find decimal approximations to the nearest tenth of the other two sides in the following special right triangles.

32.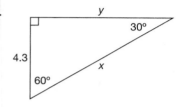

33.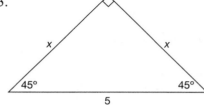

34.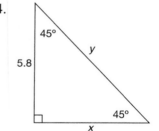

35.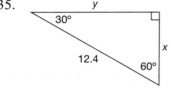

■C. Exercises

Find the other two sides in the following 30-60 right triangles. Express answers in radical form, and then use a calculator to calculate the lengths of all three sides to the nearest tenth.

36. short leg of $\sqrt{5}$

37. short leg of $2\sqrt{7}$

38. long leg of $20\sqrt{3}$

■ Dominion thru Math

Big, heavy ships float because of Archimedes' principle: An object in water is buoyed up by a force equal to the weight of the water it displaces. Actually, water is quite heavy; each cubic foot of water weighs 62.4 lb., and each gallon weighs 8.34 lb. The displacement of a ship can be expressed as volume in cubic feet or cubic meters and as weight in tons (2,000 lb.) or metric tons (1,000 kg). A ship that displaces 2,000,000 ft.^{3} of water has 62,400 tn. to distribute between the ship's weight and the cargo. In the following exercises we will assume the hull of the ship has the shape of a giant shoebox, even though the bow and stern actually have a certain amount of curvature.

39. The 3,000 TEU container ship *Manukai*, operated by Matson Navigation in Hawaii, has a gross weight of about 87,000 tn. when fully loaded. The ship itself weighs 32,600 tn. and carries 4,100 tn. of fuel and 12,800 tn. of water ballast.

    a. How many tons of container cargo can the ship carry?

    b. What is the average weight of each of the 3,000 TEUs?

    c. If the ship is 655 ft. long and has a draft of 36 ft., what is the approximate width of the ship? (Draft is the depth of the ship in the water.)

40. The 1,043 ft. long by 137 ft. wide container ship *Regina Maersk*, operated by Maersk Sealand of Denmark, can transport 6,000 TEUs containing 88,550 tn. of containerized cargo with a loaded displacement of 6,787,300 ft.^{3}.

    a. Find an approximation of the draft of the ship.

    b. What is the average weight of each TEU this ship will carry?

CUMULATIVE REVIEW

Use the following equation for the next two exercises: $y = -\frac{2}{3}x + 1$. [9.6]

41. Find the rise and run and the y-intercept.

42. Use the y-intercept and slope to graph the line.

Use the following equation for the next two exercises: $x - 2y = 6$. [9.6]

43. Change the equation to slope-intercept form and find the slope and y-intercept.

44. Use the y-intercept and slope to graph the line.

Find the consecutive integers between which the following square roots lie. [11.1]

45. $\sqrt{27}$

46. $\sqrt{120}$

Estimate the following square roots to the nearest tenth. [11.1]

47. $\sqrt{58}$

48. $\sqrt{12}$

Solve and check the following equations. If no answer exists, state "no real solution." [11.2]

49. $5 - \sqrt{x} = -4$

50. $2\sqrt{x} + 7 = 3$

M. C. Escher, Mathematical Artist

Mauritis Cornelius Escher (1898–1972), or Mauk, as he liked to be called, was not a very good student. In 1918 he barely passed the Dutch version of high school, and the following year he was forced to withdraw from technical school. Although he struggled academically, Mauk excelled in art.

After dropping out of technical school, Escher devoted his time to art. He was accepted as a student at the School for Architecture and Decorative Arts in the Dutch city of Haarlem. Upon seeing Escher's drawings, Samuel Jessum de Mesquita, the professor of graphic arts, suggested that Escher continue as a graphic arts student.

This art professor soon became Escher's mentor. The two artists stayed in touch until the Germans sent Professor de Mesquita, a Jew, to a Nazi concentration camp. Escher never saw his friend again; but he kept one of the professor's paintings, imprinted with a German soldier's boot, tacked to a cupboard in his studio.

As a teenager Escher had learned to carve scenes out of a piece of linoleum. He would then ink them and imprint them on sheets of paper. Over the years, he had perfected this technique until he could produce highly detailed black-and-white prints of people, landscapes, and animals. His linocuts won him recognition in art shows throughout the Netherlands and sparked his interest in transferring his techniques to wood.

In 1936 Escher took a trip through several Mediterranean countries. While in Spain, he was fascinated by the geometrical mosaics created by Moorish artists and decided to create the same effect in his woodcuts.

To accomplish this goal, Escher turned to mathematics. Although he had barely passed his math courses in school, Escher later remarked, "I seem to have more in common with mathematicians than with my fellow artists." Escher used mathematical principles to design a motif. He would then duplicate the motif many times over and fit the pieces together like a jigsaw puzzle.

Escher liked to create visual riddles that play tricks on the eye. One of his most famous prints, *Waterfall*, looks at first glance like a normal scene of a waterfall and a waterwheel. However, a closer look reveals that the path taken by the water to the pool underneath the water wheel is on the same level as the waterfall. Since the water does not go either uphill or downhill, it would be impossible for the water to fall. A person could sit for hours trying to figure out how the scene could be visually logical and yet impossible.

Escher's prints became enormously popular throughout the world. His designs have been printed on posters, book covers, wrapping paper, and even neckties. Mathematicians, scientists, and artists have all applauded his whimsical ability to depict the world around him in artistic and mathematical ways.

12.7 Coordinate Geometry

In this section we will apply some geometric principles to the coordinate plane. These principles include calculating distances between points and determining the coordinates of the midpoint of a segment.

Suppose you want to find the distance between the points A (3, 1) and B (7, 1) or the points C (2, −1) and D (2, 5).

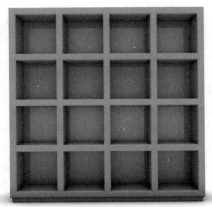

The horizontal and vertical pieces of this shelving unit are similar to the lines used to measure the location of points in a coordinate plane.

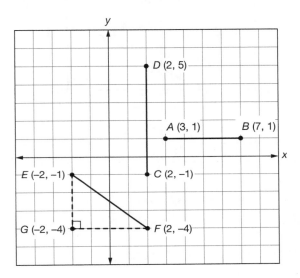

Since A (3, 1) and B (7, 1) lie on a horizontal line, you need only subtract the smaller x-coordinate from the larger x-coordinate to find the length of $\overline{AB}$.

$$AB = 7 - 3 = 4 \text{ units}$$

The points C (2, −1) and D (2, 5) lie on a vertical line, so the length of $\overline{CD}$ can be found by subtracting the smaller y-coordinate from the larger y-coordinate.

$$CD = 5 - (-1) = 5 + 1 = 6 \text{ units}$$

Horizontal and vertical distances are easy to calculate. But suppose the two points do not lie on a horizontal or a vertical line. Consider points E (−2, −1) and F (2, −4). To find the distance between them, drop a vertical segment from E down to a point G, such that G and F lie on the same horizontal line. Point G has coordinates (−2, −4). Draw a horizontal line segment from point F to G. You can see that $\angle G$ is a right angle and $\triangle EFG$ is a right triangle, which means that the Pythagorean theorem applies.

To calculate the length of the vertical segment $\overline{EG}$, subtract the smaller y-coordinate from the larger y-coordinate. Then find the horizontal length, FG, by subtracting the smaller x-coordinate from the larger x-coordinate.

$$EG = -1 - (-4) = -1 + 4 = 3 \text{ units}$$
$$FG = 2 - (-2) = 2 + 2 = 4 \text{ units}$$

Now use the Pythagorean theorem to calculate EF.

$$(EF)^2 = (EG)^2 + (FG)^2$$ 1. Apply the Pythagorean theorem.

$$= 3^2 + 4^2$$ 2. Substitute the calculated values into the formula.

$$= 9 + 16$$ 3. Simplify.

$$= 25$$

$$EF = \sqrt{25}$$ 4. Take the square root of both sides.

$$= 5 \text{ units}$$ 5. Use the positive root only since distance is always a positive number.

Following these same steps, we can develop a general formula for finding the distance, d, between any two points in a coordinate plane. Let the points be $A\ (x_1, y_1)$ and $B\ (x_2, y_2)$.

Let C be the point where the vertical and horizontal lines drawn from A and B intersect to form a right angle. Notice that C has the same x-coordinate as A and the same y-coordinate as B.

The length of $\overline{AC}$ is $y_1 - y_2$, and the length of $\overline{BC}$ is $x_1 - x_2$.

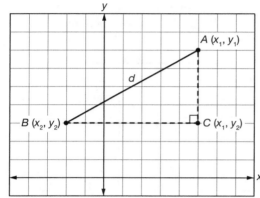

$$d^2 = (BC)^2 + (AC)^2$$ 1. Apply the Pythagorean theorem.

$$d^2 = (x_1 - x_2)^2 + (y_1 - y_2)^2$$ 2. Substitute the calculated values into the formula.

$$d = \sqrt{(x_1 - x_2)^2 + (y_1 - y_2)^2}$$ 3. Find the square root of both sides of the equation to obtain d.

Distance Formula

$d = \sqrt{(x_1 - x_2)^2 + (y_1 - y_2)^2}$, where d is the distance between the points (x_1, y_1) and (x_2, y_2).

Example 1   Find the distance between the points $(-3, 5)$ and $(2, -6)$. Round to the nearest tenth.

Answer

$$d = \sqrt{(x_1 - x_2)^2 + (y_1 - y_2)^2}$$ 1. Apply the distance formula.

$$= \sqrt{(-3 - 2)^2 + [5 - (-6)]^2}$$ 2. Substitute the coordinates of the points.

$$= \sqrt{(-5)^2 + 11^2}$$ 3. Simplify.

$$= \sqrt{25 + 121}$$

$$= \sqrt{146}$$ 4. This radical cannot be simplified further.

$$\approx 12.1 \text{ units}$$ 5. Find the answer to the nearest tenth.

Skill Check 1

Find the distance between the following points. Use a calculator and round to the nearest tenth.

1. (2, 9) and (5, –6)

2. (–3, 0) and (4, 7)

Another useful formula is the midpoint formula, which gives the coordinates of the midpoint of a segment when the coordinates of its endpoints are known. It is only necessary to average the respective coordinates of the endpoints to get the coordinates of the midpoint.

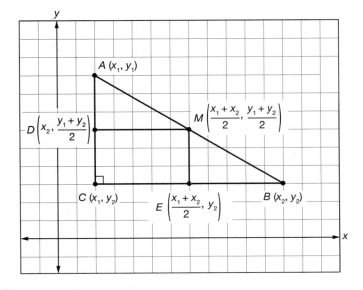

Midpoint Formula

The midpoint of the segment with endpoints (x_1, y_1) and (x_2, y_2) is $\left(\dfrac{x_1 + x_2}{2}, \dfrac{y_1 + y_2}{2} \right)$.

Example 2   Find the midpoint of the segment extending from (–8, –2) to (–1, 5).

Answer

$\left(\dfrac{x_1 + x_2}{2}, \dfrac{y_1 + y_2}{2} \right) = \left(\dfrac{-8 + (-1)}{2}, \dfrac{-2 + 5}{2} \right)$ 1. Substitute the coordinates into the midpoint formula.

$= \left(\dfrac{-9}{2}, \dfrac{3}{2} \right)$ 2. Simplify.

$= (-4.5, 1.5)$ 3. The result is the coordinates of the midpoint.

Skill Check 2

Find the midpoint of the segments with the following endpoints.

1. (–6, 8) and (0, 4)

2. (–4, –4) and (9, 6)

3. (5, –1) and (1, –7)

It is possible to calculate the lengths of the sides of a polygon and the length of any of its diagonals from the coordinates of its vertices, even without having a figure to go by.

Example 3   Parallelogram *ABCD* has vertices at *A* (3, 0), *B* (7, 1), *C* (7, 4), and *D* (3, 3). Find the length of each side and the midpoint of each diagonal.

Answer

$AD = y_1 - y_2 = 3 - 0 = 3$ units

$BC = y_1 - y_2 = 4 - 1 = 3$ units

$CD = \sqrt{(7-3)^2 + (4-3)^2} = \sqrt{16+1} = \sqrt{17} \approx 4.1$ units

$AB = \sqrt{(7-3)^2 + (1-0)^2} = \sqrt{16+1} = \sqrt{17} \approx 4.1$ units

Midpoint of $AC = \left(\frac{3+7}{2}, \frac{0+4}{2} \right) = \left(\frac{10}{2}, \frac{4}{2} \right) = (5, 2)$

Midpoint of $BD = \left(\frac{7+3}{2}, \frac{1+3}{2} \right) = \left(\frac{10}{2}, \frac{4}{2} \right) = (5, 2)$

1. *A* and *D* have the same *x*-coordinate, so $\overline{AD}$ is vertical. The same is true for $\overline{BC}$.

2. Find the lengths of the other two sides by using the distance formula.

3. Find the midpoints of the diagonals.

Notice that the opposite sides of the parallelogram are equal in length (congruent). Also, the midpoints of the two diagonals are the same point, meaning that they bisect each other. Both these observations are true of all parallelograms.

■ A. Exercises

Find the distance between the following points.

1. (2, 7) and (2, 3)
2. (–3, –2) and (–8, –2)
3. (3, 5) and (–4, 5)
4. (4, –6) and (4, 3)
5. (2, 0) and (–4, 0)
6. (0, –4) and (0, –9)

Find the midpoint of the segments with the following endpoints.

7. (2, 7) and (2, 3)
8. (–3, –2) and (–9, –2)
9. (4, –6) and (4, 10)
10. (3, 5) and (–7, 5)
11. (2, 0) and (–4, 0)
12. (0, –4) and (0, –8)

■ B. Exercises

Find the distance between the following points. Give your answer as both a simplified radical and a decimal rounded to the nearest tenth.

13. (2, 7) and (5, 12)
14. (3, 8) and (9, 6)
15. (0, 3) and (8, 9)
16. (–4, 7) and (–3, 10)
17. (–5, 6) and (–12, –4)
18. (4, –8) and (5, –7)
19. (–3, –3) and (14, –7)
20. (3, 9) and (–9, 7)

Find the midpoint of the segments with the following endpoints.

21. (2, 7) and (5, 12)
22. (3, 8) and (9, 6)
23. (0, 3) and (8, 9)
24. (–4, 7) and (–3, 10)
25. (–5, 6) and (–12, –4)
26. (4, –8) and (5, –7)
27. (–2.5, 7) and (5.1, 9.2)
28. (4, –2.3) and (4.4, 6.1)

29. Find the lengths of the sides (to the nearest tenth) of $\triangle ABC$, whose vertices are A (–3, 5), B (–1, –7), and C (2, –3).

30. Use the distance formula to find the lengths of the diagonals $\overline{AC}$ and $\overline{BD}$ of rectangle $ABCD$, whose vertices are A (–1, 4), B (7, –2), C (4, –6), and D (–4, 0). How do these two lengths compare?

31. Find the lengths of the sides (to the nearest tenth) of $\triangle ABC$, whose vertices are A (0, 3), B (4, 3), and C (2, –3). What kind of triangle is it?

■ C. Exercises

A triangle has vertices at A (6, 4), B (3, 0), and C (1, 4). Draw the figure in a coordinate plane.

32. What kind of triangle is it? Support your answer with calculations.

33. Find the midpoints of all three sides of the triangle in exercise 32.

34. Connect the three midpoints in the previous problem to make a new triangle. What kind of triangle is it? Support your answer with calculations.

35. Make a conjecture about triangles based on your figure and calculations from exercises 32–34.

■ Dominion thru Math

36. The 9,200 TEU container ship MSC *Pamela*, operated by the Mediterranean Shipping Company, is 1,105 ft. long by 151 ft. wide. The *Pamela* has a gross tonnage of 108,200 tn. plus a design load of 9,200 TEUs. Using an average TEU weight of 15.4 tn., find the approximate draft of this ship.

37. Looking at the future construction of a 12,500 TEU container ship, what overall length should it be if the draft can be no more than 46 ft. and the width 164 ft.? Assume the same average weight of a TEU is 15.4 tn. and that the gross tonnage will be 25% more than the ship in exercise 36.

CUMULATIVE REVIEW

Graph the solutions to the following inequalities. [9.8]

38. $y \geq x + 1$

39. $y < -\dfrac{3}{4}x - 2$

Answer the following exercises from the given equation and domain: $y = x^2$; $D = \{-2, -1, 0, 1, 2\}$. [9.2–9.3]

40. Determine the set of ordered pairs for the relation.

41. Give the range of the relation.

42. Graph the relation.

43. Determine whether the relation is a function. Explain your answer.

Solve. Leave answers in radical form if the radicand is not a perfect square. If no answer exists, state "no real solution." [11.3]

44. $6x^2 = 54$

45. $x^2 - 9 = 22$

46. $3x^2 + 32 = -4$

47. $\dfrac{x^2}{12} - 8 = 4$

12.8 Symmetry and Transformations

In Romans 12:2, Christians are commanded to be transformed by the renewal of their minds. They are exhorted to fulfill God's will for their lives by being changed from their current condition through the application of the Word of God, in order to become more like His Son, Jesus Christ.

In mathematics, a transformation causes a geometric figure to be changed into another figure according to a predefined rule.

A vertical line through the body of the butterfly indicates that it has two symmetric halves.

> ### Definition
>
> A **transformation** is the movement of an original geometric shape to another according to a predefined rule.

Reflection	Translation	Rotation

The *preimage* of a transformation is the figure's position before the transformation, while the *image* is the position of the figure after the transformation. When a transformation occurs, every preimage point *A* in the plane moves to its image point, *A'*. Each of the three transformations in this section requires the use of a perpendicular bisector.

> ### Definitions
>
> A **perpendicular bisector** is a line perpendicular to a segment that intersects the segment at its midpoint.
> A **reflection** is a transformation in which each point of the figure's image is the same distance from the line of reflection as the corresponding point of the preimage.

To reflect a point X through a line l, draw a line from X perpendicular to l and label the point of intersection P. Extend the line the same distance beyond l as it is from X to point P. Call the new point X'. Then $XP = PX'$.

To reflect a segment through a line, reflect the endpoints of the preimage and connect them. The reflection of $\overline{AB}$ is $\overline{A'B'}$.

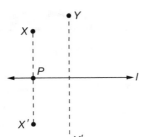

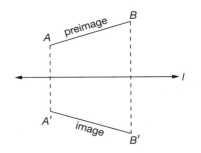

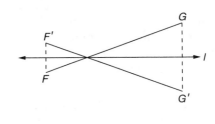

To reflect a polygon, such as a triangle, reflect all the vertices and connect them in order to get the entire figure. The reflection of $\triangle CDE$ is $\triangle C'D'E'$.

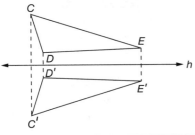

The line of reflection is a perpendicular bisector of the segment drawn from any preimage point to its image. Notice that the image of a point on the line of reflection is the original point.

Example 1 Reflect the following figures through line j.

a. point A

b. $\triangle BCD$

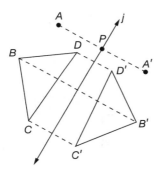

Answer

a. Draw a line from A perpendicular to j. Extend the line the same distance beyond j as it is from A. Call the new point A'. Then $AP = PA'$.

b. Reflect points B, C, and D to find B', C', and D'. Connect these in order to construct $\triangle B'C'D'$.

In a reflection, the figure appears to flip over the line of reflection to produce an image with the same shape and size as the preimage, but with its orientation reversed. Think in terms of a reflection in a mirror. The figure being reflected can be just a set of points, a geometric figure, or even a picture.

Have you wondered why the word "ambulance" is written backwards on the hood of emergency vehicles? This is done so motorists in front of the ambulance can read the word correctly when it is reflected in their rearview mirror.

Points on the Cartesian coordinate system are often reflected across an axis. The point A (5, 3) can be reflected across the x-axis to produce A' (5, –3). A segment connecting the two points would be perpendicular to and bisected by the x-axis. The reflection of B (–2, 4) across the y-axis produces B' (2, 4).

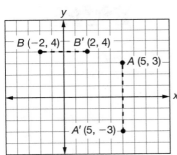

Humans were created to reflect God's image. Genesis 1:27 says, "So God created man in his own image, in the image of God created he him; male and female created he them." Sin marred this image, but a Christian is to reflect the characteristics of Christ to the unsaved so that they may be drawn to Him.

Definition

A reflection through a pair of parallel lines is a **translation**.

The figure is reflected through one of the lines, and then its image is reflected through the second line. The reflection of $\overline{AB}$ through the first line is $\overline{A'B'}$, and its reflection through the second is $\overline{A''B''}$. The first reflection reverses the figure, and the second restores it to the same relative orientation as before. In a translation, it appears that the figure slides across the surface without turning in any way.

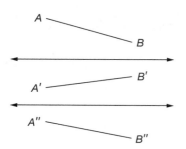

| **Example 2** | Translate the following figures by reflecting them first through line *k* and then through line *l*. |

a. point *E*

b. ΔFGH

Answer

a. Reflect *E* through line *k* to find *E′*. Then reflect *E′* through line *l* to find *E″*, the result of the translation.

b. Reflect points *F*, *G*, and *H* through line *k* to determine ΔF′G′H′. Then reflect points *F′*, *G′*, and *H′* through line *l* to determine ΔF″G″H″, the result of the translation.

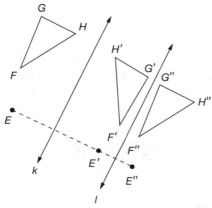

Definition

Reflecting a figure through each of two intersecting lines in succession produces a **rotation**.

A figure is rotated about the point of intersection of the two lines. This point is called the *center of rotation* and can be outside, within, or on the figure being rotated.

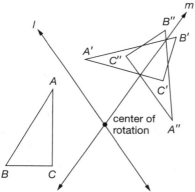

| **Example 3** | Rotate the following figures around *X* by reflecting them first through line *k* and then through line *l*. |

a. point *M*

b. ΔNOP

Answer

a. Reflect *M* through line *k* to find *M′*. Then reflect *M′* through line *l* to find *M″*, the result of the rotation.

b. Reflect points *N*, *O*, and *P* through line *k* to determine ΔN′O′P′. Then reflect points *N′*, *O′*, and *P′* through line *l* to determine ΔN″O″P″, the result of the rotation.

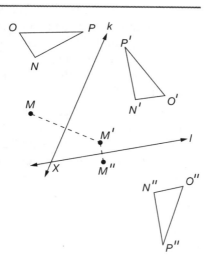

Skill Check 1

Perform the following transformations. Use a ruler, preferably metric, to draw lines of reflection and to measure distances.

1. Draw line l with two points A and B on the same side of the line and point C on the line. Reflect these points through l.

2. Draw line of reflection l and $\overline{DE}$ entirely on one side of l. Reflect $\overline{DE}$ through l.

3. Draw parallel lines of reflection l and m. Draw $\overline{FG}$ (not parallel to l and m) on the side of l away from m. Translate the segment by reflecting the segment first through l and then through m.

4. Draw two lines of reflection l and m intersecting at P. Make the angle between l and m between 60° and 75°. Draw $\triangle HIJ$ so that it is clearly scalene and so that neither l nor m intersects it. First reflect the triangle through l; then reflect its image through m.

Describe the image after the following reflections.

5. the point (7, 2) across the y-axis

6. the segment with endpoints (–4, –2) and (0, 3) across the x-axis

A figure that is a reflection of itself in a line is said to be *symmetric* about the line.

Definition

A figure has **line symmetry** if and only if each half of the figure is the image of the other half under a reflection in some line.

A figure may have more than one line of symmetry. For instance, a rectangle has two and a circle has an infinite number (every possible diameter).

If you reflect one side of any of these figures across the line shown, it will coincide with the other side. Each line drawn in these figures is called a *line of symmetry*.

Two other types of symmetry do not directly involve a reflection but do result in the image of a figure coinciding with the original figure. These other two types are called *rotational symmetry* and *point symmetry*.

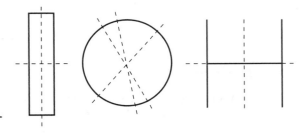

Definitions

A figure has **rotational symmetry** if and only if there is a rotation of less than 360° around a center point such that the image of the figure coincides with the original figure.

A figure has **point symmetry** if and only if it has 180° rotational symmetry.

In the propeller-like figure, the center of rotation is the center of the figure. If you trace the figure on a piece of paper, hold the center fixed, and rotate the paper 120°, then the rotated image of the figure coincides with the original figure. Thus, this figure has 120° rotational symmetry. If the figure is rotated 240°, it will coincide with the original figure as well. Multiples of a smaller rotational symmetry such as this one are often not stated.

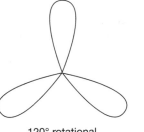
120° rotational

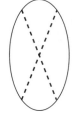
180° rotational and point

Doing a similar exercise with the second figure shows that it has 180° rotational symmetry, which means that it also has point symmetry. Connecting every point on the figure with its image gives a set of concurrent lines through the center of rotation. Two such lines are shown as dashed lines.

Skill Check 2

Which kinds of symmetry do the following figures have?

1.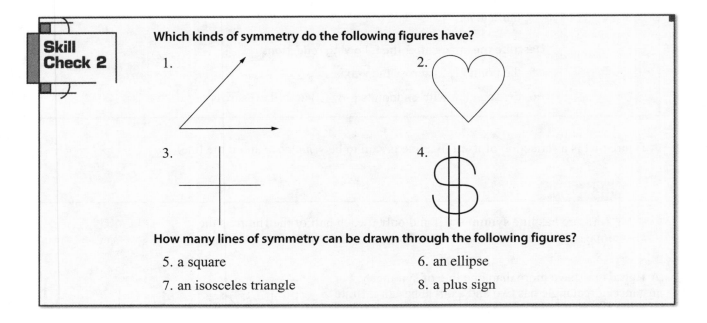

2.

3.

4.

How many lines of symmetry can be drawn through the following figures?

5. a square

6. an ellipse

7. an isosceles triangle

8. a plus sign

■ A. Exercises

Give the number of lines of symmetry for each figure. If the figure has rotational symmetry, write the minimum number of degrees followed by "rotational." If the figure has point symmetry, write "point."

1.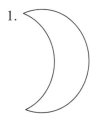

2.

3.

4.

5.

6.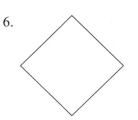

7.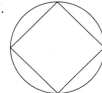

8.

9.

10.

11.

12.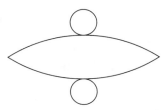

■ B. Exercises

Describe the image after the following reflections.

13. the point D (–3, 5) across the x-axis

14. the point F (2, –4) across the y-axis

15. the segment with endpoints A (1, 5) and B (3, –1) across the x-axis

16. the segment with endpoints C (2, 4) and D (3, 2) across the y-axis

17. the segment with endpoints R (–1, 5) and S (–3, –1) across the y-axis

18. the segment with endpoints T (–2, 4) and V (1, 1) across the x-axis

19. a 25° angle in quadrant 4 across the y-axis

How many lines of symmetry can be drawn through the following figures?

20. a five-pointed star

21. a soccer field

22. a basketball court

23. a circle with a single diameter drawn

24. a regular heptagon

25. a regular hexagon

Do the following have rotational symmetry in a plane? If so, state all degrees of rotational symmetry less than 360°.

26. a rectangle

27. an ellipse

28. a butterfly

29. an isosceles trapezoid

30. a square

31. a regular octagon

Perform the following transformations. Use a ruler, preferably metric, to draw lines of reflection and to measure distances.

32. Draw line l and $\overline{AB}$ with A on l. Reflect $\overline{AB}$ through l.

33. Draw line m and obtuse $\triangle CDE$. Reflect $\triangle CDE$ through m.

34. Draw line k and rectangle $FGHI$. Reflect $FGHI$ through k.

35. Draw two lines, $l \parallel m$, and right $\triangle ABC$. Translate $\triangle ABC$.

36. Draw two lines, $j \parallel k$, and right $\triangle MNO$ such that $\triangle MNO$ is between j and k. Reflect $\triangle MNO$ through j and its image through k.

37. Draw two lines, $l \perp m$, and obtuse $\triangle PQR$ in one of the quadrants formed. Reflect $\triangle PQR$ through one of the lines and its image through the other line.

38. Draw lines j and k intersecting at Q. Place $\triangle STU$ in one of the quadrants. Reflect $\triangle STU$ through j and its image through k.

■ C. Exercises

Investigate the number of lines of symmetry in regular *n*-sided polygons.

39. If n is even, how many lines of symmetry can be drawn through a regular n-gon? Describe where they pass.

40. If n is odd, how many lines of symmetry can be drawn through a regular n-gon? Describe where they pass.

CUMULATIVE REVIEW

Determine whether each table of values represents a direct variation. If it does, find the constant of variation and write an equation for the variation. [9.7]

41.

x	y
8	2
16	4
24	6
32	8

42.

x	y
1	2
2	−4
3	6
4	−8

Find *y* if *y* varies directly with *x*. [9.7]

43. If $y = 15$ when $x = 10$, find y when $x = 24$.

44. If $y = 8$ when $x = 10$, find y when $x = 3$.

45. Graph the direct variation $y = 2x$. [9.7]

Find the missing side of the following right triangles. Simplify irrational roots. [11.4]

46.

47.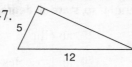

48.

Simplify the following radical expressions. [11.5]

49. $\sqrt{6}\sqrt{4}$

50. $3\sqrt{20}\left(2\sqrt{30}\right)$

MATH & SCRIPTURE

Building the Walls and Gates

While the book of Ezra portrays the restoration of the temple and worship, the focus of the book of Nehemiah is twofold: the restoration of the infrastructure of the city of Jerusalem and the restoration of the spiritual integrity of the people—especially their consecration to the Mosaic Covenant. The vision and concern of Nehemiah and his brothers was to rid the city of the heart-rending marks of conquest by rebuilding the wall and its gates. The key step forward in the rebuilding project is aptly expressed in Nehemiah 2:18, when the leaders of the people catch the vision and proclaim with great confidence: "Let us rise up and build." The following questions will help you grasp the extent of this awe-inspiring building project, completed in less than two months.

1. To the nearest 1,000, what was the population of Jerusalem and its surrounding villages (Neh. 7:66–67)?

2. If we assume that 40% of the population could do some type of work on the building project, what was the size of the workforce available? (This number would exclude children, the aged, and many of the wives and women servants who were providing food.)

3. Use an atlas of the Bible to find a map of Nehemiah's Jerusalem, and use the scale to find the approximate distance around the city (and hence the length of the wall). Approximately how long was the wall in feet?

4. Read carefully through Nehemiah 3 and list the gates mentioned. How many gates were there?

5. You may have been surprised that the names of twelve gates were not mentioned in Nehemiah 3 as they were in Revelation 21 for the New Jerusalem. What additional gates are given in Nehemiah 12:39?

6. The Scriptures do not give the thickness or height of the walls, but from archeology we know they may have been 6 to 10 ft. thick and 20 to 25 ft. high. What evidence is there that some significant parts of the wall may have been standing, even though all the gates had been destroyed by fire (Neh. 4:7)?

7. What kind of opposition did the builders face as they undertook the restoration of the walls of Jerusalem (Neh. 4:7–10; 6:2–3, 9)?

8. What does Nehemiah say that indicates the magnitude of the construction project (Neh. 4:19)?

9. How long did it take to restore the walls of Jerusalem (Neh. 6:15)?

10. What did the enemies of the Israelites conclude about the construction project (Neh. 6:16)?

11. Nehemiah's account clearly indicates that the people worked from dawn to dark every day to the point of exhaustion, much of the time under the threat of an enemy attack. Yet their enemies attributed the work to God. What conclusion can we make about how God does His work among His people?

Infinite Truths

So the wall was finished in the twenty and fifth day of the month Elul, in fifty and two days. And it came to pass, that when all our enemies heard thereof, and all the heathen that were about us saw these things, they were much cast down in their own eyes: for they perceived that this work was wrought of our God. *Nehemiah 6:15–16*

Chapter 12 Review

Vocabulary

acute angle	corresponding angles	perimeter	rotational symmetry
acute triangle	corresponding sides	perpendicular bisector	scale factor
adjacent angles	curve	perpendicular lines	scalene triangle
alternate exterior angles	diagonal	plane	segment
alternate interior angles	diameter	point	side
angle	equiangular	point symmetry	similar polygons
center	equilateral triangle	polygon	simple curve
center of rotation	geometry	preimage	square
chord	image	quadrilateral	straight angle
circle	intersecting lines	radius	supplementary angles
circumference	isosceles triangle	ray	symmetric
closed curve	line	rectangle	transformation
complementary angles	line of symmetry	reflection	translation
concave	line symmetry	regular polygon	transversal
congruent angles	obtuse angle	rhombus	trapezoid
congruent polygons	obtuse triangle	right angle	vertex
congruent segments	parallel lines	right triangle	vertical angles
convex	parallelogram	rotation	

Use proper notation to name each colored set of points in the diagram.

1. blue

2. green

3. purple

4. red

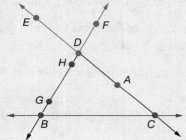

Draw angles having the following measures and classify each according to its angle measure.

5. 90°

6. 130°

Find the measure of the following angles and classify each according to its angle measure.

7.

8.

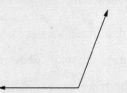

Match each pair of angles to its classification. All answers will be used once.

9. ∠1 and ∠2   a. alternate interior

10. ∠1 and ∠5   b. alternate exterior

11. ∠5 and ∠6   c. corresponding

12. ∠2 and ∠3   d. vertical

13. ∠4 and ∠5   e. supplementary

14. ∠1 and ∠8   f. complementary

Given line *a* is parallel to line *b* and *m*∠1 = 40° in the previous figure, find the measure of the following angles.

15. ∠4   16. ∠3   17. ∠5   18. ∠9   19. ∠7   20. ∠6

Classify the following triangles according to the measures of their angles and the lengths of their sides.

21.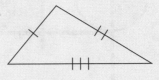

22.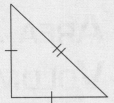

23.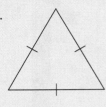

24. What is a simpler name for a rectangular rhombus?

25. Name the polygon and find the sum of the measures of its angles.

26. Find the measure of each angle in a regular pentagon.

27. Find the perimeter of an equilateral triangle with sides of 6 in.

28. Find the side lengths of a parallelogram with one side three times as long as an adjacent side if its perimeter is 48.

29. The center circle of a soccer field has a radius of 10 yd. Determine, to the nearest yard, the distance around the center circle.

30. In the Chicago area, a larger 16 in. softball is often used instead of the usual 12 in. softball. Determine the diameter of a "Chicago" softball if its circumference is 5π in.

31. If △*HDZ* ≅ △*NEP*, then ∠*Z* ≅ ____ and $\overline{NP}$ ≅ ____.

△*ABC* ~ △*DEF*. Use proportions to find the following.

32. *y*

33. *x*

34. *z*

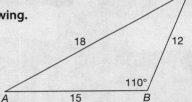
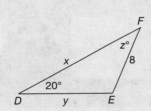

35. Find the length of the hypotenuse of a 45-45 right triangle if the length of each leg is 3.

36. Find the long leg and hypotenuse of a 30-60 right triangle whose short leg is 8.

37. Find the distance between the points (–2, 5) and (2, 8).

38. Find the midpoint of the segment extending from (–2, 5) to (2, 8).

39. What is the image of the segment with endpoints (3, 4) and (–1, 3) after it has been reflected across the *y*-axis?

40. What is the image of a triangle with vertices at (–2, 3), (0, 3), and (0, 0) after it has been reflected across both the *x*-axis and the *y*-axis?

41. A translation is two reflections through ____ lines, and a rotation is two reflections through ____ lines.

42. Give the number of lines of symmetry, write the minimum number of degrees for rotational symmetry, and write "point" if the figure has point symmetry.

43. Give the mathematical significance of Nehemiah 6:15–16.

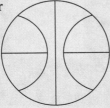

13 AREA AND VOLUME

Look! Geometry is all around you. Think of the food containers in a grocery store. Notice how much geometry goes into their construction. In the store you will see mostly prisms and cylinders since most grocery items on the shelves are in boxes, jars, or cans. Engineers design all of these containers so they are economical to make and work well with high-speed packaging equipment. The cans and boxes must also be sized to fit the product they contain. For instance, peaches come in bigger, fatter cans than peas or tomato sauce.

Look around! You can see a cylinder to store the hot water, a cylinder or a prism for the garbage, a cylinder and sphere combination for propane storage, and a prism to store the frozen food in your house. Look around! Out in your neighborhood you may see a cylinder or a sphere to store the water for your community. Many water storage tanks are spheres sitting on top of a tall cylinder. These tanks are elevated in order to provide additional pressure for the water system. The local fuel distributor will have a great number of storage tanks, mostly cylinders. Fuel or chemical storage areas are called tank farms. The name fits because it looks like the tanks have been planted and are growing out of the ground, some faster than others. Take a drive in the country or through a rural Midwestern town and you will see large grain elevators—tall blue cylinders with hemispherical tops, or maybe tall silver prisms alongside the railroad. Cones and pyramids also have important roles to play because of their geometry. They serve as chutes or hoppers for loading and unloading the storage tanks. In fact, you may have seen an upside-down pyramid on the bottom of a bulk material railroad car that helps unload the car at its destination.

After this chapter you should be able to
1. compute areas of geometric regions.

2. find the ratio of the perimeters and areas of similar polygons.

3. find the surface area of three-dimensional objects.

4. find the volume of three-dimensional objects.

5. determine the missing dimension when given the area or volume of a figure and its other dimensions.

13.1 ☐ Areas of Parallelograms

In Section 12.3 a Venn diagram showed the relationships among the various types of special quadrilaterals. That Venn diagram is presented here with the general quadrilateral removed. Notice that rectangles and squares are included in the set of parallelograms. They are special cases of the more general parallelograms. Every rectangle is a parallelogram, and every square is both a rectangle and a parallelogram. Knowing the relationships among these figures will help you understand the development of the formulas for finding their areas.

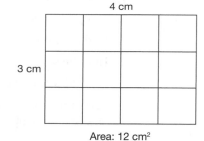

Notice the parallelograms in this decorative wallpaper.

Consider the square at the right. Since each of its sides is 1 cm long, it is called a unit square. The area of the figure is one square centimeter (1 cm²). This is an example of a unit used to measure area. A few other unit squares used to measure area are square inch, square foot, square mile, square meter, and so on.

Definition

Area is the number of unit squares needed to cover a region or surface.

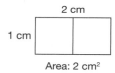

Area: 2 cm²

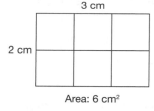

The rectangles in these figures have been divided into square centimeters. The easiest way to find the area is to count the squares horizontally and vertically and then multiply the two results. One of the sides is called the *base*, and its length is represented by *b*. The other side is the *altitude* of the polygon, and its length is called the *height*. For this reason, the length of an altitude is represented by *h*. The base and altitude are always perpendicular.

Definitions

An **altitude** of a polygon is the segment from a vertex perpendicular to the opposite side.

Height is the length of an altitude of a polygon and is represented by *h*.

The resulting equation for the area of a rectangle is $A = bh$.

Formula: Area of a Rectangle	
$A = bh$	The area of a rectangle (A) is equal to the base (b) times the height (h). This formula is often written as $A = lw$, where l is the length and w is the width.

Since the base and the height are the same value in a square, the letter s is usually used for the length of a side and the area formula is written using $s \times s$ or s^2 rather than bh.

Formula: Area of a Square	
$A = s^2$	The area of a square (A) is equal to the square of a side (s).

Any parallelogram can be transformed into a rectangle by the process shown below.

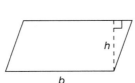 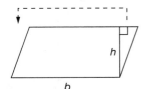 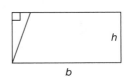

The area of the above parallelogram is equal to the area of the rectangle formed with base b and height h. The height is the perpendicular distance between the base and the side opposite it. In nonrectangular parallelograms, the height h is not a side of the parallelogram.

You can use the following formula to find the area of any parallelogram, including squares and rectangles.

Formula: Area of a Parallelogram	
$A = bh$	The area of a parallelogram (A) is equal to the base (b) times the height (h).

Altitudes are always $\perp$ to the base.

Example 1 Find the area of the following quadrilaterals.

a. a square 4.2 cm on a side

b. a rectangle with sides of 8.5 in. and 4 in.

Answer

a. $A = bh$ or s^2 1. Write the area formula for a square.

   $= 4.2(4.2)$ 2. Substitute known values for b and h.

   $= 17.64$ cm²

b. $A = bh$ 1. Write the area formula for a rectangle.

   $= 8.5(4)$ 2. Substitute known values for b and h.

   $= 34$ in.²

Example 2 Find the area of the parallelogram.

Answer

$A = bh$ 1. Write the area formula for a parallelogram.

   $= 12(6.6)$ 2. Substitute known values for b and h.

   $= 79.2$ m²   Notice that $h \neq 8$ ($h = 6.6$).

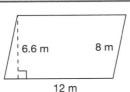

Find the area of the following quadrilaterals.

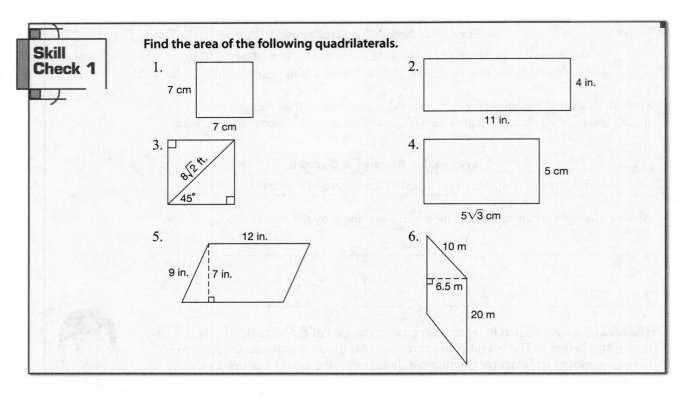

1. 7 cm, 7 cm (square)
2. 4 in., 11 in. (rectangle)
3. $8\sqrt{2}$ ft., 45°
4. 5 cm, $5\sqrt{3}$ cm
5. 12 in., 9 in., 7 in.
6. 10 m, 6.5 m, 20 m

A missing length can often be determined if the area and other lengths are known. Sketch a diagram of the situation, label all known information, and assign a variable to any unknown quantity. Use area formulas to write an equation that can be solved in order to calculate the missing length. Always check your results in the original equation.

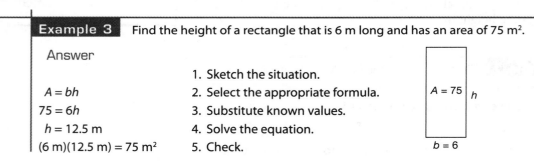

Example 3 Find the height of a rectangle that is 6 m long and has an area of 75 m².

Answer

$A = bh$ 1. Sketch the situation.
$75 = 6h$ 2. Select the appropriate formula.
$h = 12.5$ m   3. Substitute known values.
$(6 \text{ m})(12.5 \text{ m}) = 75 \text{ m}^2$ 4. Solve the equation.
                            5. Check.

$A = 75$ h
$b = 6$

■ A. Exercises

Find the area of the following quadrilaterals.

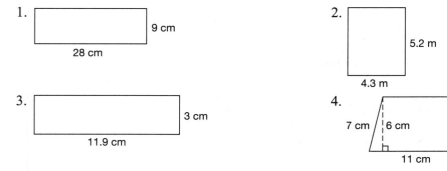

1. 9 cm, 28 cm (rectangle)
2. 5.2 m, 4.3 m (rectangle)
3. 3 cm, 11.9 cm (rectangle)
4. 7 cm, 6 cm, 11 cm (parallelogram)

5.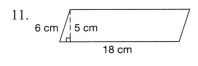

6.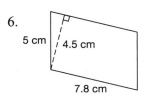

Find the area of the following rectangles or parallelograms.

7. length: 168 mm
   width: 24 mm

8. length: 5.83 m
   width: 7 m

9. base: 175 mm
   height: 34 mm

10. base: 8.76 m
    height: 0.9 m

Find the area of the following parallelograms.

11.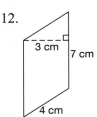

12.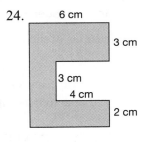

13.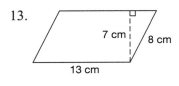

■ B. Exercises

Find the base or height of the following rectangles.

14. area: 56 in.^{2}
    base: 8 in.

15. area: 198 ft.^{2}
    height: 11 ft.

16. area: 42.6 mm^2
    height: 7.1 mm

17. area: 60.3 km^2
    base: 6.7 km

Find the base or height of the following parallelograms.

18. area: 105 cm^2
    height: 7 cm

19. area: 3,441 m^2
    base: 37 m

20. area: 210.6 m^2
    base: 9 m

21. area: 247.5 cm^2
    height: 19.8 cm

Find the area of the following colored regions.

22.

23.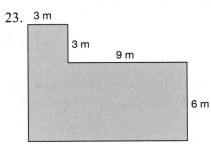

24.

25.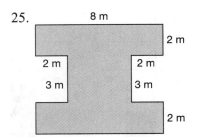

26.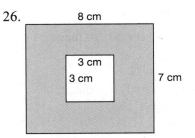

27.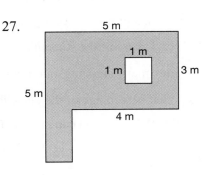

Solve.

28. A hallway is 20 ft. long and 6 ft. wide. Find the area of the hallway.

29. A swimming pool is 29 m long and 23 m wide. Find the area of the water surface when the pool is full.

30. An interior wall of a house is 8.5 ft. high and 15 ft. long. What is the area of the wall?

31. A school is putting sod on its football field from goalpost to goalpost. It is 120 yd. long and 53.3 yd. wide. How many square yards of sod will be needed?

■ C. Exercises

Write expressions for the area of the following figures.

32.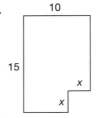

33.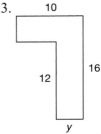

■ Dominion thru Math

If you take a cereal box apart and lay it out flat, you will see that it is made from a rectangle of light cardboard with the printing on one side. The flaps that close the top and bottom are extensions of the large sides, folded to reach most of the way across the narrow dimension. The small flaps are extensions of the narrow sides; they fold under the large flaps and serve as glue tabs for the large flaps. One other flap, about a half-inch wide, runs along the long dimension and serves as a glue tab to close up the sides of the box.

In the following exercises you will figure out the dimensions of the cardboard rectangle used to make the given box. Use a calculator as needed to solve these problems efficiently.

34. Find the dimensions of the rectangular cardboard stock used to make a cereal box 2" wide by 8" long by 10" high.

35. Cereal box cardboard comes in rolls 4 ft. wide by 150 ft. long. What is the least number of rolls of cardboard it will take to make 10,000 boxes the size of the box in exercise 34?

CUMULATIVE REVIEW

Use the histogram to answer exercises 36–38. [10.3]

36. How many of the students' scores were in the 80–90 range?

37. How many students took the test?

38. What percentage of the class scored in the 90–100 range?

Simplify the following cube roots. [11.7]

39. $\sqrt[3]{216}$ 40. $\sqrt[3]{1,728}$

41. $\sqrt[3]{108}$ 42. $\sqrt[3]{1,125}$

Simplify the following radical expressions. [11.5]

43. $\dfrac{\sqrt{225}}{\sqrt{25}}$ 44. $\dfrac{5\sqrt{150}}{\sqrt{2}}$ 45. $\dfrac{\sqrt{48}}{6}$ 46. $\sqrt{\dfrac{125}{64}}$

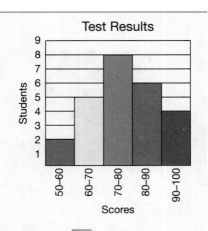

13.2 Areas of Triangles and Trapezoids

Any parallelogram (including squares and rectangles) can be divided into two congruent triangles by drawing one of its diagonals.

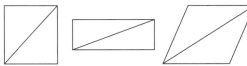

Conversely, any triangle is one-half of a parallelogram. You can form this parallelogram by drawing a line through a vertex of the triangle parallel to its opposite side. Then choose another vertex and draw a line parallel to its opposite side. One side of the given triangle forms the diagonal, and the triangle has one-half of the area of the derived parallelogram. Two different parallelograms are formed on $\triangle ABC$ in the figures at the right.

Therefore, the area of any triangle is one-half the area of a parallelogram.

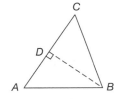

Notice the trapezoidal sides of this lampshade.

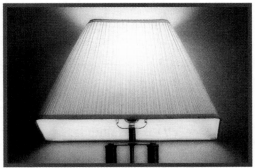

▱ ACBE

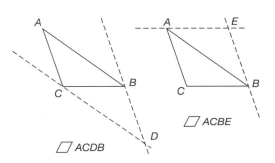

▱ ACDB

Formula: Area of a Triangle	
$A = \dfrac{1}{2}bh$	The area of a triangle (A) is half the base (b) times the height (h).

A segment drawn from any vertex of a triangle perpendicular to the line containing the opposite side is an *altitude* of the triangle. Every triangle has three altitudes, one from each vertex. The length of the altitude is the triangle's height. When the area formula is applied, any side of a triangle can be considered its base as long as the corresponding altitude is used as its height.

The area for any given triangle will be the same regardless of the side that is chosen as the base.

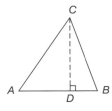

If $\overline{AB}$ is the base, $\overline{CD}$ is the altitude.

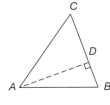

If $\overline{BC}$ is the base, $\overline{AD}$ is the altitude.

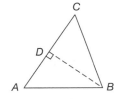

If $\overline{AC}$ is the base, $\overline{BD}$ is the altitude.

In an acute triangle, all three altitudes are within the interior of the triangle. In a right triangle, the legs are perpendicular, so either leg can be chosen as the base and the other as the height. In an obtuse triangle, only the altitude from the obtuse angle to its opposite side is within the triangle. To find the other two altitudes, you will need to extend one of the sides adjacent to the obtuse angle to the point where a perpendicular can be drawn from the acute angle opposite it to the extended side.

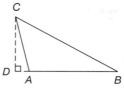 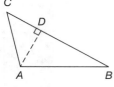 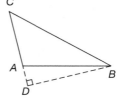

If $\overline{AB}$ is the base, $\overline{CD}$ is the altitude.   If $\overline{BC}$ is the base, $\overline{AD}$ is the altitude.   If $\overline{AC}$ is the base, $\overline{BD}$ is the altitude.

Example 1   Find the area of $\triangle XYZ$.

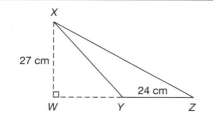

Answer

$A = \frac{1}{2}bh$ 1. Write the area formula for a triangle.

$= \frac{1}{2}(24)(27)$ 2. Substitute known values for b and h.

$= 324 \text{ cm}^2$

Skill Check 1

Find the area of the following triangles.

1.

2.

3. a triangle with a 13 cm base and 4 cm height

4. a 45-45 triangle with 7 in. legs

Recall that a trapezoid has at least one pair of parallel sides. These two parallel sides are called the bases of the trapezoid, and their lengths are labeled b_1 and b_2. The perpendicular distance between these two parallel sides is the height, labeled h.

If a second trapezoid that is congruent to the given one is turned upside down, translated to the right, and joined to the original one, a parallelogram is formed. In the figure at the right, the parallelogram formed has a base with length $b_1 + b_2$ and height h.

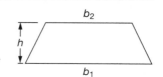

The area of this parallelogram is $A = (b_1 + b_2)h$, which is twice the area of the original trapezoid. This value must be multiplied by one-half to get the area of the trapezoid.

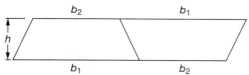

Formula: Area of a Trapezoid	
$A = \frac{1}{2}(b_1 + b_2)h$	The area of a trapezoid (A) is half the sum of the bases (b) times the height (h).

Expressed in a different way, the area of a trapezoid is the average of its two bases times its height.

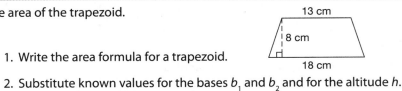

Example 2   Find the area of the trapezoid.

Answer

$A = \frac{1}{2}(b_1 + b_2)h$ 1. Write the area formula for a trapezoid.

$= \frac{1}{2}(18 + 13)(8)$ 2. Substitute known values for the bases b_1 and b_2 and for the altitude h.

$= \frac{1}{2}(18 + 13)(\overset{4}{\cancel{8}})$ 3. Calculate the area.

$= 31(4)$

$= 124$ cm^2

Skill Check 2

Find the area of the following trapezoids.

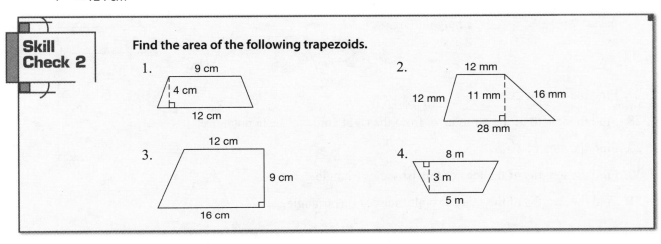

1.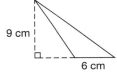

2.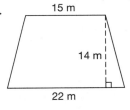

3.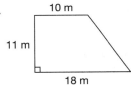

4.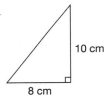

A. Exercises

Find the area of the following figures.

1. 9 cm, 6 cm

2. 10 m, 11 m, 18 m

3. 10 cm, 8 cm

4. 15 m, 14 m, 22 m

Find the area of the following triangles.

5. $b = 8$ cm, $h = 12$ cm   6. $b = 14$ cm, $h = 9$ cm   7. $b = 18$ cm, $h = 13$ cm   8. $b = 38$ cm, $h = 54$ cm

Find the area of the following trapezoids.

9. $b_1 = 6$ cm, $b_2 = 9$ cm, $h = 6$ cm

10. $b_1 = 5$ cm, $b_2 = 13$ cm, $h = 8$ cm

11. $b_1 = 8$ cm, $b_2 = 15$ cm, $h = 11$ cm

12. $b_1 = 14$ cm, $b_2 = 9$ cm, $h = 12$ cm

B. Exercises

Find the area of the following colored regions.

13.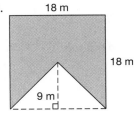

14.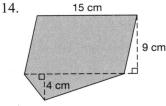

15.

16.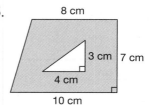

17.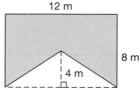

18.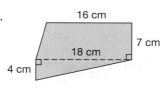

Find the base or height of the following triangles.

19. area: 35 cm²
    height: 7 cm

20. area: 24 m²
    base: 6 m

21. area: 12.75 m²
    base: 3.4 m

22. area: $1\frac{35}{64}$ ft.²
    height: $2\frac{1}{4}$ ft.

Find the other base or height of the following trapezoids.

23. area: 88 in.²
    bases: 9 in.
    and 13 in.

24. area: 35 m²
    height: 5 m
    base: 8 m

25. area: 300 cm²

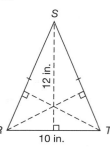

26. area: 54 yd.²

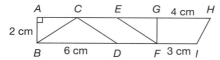

27. Find the area of △ABC.

28. Find the length of the altitude, a, from the right angle to the hypotenuse.

29. Find the area of △RST.

30. Find the lengths of the legs of this isosceles triangle.

31. Find the lengths of the other two altitudes of this triangle.

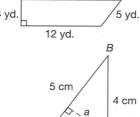

■ C. Exercises

Use the figure at the right for exercises 32–37. $\overline{AH} \parallel \overline{BI}$; $\overline{CD} \parallel \overline{EF}$; $\overline{AB} \parallel \overline{GF}$; and $\overline{AC} \cong \overline{CE} \cong \overline{EG} \cong \overline{DF} \cong \overline{FI}$.
Find the area of the following polygons.

32. △ABC

33. △BCD

34. FGHI

35. CEFD

36. CDFG

37. CEFB

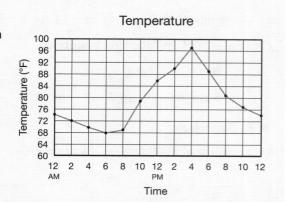

CUMULATIVE REVIEW

Use the line graph of temperatures throughout a typical summer day to answer the following questions. Times are listed in a 24-hour format. [10.4]

38. During which two-hour period did the greatest increase in temperature occur?

39. During which two-hour period did the greatest decrease in temperature occur?

40. What was the range of recorded temperatures for the day?

41. What was the approximate temperature at 9:00 AM?

Estimate the following square roots to the nearest tenth and then write them as simplified radicals. [11.1, 11.5]

42. $\sqrt{76}$

43. $\sqrt{50}$

44. $\sqrt{12}$

Find the following dimensions. [12.4]

45. the circumference of a circle with a radius of 5 in.

46. the diameter of a circle with a circumference of 62.8 m

47. the perimeter of a rhombus whose sides are 24 cm long

48. the length and width of a rectangle whose perimeter is 24 cm and whose length is 2 cm more than its width

Consider the sections of chain in the diagram below. It costs one cent to break a link and two cents to weld it again. What is the least that it would cost to join the five sections of chain into one chain?

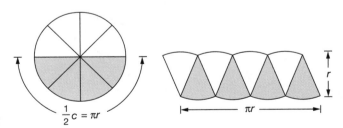

13.3 Areas of Circles

Recall that the distance around a circle is its circumference, c. To find the circumference of a circle with radius r, use the formula

$$c = 2\pi r.$$

You can use this formula to derive a formula for the area of a circle. In the figure below, the circle is divided into eight congruent pie-shaped parts. These pie-shaped parts are then arranged to form a curved figure resembling a parallelogram.

The area of the lid is a measure of how much tin is needed to make it.

Each of the horizontal sides of the "parallelogram" is formed by four of the curved pie slices and has a length of half the circumference of the circle. The height of the figure is approximately the radius of the circle. If the circle is cut into sixteen slices instead of eight, the shape of the "parallelogram" becomes closer to a true parallelogram and the height becomes closer to the radius of the circle. As the circle is cut into increasingly more congruent pieces that are spread into parallelogram form, the shape approaches the shape of a true parallelogram, the height approaches the radius of the circle (r), and the base approaches the length of half the circumference. We can use the formula for the circumference of a circle to determine the length of the base: $\frac{1}{2}c = \frac{1}{2}(2\pi r) = \pi r$. The base of the parallelogram is approaching the product of π and the radius.

Since the formula for finding the area of a parallelogram is $A = bh$, this suggests that the area of the "parallelogram," and therefore of the circle, is $A = \pi r \times r = \pi r^2$.

Formula: Area of a Circle	
$A = \pi r^2$	The area of a circle (A) is the product of π and the square of the radius (r).

For any circle,

$$\frac{\text{circumference}}{\text{diameter}} = \pi.$$

Example 1 Find the area of a circle whose radius is 3 km.

Answer

$A = \pi r^2$ 1. Write the area formula for a circle.

$= \pi(3^2)$ 2. Substitute the known value for r.

$= 3.14(9)$

$\approx 28.3 \text{ km}^2$ 3. Round the product to the nearest tenth.

All text answers will be based on the use of 3.14 for π. All answers to exercises and examples will be rounded to the nearest tenth unless otherwise specified.

Example 2 Find the area of a circle whose diameter is 5 m.

Answer

$r = \dfrac{d}{2} = \dfrac{5}{2} = 2.5$ 1. The radius is one-half the diameter.

$A = \pi r^2$ 2. Write the area formula for a circle.

$= \pi(2.5^2)$ 3. Substitute the known value for r.

$= 3.14(6.25)$

$\approx 19.6 \text{ m}^2$ 4. Round the product to the nearest tenth.

Skill Check 1

Find the area of the following circles.

1. 2 cm

2. 8 m

3. 10 cm

4. a circle with a diameter of 14 mm

5. a circle with a radius of 0.8 m

6. a circle with a diameter of 7 cm

Example 3 — Find the area of the colored region.

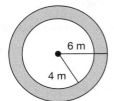

Answer

$A = \pi R^2 - \pi r^2$ 1. Subtract the area of the smaller circle from the area of the larger circle.

$= \pi(6^2) - \pi(4^2)$ 2. Substitute the known values for r.

$= 36\pi - 16\pi$

$= (36 - 16)\pi$ 3. Apply the Distributive Property.

$= 20\pi$

$= 20(3.14)$

$\approx 62.8 \text{ m}^2$ 4. Round the product to the nearest tenth.

Example 4 — Find the area of the figure.

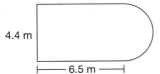

Answer

$A = bh + \dfrac{1}{2}\pi r^2$ 1. Write the area formulas for the combined area.

$= 6.5(4.4) + 0.5(3.14)(2.2^2)$ 2. Substitute known values.

$= 28.6 + 0.5(3.14)(4.84)$

$= 28.6 + 7.5988$

$= 36.1988$

$\approx 36.2 \text{ m}^2$ 3. Round the product to the nearest tenth.

Skill Check 2

1. Find the area of the colored region.

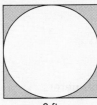

8 ft.

2. Find the area of the combined figure to the nearest whole number.

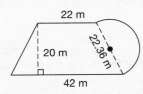

22 m   20 m   22.36 m   42 m

■ A. Exercises

Find the area of the following circles to the nearest hundredth.

1. 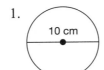 10 cm

2. 4 in.

3. 24 ft.

4. 9 m

5. $r = 6$ in.

6. $r = 15$ m

7. $d = 60$ ft.

8. $d = 17$ cm

9. $r = 0.3$ cm

10. $d = 44$ mm

11. $r = 2.4$ m

12. $d = 11.8$ cm

■ **B. Exercises**

Find the area of the following colored regions.

13.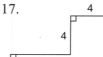

14.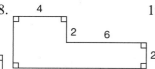

15.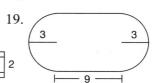

16.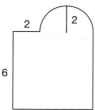

Find the area of the following figures. Dimensions are in centimeters.

17.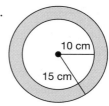

18.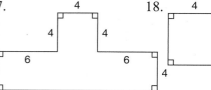

19.

20.

A circle has an area of 314 m². Find the following measures.

21. the radius of the circle   22. the diameter of the circle   23. the circumference of the circle

Find the following measures.

24. the radius of a circle with an area of 25π in.²

25. the diameter of a circle with an area of 64π m²

26. the circumference of a circle with an area of 16π ft.²

27. the area of a circle with a circumference of 4π ft.

■ **C. Exercises**

Find the area of the following colored regions. Dimensions are in centimeters.

28.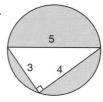

29.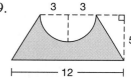

30. Find the diameter of a circle whose area is 452.16 cm².

31. If the circumference of a circle is 18.84 mi., find the area to the nearest hundredth.

■ **Dominion thru Math**

32. A case of canned goods contains 48 cans in two layers of 24 and comes in a box 12" wide by 18" long by 9" high. The long side flaps for the top and bottom reach halfway across the box, the short side flaps match the width of the long ones, and the vertical glue tab is 1" wide. What are the dimensions of the rectangular cardboard stock used to make this box?

33. A flat case of 12 oz. canned soft drinks holds one layer of 24 cans arranged in a 4 × 6 array. The box has no lid but is shrink-wrapped. The cans are 6.7 cm in diameter and 12.5 cm high. As pictured at the right, the bottom of the box is a solid sheet, its sides reach up to the top of the cans, and there is a vertical glue tab in each corner. Allowing 0.1 cm per can of horizontal space so that the cans are snug but not too tight, find the dimensions of the rectangular cardboard stock used to make this box.

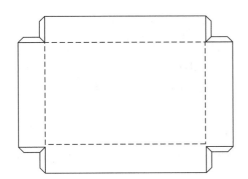

CUMULATIVE REVIEW

Identify each of the following as a permutation or a combination; then evaluate. [10.6–10.7]

34. Determine the number of ways you can choose four books from a shelf containing nine books.

35. Determine the number of ways you can arrange four out of nine books on your desk.

36. Determine the number of ways to fill four distinct class offices from a class of thirty students.

37. Determine the number of ways to choose a decorating committee of four people from a class of thirty.

Solve and check the following equations. If no answer exists, state "no real solution." [11.2]

38. $5\sqrt{x} - 2 = 8$

39. $\sqrt{5x - 6} = 7$

40. $\sqrt{x} + 10 = 7$

Complete each statement. [12.5]

41. $\triangle ABC \sim \triangle$ ____

42. $x =$ ____

43. $m\angle E =$ ____

44. perimeter of $\triangle DEF =$ ____

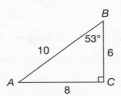

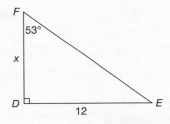

13.4 Lengths and Areas of Similar Regions

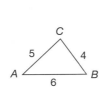

Recall that the sides of similar triangles are proportional. Consider two such triangles, $\triangle ABC \sim \triangle XYZ$, where the first has sides of 4, 5, and 6 units and the second has sides of 8, 10, and 12 units. Since every side of $\triangle XYZ$ is twice the length of its corresponding side in $\triangle ABC$, the scale factor is 2. The perimeters of the triangles are $4 + 5 + 6 = 15$ and $8 + 10 + 12 = 30$.

There are two similar triangular figures in this serving dish.

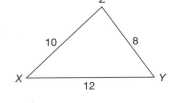

What is the ratio of the perimeter of the larger triangle to the perimeter of the smaller triangle? It is also 2, since $2 \times 15 = 30$.

More generally, if the sides of the smaller triangle are 4, 5, and 6 units, and the second triangle has sides of $4a$, $5a$, and $6a$, then their respective perimeters are $4 + 5 + 6 = 15$ and $4a + 5a + 6a = 15a$. Therefore, the perimeters are in the same ratio as the corresponding sides of the triangles: $\frac{4a}{4} = a$ and $\frac{15a}{15} = a$.

This property applies to any pair of similar polygons, not just triangles.

Ratio of the Perimeters of Similar Polygons
The ratio of the perimeters is equal to the ratio of the corresponding sides.

Example 1   The corresponding sides of two similar triangles are 16 in. and 12 in. The perimeter of the first triangle is 55 in. Find the perimeter of the second triangle, p_2.

Answer

$\dfrac{16}{12} = \dfrac{4}{3}$ 1. The ratio of the sides can be reduced; this is the scale factor. The order in the ratio is larger to smaller.

$\dfrac{4}{3} = \dfrac{55}{p_2}$ 2. The ratio of the sides equals the ratio of the perimeters. Since 16 is in the numerator, the perimeter of the triangle with the 16 in. side, 55 in., must be in the numerator.

$4p_2 = 3(55)$ 3. Apply the Property of Proportions.

$4p_2 = 165$

$\dfrac{4p_2}{4} = \dfrac{165}{4}$ 4. Divide both sides of the equation by the coefficient of the variable p_2.

$p_2 = 41.25$ in.   5. The result is the perimeter of the smaller triangle.

Example 2   The perimeters of two similar hexagons are 20 ft. and 180 ft. The smaller hexagon has one side of 2 ft. Find the corresponding side of the larger hexagon.

Answer

$\dfrac{2}{s} = \dfrac{20}{180}$ 1. The ratio of the sides equals the ratio of the perimeters. Both are ratios of the smaller measurement to the larger measurement.

$\dfrac{2}{s} = \dfrac{1}{9}$ 2. Since $\frac{20}{180}$ is easily reduced, divide the numerator and denominator by 20.

$s = 2(9)$ 3. Apply the Property of Proportions.

$s = 18$ ft.   4. The result is the length of the corresponding side of the larger hexagon.

Skill Check 1

Use proportions to find the missing measure in similar figures 1 and 2. The subscripts designate which figure a measure is from. The variable s represents a side length, and p represents a perimeter. Find the perimeter of the second figure. Round answers to the nearest tenth.

1. $s_1 = 10$, $p_1 = 47$, $s_2 = 7$ 2. $s_1 = 8$, $p_1 = 33$, $s_2 = 5$

Find the corresponding side of the second figure. Round answers to the nearest tenth.

3. $s_1 = 5$, $p_1 = 12$, $p_2 = 70$ 4. $s_1 = 25$, $p_1 = 120$, $p_2 = 70$

We have seen that perimeters of similar polygons have the same scale factor as the corresponding sides. Now consider two similar rectangles, the first with sides of 4 and 6 and the second with sides of $4a$ and $6a$. Using the formula $A = bh$, the areas are, respectively, $4 \times 6 = 24$ square units and $4a \times 6a = 24a^2$ square units.

 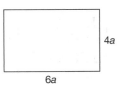

Therefore, the areas are not in the same ratio as the corresponding sides: $\frac{4a}{4} = a$ and $\frac{24a^2}{24} = a^2$. The areas are in the same ratio as the square of the scale factor. This property is true of any pair of similar polygons, not just rectangles.

Ratio of the Areas of Similar Polygons
The ratio of the areas of similar polygons is equal to the ratio of the squares of the corresponding sides.

Example 3   The first of two regular pentagons has a side of 4 cm, and the second has a side of 3 cm. What is the ratio of their areas?

Answer

$$\left(\frac{4}{3}\right)^2 = \frac{4}{3} \times \frac{4}{3} = \frac{4^2}{3^2} = \frac{16}{9}$$

It is not necessary to say that the polygons in this problem are similar because all regular polygons with the same number of sides have the same shape. All squares are similar to all other squares. All equilateral triangles are similar to one another. All 30-60 right triangles have the same shape, so they are similar to one another.

Example 4   The first of two similar polygons has a side of 3 cm and an area of 10 cm². The corresponding side of the second is 5 cm. What is the area of the second polygon?

Answer

$$\frac{10}{A_2} = \left(\frac{3}{5}\right)^2$$

$$\frac{10}{A_2} = \frac{9}{25}$$

$$9A_2 = (10)25$$

$$9A_2 = 250$$

$$\frac{9A_2}{9} = \frac{250}{9}$$

$$A_2 \approx 27.8 \text{ cm}^2$$

1. The ratio of the areas equals the square of the ratio of the corresponding sides. Since 3 is in the numerator, the area of the polygon with a side of 3 cm must be in the numerator.

2. Apply the Property of Proportions.

3. Divide both sides by the coefficient of the variable.

4. The result is the area of the second polygon.

Example 5   The areas of two similar pentagons are 400 mm² and 100 mm². One side of the smaller pentagon is 9 mm. Find the length of the similar side of the larger pentagon.

Answer

$$\frac{400}{100} = \left(\frac{s}{9}\right)^2$$

$$\frac{4}{1} = \frac{s^2}{81}$$

$$s^2 = 4(81)$$

$$s^2 = 324$$

$$s = \sqrt{324} = 18 \text{ mm}$$

1. The ratio of the areas is equal to the square of the ratio of the corresponding sides.

2. Since $\frac{400}{100}$ is easily reduced, divide the numerator and denominator by 100. Also, square the fraction.

3. Apply the Property of Porportions.

4. The result is the length of the corresponding side of the larger polygon.

Skill Check 2

Use proportions to find the missing areas in the following similar figures. Round answers to the nearest tenth.

1. $s_1 = 6$, $A_1 = 30$, $s_2 = 7$

2. $s_1 = 3$, $A_2 = 20$, $s_2 = 9$

Use proportions to find the corresponding sides in the following similar figures. Round answers to the nearest tenth.

3. $s_1 = 6$, $A_1 = 40$, $A_2 = 90$

4. $s_1 = 16$, $A_1 = 400$, $A_2 = 150$

■ A. Exercises

ABCD is 40 mm by 20 mm. *AFGE* is 20 mm by 10 mm. Write the multiplier in the blank that establishes the equality.

1. $AF =$ ___ AB

2. $AE =$ ___ AD

3. area of $AFGE =$ ___ area of $ABCD$

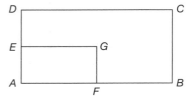

4. A section of land is a square 1 mi. by 1 mi. When a section is divided into four equal parts, each part is known as a quarter section. What are the dimensions of a quarter section?

5. How many feet are in a yard? How many square feet are in a square yard?

6. How many inches are in a foot? How many square inches are in a square foot?

7. Corresponding sides of two regular pentagons are in the ratio of 5 to 7. What is the ratio of their areas?

8. Corresponding sides of two regular octagons are in the ratio of 2 to 7. What is the ratio of their areas?

9. Corresponding sides of two squares are in the ratio of 13 to 19. What is the ratio of their perimeters?

10. The perimeters of two similar polygons are in the ratio of 6 to 5. What is the ratio of their areas?

■ B. Exercises

11. The perimeters of two similar rectangles are in the ratio of 7 to 4. What is the ratio of their diagonals?

12. If the ratio of the areas of two similar polygons is 25 to 36, what is ratio of their corresponding sides?

13. If the ratio of the diagonals of two squares is $\sqrt{2}$ to 1, what is the ratio of their areas?

14. If the ratio of the sides of two similar polygons is $\sqrt{3} : \sqrt{2}$, what is ratio of their areas?

For exercises 15–26, find the missing measures in the following pairs of similar figures.

$\triangle ABC \sim \triangle DEF$. Dimensions are in inches.

15. ratio of corresponding sides

16. perimeter of $\triangle DEF$

17. area of $\triangle DEF$

18. DE

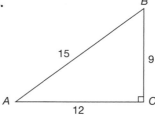
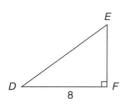

Rectangle *GHIJ* ~ **rectangle** *KLMN*. **Dimensions are in meters.**

19. ratio of corresponding sides

20. area of rectangle *KLMN*

21. perimeter of rectangle *KLMN*

22. *LM*

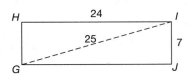

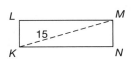

Parallelogram *PQRS* ~ **parallelogram** *UVWX*. **Dimensions are in millimeters.**

23. ratio of the corresponding sides

24. *UX*   25. *VY*

26. perimeter of *UVWX*

27. Doubling the radius of a circle has what effect on the area? What is the percent increase in area?

28. Tripling the sides of a square has what effect on the area? What is the percent increase in area?

29. The area of a square can be doubled by multiplying each side by what factor?

30. The area of a circle can be tripled by multiplying the radius by what factor?

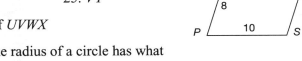

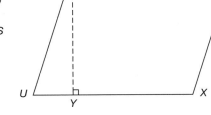

■ C. Exercises

31. Find the ratio between the volumes of two cubes whose edges are 6 in. and 3 in. respectively.

32. What is the ratio between the volumes of two similar solids if a length in the first solid is three times the corresponding length in the second?

33. If the ratio of the corresponding edges of two similar solids is 5 to 2, what is the ratio of their volumes?

■ CUMULATIVE REVIEW

A package of candy contains six orange, two blue, two brown, four yellow, one green, and three red candies. Find each of the following probabilities. [10.8–10.9]

34. The first piece of candy chosen is orange.

35. The first piece of candy chosen is a color besides orange.

36. The first piece of candy chosen is red or orange.

37. The first two pieces of candy chosen are blue.

Solve. Leave answers in radical form if the radicand is not a perfect square. [11.3]

38. $x^2 = 72$ 39. $7x^2 = 63$ 40. $\dfrac{x^2}{16} - 5 = 4$

Using the numbered angles, name an example of the following types of angles and angle relationships from the given figure. [12.1–12.2]

41. obtuse angle   42. alternate interior angles

43. supplementary angles   44. corresponding angles

45. complementary angles

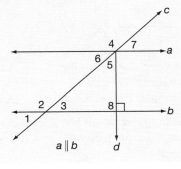

Surface Areas of Prisms and Cylinders

A *three-dimensional figure* is a shape whose points do not all lie in the same plane. Examples of three-dimensional figures follow.

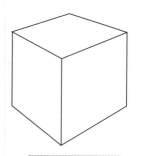
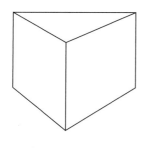
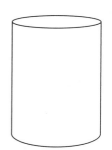

This gas can has the shape of a rectangular prism.

Definitions

A **polyhedron** is a closed three-dimensional figure with flat faces that are polygons. The first two figures above are polyhedra (plural form).
A **face** is any of the polygons making up a polyhedron.
An **edge** is a line of intersection of two faces of a polyhedron.
A **vertex** is any point where three or more faces of a polyhedron intersect (plural form: vertices).
A **prism** is a polyhedron with two congruent parallel faces.
Bases are the congruent parallel faces of a prism.
Lateral faces are all the faces of a prism or pyramid except the bases.

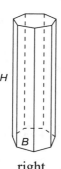
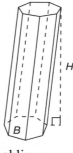

right
prism

oblique
prism

If the lateral edges of a prism are perpendicular to the plane of the base, the prism is called a *right prism*, and all its lateral faces are rectangles. If the lateral edges of a prism are not perpendicular to the plane of the base, the prism is called an *oblique prism*, and its lateral faces are parallelograms that are not rectangular.

Prisms are named for the shape of their bases. Since a rectangular prism has three pairs of parallel faces, any parallel pair can be considered the bases. This is not true of a triangular prism (since it has only one pair of parallel faces) or of any prism whose base has more than four sides.

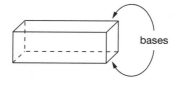
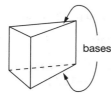

A *rectangular prism* has two parallel congruent rectangular bases.

A *triangular prism* has two parallel congruent triangular bases.

A *cube* is a special type of rectangular prism with six square congruent faces.

A rectangular prism has six faces: the two bases and four lateral faces. It has twelve edges: four on each base and four connecting the lateral faces. It has eight vertices: four on each base.

The *lateral surface area*, L, of a prism is the sum of the areas of its lateral faces. The *surface area*, S, of a prism is the sum of the areas of all its surfaces. If you unfold a rectangular prism, forming a *net*, you will see the six surfaces as separate rectangles. To find the surface area of the prism, find the areas of all the rectangles and take their sum.

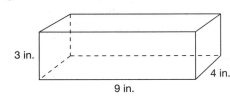

area of bottom base: $bh = 9 \times 4 = 36$ in.^{2}

area of right side: $bh = 4 \times 3 = 12$ in.^{2}

area of front: $bh = 9 \times 3 = 27$ in.^{2}

S = area of both bases + area of both sides
     + area of front and back

$S = 2(36) + 2(12) + 2(27)$

  $= 72 + 24 + 54$

  $= 150$ in.^{2}

The surface area of the rectangular prism is 150 in.^{2}

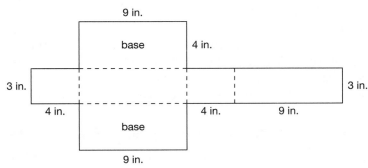

Examining the net, you will notice that when a prism unfolds, it forms a large rectangle with two flaps that form the two bases of the prism. The area of the long rectangle comprises the four lateral faces of the prism and, therefore, the lateral surface area (L) of the prism. The rectangles' dimensions are the perimeter of the base (p) and the height of the prism (H). So

$$L = pH = 26 \times 3 = 78 \text{ in.}^2.$$

The total surface area (S) can be determined by adding the lateral surface area (L) and the combined area of the two bases ($2B$).

$$2B = 2[9(4)] = 72 \text{ in.}^2 \text{ and}$$
$$S = L + 2B = 78 + 72 = 150 \text{ in.}^2.$$

Formula: Lateral Surface Area of a Prism	
$L = pH$	The lateral surface area of a prism (L) is equal to the product of the perimeter of the base (p) and the height of the prism (H).

Formula: Surface Area of a Prism	
$S = L + 2B$	The surface area of a prism (S) is equal to the sum of the lateral surface area (L) and the combined area of the two bases (B).

Example 1   Find the lateral surface area and surface area of the prism.

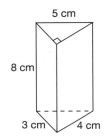

Answer

$L = pH$

$H = 8$ cm

$p = 3 + 4 + 5 = 12$

$L = 12(8)$

  $= 96$ cm^2

$S = L + 2B$

  $= 96 + 2(6)$

  $= 96 + 12$

  $= 108$ cm^2

1. Write the lateral surface area formula and determine the height of the prism, H, and the perimeter of the base, p.

2. Substitute known values into the formula and evaluate.

3. Use the surface area formula. B is the area of the triangular base: $A = \frac{1}{2}bh = \frac{1}{2}(4)(3) = 6$ cm.

4. Substitute known values into the formula and evaluate.

Skill Check 1

Find the surface area of the following prisms. Drawing a net may be helpful.

1. rectangular prism: 5 cm × 12 cm × 8 cm

2. cube with an edge of 5.5 ft.

3. triangular prism with 5 ft. × 12 ft. × 13 ft. bases and a height of 10 ft.

A *circular cylinder* is a three-dimensional figure with two parallel bases that are congruent circles. The curved surface is the *lateral surface*.

If you unfold a cylinder to form a net, the lateral surface will form a rectangle. The base of the rectangle is the circumference of the base of the cylinder, and the height of the rectangle is the height of the cylinder. The area of this rectangle is the lateral surface area of the cylinder. The sum of the lateral surface area and the combined area of the two circular bases is the surface area of a cylinder.

bases

Formula: Lateral Surface Area of a Cylinder	
$L = cH$ $\quad = 2\pi rH$	The lateral surface area of a cylinder (L) is equal to the product of the circumference of the base (c) and the height of the cylinder (H). Substitute for c.

Formula: Surface Area of a Cylinder	
$S = L + 2B$ $\quad = 2\pi rH + 2\pi r^2$	The surface area of a cylinder (S) is equal to the sum of the lateral surface area (L) and the combined area of the two circular bases (B). Substitute for L and B.

Example 2 Find the surface area of the cylinder.

Answer

$L = 2\pi rH$
$\quad = 2\pi(3)(9)$
$\quad = 54\pi$
$B = \pi r^2$
$\quad = \pi(3^2)$
$\quad = 9\pi$
$S = L + 2B$
$\quad = 54\pi + 2(9\pi)$
$\quad = 72\pi$
$\quad = 72(3.14)$
$\quad \approx 226.1 \text{ in.}^2$

1. Find the lateral surface area. Leave the answer as a multiple of π.

2. Find the area of the bottom base. Leave the answer as a multiple of π.

3. Substitute the values for the lateral surface area and for the area of one base into the surface area formula. Round the answer to the nearest tenth.

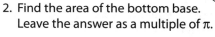

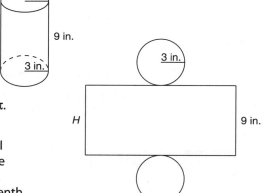

Find the surface area of the following cylinders. Round answers to the nearest whole number.

1. $r = 4$ m, $H = 10$ m
2. $r = 6.2$ in., $H = 22$ in.
3. $d = 6$ ft., $H = 6$ ft.
4. $d = 5$ cm, $H = 25$ cm

■ A. Exercises

Find the surface area of the following cubes, where *e* represents the length of an edge.

1. $e = 5$ in.
2. $e = 7.5$ ft.
3. $e = 120$ cm
4. $e = 2.5$ m

Find the surface area of the following prisms.

5.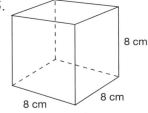
8 cm
8 cm
8 cm

6.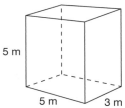
5 m
5 m
3 m

7.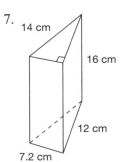
14 cm
16 cm
12 cm
7.2 cm

8.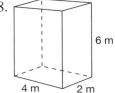
6 m
4 m
2 m

9.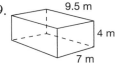
9.5 m
4 m
7 m

10.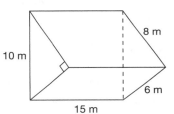
8 m
10 m
6 m
15 m

■ B. Exercises

Find the length of an edge of the cubes with the following surface areas.

11. 24 in.²
12. 96 in.²
13. 600 cm²

Find the lateral surface area of the triangular prisms with the following measures.

14. base: 6, 7, 8; $H = 10$
15. base: 12, 10, 8; $H = 2.5$
16. base: 20, 10, 13; $H = 8$
17. base: 5.5, 6.5, 8; $H = 15$

Find the surface area of the following cylinders.

18.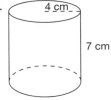
4 cm
7 cm

19.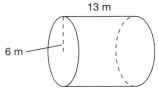
13 m
6 m

20.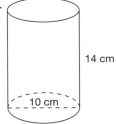
14 cm
10 cm

21. $r = 3$ m, $H = 16$ m
22. $r = 2$ m, $H = 8$ m
23. $d = 12$ cm, $H = 20$ cm

Find the surface area of the following.

24. If a soup can is 10 cm tall and 6 cm across, how many square centimeters of metal (to the nearest whole square centimeter) are used to make the can?

25. A box of cereal is 11 in. tall, 8 in. wide, and 2 in. thick. What is the surface area of the box?

26. How many square inches of cardboard comprise the tube for a roll of paper towels if the tube is 1 ft. long and 1 in. in diameter?

27. A building has the shape of a rectangular prism with outer walls made of glass. How many square feet of glass are required if each floor is 100 ft. by 150 ft. and the building is 50 ft. tall?

28. How many square inches of metal are required to make the illustrated drywall mud pan?

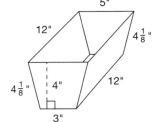

■ C. Exercises

29. The diagram is a cross section of a column to be used in front of a museum. The semicircles are 2 in. across and are connected by a flat 0.25 in. surface. How many square feet of column are to be covered by paint if the column is 20 ft. tall? How many columns can be painted with 1 gal. of paint if 1 gal. covers 400 ft.²?

30. Under what condition would the lateral surface area of a circular cylinder equal the combined area of its bases?

■ Dominion thru Math

31. Boxes for shipping large garden wagons are made of two open-top boxes, with one slightly larger to slide down over the other. These two halves are held together with two plastic bands around the narrower dimensions. The material for a band must be 4 in. longer than the girth of the box so the two ends will overlap for a crimped connector. How much banding is needed for a wagon box with outside dimensions of 36" × 18" × 12"?

32. Long, narrow tools are sometimes packed in boxes that are triangular prisms, saving cardboard and eliminating a four-piece lid. This is done by forming four long rectangles side by side and attaching an equilateral triangle to both ends of one of the rectangles. Three rectangles form the sides of the box; and when the box is folded, the fourth rectangle completely overlaps one of the other rectangles. Two glue tabs are necessary on the unattached sides of each triangular end. Tapering the ends of the glue tabs slightly makes it unnecessary to increase the size of the sheet of cardboard from which they are made and makes it easier to fold the box. Find the size of the cardboard stock used to make a box 3 ft. long if the ends are equilateral triangles 6 in. on a side with an altitude whose height is $5\frac{3}{16}$ in. Sketch a way to save material by placing the boxes end to end so the triangles are staggered.

Use prime factorizations to find the LCM of each pair of numbers. [4.4]

33. 9, 12   34. 8, 22   35. 5, 16   36. 21, 18   37. 36, 15

Find the unknown lengths in the following right triangles. [11.4]

38.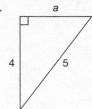

39.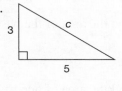

40.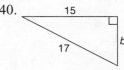

Find the unknown lengths in the following special right triangles. [12.6]

41. *n* and *h*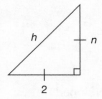

42. *s* and *g*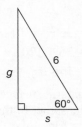

Surface Areas of Pyramids, Cones, and Spheres

13.6

There are two key differences between prisms and pyramids. Pyramids have only one base instead of two, and the faces that make up the lateral surface are triangular instead of rectangular.

> ### Definition
>
> A **pyramid** is a three-dimensional figure with a single polygonal base and triangular lateral faces that meet at a common point, known as the vertex of the pyramid.

Khafre pyramid on the Giza plateau at Cairo

The length of the *altitude of a pyramid*, H, is the perpendicular distance from the vertex to the base. Each triangular face has its own altitude, but with respect to the pyramid it is known as the *slant height, l.*

The base of a pyramid can be any polygon. The most common bases are triangles and squares. The *lateral surface area, L,* of a pyramid is the sum of the triangular faces. The *surface area, S,* of a pyramid is the sum of the areas of all its faces, including the base. To find the surface area, find the areas of all the faces and add them together.

A *regular pyramid* has a regular polygon as its base, and its vertex is directly above the center of the base. Pyramids with squares or equilateral triangles for bases are examples of regular pyramids.

The pyramid below has a square base and four faces that are congruent triangles. Notice that the heights, *h*, of the triangles are not the height, *H*, of the pyramid, but rather the slant heights, *l*, of the lateral faces.

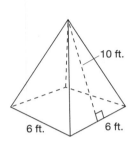

$B = s^2$

$\quad = 6^2$

$\quad = 36 \text{ ft.}^2$

1. Find the area of the base, *B*.

$A = \frac{1}{2}bl$

$\quad = \frac{1}{2}(6)(10)$

$\quad = 30 \text{ ft.}^2$

2. Find the area of one triangle.

$S = 36 + 4(30)$

$\quad = 36 + 120$

$\quad = 156 \text{ ft.}^2$

3. Add the areas of the base and the four identical lateral faces to get the surface area.

A specific formula for the lateral surface area of a regular pyramid can be developed since all slant heights are the same. In the net below, the height of the row of triangles is the slant height of the triangular faces, and the length of the row of triangles is the perimeter of the base.

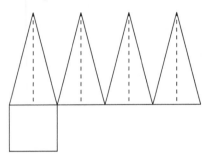
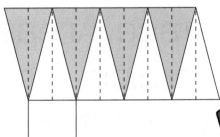

A parallelogram can be made by inverting the row of triangles and combining the result with the original row of triangles. The area of this parallelogram would be the perimeter of the pyramid's base (*p*) times the slant height (*l*). Therefore, the lateral surface area (*L*) would be half the area of the parallelogram.

$$L = \frac{1}{2}pl$$

The total surface area (*S*) can be determined by adding the lateral surface area (*L*) and the area of the base (*B*).

$$S = L + B$$

L = lateral surface area
S = total surface area
B = area of the base
H = altitude
(prism, cylinder)
l = slant height
(pyramid, cone)

Formula: Lateral Surface Area of a Regular Pyramid	
$L = \frac{1}{2}pl$	The lateral surface area of a regular pyramid (*L*) is equal to half the product of the perimeter of the base (*p*) and the slant height of the lateral faces (*l*).

Formula: Surface Area of a Regular Pyramid	
$S = L + B$	The surface area of a regular pyramid (*S*) is equal to the sum of the lateral surface area (*L*) and the area of the base (*B*).

Example 1 Find the lateral surface area and surface area of the square pyramid.

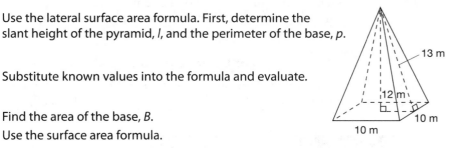

Answer

$L = \frac{1}{2}pl$

$l = 13$ m

$p = 4(10) = 40$ m

$L = \frac{1}{2}(40)(13)$

$= 260$ m²

$B = s^2 = 10^2 = 100$ m²

$S = L + B$

$= 260 + 100$

$= 360$ m²

1. Use the lateral surface area formula. First, determine the slant height of the pyramid, l, and the perimeter of the base, p.

2. Substitute known values into the formula and evaluate.

3. Find the area of the base, B.

4. Use the surface area formula.

The altitude of a pyramid (H), the slant height (l), and the perpendicular distance from the center of the base to a side of the base form a right triangle. If you know two of these quantities, you can apply the Pythagorean theorem to find the third.

Example 2 Find the slant height of the square pyramid.

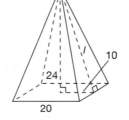

Answer

$a = 10$ and $H = 24$

$l^2 = a^2 + H^2$

$= 10^2 + 24^2$

$= 100 + 576$

$= 676$

$\sqrt{l^2} = \sqrt{676}$

$l = 26$ units

1. Identify the two known quantities.

2. Apply the Pythagorean theorem.

3. Substitute known values into the formula and evaluate.

4. Take the square root of both sides of the equation.

Skill Check 1

Find the lateral surface area and total surface area of the following pyramids. Drawing a net may be helpful.

1. square pyramid with base $s = 12$ cm, $l = 8$ cm

2. square pyramid with base $s = 18$ cm, $H = 16$ cm

3. triangular pyramid with all faces congruent equilateral triangles having $s = 3$ ft., $l = 2.6$ ft.

A *circular cone* is similar to a pyramid but has a circular base. The curved surface is the *lateral surface*.

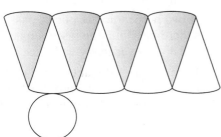

The lateral surface has been sliced into four congruent pie-shaped pieces and arranged as the triangles were arranged previously for the pyramid. As the lateral surface is cut into smaller slices, the base and height of the parallelogram-like area become closer to the circumference of the base and the slant height of the cone. As with the pyramid, we can insert four more pie-shaped pieces, forming a parallelogram-like figure.

Again, we want only half the area of the parallelogram, so the formula for the lateral surface area of a cone is similar to the formula for pyramids (with circumference replacing perimeter).

$$L = \frac{1}{2}cl$$

Substitute for the circumference, c.

$$L = \frac{1}{2}(2\pi r)l = \pi r l$$

<table>
<tr><td colspan="2">Formula: Lateral Surface Area of a Circular Cone</td></tr>
<tr><td>$L = \dfrac{1}{2}cl$
$\quad = \pi rl$</td><td>The lateral surface area of a circular cone (L) is equal to half the product of the circumference of the base (c) and the slant height (l). Substitute for c.</td></tr>
</table>

<table>
<tr><td colspan="2">Formula: Surface Area of a Circular Cone</td></tr>
<tr><td>$S = L + B$
$\quad = \pi rl + \pi r^2$</td><td>The surface area of a circular cone (S) is equal to the sum of the lateral surface area (L) and the area of the circular base (B). Substitute for L and B.</td></tr>
</table>

Example 3   Find the surface area of the cone.

Answer

$L = \pi rl$
$\quad = \pi(3)(10)$
$\quad = 30\pi$

1. Find the lateral surface area. Leave the answer as a multiple of π.

$B = \pi r^2$
$\quad = \pi(3^2)$
$\quad = 9\pi$

2. Find the area of the base. Leave the answer as a multiple of π.

$S = L + B$
$\quad = 30\pi + 9\pi$
$\quad = 39\pi$
$\quad = 39(3.14)$
$\quad \approx 122.5$

3. Substitute the values for the lateral surface area and for the area of the base into the surface area formula. Round the answer to the nearest tenth.

10

3

Skill Check 2

Find the surface area of the following cones to the nearest whole number.

1. $r = 2$ m, $l = 10$ m
2. $r = 3.2$ in., $l = 11$ in.
3. $d = 10$ ft., $l = 8$ ft.

Definition

A **sphere** is a three-dimensional closed surface, every point of which is equidistant from a given point called the center.

A diameter is a chord passing through the center. The chord $\overline{AD}$ is a diameter of sphere O. A radius is a segment that connects the center with any point on the sphere. $\overline{OB}$ is a radius.

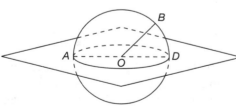

Any plane passing through a sphere intersects it in a circle. The farther the plane is from the center, the smaller the circle. The largest circle occurs when a plane passes through the center of the sphere. This circle is called a *great circle*. The great circle and the sphere have the same radius.

If two perpendicular planes pass through the center of a sphere, they divide the sphere into four equal sections called *lunes*. Visualize quartering an orange by slicing it once vertically and once horizontally. The figure shows such a quartering.

It can be proved that the area of a great circle is equal to the surface area of one of the lunes, though the proof is beyond the scope of this book. The area of a great circle is just the familiar $A = \pi r^2$; thus, the surface area of a sphere is $4\pi r^2$.

Formula: Surface Area of a Sphere	
$S = 4A$ $= 4\pi r$	The surface area of a sphere (S) is equal to four times the area of a great circle (A). Substitute for A.

Example 4   Find the surface area of the sphere.

Answer

$S = 4\pi r^2$ 1. Write the formula.

$\quad = 4\pi(8^2)$ 2. Substitute known values into the formula.

$\quad = 4\pi(64)$ 3. Simplify.

$\quad = 256\pi$

$\quad = 256(3.14)$

$\quad \approx 803.8 \text{ ft.}^2$ 4. Round the answer to the nearest tenth.

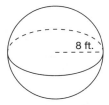

Skill Check 3

Find the surface area of the following spheres to the nearest whole number.

1. $r = 2$ cm   2. $r = 4.1$ m   3. $d = 10$ ft.

■ A. Exercises

Complete the following table to summarize the most specific formulas for lateral and total surface areas.

	Lateral Surface Area	**Total Surface Area**
Prism	1.	2.
Circular Cylinder	3.	4.
Regular Pyramid	5.	6.
Circular Cone	7.	8.
Sphere	Not applicable	9.

Use the square pyramid for exercises 10–12. Dimensions are in meters.

10. Find the lateral surface area.

11. Find the area of the base.

12. Find the total surface area.

Use the cone for exercises 13–15. Dimensions are in feet. Express answers both in terms of π and rounded to the nearest tenth.

13. Find the lateral surface area.

14. Find the area of the base.

15. Find the total surface area.

16. Find the surface area of the sphere to the nearest whole unit.

■ B. Exercises

Draw a net and find the total surface area of the following pyramids.

17.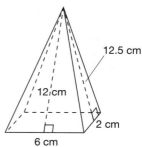

12.5 cm

12 cm

2 cm

6 cm

18.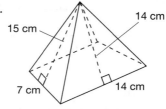

15 cm

14 cm

7 cm

14 cm

19.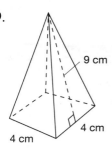

9 cm

4 cm

4 cm

Find the lateral surface area and total surface area of the following regular pyramids.

20. $B = 22$ ft.²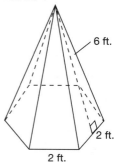

6 ft.

2 ft.

2 ft.

21.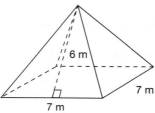

6 m

7 m

7 m

22. $B = 84$ cm²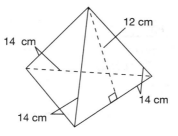

12 cm

14 cm

14 cm

14 cm

Draw pyramids with the following dimensions and find the total surface area.

23. square pyramid with base $s = 5.2$ in., $l = 7$ in.

24. rectangular pyramid with base 4 ft. by 7 ft., $l = 10$ ft. to the 7 ft. sides of the base, $l = 10.4$ ft. to the 4 ft. sides of the base

Find the lateral surface area and total surface area of the following cones. Express answers both in terms of π and rounded to the nearest tenth.

25.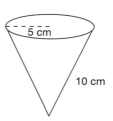

5 cm

10 cm

26.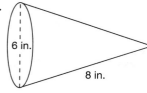

6 in.

8 in.

Draw cones with the following dimensions and find the total surface area. Express answers both in terms of π and rounded to the nearest tenth.

27. $r = 3$ cm, $l = 7$ cm

28. $d = 16$ m, $l = 16$ m

29. How many square inches of paper are required to line a funnel that has a slant height of 5 in. and an opening that is 8 in. wide?

Find the surface area of the following spheres. Express answers both in terms of π and rounded to the nearest whole number.

30. $r = 4$ m   31. $r = 24$ cm   32. $d = 6$ ft.   33. $d = 12$ ft.

■ C. Exercises

34. Each side of the Great Pyramid at Giza, Egypt, is approximately 250 yd. long. The 160 yd. climb straight up a side to the top of the pyramid is now forbidden without special permission. What is the exposed surface area of the pyramid in square yards?

35. Describe a general method for finding the lateral surface area of an obelisk. Include variables for any information needed to compute the surface area.

36. Under what condition would the lateral surface area of a square pyramid equal the area of its base? Is this possible?

■ Dominion thru Math

37. An oatmeal box is a cylinder made of cardboard with a circular cardboard bottom and a circular plastic lid. How many square inches of cardboard will it take to make an oatmeal box that is 13 cm in diameter and 24 cm tall? Draw the pattern needed to make this box. What are the dimensions of the piece of cardboard needed to make the box?

38. A cocoa can is a cylinder with cardboard sides and aluminum ends. The end that opens has a pull tab to remove it, and then a plastic lid is used to close the can. How much cardboard and aluminum are used to make the can if it is 10 cm in diameter and 9 cm tall?

CUMULATIVE REVIEW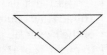

Simplify the following radical expressions. [11.5–11.7]

39. $\sqrt{27}$ 40. $7\sqrt{6}\left(2\sqrt{15}\right)$ 41. $\sqrt{18} - \sqrt{50}$

42. $\sqrt[3]{81} - \sqrt[3]{24}$ 43. $\sqrt{\dfrac{72}{50}}$

Use the figure at the right for exercises 44–45. [12.3]

44. Classify the triangle according to the measures of its angles.

45. Classify the triangle according to the lengths of its sides.

46. Find the sum of the measures of the angles in a regular decagon. [12.3]

47. Find the measure of each angle in a regular decagon. [12.3]

48. Give the common name used for a "rhombuscular" rectangle. [12.3]

PROBLEM SOLVING

Use Multiple Strategies

You have already seen some examples of using multiple strategies during the problem-solving process. It is wise to carefully read a problem and then determine one or more strategies that might help you solve the problem. Sometimes it will help to draw a diagram and make a table, or draw a diagram and write an equation. Diagrams often help you to get a better grasp of the meaning of the problem and to interpret it correctly. It is always wise to make an estimate of the answer before you begin the problem-solving process. This way, when you look back to check your answer, you already have an idea of what to expect for a reasonable answer.

The following example gives an illustration of using more than one strategy to solve a problem. The goal is to find a correct, efficient method. Remember that different people will solve the same problem in different ways. Do not be concerned if you solve a problem differently from how your classmate does. However, make sure the answer is correct; then compare the processes to see which is more efficient.

Example Mr. Tirado has boxes that measure 20" × 13" × 9" high. He wants to store them in a room 12' × 10' × 9'. If he stacks the boxes side by side and on top of each other but cannot stack the boxes on their sides, how many boxes can he store in this room?

Answer

Think: Determine what you are trying to find.

We want to know the number of boxes that he can store in the room.

Think: How can you organize this information to find the number of boxes? Would a picture help? Would it help to solve a simpler problem first? How many boxes will fit in one layer on the floor of the room?

Convert the dimensions of the floor into inches and draw a diagram of it.

$$12 \text{ ft.} \left(\frac{12 \text{ in.}}{\text{ft.}} \right) = 144 \text{ in. long}$$

$$10 \text{ ft.} \left(\frac{12 \text{ in.}}{\text{ft.}} \right) = 120 \text{ in. wide}$$

The dimensions of the room in inches are 144" × 120".

Think: How could the boxes fit into the room? Should the length of the boxes be placed along the length of the room or the width of the room? What operation should be used to determine the number of boxes that can be placed lengthwise along the length of the room?

Divide the length of a box into the length of the room to determine how many boxes one layer deep can fit in the room.

$144 \div 20 = 7.2$

Seven boxes can be placed along the length of the room. There will be $144 - 7(20) = 4$ in. of space at one end of the room.

Think: How many boxes will fit this way on the floor if the width of a box is 13 in. and the width of the room is 120 in.?

$120 \div 13 = 9.23$

Nine boxes will fit along the width of the room. There will be 120 − 9(13) = 3 in. of space on one side of the room.

Think: How many boxes will fit on the floor of the room?

7(9) = 63

If the boxes are placed in the room in this manner, there will be 63 boxes per layer with little wasted space.

Think: How high can the boxes be stacked?

The room is 9 ft. high, which is 9(12) = 108 in. Each box is 9 in. tall, so a stack of exactly 12 layers of boxes should fit into the room, assuming the door allows you to stack them all the way to the ceiling.

Think: How many boxes can be stored in the room in this configuration?

63(12) = 756 boxes can be stored in the room.

Think: Is this the most efficient way to use the room? Is there any way more boxes could be stored in the room? What problem-solving processes were used to solve this problem?

There is little wasted space in this configuration. This seems to be a very efficient method. Several processes were used, including drawing a diagram, selecting correct operations, and guess and check.

144 in.

120 in.

■ Exercises

For each of the following exercises, devise a plan for finding the solution. Then carry out the plan and check to determine whether your answer is correct. Finally, look for any methods that are more efficient.

1. Use the information in the example problem and determine how many boxes could be placed in the room if the length of each box were placed along the width of the room. How many inches of space are wasted in each direction? Which method allows more boxes to be stored in the room?

2. A bicycle shop had 72 bicycles with a price tag of $149.95. Before Christmas, the shop reduced the price by $32.99 and sold 49 of the bicycles. The rest of the bicycles were sold at the original price. How much money did the bicycle shop receive from the sale of all 72 bicycles?

3. The Kingsbury Middle School eighth-grade class is planning a class trip to an amusement park. There are 174 students in the eighth grade, and the total cost of the trip is $7,482. This amount includes the total cost of admission to the amusement park and $870 for bus tranportation. How much is admission for each student, how much will each student have to pay to cover the bus expenses, and what is the total cost for each student?

4. One family has six members who all give Christmas gifts to one another. If they have been doing this for eight years, how many gifts have been exchanged? If they have a $10 price limit on the gifts, what is the maximum amount of money spent by the family members over those eight years?

5. Sahara watches the temperature of a solution during a science experiment. She is to allow the solution to cool and heat several times throughout the project. The first reading is half the temperature of the final reading. During the experiment the solution's temperature rises 12°, falls 4°, rises 33°, falls 11°, and rises 26°. What are the initial and final temperatures of the solution?

6. The house numbers along the south side of Elm Street are numbered by consecutive odd numbers. The first number on the block is 201. If the last number on the block is 231, how many houses are on the south side of Elm Street in this block?

7. Mrs. Koto drives her car at an average speed of 48 mi./hr. for 30 min. and then increases her speed to an average of 64 mi./hr. for 2 hr. to arrive at her daughter's house. If construction work slows her down on the way home along the same route and it takes her 4 hr. to get home, what is her average speed on the way home?

8. A soda can display has 105 cans. There is one fewer can in each row than in the row below, with a single can in the top row. How many cans are in the bottom row? How many rows are there? If each soda can is 5 in. tall, how high does the display reach?

13.7 Volumes of Prisms and Cylinders

The figure on the right is a unit cube. Since each of its sides is 1 cm long, the volume of the figure is one cubic centimeter, written 1 cm³.

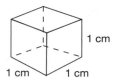

Definition

The **volume** of a three-dimensional figure is the number of cubic units needed to fill the figure.

Since the rectangular prism at the right has two layers of cubes and each layer contains six cubes, the volume of the figure is 12 cm³.

To find the volume of a prism, use the following formula.

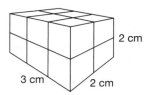

The formula for the volume of a cylinder is used to find the tank's capacity.

Formula: Volume of a Prism	
$V = BH$	The volume of a prism (V) is equal to the area of the base (B) times the height (H).

Example 1 Find the volume of a rectangular prism that has a 5 ft. × 9 ft. rectangular base and whose height is 2.5 ft.

Altitude H is $\perp$ to the plane of the base.

Answer

$V = BH$

$B = 5(9)$

   $= 45$

$V = BH$

   $= 45(2.5)$

   $= 112.5$ ft.³

1. Write the volume formula for a prism.
2. Find the area of the rectangular base by using the area formula $B = bh$, where $b = 5$ and $h = 9$.
3. Do not confuse the H of the prism, which is 2.5 ft., with the height of the base of the prism, which is symbolized by h in the area formula for a rectangle.

Example 2 Find the volume of the triangular prism.

Answer

$V = BH$

$B = \frac{1}{2}(12)(9)$

   $= 54$

$V = BH$

   $= 54(10)$

   $= 540$ cm³

1. Write the volume formula for a prism.
2. Find the area of the triangular base by using the area formula $B = \frac{1}{2}bh$, where $b = 12$ and $h = 9$.
3. Substitute known values into the volume formula and evaluate.

Skill Check 1

Find the volume of the following prisms. Round answers to the nearest whole unit.

1.

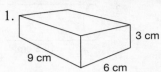

9 cm
6 cm
3 cm

2.

7 m
5 m
8 m

Draw prisms with the following dimensions and find the volume.

3. rectangular base 8.5 cm × 4 cm and height of 6 cm

4. right triangular base with legs of 2 ft. and 3 ft. and prism height of 2.5 ft.

A similar formula can be used to find the volume of a circular cylinder. Since the base is a circle, we use the formula for the area of a circle, $B = \pi r^2$.

Formula: Volume of a Circular Cylinder	
$V = BH$ $= \pi r^2 H$	The volume of a circular cylinder (V) is equal to the area of the base (B) times the height (H). Substitute for B.

Example 3   Find the volume of the cylinder.

Answer

$V = BH$

$= \pi r^2 H$

$= \pi(4^2)(7)$

$= 112\pi$

$= 112(3.14)$

≈ 351.7 cm^3

1. Write the volume formula for a cylinder.

2. Substitute known values into the formula and evaluate.

3. Round the answer to the nearest tenth.

4 cm

7 cm

When the volume of a prism or cylinder is known, the formula provides an equation that can be used to find a missing length. Substitute the known quantities into the formula and solve for the unknown measurement.

Example 4   Find the radius of a cylinder with a height of 12 ft. and a volume of 432π ft.^{3}.

Answer

$V = \pi r^2 H$

$432\pi = \pi r^2(12)$

$36 = r^2$

$\pm 6 = r$

$r = 6$ ft.

1. Substitute known values into the formula for the volume of a cylinder.

2. Divide both sides by 12π.

3. Take the square root of both sides.

Find the volume of the following cylinders. Round answers to the nearest whole unit.

1.  8 cm 2 cm

2. 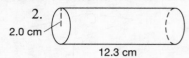 2.0 cm 12.3 cm

3. radius of 6 ft. and height of 10 ft.   4. diameter of 10 m and height of 12 m

Find the missing measure.

5. height of a cylinder with a volume of 12π m^3 and a radius of 2 m

6. width of a 6 cm tall square prism with a volume of 150 cm^3

⊕ Invention

The famous *Rubik's cube* puzzle has 4.325×10^{19} different combinations, but in June of 2003 Dan Knights of San Francisco did it in just 20 sec. The official world record, based on average time for several cubes, is 13.22 sec. and was set on March 20, 2006. Without a very keen understanding of how to put a scrambled cube back in its original position, one could spend several lifetimes working at it. The original puzzle invented by Hungarian architect Erno Rubik in 1974 was a plastic cube measuring 2.25 in. on a side. Each outer face was a 3×3 square made up of nine small cubes, each in one of six different colors: blue, green, red, orange, white, and yellow. Once the layers of the cube were scrambled in all different directions, the colors would be mixed on each side. The puzzle consists of unscrambling the cube back to its original position with one color per face. This toy became so popular that in the three years from 1980 through 1982 over 100,000,000 were sold. It easily ranks as the fastest-selling puzzle of all time.

■ A. Exercises

Find the volume of the following prisms.

1. 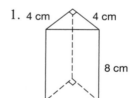 4 cm 4 cm 8 cm

2. 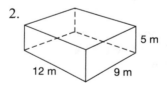 5 m 12 m 9 m

3. 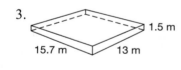 1.5 m 15.7 m 13 m

Find the volume of the rectangular prisms with the given dimensions. Use the formula $V = lwH$.

4. $l = 9$ cm
   $w = 5$ cm
   $H = 3$ cm

5. $l = 17$ m
   $w = 8$ m
   $H = 12$ m

6. $l = 7.3$ m
   $w = 4.8$ m
   $H = 10$ m

Find the volume of the following cylinders to the nearest whole unit.

7. 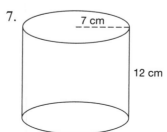 7 cm 12 cm

8. 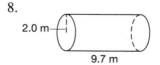 2.0 m 9.7 m

9. 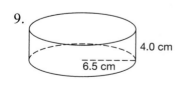 4.0 cm 6.5 cm

Find the volume of the following cylinders to the nearest whole unit.

10. $r = 13$ cm
    $H = 8$ cm

11. $r = 12$ m
    $H = 19.5$ m

12. $r = 4.8$ cm
    $H = 6.5$ cm

13. $r = 6$ in.
    $H = 12$ in.

■ B. Exercises

Find the missing measure. Round answers to the nearest tenth.

14. volume: 36 m³, height: ?

15. volume: 175.5 cm³, height: ?

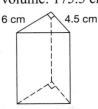

16. volume: 387.6 cm³, area of base: ?

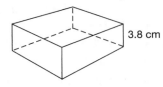

17. volume: 628 m³, height: ?

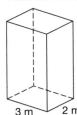

18. volume: 70.65 m³, height: ?

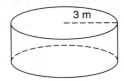

19. volume: 157 m³, area of base: ?

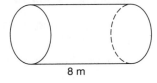

20. volume: 250 m³, length: ?

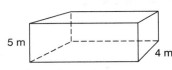

21. volume: 116.2 cm³, width: ?

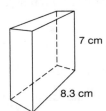

22. volume: 84.78 m³, height: ?

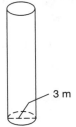

Find the missing measure.

23. height of a prism with a rectangular base of 28 m × 15 m and a volume of 5,040 m³

24. radius of a circular cylinder with a volume of 1,570 ft.³ and a height of 20 ft.

25. Derive the formula for the volume of a cube with edges of length e.

26. Find the volume of a cube with edges of 3 ft.

27. Find the volume of a cube with edges of 10 cm.

28. Express the volume of a circular cylinder as a function of its radius when the cylinder's height is equal to the diameter of its base.

29. A box is made from an 8 in. × 12 in. piece of cardboard by cutting out a 2 in. × 2 in. piece from each corner and then folding up the edges to make the sides of the box. What is the volume of the box?

30. Write an expression for the length, width, and height of the box from exercise 29 when the square that is cut off is a variable amount x.

■ C. Exercises

31. What size cube would have a surface area numerically equal to its volume?

32. The volume of a cylinder is 207.711 cm³. The area of its base is 38.465 cm². What is its height?

33. The height of a cylinder is 2.6 m. Its volume is 18.369 m³. What is the area of its base?

34. How many cubic feet of sand are needed to fill a 10 ft. × 10 ft. playground sandbox 6 in. deep? A ton of sand occupies 16 ft.³. Assume sand costs $30/tn. and can be bought only in tons and half tons. How much will the buyer have to purchase, and how much will it cost?

35. A pot has a circular base with a diameter of 6 in. and a height of 3 in. How much soup will the pot hold? Give your answer in cubic inches and then convert it to quarts. (1 in.³ = 0.55414 oz.; 32 oz. = 1 qt.)

■ Dominion thru Math

One constant is very important in determining the amount of storage in gallons that a tank can hold: a cubic foot holds 7.48 gal. of water. This number can also be used for other liquids. In the International System, a liter of water is 1,000 cm³. This means that a cubic meter of water is 1,000 L. In terms of weight, a cubic foot of water weighs 62.4 lb., and a cubic meter weighs 2,200 lb. A cubic meter has a mass of 1,000 kg, which is also a metric ton (tonne). The stated capacity of a big storage tank is usually a few hundred gallons less than its actual volume, since tanks are seldom completely filled due to expansion and other physical factors. One notable exception is a household hot-water heater, where the contents fill the tank and are under pressure.

Use a calculator and volume formulas to find the answers to the following exercises.

36. The glass-lined cylindrical tank that holds the hot water in an electric hot-water heater has a diameter of 16" and is 4' 9" high. How many gallons does this tank hold? If hot-water heaters are sold by the number of gallons they hold in round numbers, what size would this unit be?

37. For an energy-efficient unit, the actual cylindrical cabinet that holds the hot-water tank is separated by 2 in. of insulation on all sides. What are the diameter and height of the outside cabinet of the hot-water tank in exercise 36?

38. The inside dimensions of an upright home freezer are 24" × 18" × 62". What is its capacity in cubic feet?

39. How many liters of water are in a swimming pool 50 m long by 25 m wide with a water depth of 2 m?

40. A tank farm has ten rows of identical cylindrical fuel tanks with ten tanks in each row. The tanks are sitting in a square leak-proof containment "pond" (enclosure large enough to contain all possible leakage from all the tanks) that is 1 m deep. If the tanks are 4 m in diameter and 6 m tall, what are the dimensions of the enclosure?

CUMULATIVE REVIEW

The following high temperatures were recorded in several cities: {83, 80, 79, 75, 90, 77, 82, 81, 82}. [10.1–10.2]

41. Find the minimum, lower quartile, median, upper quartile, and maximum values.

42. Construct a box-and-whisker diagram for the data.

43. Find the range and interquartile range.

44. Find the mean.

45. Find the mode.

Find the distance between the following points. [12.7]

46. (3, 5) and (–4, 5)   47. (0, 3) and (8, 9)

Find the midpoint of the segments with the following endpoints. [12.7]

48. (3, 5) and (–4, 5)   49. (0, 3) and (8, 9)

50. Find the midpoint, M, of the segment with the endpoints A (–1, 2) and B (5, –4), and then use the distance formula to show that this point is an equal distance from both endpoints of the segment.

Ruth, Loyal Daughter-in-Law

Did you know that only two books in the Bible are named for women? One is Esther and the other is Ruth (circa 1280–1220 BC). Ruth has the additional honor of being the great-grandmother of David and an ancestor of the Messiah. She received these blessings from the Lord as a result of her faithfulness and loyalty to her mother-in-law, Naomi, and to the God of Israel.

During a time of famine in Israel, a Jewish man took his wife, Naomi, and his two sons into the land of Moab. Both sons married Moabite women, one of whom was Ruth. Then Naomi's husband and both sons died there. When Naomi decided to return to Bethlehem, Ruth displayed her loyalty by insisting "whither thou goest, I will go …; thy people shall be my people, and thy God my God" (Ruth 1:16). With an uncertain future before her, Ruth left home to accompany her mother-in-law to what was for her a new land.

Understanding biblical units of volume will help us better appreciate Ruth's diligence and Boaz's generosity. Upon her arrival in Bethlehem, Ruth went to work to support herself and her mother-in-law. She gleaned "an ephah of barley" (Ruth 2:17) in the fields, picking up the grain the workers dropped. An ephah is a measure of dry volume of about 0.6 bu. (almost 30 lb.). There she found favor with the owner of the field, Naomi's rich relative Boaz. He had heard about her loyalty to Naomi and seen her diligence in the fields. To understand the size of Boaz's gift to Ruth and Naomi of "six measures of barley" (Ruth 3:15, 17), we can estimate that a "measure" (probably a seah) is a third of an ephah, or about two and a half gallons of barley. His gift can then be pictured as three five-gallon buckets full of grain. In time, Boaz took Ruth to be his wife.

Ruth's testimony was such that she was recognized by the entire city as a woman of virtue (Ruth 3:11). According to Solomon, a virtuous woman "looketh well to the ways of her household" (Prov. 31:27). As a Christian, you ought to do all you can to ensure that your home runs well. Your loyalty to your parents and your love for the Lord should motivate you to help out any way you can. As you seek to please your heavenly Father, knowledge of volume and measurements will help you at home and in your understanding of the Bible.

13.8 Volumes of Pyramids, Cones, and Spheres

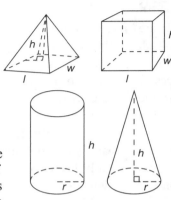

Notice that this pyramid and rectangular prism have congruent bases and the same height. Suppose you filled the pyramid with water and poured it into the prism. After you did this three times, the prism would be full. This demonstrates that the volume of the pyramid is one-third that of the rectangular prism. The same is true for a cylinder and a cone with congruent bases and the same height.

To find the volume of a pyramid or cone, use the following formula.

Formula: Volume of a Pyramid or Cone	
$V = \frac{1}{3}BH$	The volume of a pyramid or cone (V) is equal to one-third the area of the base (B) times the height (H).

The bushels of grain in this pile can be estimated using the formula for the volume of a cone.

The height of a cone or pyramid is the distance from the vertex perpendicular to the base.

Example 1 Find the volume of the square pyramid.

Answer

$V = \frac{1}{3}BH$ 1. The area of a square base is $B = s^2$.

$= \frac{1}{3}(8^2)(12)$ 2. Substitute known values into the formula and evaluate. Take $\frac{1}{3}$ of 12 first.

$= 256 \text{ cm}^3$

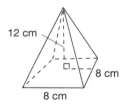

12 cm

8 cm

8 cm

Example 2 Find the volume of the cone.

Answer

$V = \frac{1}{3}BH$ 1. The area of a circular base is $B = \pi r^2$.

$= \frac{1}{3}\pi(4^2)(6)$ 2. Substitute known values into the formula and evaluate.

$= 32\pi$

$= 32(3.14)$

$\approx 100.5 \text{ cm}^3$ 3. Round the answer to the nearest tenth.

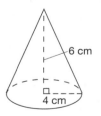

6 cm

4 cm

Find the volume of the following cones and pyramids to the nearest whole number.

1.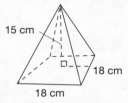
15 cm
18 cm
18 cm

2.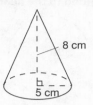
8 cm
5 cm

Find the volume of the following figures to the nearest tenth.

3. cone: $d = 12$ in., $H = 5$ in.

4. square pyramid: $s = 6.5$ ft., $H = 10$ ft.

5. rectangular pyramid: $B = 5$ m $\times$ 8 m; $H = 6$ m

Just as for the surface area of a sphere, the mathematics to demonstrate the formula for the volume of a sphere is beyond the scope of this book. Since all spheres are similar to all other spheres, the only measurement needed is the radius.

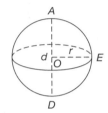

Formula: Volume of a Sphere	
$V = \dfrac{4}{3}\pi r^3$	The volume of a sphere (V) is equal to the product of $\dfrac{4}{3}$, π, and the radius cubed (r).

Example 3 Find the volume of a sphere with a diameter of 15 ft. to the nearest hundredth. Find the number of gallons it will hold. (1 ft.^{3} = 7.48 gal.)

Answer

$r = \dfrac{15}{2} = 7.5$ ft. 1. Find the radius.

$V = \dfrac{4}{3}\pi r^3$ 2. Find the volume.

$\quad = \dfrac{4}{3}\pi(7.5^3)$ 3. Substitute the known value into the volume formula and evaluate.

$\quad = \dfrac{4}{3}\pi(421.875)$

$\quad = \dfrac{1{,}687.5}{3}\pi$

$\quad = 562.5(3.14)$

$\quad \approx 1{,}766.25$ ft.^{3} 4. Round to the nearest hundredth.

$7.48(1{,}766.25) \approx 13{,}212$ gal. 5. Find the capacity to the nearest gallon.

Example 4 Find the radius of a sphere with a volume of 288π m^3.

Answer

$V = \dfrac{4}{3}\pi r^3$ 1. Write the volume formula for a sphere.

$\dfrac{4}{3}\pi r^3 = 288\pi$ 2. Substitute the known value.

$\dfrac{3}{4}\left(\dfrac{4}{3}\right)\pi r^3 = \dfrac{3}{4}(288\pi)$ 3. Multiply both sides by $\dfrac{3}{4}$.

$\pi r^3 = 216\pi$

$r^3 = 216$ 4. Divide both sides by π.

$r = 6$ m 5. Take the cube root of both sides.

Volume Formulas

Prism/Cylinder: $V = BH$

Pyramid/Cone: $V = \dfrac{1}{3}BH$

Sphere: $V = \dfrac{4}{3}\pi r^3$

Find the volume of the following spheres. Express answers both in terms of π and rounded to the nearest whole number.

1.
7 m

2. $r = 3$ ft.

3. $d = 10$ m

■ A. Exercises

Find the volume of the following pyramids.

1.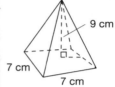
9 cm
7 cm
7 cm

2.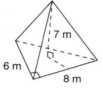
7 m
6 m
8 m

3.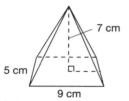
7 cm
5 cm
9 cm

Find the volume of the following pyramids with the given base area B and height H.

4. $B = 38$ m²
   $H = 7$ m

5. $B = 290$ cm²
   $H = 35$ cm

6. $B = 7.6$ m²
   $H = 5$ m

Find the volume of the following cones.

7.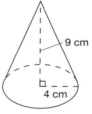
9 cm
4 cm

8.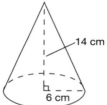
14 cm
6 cm

9.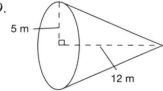
5 m
12 m

Find the volume of the following cones with the given radius r and height H.

10. $r = 2$ m
    $H = 8$ m

11. $r = 13$ in.
    $H = 4$ in.

12. $r = 7$ cm
    $H = 6.5$ cm

Find the volume of the following spheres to the nearest whole unit.

13.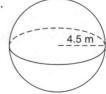
4.5 m

14.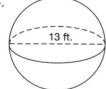
13 ft.

15.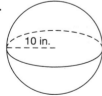
10 in.

Find the volume of the following spheres. Express answers in terms of π.

16. $r = 2$ cm

17. $r = 3$ m

18. $r = 4$ ft.

19. $d = 12$ in.

In the table below, *V* represents the volume of a cone or pyramid, *B* represents the area of the base, and *H* represents the height. Find the unknown variable in each row.

	V (volume)	B (area of base)	H (height)
20.		8	9
21.	26		6
22.	15π	9π	
23.	68π		12

In the table below, *V* represents the volume of a sphere, *r* represents the radius of the sphere, and *d* represents the diameter of the sphere. Find the unknown variables in each row.

	V (volume)	r (radius)	d (diameter)
24.			9
25.	36π		
26.	972π		
27.		6	

Find the following measures of the circular cone. Dimensions are in centimeters. Express answers in terms of π.

28. volume

29. slant height

30. surface area

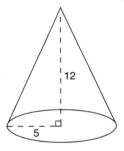

Find the following measures of the square pyramid with a volume of 384 in.³.

31. length of each side of the base

32. slant height

33. surface area

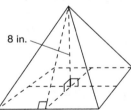

■ **C. Exercises**

34. Find the formula for the volume between the hourglass and the circular cylinder. Simplify the formula if possible.

35. Two polyhedra are similar; the ratio of their corresponding lengths is $a : b$. What is the ratio of their volumes?

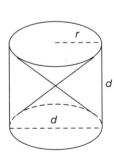

■ Dominion thru Math

36. An elevated water storage tank is a 32' diameter steel sphere sitting on top of a cylindrical steel supporting structure. How many gallons of water can the spherical tank hold? Remember that 1 ft.³ ≈ 7.48 gal., and round the result to the nearest gallon.

37. A grain storage bin is a steel cylinder with a conical top. One company markets a bin that is 18' in diameter, 16' high at the eaves, and 21' high at the peak. What is the maximum number of bushels of wheat (rounded to the nearest bushel) that can be stored in the bin? There are 0.8 bushels in one cubic foot.

38. In some areas where the rains are seasonal and there is no underground water for wells, people store water in large covered cisterns under their houses. Find the number of gallons of water that must be stored for four occupants to use an average of 50 gal. each per day during the five-month dry season (use thirty-day months in your calculations). Then find the minimum depth of the cistern if it has the same length and width as the house, 32' × 56'.

All water towers have a curved shape, and some are completely spherical.

39. Another family in the same area as the one in exercise 38 has a 22' × 24' cistern under their garage. If the five occupants use an average of 60 gal. each per day, find how many gallons should be stored and the minimum depth of the cistern.

CUMULATIVE REVIEW

Use the Fundamental Principle of Counting to find the number of possible outcomes. [10.5]

40. A shoe company offers soccer cleats with indoor, turf, firm ground, and soft ground models that are available in white, black, or silver leather.

41. A license plate number consists of two letters followed by three nonzero digits.

42. Any of the following may be added to a hamburger: lettuce, tomato, pickles, onions, ketchup, mustard, and mayonnaise. How many combinations of three condiments can be ordered? [10.7]

If $f(x) = 6x - 4$, find the following values. [9.3]

43. $f(-2)$ 44. $f(12)$ 45. $f(0)$ 46. $f(a)$

47. Which kinds of symmetry are found in any regular polygon? [12.8]

48. What is the result of reflecting a line segment with endpoints (2, 7) and (5, 4) across the x-axis? [12.8]

49. Draw two lines, $j \perp k$, and right △ABC in one of the quadrants formed. Reflect △ABC through j and its image through k. How many degrees is the final image rotated from the original triangle? [12.8]

MATH & SCRIPTURE

God's Wisdom and Noah's Faithful Work

Two short verses in Genesis 6 put everything about the judgment of the universal Flood in proper perspective. Genesis 6:8 says, "But Noah found grace in the eyes of the Lord." The next verse notes that Noah was just and perfect (blameless) and walked with God. God then gave Noah instructions for building the ark and told Noah of His plan to save life on the earth.

The second short verse is Genesis 6:22. "Thus did Noah; according to all that God commanded him, so did he." Second Peter 2:5 calls Noah a preacher of righteousness. Noah's ark was a testimony to the ungodly who watched him build it, but for Noah personally it was an object of worship and service to God as he used his mathematics and building skills to carry out God's command.

1. Using Genesis 6 and assuming a cubit to be 18 in., find the length, width, and height of Noah's ark in feet.

2. We are not told in the Scriptures whether the ark was box-shaped or if it had a pointed bow or a keel. Many creationary scientists think it probably had a keel. However, if it were box-shaped, what was its volume in cubic feet?

3. One interesting parameter of the ark is its cargo capacity in pounds or tons. For the sake of stability in the water, assume the waterline fell at 25 ft. from the bottom so that slightly more of the ark was in the water than above the water. Using the weight of water as 8.34 lb. per cubic foot, find the displacement of that part of the ark in the water in both pounds and tons. By Archimedes' principle this would be the weight of the ark and its cargo when the draft is 25 ft.

4. Find the dimensions and displacement of a modern ship, such as a destroyer. What are the size and displacement of a US Navy *Arleigh Burke* class, Flight I, guided missile destroyer? (Look online by searching on US Navy ships.)

5. Did you find the ark larger or smaller than a destroyer?

6. Besides the dimensions, what other instructions about the ark did God give Noah?

7. As Noah wisely used his mathematics and building skills to complete a task that would take decades, what do you think kept him faithful to the task?

8. List ways that people in different professions can use their skills to worship and serve God.

Infinite Truths
Thus did Noah; according to all that God commanded him, so did he. *Genesis 6:22*

Chapter 13 Review

Vocabulary

altitude	face	oblique prism	surface area
altitude of a pyramid	great circle	polyhedron	three-dimensional figure
area	height	prism	triangular prism
base	lateral face	pyramid	vertex
circular cone	lateral surface	rectangular prism	volume
circular cylinder	lateral surface area	right prism	
cube	lunes	slant height	
edge	net	sphere	

Formulas

Area	Lateral Surface Area	Surface Area	Volume
Circle	Circular Cone	Circular Cone	Circular Cylinder
Parallelogram	Cylinder	Cylinder	Prism
Rectangle	Prism	Prism	Pyramid or Cone
Square	Regular Pyramid	Regular Pyramid	Sphere
Trapezoid		Sphere	
Triangle			

Find the area of the following figures.

1. rectangle: $l = 36$ cm, $w = 9$ cm

2. parallelogram: $b = 6.93$ m, $h = 7$ m

3. triangle: $b = 23$ cm, $h = 14$ cm

4. trapezoid: $b_1 = 6$ m, $b_2 = 18$ m, $h = 13$ m

5. circle: $r = 12$ cm

6. circle: $d = 9$ m

Find the following measures.

7.
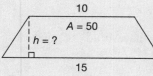

8.
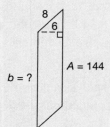

9.
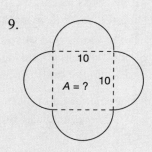

10.
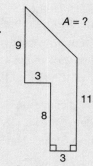

11.
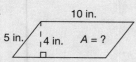

12.
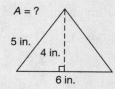

13.
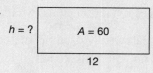

14.
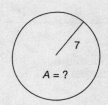

15.

16.
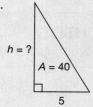

Find the area of the following colored regions.

17.

2 cm

8 cm   4 cm

3 cm

18.
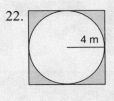

7 cm

5 cm

5 cm

7 cm

19.
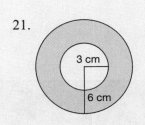

11 cm

8 cm

4 cm

20.

10 m

9 m   2 m   6 m

13 m

21.

3 cm

6 cm

22.

4 m

Use the similar triangles to find the following measures.

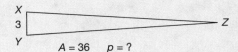

23. perimeter of △XYZ

24. area of △ABC

A
2
B
$A = ?$ $p = 34$
C

X
3
Y
$A = 36$ $p = ?$
Z

25. At Fermilab in Batavia, Illinois, nuclear particles are accelerated around a circle that is 2 km in diameter. Determine the number of acres within this circular ring if 1 km² = 247 acres. Round to the nearest acre.

26. A restaurant owner claims that his 16" (per side) square pizza is actually larger than his competitor's 18" (diameter) circular pizza. Determine which pizza has the greater area and by how much it is larger.

27. If the sides of polygon *A* are twice the length of the sides in a similar polygon *B*, what is the ratio of their perimeters? their areas?

28. Find the length of an edge of a cube with a surface area of 294 in.²

Find the surface area and volume of the following figures.

29.

7 cm

7 cm   7 cm

30.
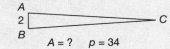

2 cm

8 cm   5 cm

31.

4 m

7 m

32.
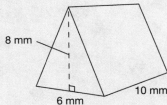

8 mm

6 mm   10 mm

33. 5 cm
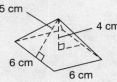

4 cm

6 cm

6 cm

34.
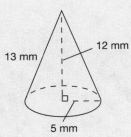

12 mm

13 mm

5 mm

35. What is the volume of a cereal box 12 in. tall, 8 in. wide, and 2 in. thick?

36. The volume of a cylinder 5 cm tall is 180π cm³. What is the diameter of the circular base of the cylinder?

37. Find the volume of a waffle cone that is 15 cm tall and has a radius of 4 cm.

38. Give the mathematical significance of Genesis 6:22.

14 POLYNOMIALS

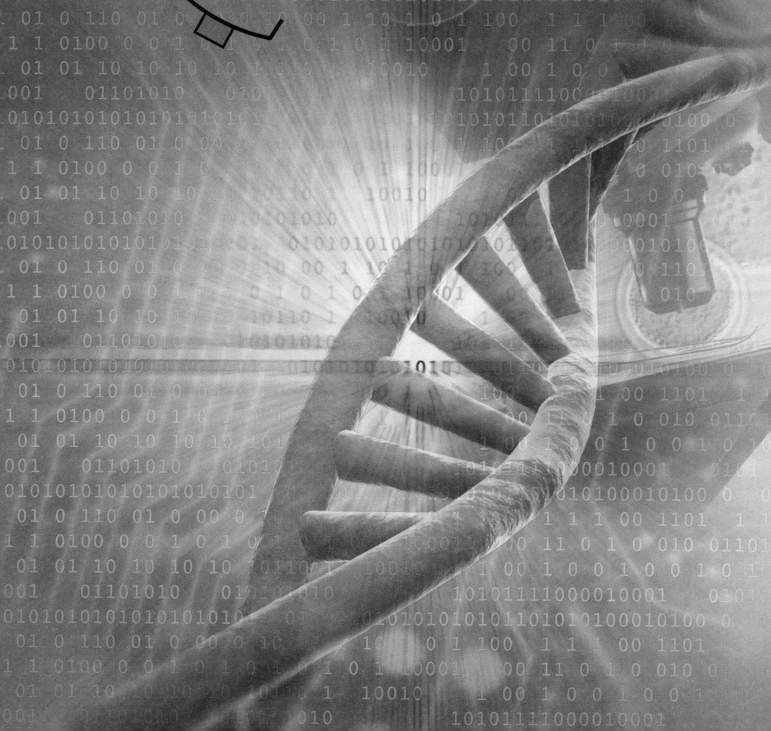

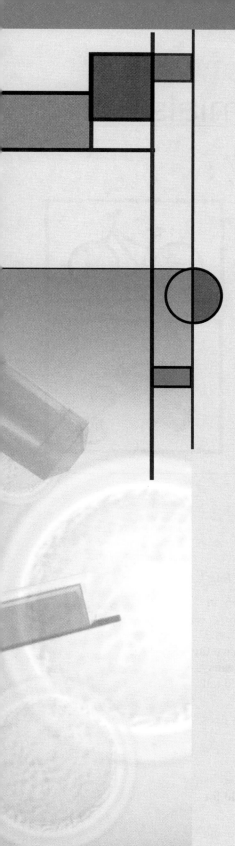

Certainly computers have been around for some time, but why have we now seen digital media replace most analog media? "Digital" means the information is stored and retrieved as computer-generated *bits* of information expressed in binary code as 0s or 1s. Electronically, a 0 means the "switch" is off, and a 1 means the "switch" is on. Our cameras, cell phones, TVs, CDs, e-mail, watches, and speedometers are all digital. But in the analog world of earlier technology cameras used film or tape, TVs used cathode-ray tubes, and music was on grooved plastic records or magnetic-tape cassettes. People talked on phones connected by wires, could send only letters written on paper, and had watches and clocks with hour, minute, and second hands that rotated.

The digital blitz flows out of rapid advances in processor speed and storage ability. Computers now operate at gigahertz speeds; and hard drives, CDs, DVDs, and flash memory may hold many gigabytes or terabytes of information. A *byte* is a collection of eight bits and can express 256 different "characters." The letter A becomes 01000001, while the number 6 looks like 00110110. A megabyte (MB) contains one million bytes, and a gigabyte (GB) contains one billion bytes (or 1,000 MB). If you really want to think big, a terabyte (TB) contains one million MB.

All of human advancement in information storage cannot compare to God's creation. Even just enough human DNA to cover the head of a straight pin contains an astronomical amount of information. The information in this amount of DNA would fill about 15 trillion books of 160 pages each. That is a staggering 36 million terabytes. "O Lord, how manifold are thy works! in wisdom hast thou made them all: the earth is full of thy riches" (Ps. 104:24).

After this chapter you should be able to

1. identify whether or not an algebraic expression is a polynomial.

2. state the degree of and classify the types of polynomials.

3. evaluate polynomials for given values.

4. find the additive inverse of a polynomial.

5. add and subtract polynomials.

6. multiply polynomials by monomial multipliers.

7. multiply binomials using the FOIL method.

8. divide a polynomial by a monomial divisor.

9. use algebra to solve word problems involving coins and bills.

14.1 Types of Polynomials

Do you remember what a term is in mathematics? In Chapter 2 a term was defined as the parts of an algebraic expression separated by a plus or minus sign. An expression containing a single term is a *monomial*.

> ### Definition
>
> A **monomial** is a real number, a variable, or the product of a real number and variable(s) with nonnegative integer exponents.

Cycles are classified by the number of wheels; polynomials, by the number of terms.

The following expressions are monomials.

$6x^2 \qquad -\dfrac{2}{3}x \qquad y \qquad xy^2 \qquad xyz \qquad \sqrt{2}z^3 \qquad 5$

> ### Definition
>
> A **polynomial** is a monomial or the sum or difference of two or more monomials.

The following expressions are polynomials.

$3x + 2$ (two terms) $\qquad 2x^2 - 5x + 9$ (three terms) $\qquad x^4 + 1$ (two terms)

$\dfrac{1}{3}x$ (one term) $\qquad -2x^2y + 9$ (two terms) $\qquad x^3y^2 + 3x - 2y - 8$ (four terms)

The prefix in the names of polynomials explains the meaning of the word. *Poly* in the word polynomial means "many," while *nomial* means "name" or "term." So *polynomial* literally means "many terms." Likewise, *monomial* means "one term." These prefixes are also used in the words *monotheistic* and *polytheistic* and have the same meaning. *Monotheistic* means the belief in one God, and *polytheistic* means the belief in many gods. The Christian religion is monotheistic, since the Bible tells us in Deuteronomy 6:4, "The Lord our God is one Lord."

The Commutative Property of Addition guarantees that the order of the terms does not affect the value of the polynomial.

Consider two of the polynomials above.

$3x + 2 = 2 + 3x$ and $2x^2 - 5x + 9 = -5x + 2x^2 + 9 = 9 - 5x + 2x^2$.

However, polynomials are usually written in descending powers of the variable for the sake of organization. $3x + 2$ and $2x^2 - 5x + 9$ are better form.

Because they are used so often, we have special names for polynomials of two and three terms.

> ### Definition
>
> A **binomial** is a polynomial consisting of exactly two terms.

The following expressions are binomials.

$3x + 2$ $x^4 + 1$ $-2x^2y + 9$

Definition

A **trinomial** is a polynomial consisting of exactly three terms.

The following expressions are trinomials.

$2x^2 - 5x + 9$ $3x^2 - 4xy - 8y^2$ $x^3 + 7x^2y - 8xy^2$

No special name is attached to polynomials of more than three terms.

The following expressions are not polynomials.

$\dfrac{5}{x} - 3$ The variable is in the denominator. This expression is equal to $5x^{-1} - 3$, which has a negative exponent.

$x^{\frac{2}{3}}$ The exponent is not a positive integer.

Monomial: $3x$
Binomial: $3x + 4$
Trinomial: $2x^2 + 3x + 4$

Skill Check 1

Are the following polynomials? If not, why not?

1. $3x^4 + x^2$
2. 2^{-1}
3. $-2x^5 + 19$
4. $-\dfrac{4x^2}{5} + x$
5. $\dfrac{8}{x^2}$
6. $\sqrt{3}m$
7. $2m^{\frac{1}{2}}$

Definitions

The sum of the exponents of the variables contained in a term is the **degree of the term**.
The highest degree of any of the individual terms of a polynomial is the **degree of the polynomial**.

Polynomial	Degree	
2	0	2 is the same as $2x^0$, since $x^0 = 1$.
$3x$	1	The variable x is the same as x^1.
$-2x^2y$	3	The variable y has an exponent of 1; $2 + 1 = 3$.
$x^3y^2 + 3x^2 + 2y^4 - 8$	5	The term x^3y^2 has a degree of 5. This is the highest-degree term in the polynomial.

Skill Check 2

Give the degree of the following polynomials.

1. $3x^2$
2. $-4xy^2z^4$
3. $x^2 + 4x - 3$
4. $-7x^8 + 5x^6 - 3x^4 + x^2$
5. $-7a^5 + a^4b^4 + 3ab^6$
6. $6x^2y + xy^3 - 2y^6$

In Chapter 2 we evaluated simple algebraic expressions by substituting values for the variable. We evaluate polynomials in the same way.

Example 1   Evaluate $x^2 - 6x - 18$ when $x = 7$.

Answer

$$x^2 - 6x - 18 = 7^2 - 6(7) - 18$$
$$= 49 - 42 - 18$$
$$= 7 - 18$$
$$= -11$$

Example 2   Evaluate $-3x^3y + 4x^2y^2$ when $x = 6$ and $y = -2$.

Answer

$$-3x^3y + 4x^2y^2 = -3(6)^3(-2) + 4(6)^2(-2)^2$$
$$= -3(216)(-2) + 4(36)(4)$$
$$= 1{,}296 + 576$$
$$= 1{,}872$$

Skill Check 3

Evaluate.

1. $x^4 + 1$ when $x = -3$
2. $2x^2 - 5x + 9$ when $x = -3$
3. $x^3y^2 + 3x - 2y - 8$ when $x = -1$ and $y = 2$
4. $-2x^2y + 9$ when $x = 3$ and $y = -4$

■ **A. Exercises**

Are the following polynomials? If not, why not?

1. $7x^5 - 4x^3$
2. $-3x^2 + 8$
3. $\dfrac{5}{x^3} + 8x$
4. $\dfrac{3}{7}x^2$

5. $7x^{-2}$
6. $\sqrt{2}x^2$
7. $4x^{\frac{3}{2}}$
8. $4x^2 - 6x$

9. $\dfrac{5x}{8}$
10. $6x^3 - 8x^2 + 7x - 9$

Give the degree of the following polynomials and identify the type of polynomial by special name. If no special name applies, write "polynomial."

11. $3x + 4y$
12. $\dfrac{5x^2y}{\sqrt{2}}$
13. $7x^2 - 9x + 4$
14. 3

15. $\dfrac{x^2}{5} - 3x$
16. $7 - 8x$
17. $4x^3 + x - 1$
18. $\dfrac{1}{4}xy - z^2$

19. $8x^3y^2 + y + 1$
20. $x^5 + 7x^3 - 2x + 14$

■ **B. Exercises**

Give the degree of the following polynomials.

21. $4x^3 + 7x^2 - 6x + 9$
22. $8x^4y^2$
23. xy^4z^2
24. $2x^2y + 6xy^2 - 9y^2$

Evaluate the following polynomials when $x = 5$ and $y = 2$.

25. $-8x + 7$
26. $-3x + 4y$
27. $4x^3 + x - 1$
28. $7x^2 - 9x + 4y$

Evaluate the following polynomials when $x = -4$ and $y = 3$.

29. $2x^2 - 8x + 9$
30. $-x^2 + 3x + 2$
31. $x^3 + y^3$
32. $-3x + 2y$

■ C. Exercises

Evaluate the following polynomials when $x = \frac{-4}{5}$, $y = -1$, and $z = 4$.

33. $x^2(5 - y)$

34. $\frac{3z}{2} - 6$

35. $x - 2y^2$

36. $3z - \frac{2y}{5}$

■ Dominion thru Math

Use a calculator to help you solve the following exercises involving large numbers.

37. Express one megabyte, one gigabyte, and one terabyte as bytes using powers of ten. (Refer to the chapter introduction if needed.)

38. Matthew has a computer with an 80 GB hard drive. How many megabytes does his hard drive hold?

39. The network storage capacity for a publishing company has fifteen hard drives, each rated at 160 GB. How many terabytes does the system have?

40. If an internet server system needs to handle 25 TB of information, how many 250 GB hard drives will it need?

41. If a computer database adds about 164 MB per day, how long will a 250 GB hard drive provide storage before it is full?

42. A 754 page textbook averages 18 KB (kilobytes) per page. How many megabytes of digital media will it take to store this book?

CUMULATIVE REVIEW

Convert each number to scientific notation, and then perform the indicated operations. Leave answers in scientific notation. [6.8]

43. $126,000,000 + 391,000,000$

44. $42,800,000 - 9,100,000$

45. $4,800 \times 2,900$

46. $0.0000042 \times 320,000,000$

Find the interest and the amount to pay back on the following simple interest loans. [7.7]

47. $32,000 at 11% for 15 yr.

48. $850 at 21% for 24 mo.

Find the area of the following figures. [13.1–13.3]

49.
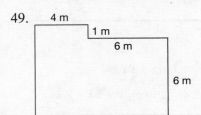

50.
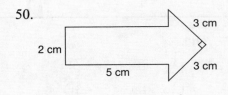

51.
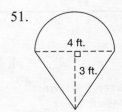

52.
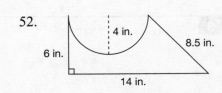

14.2 ∃ Adding Polynomials

When you add polynomials, the Commutative and Associative Properties allow you to group like terms. The Distributive Property then allows you to add the like terms. Study the following example.

Example 1   Add $(3x + 4) + (2x - 6)$.

Answer

$(3x + 4) + (2x - 6)$

$(3x + 2x) + (4 - 6)$ 1. Reorder and group like terms. Be sure to keep the correct sign with each term. $4 + (-6)$ is expressed as $4 - 6$.

$(3 + 2)x + (-2)$ 2. Use the Distributive Property to simplify the x terms. Combine the constants.

$5x - 2$ 3. Simplify.

Example 2   Add $(-5y + 9z) + (-y - 5z)$.

Answer

$(-5y + 9z) + (-y - 5z)$

$(-5y - y) + (9z - 5z)$ 1. Reorder and group like terms. Adding $-y$ is the same as subtracting y, and adding $-5z$ is just subtracting $5z$.

$(-5 - 1)y + (9 - 5)z$ 2. Apply the Distributive Property. Remember that $-y$ is the same as $-1y$:

$-6y + 4z$ $-5y - y = -5y + (-1y)$.

Applying the Distributive Property is a mental exercise that is not usually written in the process of adding polynomials. In future examples, the step will not be shown.

Skill Check 1

Add.

1. $(4y + 5) + (-2y + 6)$ 2. $(3x - 6) + (-7x + 9)$

3. $(2x + 4y) + (6x - 3y)$ 4. $(a - b + 2) + (4a - 3b + 8)$

Example 3   Add $(3x^2 - 10x + 9) + (-8x^2 + 17x - 2)$.

Answer

$(3x^2 - 10x + 9) + (-8x^2 + 17x - 2)$

$(3x^2 - 8x^2) + (-10x + 17x) + (9 - 2)$ 1. Reorder and group like terms. Be sure to keep the correct sign with each term (the sign that precedes it).

$-5x^2 + 7x + 7$ 2. Simplify.

Example 4 Add $(3a^3 - 8a - 9) + (5a^3 + 10a^2 + 8)$.

Answer

$(3a^3 - 8a - 9) + (5a^3 + 10a^2 + 8)$

$(3a^3 + 5a^3) + 10a^2 - 8a + (-9 + 8)$ 1. Reorder and group like terms.

$8a^3 + 10a^2 - 8a - 1$ 2. Simplify.

Skill Check 2

Add.

1. $(4x^2 - 6x + 9) + (-3x^2 - 2x - 8)$ 2. $(4a^2 + 3ab - 2b^2) + (-7a^2 - 10ab - 7b^2)$

3. $(x^4 - 3x^2 - 3) + (2x^3 - x^2 + 8x - 19)$ 4. $(7x^3 + 13x) + (-8x^5 + 4x^3 - 3x + 9)$

The following examples contain decimal and fractional coefficients. Polynomials can have any type of real number coefficients.

Example 5 Add $(2.5x^2 + 8.2xy - 4y^2) + (3x^2 - 0.4xy - 1.5y^2)$.

Answer

$(2.5x^2 + 8.2xy - 4y^2) + (3x^2 - 0.4xy - 1.5y^2)$

$(2.5x^2 + 3x^2) + (8.2xy - 0.4xy) + (-4y^2 - 1.5y^2)$ 1. Reorder and group like terms.

$5.5x^2 + 7.8xy - 5.5y^2$ 2. Simplify.

Example 6 Add $\left(\dfrac{1}{5}x + \dfrac{3}{10}\right) + \left(\dfrac{1}{10}x - \dfrac{3}{5}\right)$.

Answer

$\left(\dfrac{1}{5}x + \dfrac{3}{10}\right) + \left(\dfrac{1}{10}x - \dfrac{3}{5}\right)$

$\left(\dfrac{1}{5}x + \dfrac{1}{10}x\right) + \left(\dfrac{3}{10} - \dfrac{3}{5}\right)$ 1. Reorder and group like terms.

$\left(\dfrac{2}{10}x + \dfrac{1}{10}x\right) + \left(\dfrac{3}{10} - \dfrac{6}{10}\right)$ 2. Rename with common denominators for addition and subtraction.

$\dfrac{3}{10}x - \dfrac{3}{10}$ or $0.3x - 0.3$ 3. Simplify.

Skill Check 3

Add.

1. $\left(\dfrac{1}{4}x + 2y\right) + \left(\dfrac{1}{2}x - 5y\right)$

2. $(1.5x^2 - 2x + 4) + (3x^2 + 4.4x - 2)$

3. $(12x^2y - 13xy) + (-4xy^2 + 2xy) + (16x^2y + 4xy^2)$

4. $(2.5x^2 - 7xy + 0.4y^2) + (3x^2 + 2xy + 1.6y^2)$

A. Exercises

Add.

1. $(3x + 4) + (2x + 1)$

2. $(7x + 3) + (4x - 9)$

3. $(10x^2y - 6) + (-4x^2y - 3)$

4. $(3y - 7) + (5y + 18)$

5. $(-5y - 7) + (9y + 2)$

6. $3a + (-6a + 4b) + (a - 7b)$

7. $(6a - 8b) + b$

8. $(x + 1) + (3x - 2) + (5x - 3)$

9. $(4x - 9) + (2x - 3) + (x + 1)$

10. $(x + 8) + (x + 4) + (x - 7)$

B. Exercises

Add.

11. $(2x^2 + 1) + (3x - 4)$

12. $(x^4 + 1) + (x^4 - 1)$

13. $(2x^2 - 4x + 1) + (x^2 + 7x - 3)$

14. $(x^2 - 2x + 1) + (5x^2 - 8x + 7)$

15. $(3x^2 - 8x) + (7x^2 - 5x + 12)$

16. $(-x^2 + 3x - 6) + (5x^2 - 5x - 8)$

17. $(8x^2 - 6x + 4) + (3x^2 + 6x - 7)$

18. $(x^3 + 3x) + (7x^2 - 4)$

19. $(-7x^2 + x) + (5x^2 - 9x)$

20. $(4z - 5) + (-2.5z + 1)$

21. $(7.2x - 4) + (2x - 5.1)$

22. $(3y - 10) + (4.7y - 8)$

23. $\left(\frac{1}{3}x + 6 \right) + \left(x - \frac{1}{2} \right)$

24. $\left(\frac{5}{2}x - 7 \right) + \left(\frac{1}{2}x + \frac{3}{2} \right)$

25. $(2.5x - 9) + (4.32x + 5.4)$

26. $(1.7x^2 + 3.35x) + (4x^2 + 5.8x)$

27. $(7x^4 - 8x^2 + 3) + (-9x^4 + 7x^2 - 9)$

28. $(2.7x + 3) + (x - 7.1) + (4x - 3.4)$

29. $\left(\frac{1}{2}x^2 - 4x + \frac{2}{3} \right) + \left(\frac{5}{2}x^2 - 3x + \frac{7}{3} \right)$

30. $\left(\frac{5}{7}x^2 - 8x + 1 \right) + \left(\frac{1}{7}x^2 - \frac{1}{2}x + \frac{3}{2} \right)$

C. Exercises

Polynomials can be added either horizontally or vertically. The following example shows how like terms are lined up vertically and then added down vertically similar to the addition of numbers.

$$
\begin{array}{l}
 4a^2 + 9ab - 6b^2 \\
+ 3a^2 + 8b^2 - 9 \\
\hline
 7a^2 + 9ab + 2b^2 - 9
\end{array}
$$

Use the vertical addition method on the following problems.

31. $(9x^3 - 7xy^3 + y^2) + (3xy^3 - 5y^2 + 12)$

32. $(-8a^2 + 7ab - 9b^2) + (6a^2 - 4ab - 14b^2)$

33. $(y^3 + 7y^2 - 6) + (6y^2 - 2y - 5)$

34. $(4m^3n + 6m^2n^2 - 13mn^3) + (9m^2n^2 - 4mn^3)$

35. Do you prefer the horizontal method or the vertical method of addition of polynomials? Explain why you prefer one over the other.

36. Given two polynomials of different degrees, how do you determine the degree of the sum of these two polynomials?

Find the following. [7.2]

37. 460 is what percent of 80?

38. 54 is 60% of what number?

39. What is 80% of 834?

40. What percent of 250 is 184?

Use the following figures for exercises 41–46. Dimensions are in meters. [13.6, 13.8]

41. volume

43. surface area

45. volume

42. surface area

44. volume

46. surface area

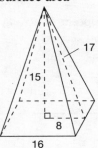

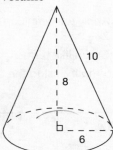

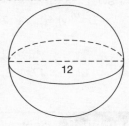

14.3 ⌐ Subtracting Polynomials

Recall that in Section 1.3 subtraction was defined as adding the opposite. That is, $a - b = a + (-b)$. This definition holds for polynomials as well. Two polynomials are opposites (additive inverses) if their sum is zero.

Polynomial	Additive Inverse
$3x + 4$	$-3x - 4$
$2y - 6$	$-2y + 6$
$-x^2 + 2x - 5$	$x^2 - 2x + 5$

$3x - 5$
Additive inverse: $-3x + 5$
Multiplicative inverse: $\dfrac{1}{3x - 5}$

To find the additive inverse or opposite of a polynomial, find the opposite of each term of the polynomial.

Example 1 Find the opposite of $x^2 - 3x + 4$.

Answer

$-(x^2 - 3x + 4) = -x^2 + 3x - 4$ Find the opposite of each term in the polynomial.

Skill Check 1   **Find the opposite (additive inverse) of each polynomial.**

1. $4a + b$ 2. $-3x + 4y$ 3. $2x^2 - 5x - 6$ 4. $-3x^2 + 4xy - 7y^2$

To subtract polynomials, write the subtraction problem as an addition problem.
To do this, apply the definition of subtraction as shown.

$$2x - 8x = 2x + (-8x) = -6x$$

and

$$-4y - 7y = -4y + (-7y) = -11y$$

The following examples show how to subtract a binomial.

Example 2 Subtract $15x - (-2x - 8y)$.

Answer

$15x - (-2x - 8y) = 15x + (2x + 8y)$	1. Apply the definition of subtraction. The opposite of $-2x - 8y$ is $2x + 8y$.
$= (15x + 2x) + 8y$	2. Group like terms.
$= 17x + 8y$	3. Simplify, using the Distributive Property.

Example 3 Subtract $(5x - 2y) - (3x + 4y)$.

Answer

$(5x - 2y) - (3x + 4y) = (5x - 2y) + (-3x - 4y)$	1. Apply the definition of subtraction.
$= (5x - 3x) + (-2y - 4y)$	2. Reorder and group like terms.
$= 2x + (-6y)$	3. Simplify, using the Distributive Property.
$= 2x - 6y$	4. Adding a negative is the same as subtracting.

Skill Check 2

Subtract.

1. $21x - (15x + 3)$

2. $(3x + 5) - 13$

3. $(4x + 1) - (2x - 5)$

4. $(-3x + 3) - (x + 9)$

Example 4 Subtract $(8x^2 - 9x - 3) - (2x^2 + 6x - 4)$.

Answer

$(8x^2 - 9x - 3) - (2x^2 + 6x - 4)$	
$(8x^2 - 9x - 3) + (-2x^2 - 6x + 4)$	1. Apply the definition of subtraction.
$(8x^2 - 2x^2) + (-9x - 6x) + (-3 + 4)$	2. Reorder and group like terms.
$6x^2 + (-15x) + 1$	3. Simplify, using the Distributive Property.
$6x^2 - 15x + 1$	4. Adding a negative is the same as subtracting.

Example 5 Subtract $(x^3 + 2x^2 - 9x + 14) - (7x^2 - 6x - 4)$.

Answer

$(x^3 + 2x^2 - 9x + 14) - (7x^2 - 6x - 4)$	
$(x^3 + 2x^2 - 9x + 14) + (-7x^2 + 6x + 4)$	1. Apply the definition of subtraction.
$x^3 + (2x^2 - 7x^2) + (-9x + 6x) + (14 + 4)$	2. Reorder and group like terms. There is only one x^3 term, so nothing is grouped with it.
$x^3 + (-5x^2) + (-3x) + 18$	3. Simplify, using the Distributive Property.
$x^3 - 5x^2 - 3x + 18$	4. Adding a negative is the same as subtracting.

| Example 6 | Subtract $(2x^3 - 1) - (6x^2 + 8x)$. |

Answer

$(2x^3 - 1) - (6x^2 + 8x)$

$(2x^3 - 1) + (-6x^2 - 8x)$ 1. Apply the definition of subtraction.

$2x^3 - 6x^2 - 8x - 1$ 2. There are no like terms. Arrange the polynomial in descending powers of the variable.

Skill Check 3

Subtract.

1. $(4x^2 + 7x + 9) - (2x^2 + 5x + 2)$ 2. $(9x^2 + 6x + 2) - (4x^2 + 8x + 5)$

3. $(-3x^2 - 5x + 17) - (7x^2 + 6x - 23)$ 4. $(7a^2 + 8a - 5) - (6a^2 - 12)$

5. $(6z^3 - 5z^2 - 8z + 5) - (3z^3 + 2z - 6)$ 6. $a^4 - (3a^3 + 2a^2 - 5a + 1)$

7. $(6x^4 - 8x^3 - 5x^2 + 13x - 6) - (4x^3 - 8x^2 + 15x)$

■ A. Exercises

Find the opposite (additive inverse) of each polynomial.

1. $-2x + 9$ 2. $7x + 4$ 3. $3a - 2b + 1$ 4. $2x^2 - 8x - 2$ 5. $-4x^3 + 7x - 1$ 6. $4x - 7y$

Subtract.

7. $(7x - 4) - 8$ 8. $9x - (2x + 4)$ 9. $(2y - 5) - 7y$ 10. $(4a - 5) - (2a - 3)$

11. $(2b - 3c) - (5b + 8c)$ 12. $(-5x + 4) - (2x - 3)$ 13. $(2x + 4) - (4x + 12)$ 14. $(x - 5y) - (x + 5y)$

15. $(2x - 3y) - (4x + y)$ 16. $(5y - 3z) - (-5y + 3z)$ 17. $(7x - 9) - (4x - 5)$ 18. $(8x - 5) - (-4x - 10)$

■ B. Exercises

Subtract.

19. $(8x^2 + 6x + 9) - (x^2 + 6x + 8)$ 20. $(7x^2 + 6x + 6) - (3x^2 + 9x + 2)$ 21. $(-4x^2 - 5x + 7) - (7x^2 + 10x - 20)$

22. $(8a^2 + 7a - 2) - (3a^2 - 5)$ 23. $(7x^2 + 4x + 6) - (x^2 + 8x + 9)$ 24. $(11x^2 + 4x + 5) - (2x^2 + 9x + 4)$

25. $7x^2 - (8x - 9)$ 26. $(5x^2 + 4x + 1) - (2x^2 - 4)$ 27. $(x^4 - 2x^2 + 6) - (4x^4 - 5x^2 + 13)$

28. $(15x^4 - 8x^2 - 1) - (3x^4 + 7x^2 - 1)$

29. $(5x^4 - 7x^3 - 4x^2 + 3x - 5) - (3x^3 - 10x^2 + 12x)$

30. $(9z^3 - 6z^2 - 4z + 3) - (2z^3 + 4z - 7)$

■ C. Exercises

Arrange the polynomials in descending order of powers, and then subtract.

31. $(2x - 8x^4 + 7x^2 - 9x^3) - (8x^2 - 4x^3 - 3x + x^4)$ 32. $(5 - x^3 + 8x - 2x^2) - (4x^2 - 7 + 9x - 5x^3)$

Set up the following problems vertically and subtract by using the definition of subtraction.

33. $(4a + 2b - 7c) - (-6a + 3b + 9c)$ 34. $(6x^2 - 9x + 4) - (-3x^2 - 12x - 5)$

■ Dominion thru Math

Digital cameras, digital TVs, cell phones, and PC monitors all display text and graphics using "picture elements" called *pixels*. Pixels are dots that make up the images you see on the display. In black and white bit maps, 0 displays a white pixel and 1 displays a black pixel, but color displays require combinations of several bits. *Resolution* describes the clarity and sharpness of focus of an image. Resolution increases with the number of pixels displayed. Choosing a PC monitor with 900 × 600 pixels gives only 540,000 pixels, compared to a monitor displaying 1,280 × 1,024 pixels, which gives 1,310,720 pixels, or about 1.3 megapixels. Of course, the more pixels displayed, the more memory and RAM needed to store and retrieve the image. A top-quality photo print of a digital picture needs at least 200 pixels per linear inch. So to determine the number of megapixels a 5" × 7" print will need, convert the dimensions to pixels and then to megapixels. To do this on the calculator, complete the following steps.

Digital cameras provide the flexibility of electronic images.

1. $5 \boxed{\times} 200 \boxed{=}$ and $7 \boxed{\times} 200 \boxed{=}$, resulting in 1,000 × 1,400.

2. $1,000 \boxed{\times} 1,400 \boxed{=} \boxed{\div} 1,000$, resulting in the answer 1.4 megapixels.

Use a calculator to solve the following exercises.

35. How many megapixels will a top-quality 8" × 10" photo need?

36. A 19 in. color monitor producing extended graphics array has approximately 768 vertical pixels. If the monitor can display 0.786 megapixels, how many pixels are needed for the horizontal resolution?

37. The resolution of a digital camera can be indicated in dots per inch (dpi) on its LCD monitor. If a camera is identified as a 640 × 480 dpi model, it will produce images at 640 pixels per horizontal inch by 480 pixels per vertical inch for a total of 307,200 dots per square inch. Using the standard for top-quality prints, what is the largest photo you would want to print from a 640 × 480 dpi camera with a 2" × 1.5" LCD monitor?

38. At a camera resolution of 1,704 pixels × 2,272 pixels, what is the largest size print that will still retain at least 200 pixels per inch?

39. How many megapixels are used for a resolution of 1,704 × 2,272?

▬ CUMULATIVE REVIEW ▬

Solve. [8.1]

40. $12(x + 7) = 180$

41. $-9(x - 8) = 32$

42. $3(6y + 14) = -30$

Using a table, find three ordered pairs that satisfy the given function rules. Graph each linear equation. [9.4]

43. $y = 2x - 3$

44. $y = -5x - 1$

45. $y = -\dfrac{1}{2}x + 4$

Use the following figures for exercises 46–49. Dimensions are in feet. [13.5, 13.7]

46. volume of the cylinder

47. surface area of the cylinder

48. surface area of the prism

49. volume of the prism

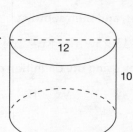

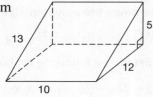

PROBLEM SOLVING

Mixed Review

In each chapter of this book you have looked at problem-solving strategies. Use these to solve the following problems. Try to recognize which strategy would be the best and most efficient to use while you are carefully reading the problem. Spend some extra time reading the problem a second time and determining whether it is like any of the problems you have solved before in previous chapters. This extra minute of thinking might help you determine which strategy would be best to use. Remember, there is often more than one problem-solving strategy that will lead you to the correct solution, but there is generally a most efficient strategy.

Problem-Solving Strategies		
Select the operations	Divide and conquer	Work backwards
Guess and check	Write an equation	Organize data with diagrams
Look for a pattern	Make a table	Use multiple strategies
Draw a picture	Make a graph	

Like playing chess, problem solving requires a strategy.

■ Exercises

For each of the following problems, devise a plan for finding the solution. Then carry out the plan and write a check to determine whether your answer is correct. Look for a more efficient method of solving the problem.

1. The chess club at Colonial Christian School has five members. They are planning their annual tournament, in which every member plays every other member one time. How many matches will be played in all?

2. One angle of a triangular piece of land is 26°; a second angle is a right angle. What is the measure of the third angle?

3. Fifteen coins have a value of $1.05. There are at least one each of quarters, dimes, nickels, and pennies. How many of each type of coin are there?

4. Joan bought 8 gal. of gasoline. She also spent $2.25 for a quart of oil and $0.65 for a candy bar. She spent a total of $35.54. What was the cost per gallon for the gasoline?

Estimate the cost of building each new house.

5. cost factor: $82 per square foot
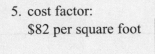
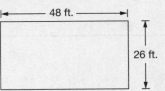

6. cost factor: $95 per square foot
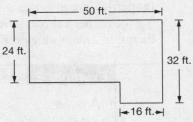

7. How many different ways can the letters in the word CAT can be arranged? List the arrangements.

8. Find the next three terms of the following sequence of rational numbers (all in lowest terms):
$2, \dfrac{7}{10}, \dfrac{1}{5}, \dfrac{13}{250}, \dfrac{8}{625}, \cdots$

9. The cost of an item was $63.84. If it was reduced by 20% and then by another 30% before it sold, find the original price. Determine what percent the buyer saved by buying it on sale.

10. Does the graph represent a direct variation? If yes, write its equation. If not, state why not.

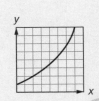

14.4 Multiplying by a Monomial

Recall from Section 1.6 that exponents indicate repeated multiplication, with the exponent showing the number of factors.

$$2^3 = 2 \cdot 2 \cdot 2 \text{ and } 2^4 = 2 \cdot 2 \cdot 2 \cdot 2$$

When 2^3 is multiplied by 2^4, there are seven factors of 2. This can be written as 2^7.

$$2^3 \cdot 2^4 = (2 \cdot 2 \cdot 2) \cdot (2 \cdot 2 \cdot 2 \cdot 2) = 2^7$$

To multiply numbers with like bases, you add the exponents.

$$2^3 \cdot 2^4 = 2^{3+4} = 2^7$$

This illustrates the Multiplication Property of Exponents, which is repeated below.

Multiplication Property of Exponents
For any number x and integers a and b, $x^a \cdot x^b = x^{a+b}$.

Example 1 Multiply. Leave answers in exponential form.

a. $5^2 \cdot 5^4 \cdot 5^3$

b. $x^5 \cdot x$

c. $y^4 \cdot y^7 \cdot z^2$

Answer

a. $5^2 \cdot 5^4 \cdot 5^3 = 5^{2+4+3} = 5^9$

b. $x^5 \cdot x = x^{5+1} = x^6$

c. $y^4 \cdot y^7 \cdot z^2 = y^{4+7} \cdot z^2 = y^{11}z^2$

The Multiplication Property of Exponents is used for multiplying monomials. The properties of addition and multiplication, such as the Commutative and Associative Properties, are also needed. The monomials $2a^3$ and $5a^2$ are multiplied by grouping the numerical coefficients together and grouping the variable factors together. Example 2 shows the product.

Example 2 Multiply $2a^3$ times $5a^2$.

Answer

$2a^3(5a^2) = (2 \cdot 5)(a^3 \cdot a^2)$ 1. Apply the Commutative and Associative Properties of Multiplication to group the coefficients and the variables.

$\qquad = 10a^{3+2}$ 2. Multiply the coefficients. Apply the Multiplication Property of Exponents.

$\qquad = 10a^5$ 3. Add the exponents.

Skill Check 1

Multiply. Leave answers in exponential form.

1. $3^4 \cdot 3^6$

2. $2^2 \cdot 2^6 \cdot 5^3 \cdot 5$

3. $x^3 \cdot x^6 \cdot x^2$

4. $x^5 \cdot y^3 \cdot x \cdot y^5$

Multiply.

5. $5x^4(7x^2)$

6. $-7x^3(-8x^5)$

7. $4a^3(-7a^3)$

8. $3y^4(13y)$

If a polynomial has more than one variable factor, like variables must be grouped together when multiplying.

Example 3 Multiply $-4x^3y^2$ times $15xy^2$.

Answer

$-4x^3y^2 \cdot 15xy^2 = (-4 \cdot 15)(x^3 \cdot x^1)(y^2 \cdot y^2)$ 1. Group the coefficients and the like variable factors.

$= -60x^{3+1}y^{2+2}$ 2. Apply the Multiplication Property of Exponents.

$= -60x^4y^4$ 3. Add the exponents for each variable.

In Example 3, it is important to understand that the x in the second monomial has an unwritten exponent of 1.

Multiplying a polynomial by a monomial requires use of the Distributive Property, $a(b + c) = ab + ac$. This property can be extended to any number of terms within the parentheses. For example, if there are three terms within the parentheses, each term is multiplied by the factor outside the parentheses:

$$a(b + c + d) = ab + ac + ad.$$

Example 4 Multiply.

a. $6(5x^2 + 3x)$

b. $-2(9x^2 - 8x - 3)$

Answer

a. $6(5x^2 + 3x) = 6(5x^2) + 6(3x)$ 1. Apply the Distributive Property.

$= (6 \cdot 5)x^2 + (6 \cdot 3)x$ 2. Group the coefficients and variables.

$= 30x^2 + 18x$ 3. Multiply the coefficients.

b. $-2(9x^2 - 8x - 3) = -2(9x^2) + (-2)(-8x) + (-2)(-3)$ 1. Apply the Distributive Property.

$= (-2 \cdot 9)x^2 + (-2)(-8)x + (-2)(-3)$ 2. Group the coefficients.

$= -18x^2 + 16x + 6$ 3. Simplify.

Skill Check 2

Multiply.

1. $5(7x^2y)$

2. $2ab(3abc)$

3. $-3abc(4a^2b)$

4. $-4ab^4(-12a^3b^2)$

5. $5(x^4 - 2x^2)$

6. $-9(4x^2 - 2x + 8)$

7. $2(3y^4 - 8y^2 + 3)$

8. $3x(x^2 - 2x + 4)$

The Multiplication Property of Exponents applies only to quantities with the same base. You cannot multiply the variable parts for monomials such as x^4 and y^2. You can write the product only as x^4y^2. Therefore, when $5x^4$ is multiplied by $3y^2$, only the product of the constants can be simplified, producing the product $15x^4y^2$. Example 5 is a product of a monomial and a polynomial with more than one variable.

> **Example 5**   Multiply $3z(4x^2y - 7xy^2)$.
>
> Answer
>
> $3z(4x^2y - 7xy^2)$
>
> $3z(4x^2y) - 3z(7xy^2)$ 1. Apply the Distributive Property.
>
> $12x^2yz - 21xy^2z$ 2. Multiply the constants.

Example 6 shows a product with each term having a constant and two variable factors. When multiplying quantities such as x^4y^2 and xy^3, you can multiply the two factors containing the base x and the two factors containing the base y. This product would be $x^{4+1}y^{2+3} = x^5y^5$. Of course, if they are preceded by constants, you can also multiply those.

> **Example 6**   Multiply $-3a^3b(13a^2b + 4ab)$.
>
> Answer
>
> $-3a^3b(13a^2b + 4ab)$
>
> $-3a^3b(13a^2b) + (-3a^3b)(4ab)$ 1. Apply the Distributive Property.
>
> $-39(a^{3+2})(b^{1+1}) + (-12)(a^{3+1})(b^{1+1})$ 2. Group and multiply the coefficients. Apply the Multiplication Property of Exponents to the like variable factors.
>
> $-39a^5b^2 - 12a^4b^2$ 3. Simplify.

Skill Check 3

Multiply.

1. $-5x^2(xy - 2y^2)$ 2. $2xy(-2x^2y + 3xy^2)$

3. $-3a^2b(5a^2b^2 - ab + 2a)$ 4. $ab^2c(2a^2 + 3ab - 6b^2)$

⊕ Invention

Although the first computers were driven by vacuum tube technology and the next generation by transistor technology, both schemes were far too large. What the computer industry needed for faster processing was a way to have thousands of transistors in a very small package. In 1959 the first integrated circuits were patented by two different inventors—Jack Kilby of Texas Instruments and Robert Noyce of Fairchild Semiconductor. The result was a very small wafer of silicon that contained thousands of transistors. These miniaturized integrated circuits are typically referred to these days as *microchips*. They are the reason our computers, PDAs, cell phones, cameras, and automobiles can have microprocessors that are not the size of a freight truck.

■ A. Exercises

Multiply. Leave answers in exponential form.

1. $4^3 \cdot 4^5$ 2. $7 \cdot 7^3$ 3. $5^4 \cdot 5^2 \cdot 5$

4. $x^2 \cdot x^9$ 5. $y^5 \cdot y^7$ 6. $a^4 \cdot a^3 \cdot b^2 \cdot b^5$

Multiply.

7. $4x^3(2x^4)$

8. $-2y^2(-3y^5)$

9. $8z^3(-12z^2)$

10. $-a^4(15a^9)$

11. $-9b^3(-3b^3)$

12. $15c^4(-9c)$

13. $-6x^2y(3xy^3)$

14. $6x^2y^4(5xy^5)$

■ B. Exercises

Multiply.

15. $-8x^7y^4(3x^2y^2)$

16. $5w^5z^4(-7w^9z)$

17. $-3w^4z(-8w^4z)$

18. $12a^2b^3(5a^3b^5)$

19. $(4a^3b^4)^2$

20. $(3ab^2)^3$

Multiply.

21. $2x(3x^2 - x)$

22. $-5x^3(x^5 + 2x^3)$

23. $3y^3(y^4 + 2y^3)$

24. $-2x^3(5y^2 - 2z)$

25. $m^4n^2(4m^6 - 7n^3)$

26. $2m^2n(-3m^6n + 7mn^3)$

27. $-9x^2(4x^2 - 2x - 3)$

28. $7x^2(5x^2 - x + 4)$

29. $2x^2(-6x^5 + 5x^3 + 1)$

30. $-6a^3(2a^2 - 6a + 10)$

31. $2x^2(x^2y - 5xy + 3y)$

32. $-3xy(4x^2 + 4xy + y^2)$

33. $5x^2y^2(9x^2 + 6x + 1)$

34. $14a^2b(2ab^2 + 3ab - 4b^3)$

35. $3xy^2(-10x^2y^3 + 5xy^3 - xy)$

■ C. Exercises

Perform the indicated operations.

36. $2(x^2 - 3x + 9) + 4(3x^2 - x + 6)$

37. $3x(x + 5) - 4(5x^2 - 8x + 1)$

38. Show how the multiplication of a monomial and a polynomial in exercise 34 could be set up vertically.

CUMULATIVE REVIEW

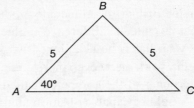

Solve. [7.3]

39. Terrianne took 41 free throws during the season and made 16 of them. What was her shooting percentage from the free-throw line?

40. Twenty-five percent of the pastries made at the K&E Bakery are bear claws. If a total of 160 pastries are made each day, how many bear claws are made?

41. Jed paid a total of $87.50 for a new baseball glove. If the tax rate is 7.5%, what was the price of the glove before tax?

42. A local school board surveyed 150 parents. Forty-two favored a new writing curriculum. What percent of the parents supported it? The school board had said if at least 40% of the parents favored it, it would be implemented. Will it be implemented?

Solve the following inequalities. Round decimal answers to the nearest hundredth. [8.4]

43. $12y + 32 < 16$

44. $-7.2x + 9.8 < 10.6$

45. $9y - 51 \geq 26$

Use the figure to complete the following statements. [12.1, 12.3]

46. $\angle BAC$ is classified as a(n) ____ angle.

47. When classified by angle measures, the triangle is ____.

48. When classified by side measures, the triangle is ____.

Charles Babbage, Computer Pioneer

Charles Babbage was an Englishman who lived from 1791 to 1871. He was both a mathematician and an inventor. His best-known invention was a device that he never completed—the computer. Often referred to as the "Father of Computers," he developed a detailed set of plans for an advanced calculating machine. The design of this machine foreshadowed many of the features of modern-day computers, including the ability to program the computer to perform mathematical operations.

Babbage attended a private academy, where his learning was hindered by ill health. After leaving the academy, he engaged in self-study with the help of tutors to reach university level. He was then accepted at England's renowned Cambridge University. By this time he had already mastered the principles of calculus. At Cambridge he discovered that his mathematical ability surpassed that of many of his classmates. Disappointed with the type of notation used for calculus, he, along with others, founded Cambridge's Analytical Society. The purpose of the society was to analyze and study the mathematical developments in calculus promoted by the top European mathematicians in continental Europe, and then to bring them across the English Channel to Cambridge. It was during one of these meetings that Babbage first considered the possibility of using a machine to calculate. After studying a set of tables that were riddled with errors, Babbage turned to a classmate and exclaimed, "I am thinking that all these mathematical tables might be calculated by machinery!"

This idea became an obsession with Babbage for the rest of his life. In 1822 he developed a small machine powered by a hand crank that could perform mathematical calculations rapidly and accurately. Using this invention as a springboard, he secured financial backing from the British government to produce a large machine that he called a "difference engine."

Ten years later, he abandoned work on this project to begin work on an even more complicated device. This forerunner of the computer, called an "analytical engine," would be capable of storing numbers. It would also be programmable by punched cards, an idea he borrowed from the Jacquard loom, which used a series of punched cards to program the loom to weave a pattern in cloth.

Although Babbage spent thirty-seven years and much of his personal fortune on perfecting the analytical engine, he never lived to see his dream realized. The machine was just too complicated to be constructed in the nineteenth century. However, Babbage's plans for the computer were sound. In fact, they later served as the foundation for the Harvard Mark I computer, which was invented in 1944 by Howard Aiken.

14.5 Multiplying Binomials

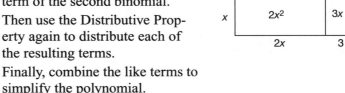

Finding the area of an enlarged circuit board illustrates the use of multiplying binomials. The length of the original circuit board is twice the width of the circuit board. If x represents the width, then $2x$ would represent the length. The area of the original circuit board is length times width, or $x(2x) = 2x^2$. Suppose the circuit board is enlarged by increasing the length by 3 cm and the width by 2 cm. The new dimensions would be $2x + 3$ by $x + 2$. To find the area of this board, you would multiply the length times the width, or $(2x + 3)(x + 2)$. From the figures at the right, you can see that the new area is the sum of the areas of the parts, or $2x^2 + 4x + 3x + 6$.

Multiplying binomials is an extension of the Distributive Property, which is written as $a(b + c) = ab + ac$.

$(2x + 3)(x + 2) = (2x + 3)x + (2x + 3)2$ Rather than distributing a single quantity, you must distribute the binomial $(2x + 3)$ times each term of the second binomial.

$= 2x^2 + 3x + 4x + 6$ Then use the Distributive Property again to distribute each of the resulting terms.

$= 2x^2 + 7x + 6$ Finally, combine the like terms to simplify the polynomial.

In the multiplication of two binomials, there are always four products to be taken before simplifying. The order in which they are taken does not matter. These four products can be remembered using the acronym FOIL. Each letter tells you which parts of the binomials to multiply to get one of the four partial products.

Using FOIL, the binomials $(2x + 3)(x + 2)$ are multiplied as follows.

F	first × first: multiply $2x$ times x	$2x^2$
O	outer × outer: multiply $2x$ times 2	$4x$
I	inner × inner: multiply 3 times x	$3x$
L	last × last: multiply 3 times 2	6

The final product is the sum of the four partial products. Be sure to combine all like terms.

Example 1   Multiply $(x + 5)(x + 3)$.

Answer

F	O	I	L	
$x \cdot x$	$x \cdot 3$	$5 \cdot x$	$5 \cdot 3$	$x^2 + 3x + 5x + 15$
				$x^2 + 8x + 15$

Example 2   Multiply $(x - 6)(x + 5)$.

Answer

F	O	I	L	$x^2 + 5x - 6x - 30$
$x \cdot x$	$x \cdot 5$	$-6 \cdot x$	$-6 \cdot 5$	$x^2 - x - 30$

Skill Check 1

Multiply.

1. $(x + 2)(x + 1)$ 2. $(x - 7)(x + 2)$ 3. $(x + 3)(x - 9)$ 4. $(x - 2)(x - 8)$

Example 3   Multiply $(2x - 3)(3x - 4)$.

Answer

$(2x - 3)(3x - 4)$

$2x(3x) = 6x^2$	1. Multiply the first terms.
$2x(-4) = -8x$	2. Multiply the outer terms.
$-3(3x) = -9x$	3. Multiply the inner terms.
$-3(-4) = 12$	4. Multiply the last terms.
$6x^2 - 8x - 9x + 12$	5. Add the products.
$6x^2 - 17x + 12$	6. Combine like terms.

Example 4   Expand $(2x + 5)^2$.

Answer

$(2x + 5)^2 = (2x + 5)(2x + 5)$	1. Squaring a quantity means to multiply it times itself.
$2x(2x) = 4x^2$	2. Multiply the first terms.
$2x(5) = 10x$	3. Multiply the outer terms.
$(2x) = 10x$	4. Multiply the inner terms.
$5(5) = 25$	5. Multiply the last terms.
$4x^2 + 10x + 10x + 25$	6. Add the products.
$4x^2 + 20x + 25$	7. Combine like terms.

Skill Check 2

Multiply.

1. $(x + 2)(2x - 3)$ 2. $(3x - 5)(5x - 8)$ 3. $(x - 4)^2$ 4. $(3x - 2)^2$

■ A. Exercises

Multiply.

1. $(x + 4)(x + 6)$ 2. $(x - 3)(x - 5)$ 3. $(x + 4)(x - 7)$ 4. $(x - 5)(x - 8)$

5. $(x - 7)(x + 8)$ 6. $(x + 10)(x + 6)$ 7. $(x - 7)(x - 6)$ 8. $(x + 14)(x - 3)$

9. $(x - 9)(x - 8)$ 10. $(x - 9)(x + 8)$ 11. $(x + 12)(x - 8)$ 12. $(x - 6)(x - 9)$

13. $(x + 6)^2$ 14. $(x - 3)^2$

■ B. Exercises

Multiply.

15. $(2x + 1)(x - 8)$ 16. $(5x + 6)(x - 4)$ 17. $(x + 4)(3x + 8)$ 18. $(2x - 1)(3x - 5)$

19. $(5x + 2)(x + 3)$ 20. $(4x + 1)(x - 7)$ 21. $(x + 2)(7x - 8)$ 22. $(x - 6)(4x - 5)$

23. $(3x + 11)(x - 6)$ 24. $(x - 5)(3x - 4)$ 25. $(2x + 1)^2$ 26. $(3x - 5)^2$

27. $(2x + 3)(3x - 8)$ 28. $(4x - 12)(5x - 6)$ 29. $(5x + 12)(7x - 9)$ 30. $(4x - 9)(2x + 7)$

■ C. Exercises

Perform the indicated operations.

31. $2(x - 5)^2$ 32. $3(x + 4)^2$ 33. $(x - 7)^2 + (x + 3)^2$ 34. $(x + 5)^2 - (x + 4)^2$

■ Dominion thru Math

Television screens and PC monitors are usually sized by their diagonal measurement in inches. A 15 in. PC monitor measures 15 in. diagonally across the screen. The relationship between width and height of the screen is called the aspect ratio and is notated as

$$\text{aspect ratio} = \text{horizontal : vertical.}$$

Knowing the aspect ratio, we can find the width and height of a 15 in. monitor using the Pythagorean theorem. For a 15 in. monitor with a 4 : 3 aspect ratio, we would solve the following for x: $(3x)^2 + (4x)^2 = 15^2$. Here $x = 3$, so the height is $3(3) = 9$ in. and the width is $4(3) = 12$ in.

Use a calculator to solve the following exercises.

35. A large 60 in. flat-screen TV has an aspect ratio of 16 : 9. Find the horizontal and vertical dimensions of the screen.

36. What are the dimensions of a 19 in. monitor with an aspect ratio of 4 : 3?

37. What is the diagonal size of a monitor that measures 11.9" × 14.9"?

38. What is the aspect ratio of the monitor in exercise 37?

39. If the monitor in exercise 37 has an effective screen size of 11" × 14" and has a resolution of 1,024 × 768 pixels, what is its dpi?

CUMULATIVE REVIEW

Find the size of the picture produced if a 120 mm × 180 mm picture is copied using the following settings. [7.4]

40. 35%   41. 70%   42. 110%   43. 300%

44. What is the ratio of the area of the new picture in exercise 43 to the original picture? [13.4]

45. If the ratio of the areas of the copy and the original picture is to be 2 : 1, what percentage setting should be used on the copier? [13.4]

Change the following equations to slope-intercept form and find the slope and y-intercept. [9.6]

46. $9x + 2y = 24$ 47. $-6x + y = 18$

48. $6x - 4y = -15$ 49. $-7x - 5y = 75$

14.6 Dividing by a Monomial

When dividing a monomial by a monomial, divide the coefficients and divide like variables. Remember that the division of variables with exponents uses the Division Property of Exponents, introduced in Section 1.6. In Example 1 the division of variables is shown as cancellation. In Example 2 it is shown by taking the difference of the exponents.

Example 1 Divide $\dfrac{6x^5}{2x^2}$.

Answer

$$\frac{6x^5}{2x^2} = \frac{6}{2} \cdot \frac{\cancel{x} \cdot \cancel{x} \cdot x \cdot x \cdot x}{\cancel{x} \cdot \cancel{x}}$$
$$= 3x^3$$

Split the quotient of the coefficients from the quotient of the variables. Cancel variable terms in the denominator with those in the numerator.

Example 2 Divide $-45x^3y^5$ by $5xy^3$.

Answer

$$\frac{-45x^3y^5}{5xy^3} = \frac{-45}{5} \cdot \frac{x^3}{x} \cdot \frac{y^5}{y^3}$$
$$= -9 \cdot x^{3-1} \cdot y^{5-3}$$
$$= -9x^2y^2$$

1. Express the division as three separate divisions, each the quotient of like terms.
2. Divide the coefficients. Then divide like variables by subtracting exponents.

When the larger power of the variable is in the denominator, subtracting the exponents produces a negative power of the variable. Applying the definition of a negative exponent allows us to write the expression using variables with positive exponents in the denominator.

$$\frac{x^3}{x^5} = x^{3-5} = x^{-2} = \frac{1}{x^2}$$

Example 3 Divide $\dfrac{-16a^5bc^3}{8a^4bc^4}$.

Answer

$$\frac{-16a^5bc^3}{8a^4bc^4} = \frac{-16}{8} \cdot \frac{a^5}{a^4} \cdot \frac{b}{b} \cdot \frac{c^3}{c^4}$$
$$= -2 \cdot a^{5-4} \cdot b^{1-1} \cdot c^{3-4}$$
$$= -2 \cdot a^1 \cdot b^0 \cdot c^{-1}$$
$$= -2 \cdot a \cdot 1 \cdot \frac{1}{c}$$
$$= -\frac{2a}{c}$$

1. Split the division into four separate divisions.
2. Divide the coefficients. Then divide like variables by subtracting exponents.
3. Recall the definition of a negative exponent and that $b^0 = 1$.

Divide.

1. $\dfrac{-25x^8}{-5x^5}$

2. $\dfrac{-20x^7}{5x^6}$

3. $\dfrac{60x^2y^6}{10xy^3}$

4. $\dfrac{-144m^4n^6p}{16m^4n^4}$

5. $\dfrac{18a^5b^3}{6ab^4}$

6. $\dfrac{-9a^3b^6c^9}{9a^5b^4c^6}$

Dividing a polynomial by a monomial uses a fundamental principle of fractions. Remember that it is necessary to have a common denominator when adding fractions. To add fractions that have a common denominator, the following principle is used: $\dfrac{a}{b} + \dfrac{c}{b} = \dfrac{a+c}{b}$. When dividing a polynomial by a monomial, we use the principle in reverse: $\dfrac{a+c}{b} = \dfrac{a}{b} + \dfrac{c}{b}$. This simplifies the division of a polynomial by a monomial into a series of divisions of a monomial by a monomial.

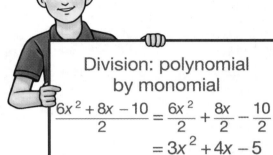

Division: polynomial by monomial

$$\frac{6x^2 + 8x - 10}{2} = \frac{6x^2}{2} + \frac{8x}{2} - \frac{10}{2}$$
$$= 3x^2 + 4x - 5$$

Example 4   Divide $(10x^2 + 5x - 20)$ by 5.

Answer

$\dfrac{10x^2 + 5x - 20}{5} = \dfrac{10x^2}{5} + \dfrac{5x}{5} - \dfrac{20}{5}$ 1. Write the division as a fraction and change it to a series of simple divisions.

$\qquad\qquad\qquad = 2x^2 + x - 4$ 2. Divide each of the parts to find the quotient of the original division problem.

Example 5   Divide $(9x^4 + 12x^3 - 3x^2)$ by $3x^2$.

Answer

$\dfrac{9x^4 + 12x^3 - 3x^2}{3x^2} = \dfrac{9x^4}{3x^2} + \dfrac{12x^3}{3x^2} - \dfrac{3x^2}{3x^2}$ 1. Write the division as a fraction and change it to a series of divisions by the monomial divisor $3x^2$.

$\qquad\qquad\qquad = 3x^2 + 4x - 1$ 2. Divide the coefficients and use the Division Property of Exponents by subtracting exponents on the variable.

Example 6   Divide $(8a^5b^4 - 16a^4b^2 + 8a^2b)$ by $4a^2b$.

Answer

$\dfrac{8a^5b^4 - 16a^4b^2 + 8a^2b}{4a^2b}$ 1. Write the division as a fraction.

$\dfrac{8a^5b^4}{4a^2b} - \dfrac{16a^4b^2}{4a^2b} + \dfrac{8a^2b}{4a^2b}$ 2. Change it to a series of divisions by the monomial divisor $4a^2b$.

$2a^3b^3 - 4a^2b + 2$ 3. Divide the coefficients. Then divide like variables by subtracting exponents.

Skill Check 2

Divide.

1. $\dfrac{8x^4 + 16x^3 - 20x^2}{4}$

2. $\dfrac{9y^8 - 18y^4 - 3}{3}$

3. $\dfrac{5x^6 - 15x^5 - 35x^4}{5x^3}$

4. $\dfrac{9a^{10} - 36a^6 - 81a^3}{9a^2}$

5. $\dfrac{16x^6y - 8x^5y + 4x^3y}{2xy}$

6. $\dfrac{-7a^5b^3 + 14a^4b^4 + 21a^3b^5}{7a^3b^3}$

■ A. Exercises

Divide.

1. $\dfrac{18x^5y}{6x^2}$

2. $\dfrac{24x^7y^3}{6x^2y}$

3. $\dfrac{44a^4b^7}{11a^3b^5}$

4. $\dfrac{-68x^5y^3}{4x^3y^3}$

5. $\dfrac{-24b^3c^2}{-8b^2c^2}$

6. $\dfrac{150y^7z^4}{25y^3z^2}$

7. $\dfrac{-81x^5y^{10}}{3x^5y^9}$

8. $\dfrac{13a^6b^4c^5}{26a^5b^3c^5}$

9. $\dfrac{27x^{10}y^2z^8}{9x^5yz^4}$

10. $\dfrac{-74a^4b^3c^4}{37a^4b^3c^4}$

Divide.

11. $\dfrac{4x^4 - 8x^3}{2}$

12. $\dfrac{8x^2 + 4x - 2}{2}$

13. $\dfrac{6x^2 - 12xy + 6y^2}{6}$

14. $\dfrac{36a^2b^5 - 6a^3b^3}{2}$

15. $\dfrac{6a^2 - 15b^2 + 21}{3}$

16. $\dfrac{16b^3 + 8b^2 - 4b}{4}$

■ B. Exercises

Divide.

17. $\dfrac{12x^3 + 4x^2}{4x}$

18. $\dfrac{14a^2 - 49a}{7a}$

19. $\dfrac{62y^4z^3 - 124y^3z^5}{31y^2z^2}$

20. $\dfrac{3x^5 - 6x^4 + 9x^3}{3x^2}$

21. $\dfrac{-20y^8z - 12y^6z + 4y^4z}{2y^4z}$

22. $\dfrac{12a^6b - 6a^4b + 2a^2b}{2a^2b}$

23. $\dfrac{32x^3y - 64x^2y^2 + 54xy^3}{2xy}$

24. $\dfrac{25x^4y^3 + 15x^3y^4 - 25x^2y^5}{5x^2y^3}$

25. $\dfrac{-54a^3b^2 + 18a^2b^4 - 9ab^6}{9ab^2}$

26. $\dfrac{12c^4d^4 - 30c^3d^4 + 42c^2d^4}{6c^2d}$

27. $\dfrac{21x^4y^3 - 84x^3y^2 - 18x^2y}{3x^3y}$

28. $\dfrac{28a^3b - 24a^2b - 4ab}{4a^2b}$

29. $\dfrac{15a^2 - 18ab + 39b^2}{3a^2b^2}$

30. $\dfrac{20a^4b^2c - 15a^2b}{5ab^2c^3}$

■ C. Exercises

31. Explain why a variable with a negative exponent is equal to 1 over the variable with the opposite exponent. For example, $x^{-3} = \dfrac{1}{x^3}$.

32. Is the following statement true: $x^5 = \dfrac{1}{x^{-5}}$? Explain why.

33. The illustrated vertical form is often used for dividing numbers. Represent the division of $(8x^4 + 4x^3 - 10x^2)$ by $2x$ in a similar vertical format.

$$
\begin{array}{r}
23 \\
6\overline{)138} \\
12 \\
\hline
18 \\
18 \\
\hline
0
\end{array}
$$

Write an equation and solve. [3.5]

34. A school is starting a new sixth-grade girls' volleyball team. The principal has allotted $450 to outfit a ten-girl team. If each uniform costs $22 and $100 will be used for travel expenses, how much money is left for equipment?

35. The Johnston family likes to spend family evenings at the Fun Park. There are three children and two adults in the family. Each adult admission costs $6, and each child admission costs $4. If the family budget allows $125 for family entertainment per month, how many times can the family plan to attend the Fun Park each month?

36. A science project requires beakers, solution, and safety equipment. If each beaker costs $3, the solution costs $8, and the safety equipment costs $26, how many beakers can be purchased if $45 can be spent on the project?

Find k if y varies directly with x. [9.7]

37. $y = 16$ when $x = 2$ 38. $y = 74$ when $x = 10$ 39. $y = 9$ when $x = 27$

Given parallel lines m and n are cut by transversal k, answer the following questions from the figure below. [12.2]

40. Which angle forms a pair of corresponding angles with $\angle 1$?

41. Which angle forms a pair of alternate exterior angles with $\angle 1$?

42. If $m\angle 1 = 135°$, what is $m\angle 7$?

43. If $m\angle 6 = 37°$, what is $m\angle 3$?

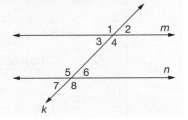

MIND OVER MATH

When Alan and Brady stood together on the scale, their total weight was 250 lb. Brady and Charles were weighed together, and their total weight was 300 lb. Charles and Damian weighed 280 lb. when they stood on the scale together. Initially, when Charles, Damian, and Brady all stood on the scale together, it registered 420 lb. How much does each of the four boys weigh?

14.7 Applying Algebra

In this section we will cover two types of problems involving money. The object in both is to find the total number of coins or bills of different denominations.

In the first type of problem, the total number of coins is known. The total value of the money is not.

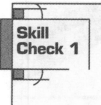

Example 1 Ivan has been saving money and has 351 coins. He has three more quarters than twice the number of dimes. How many of each coin does he have? How much money does he have?

Answer

Since the number of quarters is expressed in terms of the number of dimes, let d represent the number of dimes, as shown below. Then express the number of quarters in terms of d.

Coin	Number of coins
Dimes	d
Quarters	$2d + 3$

$d + (2d + 3) = 351$ 1. Write an equation.

$(d + 2d) + 3 = 351$ 2. Apply the Associative Property of Addition.

$3d + 3 = 351$ 3. Solve the equation.

$3d + 3 - 3 = 351 - 3$

$3d = 348$

$\dfrac{3d}{3} = \dfrac{348}{3}$

$d = 116$ dimes

$351 - 116 = 235$ quarters   4. Find the number of quarters.

$116(0.10) + 235(0.25) = \$70.35$ 5. Calculate the amount of money he has.

Skill Check 1

1. Brenda has thirty-six bills. Some are ones, some fives, and some tens. The number of fives is one less than three times the number of tens, and she has two more ones than tens. How many of each bill does she have? How much money does she have?

2. Edgar saved 226 coins consisting of quarters, dimes, and nickels. He has thirty more dimes than quarters and five times as many nickels as quarters. How many of each coin does he have?

In the second type of money problem, the total value of the money is known, but the number of coins (or bills) of each denomination is not. In this type of problem, express the total value for each type of coin (or bill) as the product of the value of the coin (or bill) and the number of that type of coin.

Example 2 Steve saves money by putting his dimes, nickels, and pennies in a jar. He has three times as many dimes as pennies and 18 more nickels than dimes. If he has a total of $14.24, find the number of dimes, nickels, and pennies he has.

Answer

Notice that the number of dimes is described in terms of the number of pennies, and the number of nickels is described in terms of the number of dimes. It would be best to know the number of pennies first. Let p = the number of pennies.

Coin	Number of coins	Value of each coin (in cents)	Total value
Pennies	p	1	$1p$
Nickels	$3p + 18$	5	$5(3p + 18)$
Dimes	$3p$	10	$10(3p)$

Each dollar is 100 cents, so he has $14.24(100) = 1,424$ cents. This number will be used in the equation since the values of the coins in the table are given in cents.

$p + 5(3p + 18) + 10(3p) = 1,424$ 1. Write an equation expressing the value of the coins in cents.

$p + 15p + 90 + 30p = 1,424$ 2. Solve the equation to find the number of pennies.

$46p + 90 = 1,424$ 3. Combine like terms.

$46p + 90 - 90 = 1,424 - 90$ 4. Apply the Addition Property of Equality.

$46p = 1,334$

$\dfrac{46p}{46} = \dfrac{1,334}{46}$ 5. Apply the Multiplication Property of Equality.

$p = 29$ pennies

$3p = 3(29) = 87$ dimes   6. Find the number of dimes.

$3p + 18 = 3(29) + 18 = 105$ nickels   7. Find the number of nickels.

Steve has 29 pennies, 87 dimes, and 105 nickels. His pennies are worth $0.29; his dimes are worth $8.70; and his nickels are worth $5.25. These total to the correct amount of $14.24.

When solving coin problems, use the table format shown in Examples 1 and 2. This organizes problem solving.

Example 3 Shyla has twice as many dimes as nickels, and she has three more quarters than nickels. If her coins total $4.75, how many of each coin does she have?

Answer

Coin	Number of coins	Value of each coin	Total value
Nickels	n	5	$5n$
Dimes	$2n$	10	$10(2n)$
Quarters	$n + 3$	25	$25(n + 3)$

$5n + 10(2n) + 25(n + 3) = 475$ 1. Find the sum of the total values of the coins, and set it equal to the total amount in cents.

$5n + 20n + 25n + 75 = 475$ 2. Apply the Distributive Property.

$50n + 75 = 475$ 3. Combine like terms.

$50n + 75 - 75 = 475 - 75$ 4. Apply the Addition Property of Equality.

$50n = 400$

$\dfrac{50n}{50} = \dfrac{400}{50}$ 5. Apply the Multiplication Property of Equality.

$n = 8$ nickels

$2n = 2(8) = 16$ dimes   6. Find the number of dimes and quarters that Shyla has.

$n + 3 = 8 + 3 = 11$ quarters

Example 4   George has 29 coins, made up of quarters and nickels. If their total value is $4.85, how many of each coin does he have?

Answer

Choose a variable for the number of nickels or quarters. We will let q = the number of quarters. The number of nickels would then be represented as the difference between the total number of coins, 29, and the number of quarters, q.

Coin	Number of coins	Value of each coin	Total value
Nickels	$29 - q$	5	$5(29 - q)$
Quarters	q	25	$25q$

$5(29 - q) + 25q = 485$ 1. Find the sum of the total values of the coins, and set it equal to the total amount in cents.

$145 - 5q + 25q = 485$ 2. Apply the Distributive Property.

$145 + 20q = 485$ 3. Combine like terms.

$145 - 145 + 20q = 485 - 145$ 4. Apply the Addition Property of Equality.

$20q = 340$

$\dfrac{20q}{20} = \dfrac{340}{20}$ 5. Apply the Multiplication Property of Equality.

$q = 17$ quarters

$29 - q = 12$ nickels   6. Find the number of nickels.

Skill Check 2

1. Casson has a collection of coins in his bank. Only pennies, dimes, and nickels will fit in the slot of the bank. There are twice as many pennies as nickels and eight more nickels than dimes. If the total value in the bank is $3.62, how many of each coin are in the bank?

2. The teen group at church decided to start taking a loose-change offering during the teen meetings. In the first offering there were twice as many dimes as quarters, two more nickels than quarters, and twice as many pennies as nickels. If the total offering was $3.26, how many of each coin was in the offering?

■ A. Exercises

In exercises 1–3, write a simplified expression representing the number of dimes if the expression $x + 5$ represents the number of quarters and the following is true.

1. There are seven more dimes than quarters.   2. There are three times as many dimes as quarters.

3. The number of dimes is three less than twice the number of quarters.

In exercises 4–6, write a simplified expression representing the number of nickels if the expression $3x + 1$ represents the number of quarters and the following is true.

4. There are four fewer nickels than quarters.   5. There are twice as many nickels as quarters.

6. The number of nickels is five more than three times the number of quarters.

7. Shawna has four fewer than twice as many quarters as dimes. She has one-half as many nickels as quarters. If you let d = the number of dimes, how would you represent the number of quarters and how would you represent the number of nickels?

8. How could you avoid using common fractions when representing the following information? Tina has one-ninth as many quarters as dimes and one-fifth as many nickels as quarters.

Write an equation and solve.

9. Elena has a total of 204 coins. She has twice as many quarters as nickels and three times as many dimes as nickels. How many of each coin does she have?

10. Alex has 66 bills. There are four times as many tens as there are ones and 1.5 times as many fives as there are tens. How many of each denomination does he have?

11. Ismael has five more quarters than dimes, six fewer nickels than dimes, and seven fewer pennies than nickels. He has 146 coins. How many of each coin does he have?

12. Johnette has two more quarters than nickels and three times as many dimes as quarters. If she has a total of 98 coins, how many of each coin does she have?

13. Alyssa has twelve more nickels than dimes and eight fewer quarters than nickels. She has 67 coins. How many of each coin does she have?

14. Nathan has a coin collection containing 85 coins, of which there are 16 more US coins than Canadian ones and 12 fewer Romanian coins than Canadian. How many of each country's coins does he have?

■ B. Exercises

Write an equation and solve.

15. When Margaret broke her piggy bank, she found an equal number of nickels and dimes. She also noticed that the number of pennies was five less than three times the number of dimes. If there were no quarters among the 85 coins, how much had she saved in the piggy bank?

16. Sue has twice as many quarters as dimes. Yolanda has three times as many quarters as dimes. Both have the same number of dimes, and together they have $14.50. Find the number of coins each girl has.

17. Andy has $201. He has twice as many fives as tens. The number of ones is one more than five times the number of tens. How many of each bill does he have?

18. Angela has two more than twice as many quarters as dimes, one fewer than three times as many nickels as dimes, and eight more pennies than dimes. She has $7.37. How many of each coin does she have?

19. Esther and Rachel have both been saving quarters. Together they have 47 quarters, and Esther has $3.75 less than Rachel. How much money does each one of them have?

20. Josef, Jacqueline, and Joni are saving quarters. Together they have 117 quarters. Jacqueline has twenty-five more quarters than Josef and eight more than Joni. How much money does each have?

21. Omar has three times as many quarters as dimes and one more than twice as many nickels as dimes. If he has $5.75, how many of each coin does he have?

22. Jack has a total of $32.15. He has twice as many quarters as dimes, one more than three times as many nickels as dimes, and eighteen more pennies than dimes. How many of each coin does he have?

23. Laura has equal numbers of dollar bills and quarters. The number of dimes she has is equal to the sum of the number of dollar bills and quarters. She has $17.40. How many of each does she have?

24. Mr. Mont has three CDs (certificates of deposit). One has twice as much invested in it as another. The third one has $1,750 less than the larger one. If he has $23,250 invested, how much is invested in each CD?

25. A company is buying three vehicles as company cars. The least expensive one costs one-third as much as the most expensive one, and the third car costs one-half as much as the most expensive one. If the total cost of all three cars combined is $110,000, how much does each car cost?

26. Jared has thirty-five coins, composed of quarters and nickels. The total amount of money is $7.15. How many of each coin does he have?

■ C. Exercises

Write an equation and solve.

27. Mr. Cohen's net worth is twice as much as Mr. Hall's and three times as much as Mr. Chang's. They claim that their combined net worth is a million dollars. Find the net worth of each one to the nearest dollar.

28. A roll of 36 bills contains two more twenties than fifties, eight fewer tens than twenties, and twice as many fives as fifties. How many of each bill are in the roll? How much money is in the roll of bills?

■ Dominion thru Math

A digital camera set at a high resolution of 3,264 × 2,448 can store 582 photos on a 2 GB (2,048 MB) memory card. At a medium resolution of 2,560 × 1,920, it can store 800 images on the same memory card. Assume that only 95% of the memory card is usable for storing images because formatting uses some of the storage.

Use a calculator to solve the following exercises.

29. How many megapixels are contained in a high-resolution photo? Round to the nearest tenth.

30. How many megapixels are contained in a medium-resolution photo? Round to the nearest tenth.

31. What is the aspect ratio of the camera?

32. How many megabytes are needed to store an image at high resolution? Round to the nearest hundredth.

33. How many megabytes are needed to store an image at medium resolution? Round to the nearest hundredth.

34. If a CD-RW holds about 800 MB of information, how many high-resolution images can be stored on a CD if it can be filled to 95% of capacity?

35. If a DVD holds about 4.7 GB of information, how many medium-resolution images can be stored on a DVD if it can be filled to 95% of capacity?

CUMULATIVE REVIEW

$\triangle ABC \sim \triangle FED$. **Complete each statement.** [12.5, 13.4]

36. $EF =$ _____

37. $DF =$ _____

38. If the area of $\triangle ABC$ is 27 cm², what is the area of $\triangle FED$?

39. What is the perimeter of $\triangle FED$?

Find the unknown lengths in the following special right triangles. [12.6]

40. $b =$ _____

$a =$ _____

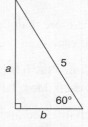

41. $a =$ _____

$c =$ _____

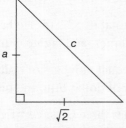

Find the distance between the following points. Give your answer as both a simplified radical and a decimal rounded to the nearest tenth. [12.7]

42. (−9, 3) and (1, 8)

43. (2, 0) and (0, 8)

Find the midpoint of the segments with the following endpoints. [12.7]

44. (−9, 3) and (1, 8)

45. (2, 0) and (0, 8)

MATH & SCRIPTURE

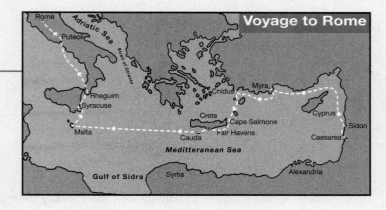

Shipwrecked

The account in Acts 27 of Paul's shipwreck provides a fascinating glimpse of God's sovereign control in the midst of a raging storm on the Mediterranean Sea. As the trip begins, Luke, Paul, and Aristarchus are probably the only believers on the Alexandrian ship bound for Italy. By the end of the perilous voyage that everyone survives, the gospel has no doubt found entrance into many hearts—not only among the ship's passengers but also among the residents of the island of Malta (also called Melita), where the shipwreck took place.

The dramatic account of Paul's shipwreck begins along the coast of Crete, located at 35° N latitude and 24° E longitude, and ends on the island of Malta, located at 35°50' N latitude and 14°35' E longitude. There is mostly open sea between these islands. The Gulf of Sidra, Libya, is about 600 km southwest of Crete and 650 km southeast of Malta. The entrance to the Adriatic Sea (Strait of Otranto) between Italy and Greece is about 800 km northwest of Crete and 650 km northeast of Malta. Acts 27 indicates that the ship may have been driven about in the Adriatic Sea.

Read Acts 27:1–28:1 and answer the following questions.

1. At three different times the sailors made the ship lighter by throwing items overboard. Two specific items were mentioned. What were they?

2. For how many days was the ship driven before the fierce wind of the storm?

3. How did the sailors determine that the ship was approaching land?

4. Research the method sailors used to measure the depth of the water and describe how it works.

5. One minute of longitude on an arc of a great circle on the earth's surface measures a nautical mile (1,852 m). Approximately how many kilometers on a straight line are Crete and Malta apart? You may ignore the difference in latitudes.

6. Calculate the average speed of the ship in km/hr. for two possible routes: first, if the ship traveled in a straight line from Crete to Malta; second, if the ship traveled from Crete to the Adriatic Sea to Malta.

7. What did Paul encourage the people on the ship to do that was necessary for their well-being? Why do you think they neglected to take care of this important matter?

8. How many people were aboard the ill-fated Alexandrian ship?

9. Why did Paul know that no one would die when the ship ran aground and was destroyed on the coast of Malta?

10. What condition did Paul impose on the sailors and soldiers in order for everyone to be kept alive?

11. How is the foolishness of men portrayed in this account of the storm and shipwreck?

12. In spite of the foolishness of men, what purposes do you think God intended as this drama unfolded?

Infinite Truths

And now I exhort you to be of good cheer: for there shall be no loss of any man's life among you.
Acts 27:22

Chapter 14 Review

Vocabulary

binomial	degree of the term	polynomial
degree of the polynomial	monomial	trinomial

Are the following polynomials? If not, why not?

1. $2x^5 - 9x^{-6}$

2. $-5x^2 - 6x + 8$

Give the degree of the following polynomials and identify the type of polynomial by special name. If no special name applies, write "polynomial."

3. $3x^3y + 4xy$

4. $6a^4b^6$

Evaluate the following polynomials when $x = -9$ and $y = 6$.

5. $19 - 3x$

6. $-8x + y^2$

7. $2x^2 + xy + y$

Add.

8. $(-9x^2 + 14) + (7x - 2)$

9. $(x^2 + 5xy - 9) + (x^2 - 3xy)$

10. $(-6a^2 - ab + 6b^2) + (a^2 + 4ab - 11b^2)$

11. $(x^2 - y) + (-7x^2 + 9y^2 - 8y)$

12. $(14x^2 - 9x) + (6x^2 - 3x + 28)$

13. $\left(\frac{2}{9}m^3 + 6m^2 - \frac{1}{5}m + \frac{3}{8}\right) + \left(\frac{3}{2}m^2 - \frac{4}{5}m - 6\right)$

14. $(5.8x + 2.4y - 5.7) + (-8.2y + 12.4)$

Find the opposite (additive inverse) of each polynomial.

15. $-7x + 8$

16. $21x - 9$

17. $10a - 6b + 14$

Subtract.

18. $(-9x - 7) - 15$

19. $6x - (5x + 18)$

20. $(2y - 12) - y$

21. $(-8x^2 - 2x + 9) - (5x^2 + 16x - 3)$

22. $(-4a^2 + 3a - 8) - (9a^2 - 7)$

Multiply.

23. $-7x^5(8x^{10})$

24. $9y(-16y^8)$

25. $3z^8(8z^2)$

26. $-3x^2(7x^2 - x - 17)$

27. $2x^4(9x^2 - 3x + 5)$

28. $x(-8x^5 + 13x^3 + 21)$

29. $-5a^2(4a^4 - 9a^2 + 7)$

Multiply.

30. $(x + 8)(x - 2)$

31. $(x - 12)(x - 3)$

32. $(x + 5)(x - 3)$

33. $(x - 9)(x - 6)$

34. $(x - 10)(x + 7)$

35. $(6x - 3)(9x - 1)$

36. $(-4x + 6)(2x + 7)$

37. $(8x + 3)(5x - 2)$

Divide.

38. $\dfrac{12x^9y^3}{4x^6y}$

39. $\dfrac{15x^3y^8}{5x^5y^7}$

40. $\dfrac{96a^6b^3}{12a^9b^2}$

41. $\dfrac{7x^5 + 28x^4}{7x^2}$

42. $\dfrac{84a^8 - 28a}{14a^5}$

43. $\dfrac{4x^5 - 16x^4 + 36x^3}{2x^3}$

44. $\dfrac{-200x^4y^4z^2 - 150x^2y^6z^8 + 25xy^2z^5}{5xy^4z}$

45. Neil has four more quarters than dimes in his pocket. If you let d = the number of dimes, how would you represent the number of quarters?

46. Jerry's collection of nickels totals $6.40. Write an equation to find the number of nickels he has in his collection. Do not solve.

Write an equation and solve.

47. Abe has six more quarters than nickels and five times as many dimes as quarters. If he has a total of 141 coins, how many of each coin does he have?

48. Charity has 42 more pennies than dimes. Hope has seven times as many pennies as dimes. Both of them have the same number of dimes, and together they have $5.46. Find the number of dimes and pennies each has.

49. Dustan has $1,380. He has three times as many fives as twenties. He has six more than two times as many fifties as twenties. How many of each bill does he have?

50. State the mathematical significance of Acts 27:22.

SYMBOLS

$\|x\|$	absolute value of x		$\neq$	not equal to
$\angle A$	angle A		$\not>$	not greater than
$\approx$	approximately equal to		$\ngeq$	not greater than or equal to
$_nC_r$	combination of n things taken r at a time		$\not<$	not less than
$\cong$	congruent to		$\nleq$	not less than or equal to
$^\circ$	degrees		$-x$	opposite of x
AB	distance between points A and B		(a, b)	ordered pair
$\in$	element of		$\|\|$	parallel to
$\ldots$	ellipses		$\%$	percent
$\varnothing$	empty set		$_nP_r$	permutation of n things taken r at a time
$=$	equal to		$\perp$	perpendicular to
$!$	factorial		π	pi
$>$	greater than		$\pm$	plus or minus
$\geq$	greater than or equal to		$a : b$	ratio of a to b
A'	image of A (read A prime)		$\overrightarrow{AB}$	ray AB
$\cap$	intersection		$\overline{AB}$	segment AB
$<$	less than		$\sim$	similar to
$\leq$	less than or equal to		$\sqrt{x}$	square root
$\overleftrightarrow{AB}$	line AB		$\subseteq$	subset of
$m\angle A$	measure of angle A		$\triangle ABC$	triangle ABC
$\notin$	not an element of		$\cup$	union
$\nsubseteq$	not a subset of		y^n	y to the nth power

SKILL CHECK ANSWERS

Chapter 1—Integers

1.1 Opposites and Absolute Value

Skill Check 1

1–3.

Skill Check 2

1. −14   2. 52   3. 1,422

Skill Check 3

1. 24   2. 2   3. 150

Skill Check 4

1. <   2. >   3. >

Skill Check 5

1. $−7 < −3 < 5$
2. $8 > 0 > −1 > −6$

1.2 Adding Integers

Skill Check 1

1. 8

2. −9

3. −8   4. 11   5. −14

Skill Check 2

1. −6   2. 13   3. −8

1.3 Subtracting Integers

Skill Check 1

1. $4 + (−9)$ 2. $9 + 8$
3. $−8 + 4$ 4. $−6 + (−3)$

Skill Check 2

1. −12   2. 2
3. −6   4. 10
5. −3   6. −1
7. 230 points   8. −$555

1.4 Multiplying Integers

Skill Check 1

1. −12   2. −30   3. −7

Skill Check 2

1. negative   2. positive
3. negative   4. −40
5. −35   6. 24

7. −12   8. 22
9. 27

Skill Check 3

1. positive   2. negative
3. 30   4. −432
5. 0   6. −48

1.5 Dividing Integers

Skill Check 1

1. 5   2. 8   3. −9
4. −141   5. 3   6. −6

Skill Check 2

1. 12   2. −1   3. 7
4. −32   5. 8   6. −250

1.6 Exponents

Skill Check 1

1. c^4
2. $(−1)^7$
3. $10(10)(10) = 1,000$
4. $b(b)(b)(b)(b)$
5. $7(7)(7)(7) = 2,401$
6. $−[2(2)(2)(2)(2)(2)] = −64$

Skill Check 2

1. 25   2. 26
3. 26   4. −5

Skill Check 3

1. 2^6 2. 7^{15} 3. d^4
4. x^{10} 5. b^{18} 6. 10^{13}

Skill Check 4

1. 7^3 2. 5^5
3. x^4 4. y^7

Skill Check 5

1. $(−4)^2$ 2. $7^{−4}$ 3. $9^{−3}$
4. c^4 5. $3^3 \times 5^2$ 6. 7^4
7. $\frac{1}{9}$ 8. $\frac{1}{16}$ 9. −125

1.7 Order of Operations

Skill Check 1

1. multiplication
2. multiplication
3. division
4. division
5. subtraction
6. exponent

Skill Check 2

1. 27   2. −64   3. 19
4. 4   5. −16   6. 35

Skill Check 3

1. −26   2. $\frac{1}{2}$
3. 72   4. 1,900

1.8 Scientific Notation

Skill Check 1

1. 4   2. −4
3. 7.25   4. 9
5. $3.21 \times 10^{−6}$ 6. 6.4×10^8

Skill Check 2

1. 4,900   2. 0.031
3. 6,000,000

Chapter 2—Expressions

2.1 Properties of Addition

Skill Check 1

1. Commutative
2. Commutative
3. Associative
4. Associative and Commutative
5. No; $2 − 6 = −4$, which is not a whole number.
6. Yes; if you add two negative numbers, you get a negative number.
7. $h + 7$
8. $8 + (m − 4)$

Skill Check 2

1. 54   2. 6   3. −114
4. $a = 8$ 5. $b = 4$ 6. $c = 0$
7. $d = 12$

Skill Check 3

1. Associative
2. Commutative
3. Identity
4. Inverse
5. $a = 0$; Identity
6. $b = 4$; Associative
7. $c = 7$; Commutative
8. $d = −32$; Inverse

2.2 Properties of Multiplication

Skill Check 1

1. $-4(8)$ 2. $(mn)t$

Skill Check 2

1. Commutative
2. Identity
3. Associative
4. Zero
5. Associative and Commutative
6. $5(4)$
7. $(18 \cdot 7)n$
8. $[5(4)](-130)$

2.3 Distributive Property

Skill Check 1

1. $-5x + (-5)(6) = -5x - 30$
2. $-4(3) - (-4y) = -12 + 4y$
3. $8(12) - 8(4) = 96 - 32 = 64$
4. $6(-4) + 6(2) = -24 + 12 = -12$
5. $5(70 + 6) = 350 + 30 = 380$
6. $9(60 - 2) = 540 - 18 = 522$

Skill Check 2

1. $5\underline{x} + 5\underline{y}$ 2. $\underline{4}(3 + 5)$
3. $3(\underline{2} + \underline{7})$ 4. $(\underline{9} + \underline{2})x$
5. $2y + 3y$ 6. $(4 + 6)3$

2.4 Evaluating Expressions

Skill Check 1

1. -7 2. -17

Skill Check 2

1. 11 2. -4
3. 14 4. 19

2.5 Simplifying Expressions

Skill Check 1

1. $35b$ 2. $54n$ 3. $52r$
4. $m + 13$ 5. $a + 23$ 6. $s + 16$

Skill Check 2

1. 4 2. 1 3. -7
4. $-4y$ 5. $9xy$ 6. $2z$
7. $10x$

Skill Check 3

1. $7x$ 2. $9a + 11$
3. $6b + 12$ 4. $9y - 15$
5. $-10m + 1$ 6. $12p + 6$
7. $3r - 15s$
8. $-4w + 12x + 3$

2.6 Translating Word Phrases

Skill Check 1

1. $6 + 31$
2. $54 - 14$
3. $\frac{75}{3}$, or $75 \div 3$
4. $5 + 2$
5. 17×61

Skill Check 2

1. $n + 12$ 2. $n - 4$
3. $8x$ 4. $11 - n$
5. $81 \div x$, or $\frac{81}{x}$

Skill Check 3

1. $m + 15$ 2. $2n$

Skill Check 4

1. $6(7 + 4)$
2. $\frac{15}{n - 3}$, or $15 \div (n - 3)$
3. $8n - 7$
4. $\frac{n}{7} + 6$

2.7 Estimating

Skill Check 1

1. 80 2. 628.06
3. $25,000$ 4. 0.30522

Skill Check 2

1. 100 2. $7,500$
3. $3,000$ 4. $3,000$
5. $12,000$ 6. $36,000$
7. 3.8 8. 7.2

Skill Check 3

1. $2,400$ 2. 3
3. $56,000$ 4. 30

Skill Check 4

1. $12,000; 13,200$
2. $20,000; 23,000$

Chapter 3—Basic Equations and Inequalities

3.1 Solving Equations by Adding or Subtracting

Skill Check 1

1. subtract 18   2. add 25
3. subtract 87   4. add 48
5. $x = -64$ 6. $b = 112$
7. $s = 38$ 8. $c = -114$

Skill Check 2

1. $n = 45$ 2. $v = 81$
3. $m = 128$ 4. $r = 167$

Skill Check 3

1. $3 - n$ 2. $n + 9$ 3. $m + 5$
4. $x + 12$ 5. $n - 45$

Skill Check 4

1. $n + 18 = 31$
2. $n - 23 = 6$
3. $x + 8 = 76$
4. $d + d + 12 = 118$

3.2 Solving Equations by Multiplying or Dividing

Skill Check 1

1. divide by 12
2. multiply by 35
3. divide by -27
4. multiply by -3
5. $b = 2$ 6. $r = -315$
7. $n = -3$ 8. $x = -18$

Skill Check 2

1. $3n$ 2. $\frac{60}{n}$
3. $12m$ 4. $\frac{x}{5}$ or $\frac{1}{5}x$
5. $61 - v$ 6. $\frac{2x}{3}$ and $\frac{2}{3}x$

Skill Check 3

1. $\frac{x}{12} = 8$; $x = 96$
2. $7x = 42$; $x = 6$ lb.
3. $2,107x = 8,428$; $x = 4$ families

3.3 Solving Two-Step Equations

Skill Check 1

1. subtract 7
2. multiply by 12
3. add 9
4. add 5

Skill Check 2

1. $n = 7$ 2. $x = -2$
3. $x = -19$ 4. $t = -56$
5. $a = 216$ 6. $x = -5$

Skill Check 3

1. $2B - 2,500 = 20,800$;
  $B = \$11,650$
2. $\frac{1}{3}p + 10 = 19$; $p = 27$ ft.

3.4 Simplifying Before Solving

Skill Check 1

1. $8m$ 2. $-4x + 2y + z$
3. 8 4. $-37n - 2$

Skill Check 2

1. $x = -23$ 2. $x = -1$
3. $x = 2$ 4. $x = -3$

3.5 Using Equations

Skill Check 1

1. 9 lb. of cashews; 18 lb. of peanuts
2. 118 children

Skill Check 2

1. 36 mi./hr.

3.6 Sets of Numbers and Inequalities

Skill Check 1

1–6.

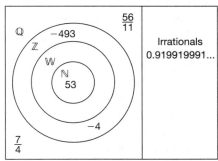

Skill Check 2

1. yes; –7 **2.** yes; 17 **3.** no
4. no **5.** no **6.** yes; 5

Skill Check 3

1. –3, 5, 18 **2.** –2, 0, 2
3. –4, –2 **4.** –6

3.7 Solving Linear Inequalities

Skill Check 1

1. [number line: open circle at 7, shading left; marks –2, 0, 2, 4, 6, 8]
2. [number line: open circle at –4, shading right; marks –8, –6, –4, –2, 0]
3. [number line: closed circle at 2, shading right; marks –4, –2, 0, 2, 4, 6]
4. $y \geq -3$ [number line: closed circle at –3, shading right; marks –8, –6, –4, –2, 0, 2, 4]
5. $y < -7$ [number line: open circle at –7, shading left; marks –12, –10, –8, –6, –4, –2, 0]

Skill Check 2

1. yes **2.** no
3. no **4.** no
5. $x \neq -11$ **6.** $x \geq 3$
7. $x > 18$ **8.** $x \geq -14$

Skill Check 3

1. $x \leq 14$ **2.** $x \geq 32$
3. $x < -4$ **4.** $x > -40$

3.8 Using Inequalities

Skill Check 1

1. $x - 25 > 82$ **2.** $60t \leq 720$
3. $x \geq 8.5$ **4.** $x < 40$

Skill Check 2

1. $x + 800 \leq 2{,}300$; $x \leq 1{,}500$; at most 1,500 more calories
2. $-5x \geq 360$; $x \leq -72$; –72 or any integer less than it
3. $3x \geq 135$; $x \geq 45$; at least $45

Chapter 4—Number Theory

4.1 Prime and Composite Numbers

Skill Check 1

1. true **2.** false
3. true **4.** false
5. 3, 6, 9, 12 **6.** 8, 16, 24, 32
7. yes **8.** no
9. 1, 2, 3, 4, 6, 12
10. 1, 2, 3, 5, 6, 10, 15, 30

Skill Check 2

1. 1, 11
2. 1, 2, 4, 8, 16
3. 1, 23
4. 1, 2, 3, 4, 6, 8, 12, 24
5. composite **6.** prime
7. composite **8.** composite
9. prime **10.** composite

4.2 Prime Factorization

Skill Check 1

1. $2 \cdot 3 \cdot 5$ **2.** $2 \cdot 7^2$
3. $3^2 \cdot 5^2$ **4.** $2^2 \cdot 3 \cdot 5$
5. $2 \cdot 3 \cdot 5^2$ **6.** $2 \cdot 3^2 \cdot 13$
7. $2^3 \cdot 5^2$ **8.** $3 \cdot 5 \cdot 11$

4.3 Greatest Common Factor

Skill Check 1

1. 3 **2.** 2
3. 4 **4.** 10

Skill Check 2

1. 20 **2.** 3 **3.** 6
4. 6 **5.** $3xy^3$ **6.** $12yz$

4.4 Least Common Multiple

Skill Check 1

1. 6 **2.** 24
3. 30 **4.** 45

Skill Check 2

1. 30 **2.** 100 **3.** 36
4. 21 **5.** $24x^2y^2z$ **6.** $70a^3bc$

4.5 Arithmetic Sequences

Skill Check 1

1. $d = 3$; $a_1 = 5$; $a_4 = 14$; $a_7 = 23$
2. $d = 4$; $a_1 = -9$; $a_4 = 3$; $a_7 = 15$
3. $d = -3$; $a_1 = 22$; $a_4 = 13$; $a_7 = 4$

Skill Check 2

1. –8, –2, 4, 10, 16
2. 3, –6, –15, –24, –33
3. –3, –7, –11, –15, –19
4. $a_1 = 7$; $a_n = a_{n-1} + 5$
5. $a_1 = -15$; $a_n = a_{n-1} + 8$

Skill Check 3

1. 26 **2.** 197 **3.** –72

4.6 Geometric Sequences

Skill Check 1

1. 4, –8, 16, –32, 64
2. 972, 324, 108, 36, 12
3. $a_1 = 2$; $r = 3$; $a_4 = 54$; $a_6 = 486$
4. $a_1 = -7$; $r = -2$; $a_4 = 56$; $a_6 = 224$
5. $a_1 = 256$; $r = \frac{1}{2}$ or 0.5; $a_4 = 32$; $a_6 = 8$

Skill Check 2

1. $a_n = 6a_{n-1}$
2. $a_n = -3a_{n-1}$
3. $12, 6, 3, \frac{3}{2}, \frac{3}{4}$
4. –10, 20, –40, 80, –160

Skill Check 3

1. $a_n = 2(4)^{n-1}$
2. $a_n = -250\left(-\frac{1}{5}\right)^{n-1}$
3. geometric
4. arithmetic
5. neither

4.7 Bases

Skill Check 1

1. 125 **2.** 116
3. 2,880 **4.** 293
5. 1, 10, 11, 100, 101, 110, 111, 1000, 1001, 1010

Skill Check 2

1. 11101_2 **2.** 322_5 **3.** 1212_8

4.8 Operations in Bases

Skill Check 1
1. 1141_5 2. 7260_8 3. 10000_2

Skill Check 2
1. 153_8 2. 1424_5
3. 110_2 4. $22D7_{16}$

Chapter 5—Rational Numbers

5.1 Forms of Rational Numbers

Skill Check 1
1. $\frac{3}{14}$ 2. $\frac{3}{8}$
3. $\frac{3}{5}$ 4. $\frac{7}{12}$

Skill Check 2
1. $\frac{5}{4}$, $1\frac{1}{4}$ 2. $\frac{5}{3}$, $1\frac{2}{3}$ 3. $4\frac{5}{6}$
4. $-6\frac{1}{3}$ 5. 13 6. $5\frac{4}{7}$

Skill Check 3
1. $\frac{9}{7}$ 2. $\frac{26}{3}$ 3. $\frac{77}{8}$
4. $\frac{100}{3}$ 5. $-\frac{23}{3}$ 6. $-\frac{71}{4}$

5.2 Comparing Rational Numbers

Skill Check 1
1. $\frac{6}{16}$ 2. $\frac{6}{7}$ 3. $\frac{6}{11}$
4. $\frac{5}{6} \rhd \frac{3}{4}$; $\frac{10}{12} \rhd \frac{9}{12}$
5. $-\frac{5}{8} \lhd -\frac{1}{2}$; $-\frac{5}{8} \lhd -\frac{4}{8}$
6. $\frac{2}{5} = \frac{6}{15}$; $\frac{6}{15} = \frac{6}{15}$

Skill Check 2
1. $\frac{7}{12} \lhd \frac{8}{13}$; $91 < 96$
2. $\frac{5}{6} \rhd \frac{7}{11}$; $55 > 42$
3. $\frac{9}{13} \lhd \frac{11}{15}$; $135 < 143$
4. yes   5. no   6. yes

Skill Check 3
1. $\frac{1}{3}$ 2. $-\frac{5}{3}$
3. 2 4. $-\frac{7}{3}$
5. $-2\frac{1}{4} < -\frac{3}{4} < 1\frac{1}{2} < 2\frac{2}{3}$

![number line from -2 to 4 with points at -2, -3/4, 1 1/2, 2 2/3]

5.3 Decimal Equivalents

Skill Check 1
1. 0.375 2. $0.\overline{2}$ 3. 0.16

Skill Check 2
1. $\frac{4}{5}$ 2. $\frac{3}{20}$
3. $\frac{4}{11}$ 4. $\frac{1}{6}$

5.4 Ratio and Rate

Skill Check 1
1. $1 : 4$ 2. $3 : 2$
3. $2 : 4$ 4. $4 : 5$

Skill Check 2
1–4. Answers will vary.
1. travel
2. keyboarding
3. wages
4. engine, pedaling
5. 56 mi./hr.
6. 48 words/min.
7. 20 mi./gal.
8. 300 rev./min.

5.5 Proportions

Skill Check 1
1. $\frac{9}{5} = \frac{27}{15}$; $\frac{5}{15} = \frac{9}{27}$
2. $\frac{y}{x} = \frac{15}{6}$; $\frac{x}{6} = \frac{y}{15}$

Skill Check 2
1. $b = 10$ 2. $n = 14$
3. $s = 5$ 4. $x = 15\frac{3}{4}$

Skill Check 3
1. $\frac{2}{0.27} = \frac{c}{1.35}$; $c = 10$
2. $\frac{7}{15} = \frac{14}{n}$; $n = 30$

5.6 Real Numbers

Skill Check 1
1. rational   2. whole
3. integer   4. rational
5. natural   6. rational

Skill Check 2
1–6.

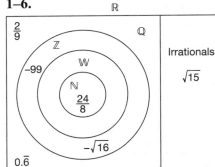

Skill Check 3
1. Commutative Property of Addition
2. Identity Property of Multiplication
3. Inverse Property of Addition
4. Zero Property of Multiplication
5. Associative Property of Addition
6. Inverse Property of Multiplication

Chapter 6—Operations on Rational Numbers

6.1 Addition and Subtraction

Skill Check 1
1. 1 2. $\frac{1}{2}$ 3. $\frac{5}{7}$
4. $\frac{2}{3}$ 5. $\frac{2}{3}$ 6. $\frac{1}{3}$

Skill Check 2
1. $1\frac{1}{4}$ 2. $-\frac{1}{15}$
3. $-\frac{7}{12}$ 4. $\frac{1}{40}$

Skill Check 3
1. $3\frac{1}{9}$ 2. 12.885
3. $6\frac{23}{40}$ 4. 9.37

6.2 Multiplication

Skill Check 1
1. $\frac{10}{21}$ 2. $\frac{20}{9}$ 3. $-\frac{21}{55}$
4. $\frac{63}{220}$ 5. $\frac{125}{64}$ 6. $-\frac{8}{343}$

Skill Check 2

1. $\frac{23}{10}$ 2. $-\frac{1}{15}$

3. $\frac{45}{2}$ 4. $\frac{7}{30}$

Skill Check 3

1. 0.945   2. −0.7942

3. 0.0007   4. 29.7778

6.3 Division

Skill Check 1

1. $\frac{1}{10}$ 2. −10

3. $\frac{9}{2}$ 4. $\frac{75}{2}$

Skill Check 2

1. 16.3   2. $6.03\overline{39}$

3. $0.41\overline{6}$ 4. −6.23

6.4 Evaluating Algebraic Expressions

Skill Check 1

1. $\frac{34}{15}$ 2. −166

3. $\frac{65}{9}$ 4. $\frac{7}{4}$

Skill Check 2

1. $\frac{601}{64}$ 2. $\frac{13}{6}$ 3. 18.495

4. 65   5. −11.4

6.5 Simplifying Algebraic Expressions

Skill Check 1

1. $\frac{42}{5}x - \frac{5}{3}$ 2. $-\frac{11}{3}x + 11y$

3. $6.92x^2 - 9.4x$ 4. $7.03a + 7.2b$

Skill Check 2

1. $\frac{32}{5}y + 4$

2. $-1.88x^2 + 3.4x + 5$

3. $\frac{5}{6}x^3 + \frac{4}{9}x$

4. $1.75a^4 + 2a^2$

6.6 Solving Equations with Rational Numbers

Skill Check 1

1. $x = 7.15$ 2. $x = \frac{14}{9}$

3. $x = 1.44$ 4. $x = \frac{17}{10}$

Skill Check 2

1. $x = \frac{6}{7}$ 2. $x = 6$

3. $y = \frac{11}{5}$ 4. $x = 1.11$

6.7 Using Algebra

Skill Check 1

1. n = the number;
   $(n + 4) - 5\frac{1}{3} = 43$

2. n = the second number,
   $\frac{n}{3}$ = the first number;
   $n + \frac{n}{3} = -16$

3. x = games won, $\frac{1}{5}x$ = games
   lost; $x + \frac{1}{5}x = 84$

Skill Check 2

1. 24 students   2. $2,780

6.8 Operations with Scientific Notation

Skill Check 1

1. 1.116×10^8
2. -2.93×10^{14}
3. 2.09×10^{-5}

Skill Check 2

1. 5.39×10^4
2. 1.0558×10^5

Skill Check 3

1. 4.6656×10^{-11}
2. 2×10^{-13}
3. 1.86×10^5; 2.83×10^{-1};
   6.57×10^5

Chapter 7—Percents

7.1 Forms of Percents

Skill Check 1

1. $\frac{2}{25}$ 2. $\frac{1}{8}$ 3. $3\frac{13}{20}$

4. $\frac{1}{150}$ 5. true   6. false

7. false   8. 0.6   9. 0.1325

10. 1.53

Skill Check 2

1. 54%   2. 0.9%   3. 230%
4. 53.5%   5. 107%   6. 1,130%

Skill Check 3

1. 80%   2. 12%   3. 86%
4. 150%   5. 400%   6. 0.5%

7. $66\frac{2}{3}\%$

7.2 Solving Percent Equations

Skill Check 1

1. $10.20   2. 42   3. 88
4. 40   5. 20   6. 24
7. 880

Skill Check 2

1. 20%   2. 16.7%
3. 250%   4. 4.5%

Skill Check 3

1. 50   2. 150
3. 7.2   4. 2

7.3 Using Percents

Skill Check 1

1. $0.15w = 12$; 80 lb.
2. $m = 0.35(20)$; 7 shots made
3. $75p = 69$; $p = 0.92 = 92\%$

Skill Check 2

1. 13 oz. water; 81.25%
2. 36 seats
3. $5,400

7.4 Scales

Skill Check 1

1. 45 km   2. 78 km
3. 190.5 km   4. 50 km
5. 42.5 km

Skill Check 2

1. 2.5 in. or $2\frac{1}{2}$ in.

2. 0.25 in. or $\frac{1}{4}$ in.

3. 1 in. : 4 ft.

Skill Check 3

1. 150%   2. 6 in.

3. $2\frac{1}{4}$ in. × 3 in.   4. 56 ft.

7.5 Discount and Markup

Skill Check 1

1. $0.90; $8.10
2. $6.45; $19.35
3. $690; $2,760
4. $73.75; $516.25
5. 24%
6. 25%

Skill Check 2

1. $5; $30   2. $35; $135
3. $10; 50%   4. $2.70; 18%

7.6 Commissions and Tips

Skill Check 1

1. $212.50   2. $1,200
3. 15%   4. 17%
5. $18,500   6. $2,150

Skill Check 2

1. $7.25   2. $19.80
3. 12%   4. 18%

7.7 Interest

Skill Check 1

1. $300   2. $270
3. $750; $5,750   4. $180; $3,180

Skill Check 2

1. $6,242.40; $242.40
2. $9,738.98; $238.98

Skill Check 3

1. $8,671.77; $1,671.77
2. $2,007.34; $507.34

7.8 Percent Change

Skill Check 1

1. 26
2. 34
3. 30% increase
4. 76% decrease
5. 5% increase
6. 8% decrease

Skill Check 2

1. 60% increase
2. 15% decrease
3. 20% increase
4. 42% decrease

Chapter 8—Applying Equations and Inequalities

8.1 Simplifying Equations

Skill Check 1

1. $-11b - 3$ 2. $10r + 9$
3. $x = 13$ 4. $x = -2$
5. $x = -2$ 6. $x = -22$

Skill Check 2

1. $x = 7$ 2. $x = -2$
3. $x = 15$ 4. $x = \frac{1}{3}$

8.2 Variables on Both Sides

Skill Check 1

1. subtract $4c$ 2. add $2x$
3. subtract $3n$ 4. subtract $5y$
5. $x = 9$ 6. $r = 3$

Skill Check 2

1. $m = 6$ 2. $s = 1$ 3. $x = 10$
4. $y = -\frac{1}{2}$ or -0.5

8.3 Applying Equations

Skill Check 1

1. $2x + 3 = \frac{1}{2}x$; $x = -2$
2. $5(n + 3) = 2n - 6$; $n = -7$

Skill Check 2

1. $x + (x + 1) = 91$; 45 and 46
2. $x + (x + 2) = 94$; 46 and 48
3. $2x = (x + 4) + 7$; 11, 13, and 15

Skill Check 3

1. $9.8r = 100$; $r = 10.20$ m/sec.
2. $(25 - c)5 = 110$; $c = 3$ mi./hr.
3. $(r - 65)2 = 680$; $r = 405$ mi./hr.

8.4 Solving Inequalities

Skill Check 1

1. $x > 2$

2. $n \le 6$

3. $a \le -4$

4. $x > 5$

Skill Check 2

1. $x \le -3$ 2. $x > -9$
3. $x < -2$ 4. $y \le 4$

8.5 Applying Inequalities

Skill Check 1

1. $0.7x - 1.50 > 42$; at least 63 customers
2. $3(n + 1) > 70$; since $n > 22\frac{1}{3}$ and an integer, $n \ge 23$ and $n + 1 \ge 24$

Skill Check 2

1. $6n \le 5(n + 1) + 35$; $n \le 40$ and $n + 1 \le 41$
2. $5n \ge (n + 2) + 50$; $n \ge 13$ and $n + 2 \ge 15$
3. $m\angle B + 2m\angle B + (2m\angle B + 1) \ge 61$; $m\angle B \ge 12°$

Chapter 9—Relations and Functions

9.1 The Coordinate Plane

Skill Check 1

1. II   2. x-axis   3. I
4. II   5. IV   6. II
7. y-axis   8. III

Skill Check 2

1–4.

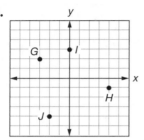

9.2 Relations

Skill Check 1

1. $D = \{-3, 1, 2, 4\}$;
   $R = \{-3, 5, 9, 10\}$
2. $D = \{-7, -6, -4, 3\}$;
   $R = \{-1, 7, 8\}$
3. $D = \{-4, -3, 8\}$;
   $R = \{-6, 5, 6, 10\}$
4. $D = \{-6, -3, 0, 2, 3\}$;
   $R = \{8\}$

Skill Check 2

1. $\{(-4, 6), (5, -7), (-6, 5)\}$
2. $\{(-4, -8), (-3, -7), (-6, 0), (-8, -3)\}$
3. $H = \{(-3, -4), (1, 0), (5, 4)\}$

Skill Check 3

1.

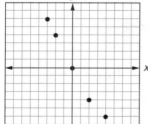

2.

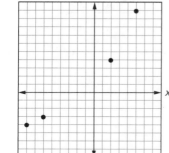

3.

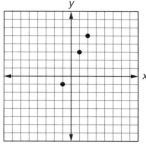

4.

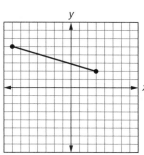

$D = -7 \le x \le 3;$
$R = 2 \le y \le 5$

9.3 Functions

Skill Check 1

1. yes

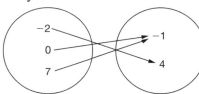

2. no

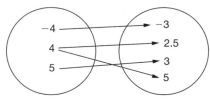

3. yes

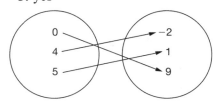

Skill Check 2

1. −4   **2.** −10
3. 2   **4.** 8

Skill Check 3

1. $R = \{3, 6, 7, 8.5\}$
2. yes   **3.** no
4. yes   **5.** no

9.4 Graphing Linear Functions

Skill Check 1

1. no   **2.** yes
3. yes   **4.** no

Skill Check 2

Answers will vary.

1. (0, 0), (2, 6), (4, 12)

x	$3x$	y
0	3(0)	0
2	3(2)	6
4	3(4)	12

2. (0, −8), (2, 2), (4, 12)

x	$5x - 8$	y
0	5(0) − 8	−8
2	5(2) − 8	2
4	5(4) − 8	12

3. (0, 1), (2, 0), (4, −1)

x	$-\frac{x}{2} + 1$	$f(x)$
0	$-\frac{0}{2} + 1$	1
2	$-\frac{2}{2} + 1$	0
4	$-\frac{4}{2} + 1$	−1

Skill Check 3

1.

x	$-x + 7$	y
−1	−(−1) + 7	8
0	−0 + 7	7
1	−1 + 7	6

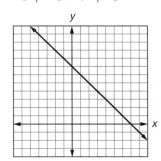

2.

x	$3x + 1$	y
−1	3(−1) + 1	−2
0	3(0) + 1	1
1	3(1) + 1	4

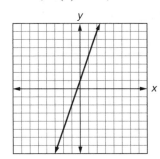

9.5 Slope

Skill Check 1·

1. $m = \frac{2}{3}$ **2.** $m = -\frac{3}{2}$

Skill Check 2

1. $m = \frac{7}{4}$ **2.** $m = \frac{11}{2}$

3. $m = 0$ **4.** $m = -\frac{7}{9}$

5. undefined   **6.** $m = -4$

9.6 Slope-Intercept Form

Skill Check 1

1. (4, 0), (0, −6)
2. (10, 0), (0, −2.5)
3. (5, 0), (0, 3)

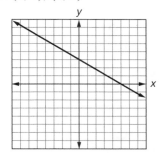

4. (−5, 0), (0, −2)

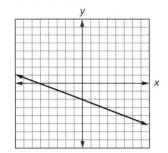

Skill Check 2

1. $y = -x + 7$; $m = -1$; (0, 7)
2. $y = 3x + 2$; $m = 3$; (0, 2)
3. $y = x + 2$; $m = 1$; (0, 2)
4. $y = 2x - 4$; $m = 2$; (0, −4)

Skill Check 3

1.

2.

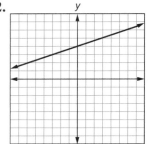

3. $y = 4x - 5$

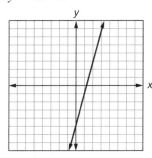

4. $y = \frac{2}{3}x + 2$

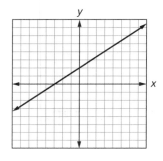

9.7 Direct Variations

Skill Check 1
  1. no
  2. yes; $k = 6$; $y = 6x$

Skill Check 2
  1. yes; $k = 3.5$ 2. yes; $k = \pi$
  3. no   4. no

Skill Check 3

  1.

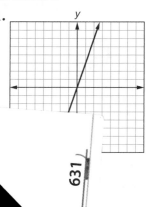

2.

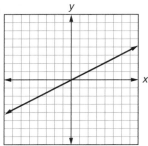

Skill Check 4
  1. $k = 4.5$ 2. $k = 8$
  3. $y = 11$ 4. $y = 8.8$

9.8 Graphing Linear Inequalities

Skill Check 1
  1. below; solid
  2. above; dashed
  3. above; dashed
  4. above; solid

Skill Check 2

  1.

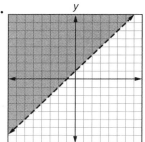

  2.

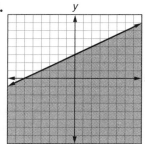

  3.

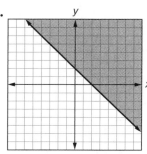

4.

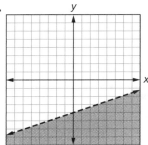

Chapter 10—Statistics and Probability

10.1 Statistical Measures

Skill Check 1
  1. sample
  2. sample
  3. population
  4. c (mail survey)

Skill Check 2
  1. convenience
  2. systematic
  3. random
  4. cluster

Skill Check 3
  1. 34   2. 25.6
  3. 30.5   4. 31

10.2 Diagramming Data

Skill Check 1
  1. quartiles: 12.5, 17, and 25;
     interquartile range: 12.5
  2. quartiles: 199, 220, and 233;
     interquartile range: 34
  3.

18	45	55	75	90

  4.

45	52	64	70	77

Skill Check 2
  1.
1	0 2 3 3
2	1 1 9
3	2

  2.
18	1
19	9
22	0 0 5
23	3
24	0

Skill Check 3

1. positive correlation

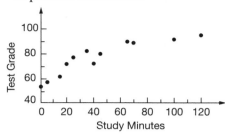

10.3 Histograms

Skill Check 1

1.

Data	Tally	Freq.	Prod.
10	||	2	20
11	|	1	11
12	||	2	24
13	||	2	26
14	|||	3	42
15	||	2	30
16	|	1	16
17	|||	3	51
18	|	1	18
19	|	1	19
20	|	1	20
Total		19	277

2. range: 10; mean: 14.6;
median: 14; mode: 14 and 17

Skill Check 2

1.

Interval	Mid.	Freq.	Prod.
10–14	12	6	72
15–19	17	15	255
20–24	22	20	440
25–29	27	10	270
30–34	32	3	96
Total		54	1,133

range: 24; mean: 21.0;
median interval: 20–24;
modal interval: 20–24

2.

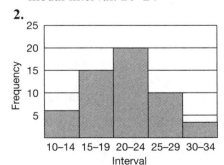

10.4 Graphing Data

Skill Check 1

1.

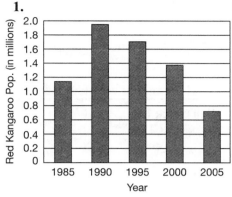

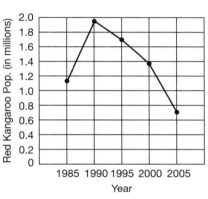

Skill Check 2

1.

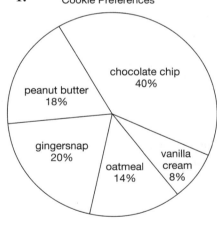

Cookie Preferences

10.5 Fundamental Principle of Counting

Skill Check 1

1.

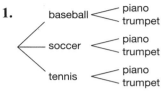

6; baseball and piano, baseball and trumpet, soccer and piano, soccer and trumpet, tennis and piano, tennis and trumpet

2.

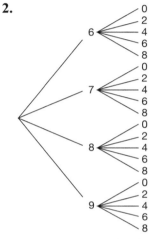

20; 60, 62, 64, 66, 68, 70, 72, 74, 76, 78, 80, 82, 84, 86, 88, 90, 92, 94, 96, 98

Skill Check 2

1. 6   **2.** 12

10.6 Permutations

Skill Check 1

1. 5!   **2.** 8!   **3.** 24
4. 5,040   **5.** 360   **6.** 4,320

Skill Check 2

1. 120   **2.** 40,320

10.7 Combinations

Skill Check 1

1. permutation
2. combination
3. combination
4. permutation

Skill Check 2

1. 330 committees
2. 1,716 squads

10.8 Probability

Skill Check 1

1. heads, tails
2. red, white, blue
3. $\frac{1}{5}$, or 0.2
4. 0
5. $\frac{3}{5}$, or 0.6

Skill Check 2

1. $\frac{1}{3} \approx 0.33$ 2. $\frac{5}{6} \approx 0.83$
3. $\frac{2}{3} \approx 0.67$ 4. $\frac{2}{3} \approx 0.67$
5. 1   6. $\frac{1}{2} = 0.5$

10.9 Independent and Dependent Events

Skill Check 1

1. $\frac{15}{76} \approx 0.20$ 2. $\frac{15}{76} \approx 0.20$
3. $\frac{21}{38} \approx 0.55$ 4. $\frac{1}{19} \approx 0.05$

Skill Check 2

1. $\frac{1}{12} \approx 0.08$ 2. $\frac{1}{3} \approx 0.33$
3. $\frac{9}{64} \approx 0.14$ 4. $\frac{15}{64} \approx 0.23$
5. $\frac{15}{64} \approx 0.23$

Chapter 11—Radicals

11.1 Square Roots

Skill Check 1

1. 5   2. not real
3. 6   4. −8
5. not real   6. −10

Skill Check 2

1. 8 and 9   2. 11 and 12
3. −5 and −4   4. −10 and −9

Skill Check 3

1. 2.6   2. 4.8   3. −3.3

Skill Check 4

1. 3   2. 2
3. −3   4. 36

11.2 ... tions

Skill Check 2

1. $x = 27$
2. no real solution
3. $x = 2$
4. $x = -4$
5. no real solution
6. $x = 17.5$

11.3 Equations with Exponents

Skill Check 1

1. $x = \pm 9$ 2. $x = \pm 6$
3. $x = \pm 5$ 4. $x = \pm 3$

Skill Check 2

1. $x = \pm\sqrt{43}$
2. no real solution
3. $x = \pm 3$
4. $x = \pm\sqrt{11}$

11.4 The Pythagorean Theorem

Skill Check 1

1. 13
2. 26
3. $\sqrt{149} \approx 12.2$

Skill Check 2

1. 15
2. $\sqrt{24} \approx 4.9$
3. 11

Skill Check 3

1. yes   2. no   3. yes

11.5 Products and Quotients of Radicals

Skill Check 1

1. 40   2. 90   3. 110

Skill Check 2

1. $2\sqrt{3}$ 2. $5\sqrt{5}$
3. $11\sqrt{2}$ 4. $3\sqrt{7}$

Skill Check 3

1. $5\sqrt{2}$ 2. $6\sqrt{7}$

Skill Check 4

1. 2   2. 7
3. $\frac{9}{4}$ 4. $\sqrt{3}$

11.6 Sums and Differences of Radicals

Skill Check 1

1. $6\sqrt{3}$ 2. $3\sqrt{6}$
3. no like terms   4. $-3\sqrt{2} + 3\sqrt{5}$

Skill Check 2

1. $-4\sqrt{2}$ 2. $11\sqrt{6}$
3. $10\sqrt{3}$ 4. $8\sqrt{2} + 6\sqrt{3}$

11.7 Cube Roots

Skill Check 1

1. 1,728   2. −343
3. −12   4. 8
5. 3 and 4   6. −5 and −4

Skill Check 2

1. 2.2   2. 1.7
3. $2\sqrt[3]{25}$ 4. $10\sqrt[3]{3}$

Chapter 12—Geometry

12.1 Basic Geometric Figures

Skill Check 1

1. $A \bullet\!\!\longleftrightarrow\!\!\bullet B$
2. (line through M and N)
3. (ray from X through Y)
4. $\overleftrightarrow{AB}$ or $\overleftrightarrow{AC}$
5. $\overrightarrow{BA}$ or $\overrightarrow{BC}$
6. $\overrightarrow{CA}$ and $\overrightarrow{CB}$

Skill Check 2

1. 39°; acute
2. 120°; obtuse
3. 90°; right
4. $m\angle ABD + 33 = 48$; $m\angle ABD = 15°$
5. $m\angle PQS + 39 = 136$; $m\angle PQS = 97°$

12.2 Pairs of Angles

Skill Check 1

1. 66°; complement: 24°; supplement: 114°
2. 39°; complement: 51°; supplement: 141°
3. 114°; supplement: 66°
4. $m\angle XYW + 22 = 180$; $m\angle XYW = 158°$
5. $c + 17 = 90$; complement: 73°

Skill Check 2

1. 7   2. 7 or 9   3. 8
4. 62°   5. 118°   6. 62°

Skill Check 3

1. $\angle 2$ and $\angle 3$, $\angle 4$ and $\angle 5$
2. $\angle 1$ and $\angle 6$, $\angle 7$ and $\angle 8$
3. any two: $\angle 1$ and $\angle 5$, $\angle 3$ and $\angle 7$, $\angle 8$ and $\angle 2$, $\angle 4$ and $\angle 6$
4. $115°$ 5. $65°$ 6. $65°$
7. $115°$ 8. $115°$ 9. $115°$
10. $65°$

12.3 Polygons

Skill Check 1

1. isosceles 2. scalene
3. obtuse 4. acute
5. $m\angle X + 110 + 30 = 180$; $m\angle X = 40°$
6. $m\angle X + 37 + 22 = 180$; $m\angle X = 121°$

Skill Check 2

1. hexagon; $720°$
2. $108°$
3. $m\angle A + 95 + 70 + 115 = 360$; $m\angle A = 80°$

12.4 Perimeter and Circumference

Skill Check 1

1. 32 m   2. 29 m   3. 3.1 in.
4. 14 cm by 7 cm

Skill Check 2

1. 20π in. ≈ 62.8 in.
2. 100π yd. ≈ 314 yd.
3. 3 ft.
4. 1 m

12.5 Congruence and Similarity

Skill Check 1

1. $\angle T$ 2. $\overline{UV}$ 3. $m\angle V$
4. TU 5. $\angle R$ 6. $\overline{QS}$

Skill Check 2

1. $\overline{ST}$ 2. $\overline{PR}$ 3. $\overline{TU}$
4. $\angle P$ 5. $\angle T$ 6. $\angle R$
7. 4   8. 9

12.6 Special Right Triangles

Skill Check 1

1. 10   2. 3
3. $8\sqrt{2}$ 4. $12\sqrt{2}$

Skill Check 2

1. $x = 5$, $y = 10$
2. $x = 6$, $y = 3\sqrt{3}$
3. $x = 4$, $y = 4\sqrt{3}$

4. $9\sqrt{3}$ and 18
5. 7.5 and $7.5\sqrt{3}$
6. 14 and 28

12.7 Coordinate Geometry

Skill Check 1

1. $\sqrt{234} \approx 15.3$ 2. $\sqrt{98} \approx 9.9$

Skill Check 2

1. $(-3, 6)$ 2. $(2.5, 1)$ 3. $(3, -4)$

12.8 Symmetry and Transformations

Skill Check 1

1–4. Answers will vary. Sample answers are provided.

1.

2.

3.

4.

5. the point $(-7, 2)$
6. the segment with endpoints $(-4, 2)$ and $(0, -3)$

Skill Check 2

1. line
2. line
3. line, rotational, point
4. rotational, point
5. 4
6. 2
7. 1 (or 3 if equilateral)
8. 4

Chapter 13—Area and Volume

13.1 Areas of Parallelograms

Skill Check 1

1. 49 cm^2
2. 44 in.^{2}
3. 64 ft.^{2}
4. $25\sqrt{3}$ cm$^2 \approx 43.3$ cm^2
5. 84 in.^{2}
6. 130 m^2

13.2 Areas of Triangles and Trapezoids

Skill Check 1

1. 6 cm^2 2. 22.5 m^2
3. 26 cm^2 4. 24.5 in.^{2}

Skill Check 2

1. 42 cm^2 2. 220 mm^2
3. 126 cm^2 4. 19.5 m^2

13.3 Areas of Circles

Skill Check 1

1. 12.6 cm^2 2. 50.2 m^2
3. 314 cm^2 4. 153.9 mm^2
5. 2.0 m^2 6. 38.5 cm^2

Skill Check 2

1. 13.8 ft.^{2} 2. 836 m^2

13.4 Lengths and Areas of Similar Regions

Skill Check 1

1. $p_2 = 32.9$ units
2. $p_2 \approx 20.6$ units
3. $s_2 \approx 29.2$ units
4. $s_2 \approx 14.6$ units

Skill Check 2

1. $A_2 \approx 40.8$ units^2
2. $A_1 \approx 2.2$ units^2
3. $s_2 = 9$ units
4. $s_2 = \sqrt{96} \approx 9.8$ units

13.5 Surface Areas of Prisms and Cylinders

Skill Check 1

1. 392 cm^2 2. 181.5 ft.^{2}
3. 360 ft.^{2}

Skill Check 2

1. 352 m^2 2. 1,098 in.^{2}
3. 170 ft.^{2} 4. 432 cm^2

13.6 Surface Areas of Pyramids, Cones, and Spheres

Skill Check 1
1. $L = 192$ cm^2; $S = 336$ cm^2
2. $l = 18.4$ cm; $L = 662.4$ cm^2; $S = 986.4$ cm^2
3. $L = 11.7$ ft.^{2}; $S = 15.6$ ft.^{2}

Skill Check 2
1. 75 m^2 2. 143 in.^{2} 3. 204 ft.^{2}

Skill Check 3
1. 50 cm^2 2. 211 m^2 3. 314 ft.^{2}

13.7 Volumes of Prisms and Cylinders

Skill Check 1
1. 162 cm^3 2. 140 m^3
3. 204 cm^3 4. 7.5 ft.^{3}

Skill Check 2
1. 402 cm^3 2. 154 cm^3
3. 1,130 ft.^{3} 4. 942 m^3
5. 3 m   6. 5 cm

13.8 Volumes of Pyramids, Cones, and Spheres

Skill Check 1
1. 1,620 cm^3 2. 209 cm^3
3. 188.4 in.^{3} 4. 140.8 ft.^{3}
5. 80 m^3

Skill Check 2
1. $\frac{1,372}{3}\pi$ m$^3 \approx 1,436$ m^3
2. 36π ft.$^3 \approx 113$ ft.^{3}
3. $\frac{500}{3}\pi$ m$^3 \approx 523$ m^3

Chapter 14—Polynomials

14.1 Types of Polynomials

Skill Check 1
1. yes
2. yes (the constant monomial $\frac{1}{2}$)
3. yes
4. yes
5. no; negative exponent (equivalent to $8x^{-2}$)
6. yes
7. no; fractional exponent

Skill Check 2
1. 2   2. 7   3. 2
4. 8   5. 8   6. 6

Skill Check 3
1. 82   2. 42
3. −19   4. 81

14.2 Adding Polynomials

Skill Check 1
1. $2y + 11$ 2. $-4x + 3$
3. $8x + y$ 4. $5a - 4b + 10$

Skill Check 2
1. $x^2 - 8x + 1$
2. $-3a^2 - 7ab - 9b^2$
3. $x^4 + 2x^3 - 4x^2 + 8x - 22$
4. $-8x^5 + 11x^3 + 10x + 9$

Skill Check 3
1. $\frac{3}{4}x - 3y$
2. $4.5x^2 + 2.4x + 2$
3. $28x^2y - 11xy$
4. $5.5x^2 - 5xy + 2y^2$

14.3 Subtracting Polynomials

Skill Check 1
1. $-4a - b$
2. $3x - 4y$
3. $-2x^2 + 5x + 6$
4. $3x^2 - 4xy + 7y^2$

Skill Check 2
1. $6x - 3$ 2. $3x - 8$
3. $2x + 6$ 4. $-4x - 6$

Skill Check 3
1. $2x^2 + 2x + 7$
2. $5x^2 - 2x - 3$
3. $-10x^2 - 11x + 40$
4. $a^2 + 8a + 7$
5. $3z^3 - 5z^2 - 10z + 11$
6. $a^4 - 3a^3 - 2a^2 + 5a - 1$
7. $6x^4 - 12x^3 + 3x^2 - 2x - 6$

14.4 Multiplying by a Monomial

Skill Check 1
1. 3^{10} 2. $2^8 \cdot 5^4$ 3. x^{11}
4. x^6y^8 5. $35x^6$ 6. $56x^8$
7. $-28a^6$ 8. $39y^5$

Skill Check 2
1. $35x^2y$ 2. $6a^2b^2c$
3. $-12a^3b^2c$ 4. $48a^4b^6$
5. $5x^4 - 10x^2$
6. $-36x^2 + 18x - 72$
7. $6y^4 - 16y^2 + 6$
8. $3x^3 - 6x^2 + 12x$

Skill Check 3
1. $-5x^3y + 10x^2y^2$
2. $-4x^3y^2 + 6x^2y^3$
3. $-15a^4b^3 + 3a^3b^2 - 6a^3b$
4. $2a^3b^2c + 3a^2b^3c - 6ab^4c$

14.5 Multiplying Binomials

Skill Check 1
1. $x^2 + 3x + 2$
2. $x^2 - 5x - 14$
3. $x^2 - 6x - 27$
4. $x^2 - 10x + 16$

Skill Check 2
1. $2x^2 + x - 6$
2. $15x^2 - 49x + 40$
3. $x^2 - 8x + 16$
4. $9x^2 - 12x + 4$

14.6 Dividing by a Monomial

Skill Check 1
1. $5x^3$
2. $-4x$
3. $6xy^3$
4. $-9n^2p$
5. $\frac{3a^4}{b}$ or $3a^4b^{-1}$
6. $-\frac{b^2c^3}{a^2}$ or $-a^{-2}b^2c^3$

Skill Check 2
1. $2x^4 + 4x^3 - 5x^2$
2. $3y^8 - 6y^4 - 1$
3. $x^3 - 3x^2 - 7x$
4. $a^8 - 4a^4 - 9a$
5. $8x^5 - 4x^4 + 2x^2$
6. $-a^2 + 2ab + 3b^2$

14.7 Applying Algebra

Skill Check 1
1. 7 tens, 20 fives, and 9 ones; $179
2. 28 quarters, 58 dimes, and 140 nickels

Skill Check 2
1. 52 pennies, 26 nickels, and 18 dimes
2. 6 quarters, 12 dimes, 8 nickels, and 16 pennies

GLOSSARY

absolute value The distance of a number from zero on a number line.

acute angle An angle that measures less than 90°.

acute triangle A triangle in which all three angles are acute.

addend Any of the two or more numbers being added together.

additive inverse If $a + b = 0$, then b is the additive inverse of a, denoted $-a$.

Addition Property of Equality For all integers a, b, and c, if $a = b$, then $a + c = b + c$.

Addition Property of Inequality If a and b are real numbers such that $a < b$, and c is any real number, then $a + c < b + c$.

adjacent angles Angles that have a common vertex and a common ray between them.

algebraic expression A mathematical expression containing numbers, variables, and operational signs.

alternate exterior angles A pair of angles outside two lines intersected by a transversal and on opposite sides of the transversal.

alternate interior angles A pair of angles inside two lines intersected by a transversal and on opposite sides of the transversal.

altitude (1) A segment drawn from any vertex of a triangle perpendicular to the line containing the opposite side. (2) The perpendicular segment between parallel sides of a parallelogram or trapezoid. (3) The perpendicular segment from the vertex of a pyramid or cone to its base. (4) The perpendicular segment between parallel bases in a prism or cylinder.

angle Two rays with a common endpoint.

arc Any continuous section of a curve.

area The number of square units needed to cover a region.

arithmetic sequence A sequence of numbers, each differing by a constant amount from the preceding number.

Associative Property of Addition For all real numbers a, b, and c, $a + (b + c) = (a + b) + c$.

Associative Property of Multiplication For all real numbers a, b, and c, $a \times (b \times c) = (a \times b) \times c$.

axis (plural, *axes*) Either of two perpendicular number lines on a coordinate plane.

bar graph A graph containing a sequence of vertical or horizontal bars whose heights (or lengths) are proportional to the variables they represent.

base (1) The number used as the factor in exponential form. (2) The number used for place values in a number system. (3) Either of two congruent and parallel faces of a prism or cylinder. (4) The circular or polygonal face of a cone or pyramid.

binary A base 2 system of numbers.

binomial A polynomial consisting of exactly two terms.

box-and-whisker diagram A line segment showing the highest and lowest numbers, upper and lower quartiles, and median of a set of data.

capacity The amount of fluid or dry measure a container will hold.

Cartesian coordinate plane See *coordinate plane*.

center of rotation A point in a plane about which a plane figure is rotated.

central angle An angle with its vertex at the center of a circle.

chord A segment with its endpoints on a circle.

circle The set of points in a plane that are the same distance from a given point.

circular cone A cone with a circular base.

circular cylinder A cylinder with circular bases.

circumference The distance around a circle.

closed curve A two-dimensional curve that starts and ends at the same point.

Closure Property of Addition A set S is closed for addition if $a + b$ is in S for any numbers a and b in S.

Closure Property of Multiplication A set S is closed for multiplication if $a \times b$ is in S for any numbers a and b in S.

coefficient See *numerical coefficient*.

combination A selection of a subset of objects from a set without regard to the order in which they are selected.

commission A percent multiplied by the dollar value of sales to determine an employee's earnings.

common difference The difference between any two consecutive terms of an arithmetic sequence.

common ratio The constant multiplier for a geometric sequence.

Commutative Property of Addition For any real numbers a and b, $a + b = b + a$.

Commutative Property of Multiplication For any real numbers a and b, $a \times b = b \times a$.

complementary angles Two angles with measures whose sum is 90°.

composite number A natural number greater than 1 with factors other than 1 and itself.

compound interest Interest that is calculated at set intervals on the sum of the principal and any previously earned interest.

compound interest formula $S = P(1 + i)^n$, where S is the amount in the savings account, P is the principal, i is the interest rate per period, and n is the number of interest payments.

concave polygon A polygon in which at least one interior angle has a measure greater than 180°.

cone A closed curve or polygonal base connected to a point not in the plane of the base. (All pyramids are cones.)

congruent Two figures with the same size and shape.

conjecture A generalized statement that seems to be true at all times.

constant A fixed number.

constant of proportionality The constant k in the equation for a direct variation.

constant of variation See *constant of proportionality*.

converse The statement resulting when the "if" part and the "then" part of a conditional statement are switched.

convex polygon A polygon in which all interior angles have measures less than 180°.

coordinate plane A graph formed by two perpendicular number lines, one horizontal and one vertical. The point of intersection is zero on both number lines.

correlation A measure of how well data fits a function.

corresponding angles A pair of angles, both of which lie on the same side of a transversal intersecting two lines, with one being an exterior angle and the other an interior angle.

cost The price a retailer pays for his merchandise from a wholesaler or manufacturer.

cross multiplication The process of multiplying the numerator of the first fraction times the denominator of the second and multiplying the denominator of the first times the numerator of the second.

cube A rectangular prism with six square congruent faces.

cubed Any expression taken to the third power.

curve A continuous set of points. (Lines are curves.)

cylinder A three-dimensional figure with two parallel congruent bases. (All prisms are cylinders.)

data Recorded observations that can be measured or counted.

decagon A polygon with ten sides.

decimal A number expressed using a decimal point rather than as a ratio of integers.

deductive reasoning Reasoning such that the premises guarantee the conclusion.

degree of a polynomial The degree of the highest term in the polynomial.

degree of a term The sum of the exponents of the variables contained in the term. Variables with no exponent have an unwritten exponent of 1.

denominator The bottom number in a fraction.

dependent events Two events in which the occurrence of one changes the probability of the occurrence of the other.

diagonal A line segment that joins two vertices of a polygon but is not one of the sides.

diameter A chord that passes through the center of a circle or sphere.

difference The answer to a subtraction problem.

directly proportional See *direct variation*.

direct variation The relationship between the variables x and y when there is a positive constant k such that $y = kx$.

discount The amount by which a product is reduced below its retail price.

discount rate The percentage by which a product is reduced below its retail price.

disjoint sets Two sets whose intersection is the empty set.

Distributive Property For any real numbers a, b, and c, $a(b + c) = ab + ac$.

dividend The number in a division problem being divided into parts.

divides (1) The number a divides b, written $a|b$, if there is an integer c such that $b = ac$. (2) a divides b if b is a multiple of a.

divisible If the remainder is zero when b is divided by a, then b is divisible by a.

divisor The number in a division problem that divides another number.

domain The set of all first coordinates of a relation.

earnings The dollar amount a salesperson earns as a percentage of his sales.

edge The line of intersection of two faces of a polyhedron.

element An object or quantity included in a set.

empty set A set with no elements.

equation A mathematical sentence stating that two expressions are equal.

equilateral triangle A triangle with three congruent sides.

equivalent fractions Fractions that represent the same rational number.

event A subset of the sample space.

experiment A process used to obtain a statistical measurement or observation.

explicit formula A formula that gives the nth term of a sequence in terms of n.

exponent A superscript that indicates how many times a base is used as a factor.

extremes The first and fourth terms of a proportion.

face Any of the polygons making up a polyhedron.

factor (1) A number that is being multiplied. (2) Any integer that divides a given integer with no remainder. (3) The number a is a factor of b if there is another integer c such that $ac = b$.

factorial See n *factorial*.

finite set A set whose elements can be counted using whole numbers.

fraction A ratio expressed with one number over another number.

frequency distribution table A table used to organize a large set of data.

function A relation in which no two ordered pairs have the same first coordinate.

function rule An equation or property that describes a function.

function value An element of the range of a function.

Fundamental Principle of Counting If one step can be done in p ways and another step in q ways, then the two-step process can be done in $p \cdot q$ ways.

Fundamental Theorem of Arithmetic Every composite number can be expressed in exactly one way as a product of prime numbers (though the order of the factors may vary).

geometric sequence A sequence of numbers whose successive terms differ by a constant multiplier.

geometry The study of shapes formed by points in a plane or in space.

graph The set of points that are elements of a relation.

great circle The intersection of a sphere with a plane that passes through the center of the sphere.

greater than The number a is greater than b, denoted $a > b$, if a is to the right of b on the number line.

greatest common factor (GCF) The largest number that evenly divides each of the given numbers or algebraic expressions.

heptagon A polygon with seven sides.

hexadecimal A base 16 system of numbers.

hexagon A polygon with six sides.

histogram A bar graph representing equal intervals, with no space between the bars.

hypotenuse The side opposite the right angle in a right triangle.

Identity Property of Addition For any real number a, $a + 0 = 0 + a = a$.

Identity Property of Multiplication For any real number a, $a \times 1 = 1 \times a = a$.

image If a transformation maps a point P to a point P', then P' is the image of P.

improper fraction A fraction whose numerator is equal to or greater than its denominator.

independent events Two events in which the occurrence of one has no effect on the probability of the occurrence of the other.

index of a radical In $\sqrt[n]{x}$, n is the index.

inequality A mathematical sentence expressing the relative size of two quantities that may or may not be equal.

infinite set A set that is not finite.

integers The set of whole numbers and their opposites.

interest Payment for the use of money.

interquartile range The difference between the upper and lower quartiles of a set of data.

intersecting lines Lines that share a common point.

intersection The set of elements contained in two or more given sets.

inverse operations Operations that undo each other (e.g., addition and subtraction, multiplication and division).

Inverse Property of Addition For any real number a, there exists another real number denoted $-a$, such that $a + (-a) = 0$.

Inverse Property of Multiplication For any real number a, where $a \neq 0$, there exists another real number denoted $\frac{1}{a}$, such that $a \times \frac{1}{a} = 1$.

irrational number A real number that cannot be written as a fraction (the decimal neither repeats nor terminates).

isosceles triangle A triangle with at least two congruent sides.

lateral faces All the faces of a prism or pyramid except the base(s).

lateral surface area (1) The combined area of the lateral faces of a prism or pyramid. (2) The area of the curved surface of a cylinder or cone.

least common multiple (LCM) The smallest positive number that is evenly divided by each of the given numbers or algebraic expressions.

legs The two sides of a right triangle that form the right angle.

less than The number a is less than b, denoted $a < b$, if a is to the left of b on the number line.

like terms Terms that contain an identical variable or variables all raised to the same respective powers.

line A set of points along a straight path with no endpoints.

linear function A function whose graph is a line.

linear inequality Any inequality of one of the following forms: $ax + by < c$, $ax + by > c$, $ax + by \leq c$, or $ax + by \geq c$.

line graph A graph in which line segments connect a series of ordered pairs from left to right to show the relationship between two variables.

line segment A subset of a line, consisting of two points and all the points between them.

line symmetry A characteristic of a figure in which each half of the figure is the image of the other half under a reflection in some line, which is called the line of symmetry.

lower quartile The median of the lower half of a set of data.

lowest terms A rational number $\frac{a}{b}$ is in lowest terms if the GCF of a and b is 1.

lunes The four sectors of a sphere obtained by passing two perpendicular planes through the center of the sphere.

markup The amount a retailer adds to his cost to arrive at the retail price; the difference between the retail price and the cost.

markup rate The percent increase of markup over cost (markup = markup rate × cost).

mean The sum of the numbers in a finite data set divided by the quantity of numbers in the set.

means The second and third terms of a proportion.

median The middle number in an ordered set of data, or the average of the two middle numbers if the quantity of numbers is even.

middle quartile A term sometimes used to refer to the median of a set of data.

minuend The number in a subtraction problem from which another number is subtracted.

mixed number The sum of a whole number and a proper fraction.

mode The number or numbers that appear most frequently in a set of data.

monomial A real number, a variable, or the product of a real number and one or more variables with nonnegative integer exponents.

multiple of an integer Any product of that integer and any natural number.

Multiplication Property of Equality For all integers a, b, and c, if $a = b$, then $ac = bc$.

Multiplication Property of Exponents For all integers x, a, and b, $x^a \cdot x^b = x^{a+b}$.

Multiplication Property of Inequality If a and b are real numbers such that $a < b$, then for any positive real number c, $ac < bc$; and for any negative real number c, $ac > bc$.

multiplicative inverse If $a \times b = 1$, then b is the multiplicative inverse of a, denoted $\frac{1}{a}$.

mutually exclusive events Events in which the occurrence of one event makes the occurrence of another event impossible.

mutually exclusive sets Sets whose intersection is empty.

natural numbers The set of counting numbers: $\{1, 2, 3, \ldots\}$.

negation The denial of a statement.

negative exponent For any nonzero real number x and any integer a, $x^{-a} = \frac{1}{x^a}$.

negative integer An integer whose value is less than zero.

n factorial The product of the natural numbers from n down to 1. Denoted $n!$

nonagon A polygon with nine sides.

numerator The top number in a fraction.

numerical coefficient The constant factor of a term.

numerical expression A mathematical phrase containing numbers and operations, but no variables.

oblique prism A prism in which the lateral faces are not perpendicular to the bases.

obtuse angle An angle that measures greater than 90° but less than 180°.

obtuse triangle A triangle with one obtuse angle.

octagon A polygon with eight sides.

octal A base 8 system of numbers.

one-to-one correspondence Two sets have a one-to-one correspondence if every element in one set is paired with one and only one element in the other set and no elements in either remain unpaired.

opposites Two numbers an equal distance from zero on a number line but in opposite directions (additive inverses).

ordered pair A pair of numbers used to locate a point in a coordinate plane.

origin The point where the axes intersect in the coordinate plane.

outcome The result of a single trial in a statistical experiment.

parallel lines Lines in the same plane that never intersect.

parallelogram A quadrilateral with both pairs of opposite sides parallel.

parameter A measure calculated from data for an entire population.

pentagon A polygon with five sides.

percent A ratio that compares a number to 100.

percent change The amount of increase or decrease expressed as a percent of the original amount.

percent change formula

$$\text{Percent change} = \frac{\text{amount of change}}{\text{original amount}} \times 100\%.$$

percent formula The percent of the whole is equal to the part: percent × whole = part.

perfect cube An integer b is a perfect cube if $b = a^3$, where a is an integer.

perfect square An integer b is a perfect square if $b = a^2$, where a is an integer.

perimeter The distance around a plane geometric figure.

permutation A way of arranging a set of objects in a particular order.

perpendicular bisector A line intersecting a segment at its midpoint, which is perpendicular to the segment.

perpendicular lines Lines that intersect to form right angles.

pie chart A circle divided into sectors whose areas are proportional to the quantities they represent.

place value A digit's position in a numeral.

plane A flat surface that extends infinitely in all directions.

point An exact location in space having no length, width, or thickness.

point symmetry A characteristic of a figure that has 180° rotational symmetry.

polygon A simple closed curve in a plane made up of line segments.

polyhedron A closed three-dimensional figure with flat faces that are polygons.

polynomial A monomial or the sum or difference of two or more monomials.

population The entire set of objects sharing similar characteristics from which data can be collected and analyzed.

positive integer An integer whose value is greater than zero.

preimage If a transformation maps a point P to a point P', then P is the preimage of P'.

prime factorization The factoring of a positive integer into a product of primes.

prime number A natural number greater than 1 with exactly two factors: 1 and itself.

principal An amount of money that is deposited or borrowed.

principal square root The positive square root.

prism A polyhedron with two parallel congruent faces.

probability The ratio of successes to possible outcomes in an experiment.

product The answer to a multiplication problem.

proper fraction A fraction whose numerator is less than its denominator.

Property of Proportions The product of the extremes is equal to the product of the means.

proportion A statement of equality between two ratios.

proportion method The part is to the whole as the percent is to 100.

pyramid A three-dimensional figure with a polygonal base and triangular lateral faces that meet at a common point called the vertex.

Pythagorean theorem If the hypotenuse of a right triangle has length c and the legs have lengths a and b, then $a^2 + b^2 = c^2$.

quadrant One of four regions of the coordinate plane determined by the intersection of the x- and y-axes.

quadrilateral A polygon with four sides.

quartile Any one of the three values that divide a set of data into four equal-size groups.

quotient The answer to a division problem.

radical equation An equation that contains a variable in the radicand (e.g., $\sqrt{x} = 5$).

radical sign In $\sqrt[n]{x}$, $\sqrt{\ }$ is the radical sign.

radicand In $\sqrt[n]{x}$, x is the radicand.

radius A segment extending from the center of a circle to a point on the circle.

random sample A sample in which each element in the population has an equally likely chance of being included.

range (1) The difference between the greatest number and the least number in a set of data. (2) The set of all second coordinates of a relation.

rate A ratio comparing measures with different units.

ratio A comparison of two numbers by division, often written as a fraction.

rational numbers The set of all numbers that can be written as a ratio of integers.

ray Part of a line extending endlessly in one direction from an endpoint.

real numbers The combined set of all rational and irrational numbers.

reciprocal See *multiplicative inverse*.

rectangle A parallelogram with four right angles.

rectangular coordinate plane See *coordinate plane*.

rectangular prism A prism that has two parallel congruent rectangular bases.

recursive definition A formula specifying the steps by which each successive term of the sequence is generated from the preceding term or terms.

reflection A transformation that maps each point A of a plane onto point A' such that the following conditions are met: (1) If A is on line l, then $A = A'$. (2) If A is not on line l, then l is the perpendicular bisector of $\overline{AA'}$.

regular polygon A polygon in which all the sides have the same length and all the angles have the same measure.

regular pyramid A pyramid whose base is a regular polygon and whose vertex is directly above the center of the base.

relation A set of ordered pairs.

relatively prime Two positive integers are relatively prime if they have a GCF of 1.

repeating decimal A decimal with a digit or a group of digits that repeats endlessly.

retail price The price of a product before it is discounted.

rhombus A parallelogram with four congruent sides.

right angle An angle that measures 90°.

right cylinder A cylinder in which the curved surface is pependicular to its bases.

right prism A prism in which all the lateral faces are perpendicular to the bases.

right triangle A triangle with one right angle.

rise The vertical change from point P_1 to point P_2 on a line.

rotation (1) The turning of a plane figure about a point in the same plane. (2) The reflection of a figure through two intersecting lines.

rotational symmetry A characteristic of a figure that has a rotation of less than 360° around a center point such that the image of the figure coincides with the original figure.

run The horizontal change from point P_1 to point P_2 on a line.

sale price The retail price less a discount.

sample A portion of a population from which data is collected to estimate the characteristics of the entire population.

sample space The set of all possible outcomes of an experiment.

scale The ratio of a drawing's dimensions to the actual dimensions of the figure.

scale drawing A drawing in which all the lengths are at the same scale, or ratio, to the actual lengths of the object it represents.

scale factor The ratio of corresponding dimensions in similar figures.

scalene triangle A triangle with no two sides equal in length.

scatterplot A graphical representation of the relationship of two variables in the form of ordered pairs of points plotted in a coordinate plane.

scientific notation The expression of a number as the product of a number from 1 to 10 and a power of ten.

segment The part of a line consisting of two endpoints and all the points between them.

sequence A finite or infinite set of numbers determined by a pattern.

set A group or collection of objects.

similar figures Two figures with the same shape (but not necessarily the same size).

simple curve A curve that does not intersect itself.

simple interest Interest that is proportional to the length of a loan.

simple interest formula $I = Prt$, where I is the interest earned, P is the principal, r is the annual interest rate, and t is the time in years that the money is invested or borrowed.

slope The ratio of the rise of a line to its run.

slope-intercept form The equation of a line written in the form $y = mx + b$, where m is the slope and the y-intercept is $(0, b)$.

solution A number or ordered pair that makes a mathematical sentence (equation or inequality) true when substituted for the variable(s).

solution set The set of all solutions to an equation or inequality.

sphere A three-dimensional closed surface, every point of which is equidistant from a given point called the center.

square A rectangle with all sides congruent.

squared A number or algebraic expression multiplied by itself, as indicated by an exponent of two.

square root One of a number's two equal factors.

standard form An equation of a line written in the form $ax + by = c$.

statistic A measure calculated from a sample of data.

statistics The branch of mathematics that deals with collecting, organizing, analyzing, and reporting quantitative information.

stem-and-leaf diagram A type of bar graph in which the data points in each interval are listed in order.

straight angle An angle that measures 180°.

subset A set, all of whose elements are contained in another set.

subtraction Adding the opposite.

subtrahend The number in a subtraction problem being subtracted.

sum The answer to an addition problem.

supplementary angles Two angles with measures whose sum is 180°.

surface area The sum of the areas of a closed three-dimensional figure's surfaces.

symmetric A characteristic of a figure that is a reflection of itself in a line.

Symmetric Property of Equality If $a = b$, then $b = a$.

term (1) A number in a sequence. (2) A constant, variable, or product of a constant and one or more variables in a polynomial. (3) One of the four numbers in a proportion.

terminating decimal A decimal that contains a finite number of digits.

three-dimensional figure A shape whose points do not all lie in the same plane.

transformation The movement of an original geometric shape to another location or shape according to a predefined rule.

translation (1) The action of sliding a figure across a plane. (2) The reflection of a figure through a pair of parallel lines.

transversal A line that intersects two or more other lines.

trapezoid A quadrilateral with at least one pair of parallel sides.

tree diagram A segmented graph in the shape of a tree in which no branch leads from any vertex back to itself. Each path through it represents a mutually exclusive event.

trial A single observation.

triangle A polygon with three sides.

triangular prism A prism that has two parallel congruent triangular bases.

trichotomy axiom For all real numbers a and b, $a > b$, $a < b$, or $a = b$.

trinomial A polynomial consisting of exactly three terms.

union The set of elements that belong to either one or both of two given sets.

unit rate A ratio that compares a quantity to 1.

upper quartile The median of the upper half of a set of data.

variable A letter used to represent an unknown number.

vertex (1) The common endpoint of the two rays that form an angle. (2) The common endpoint of a pair of sides of a polygon. (3) The corners of a polyhedron.

vertical angles Two angles with no sides in common formed by intersecting lines.

vertical line test A test of whether a graph represents a function. If a vertical line can intersect a graph in more than one point, the graph does not represent a function. If all vertical lines drawn through the graph intersect the graph in only one point, the graph represents a function.

volume The number of cubic units contained in a closed three-dimensional figure.

whole numbers The set of counting (natural) numbers and zero.

x-axis The horizontal number line in the coordinate plane.

x-coordinate The first coordinate of an ordered pair.

x-intercept A point where a graph crosses the x-axis.

y-axis The vertical number line in the coordinate plane.

y-coordinate The second coordinate of an ordered pair.

y-intercept A point where a graph crosses the y-axis.

zero power Any nonzero number to the zero power equals 1.

Zero Property of Multiplication The product of zero and any other number is zero.

INDEX